A Guide & Checklist 2nd Edition

World Notgeld

1914 - 1947

And other Local Issue Emergency Money

Courtney L. Coffing

DEDICATION

To our Giessen, Germany-born
daughter
Catharine Elizabeth

Published by

700 E. State Street • Iola, WI 54990-0001
Telephone: 715/445-2214

Please, call or write us for our free catalog of publications. To place an order or receive our free catalog, call 800-258-0929. For editorial comment and further information, use our regular business telephone at (715) 445-2214 or www.krause.com

Library of Congress Catalog Number: 90-63918
ISBN: 0-87341-810-7

Portions of the city listings presented in this work are incorporated with the permission of "Coin World", in which they were first published between Feb. 13, 1980, and July 27, 1983.

Printed in the United States of America

Table of Contents

Introduction

A summary of the German emergency money can perhaps best be viewed through experiences and remarks of two men, one at the beginning of the period when World War I started, and the other at the end, when the hyperinflation inferno was snuffed out.

Dr. Arnold Keller was born in Freiburg/Breisgau on Jan. 31, 1897. In 1904 his father took a job in Frankfurt/Main and the lad attended schools there. One of his high school teachers was Dr. Carl Hahn, brother of physicist Otto Hahn. Teacher Hahn was a numismatist and showed coins in connection with his lectures. Dr. Keller commented, "During this period the whole school collected coins, but I was the only member of the class who continued collecting after graduation."

In 1915 he attended the university in Munich; later he attended the university in Leipzig, and then returned to Munich. He majored in oriental languages and numismatics. Dr. Keller recalled, "My principal professor was the famous numismatist, Professor Heinrich Buchenau. He gave me the theme for my dissertation, "The Coinage Treaty of 1572 between the Rhenish electors and the Landgraves of Hesse."

Beginning as a collector of emergency money in 1914, as it was being issued, Dr. Keller became the editor of a magazine, *Das Notgeld,* later a dealer in coins and paper money, and finally the author of numerous emergency money catalogs. In 1959 he sold his collection, about 200,000 notes, including paper money from around the world, to the Bundesbank of the Federal Republic of Germany. He died in Berlin on Dec. 13, 1972.

The first emergency money apeared in Germany on July 31, 1914, issued by the Buergerliches Brauhaus GmbH, Bremen, in values of one, two and 2.5 mark, produced on heavy paper by the hectograph method. The money had no control numbers and one handwritten signature. The total value of the three denominations was 100 mark.

Dr. Keller grouped the different and mostly unrelated waves of emergency money, appearing between 1914 and 1924, into "periods." Individual catalogs for each of these periods give collectors today the tools to pursue their special collecting interests.

Several explanations were given for change shortages in the early years of the war. Expansion into other lands created a need for change, some said; others blamed the players of the three-hand card game, skat, for hoarding change. A more probable explanation was an increase in the value of silver. Silver coins quickly disappeared from circulation, fewer coins were struck in the mints due to fewer workers and product shortages. Later nickel and copper coins disappeared into the cauldrons of war, further tightening the shortage. Some large cities hoarded coins for unknown and unforeseen contingencies.

In 1917, postmen were accepting as 5.30 mark coins totaling five mark. No more copper coins were minted after 1916; one and two-pfennig paper notes were issued to replace them, particularly in Bavaria. Many retailers resorted to their own private forms of money. Various states tried to prohibit local issues of Notgeld, from requiring a deposit of funds equal to the proposed Notgeld issue, to "tacit toleration," to permitting issues only by major cities.

A compact summary of Notgeld was supplied by Dr. Keller, which indicates to the reader today characteristics of notgeld issues, and how the numismatists divided their collections. In 1914, 452 localities issued 5,500 notes.

Large notes, called Grossgeld, one mark or more denominations, from 1918 to 1921, were from 579 places, some 5,000 notes.

Inflation notes of 1922, values 100 to 1,000 Mark, were from 800 places, 4,000 notes. The inflation of 1923 saw above 6,000 places issue 70,000 notes. Notes of constant value in 1923 and 1924 were from 562 places, totaling 3,660 notes. Prisoner of War camps saw 600 issuing locations, about 3,000 notes. In the 1935-1945 period, 20 concentration camps issued 90 notes.

Notgeld of 1945 comprises 20 places with 150 notes and notgeld of 1947-1948, 270 issuers with about 1,000 notes. The German Reichsbank issued between 1874 and the end of inflation 141 basic types of notes, augmented by a large number of sub-types and variations. From the various German colonies came about 80 different types of notes, many of these with varieties.

One cannot total the number of issuing places above to arrive at the total number of issuing places because of duplication. As collector demand increased, so too did available note issues, spawned by greed and opportunistic cities. Abuses learned by the cities included: charges in excess of value; a termination date for redemption which had passed by the time the notes were mailed; mass production of notes engineered by entrepreneurs, such as the so-called Pinneberg set of 40 communities northwest of Hamburg and the 70 communities of Mecklenburg carrying themes of Fritz Reuter designed by five artists. Finally, there were issues that are pure swindle (Ebstorf-Soldatenrat, Fockbeck, POW camp Lichtenhorst and many others).

Profit-minded entrepreneurs produced even notes from non-existing towns (cities of Neukirch, Knivsberg, Gaansager). In many cases groups and societies issued "Notgeld" disguised as admission tickets, donation receipts and others. Notgeld exhibitions in 10 cities (we would call them coin shows) issued their own "Exhibition Notgeld," described by Dr. Keller as "making a mockery of real Notgeld."

Today, collectors care little which notes were spurious, issued to take advantage of collectors or were less than legitimate in their issues. Many of these notes are in the Keller volume *Serienscheine.*

As Dr. Keller had followed the development of Notgeld from the outset, as a collector, editor and later dealer, he deeply resented the intrusion of fantasy notes. He handled these undesirable aspects of the hobby in a manner which would make the libel-conscious publisher today throw up his hands in horror. He established "Black Lists" (Schwarze Listen) in his publication *Das Notgeld.*

If a collector had corresponded with another, and was owed some money or the person had made some deceptive trades, all that was needed was that the unhappy collector write Dr. Keller. The culprit's name immediately appeared in Dr. Keller's magazine. If a city bilked collectors by selling their notgeld for too much, the Blacklist was waiting for them. For instance, in the October 1921 issue, *Das Notgeld,* in the Schwarze Liste, Keller accused the city of Langenschwalbach of selling notes with a face value of 50-pfennig for one mark; Lindenberg/A, 1.45 mark face value notes sold for 3.45 mark; and from Pyrmont, a note of 75 pfennig was selling for five mark!

With most collectors of notgeld, paper or metal, the day of reckoning must come when one realizes he cannot collect it all, and must decide to specialize. In a half century of collecting, starting with the first issues in August 1914, Dr. Keller obtained some 109,860 pieces of an estimated 163,000 total of all German emergency paper money.

Dr. Hjalmar Horace Greeley Schacht

Responsible for restoring financial sanity to Germany was Hjalmar Horace Greeley Schacht, born Jan. 31, 1899, in Tingleff, now Denmark. His parents, both German, married in New York City. Schacht was named Commissioner of National Currency on Nov. 13, 1923, when he was given a free hand in all questions of money and credit. His job was to snuff the candle of inflation that had become a blowtorch. He formulated a plan to return to a mark valued at 4.2 to the dollar, first freezing the inflation at the rate of 4.2 trillion mark on Nov. 20, 1923. At the time one U.S. cent would have bought more German mark notes than the entire German mortgaged indebtedness of 1914.

There is a relationship between the rate of inflation in Germany and the reparation payments demanded by France under the Treaty of Versailles. In April 1921 the Reparations bill was assessed at $33 billion. On June 24, 1923, the mark sank to 300 to $1 with news of the assassination of Dr. Walter Rathenau, German's foreign minister.

In July 1922 the mark was 500 to the $1, with the first reparations payment due. In late October 1922 with the second reparations payment due, the mark fell to 4,500 to $1.

In January 1923, the Allies marched in the Ruhr region, with the mark standing at 10,200 to the $1. And in April 1923, hyperinflation started! By the end of 1923, on the black market, the rate rose to 12 trillion to the $1, but the losers were the speculators who kept the flames of inflation white hot, despite the admonition of Schacht that the official rate was pegged at 4.2 trillion to $1. Schacht wrote in his memoirs, *Confessions of 'The Old Wizard,'* "theoretically, in circulation in late November 1923, were the gold mark of the empire; the paper mark; and the Rentenmark."

By simply declaring four percent of public lands, including the railroads, as the backing of the new German unit, the Rentenmark, Schacht exuded a sense of confidence to the public and brought an end to the senseless hyperinflation which was spawned by war and nurtured by reparation demands. His solution could easily have gone the way of the old mark, but desperate Germans were clutching at straws. Two enemies to be overpowered: The black market and the emergency money floating around. For a short while there was a redemption period when 4.2 trillion inflated mark would bring $1 or 4.2 Rentenmark. The black market speculators were wiped out in one fell swoop. The Rentenmark was issued as a legal measure, but was not legal tender, and Rentenmark loans were distributed through the Reichsbank to give confidence to that institution.

Schacht became president of the Reichsbank, appointed for life on Dec. 22, 1923. He served until 1930, and again, from 1933 to 1939. He served with the German central bank into the Hitler era. A famous photograph showed Schacht walking at the side of Hitler. He was a conspirator in the plot to assassinate Hitler with a bomb.

Schacht was imprisoned by the Gestapo on July 23, 1944, was then held by the Allies for two years, and placed in 32 prison camps in that time. The Nuernberg tribunal sentenced him to eight years in 1946, but he was later acquitted and released Sept. 2, 1948. He wrote, "I was imprisoned for hating Hitler. After Hitler was dead I was imprisoned for helping him." Schacht died on June 4, 1970, in Munich.

Metal Notgeld

Metal tokens did not appear until 1916, issued by cities and private firms; also, they were used in prisoner of war camps and firms employing prisoners. Later, as shortages continued, metal gas tokens, streetcar tokens and encased and unencased postage stamps were used for money. While more than 40 firms have been reported as having struck metal pieces, the bulk of these were struck by L. Christian Lauer in Nuernberg.

In many cases, the reverse of the piece carried the value; the obverse carried the name of the town and coat of arms. Hence,it was required to only make a die for each new obverse and use a standard "house" die as the reverse. One must struggle with the classification of these pieces. The private issues and POW pieces are irrefutably tokens. But according to the American Numismatic Association definition of a coin: "Usually a piece of metal, marked with a device, issued by a governing authority and intended to be used as money," requires that the city-issued metal pieces, including streetcar metal pieces, be called coins, since they are issued by a governmental body.

Contracts calling for the purchase of metal notgeld were interesting; the sale was not by number of pieces but by weight, a certain number of kilograms. So size, metal and thickness of a planchet would help determine the number struck per kilogram. In cases where mintages are reported, they are more likely to have an odd number rather than a nice round number.

For the collector with patience and a magnifying glass that divides a millimeter into tenths, endless hours of pleasure can come by picking out varieties with die differences. A collection of metal notgeld from more than 600 places, totaling some 3,600 coins, is possible for the municipal issues; a similar number of private issues is feasible.

Forms Of Notgeld

One volume of Dr. Keller's work, titled *Notgeld besonderer Art,* was devoted to objects, other than paper or metal, which passed for money. Included were linen, silk, leather, wood , porcelain, coal, aluminum foil, cotton, playing cards, celluloid and gelatin. But more bizzare, and showing the economic tenor of the times, were paper notes denominated in products of constant value, such as wood, water, wheat, rye, sugar and electricity.

Less successful was the sham of the "gold mark," denominations based on the 4.2 mark to the dollar of 1914, which, despite the name, were not exchangeable for gold.

Ways To Collect

Even Dr.Keller, before all the notgeld was issued, said no one could collect it all.

Thus, the collector must define his parameters and work toward limited goals. As targets are achieved, the goals can be expanded. Among choices are collecting the notes from one state, perhaps Bavaria or Brandenburg. One note from each town would be a beginning. Another is by topics shown on notes: maps, ships, animals, sports, Christmas, windmills, musical instruments, weapons, trains or a theme, such as the plebiscite issues. An interesting display would be exammples of notes in denominations from one pfennig to 10 mark, showing as many values as possible.

The collector seeking just one note or metal piece from each issuing place will encounter little difficulty in the first 500 towns. The towns up to number 1,000 will be a bit slower, and after that the gains come slowly.

In this area, one is working to a goal of about 3,600 towns, both in the metal series and in paper. For this reason, early on the collector should set his collecting areas, and decided to collect municipal or private issues, from a single area or a particular theme.

Notgeld Literature

Literature from various countries, pricelists from early dealers, periodicals from clubs devoted to collecting notgeld and contemporary newspaper accounts could all contribute to exhibits of either metal or paper notgeld. Notgeld collectors have available to them today several segments of literature, each with its own individuality. More than 30 volumes were written by Dr. Keller. Some were revised several times, between 1920 and 1962.

His early catalogs began as installments in *Das Notgeld,* and once they were published as books, revisions appeared in the periodical. Reprint editions of his catalogs, some revised and supplemented by Albert Pick and Carl Siemsen, were published by Battenberg Publishers, Munich, in the 1970s.

Through the efforts of Hans Meyer, Manfred Mehl, Heinz Jansen and others, Berlin publisher Erich Proeh released a series of books which detailed the metal and paper issues, province by province. This series was supplemented by monthly publications, *Die Muenz,* and briefly for paper money collectors only, *Der Geldschein.* The publication effort was later sold to a firm in Braunschweig and the series stopped.

Beginning in 1982, Hartmut Schoenawa and Hans Meyer have published from Werlaburgdorf, Germany, paper notgeld books by areas, from notes of Brandenburg and Berlin (revised in 1985 and 1995); in 1983, Niedersachsen and Bremen (revised in 1984 and 1987); in 1984, Provinz Sachsen and Anhalt, (revised in 1988); in 1985, Mecklenburg and Pommern (revised in 1993); in 1986, Westfalen and Lippe; in 1987, Hessen and Pfalz; in 1991, Sachsen (revised in 1997); in 1990, Schneidemuehl and in 1999, Thueringen.

In 1987, Kai Lindman, Sassenburg, Germany, published *Katalog der Serienscheine, Spendenquittung und Bausteine 1918-1922;* a second edition was published in 1989, and a third edition in 2000. Mehl published *Deutsche Serienscheine von 1918-1922* in 1998, with illustrations in color.

More recent notgeld books published on a regional basis include *Baden,* by Guenter Rupertus, 1988; *Bayern*, in 1989, by Albert Pick; and *Westfalen,* in 1998, by Jochen Jos. Topp. For other nations issuing notgeld, there are catalogs from Czechoslovakia, Austria, Yugoslavia, France, Portugal, Spain, Hungary and Poland.

Since Novembesr 1986 there has been published in Regenstauf, Germany, *Der Geldscheinsammler,* edited by Dr. Alexander Persijn. It is published nine times a year, with many references to notgeld.

Valuations in each category in the town listings are estimated in five stages, most common to most scarce, by letters A, to $25; B, to $60; C, to $125; D, to $200; and E, $350 and more. The letter designation represents the most inexpensive note or coin in the best condition of any category.

EINLEITUNG

Eine Gesamtdarstellung des deutschen Notgeldes spiegelt sich nicht zuletzt in den Leistungen und Meinungen zweier Maenner - beim einen zur Zeit des Ausbruchs des 1. Weltkrieges, beim andern am Ende, als das Inferno der Hyperinflation erlosch.

Dr. Arnold Keller wurde am 31. Januar 1897 in Freiburg/Breisgau geboren. Im Jahr 1904 zog die Familie nach Frankfurt/Main, wo der junge Arnold die Schule besuchte. Einer seiner Lehrer auf dem Gymnasium war Dr. Carl Hahn, ein Bruder des Physikers Otto Hahn, der als Numismatiker seinen Schuelern gelegentlich Muenzen zeigte. "Waerend dieser Zeit sammelte die ganze Klasse Muenzen, aber ich war der einzige, der damit auch nach dem Abitur noch fortfuhr," erzaehlte Dr. Keller spaeter.

1915 begann das Studium an der Universitaet zu Muenchen, gefolgt von Leipzig und dann wieder Muenchen. Arnold Keller studiert Orientalistik und Numismatik und spaeter einnerte er sich "Mein Professor war der beruhmte Numismatiker Professor Heinrich Buchenau. Das Thema, das er mir fuer meine Dissertation gab, lautete "Der Muenzvertrag zwischen den rheinischen Kurfuersten und den Landgrafen von Hessen."

Dr. Keller begann mit dem Sammeln von Notgeld im Jahr 1914, als die ersten Scheine ausgegeben wurden. Spaeter gab er die Zeitschrift *Das Notgeld* heraus, eroeffnete eine Handlung fuer Muenzen und Papiergeld, und wurde schliesslich der verfasser zahlreicher Katalog. 1959 verkaufte er seine etwa 200,000 Scheine umfassende Sammlung - ausser deutschem Notgeld enthielt sie Papiergeld aus aller Welt - an die Deutsche Bundesbank in Frankfurt/M. Er starb in Berlin am 13 Dezember 1972.

Das erste deutsche Notgeld wurde am 31. Juli 1914 vom Buergerlichen Brauhaus GmbH in Bremen verausgabt. Die drei Werte zu 1, 2 und 2.5 Mark wurden auf dickem Papier hektographiert und trugen zwar eine Unterschrift, aber keine Kontrollziffern. Der Gesamtwert aller ausgegebenen Scheine betrug 100 Mark.

Dr. Keller teilte das zwischen 1914 und 1924 erschienene Notgeld in "Perioden" ein. Fuer jede dieser Perioden gibt es individuelle Kataloge.

Fuer den Mangel an Kleingeld waehrend des 1. Weltkrieges gibt es verschiedene Theorien. Die Besetzung anderer Laender erfordere angeblich einen zusaetzlichen Bedarf an Muenzen, sagen die einen-oder selbst das Skatspiel mit dem dafuer beiseite gelegten Kleingeld sei Schuld am Mangel, sagen die anderen.

Der wahrscheinlichere Grund ist, dass Muenzen aus Silver, Kupfer und Nickel von der Bevoelkerung gehortet wurden. Und wegen des Mangels an Arbesitskraeften und Material wurden in den staatlichen Muenzen auch weniger Geldstueck gepraegt. Einige groessere staedte horteten Muenzen fuer "unvorhergesehene Faelle."

Fuer fuenf Mark in Muenzen vergueteten Postbeamte 1917 5.30 Mark.

Nach 1916 bereits wurden keine Kupfermuenzen mehr gepraegt und zahlreiche Notgeldscheine zu ein und zwei Pfennig traten an ihre Stelle, besonders in Bayern. Viele kleine Geschaeftsleute schufen ihr eigenes Geld.

Von Dr. Keller stammt eine aufstellung der einzelnen charakteristischen Notgelderioden und ihre ausgaben:

Notgeld 1914: 452 Ausgebestellen mit insgesamt 5,500 Scheinen. Kleingeldscheine (Nennwerte unter eine Mark) 1916-1922: 3,658 Ausgabestellen, 36,000 scheine., Grossgeldscheine 1918-1921, Nennwerte 1 Mark bis 100 Mark: 579 Ausgabestellen, etwa 5,000 Scheine. Inflationsscheine 1922, Werte vorwiegend 100 Mark bis 1,000 Mark: rund 800 Ausgabestellen, etwa 4,000 Scheine. Inflationsscheine 1923: rund 6,000 ausgabestellen, 70,000 Scheine. Wertbestaendiges Notgeld 1923-19244: 562 Ausgabestellen mit 3,660 Scheinen. Kriegsgefangenenlagesrgeld: 600 Ausgabestellen, rund 3,000 Scheinen. KZ-Lagergeld 1935-1945: 20 Konzentrationslager, 90 Scheine. Notgeld 1945: 20 Ausgabestellen mit 150 Scheinen, und Notgeld 1947-1948: 270 Ausgabestellen mit etwa 1,000 Scheinen.

Die Deutsche Reichsbank gab von 1874 bis zum Ende der Inflation 141 Grundtypen von Banknoten heraus, dazu kommt noch eine sehr grosse Zahl von Abarten und Varianten. In den verschiedenen deutschen Kolonien wurden etwa 80 Typen von Noten verausgabt; von vielen davon existieren ebenfalls varianten. Um die Anzahl aller Ausgabestellen von Notgeld zu bestimmen, darf man natuerlich nicht die oben genannten Ausgabestellen zusammenzaehlen; die Zahlen ueberschneiden sich, da viele Orte waehrend mehrer Perioden Notgeld ausgaben.

Angeregt durch wachsenden Sammlerbedarf entstanden immer neue und oftmals unnoetige Notgeldausgaben. Es gab Auswuechse und dazu gehoerten: Verkaufspreise weit ueber dem Unternehmer veranstalteten Massenproduktionen - wie etwa die Serien von rund 40 Ortschaften im Kreis Pinneberg bei Hamburg, oder das von fuenf Kuenstlern geschaffene "Reutergeld" 70 mecklenburgischer Gemeinden mit Motiven aus den Werken Fritz Reuters.

Schliesslich gab es Ausgaben, die reiner Schwindel sind (Ebstorf-Soldatenrat, Fockbeck, Gefangenenlager Lichtenhorst und viele andere), und durch geschaeftstuechtige Unternehmer wurden sogar Scheine von nicht existerenden Orten (Stadt Neukirch, Knivsberg, Gaansager) hergestellt.

Vielfach wurde "Notgeld" von Gesellschaftgen und Vereinen in Form von Eintrittskarten, Spendenquittungen usw. ausgegeben. Erwaehnenswert ist auch, dass in nicht weniger als zehn Faellen Notgeld-Ausstellunen ihr eigenes "Ausstellungs-Notgeld" hatten - eine Praxis, die von Dr. Keller als eine "Parodie" auf das wirkliche Notgeld bezeichnet wurde.

Die modernen Sammler fragen nicht mehr danach, ob eine Ausgabe zwifelhaft oder betruegerisch war. Viele der Schwindelausgaben behoeren heute zu den Seltenheiten in einer Sammlung und alle die fraglichen Stuecke sind laengst in den Band "Serienscheine" der Keller-Kataloge aufgenommen.

Dr. Keller, der die Entwicklung des Notgeldes als Sammler, "Katalogverfasser und Haendler miterlebt hatte, reagierte allen Phantasieausgaben gegenueber untwillig. In der von ihm herausgegebenen Zeitschrift *Das Notgeld,* gab eine Spalte "SCHWARZE LISTE," in der er alle ihm bekannt gewordenen Missstaende anprangerte. Sammler, die betruegerisch operierten oder Haendlerrechnungen trotz Mahnung nicht bezahlkten, wurden namentlich genannt. Auch wenn oertliche Behoerden die Sammler uebervorteilten, konnten sie ihr Vergehen in der Schwarzen Liste nachlesen. Im Oktoberheft 1921 z. B. wirst Dr. Keller der Stadt Langenschwalbach vor, ihre 50-Pfennigscheine Zum doppelten Nennwert angeboten zu haben. Lindenberg/A. verkaufte seine Scheine mit einem Nennwert von 1.45 Mark fuer 3.45 Mark, oder Pyrmont wird zitiert 75-Pfennigscheine fuer fuenf Mark verkauft zu haben.

Frueher oder spaeter aber muessen alle Sammler von Notgeld, sei es Papier oder Metall, einsehen, dass eine "komplette" Sammlung nicht moeglich ist. Ein ausweg ist die Spezialisierung., Die Gesamtzahl aller Notgeldscheine, beginnend mit den Ausgaben vom August 1914, wird auf 163,000 geschaetzt. Davon hatte Dr. Keller in seiner Sammlung, die die groesste war, 109,860 Scheine.

Dr. Hjalmar Horace Greeley Schacht

Der Mann, der fuer die finanzielle Gesundung Deutschlands verantwortlich war, war Dr. Hjalmar Horce Greeley Schacht. Er wurde am 31. Januar 1877 in Tingleff (heute Daenemark) geboren. Seine Eltern, beide waren sie Deutsche, heirateten in New York City. Schacht wurde am 13. November 1923 zum Reichswaehrungskommissar ernannt und erhielt freie Hand in allen geld- und Kreditangelegenheiten.

Seine Aufgabe war es, der Inflation Einhalt zu gebieten. Am 20. November 1923 wurde der amtliche Kurs von 4.2 Billionen Mark - 1 Dollar festgelegt. Das hiess, dass man fuer einen Cent mehr Mark kaufen konnte, als de gesamten deutschen Schuldverschreibungen 1914 betragen hatten.

Zwischen der zunehmenden Inflation und der laut Versailler Vertgrag von Frankreich geforderten Reparationszahlung besteht eine Relation. Im April 1921 wurden dir Reparationskosten mit 33 Milliarden Mark veranschlaget. Mit der Nachricht vom Attentatauf Deutschlands Aussenminister Walter Rathenau sank die Mark am 24. June 1922 auf 300 per Dollar.

In Juli 1922, beim Faelligwerden der ersten Reparationszahlung, war das Verhaeltnis der Mark zum Dollar 500:1. Ende Oktober, bei faelligkeit der zweiten Reparationsrate, war das Mark-Doillar Verhaeltnis 4,500:1.

Im Januar 1923 besetzten die Allierten das Ruhrgebiet und die Mark stand 10,200:1 Dollar. Und im April 1923 begann die Hyperinflation.

Ende November 1923 erzielte der Dollar auf dem schwarzen Markt 12 Billionen Mark. Die Verlierer aber wurden die Spekulanten, die die Flamme der Inflation geschuert hatten - trotz der Mahnung Dr.Schachts, dass der offizielle Kurs mit 4.2 Billionen Mark - 1 Dollar festgestetzt worden war. Schacht schreibt in seinen Memoiren, dass im November 1923 theoretisch die alte Goldmark des Reiches, die papiermark und die Rentenmark im Umlauf waren.

Indem Dr.Schacht vier Prozent allen oeffentlichen Landes, einschliesslich der Reichsbahn, als Deckung fuer die neue Waehrungseinheit Rentenmark erklaert, gewann er damit das vertrauen der Bevoelkerung und beendete die sinnlose, durch den Krieg gezuechtete und die Reparationsforderungen gefuetterte Hyperinflation.

Seiner Loesung haette esleicht wie der alten Mark ergeben koennen, aber das verzweifelte Volk klammerte sich an jeden Strohhalm. Zwei Gegner galt es zu bewaeltigen den schwarzen Markt und das unlaufende Notgeld.

Es gab eine kurz anberaumte Frist, um jeweils 4.2 Billionen Inflationsmark gegen einen Dollar oder 4.2 Rentenmark einzutauschen - und die Spekulanten waren mit einem Schlage erledigt. Die Rentenmark wurde als gesetzliche Massnahme eingefuerhrt, war aber kein gesetzliches Zahlungsmittel. Die Reichsbank gab Rentenmarkanleiben aus, um das Vertrauen in diese Institution zu staerken.

Dr. Schacht wurde am 22. Dezember 1923 zum Reichsbankpraesidenten auf Lebenszeit ernannt. Er fuellte diesen Posten bis 1930 aus, und dann nochmals in den Hitlerjahren von 1933 bis 1939. Eine beruehmte Photographie Zeigt ihn an der Seite Hitlers. Er gehoertezur Grupe der Verschwoerer, die das Bombenattentat auf Hitler geplant hatten. Schacht wurde am 23. July 1944 von der Gestapo verhaftet und eingekerkert Nach Kriegsende hat er als Gefangener der Allierten nicht weniger als 32-mal das Gefaengnis gewechselt. Im Nuernberger prozess wurdeer zu acht Jahren Zuchthaus verurteilt, wurde aber spaeter freigesprochen und am 2. September 1948 entlassen. Er schrieb, "Ich wurde eingekerkert, weil ich Hitler hasste. Nach Hitlers Tod wurdeich eingesperrt, weil ich ihn unterstuetzthatt." Dr.Schacht starb am 4. Juni 1970 in Muenchen.

Hartnotgeld

Notmuenze wurden etwa von 1916 ab von oertlichen Behoerden und privaten Firmen ausgegeben; teilweise waren sie auch in Gefangenenlagern oder bei Firmen, die Gefangene beschaeftigten, in gebrauch.

Da der Kleingeldmangel nicht behoben werden konnte, wurden selbst Gasmuenzen und Strassenbahnfahrmarken und in zunehmendem Masse schliesslich auch Briefmarkengeld (Kapselmarken) verwendet.

Metallnotgeld wurde von rund 40 Firmen gepraegt, der weitaus groesste Teil aber durch die Firma L. Christian Lauer in Nuernberg.

Vielfach erschien auf der rueckseite einer Muenze der Wert, waehrend die Vorderseite, den Ortsnamen und evtl. das Ortswappen zeigt. Die Prasegenstalt erleicherte sich ihre Arbeit, indem sie fuer die Muenzen verschiedener Orte die gleichen rueckseiten beibehielt.

Beim Hartgeld ist eine korrekte Terminologie nicht immer einfach. Die privaten Ausgaben und die Stuecke der Gefangenenlager sind unwiderleglich Token oder Zeichen. Eine Muenze aber - nach der Definition der American Numismatic Association - ist ueblicherweise eine metallische, mit Merkzeichen versehene Praegung, die von einer amtsausuebenden Autoritaet ausgegeben und als Zahlungsmittel bestimmt wurde. Darunter fallen also alle von Ortsbehoerden ausgegebenen Stucke.

Interessant sind die Kaufvertraegefuer Metallnotgeld. Dem Kunden wurde nicht eine bestimmte Stuckahl, sondern das Gewicht berechinet. Metall, Durchmesser and Dicke, eines Schroeltings waren also bestimmend fuer die Anzahl von Auspraegungen pro Kilogramm. In Faellen, wo Praegeahlen ueberliefert sind, handelt es sich zumeist nicht um runde Zahlen.

Sammler mit viel Geduld und einem guten Vergroesserungsglas koennen Stunden des Vergnuegens daraus ziehen, Praegevarianten festzustellen.

Eine Hartnotgeldsamlung von ueber 3,000 Stuecken, ausgegeben von reichlich 600 Ortsbehoerden, is theoretisch moeglich, dazu kaemen noch etwa die gleiche Anzahl privater Ausgaben.

Arten Des Notgeldes

Einer der Kataloge von Dr. A. Keller traegt den Titel *Notgeld besonder Art.* Er behandelt Notgeld, das nicht aus Papier oder Metall, sondern anderen Materialien hergestellt ist.

Dazu gehoeren Leinen, Seide, Leder, Holz, Porzellan, Kohle, Aluminiumfolie, Baumwolle, Spielkarten, Zelluloid und Gelatine.

Noch ungewohnlicher und die wirtschaftlichen Probleme der Zeit widerspiegelnd, war das wertbestaendige Notgeld, das auf Sachwerte wie Holz, Wasser, Weizen, Roggen, Zucker usw. ausgestellt war.

Wenigererfolgreich war das auf "Goldmark" oder Dollars (1 Dollar = 4.2 Goldmark) lautende Scheingeld, das trotz seines Namens in Wirklichkeit nicht durch Gold gedeckt war.

Moeglichkeiten Des Sammelns

Noch waehrend das Notgeld verausgabt wurde, sagte Dr. Keller, dass keiner "alles" sammeln koenne. Daher ist es fuer den Sammler ratsam, sich ein bestimmt es Ziel zu stecken und daraufhin zu arbeiten. Ist es erreich, koennen neue Zielpunkie geschaffen werden.

Man hat die Wahl, etwa nach geographischen Gesichtspunkten zu sammeln und sich aufeinen Staat oder ein gebiet - wie Bayern oder Brandenburg - zu spezialisieren. Man koennte damit beginnen, zunaechst von jedem Ort einen Schein zu erlangen.

Eine andere Moeglichkeit ist das Sammeln von Motiven: Schiffe, Landkarten, Tiere, Sport, Weihnachten, Windmuehlen, Musikinstrumente, Waffen, Eisenbahnen und vieles andere - oder von Theme, wie etwa Abstimmungsaugaben.

Ein interessantes austellungsobjekt waere es beispielsweise, aus dem Bereich von 1 Pfennig bis 10 Mark so viele Wertstufen als nur irgend moeglich zu zeigen.

Der Sammler, der sich bemueht, von jedem ausgabeort nur einen Schein zu erlangen, wird bei den ersten 500 Orten kaum Schwierigkeiten haben. Nicht ganz so einfach sind die folgenden 500, und darueber hinaus ist ein Fortschreiten nur noch langsam moeglich.

Die Gesamtzahl der ausgabestellen, fuer Metall- und fuer Papiernotgeld, belaeuft sich auf etwa 3,600. Aus diesem Grunde sollte sich der Sammler schon fruehzeitig entscheiden, auf welche Gebiete er sich spezialisieren will: amtliche oder private Ausgaben, von einem begrenzten gebiet oder einem bestimmten thema.

Arten Des Notgeldes

Einer der Kataloge von Dr. A. Keller traegt den Titel Notgeld besonderer Art. Er behandelt Notgeld, das nicht aus Papier oder Metall, sondern anderen Materialien hergestellt ist.

Dazu gehoeren Leinen, Seide, Leder, Holz, Porzellan, Kohle, Aluminiumfolie, Baumwolle, Spielkarten, Zelluloid und Gelatine.

Noch ungewoehnlicher und die wirtschaftlichen Probleme der Zeit widerspiegelnd, war das wertbestaendige Notgeld, das asuf sacherte wie Holz, wasser, Weizen, Roggen, zucker usw. lausgestellt war.

Weniger erfolgreich war das asug “Goldmark” oder Dollars (1 Dollar = 4.2 Goldmark) lautende Scheingeld, das trotz seines Namens in Wirklichkeit nicht durch Gold gedeckt war.

Moeglichkeiten Den Sammelns

Noch waehrend das Notgeld verausgabt wurde, sagte Dr. Keller, das keiner “alles” sammeln koenne. Daher ist es fer den Sammler ratsam, sich ein bestimmtes Zeit zu stecken und daraufhin zu arbeiten. Ist es erreich, koennen neue Zielpunkte geschaffen werden.

Man hat die Wahl, etwa nach geographischen Gesichtspunkten u sammeln und sich auf einen Staat oder ein Gebiet - wie Bayern oder Brandenburg - zu spezialisieren. Man koennte damit beginnen, zunaechst von jedem Ort einen Schein zu erlangen.

Eine anderer Moeglichkeit ist das Sammeln von Mortiven: Schiffe, Landkarten, Tier, Sport, Weihnachten, Windmuehlen, Musikinstrumente, Waffen, Eisenbahnen und vieles andere - oder von Themen, wie etwa Abstimmungsausgaben.

Ein interessantes austellungsobjekt waere es beispielsweise, aus dem beweich von 1 Pfennig bis 10 Mark so viele Wertstufen als nur irgend moeglich zu zeigen.

Der Sammler, der sich bemueht, von jedem Ausgabeort nur einen Schein zu erlangen, wird bei den ersten 500 Orten kaum Schwierigkeiten haben. Nicht ganz so einfach sind die folgenden 500, und darueberhinaus ist ein Fortschreiten nur noch langsam moeglich.

Die Gesamtzahl der Ausgabestellen, fuer Metall- und fuer Papiernotgeld, belaeuft sich auf etwa 3,600. Aus diesem Grunde sollte sich der sammler schoen fruehzeitig entscheiden, auf welche Gebiete er sich sezialisieren will: lastliche oder rivat Ausgaben, von einem begrenzten Gebiet oder einem bestimmten Thema.

Notgeld-Literatur

Fachliteratur aus verschiedenen Laendern, alte Haendlerpreislisten, Veroeffentlichungen von Notgeldsammlervereinen, Zeitschriften, Kataloge und zeitgenoessische Zeitungsartikel - alles kann zur Gestaltung einer Notgeldausstellung beitgragen.

Modernen Notgeldsammlern stehteine reiche Auswahl von Literatur zur Verfuegung. Dr. Keller allein veroeffentlichte mehr als 30 Baende; einige davon wurden zwischen 1920 und 1962 mehrmals revidiert.

Seine ersten Kataloge erschienen in Fortsetzungen in der Zeitschrift *Das Notgeld* und nachdem sie in Buchform herausgekommen waren, wurden revisinen in der genannten Zeitschrift veroeffentliocht. Eine Neuauflage seiner Kataloge, zum Teil ergaentzt und bearbeitet durch Albert Pick und Carl Siemsen, erschien ab 1975 im Verlag Battenberg zu Muenchen.

Eine nach deutschen Staaten unterteilte Reihe von Spezialkatalogen fuer Metall- und Papiernotgeld - zusammengestellit von Hans Meyer, Manfred Mehl, Heinz Jansen und andernbrachte der Berliner verlag Erich Proeh heraus. Die Serie wurde durch die Monatszeitschrift Die Geldschein folgte. Die Verlagsprojekte wurden spaeter an eine Braunschweiger Firma verkauft und nicht weitergefuehrt.

Seit 1982 werden von Hartmut Schoenawa und Hans Meyer in Werlaburgdorf Gebiets-Notgeld kataloge herausgegeben. Bisher erschienen: Brandenburg und Berlin (1983); Neuauflage (1985); Niedersachsen und Bremen (1983); Provinz Sachsen und Anhalt (1984); Mecklenburg und Pommern (1985); und Westfalen und Lippe (1986).

Seit November 1986 wird im Verlag H. Gietl in Regenstauf eine neue, von Dr. Alexander Persijn betreute Zeitschrift *Der Geldscheinsammler* Publiziert. Sie erscheint neunmal im Jahre und enthaelt viele beitraegeueber Notgeld.

Waehrend diese Einfuehrung nur das Notgeld von Deutschland aus dem Zeitraum 1914-1947 behandelt, gab es Notgeld verschiedener Kategorien in mindestens 60 Laendern Zu den wichtigeren Nationnen, die Notgeld ausgaben und fuer das Kataloge erhaeltlich sind, gehoeren Oesterreich, Belgien, Frankreich, Portugal und Spanien.

Seltener, aber ebenfalls zahlreiche Ausgabeorte repraesentierend, ist Notgeld von Norwegen, Daenemark und franzoesischen Kolonien in Afrika und Indien.

Sammler muessen sich bewusst sein, dass es nicht einfach

ist, Scheine von Grenzgebieten zu klassifiezieren, deutschsprachige Scheine vom modernen Frankreich (Elsass und Lothringen), Daenemark (Schleswig-Holstein), Polen mit Scheinen in deutscher und russischer Sprache, und ausserdem Laender, die nach dem 1. Weltkrieg geschaffen wurden, wie die Tschechoslowakei und das neuerstandene Polen. Beispielsweise werden die Scheine gewisser Orte in Zu den Scheinen Oesterreichis gehoeren oestertliche Ausgaben aus der Zeit deutschen und franzoesischen Verzeichnissen erscheinen, und andere wieder in nur einem von beiden.

Oesterreich-Ungarns; zahlreich Orte in Oesterreich gaben 1920 ihr eigenes Notgeld heraus, manche davon in vielen Serien und asuflagen. Der Dentist Dr. Karl Jaksch katalogisierte die oesterreichischen Ausgaben von 1916-1921, seine letzie veroeffentlichung stammt aus dem Jahre 1976. In neuerer Zeit hat Rudolf Richter das werk fortgefuehrt, bisher erschienen drei Baende und wenigstens ein weiterer ist vorgesehen.

Eine grosse Anzahl belgischerher Orte gab Papiernotgeld und einige auch Hartnotgeld heraus. Ein Manuskript mit dem Titel *Le Papier-Monnaie Belge de Necessite de la Guerre 1914-1918* wurde von Wladimir Ouchkoff (Paris) und Dr. Arnold Keller unter dem Titel *Das belgische Kriegsnotgeld 1914-1918* in Deutsche uebersetzt.

Die Reihe Monnaies de Necessite Francaises behandelt das Metall- und Papiergeld Frankreichs. Unter den Baenden aus juengerer Zeit gibt es Monnaies de Necessite francaises vom inzwischien verstorbenen Victor Gadoury und Roland Elie, Hartgeld betreffend. Fuer das Metallgeld der franzoesischien Kolonien wurde von Gadoury und Georges Cousinis Monnaies Coloniales Francaises verfasst. J.R. De Mey und Bernard Poindessault schufen Repertoire des Billets des Necessite Francais 1914-1926.

In Frankreich kannte man nicht der unten Sammlerserien, wie es sie in Deutschland gab. Viele Stuecke zeigen Gebrauchsspuren, da sietatsachlich im Umlauf waren.

1973 vesrfasste der inzwischen vesrstorbene Carl Siemsen einen Katalog *Das Notgeld Portugals 1917-1922*. Mario S. de Almeide vesroeffentlichte 1980 ueber die Sociedade Portuguesa de Numismatica den Catalogo Geral de Cedulas de Portugal und fuehrte die Orte auf, die die "Cedulas" genannten Scheine mit niedrigen Nennwerten ausgaben.

Der Katalog *Local Paper Money issued during the Spanish Civil War* kann sich ruehmen, unmittelbar an der Quelle entstanden zu sein. Das Buch wurde vom verstorbenen Kenneth Graeber verfasst und von der International Bank Note Society herausgegeben. Der in Kansas geborene Graeber war 1939 Absolvent der University of Kansas und diente vom Juni 1937 bis Dezember 1938 als Ambulanzfahrer fuer die Spanische Republik.

Fuer andere Laender, die Notgeld ausgaben, gibt es Kataloge von der Tschechoslowakei, von Oesterreich, Jugoslavien, Frankreich, Portugal, Spanien, Ungarn und Polen.

Bewertungen der einzelnen Kategorien im Ortsverzeichnis wurden in fuenf Stufen vorgenommen von haeufig bis sehr seiten, und durch Buchstaben ausgedrueckt: A = bis $25 (DM 40); B = bis $60 (DM 100); C = bis $125 (DM 200); D = bis $200 (DM 320); D = bis $350 (DM 550); und darueber). Die kennzeichnenden Buchstaben repraesentieren jeweils den billigsten Schein, bezw. die billigste Muenze, in der besten Erhaltung innerhalb jeder Kategorie.

(Translation by Hermann Krause)

Gutschein der Gemeinde Desselbrunn
50 Heller
PRAGER EISEN-INDUSTRIE-GESELLSCHAFT
Kriegsgefangenen-Lager
KÖNIGSHOF
2 HELLER
DER I. KASSIER:
WERKE ALTHÜTTEN u. KÖNIGSHOF
GUT-SCHEIN
FÜNZIG PFENNIG
GÜLTIG BIS ZUM 1.SEPT 1921
50
GAUTURN-
DEUTSCHE MACHT UND KRAFT IST GEIST UND
BARGTEHE
DIESER SCHEIN IST GÜLTIG IN ALLEN BARGTEHEIDER
FÜNFZIG PFENNIG
50
De Bieckumer Raothues-Püt.
Gegen Einlieferung dieses GUT-SCHEINES zahlt die Stadt BECKUM
Mk
Monats nach erfolgter öffentlicher Aufforderung zur Einlösung vorgelegt wird.
10 HELLER
LAGERGELD
IM KRIEGSGEFANGENEN-LAGER
GRÖDIG
VERWALTUNGS-OFFICIER
LAGER COMMANDANT
Gutschein der St
1 Mark
75
Drum-soll-es-vorwärts-zieht-man-fein-
Am-Schwänzlein-es-zurück.
Casten & Sühling, Bremen.
Die heilige Fehme in Bruchhausen
Mark
Sankt Christof, hilf mit starker Hand, Hol über!
50 Pf.
CHAMBRE DE COMMERCE
1921
DJIBOUTI
50

Issuing Cities (by Countries)

ANGLO-EGYPTIAN SUDAN

❐ WADI SEIDNA 14D

ALGERIA

❐ ALGER 1A 6A 7B
❐ AFFREVILLE (Khemis Miliana) 1A
❐ AKFADOU-EN-KABYLIE 7B
❐ ALGER 1A 2A 6A 7A 11B 12A
❐ ATTAFS Les Alger 2A
❐ AUMALE (Sour al-Ghozlane) Medea 1A
❐ BENI-SAF Tlemcen 2A
❐ BERARD 7B
❐ BERROUAGHIA 1A
❐ BLIDA Alger 1A
❐ BOGHAIR (Ksar el Boukhari) 1A
❐ BONE (Annaba) Bone 6A 7A
❐ BORD J-BOU-ARRERIDJ Setif 1A 6A
❐ BORDJ-MENAIEL Tizi-Ouzou 1A
❐ BOU-THALEB (Bou-Thale) 7B
❐ BOUFARIK (Bufarik) Alger 1A
❐ BOUGIE (Bejaia) 1A 6A
❐ BOUGIE-SETIF Constantine 1A
❐ CARNOT Alger 2A
❐ CHERCHELL (Shershell Caesarea) Al-Asnam 1A
❐ CONSTANTINE (Cirta) Constantine 1A 6A 7A
❐ DJIDJELLI Constantine 7A
❐ DOUERA 1A
❐ DRA-EL-MIZAN 1A 7A
❐ FRENDA 1A
❐ GAR-ROUBAN 7E
❐ GUERGOUR 7A
❐ HERBILLON 7B 10A
❐ ISSERVILLE 1A
❐ KENADSA 1A 7A
❐ LAFAYETTE (Bougaa) 7A
❐ MAADID 2A
❐ MAAZIZ Algerie 2A
❐ MARC-EN-OSTREVENT 1A
❐ MARENGO (Hadjout) 1A
❐ MASCARA Mostaganem 1A
❐ MEDEA Medea 1A
❐ MEKTA-EL-HADID 1A
❐ MILIANA 1A

10 Centimes, Dra-el-Mizan, Algeria, 1B

❐ MOSTAGANEM 1A 2A 7B
❐ ORAN Oran 1A 6A 7B
❐ ORLEANVILLE (El Asnam) 2A 7B
❐ ORTAFFA 1A
❐ OUED-EL-ALLEUG 1A
❐ OUENZA 7B
❐ OUM-THEBOUL 1A
❐ PHILIPPEVILLE (Skikda, Constantine) 1A
❐ RAS-EL-MA (Bedeau) 1A 7A
❐ RELIZANE (Ighil, Izane) 1A
❐ SETIF Setif 7B
❐ SIDI-BEL-ABBES Oran 1A 2A 7B
❐ TEBESSA Annaba 7B
❐ TENES (El Bayadh) 2A
❐ VIALAR (Tissemsilt) 1A
❐ ZERALDA 7B

ANGOLA

❐ BENGUELA 1E 2D
❐ LOANDA 1E
❐ LUBANGO 1E
❐ MOCAMEDES 1E

ARGENTINA

❐ BUENOS AIRES 11D

10 Heller, Abtenau, Austria, 1A

10 Heller, Ach, Austria, 2A

50 Heller, Aggsbach, NÖ, 1A

ARMENIA

❒ SARDARABAD (Oktemberyan) Yerevan prov.		1A

AUSTRALIA

❒ CAMP SEVEN INT. CAMP (Camp Hay)		14E
❒ LOVEDAY (South Australia)		14E

AUSTRIA

❒ ABETZBERG	NO	1A	
❒ ABSTETTEN	NO	1A	
❒ ABTENAU Salzburg		1A	
❒ ACH	OO	2B	
❒ ADLWANG	OO	1A	
❒ ADMONT Steiermark		1A	
❒ AFLENZ Steiermark		1A	
❒ AGGSBACH	NO	1A	
❒ AICH Kaernten		1A	
❒ AICH	OO	1A	
❒ AICHKIRCHEN	OO	1A	
❒ AIGEN	OO	1A	
❒ AIGEN Salzburg		1A	
❒ AIGEN Steiermark		1A	
❒ AISTERSHEIM	OO	1A	
❒ AISTHOFEN	OO	1A	
❒ ALBERNDORF	OO	1A	
❒ ALKOVEN	OO	1A	
❒ ALLAND	NO	1A	
❒ ALLENTSTEIG	NO	1A	
❒ ALLERHEILIGEN	OO	1A	
❒ ALTA	OO	1A	
❒ ALTAIST	OO	1A	
❒ ALTENBERG	NO	1A	2A
❒ ALTENBURG	OO	1A	
❒ ALTENFELDEN	OO	1A	
❒ ALTENMARKT Steiermark		1A	
❒ ALTENMARKT IM PONGAU Salzburg		1A	
❒ ALTENMARKT/TRIESTING	NO	1A	
❒ ALTENMARKT/YSPER	NO	1A	
❒ ALTHEIM	OO	1A	
❒ ALTLENGBACH	NO	1A	
❒ ALTMUENSTER	OO	1A	
❒ ALTSCHWENDT	OO	1A	
❒ AMPFLWANG	OO	1A	
❒ AMSTETTEN	NO	1A	2A
❒ ANDORF	OO	1A	
❒ ANDRICHSFURT	OO	1A	
❒ ANGERSBERG	OO	1A	
❒ ANIF Salzburg		1A	
❒ ANNABERG	NO	1A	
❒ ANSFELDEN	OO	1A	
❒ ANTHERING Salzburg		1A	
❒ ANTIESENHOFEN	OO	1A	
❒ ANZBACH	NO	1A	
❒ ARBING	OO	1A	
❒ ARDAGGER	NO	1A	
❒ ARTSTETTEN	NO	1A	
❒ ASCHACH	OO	1A	3A
❒ ASCHACH Steyr		1A	
❒ ASCHACH/DONAU	OO	1A	3A

50 Heller, Aistersheim, OÖ, 1A

50 Heller, Allentsteig, N.Ö., 1A

50 Heller, Allerheiligen, OÖ, 1A

20 Heller, Altenberg, 1A

10 Heller, Altenburg/Perg, Austria, 1A

50 Heller, Altenmarkt/Triesting, 1A

10 Heller, Ampflwang, OÖ, 1A

50 Heller, Anif (Salzburg), 1A

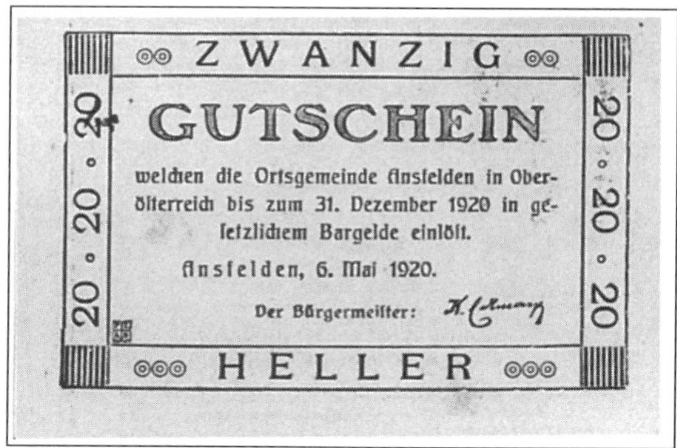

20 Heller, Ansfelden, OÖ, 1A

50 Heller, Arbing, OÖ, 1A

❐ ASCHBACH	NO	1A			
❐ ASCHBACH	OO	1A			
❐ ASPACH	OO	1A			
❐ ASPERHOFEN	NO	1A			
❐ ASTEN	OO	1A			
❐ ATTERSEE	OO	1A			
❐ ATTNANG-PUCHHEIM	OO	1A			
❐ ATZBACH	OO	1A			
❐ ATZENBRUGG	NO	1A			
❐ AU BEIM HOHEN STEG	OO	1A			
❐ AU/DONAU	OO	1A			
❐ AUBERG	OO	1A			
❐ AUEN Kaernten		1A			
❐ AUMUEHL Steiermark		9A			
❐ AURACH	OO	1A			
❐ AUROLZMUENSTER	OO	1A			
❐ AUSSEE, BAD Steiermark		1A			
❐ AUSSERFELDEN Salzburg		2D	5A		
❐ BACH Steiermark		1A			
❐ BACHMANNING	OO	1A			
❐ BADEN	NO	1A			
❐ BAUMGARTEN	OO	1A			
❐ BAUMGARTENBERG	OO	1A			
❐ BECHYNE Bohemia		1A			
❐ BEHAMBERG	NO	2A			
❐ BERG	OO	1A			
❐ BERGHEIM Salzburg		1A			
❐ BERNDORF	NO	1A	2C	3A	5A
❐ BERNHARDSLEITEN	OO	1A			
❐ BIBERBACH	NO	1A			
❐ BIECHLACH	OO	1A			
❐ BIEDERMANNSDORF	NO	1A			
❐ BISCHOFSHOFEN Salzburg		1A	2A		
❐ BISCHOFSTETTEN	NO	1A			
❐ BISTRITZ 3					
❐ BLINDENMARKT	NO	1A	2A		
❐ BLUMAU Steiermark		1A			
❐ BODENDORF	OO	1A			
❐ BOEHEIMKIRCHEN	NO	1A			
❐ BOEHMERWALD Ulrichsberg		1A			
❐ BOEHMISCHKRUT	NO	2A			
❐ BOLDOGESSZONY (Boldogaszony) Frauenkirchen		3A			
❐ BRANDENBERG Tirol		1A			
❐ BRANDSTATT	OO	1A			
❐ BRAUNAU/INN	OO	1A	2B	3A	4A
❐ BREGENZ Vorarlberg		1A	3A	9C	
❐ BREITENBERG	OO	1A			
❐ BRIXLEGG Tirol		1A			
❐ BROMBERG	NO	1A			
❐ BRUCK	OO	1A	9A		
❐ BRUCK IM PINZGAU Salzburg		1A			
❐ BRUCK-WAASEN	OO	1A			
❐ BRUCK/MUR Steiermark		9A			

20 Heller, Aschach/Donau, OÖ, 1A

20 Heller, Au/Donau, Austria, 1A

80 Heller, Bad Aussee (Steiermark), 1A

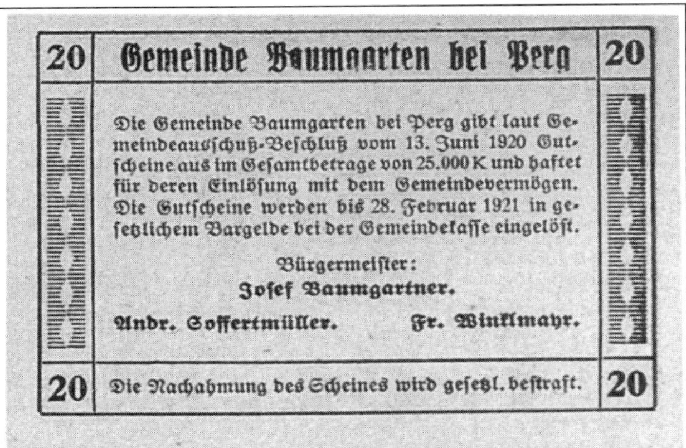

20 Heller, Baumgarten, OÖ, 1A

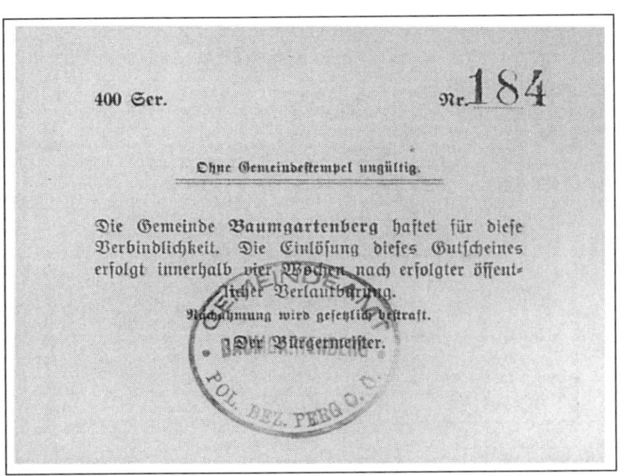

30 Heller, Baumgartenberg, OÖ, 1A

50 Heller, Bergheim (Salzburg), 1A

❒ BRUNN AM GEBIRGE	NO	1A	3A	9A
❒ BRUNNENTHAL	OO	1A		
❒ BUBENDORF, MEILERSDORF, WOLFSBACH	NO	1A		
❒ BUCH	NO	1A		
❒ BUCH	OO	1A		
❒ BUCHKIRCHEN	OO	1A		
❒ BURGKIRCHEN	OO	1A		
❒ BURGSCHLEINITZ	NO	1A		
❒ CHRISTOFEN	NO	1A	2A	
❒ CHRIZANOW Galicie		1A		
❒ DESSELBRUNN	OO	1A		
❒ DEUTSCH-ALTENBURG	NO	2A		
❒ DEUTSCH-GABEL Boehemen		3A		
❒ DEUTSCH-WAGRAM	NO	1A		
❒ DEUTSCHLANDSBERG Steiermark		9A		
❒ DIERSBACH	OO	1A		
❒ DIETERSDORF	OO	1A		
❒ DIETRICHSCHLAG BEI AIGEN	OO	1A		
❒ DIETRICHSCHLAIG BEI LEONFELDEN	OO	1A		
❒ DIMBACH	OO	1A		
❒ DIRNWAGRAM	OO	1A		
❒ DOERFL Steiermark		1A		
❒ DONAUTALNOTGELD	OO	1A		
❒ DONAWITZ Steiermark		2A	9A	
❒ DOPPL	OO	1A		

60 Heller, Bruck/Pinzgau, Austria, 1A

❒ DORF AN DER PRAM	OO	1A		
❒ DORFGASTEIN Salzburg		1A		
❒ DORNBACH	NO	1A		
❒ DRASENDORF Kaernten		1A		
❒ DROSENDORF	NO	1A		
❒ DROSS	NO	1A		
❒ DUERNAU	OO	1A		
❒ DUERNSTEIN	NO	1A		
❒ DUNKELSTEIN	NO	1A		
❒ DURRACH	OO	1A		
❒ EBELSBERG	OO	1A	2D	
❒ EBEN	OO	1A		
❒ EBEN/ACHENSEE Tirol		1A		
❒ EBENSEE	OO	1A	9A	
❒ EBENTHAL Kaernten		1A		
❒ EBERGASSING	NO	9A		
❒ EBERSCHWANG	OO	1A		
❒ EBERSTALLZELL	OO	1A		
❒ EBREICHSDORF	NO	1A	2E	
❒ ECHTSBERG	OO	1A		
❒ ECKARTSAU	NO	1A		
❒ EDLBACH	OO	1A		
❒ EDT BEI LAMBACH	OO	1A		
❒ EFERDING	OO	1A	2A	
❒ EGELSEE	NO	1A		
❒ EGG Kaernten		1A		
❒ EGGELSBERG	OO	1A		
❒ EGGENBERG	OO	1A		
❒ EGGENBURG	NO	1 A	2A	
❒ EGGENDORF	OO	1A		
❒ EGGERDING	OO	1A		
❒ EIBISWALD Steiermark		9A		
❒ EICHBERG Steiermark		1A		
❒ EIDENBERG	OO	1A		
❒ EISENERZ Steiermark		1A	2C	5A
❒ EIZENDORF	OO	1A		
❒ EMMERSDORF	NO	1A		
❒ ENGELHARTSZELL	OO	1A		
❒ ENGERWITZDORF	OO	1A		
❒ ENNS	OO	1A	2A	
❒ ENNSDORF	NO	1A		
❒ ENZESFELD	NO	1A		
❒ ERDMANNSDORF	OO	1A		
❒ ERLA	NO	1A		
❒ ERLACH	OO	1A		
❒ ERLAUF IM NIBELUNGENGAU	NO	1A	2A	
❒ ERNSTBRUNN	NO	1A		
❒ ERNSTHOFEN	NO	1A		
❒ ERTL	NO	2A		
❒ ESCHENAU	OO	1A		
❒ ESCHENAU IM PINZGAU Salzburg		1A		
❒ ESTERNBERG	OO	1A		
❒ ETSDORF	NO	1A		

50 Heller, Desselbrunn, OÖ, 1A

❒ ETZERSTETTEN	NO	2A			
❒ EURATSFELD	NO	1A			
❒ FAHRAFELD	NO	2A			
❒ FELDBACH Steiermark		3D			
❒ FELDEGG	OO	1A			
❒ FELDKIRCH Voralberg		2A	9A		
❒ FELDKIRCHEN/DONAU	OO	1A			
❒ FELDKIRCHEN/INN	OO	1A			
❒ FELDMUEHL	OO	1A			
❒ FERSCHNITZ	NO	1A	2A		
❒ FEUERSBRUNN	NO	1A			
❒ FIEBERBRUNN Tirol		1A			
❒ FIRSCHING	OO	1A			
❒ FISCHAMEND	NO	1A			
❒ FISCHLHAM	OO	1A			
❒ FOHNSDORF Steiermark		2C	9A		
❒ FORSTHUB	OO	1A			
❒ FRAHAM	OO	1A			
❒ FRANKENBURG	OO	1A	2A		
❒ FRANKENFELS	NO	1A			
❒ FRANKENMARKT	OO	1A			
❒ FRANZBERG	OO	1A			
❒ FREILAND	NO	2C			
❒ FREINBERG	OO	1A			
❒ FREISTADT	OO	1A	2A	3A	4B
❒ FURTH	NO	1A			
❒ FUSCHL/SEE Salzburg		1A			
❒ GAFLENZ	OO	1A			
❒ GAINFARN	NO	1A			
❒ GALLNEUKIRCHEN	OO	1A			
❒ GALLSPACH	OO	1A			
❒ GAMING	NO	1A			
❒ GAMPERN	OO	1A			
❒ GARS/KAMP	NO	1A	2A		
❒ GARSTEN	OO	1A			
❒ GASPOLTSHOFEN	OO	1A			
❒ GASTEIN, BAD Salzburg		1A			
❒ GEBOLTSKIRCHEN	OO	1A			
❒ GEIERSBERG	OO	1A			
❒ GEINBERG	OO	1A			
❒ GEORGENDORF Kaernten		1A			
❒ GERERSDORF	NO	1A			
❒ GERETSBERG	OO	1A			
❒ GERHARDSBRUNN	OO	1A			
❒ GEROTTEN UN POETZLES	NO	1A			
❒ GFOEHL	NO	1A			
❒ GIESSHUEBL	NO	1A			
❒ GILGENBERG	OO	1A			
❒ GLEINACH Kaernten		1A			
❒ GLEINK	OO	1A			
❒ GLOGGNITZ	NO	9A			
❒ GMUEND	NO	1A	3A		

❒ GMUDEN	OO	1A				
❒ GNEIXENDORF	NO	1A				
❒ GOELLERSDORF	NO	2A	3A			
❒ GOESING AM WAGRAM	NO	2A				
❒ GOESTLING	NO	1A	2C			
❒ GOETTWEIG	NO	2A				
❒ GOETZENDORF	NO	1A				
❒ GOISER	NO	1A				
❒ GOLDWOERTH	OO	1A				
❒ GOLLING Salzburg		1A				
❒ GONTENBACH		1A				
❒ GOSAU	OO	1A				
❒ GOSSAM	NO	1A				
❒ GOTTSDORF	NO	2A				
❒ GRAFENSCHLAG	NO	1A				
❒ GRAMASTETTEN	OO	2A				
❒ GRATKORN Steiermark		2C				
❒ GRAZ Steiermark		1A	2B	3A	9A	11B

Types of Emergency Money

Type	**Reference #**
Municipal paper	1
Private paper	2
POW paper	3
POW official metal	4
POW private metal	5
Municipal metal	6
Private metal	7
Gas tokens	8
Food; beer; konsumverein	9
Naval; military; kantine	10
Encased, unencased stamps	11
Streetcar tokens	12
Porcelain	13
World War II issues	14
Concentration, Civilian internment camps	15

Rarity grades: A, to $25; B, to $60; C, to $125; D, to $200; and E, $350

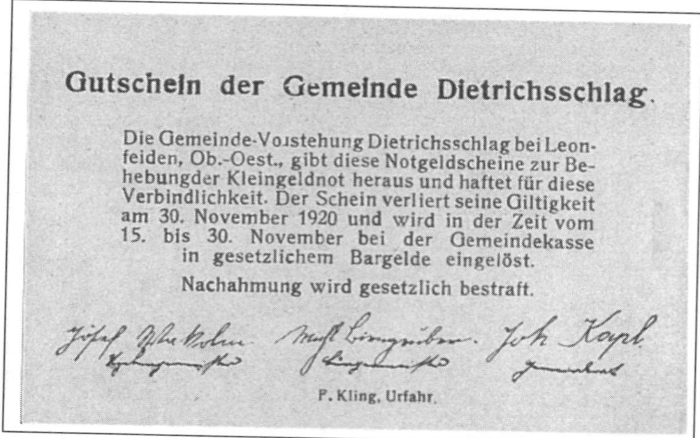

50 Heller, Dietrichschlag/L, OO, 1A

30 Heller, Ebelsberg, OO, 1A

10 Heller, Ebelsberg, Austria, 1A

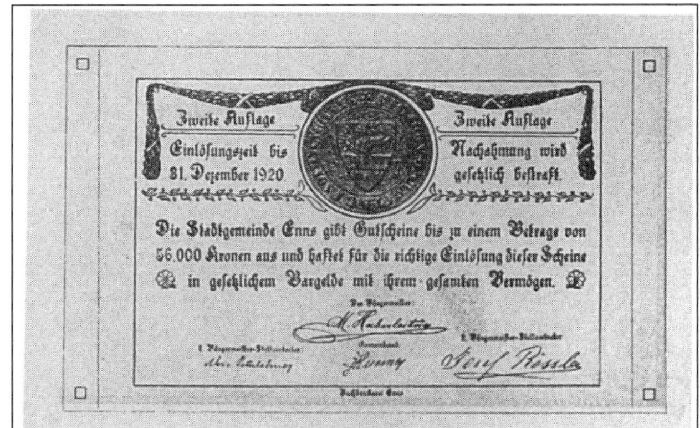

50 Heller, Enns, OÖ, 1A

20 Heller, Enzesfeld, NO, 1A

50 Heller, Erla/No, Austria, 1A

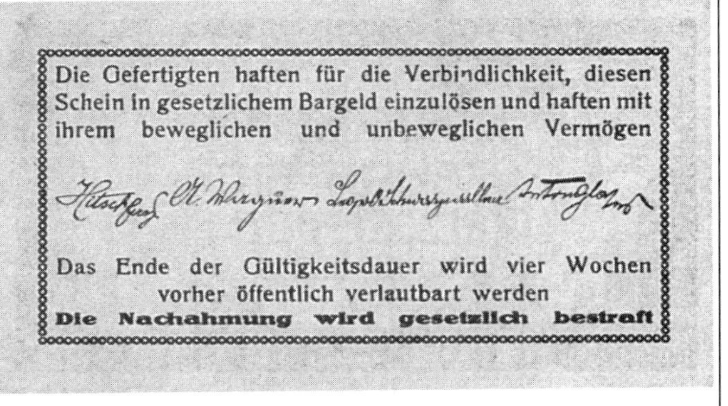

10 Heller, Fahrafeld, NO, 1A

50 Heller, Fischamend, NO, 1A

❐ GREIFENSTEIN	NO	1A			
❐ GREIN	OO	1A	2A		
❐ GRESTEN	NO	1A	2A		
❐ GRIES	OO	1A			
❐ GRIES AM BRENNER Tirol		1A			
❐ GRIESKIRCHEN	OO	1A	2A		
❐ GROEBMING Steiermark		1A			
❐ GROEDIG Salzburg		1A	2A	3A	4B
❐ GROESSGSTOETTEN	OO	1A			
❐ GROSS-PERTHOLZ	NO	1A			
❐ GROSS-SIEGHARTS	NO	1A	2C		
❐ GROSSARL Salzburg		1A			
❐ GROSSHOFEN	NO	1A			
❐ GROSSRAMING	OO	1A			
❐ GRUBEN Steiermark		1A			
❐ GRUENAU	NO	1A			
❐ GRUENAU	OO	1A			
❐ GRUENBACH AM SCHNEEBERG	NO	1A			
❐ GRUENBACH BEI FREISTADT	OO	1A			
❐ GRUENBURG	OO	1A			
❐ GSCHWANDT	OO	1A			
❐ GSTOETTENAU	OO	1A			
❐ GUGU	OO	1A			
❐ GUMPOLDSKIRCHEN	NO	1A			
❐ GUNSKIRCHEN	OO	1A			
❐ GUNTRAMSDORF	NO	1A			
❐ GURGL Tirol		1A			
❐ GURTEN	OO	1A			
❐ GUSSWERK Steiermark		9A			
❐ GUTAU	OO	1A			
❐ GUTENBRUN-HEILIGENKREUZ	NO	1A			
❐ GUTENBRUNN	NO	1A			

❐ HAAG AM HAUSRUCK	OO	1A			
❐ HAAG DORF	NO	1A	2A		
❐ HACKELBRUNN	OO	1A			
❐ HADERSDORF AM KAMP	NO	1A	2A		
❐ HADERSDORF-WEIDLINGAU	NO	1A			
❐ HADERSFELD (Wood)	NO	1A			
❐ HADRES	NO	1A	2A		
❐ HAGENBERG	OO	1A			
❐ HAGFELD	OO	1A			
❐ HAIBACH	OO	1A			
❐ HAIBACH BEI ASCHACH Salzburg		1A			
❐ HAID BEI MATUHAUSEN (1957)	OO	1A	15D		
❐ HAIDERSHOFEN	NO	1A			
❐ HAIGERMOOS	OO	1A			
❐ HAINBURG	NO	1A	2A	9A	
❐ HAINDORF	NO	1A			
❐ HAINFELD	NO	2A			
❐ HAIZENDORF	NO	1A			
❐ HALL IN TIROL Tirol		1A	2A		
❐ HALL, BAD	OO	1A			
❐ HALLEIN Salzburg		1A	2A		
❐ HALLMONSOEDT	OO	1A			
❐ HALLSTATT	OO	1A			
❐ HALLWANG Salzburg		1A			
❐ HANDENBERG	OO	1A			
❐ HARBACH Kaernten		1A			
❐ HARGELSBERG	OO	1A			
❐ HART	OO	1A			
❐ HART BEI AMSTETTEN		3A			
❐ HARTHEIM	OO	2A			
❐ HARTKIRCHEN	OO	1A			
❐ HASELBACH Steiermark		1A			
❐ HASLACH	OO	1A			
❐ HAUNOLDSTEIN	NO	1A			

50 Heller, Freinberg, OÖ, 1A

50 Heller, Freinberg, Austria, 1A

10 Heller, Geboltskirchen, OÖ, 1A

20 Heller, Gerotten, NÖ, 1A

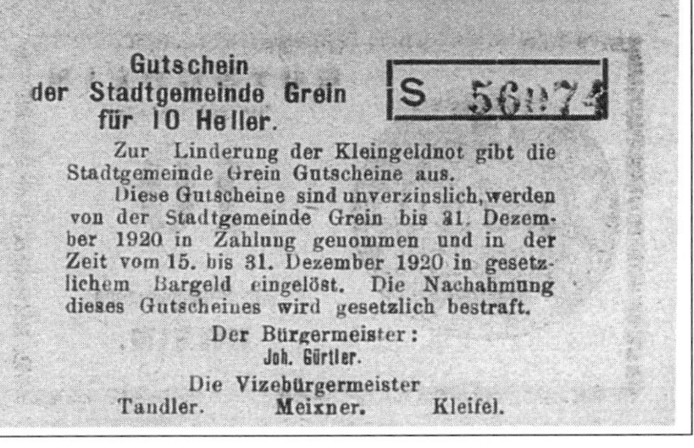

10 Heller, Grein, OO, 1A

75 Heller, Gries/Brenner, Tirol, 1A

❒ HAUSMANING	OO	1A	
❒ HAUSMENING	NO	1A	
❒ HEBETSBERG	OO	1A	
❒ HEFT Kaernten		2E	
❒ HEIDENREICHSTEIN	NO	1A	
❒ HEILIGENBERG	OO	1A	
❒ HEILIGENKREUZ Steiermark		1A	
❒ HEINRICHSGRUEN		3A	
❒ HELFENBERG	OO	1A	
❒ HELPFAU-UTTENDORF	OO	1A	
❒ HENHART	OO	1A	
❒ HERZOGENBURG	NO	1A	2A
❒ HERZOGSDORF	OO	1A	
❒ HIMBERG	NO	1A	
❒ HINTENBERG	OO	1A	
❒ HINTERBERG	OO	1A	
❒ HINTERBRUEHL	NO	1A	
❒ HINTERSTODER	OO	1A	
❒ HINZENBACH	OO	1A	
❒ HIRSCHBACH	OO	1A	
❒ HIRSCHENWIES Kaernten		1A	
❒ HOCHBURG-ACH	OO	1A	
❒ HOCHFILZEN Tirol		1A	
❒ HOCHHUB	OO	1A	
❒ HOERSCHING	OO	1A	2A
❒ HOFGASTEIN Salzburg		1A	
❒ HOFKIRCHEN AN DER TRATTNACH	OO	1A	
❒ HOFKIRCHEN IM MUEHLKREIS	OO	1A	
❒ HOFKIRCHEN IM TRAUNKREIS	OO	1A	
❒ HOHENBERG	NO	1A	
❒ HOHENZELL	OO	1A	
❒ HOLLENBURG A.D. DONAU	NO	1B	2C
❒ HOLLENSTEIN	NO	1A	
❒ HOLZHAUSEN	OO	1A	
❒ HORASITZ		3B	
❒ HORN	NO	1A	2B
❒ HUERM	NO	2A	
❒ HUETTAU Salzburg		1A	
❒ HUETTE	OO	1A	
❒ HUNDSBERG	OO	1A	
❒ HUNDSDORF	OO	1A	

❒ HURTH		3A		
❒ IGLS Tirol		1A		
❒ IMBACH	NO	1A		
❒ IMST Tirol		1A		
❒ INNERNSTEIN	OO	2A		
❒ INNERSCHWANDT	OO	1A		
❒ INNSBRUCK Tirol		1A	2A	9A
❒ INZERSDORF	OO	1A		
❒ IRDNING Steiermark		2A		
❒ IRMSTOETTEN	OO	1A		
❒ IRRINGSTORF	OO	1A		
❒ ISCHL, BAD	OO	1A		
❒ JENBACH Tirol		14E		
❒ JEUTENDORF	NO	1A		
❒ JOCHBERG Tirol		1A		
❒ JOSEFSTADT		3A		
❒ JUDENAU	NO	1A		
❒ JUDENBURG Steiermark		9B		
❒ JUDENDORF	OO	1A		
❒ JUDENDORF-LEOBEN Steiermark		9A		
❒ JUNGBUNZLAU		3A		
❒ KAERNTNER (Landes Kasse) Kaernten	1A	14D		
❒ KAISERSTEINBRUCH	NO	14B		
❒ KALLHAM	OO	1A		
❒ KALTENLEUTGEBEN	NO	9B		
❒ KALVARIENBERG Steiermark		1A		
❒ KAMMERN AM KAMP	NO	1A		
❒ KAPELLEN	NO	2A		
❒ KAPFENBERG Steiermark		9A		
❒ KARLINGBERG	OO	1A		
❒ KARNTNER LANDESKASSE Karnten		1A		
❒ KASTEN	NO	1A		
❒ KATZENAU BEI LINZ	OO	3A	4A	
❒ KEFERNMARKT	OO	1A		
❒ KEMATEN	NO	1A		
❒ KEMATEN AN DER KREMS	OO	1A		
❒ KEMATEN BEI WELS	OO	1A		
❒ KEMMELBACH	NO	1A	2A	
❒ KETTENREITH	NO	1A		
❒ KILB	NO	1A	2A	
❒ KINDBERG Steiermark		14D		
❒ KIRCHBERG AM WAGRAM	NO	1A		
❒ KIRCHBERG AM WALDE	NO	1A		
❒ KIRCHBERG AN DER DONAU	OO	1A		
❒ KIRCHBERG AN DER PIELACH	NO	1A		
❒ KIRCHBERG BEI LINZ	OO	1A		
❒ KIRCHDORF AM INN	OO	1A		
❒ KIRCHDORF AN DER KREMS	OO	1A		
❒ KIRCHHAM	OO	1A		
❒ KIRCHHEIM	OO	1A		
❒ KIRCHSCHLAG	NO	1A		
❒ KITZBUEHEL Tirol		1A		
❒ KLAFFER	OO	1A		
❒ KLAGENFURT Kaernten		1A	2A	9A

10 Heller, Groedig, POW, 3B

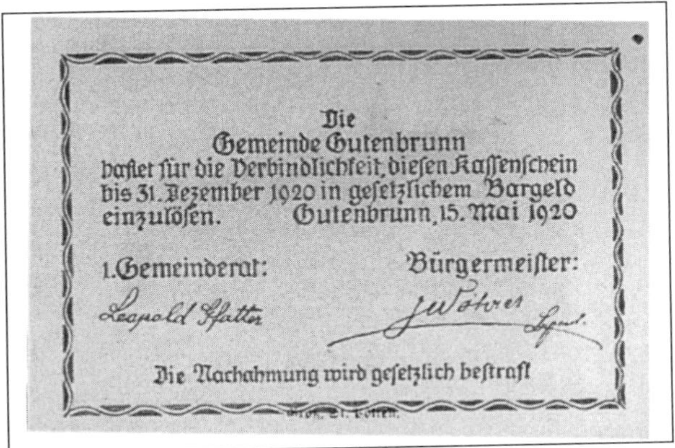

20 Heller, Gutenbrunn, NO, 1A

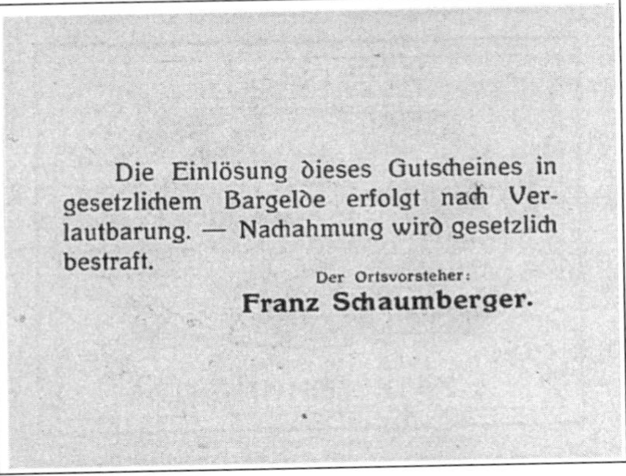

50 Heller, Hackelbrunn, OÖ, 1A

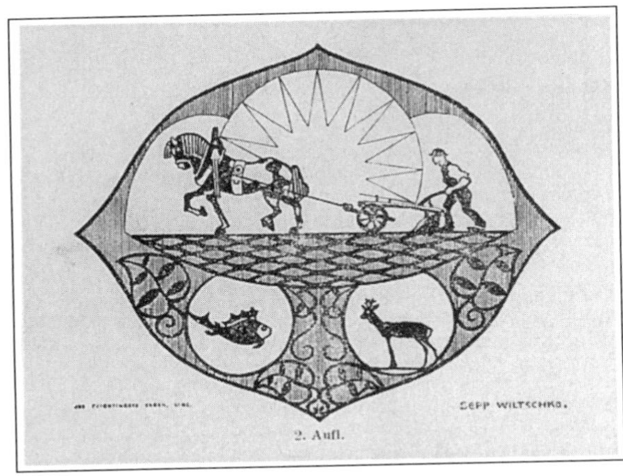

50 Heller, Hagenberg, OÖ, 1A

70 Heller, Hall/Tirol, 1A

20 Heller, Hallein (Salzburg), 1A

❒ KLAMM	OO	1A				
❒ KLAUS	OO	1A				
❒ KLAUSEN-LEOPOLDSDORF	NO	1A				
❒ KLEINMUENCHEN	OO	1A	3A	4A	5B	9A
❒ KLEINPOECHLARN	NO	1A				
❒ KLEINZELL IM MUEHLKREIS	OO	1A				
❒ KLINGET	OO	1A				
❒ KLOSTERNEUBURG	NO	2A				
❒ KNITTELFELD Steiermark		3D				
❒ KOEFLACH Steiermark		2D				
❒ KOENIGSAU	OO	1A				
❒ KOENIGSHOF Boehmen		3A				
❒ KOENIGSWIESEN	OO	1A				
❒ KOESSEN Tirol		1A				
❒ KOESTENDORF Salzburg		1A				
❒ KOGEL Steiermark		1A				
❒ KOLLMITZBERG	NO	1A				
❒ KOPFING	OO	1A				
❒ KORNEUBURG	NO	1A	9A			
❒ KREISBACH	NO	1A				
❒ KREITH Tirol		1A				
❒ KREMS	NO	1A	2A	9A		
❒ KREMSMUENSTER	OO	1A	2A			
❒ KREUZBERG Steiermark		1A				
❒ KREUZEN	OO	1A				
❒ KRIEGLACH Steiermark		1A	2A			
❒ KRIFT	OO	1A				
❒ KRIMML Salzburg		1A				
❒ KRITZENDORF	NO	1A				
❒ KROISBACH	OO	1A				
❒ KRONSTORF	OO	1A				
❒ KRUMAU AM KAMP	NO	1A				
❒ KRUMMNUSSBAUM	NO	1A				
❒ KUEHNRING	NO	1A				
❒ KUERNBERG		1A	2D			
❒ LAA A.D. THAYA	NO	1A				

❒ LAAKIRCHEN	OO	1A			
❒ LAIMBACH	OO	2A			
❒ LAMBACH	OO	1A			
❒ LAMBRECHTEN	OO	1A			
❒ LAMPRECHTSHAUSEN Salzburg		1A			
❒ LANDEGG	NO	3A			
❒ LANDERDING	OO	1A			
❒ LANDFRIEDSTETTEN	NO	1A			
❒ LANGACKER	OO	1A			
❒ LANGENLOIS	NO	1A			
❒ LANGENSTEIN	OO	1A			
❒ LANNACH Steiermark		2A			
❒ LANZENBERG	OO	1A			
❒ LASBERG	OO	1A			
❒ LAUSA BEI LOSENSTEIN	OO	1A			
❒ LAXENBURG	NO	1A			
❒ LEBING	OO	1A			
❒ LEIBEN	OO	1A			
❒ LEMBACH	OO	1A			
❒ LEND Salzburg		1A			
❒ LENGAU	OO	1A			
❒ LEOBERSDORF	NO	9A			
❒ LEONDING	OO	1A			
❒ LEONFELDEN	OO	1A	2A		
❒ LEOPOLDSCHLAG	OO	1A			
❒ LICHTENAU	OO	1A			
❒ LICHTENBERG	OO	1A			
❒ LICHTENBUCH	OO	1A			
❒ LICHTENEGG	OO	1A			
❒ LIEBENUA	OO	1A			
❒ LILIENFELD	NO	1A	2A	9A	
❒ LINDABRUNN	NO	1A			
❒ LINDBERG Kaernten		1A			
❒ LINZ	OO	1A	2A	3A	9A
❒ LITSCHAU	NO	1A			
❒ LOCHEN	OO	1A			

50 Heller, Hallstadt, OO, 1A

20 Heller, Hallwang (Salzburg), 1A

❒ LOFER Salzburg		1A		
❒ LOHNSBURG	OO	1A		
❒ LOICH	NO	1A		
❒ LOOSDORF	NO	1A		
❒ LORCH	OO	1A		
❒ LORENZENBERG Kaernten		1A		
❒ LOSENSTEIN	OO	1A		
❒ LOSENSTEINLEITHEN	OO	1A		
❒ LUCKA	OO	1A		
❒ LUFTENBERG	OO	1A		
❒ LUGHOF	OO	1A		
❒ LUNZ AM SEE	NO	1A		
❒ MAISHOFEN Salzburg		1A		
❒ MAISSAU	NO	1A		
❒ MANGLBURG	OO	1A		
❒ MANHARTSBERG	NO	1A		
❒ MANK	NO	1A		
❒ MANNERSDORF	NO	1A		
❒ MANNING	OO	1A		
❒ MARBACH	NO	1A		
❒ MARCHEGG	NO	1A		
❒ MARCHTRENK	OO	1A	3A	4A
❒ MARIA LAAB		1A		
❒ MARIALAACH	NO	1A		
❒ MARIA LAAH	OO	1A		
❒ MARIA LANZENDORF	NO	1A		
❒ MARIA SCHMOLLN	OO	1A		
❒ MARIA TAFERL	NO	1A	2A	
❒ MARIA-ENZERSDORF	NO	1A		
❒ MARIAZELL Steiermark		1A	2A	
❒ MARSBACH	OO	1A		
❒ MARTINSBERG	NO	1A		
❒ MATTIGHOFEN	OO	1A	2A	
❒ MATTSEE Salzburg		1A		
❒ MATZLEINSDORF	NO	1A		
❒ MAUER-OEHLING	NO	1A		
❒ MAUERKIRCHEN	OO	1A	9A	
❒ MAUTERN	NO	1A		
❒ MAUTHAUSEN	OO	1A	3A	14A
❒ MAXGLAN Salzburg		1A		
❒ MEDEROESTERREICH Land		1A		
❒ MEGGENHOFEN	OO	1A		
❒ MEHRNBACH	OO	1A		
❒ MEILERSDORF	NO	1A		
❒ MELK	NO	1A	2A	
❒ METTERSDORF Kaernten		1A		
❒ METTMACH	OO	1A		
❒ MICHAELNBACH	OO	1A		
❒ MICHELDORF	OO	1A		
❒ MILEVSKA		1A		
❒ MILOWITZ		3A		
❒ MINING	OO	1A		
❒ MISTELBACH	NO	1A	3A	
❒ MISTLBERG	OO	1A		
❒ MITTELBERG	NO	1A		
❒ MITTELBNERG Vorarlberg		14A		
❒ MITTENDORF		3A		
❒ MITTER-ARNSDORF	NO	1A		
❒ MITTERBACH	NO	1A	2A	
❒ MITTERHAUSLEITEN	NO	1A		
❒ MITTERNDORF Steiermark		1A	3B	
❒ MITTERSILL Salzburg		1A		
❒ MOEDLING	NO	1A	2A	9A
❒ MOERSCHWANG	OO	1A		
❒ MOLLN	OO	1A		
❒ MONDSEE	OO	1A		
❒ MOOS Kaernten		1A		
❒ MOOSBACH	OO	1A		
❒ MOOSDORF	OO	1A		
❒ MORZG Salzburg		1A		
❒ MUEHLHEIM	OO	1A		
❒ MUEHLING	OO	3A	4A	5B
❒ MUENCHHAUSEN		2A		
❒ MUENSTER Tirol		1A		
❒ MUENZBACH	OO	1A		
❒ MUENZKIRCHEN	OO	1A		
❒ MUERZZUSCHLAG Steiermark		1A	2B	9A

Types of Emergency Money

Type	Reference #
Municipal paper	1
Private paper	2
POW paper	3
POW official metal	4
POW private metal	5
Municipal metal	6
Private metal	7
Gas tokens	8
Food; beer; konsumverein	9
Naval; military; kantine	10
Encased, unencased stamps	11
Streetcar tokens	12
Porcelain	13
World War II issues	14
Concentration, Civilian internment camps	15

Rarity grades: A, to $25; B, to $60; C, to $125; D, to $200; and E, $350

20 Heller, Oberndorf/Ebene, NO, 1A

20 Heller, Herzogenburg, NO, 1A

20 Heller, Herzogenburg, NO, 1A

30 Heller, Hinzenbach, OO, 1A

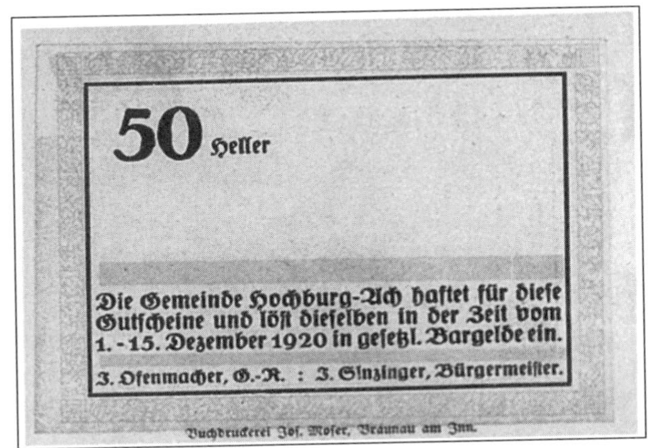

50 Heller, Hochburg/Ach, 1A

90 Heller, Hochfilzen, 1A

50 Heller, Hundsberg, OO, 1A

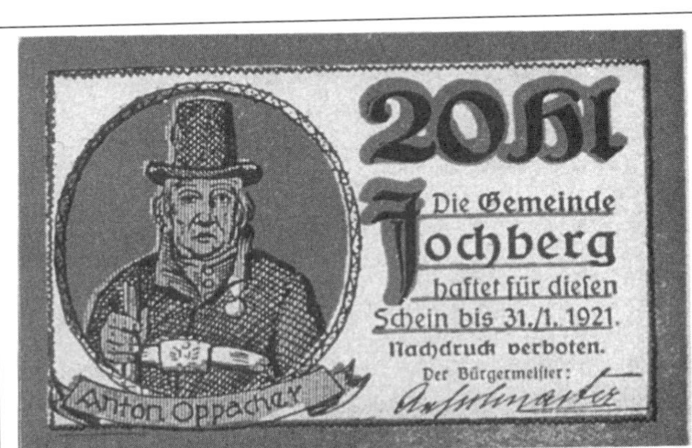

20 Heller, Jochberg, Tirol, 1A

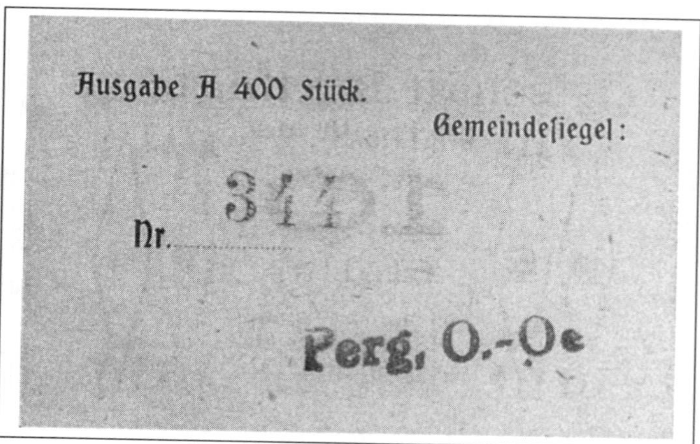

10 Heller, Karlingberg, OÖ, 1A

❒ MUNDERFING	OO	1A	2D
❒ MURAU Steiermark		1A	
❒ MUTTERS Tirol		1A	
❒ NAARN	OO	1A	
❒ NATTERNBACH	OO	1A	
❒ NEUBERG Steiermark		2E	
❒ NEUFELDEN	OO	1A	2A
❒ NEUHAUS	NO	1A	
❒ NEUHOF	OO	1A	
❒ NEUHOFEN AN DER KREMS	OO	2A	
❒ NEUHOFEN AN DER YBBS	NO	1A	
❒ NEUHOFEN IM INNKREIS	OO	1A	
❒ NEUKEMATEN	OO	1A	
❒ NEUKIRCHEN AM OSTRONG	NO	2A	
❒ NEUKIRCHEN AM WLADE	OO	1A	
❒ NEUKIRCHEN AN DER ENKNACH	OO	1A	
❒ NEUKIRCHEN BEI LAMBACH	OO	1A	
❒ NEUKIRCHEN/VOECKLA	OO	1A	
❒ NEULENGBACH	NO	1A	
❒ NEUMARKT Salzburg		1A	
❒ NEUMARKT Steiermark		1A	
❒ NEUMARKT AN DER YBBS	NO	1A	
❒ NEUMARKT IM HAUSRUCKKREIS	OO	1A	
❒ NEUMARKT IM MUEHLKREIS	OO	1A	
❒ NEUNKIRCHEN	NO	9A	
❒ NEUSTADT Schlesien		6A	
❒ NEUSTADTL A.D. DONAU	NO	1A	
❒ NEUSTIFT	OO	1A	
❒ NEUSTIFT IM STUBAL Tirol		1A	
❒ NEUSTIFT-INNERMANZING	NO	1A	
❒ NICKLASDORF	NO	1A	
❒ NIEDERLEIS	NO	1A	
❒ NIEDERNEUKIRCHEN	OO	1A	
❒ NIEDEROESTERREICH Land		1A	
❒ NIEDERTHALHEIM	OO	1A	
❒ NIEDERWALDKIRCHEN	OO	1A	
❒ NOECHLING	NO	1A	2A
❒ NUSSBACH IM KREMSTAL	OO	1A	
❒ NUSSDORF AM ATTERSEE	OO	1A	
❒ NUSSDORF AN DER TRAISEN	NO	1A	
❒ NUSSENDORF-ARTSTETTEN	NO	1A	
❒ OBERACHMANN	OO	1A	
❒ OBERALM Steiermark		1A	
❒ OBERESTERREICH Land		1A	
❒ OBER-GRAFENDORF	NO	1A	9D
❒ OBERHOLLABRUNN	NO	1A	3B
❒ OBERKAPPEL	OO	1A	
❒ OBERNBERG AM BRENNER Tirol		1A	
❒ OBERNBERG AM INN	OO	1A	2A
❒ OBERNDORF (St. Johann) Tirol			1A
❒ OBERNDORF A.D. EBENE	NO	2A	
❒ OBERNDORF AN DER SALZACH Salzburg			1A
❒ OBERNDORF, REDLHAM (& SCHLATT)	OO	1A	
❒ OBERNEUKIRCHEN	OO	1A	
❒ OBERSCHADEN	OO	1A	

10 Die Not ist groß, die Hilfe weit, Hilf dir selbst, du wirst befreit. 10

Notgeld
der Marktgemeinde Kirchberg a. Wgr.

Obige Gemeinde gibt Kassenscheine im Gesamtgetrage von 50.000 K aus. Dieselben sind unverzinslich, werden von der Gemeinde bis 31. Dezember 1920, in Zahlung genommen und in der Zeit vom 1. bis 31. Dezember 1920 eingelöst. Die Nachahmung wird gesetzlich bestraft.

10 Heller, Kirchberg/Wagram, NÖ, 1A

10 Heller, Klosterneuburg, NO, 1A

2 Heller, Koenigshof, Austria, POW 3B

10 Heller, Korneuburg, Austria, 1A

10 Heller, Kreuzen, Austria, 1A

50 Heller, Kuehnring, Austria, 1A

50 Heller, Laa/Thaya, Austria, 1A

❐ OBERSCHLIERBACH OO 1A
❐ OBERTRUM Salzburg 1A
❐ OBERVORMARKT OO 1A
❐ OBERWEISSENBACH (und Bernhardschlag) OO 1A
❐ OBERWOELBLING NO 1A
❐ OBERWOLFERN OO 1A
❐ OBLADIS Tirol 2A
❐ OBRITZBERG NO 1A
❐ OCKERT NO 1A
❐ OEBLARN IM ENNSTALE Steiermark 1A
❐ OED NO 1A
❐ OEHLING NO 1A
❐ OEPPING OO 1A
❐ OESTERREICH OB DER ENNS OO 2A
❐ OFFENHAUSEN OO 1A 2A
❐ OFTERING OO 1A
❐ OHLSTORF OO 1A
❐ OLLERSBACH NO 1A
❐ ORT IM INNKREIS OO 1A
❐ ORTMANN NO 5D
❐ OSSARN NO 1A
❐ OSTERMIETHING OO 1A
❐ OSTERNACH OO 2A
❐ OSTSTEIERMARK 2A
❐ OTTENSCHLAG NO 1A
❐ OTTENSHEIM OO 1A 2D
❐ OTTNANG OO 1A
❐ PABNEUKIRCHEN OO 1A
❐ PALTING-PERWANG OO 1A
❐ PARZ OO 1A
❐ PASCHING OO 1A
❐ PATTIGHAM OO 1A
❐ PAUDORF NO 1A
❐ PAYERBACH NO 1A
❐ PECKING OO 1A
❐ PENKING OO 1A
❐ PENNEWANG OO 1A
❐ PERCHTOLDSDORF NO 1A 2A
❐ PERG OO 1A 2A
❐ PERGKIRCHEN OO 1A
❐ PERK OO 2A
❐ PERNAU OO 1A
❐ PERNERSDORF NO 2A
❐ PERSENBEUG NO 1A
❐ PETERSKIRCHEN OO 1A
❐ PETRONELL NO 1A
❐ PETTENBACH OO 1A 2A
❐ PETZENKIRCHEN NO 1A
❐ PEUERBACH OO 1A 2A
❐ PFARRKIRCHEN BEI BAD HALL OO 1A
❐ PFARRKIRCHEN IM MUEHLKREIS OO 1A
❐ PFARRWERFEN Salzburg 1A
❐ PIBERBACH OO 1A
❐ PICHL BEI WELS OO 1A
❐ PICHL BEI WINDISCHGARSTEN OO 1A
❐ PIERBACH OO 1A
❐ PINSDORF OO 1A
❐ PIRCHHORN OO 1A
❐ PISCHELSDORF OO 1A
❐ PITZENBERG OO 1A
❐ PLAN 3A
❐ PLOCHWALD OO 1A
❐ POECHLARN NO 1A
❐ POEGGSTALL NO 2A
❐ POELFING-BRUNN Steiermark 9A
❐ POENDORF OO 1A
❐ POETTING OO 1A
❐ POTTENBRUNN NO 1A 2A
❐ POTTENDORF NO 1A 9A
❐ POTTENSTEIN NO 1A 2A 9A
❐ POXRUCK OO 1A
❐ POYSDORF NO 1A
❐ PRAEGARTEN OO 1A
❐ PRAM OO 1A
❐ PRAMBACHKIRCHEN OO 1A
❐ PRAMBERG OO 1A
❐ PRAMET OO 1A
❐ PREINSBACH NO 1A
❐ PREMING OO 1A
❐ PRERAU-WIEN NO 2A
❐ PRESSBAUM NO 1A
❐ PROTZTRUM OO 1A
❐ PUCHBERG AM SCHNEEBERG NO 1A
❐ PUCHBERG BEI WELS OO 1A
❐ PUCHBERG IM MACHLAND OO 1A
❐ PUCHENAU OO 1A
❐ PUCHKIRCHEN AM TRATTBERG OO 1A
❐ PUCKING OO 1A
❐ PUEHRET OO 1A
❐ PUERBACH NO 1A
❐ PUERNSTEIN OO 1A
❐ PUERSTLING OO 1A
❐ PUPPING OO 1A 14
❐ PURGSTALL NO 1A 2A
❐ PURKERSDORF NO 1A
❐ PUTZLEINSDORF OO 1A
❐ RAAB OO 1A
❐ RAABS NO 1A
❐ RABENSBURG NO 1A
❐ RABENSTEIN NO 1A 2A

20 Heller, Langenlois, Austria, 1A

20 Heller, Lasberg, Austria, 1A

❒ RABENTAL	OO	1A	
❒ RADLBERG	NO	1A	
❒ RADSTADT Salzburg		1A	
❒ RAFFINGS	NO	1A	
❒ RAIN Kaernten		1A	
❒ RAINBACH	OO	1A	
❒ RAINBERG	OO	1A	
❒ RAIPOLTENBACH	NO	1A	9A
❒ RANDEGG	NO	1A	
❒ RANNARIEDL A.D. DONAU	OO	1A	
❒ RANSHOFEN	OO	1A	
❒ RASTENFELD	NO	1A	
❒ RATTENBERG Tirol		1A	
❒ RATZERSDORF	NO	1A	
❒ RAURIS Salzburg		1A	
❒ RAXENDORF	NO	2A	
❒ REGAU	OO	1A	
❒ REHBERG	NO	1A	
❒ REICHENBERG Boehmen		3A	
❒ REICHENTAL IM MUEHLKREIS	OO	1A	
❒ REICHERSBERG AM INN	OO	1A	
❒ REICHERSDORF	NO	2D	
❒ REICHRAMING	OO	1A	
❒ REID BEI MAUTHAUSEN	OO	1A	
❒ REID BEI TRAUNKREIS	OO	1A	
❒ REIFENSTEIN/CILLI Steiermark		3A	

20 Heller, Leonding, Austria, 1A

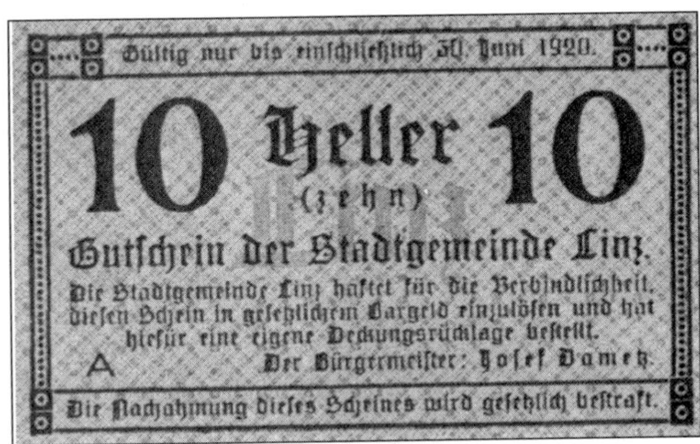

10 Heller, Linz, Austria, 1A

❒ REISGARN	NO	2A		
❒ REITERSCHLAG Kaernten		1A		
❒ REITH Tirol		1A		
❒ RETZ	NO	1A		
❒ RIED bei Mauthausen	OO	1A		
❒ RIED bei Traunkreis	OO	1A		
❒ RIED IM INNKREIS	OO	1A		
❒ RIEDAU	OO	1A		
❒ RIEDENBURG Salzburg		1A		
❒ RINDLBERG	OO	1A		
❒ RODAUN	NO	1A		
❒ ROHRBACH	OO	1A	2A	
❒ ROITHAM	OO	1A		
❒ ROSEGG Steiermark		1A		
❒ ROSENBURG	NO	1A	2D	
❒ ROSSATZ IN DER WACHAU	NO	1A		
❒ ROTHEN	OO	1A		
❒ ROTHENBACHL	OO	1A		
❒ ROTTENBACH	OO	1A		
❒ ROTTENMANN Steiermark		1A		
❒ RUEHRING	OO	1A		
❒ RUESTORF	OO	1A		
❒ RUPPERSTHAL	NO	1A		
❒ RUPRECHTSHOFEN	OO	1A		
❒ RUTE Kaernten		1A		
❒ RUTZENHAM	OO	1A		
❒ SAALBACH Salzburg		2A		
❒ SAALFELDEN Salzburg		1A		
❒ SAEUSENSTEIN	NO	1A		
❒ SALZBURG (Salzburg) Land and Stadt		1A	2A	9A
❒ SANDL	OO	1A		
❒ SANKT	OO	1A		
❒ SANKT AEGIDI 00		1A		
❒ SANKT AEGYD/NEUWALD	NO	1A		
❒ SANKT AGATHA	OO	1A		
❒ SANKT FLORIAN 00 1		2A		
❒ SANKT FLORIAN Steiermark		1A		
❒ SANKT FLORIAN/INN	OO	1A		
❒ SANKT GALLEN Steiermark		1A	9C	
❒ SANKT GEORGEN UND TOLLETT	OO	1A		
❒ SANKT GEORGEN/ATTERGAU	OO	1A	2A	
❒ SANKT GEORGEN/GUSEN	OO	1A		
❒ SANKT GEORGEN/LEYS	NO	1A		
❒ SANKT GEORGEN/REITH	NO	1A		
❒ SANKT GEORGEN/WALD	OO	1A		
❒ SANKT GEORGEN/YBBSFELDE	NO	1A		
❒ SANKT GILGEN Salzburg		1A		
❒ SANKT GOTTHARD	OO	1A	2A	
❒ SANKT JOHANN Tirol		1A		
❒ SANKT JOHANN/ENGSTETTEN	NO	1A		
❒ SANKT JOHANN/PONGAU Salzburg		1A	2A	
❒ SANKT JOHANN/WALDE	OO	1A		
❒ SANKT JOHANN/WIMBERG	OO	1A		

99 Heller, Lofer (Salzburg), 1A

20 Heller, Marialaach, Austria, 1A

20 Heller, Melk/Donau, Austria, 1A

2 Korona, Mauthner, Hungary (Mauthausen Austria), 15A

20 Heller, Muenster/Tirol, Austria, 1A

10 Heller, Neumarkt/Hausruckreis 1A

10 Heller, Oberndorf, Salkzburg, 1A

20 Heller, Obertrum, 1A

30 Heller, Oberweissenbach, OO, 1A

50 Heller, Obritzberg, OO, 1A

20 Heller, Ockert, 1A

10 Heller, OED, 1A

10 Heller, Offenhaussen, 1A

30 Heller, Parz, OO, 1A

❒ SANKT KONRAD	OO	1A		
❒ SANKT LAU RENZ	OO	1A		
❒ SANKT LEONHARD BEI FREISTADT	OO	1A		
❒ SANKT LEONHARD/FORST UND				
❒ REPRECHTSHOFEN	NO	1A		
❒ SANKT LEONHARD/WALDE	NO	1A		
❒ SANKT LORENZE/MONDSEE	OO	1A		
❒ SANKT LORENZEN Kaernten		1A		
❒ SANKT MAGDALENA BEI LINZ	OO	1A		
❒ SANKT MARIEN	OO	1A		
❒ SANKT MARIENKIRCHEN AM HAUSRUCK	OO	1A		
❒ SANKT MARIENKIRCHEN BEI SCHAERDING	OO	1A		
❒ SANKT MARIENKIR CHEN/POLSENZ	OO	1A		
❒ SANKT MARTIN BEI LINZ	OO	1A		
❒ SANKT MARTIN BEI TRAUN	OO	9A		
❒ SANKT MARTIN IM INNKREIS	OO	1A		
❒ SANKT MARTIN IM MUEHLKREIS	OO	1A		
❒ SANKT MARTIN UND KARLSBACH	NO	1A		
❒ SANKT NIKOLA/DONAU	OO	1A		
❒ SANKT OSWALD	NO	1A	2A	
❒ SANKT OSWALD BEI FREISTADT	OO	1A		
❒ SANKT OSWALDE BEI HASLACH	OO	1A		
❒ SANKT PANKRAZ	OO	1A		
❒ SANKT PANTALEON	NO	1A		
❒ SANKT PANTALEON	OO	1A		
❒ SANKT PETER Kaernten		1A		
❒ SANKT PETER IN DER AU	NO	1A		
❒ SANKT PETER/HART	OO	1A		
❒ SANKT PETER/WIMBERG	OO	1A		
❒ SANKT POLTEN	NO	1A	2E	14C
❒ SANKT ROMAN	OO	1A		
❒ SANKT SEBASTIAN BEI MARIAZELL Steiermark				1A
❒ SANKT STEFAN AM WALD	OO	1A		
❒ SANKT THOMAS AM BLASENSTEIN	OO	1A		
❒ SANKT THOMAS BEI WAIZENKIRCHEN	OO	1A		
❒ SANKT ULRICH	OO	1A		
❒ SANKT VALENTIN	NO	1A		
❒ SANKT VEIT AN DER GOELSEN	NO	1A		
❒ SANKT VEIT/MUEHLKREIS	OO	1A		
❒ SANKT VEIT/PONGAU Salzburg		1A		
❒ SANKT VEIT/TRIESTING	NO	1A		
❒ SANKT WILLIBALD	OO	1A		
❒ SANKT WOLFGANG	OO	1A		
❒ SARLEINSBACH	OO	1A		
❒ SARMINGSTEIN IM STRUDENGAU	OO	2A		
❒ SATTLERN	OO	1A		
❒ SCHAERDING/INN	OO	1A		
❒ SCHALCHEN	OO	1A		
❒ SCHANZ	OO	1A		
❒ SCHARDENBERG	OO	1A		
❒ SCHARTEN	OO	1A		
❒ SCHATTLEITEN UND				

50 Heller, Perg, OÖ, 1A

10 Heller, Persenbeug/D, NO, 1A

SCHWEINSEGG	OO	1A	
❒ SCHEIBBS	NO	1A	
❒ SCHENKENFELDEN	OO	1A	
❒ SCHILDORN	OO	1A	
❒ SCHLAEGL	OO	1A	
❒ SCHLEISSHEIM	OO	1A	
❒ SCHLIERBACH	OO	1A	
❒ SCHNEEGATTERN	OO	2E	
❒ SCHNEUZLREIT		2A	
❒ SCHOENAU	NO	1A	
❒ SCHOENAU IM MUEHLKREIS	OO	1A	
❒ SCHOENAU-SCHALLERBACH	OO	1A	
❒ SCHOENAU/TRIESTING	NO	1A	
❒ SCHOENBERG	OO	1A	
❒ SCHOENBICHL	NO	1A	
❒ SCHOENBUEHEL/DONAU	NO	1A	
❒ SCHOERFLING AM ATTERSEE	OO	1A	
❒ SCHREMS	NO	1A	
❒ SCHULTERZUCKER	OO	1A	
❒ SCHWADORF	NO	2D	
❒ SCHWALLENBACH/DONAU	NO	1A	
❒ SCHWAND IM INNKREIS	OO	2A	
❒ SCHWANENSTADT	OO	1A	
❒ SCHWARZACH IM PONGAU Salzburg		1A	
❒ SCHWARZENAU	NO	1A	
❒ SCHWARZENBERG	OO	1A	
❒ SCHWARZENTHAL	OO	1A	
❒ SCHWARZGRAEBEN	OO	1A	
❒ SCHWAZ Tirol		1A	2C
❒ SCHWECHAT	NO	9A	
❒ SCHWERTBERG	OO	1A	
❒ SCHWOEDIAU	OO	1A	
❒ SEEGRABEN Steiermark		2D	
❒ SEEKIRCHEN Salzburg		1A	
❒ SEEWALCHEN AM ATTERSEE	OO	1A	
❒ SEITENSTETTEN	NO	1A	
❒ SELZTAL Steiermark		1A	9A
❒ SENFTENBACH	OO	1A	
❒ SENFTENBERG	NO	1A	
❒ SIEDING	OO	1A	
❒ SIERNING	OO	1A	
❒ SIEZENHEIM Salzburg		1A	
❒ SIGHARTING	OO	1A	
❒ SIGMUNDSHERBERG	NO	1A	3A
❒ SINDELBURG	NO	1A	
❒ SIPBACHZELL	OO	1A	
❒ SITTENDORF	NO	1A	
❒ SITZENBERG	NO	1A	
❒ SONNBERG	OO	1A	
❒ SONNBERG Salzburg		1A	
❒ SONNTAGSBERG	NO	1A	
❒ SPARBACH	NO	1A	
❒ SPITAL/PHYRN	OO	1A	2D
❒ SPITZ/DONAU	NO	1A	
❒ SPRATZERN	NO	3C	
❒ STADL-PAURA	OO	1A	
❒ STAINZ Steiermark		9A	
❒ STANDHARDT	OO	1A	
❒ STANZTHAL Kaernten		1A	
❒ STATTERSDORF	NO	1A	
❒ STEEGEN	OO	1A	
❒ STEFANSHART	NO	1A	

10 Heller, Peuerbach, OÖ, 1A

50 Heller, Pfarrkirchen, OO, 1A

20 Heller, Pischelsdorf, OO, 1A

50 Heller, Pöndorf, OO, 1A

10 Heller, Pottenbrunn, NO, 1A

❒ STEIN Kaernten 1A
❒ STEIN AN DER DONAU NO 1A
❒ STEINAKIRCHEN AM FORST NO 1A 2A
❒ STEINAWEG NO 1A
❒ STEINBACH AM ZIEHBERG OO 1A
❒ STEINBACH/STEYR OO 1A
❒ STEINBRUCK OO 1A
❒ STEINERKIRCHEN AN DER TRAUN OO 1A
❒ STEINERKIRCHEN/INNBACH OO 1A
❒ STEINHAUS BEI WELS OO 1A
❒ STEINKLAMM NO 2A 3A
❒ STEINKREUZ OO 1A
❒ STEINWALD OO 1A
❒ STEYR OO 1A 2A 3B
❒ STEYR-SELZTHAL ST. MICHAEL OO 9A
❒ STEYREGG OO 1A
❒ STEYREMUEHL OO 2C 9A
❒ STIFTUNG BEI LEONFELDEN OO 1A
❒ STOCKERAU NO 1A 9A
❒ STOESSING NO 1A 2A
❒ STOLNBERG OO 1A
❒ STRASS Kaernten 1A
❒ STRASS NO 1A
❒ STRASS OO 1A
❒ STRASSEN Steiermark 1A
❒ STRASSWALCHEN Salzburg 1A
❒ STRENGBERG NO 1A
❒ STRETWIESEN NO 2A
❒ STROHEIM OO 1A
❒ STRONSDORF NO 2A
❒ SUBEN OO 1A
❒ SUESSENBACH NO 2A
❒ TAFELBERG OO 1A
❒ TAISKIRCHEN OO 1A
❒ TARSDORF OO 1A
❒ TAUBENBRUNN OO 1A
❒ TAUFKIRCHEN/PRAM OO 1A
❒ TAUFKIRCHEN/TRATTNACH OO 1A
❒ TAUSENBLUM NO 1A
❒ TEICHWALD OO 1A
❒ TELFS Tirol 1A
❒ TERNBERG OO 1A
❒ TERNITZ NO 9A
❒ TESCHEN (Cieszyn, Decin, Tesin) Schlesien 1A 2B
❒ TEXING NO 1A
❒ THALGAU Salzburg 1A
❒ THALHEIM BEI WELS OO 1A
❒ THANN OO 1A
❒ THANSTETTEN OO 1A
❒ THERESIENFELD NO 1A
❒ THERESIENSTADT Boehmen 3A
❒ THOMASROITH OO 2D 9A
❒ TIEFGRABEN OO 1A
❒ TIMELKAM OO 1A
❒ TIROLER Landkasse 1A
❒ TRADIGIST NO 2A
❒ TRAGWEIN OO 1A
❒ TRAISEN NO 1A 3A
❒ TRAISKIRCHEN NO 1A
❒ TRAISMAUER NO 1A
❒ TRATTEN Kaernten 1A
❒ TRAUN OO 1A
❒ TRAUNKIRCHEN OO 1A
❒ TREBITSCH (Trebic) Moravia 2A
❒ TREUBACH OO 1A
❒ TUERNITZ NO 1A
❒ TULLN NO 1A
❒ TULLNERBACH NO 1A
❒ TUMELTSHAM OO 1A
❒ UFER OO 2A
❒ ULMERFELD NO 1A 2A
❒ ULRICHSBERG OO 1A
❒ UNGENACH OO 1A
❒ UNTER-LOIBEN NO 1A
❒ UNTER-RATZERSDORF NO 2A
❒ UNTER-SCHADEN OO 1A
❒ UNTER-THUMRITZ NO 2A
❒ UNTER-VORMARKT OO 1A
❒ UNTER-WEISSENBACH OO 1A
❒ UNTER-WEITERSDORF OO 1A
❒ UNTER-WOLFERN OO 1A
❒ UNTERACH OO 1A
❒ UNTERGAISBACH OO 1A

Puchberg am Schneeberg.

Von Wien in zirka zweistündiger Bahnfahrt erreichbar, breitet sich Puchberg am Fuße des Schneebergs aus, dessen Alpenpracht sich hier in vollem Glanze zeigt. Eine Folge der nahen, ozonreichen Hochwälder, Almen und Triften ist das erfrischende, belebende Klima. Nach allen Richtungen ziehen bequeme, gut markierte Promenadenwege auf ebenem und sanft ansteigendem Gelände. Die herrlichsten Landschaftsbilder bietet jedoch die Besteigung des Hochschneebergs. Wer aber die Mühen mehrstündigen Wanderns scheut, kann die Zahnradbahn benützen, welche in einstündiger Fahrt den Berg erklimmt.

50 Heller, Puchberg (Austria), 1A

20 Heller, Puernstein (Austria), 1A

❒ UNTERHART	OO	1A				
❒ UNTERWALD	OO	1A				
❒ UNZMARKT		9A				
❒ URFAHR	OO	1A	2A			
❒ UTZENAICH	OO	1A				
❒ VICHTENSTEIN	OO	1A				
❒ VIECHTWANG	OO	1A				
❒ VIEHBERG	OO	1A				
❒ VIEHDORF	NO	1A				
❒ VIEHOFEN	NO	1A				
❒ VILLACH Kaernten		2A	9A			
❒ VILLACH-TARVIS		9A				
❒ VITIS	NO	1A				
❒ VOECKLABRUCK	OO	1A				
❒ VOECKLAMARKT	OO	1A				
❒ VOESLAU	NO	1A	9A			
❒ VOITSBERG Steiermark		9A				
❒ VORCHDORF	OO	1A				
❒ VORDENBERG Steiermark		9A				
❒ VORDERSTODER	OO	1A				
❒ VORKLOSTER (Bregenz) Voralberg		9A				
❒ WAGENHAM	OO	1A				
❒ WAIDENDORF	OO	1A				
❒ WAIDHOFEN AN DER YBBS	NO	1A				
❒ WAIDHOFEN/THAYA	NO	1A				
❒ WAIZENKIRCHEN	OO	1A				
❒ WALD IM PINZGAU Salzburg		1A				
❒ WALD Steiermark		2D				
❒ WALDBURG	OO	1A				
❒ WALDHAUSEN	OO	1A				

10 Heller, Rabenstein, NO, Austria, 1A

❒ WALDING	OO	1A				
❒ WALDKIRCHEN AM WESEN	OO	1A				
❒ WALDNEUKIRCHEN	OO	1A				
❒ WALDZELL	OO	1A				
❒ WALLERN	OO	1A				
❒ WALLSEE	NO	1A				
❒ WAMPERSDORF	NO	1A				
❒ WANG	NO	1A				
❒ WARMING	OO	1A				
❒ WARTBERG/AIST	OO	1A				
❒ WARTBERG/KREMS	OO	1A				
❒ WASCHPOINT	OO	1A				
❒ WAXENBERG	OO	1A				
❒ WECHLING	NO	1A				
❒ WEGSCHEID BEI LINZ	OO					
(Camp Maurice L. Tyler)		15E				
❒ WEIBERN	OO	1A				
❒ WEIGETSCHLAG	OO	1A				
❒ WEILBACH	OO	1A				
❒ WEINBERG Steiermark		1A				
❒ WEINVIERTEL	OO	1A				
❒ WEINZIERL AM WALDE	NO	1A				
❒ WEINZIERL BEI PERG	OO	1A				
❒ WEINZIERL BEI WIESELBURG	NO	1A				
❒ WEISSENBACH Kaernten		1A				
❒ WEISSENBACH BEI MOEDLING	NO	1A				
❒ WEISSENBACH/TRIESTING	NO	1A				
❒ WEISSENKIRCHEN BEI FRANKENMARKT	OO	1A				
❒ WEISSENKIRCHEN IN DER WACHAU	NO	1A				
❒ WEISSENSTEIN/DRAU Kaernten		1A				
❒ WEISSKIRCHEN	OO	1A				
❒ WEISTRACH	NO	1A				
❒ WEITEN	NO	2A				
❒ WEITENEGG	NO	1A				
❒ WEITERSFELDEN	OO	1A				
❒ WEITRA	NO	1A				
❒ WELS	OO	1A	2A			
❒ WENDLING	OO	1A				
❒ WENG	OO	1A				
❒ WERFEN Salzburg		1A				
❒ WERNSTEIN	OO	1A				
❒ WEYER	OO	1A	2D			
❒ WICKENDORF	OO	1A				
❒ WIEN	NO	1A	2A	9A	11B	14B
❒ WIENER-NEUDORF	NO	1A				
❒ WIENER-NEUSTADT	NO	1A	3D	5D		
❒ WIESELBURG/ERLAUF	NO	1A	2A			
❒ WILHELMSBURG	NO	1A				

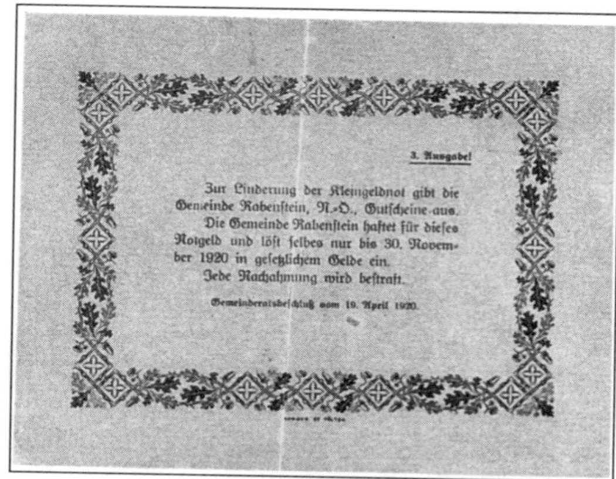

50 Heller, Rabenstein (Austria), NÖ, 1A

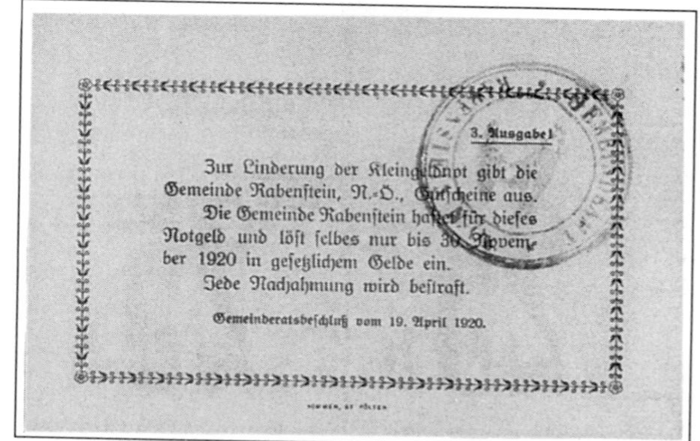

25 Heller, Rabenstein (Austria), NÖ, 1A

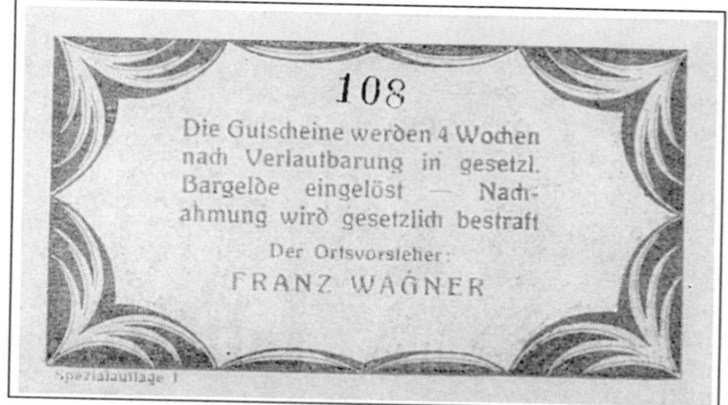

75 Heller, Rindlberg, 1A

20 Heller, Rohrbach, OO, 1A

50 Heller, Salzburg, Austria, 1A

50 Heller, St. Georgen/Tollet, OO, 1A

10 Heller, St. Johann/Tirol, Austria, 1A

30 Heller, St. Johann/Tirol, 1A

20 Heller, St. Johann/Pongau, 1A

10 Heller, St. Marienkirchen/H, OÖ, 1A

20 Heller, St. Oswald, NO, 1A

50 Heller, St. Pantaleon, 1A

10 Heller, St. Poelten, NO, 1A

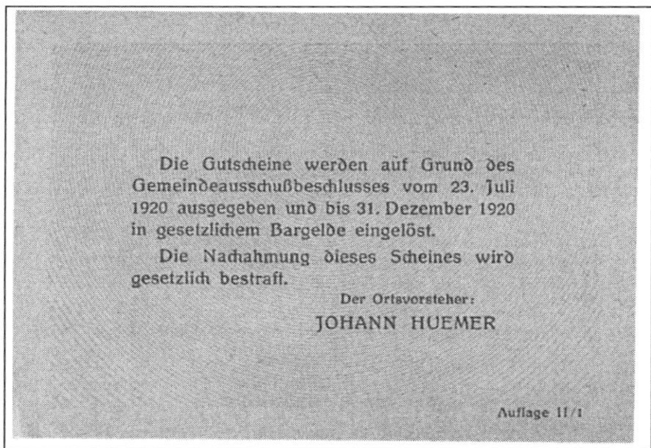

30 Heller, Schanz, OO, 1A

10 Heller, Schleissheim, OO, 1A

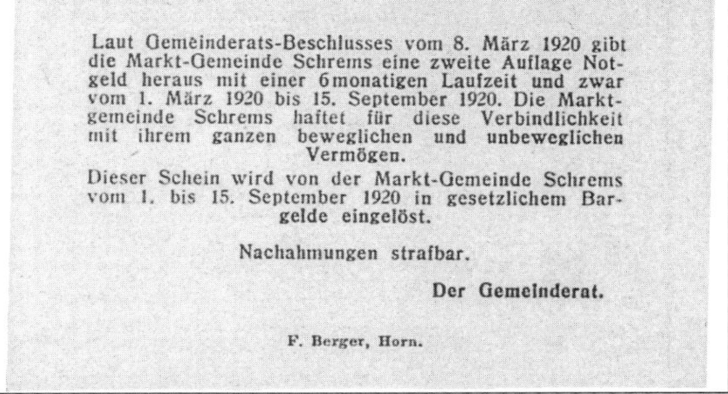

50 Heller, Schrems, NO, 1A

5 Heller, Sparbach, NO, 1A

80 Heller, Spital/Pyhrn, OO, 1A

30 Heller, Stadl-Paura, OO, 1A

60 Heller, Teles, Tirol, 1A

50 Heller, Thalgau (Salzburg), 1A

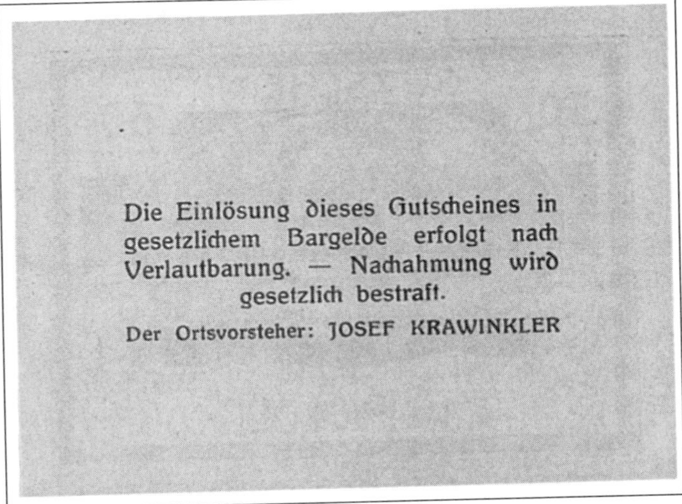

50 Heller, Thann, OÖ, 1A

20 Heller, Timelkam, OO, 1A

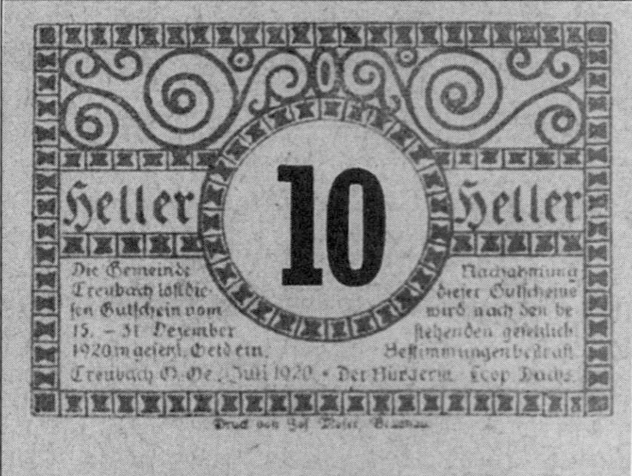

10 Heller, Treubach, OO, 1A

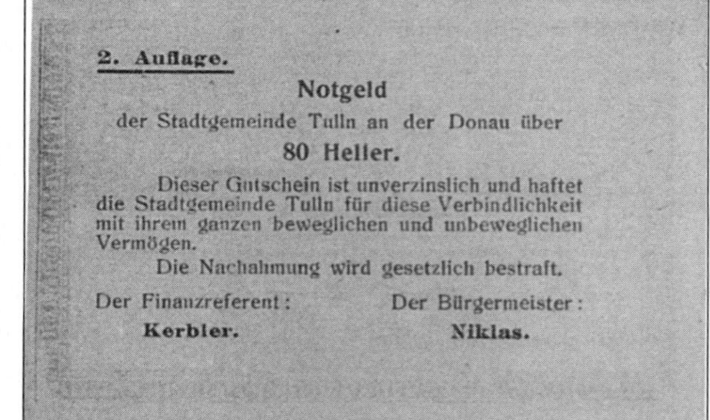

80 Heller, Tulln/D, 1A

20 Heller, Unterach, OO, 1A

10 Heller, Vichtenstein, OÖ, 1A

45 Heller, Austria, 11B

50 Heller, Wartberg/Krems, 1A

50 Heller, Wien Austria (Industrial Bank), 11A

Types of Emergency Money

Type	Reference #
Municipal paper	1
Private paper	2
POW paper	3
POW official metal	4
POW private metal	5
Municipal metal	6
Private metal	7
Gas tokens	8
Food; beer; konsumverein	9
Naval; military; kantine	10
Encased, unencased stamps	11
Streetcar tokens	12
Porcelain	13
World War II issues	14
Concentration, Civilian internment camps	15

Rarity grades: A, to $25; B, to $60; C, to $125; D, to $200; and E, $350

10 Heller Stamp, Wiegele, Wien Austria, 11B

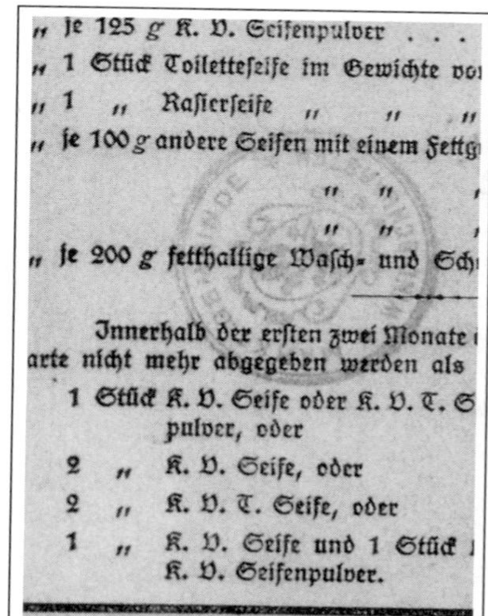

„ je 125 g K. V. Seifenpulver . . .
„ 1 Stück Toiletteseife im Gewichte vo
„ 1 „ Rasierseife „ „ „
„ je 100 g andere Seifen mit einem Fettg
„ „
„ „
„ je 200 g fetthaltige Wasch- und Sch

Innerhalb der ersten zwei Monate
arte nicht mehr abgegeben werden als
1 Stück K. V. Seife oder K. V. T. S
pulver, oder
2 „ K. V. Seife, oder
2 „ K. V. T. Seife, oder
1 „ K. V. Seife und 1 Stück
K. V. Seifenpulver.

20 Heller, Windischgarsten, OO, 1A

10 Heller, Woellersdorf, Austria, 2B

10 Heller, Woergl/Tirol, Austria, 1A

90 Heller, Woergl, Tirol, 1A

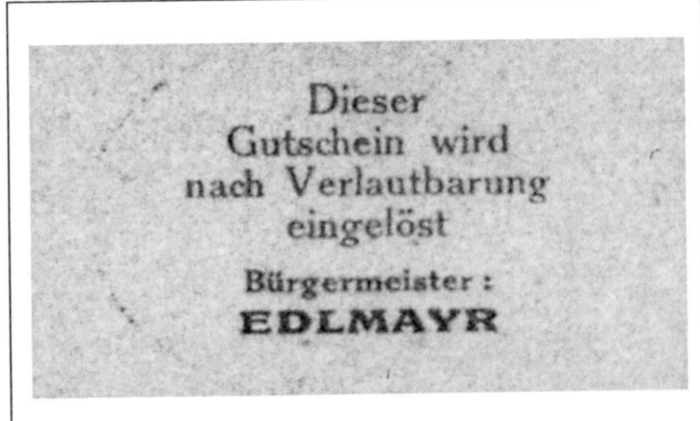

20 Heller, Wolfern, OO, 1A

10 Heller, Wolfsegg, OO, 1A

50 Heller, Zell am See (Salzburg), 1A

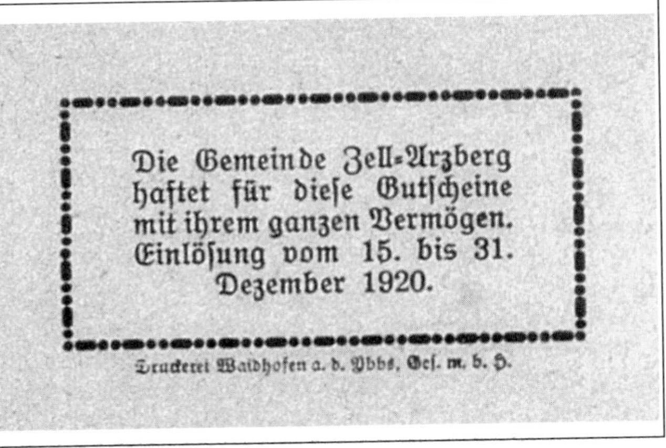

20 Heller, Zell-Arzberg, OÖ, 1A

10 Heller, Zell/Moos, Austria, 1A

❒ WILHERING	OO	1A	
❒ WIMM	OO	1A	
❒ WIMPASSING/PIELACH	NO	1A	2A
❒ WIMSBACH	OO	1A	
❒ WINDEGG	OO	1A	
❒ WINDHAAG BEI FREISTADT	OO	1A	
❒ WINDHAAG BEI PERG	OO	1A	
❒ WINDHAAG/YBBS	NO	1A	
❒ WINDISCHGARSTEN	OO	1A	
❒ WINKLARN	NO	1A	
❒ WIPPENHAM	OO	1A	
❒ WOELLERSDORF	NO	2A	
❒ WOERGL Tirol		1A	2A
❒ WOERSCHACH Steiermark		1A	
❒ WOESENDORF	NO	1A	
❒ WOLFERN	OO	1A	
❒ WOLFPASSING AM FORST	NO	1A	
❒ WOLFSBACH	NO	1A	
❒ WOLFSEGG	OO	1A	2B
❒ WUERNITZ	NO	9D	
❒ WUERNSDORF	NO	1A	
❒ YBBS	NO	1A	
❒ YBBS/DONAU	NO	2A	
❒ YBBSITZ	NO	1A	
❒ YSPER	NO	1A	
❒ ZEHETGRUB	NO	1A	
❒ ZEILLERN	NO	1A	
❒ ZEILLING	OO	1A	
❒ ZEISELMAUER	NO	1A	
❒ ZEISS	OO	1A	
❒ ZELKING	NO	1A	
❒ ZELL AM SEE Salzburg		1A	
❒ ZELL BEI ZELLHOF	OO	1A	
❒ ZELL-ARZBERG	NO	1A	
❒ ZELL/MOOS	OO	1A	
❒ ZELL/PETTENFUERST	OO	1A	
❒ ZELL/PRAM	OO	1A	
❒ ZELL/YBBS	NO	1A	
❒ ZELTWEG Steiermark		2B	
❒ ZIERSDORF	NO	1A	
❒ ZISTERSDORF	NO	1A	
❒ ZWETTL	NO	1A	
❒ ZWETTL IM MUEHLKREIS	OO	1A	
❒ ZWITTAU		1A	

AZORES

❒ CALHETA Angra do Heroismo	1C	2B
❒ HORTA Horta	1B	2E
❒ SANTA CRUZ DE GRACIOSA	2E	
❒ SAO ROQUE DO PICO Horta	2B	
❒ VELAS Angra do Heroismo	1B	

BELGIUM

❒ AALST (Alost) East Flanders	1A				
❒ AALST-HERZELE East Flanders	1B				
❒ ABEE Liege	1A				
❒ AELBEKE West Flanders	1A				
❒ AELST Limbourg	1B				
❒ AELTRE East Flanders	1A				
❒ AERTRYCKE West Flanders	10D				
❒ AISEAU Hainaut	1A				
❒ ALFERSTEG St. Vith	14B				
❒ ALTENBERG	14				
❒ AMAY Liege	1A				
❒ AMEL (Ambleve) St. Vith	14B				
❒ AMOUGIES East Flanders	1A				
❒ AMPSIN-BENDE Liege	1A	14B			
❒ ANDENNE Namur	1A	2B			
❒ ANDERLUES Hainaut	2B				
❒ ANDRIMONT Liege	1A				
❒ ANGLEUR Liege	1A	2B			
❒ ANHIERS Nord	1A				
❒ ANICHE Nord	1A	2B			
❒ ANOR Nord	1A				
❒ ANSEGHEM West Flanders	1A				
❒ ANSEREMME Namur	1A				
❒ ANSEROEUL Hainaut	1C				
❒ ANTHEIT Liege	1A				
❒ ANTOING Hainaut	1A	2B	14B		
❒ ANTWERP (Antwerpen, Anvers) Antwerp	1A	2B	9A	11B	
❒ ANVAING Hainaut	1A	2A			
❒ ANZIN	2B				
❒ ARBRE (Aubres) Hainaut	1A				
❒ ARC-AINIERES Hainaut	1A				
❒ ARDOYE West Flanders	1A				
❒ ARIMONT Malmedy	14B				
❒ ARNEY Liege	1A				
❒ ARSIMONT Namur	1A				
❒ ARVILLE Luxembourg	1B				
❒ ASSCHE Brabant	1A				
❒ ASSEBROUCK (Assebroek) West Flanders	1A	14B			
❒ ATH Hainaut	1A				
❒ ATZERATH St. Vith	14B				
❒ AUBEL Liege	1B				
❒ AUBENCHEUL-AU-BAC Nord	1B				
❒ AUBIGNY-AU-BAC Nord	1A				
❒ AUBY Nord	1A				
❒ AUCHY-LEZ-ORCHIES Nord	1A				
❒ AUDEGEM East Flanders 1	2A				
❒ AUDEMETZ	1B				
❒ AUDENARDE (Audenaerde) East Flanders	1B				
❒ AUDENARDEE-ST. GEORGES Seine	7B				
❒ AUDERGHEM Brabant	1A				
❒ AUDEWARDE I					
❒ AUTRYVE West Flanders	1A				
❒ AUVELAIN East Flanders 1					
❒ AUVELAIS Namur	1B				
❒ AVELGEM (Aveighem) West Flanders	1A	2B			
❒ AVESNES Nord	1B				
❒ AWANS Liege	2B				
❒ AWIRS, LES Liege	2B				
❒ AWOINGT	1B				
❒ AYWAILLE Liege	2A				
❒ BAELEN SUR VESDRE (Baelegen) West Flanders	14				
❒ BAILLEUL (Bailloeul) Hainaut	1B				
❒ BAISIEUX Hainaut	1A				
❒ BAISIEUX Nord	1A				
❒ BARRY Hainaut	1A				
❒ BAS-OHA Liege	1B				
❒ BAS-WARNETON West Flanders	1A				
❒ BASECLES Hainaut 1					
❒ BASEL East Flanders	1A				

❒ BASSE-BODEUX Liege 1A
❒ BASTOGNE Luxembourg 1A 2B
❒ BAUGNEZ Malmedy 14B
❒ BAUGNEZ-BAGATELLE Melmedy 14B
❒ BAUGNIES Hainaut 1A
❒ BAVICHOVE (Bavikhove) West Flanders 1A
❒ BECLERS Hainaut 1A
❒ BEERNEM West Flanders 1B
❒ BEHO Luxembourg 14A
❒ BELCELE East Flanders 1A
❒ BELLEM East Flanders 1A
❒ BELLERNAUX 14B
❒ BELLEVAUX Luxembourg 14B
❒ BELLEVAUX-LIGNEUVILLE 14B
❒ BELLEVUE Malmedy 14B
❒ BELLONE Pas-de-Calais 1B
❒ BEN-AHIN Liege 1B
❒ BERCHEM East Flanders 1A
❒ BERG Malmedy 14B
❒ BERLAER Brabant 1A
❒ BERNISSART Hainaut 1A
❒ BERNISTER Malmedy 14B
❒ BERSILLIES L'ABBAYE Hainaut 1A
❒ BERTREE Liege 1B
❒ BETECOM (Betekom, Beauvechain) Brabant 1A
❒ BEUVRY-LEZ-ORCHIES Nord 1A
❒ BEVERCE Liege 14B
❒ BEVERE-BIJ-AUDENAERDE East Flanders 1A
❒ BEVEREN-LEZ-COURTRAI (Beveren-Leie)West Flanders 1A
❒ BEVEREN-WAAS (Beveren-Waes) East Flanders 1A
❒ BEVEREN-BIJ-ROUSELARE West Flanders 1C
❒ BEVERLOO Limbourg 3B
❒ BIACHE-ST. VAAST Pas-de-Calais 1A
❒ BIERBEEK (Sint Camillus) Brabant 14
❒ BIESME (Biesmes) Namur 1A
❒ BILLY-MONTIGNY Pas-de-Calais 1A
❒ BILSTAIN Liege 1A
❒ BINCHE Hainaut 1A 2B
❒ BISSEGEM (Bisseghm) West Flanders 1A
❒ BLAESVELT (Blaasveld) Antwerp 1 2A
❒ BLANC-MISSER ON-CRESIN Nord 1A
❒ BLANDAIN Hainaut 1A
❒ BLANKENBERGE (Blankenberghe) West Flanders 1A
❒ BLATON Hainaut 1A
❒ BLEHARIES Hainaut 1A
❒ BLEHARIES, ERE, ETC. Hainaut 1C
❒ BLICQUY Hainaut 1D
❒ BOIRY-NOTRE-DAME Pas-de-Calais 1A
❒ BOMMERSHOVEN Limbourg 1B
❒ BON-SECOURS Hainaut 1B
❒ BONCELLES Liege 1A
❒ BOOM Antwerp 1A
❒ BORGLOON Limbourg 1A
❒ BORLOO (Borio) Limbourg 1B
❒ BOSSUTY/Escaut Hainaut 1A
❒ BOSSUYT (Bossuit) West Flanders 1B
❒ BOUCLE-SAINT BLAISE East Flanders 1A
❒ BOUFFIOULX Hainaut 1A 2B
❒ BOUILLON Luxembourg 1A
❒ BOURG-LEOPOLD Limbourg 1C
❒ BOUSBECQUE Nord 1B
❒ BOUSSIRE Malmedy 14B
❒ BOUVIGNIES Nord 1A
❒ BRA-SUR-LIENNE Liege 1A
❒ BRAINE-LE-COMTE Hainaut 1A
❒ BRASMENIL Hainaut 1B
❒ BRASSCHAAT (Brasschaet) Antwerp 1A 2B
❒ BREBIERES Pas-de-Calais 1A
❒ BRECHT Antwerp 1B 2A
❒ BREE Limbourg 1A
❒ BREITFELD St. Vith 14B
❒ BRESSOUX Liege 2B
❒ BRIFFOEIL 1A
❒ BROECHEM Antwerp 1B 2A
❒ BRUGES (Brugge) West Flanders 1A 2A 10B
❒ BRUILLE LES MARCHIENNES Nord 1A
❒ BRUSSELS (Bruxelles) Brabant 1A
❒ BRUYELLE (Bruyelles) Hainaut 1A
❒ BRUYERES Malmedy 14B
❒ BUELLINGEN (Bullange) Liege 14B
❒ BUETGENBACH 14B
❒ BUGGENHOUT East Flanders 1B
❒ BUIRONFOSSE Verviers 1A
❒ BUISSENAL Hainaut 1A
❒ BUISSIERE, LA Hainaut 1A
❒ BURDINNE Liege 1A
❒ BURGHT East Flanders 1A
❒ BURNENVILLE Malmedy 14A
❒ BURY Hainaut 1A
❒ BUTGENBACH Liege 14B
❒ BUZET Hainaut 1C
❒ CACHTEM West Flanders 1A
❒ CAENEGHEM West Flanders 1A
❒ CALLENELLE Hainaut 1A
❒ CALLOO East Flanders 1A
❒ CALONNE Hainaut 1A
❒ CAMBRAI Nord 1A
❒ CARNIERES Hainaut 2B
❒ CARVIN Pas-de-Calais 1A 2A
❒ CHAMPAGNE Malmedy 14B
❒ CHANXHE-POULSEUR Liege 2B
❒ CHAPELLE-A-WATTINES Hainaut 1B
❒ CHAPON-SERAING Liege 1A
❒ CHARLEROI Hainaut 2B
❒ CHARLEVILLE ET MEZIERES Ardennes 1A
❒ CHATELET Hainaut 1A 2B 14B
❒ CHATELINEAU Hainaut 1A 2B
❒ CHENEE Liege 1A
❒ CHODES Malmedy 14B
❒ CHERATTE Liege 1A
❒ CHERCQ Hainaut 1
❒ CHEVOFOSSE Malmedy 14B
❒ CHIEVRES Hainaut 1A
❒ CLERMONT-SOUS-HUY Liege 1A 2B
❒ CLERMONT-SUR-BERWINNE Liege 1A
❒ CLIGNEVAL Malmedy 14B
❒ COMBLAIN-AU-PONT Liege 1A
❒ COMINES West Flanders 1C
❒ COMINES West Flanders 1B 9A
❒ COMINES-BELGIQUE 1A
❒ CONTICH Antwerp 1A
❒ CORBEEK-LOO Brabant 1A
❒ CORBEHEM Pas-de-Calais 1A
❒ CORNESSE Liege 1A
❒ CORPHALIE-LEZ-HUY Liege 2B
❒ CORTRYCK-DUTZEL Brabant 1A
❒ COUCKELAERE West Flanders 2B
❒ COUILLET Hainaut 1A 2A
❒ COUR-SUR-HEURE Hainaut 1A
❒ COURCELLES Hainaut 2B

❒ COURCHELETTES Nord 1B
❒ COURRIERE Namur 1A 2B
❒ COURRIERES Pas-de-Calais 1A
❒ COURSEL Limbourg 1A
❒ COUTHUIN Liege 1A
❒ COUTICHES Nord 1A
❒ CROIX Lille 1A
❒ CROIX ET WASQUEHAL Lille 1A
❒ CROMBACH Liege 14B
❒ CRUYBEKE Antwerpen 1A
❒ CRUYSHAUTEM East Flanders 1A
❒ CUERNE West Flanders 1A
❒ CUINEY Nord 1A
❒ CYSOING Lille 1A
❒ DACKNAM East Flanders 1A
❒ DADIZEELE West Flanders 1A
❒ DALHEM Liege 1A
❒ DAMPREMY Hainaut 1A
❒ DAMRE Liege 2B
❒ DECHY Nord 1A
❒ DE CLINGE (Deklinge) East Flanders 1A
❒ DEERLYCK (Deerlijk) West Flanders 1A
❒ DEIDENBERG St. Vith 14B
❒ DENDERBELLE East Flanders 1A
❒ DENDERMONDE East Flanders 1B
❒ DERGNEAU Hainaut 1A
❒ DESSELGHEM (Desselgem) West Flanders 1A
❒ DEUX-ACREN Hainaut 1A
❒ DEYNZE (Deinze) East Flanders 1A
❒ DIEPENBEEK Limbourg 1C
❒ DIEST Brabant 3B 9A
❒ DIFFLOT Eupen 14B
❒ DINANT Namur 1A
❒ DISON Liege 1B
❒ DOEL East Flanders 1A
❒ DONSTIENNES Hainaut 1A
❒ DOTTIGNIES West Flanders 1B
❒ DOUAI Nord 1B
❒ DOUR Hainaut 2B
❒ DOURGES Pas-de-Calais 1A
❒ DROCOURT Pas-de-Calais 1A
❒ DRONGEN (Tronchiennes) East Flanders 1A
❒ DUFFEL Antwerp 1A 2A
❒ ECAUSSINES-D'ENGHIEN Hainaut 1A 2B
❒ ECAUSSINES-LALAING Hainaut 1A 2A
❒ EDELAERE East Flanders 1A
❒ EENAME East Flanders 1A
❒ EERNEGHEM West Flanders 1B
❒ EGHEM (Eeghem) West Flanders 1A
❒ EHEIN Liege 1A
❒ EIBERTINGEN Malmedy 14B
❒ EISDEN Limbourg 1 14B
❒ ELLEZELLES East Flanders 1B
❒ ELSENBORN Liege 14B
❒ ELSENBORN-CAMP Liege 14B
❒ ELVERSEELE (Eiverseele) East Flanders 1B
❒ EMBOURG Liege 1A
❒ EMELGHEM (Emelgem) West Flanders 1A 14B
❒ EMMELS St. Vith 14B
❒ ENSIVAL Liege 1C
❒ EPPEGHEM (Eppegem) Brabant 1A
❒ ERE (Erre) Hainaut 1A
❒ ERMETON-SUR-BIERT Namur 1A
❒ ERQUELINNES Hainaut 1A
❒ ESNEUX Liege 1A
❒ ESPIERRES West Flanders 1B
❒ ESPLECHIN Hainaut 1A
❒ ESQUELMES Hainaut 1A
❒ ESQUERCHIN Nord 1A
❒ ESTAIMBOURG Hainaut 1B
❒ ESTREES Nord 1A
❒ ETHE Luxembourg 1A
❒ EUPEN Liege 6B 14B
❒ EVREGNIES Hainaut 1B
❒ EYNATTEN East Flanders 14B
❒ EYNE East Flanders 1A
❒ FALIZE Malmedy 14B
❒ FALIZE-CLIGNEVAL Malmedy 14B
❒ FALLAIS Liege 1A
❒ FARCIENNES Hainaut 1A
❒ FAUMONT Nord 1A
❒ FAYMONVILLE Liege 14B
❒ FENAIN Nord 1A
❒ FERIN Nord 1B
❒ FLEMALLE-GRANDE Liege 1A 6B
❒ FLEMALLE-HAUTE Liege 1B 2A
❒ FLERS-EN-ESCREBIEUX Nord 1B
❒ FLINES-LEZ-RACHES Nord 1A
❒ FLOBECQ Hainaut 1A
❒ FLOREFFE Namur 1A
❒ FLORIHEID Maldedy 14B
❒ FONTAINE-L'EVEQUE Hainaut 1A 2B
❒ FONTAINE-VALMONT Hainaut 1A
❒ FONTENOY-BOURGEON Hainaut 1A
❒ FORCHIES-LA-MARCHE Hainaut 1A
❒ FOREST-LEZ-BRUXELLES Brabant 1D
❒ FOREST-LEZ-FRASNES Hainaut 1A
❒ FOSSE Namur 1A
❒ FOURMIES Nord 1A
❒ FRAITURE-EN-CONDROZ Liege 1A
❒ FRASNES-LEZ-BUISSENAL Hainaut 1B
❒ FROIDMONT Hainaut 1A
❒ FROYENNES Hainaut 1B
❒ FUMAL Liege 1A
❒ FURNEAUX (Furnaux) Namur 1A
❒ GALHAUSEN St. Viet 14B
❒ GALLAIX Hainaut 1A
❒ GAND (Guisland) East Flanders 1A 14B
❒ GAUDRAIN-RAMECROIX Hainaut 1B
❒ G'DOUMONT Malmedy 14A
❒ GEERAARDSBERGEN East Flanders 1B
❒ GEMEHRET Eupen 14B
❒ GEMMENICH Liege 1A
❒ GENK (Genck) Limbourg 1A 14B
❒ GENT (Ghent, Gant, Gand) East Flanders 1A 6B
❒ GEROMONT Malmedy 14B
❒ GHEEL Antwerp 2A
❒ GHELUWE West Flanders 1B
❒ GILLY Hainaut 1A
❒ GINGHELOM (Gingelom) Limbourg 1A
❒ GITS West Flanders 1B
❒ GLEIZE, LA Liege 1A
❒ GOEULZIN Nord 1B
❒ GOHIMONT Malmedy 14B
❒ GOSSELIES Hainaut 1A 2B
❒ GOUGNIES Hainaut 2A
❒ GOZEE Hainaut 1A
❒ GRACE-BERLEUR Liege 1A
❒ GRANDGLISE (Grandglisse) Hainaut 1B
❒ GRAND HORNU Hainaut 2A
❒ GRAND RENG Hainaut 1A
❒ GRAND-METZ Hainaut 1D
❒ GREMBERGEN East Flanders 1A

❒ GRIVEGNEE Liege 1 9A
❒ GROBBENDONCK (Grobbondonk) Antwerp 1A
❒ GROSAGE Hainaut 1A
❒ GUESNAIN Nord 1A
❒ GUEUZAINE Malmedy 14B
❒ GUIGNIES Hainaut 1A
❒ GULLEGHEM (Gullegem) West Flanders 1A
❒ GYSEGEM East Flanders 1A
❒ HAELTERT East Flanders 1A
❒ HAESDONCK East Flanders 1A
❒ HALEN East Flanders 1B
❒ HALENFELD St. Vith 14B
❒ HALLUIN Nord 1A
❒ HAM-SUR-HEURE Hainaut 1A
❒ HAM-SUR-SAMBRE Namur 1A
❒ HAMME East Flanders 1A
❒ HAMOIS-EN-CONDROZ Namur 2B
❒ HANSBEKE East Flanders 1A
❒ HANSINELLE (Hanzinelle) Namur 1A
❒ HANTES-WIHERIES Hainaut 1A
❒ HANZINNE Namur 1A
❒ HARCHIES Hainaut 1A
❒ HARELBEKE West Flanders 1A
❒ HARNES Pas-de-Calais 1A
❒ HASSELT Limbourg 1A 2B
❒ HAUSET Liege 14B
❒ HAVINNES Hainaut 1A
❒ HAVRE West Flanders 14B
❒ HECHTEL Limbourg 1A
❒ HEDIMONT 1A
❒ HEDOMONT Malmedy 14B
❒ HEESTERT West Flanders 2B
❒ HEKELGEM Brabant 1A
❒ HELCHEREN-ZOLDER East Flanders 1A 14B
❒ HELCHIN West Flanders 1A
❒ HEM Nord 1A

Types of Emergency Money

Type	Reference #
Municipal paper	1
Private paper	2
POW paper	3
POW official metal	4
POW private metal	5
Municipal metal	6
Private metal	7
Gas tokens	8
Food; beer; konsumverein	9
Naval; military; kantine	10
Encased, unencased stamps	11
Streetcar tokens	12
Porcelain	13
World War II issues	14
Concentration, Civilian internment camps	15

Rarity grades: A, to $25; B, to $60; C, to $125; D, to $200; and E, $350

❒ HEMIXEM Antwerp 1A
❒ HENIN-LIETARD Pas-de-Calais 1A
❒ HENRI-CHAPELLE Liege 14A
❒ HEPPENBACH Liege 14B
❒ HEPPIGNIES Hainaut 1A
❒ HEPSCHEID St. Vith 14B
❒ HERBESTHAL Eupen 14B
❒ HERCK-ST. LAMBERT Limbourg 1A
❒ HERENT Brabant 1A
❒ HERENTHALS (Herentals) Antwerp 1A 2A
❒ HERENTHOUT Antwerp 1A
❒ HERGENRATH Liege 14B
❒ HERINNES-LEZ-PECQ Hainaut 1A
❒ HERMALLE-SOUS-HUY Liege 1A
❒ HERMEE Liege 1C
❒ HERON Liege 1A
❒ HERSEAUX West Flanders 1C 14A
❒ HERSTAL Liege 2B
❒ HERVE Liege 1A
❒ HESTRE, LA Hainaut 1A
❒ HEUEM St. Vith 14B
❒ HEULE West Flanders 1A
❒ HEUSY Liege 1A
❒ HEVERLE (Heverlee) Barbant 1A
❒ HEX Limbourg 1A
❒ HEYST-AAN-ZEE West Flanders 1A
❒ HINDERHAUSEN St. Vith 14B
❒ HOBOKEN Antwerp 1A 2A
❒ HODIMONT Liege 1B
❒ HOEVENEN Antwerp 1A
❒ HOLLAIN (Hainaut) 1A
❒ HOMBOURG (Homburg) Liege 1A
❒ HONSFELD Malmedy 14B
❒ HORNAING Nord 1A
❒ HOUDENG West Flanders 1B
❒ HOUTAING Hainaut 1A
❒ HOUTHEM West Flanders 1A
❒ HOWARDRIES Hainaut 1A
❒ HUCCORGNE Liege 1A
❒ HUENNINGEN Malmedy 14B
❒ HULSTE West Flanders 1A
❒ HUY Liege 1A
❒ ICHTEGEM West Flanders 1A
❒ INGELMUNSTER West Flanders 1A 14B
❒ INGOYGHEM West Flanders 1A
❒ ISEGHEIM (Iseghem, Izegem) West Flanders 1A 6A 14B
❒ IVELDINGEN St. Vith 14B
❒ IWUY Nord 1A
❒ IXELLES Brabant 1A
❒ IZEL Luxembourg 1B
❒ JEMEPPE-SUR-MEUSE Liege 1A
❒ JEMPPE-SUR-SAMBRE Namur 1A
❒ JEUCK (Goyer) Limbourg 1A
❒ JOLLAIN-MERLIN Hainaut 1B
❒ JUMET Hainaut 1C 2A
❒ KAIN Hainaut 1B
❒ KEMSEKE East Flanders 1A
❒ KESSEL-LOO (Kessel-Lo) Brabant 1A
❒ KETTENIS Liege 14B
❒ KIELDRECHT West Flanders 1A
❒ KNOKE (Knokke) West Flanders 1A
❒ KOMEN (Comines) West Flanders 6A
❒ KORTENBERG Sint Jozef 14B
❒ KORTRIJK (Courtrai) West Flanders 1C
❒ KORTRIJK-DUTZEL (Cortryck-Dutzel) Brabant 1A
❒ KRINKELT Malmedy ` 14B
❒ KRUIBEKE (Cruybeke) East Flanders 1B
❒ LADEUZE Hainaut 1C
❒ LAEKEN Brabant 1A

❒ LALLAING Nord 1A
❒ LAMBERMONT Liege 1B
❒ LAMBERSART Hainaut 1B
❒ LAMBRES Nord 1A
❒ LAMONTZEE Liege 1B
❒ LAMONRIVILLE Malmedy 14B
❒ LANAYE Limbourg 1A
❒ LANDAS Nord 1A
❒ LANDELIES Hainaut 1A
❒ LANDENNE-SUR-MEUSE Liege 1A
❒ LANNOY Nord 1A
❒ LANTREMANCE (Lantremange) Liege 1A
❒ LAPLAIGNE (Bleharies, Ere, etc.) Hainaut 1A
❒ LA REID Liege 1B
❒ LASNENVILLE Malmedy 14B
❒ LATINNE Liege 1A
❒ LAUW (Lowaige) Limbourg 1A
❒ LAUWE West Flanders 1A
❒ LAUWIN-PLANQUE Nord 1A
❒ LAVOIR Liege 1A
❒ LEBBEKE East Flanders 1A
❒ LEDEBERG East Flanders 1B
❒ LEDEGHEM (Ledegem) West Flanders 1C
❒ LEERNES Hainaut 1A
❒ LEERS Nord 1A
❒ LEERS-NORD Hainaut 1B
❒ LEFOREST Pas-de-Calais 1A
❒ LEMBECQ-LEZ-HAL Barbant 1A
❒ LENDELEDE West Flanders 1A
❒ LENS Pas-de-Calais 1A
❒ LEOPOLDSBURG Limbourg 1A
❒ LE QUESNOY Nord 1A
❒ LESDAIN Hainaut 1A
❒ LESSINES Hainaut 1A 2B
❒ LEUPEGEM East Flanders 1A
❒ LEUVEN (Louvain) Brabant 1A
❒ LEUZE Hainaut 1A
❒ LEVAL-TRAHEGNIES Hainaut 1A
❒ LEWARDE Nord 1A
❒ LIBOMONT Malmedy 14B
❒ LICHTERVELDE (Lichterfelde) West Flanders 1A 14B
❒ LIEGE Liege 1A 2A 9A
❒ LIER Antwerp 1A 2A
❒ LIERNEAUX Liege 1B
❒ LIEVIN 1B
❒ LIGNE Hainaut 1C
❒ LIGNEUVILLE Malmedy 14B
❒ LILLE Nord 1A
❒ LIMBOURG Limbourg 1A
❒ LINDEN Brabant 1A
❒ LLEVIN Pas-de-Calais 1A 2A
❒ LODELINSART Hainaut 1A
❒ LOKEREN East Flanders 1A
❒ LOMMERSWEILER Liege 14B
❒ LONGFAYE Malmedy 14B
❒ LONTZEN Liege 14B
❒ LOUVAIN Brabant 1A
❒ LOUVIERE, LA Hainaut 2B
❒ LOVERVAL Hainaut 1B
❒ LOWAIGE (Lauw) Liege 1A
❒ LUINGNE West Flanders 1B 2A
❒ LYS 1A
❒ LYS-LEZ-LANNOY Nord 1A
❒ MACAMPAGNE Malmady 14B
❒ MAERKE-KERKHEM (Maarke-Kerkem) West Flanders 1A
❒ MAFFLE (Maffles) Hainaut 1A
❒ MAINVAULT Hainaut 1B
❒ MALDEGEM East Flanders 1A
❒ MALMEDY Liege 14B
❒ MANDERFELD Liege 14A
❒ MARBAIX-LA-TOUR Hainaut 1A
❒ MARCHE Luxembourg 1A
❒ MARCHE-LEZ-ECAUSSINES Hainaut 1A
❒ MARCHIENNE-AU-PONT Hainaut 1A 2B
❒ MARCHIENNES Nord 1A
❒ MARCHIENNES-CAMPAGNE Nord 1A
❒ MARCHIN Liege 1A
❒ MARCINELLE Hainaut 1A 2A
❒ MARCKE West Flanders 1B
❒ MARIEMONT Hainaut 2A
❒ MARLINNE Limbourg 1C
❒ MARNEFFE Liege 1A
❒ MARQUAIN Hainaut 1A
❒ MARTINS Liege 1A
❒ MAUBRAY Hainaut 1A
❒ MAULDE Hainaut 1B
❒ MAURAGE Hainaut 2B
❒ MECHELEN (Malines) Antwerp 1A
❒ MEENEN (Menin) 1A
❒ MEERDONCK East Flanders 1A
❒ MEIZ Malmedy 14B
❒ MELLE East Flanders 1C
❒ MELLET Hainaut 1A
❒ MELSELE East Flanders 1B 9A 14B
❒ MEMBACH Liege 1A 14B
❒ MENEN (Meenen, Menin) West Flanders 1D
❒ MERBES-LE-CHATEAU Hainaut 2B
❒ MERICOURT 1B
❒ MERXPLAS Antwerp 1A 2A
❒ MERY-TILEF (Mery-Tilff) Liege 2B
❒ MEUKERKEN-WAAS (Nieukerken) East Flanders 14B
❒ MEULEBEKE West Flanders 1A 14B
❒ MEYERODE Liege 14A
❒ MIELEN-BOVEN-AELST Limbourg 1A
❒ MIRAMONT Courcelettes 1A
❒ MIRAMONT lries 1A
❒ MIRAMONT Pys...70 Communes 1A
❒ MIRFELD St. Vith 14B
❒ MOEDERSCHEID St. Vith 14B
❒ MOEN West Flanders 1B
❒ MOERBEKE East Flanders 1A
❒ MOERKERKE West Flanders 1A
❒ MOERZEKE East Flanders 1 2A
❒ MOIGNELEE Namur 1A
❒ MOLENBEEK-ST. JEAN Brabant 1A 2A
❒ MOLL Antwerp 1A 2A
❒ MONCEAU-SUR-SAMBRE Hainaut 1A 2B
❒ MONS Hainaut 2B
❒ MONT Malmedy 14B
❒ MONT-SAINTE-ALDEGONDE Hainaut 1A
❒ MONT-SUR-MARCHIENNE Hainaut 1A 2B
❒ MONTEGNEE Liege 1A 7B
❒ MONTENAU Malmedy 14B
❒ MONTIGNIES-SAINT-CHRISTOPHE Hainaut 1A
❒ MONTIGNY-EN-GOHELLE Pas-de-Calais 1A
❒ MONTIGNY-LE-TILLEUL (Montignies-le-Tilleul) Hainaut 1A 2B
❒ MONTIGNY-SUR-SAMBRE (Montignies-sur-Sambre) 1A 2A 9A
❒ MONTZEN Liege 1A 14A

❒ MOORSELEN (Moorsele) West Flanders 1A
❒ MORESNET Liege 1A 14B
❒ MORTSEL (Sint-Amedus) Liege 14A
❒ MOULBAIX Hainaut 1B
❒ MOUSCRON West Flanders 1B 2B 14A
❒ MOUSTIER Hainaut 1A
❒ MOUVAUX 1A
❒ MUERRINGEN Malmedy 14B
❒ NALINNES Hainaut 1A
❒ NAMUR Namur 1A 9A
❒ NANDRIN Liege 1A
❒ NEDER-EENAME East Flanders 1A
❒ NEDERBRAKEL East Flanders 1A
❒ NEEROETEREN Limbourg 1A
❒ NEERPELT Limbourg 1A
❒ NEIDINGEN St. Vith 14B
❒ NEUBRUECK St. Vith 14B
❒ NEU-MORESNET Liege 14B
❒ NEUNDORF St. Vith 14B
❒ NIDRUM Malmedy 14B
❒ NIEL Antwerp 1A
❒ NIEUKERKEN-WAAS (Nieukerken, Nieuwkerken)East Flanders 1A 14B
❒ NIEUWERKERKEN East Flanders 1A
❒ NIVELLES Brabant 1A 2B
❒ NOMAIN Nord 1A
❒ NORDERWIJCK (Noorderwijk,Norderwyck) Antwerp 1A
❒ NOYELLES-GODAULT Pas-de-Calais 1A
❒ NUKERKE East Flanders 1A
❒ OHAIN Nord 1A
❒ OIGNIES-AISEAU Hainaut 2B
❒ OIGNIES Pas-de-Calais 1A
❒ OMBRET-RAUSE Liege 1A
❒ ONDENVAL Malmedy 14B
❒ ONOZ Namur 1A
❒ OOST-ROOSBEKE (Oostrozebeke) West Flanders 1A
❒ OP-BRAKEL East Flanders 1A
❒ OP-GLABBEECK Limbourg 1B
❒ ORCHIES Nord 1A
❒ ORCQ Hainaut 1A
❒ ORMEIGNIES Hainaut 1A
❒ ORP-LE-GRAND Brabant 1A
❒ ORROIR East Flanders 1A
❒ OSTENDE (Oostende) West Flanders 1A
❒ OSTRICOURT Pas-de-Calais 1A
❒ OTAIMONT Malmedy 14B
❒ OUCKENE West Flanders 1A
❒ OUGREE Liege 2A
❒ OUPEYE Liege 1A
❒ OVERMEIRE East Flanders 1B
❒ OVIFAT Malmedy 14A
❒ PAAL Limbourg 14A
❒ PAPIGNIES Hainaut 1B
❒ PATURAGES Hainaut 2B
❒ PECQ Hainaut 1B
❒ PECQUENCOURT Nord 1B
❒ PEPINSTER Liege 1A
❒ PERONNE-LEZ-ANTOING (Peronnes lez-Antoing) Hainaut 1B
❒ PETEGHEM East Flanders 1A
❒ PETERGHEM-AUDENAERDE East Flanders 1A
❒ PETIT-RECHAIN Liege 1A
❒ PHILIPPEVILLE Namur 2B
❒ PIETON Hainaut 1A
❒ PINTE, DE East Flanders 1B
❒ PIPAIX Hainaut 1A 14B
❒ PIRONCHAMPS Hainaut 1A
❒ PLANCHE Malmedy 14B
❒ POLLEUR Liege 1A
❒ PONT Malmedy 14B
❒ PONTE DE LOUP Hainaut 1A
❒ POULSEUR Liege 1A 2B
❒ POUSSET Liege 1B
❒ PREAIX Malmedy 14B
❒ PRY Namur 1A
❒ PUSSEMANGE Luxembourg 1B
❒ QUAREMONT East Flanders 1A
❒ QUIEVRAIN Hainaut 1A
❒ RACHES Nord 1A
❒ RAEREN Liege 14B
❒ RAIMBEAUCOURT Nord 1A
❒ RAMEGRIES-CHIN Hainaut 1A
❒ RAMSEL Barbant 1A
❒ RANCE Hainaut 1A
❒ RANSART Hainaut 1A
❒ RANST Antwerp 1A
❒ RECHT Liege 14A
❒ RECKEM West Flanders 1A
❒ RECULEMONT Malmedy 14A
❒ REMONVAL Malmedy 14A
❒ REMOUCHAMPS Liege 1B
❒ RENAIX (Rosne) East Flanders 1B 2B 14A
❒ RENLIES Hainaut 1A
❒ RETHY Antwerp 1A
❒ REULAND Liege 14
❒ REVES Hainaut 1A
❒ RIEUULAY Nord 1B
❒ ROBERTVILLE Liege 14B
❒ ROBERTVILLE-OUTREWARCHE Malmedy 14B
❒ ROCHERATH Liege 1A
❒ RODT Malmedy 14A
❒ ROLLEGHEM-CAPELLE (Rollegem-Kapelle) West Flanders 1A
❒ RONGY Hainaut 1A
❒ RONXHY (Ronse) Malmedy 14B
❒ ROOBORST East Flanders 1A
❒ ROOST-WARENDIN Nord 1A
❒ ROUBAIX Nord 1A
❒ ROUBAIX ET TOURCOING Nord 1A
❒ ROUCOURT Hainaut 1A
❒ ROUSSELARE (Roulers) West Flanders 2B
❒ ROUVROY Hainaut 1A
❒ ROUX Hainaut 1A 2B
❒ RUISBROEK Brabant 1A
❒ RUMAUCOURT Pas-de-Calais 1A
❒ RUMBEKE West Flanders 1A 14B
❒ RUMILLIES Hainaut 1A
❒ RUMPST Antwerp 1A
❒ RUPELMONDE East Flanders 1B
❒ RUSSEIGNIES East Flanders 1A
❒ RUTTEN (Russon) Limbourg 1A
❒ RUYEN East Flanders 1A
❒ RUYSSELEDE West Flanders 1A
❒ RYCKEVORSEL Antwerp 1A
❒ SAILLY-LEZ –LANNOY Nord 1A
❒ SAINT VITH Liege 14A
❒ SAINT-GENOIS West Flanders 1A
❒ SAINT-GEORGES-SUR-MEUSE Liege 1A
❒ SAINT-GILLES-BRUXELLES Brabant 1A
❒ SAINT-HUBERT Luxembourg 1B
❒ SAINT-LEGER Hainaut 1A
❒ SAINT-MAUR Hainaut 1A
❒ SAINT-QUENTIN Aisne 1B
❒ SAINT-REMY-GEEST Brabant 1B
❒ SAINT-SEVERIN Liege 1A

5 Centimes, Turnhout, Belgium, 1A

❒ SAMEON Nord 1B
❒ SARS-LA-BUISSIERE Hainaut 1A
❒ SART Liege 1B
❒ SCHERPENHEUVEL (Schaarbeek, Montaigu) Brabant 1A
❒ SCHLIERBACH St. Vith 14A
❒ SCHOENBERG Liege 14A
❒ SCHOORISSE East Flanders 1A
❒ SCHOOTEN Antwerp 1A
❒ SECLIN Nord 1A
❒ SEILLES Liege 1A
❒ SERAING-SUR-MEUSE Liege 1A 2B
❒ SETZ St. Vith 14B
❒ SEVENEEKEN East Flanders 1A
❒ SILENRIEUX Namur 2B
❒ SINAAI-WAAS East Flanders 1A 14B
❒ SINT-AMANDS Antwerp 1A
❒ SINT-ANDRIES West Flanders 1A
❒ SINT-BLASIUS-BOUCLE East Flanders 1B
❒ SINT-CORNELIS-HOOREBEKE East Flanders 1A
❒ SINT-GILLIS-BIJ-DENDERMONDE East Flanders 1A
❒ SINT-GILLIS-WAAS East Flanders 1B
❒ SINT-HUIBRECHTS-LILLE Limbourg 1A
❒ SINT-LENAARTS (Lenaerts) Antwerp 1A
❒ SINT-LIEVENS-HOUTEM East Flanders 1A
❒ SINT-MICHIELS West Flanders 2B
❒ SINT-NIKOLAAS-WAAS (Sint-Niklaas) East Flanders 1A 6A 14B
❒ SINT-PAUWELS-WAAS East Flanders 1A
❒ SINT-PIETERS-LEEUW Brabant 1A
❒ SINT-TRUIDEN Limbourg 1C 14B
❒ SINTE-KATHELIJNE-WAVER Antwerp 1A
❒ SINTE-KRUIS West Flanders 1A
❒ SIPPENAEKEN Liege 14A
❒ SIVRY Hainaut 1A
❒ SCHOPPEN St. Vith 14B
❒ SOHEIT-TINLOT (Soheit-Tinlet) Liege 1A
❒ SOIGNIES Hainaut 1B 2B
❒ SOLESMEN Nord 1A
❒ SOLRE-SUR-SAMBRE Hainaut 1A
❒ SOMAIN Nord 1A
❒ SOSOYE Namur 1A
❒ SOURBRODT Malmedy 14A
❒ SOUVRET Hainaut 1C
❒ SPA Liege 1A 6A 9A 14A
❒ SPRIMONT Liege 1A 2B
❒ SPY Namur 1A
❒ STAINBRUGES (Stambruges) Hainaut 1A
❒ STEINEBRUECK St. Vith 14B
❒ STAVELOT Liege 1A
❒ STEENDORP East Flanders 1B
❒ STEINBACH Malmedy 14A
❒ STEKENE East Flanders 1A
❒ STEMBERT Liege 1A
❒ STOCKHEIM Limbourg 1C
❒ SULSIQUE East Flanders 1A 2B
❒ SWEVEZEELE 14A
❒ SWEVEGHEM West Flanders 1A
❒ SYSSEELE West Flanders 1B
❒ TAMINES Namur 1A
❒ TEMPLEUVE Hainaut 1A
❒ TEMSCHE (Tamise) East Flanders 1A 2A
❒ TERHAGEN Antwerp 1A 2A
❒ TERTRE Hainaut 2B
❒ TESSENDERLOO Limbourg 1A 2A
❒ THEUX Liege 1A
❒ THIELRODE-WAAS East Flanders 1A
❒ THIELT West Flanders 1A
❒ THIENEN 9A
❒ THIEULAIN Hainaut 1A
❒ THIMISTER Liege 1B
❒ THIOX Malmedy 14B
❒ THIRIMONT Malmedy 14B
❒ THOMMEN Liege 14A
❒ THOUROUT West Flanders 1A
❒ THUIN Hainaut 1B
❒ THULIN Hainaut 1B
❒ THY-LE-BAUDHUIN (Thy-le-Baudin) Namur 1B
❒ THY-LE-CHATEAU Namur 1A
❒ TIENEN Tiense Brabant 1A 2B 14C
❒ TIHANGE Liege 1A
❒ TILLEUR Liege 2B
❒ TONGEREN Limbourg 1A
❒ TOUFFLERS Nord 1A
❒ TOURCOING Nord 1A
❒ TOURNAI Hainaut 2B
❒ TOURNAI, ANTOING, CALONNE, ETC. Hainaut 1B
❒ TOURNHOUT (Turnhout) Antwerp 1A
❒ UCCLE Brabant 1A
❒ VALENCIENNES Nord 1D

25 Francs, Turnhout, Belgium, 1A

❒ VALENDER St. Vith 14B
❒ VAULX Hainaut 1A
❒ VAULX-LEZ-TOURNAI Hainaut 1A
❒ VELAINES-LEZ-TOURNAI Hainaut 1B
❒ VERREBROECK East Flanders 1B
❒ VERVIERS Liege 1A 2B 14B
❒ VEZON Hainaut 1A
❒ VICHTE West Flanders 1A
❒ VILLERS-CAMEAU 1B
❒ VILLERS-LA-TOUR Hainaut 1B
❒ VILLERS-LE-BOUILLET Liege 2B
❒ VILLERS-LE-TEMPLE Liege 1A
❒ VILLERS-NOTRE-DAME Hainaut 1A
❒ VILLERS-SAINT-AMAND Hainaut 1A
❒ VIELSALM Luxembourg 1A
❒ VILVOORDE Brabant 1A 6A 14B
❒ VINALMONT Liege 1A
❒ VIRTON Luxembourg 1B
❒ VITRY-EN-ARTOIS Pas-de-Calais 1A
❒ VIVE-SAINT-ELOI West Flanders 1B
❒ VLEHARIES Hainaut 1A
❒ VLIERZELE East Flanders 1A
❒ VOLKEGHEM East Flanders 1A
❒ VOSSELAER Antwerp 1A 2A
❒ VRACENE East Flanders 1A
❒ VRED Nord 1A
❒ WAASMUNSTER (Waesmunster) East Flanders 1B
❒ WACHTEBEKE East Flanders 1A
❒ WACKEN (Wakken) West Flanders 1B 14A
❒ WAERGHEM West Flanders 1A
❒ WAERMAERDE West Flanders 1B
❒ WAGNES 1A
❒ WAHA Luxembourg 1A
❒ WAKKEN (Wacken) 14B
❒ WALEFFES, LES Liege 1B
❒ WALHORN-ASTENET Liege 14B
❒ WALK Malmedy 14B
❒ WANDIGMES-HAMAGE Nord 1B
❒ WANNEGEM-LEDE East Flanders 1A
❒ WANZE Liege 1A
❒ WARCHE Malmedy 14B
❒ WARCHIN Hainaut 1A
❒ WAREMME Liege 1A
❒ WARET-L'EVEQUE Liege 1B
❒ WARLAING Nord 1A
❒ WASMES-AUDEMETZ-BRIFFOEIL Hainaut 1A
❒ WASMUEL Hainaut 2B
❒ WASSEIGES Liege 1A
❒ WATERLOO Brabant 1A

10 Heller, Wetteren, 1A

❒ WATERSCHEI Limbourg 14A
❒ WATTRELOS Nord 1A
❒ WAUDREZ Hainaut 1A
❒ WAVREUMONT Malmedy 14B
❒ WAZIERS Nord 1A
❒ WEGNEZ Liege 1B
❒ WEISMES (Waimes) Liege 14B
❒ WELDEN East Flanders 1A
❒ WELKENRAEDT Liege 1B 14B
❒ WELLE East Flanders 1A
❒ WENDUYNE West Flanders 1A
❒ WEPPLER St. Vith 14B
❒ WERETH St. Vith 14B
❒ WERVICQ West Flanders 1C
❒ WETTEREN (Wetterne) East Flanders 1B
❒ WEVELGHEM (Wevelgem) West Flanders 1B
❒ WEYWERTZ Malmedy 14B
❒ WEZ-VALVAIN Hainaut 1A
❒ WEZ-VELVAIN BLEHARIES, ERE, ETC. Hainaut 1A
❒ WILLEBROEK (Wilebroeck) Antwerp 1A
❒ WILLEMS Nord 1A
❒ WILSELE Brabant 1A
❒ WINGENE (Wyngene) West Flanders 1A 14A
❒ WINKEL-SAINT-ELOI West Flanders 1B
❒ WIRTZFELD Malmedy 14B
❒ WISSELS 1A
❒ WODECQ Hainaut 1A
❒ WORTEGEM (Wortegen) East Flanders 2B
❒ XHOFFRAIX Malmedy 14B
❒ XHURDEBISE Malmedy 14B
❒ YERNEE-FRAINEUX Liege 1A
❒ YPRES West Flanders 1A
❒ YVOIR Namur 2A
❒ ZEDELGHEM (Zedelgem) West Flanders 1D
❒ ZELE East Flanders 1A
❒ ZELZATE (Sint-Jean-Baptist) Liege 14B
❒ ZOLDER-VOORT Limbourg 2A
❒ ZONHOVEN Limbourg 1B 2B
❒ ZWIJNDRECHT East Flanders 1B 2A

CAMEROONS

❒ DUALA 1E

CAPE VERDE ISLANDS

❒ SALINES DU CAP-VERT 6B
❒ SANTIAGO 1E

CEYLON

❒ DUTATAKAWA 3E
❒ RAGAMA 3E

CHINA

❒ NINGPO (Lotu) 11C
❒ SHANGHAI 11C
❒ SOOCHOW (Wuhsien, Wu-shi) 11C
❒ TSINANFU Shantung 7C

CYPRUS

❒ CYPRUS 14

CZECH and SLOVAKIA

❒ ALT ROHLAU (Stara Role) 2A
❒ ASCH (As) Boehmen 1A 2B
❒ ANTALOCZ (Antalovci) 5B
❒ AUSSIG (Usti nad Labem) Boehmen 1A 12A

20 Kronen, Aussig (Aust-Hun), 1A

❒ BARZDORF (Bozanov) 2A
❒ BECHYNE (Bechin) Boehmen 2A
❒ BENSEN (Benesov nad Ploucnici) Boehmen 1B 2B
❒ BEREHOVO (Beregszasz) 1A
❒ BIELITZ (Bilsko, Bielsko) 1A 2A
❒ BLATNA Boehmen 1A
❒ BLOTTENDORF (Polevski) Boehmen 1B
❒ BLOTTENDORF-SCHOENFELD Boehmen 1B
❒ BLOTTENDORF-TANNEBERG Boehmen 1B
❒ BOBENBACH-TETSCHEN (Podmokly-Decin) Boehmen 1A
❒ BOZKOV 3A
❒ BRATISLAVA (Pressburg) 1A 2B
❒ BRAUNAU (Broumov) Boehmen 2B 6A 9A
❒ BREZNICE (Breznicka) Boehmen 2A
❒ BRUCH (Lom u Mostu) Boehmen 1A
❒ BUCOVIC/BUTSCHOWITZ Maehren 1B 2A
❒ BRUENN (Brno) Maehren 2A
❒ BRUESAU (Brezova nad Svitavou) Maehren 1A
❒ BRUEX (Most) Boehmen 2A 3A
❒ BUCOVICE (Butschowitz) 1B 2A 3B
❒ BUERGSTEIN (Sloup) Boehmen 2A
❒ BYSTRICE nad Pernstejnem (Bysstritz/Pernstsein) Maehren 2B
❒ CASLAV (Caslau) Boehmen 2B
❒ CASTROV (Castrow) Boehmen 2A
❒ CECHTICE (Chatitz) Boehmen 2A

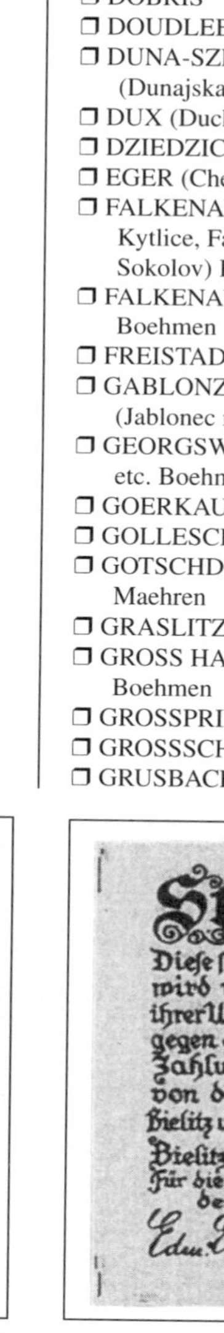

❒ CELAKOVICE (Celakowitz) Boehmen 2B
❒ CESKA TREBOVA Boehmen 2A
❒ CHOMUTOV (Komatau, Komotau) Boehmen 1A
❒ CHOTEBOR (Obcanska Zalozna) Boehme 2A
❒ CHRAST Boehmen 2B
❒ CHUDIWA (Chudenin) Boehmen 2B
❒ CHYSKY 1A
❒ CISTA U RAKOVNIKA Boehmen 2B
❒ CUKMANTL (Zuckmantel) 1A
❒ DESCHENITZ (Desenice) Boehmen 1B 2B
❒ DESTNAI Deschna Boehmen 1C
❒ DEUTSCH GABEL (Nemecke Jablonne) 3A 6A
❒ DEUTSCH WERNERSDORF (Vernerovice) Boehmen 2A
❒ DIANABERG Boehmen 2A
❒ DITTERSBACH (Jetrichov) Boehmen 2A
❒ DOBRIS Boehmen 1A 2A
❒ DOUDLEBY NAD ORLICI (Daudlieb/Adler-Kosteletz) Boehmen 2B
❒ DRAHOMISCHL (Drogomysl) 2B
❒ DOBRIS 2A
❒ DOUDLEBY U KOSTELCE 2B
❒ DUNA-SZERDAHLEY (Dunajska Streda, Dunaszerdahely) 3A
❒ DUX (Duchov, Duchcov) Boehmen 2B
❒ DZIEDZICE Dziedzitz 2A
❒ EGER (Cheb) Boehman 2A
❒ FALKENAU-KITTLITZ (Falknov-Kytlice, Falkenou-Kittlitz, Eger, Sokolov) Boehmen 2A
❒ FALKENAU/OHRI (Falknov/Eger) Boehmen 1A
❒ FREISTADT (Frystat, Frystak) 2B 3A 6A
❒ GABLONZ/NEISSE (Jablonec nad Nisou) Boehmen 1A
❒ GEORGSWALDE Gross-Schoenau), etc. Boehmen 2A
❒ GOERKAU (Jirkov) 1A
❒ GOLLESCHAU 2B
❒ GOTSCHDORF (Hostalkovy) Maehren 2A
❒ GRASLITZ (Kraslice) Boehmen 1A
❒ GROSS HAMMER (Velke Hamry) Boehmen 1A
❒ GROSSPRIESEN (Velke Brezno) 2A
❒ GROSSSCHOENAU (Velky Senov) 1A
❒ GRUSBACH Maehren 2A

20 Halerzy, Bielsko, Silesia, 1A

5 Kronen, Bobenbach, Teschen (Aust-Hun), 1A

❒ HAIDA (Hajda, Novy Bor) 2A
❒ HAINSPACH (Hanspach, Lipova) Boehmen 1A
❒ HALBSTADT (Mezimesti) Boehmen 2A
❒ HAUPTMANNSDORF (Hejtmankovice) Boehmen 2A
❒ HEINZENDORF (Hyncice) Boehmen 2A
❒ HERMANUV MESTEC Boehmen 2C
❒ HERMSDORF (Hermankovice) Boehmen 2A
❒ HOLICE 2A
❒ HOLYSOV (Holleischen) 4A
❒ HOREPNIK 2A 3B
❒ HORICE (Horitz) Boehmen 2A
❒ HOSTOMICE POD BRDY (Hostonitz) Boehmen 2C
❒ HRONOV (Hronow, Hronov) 1A 3A
❒ HUMPOLEC (Humpoletz) Boehmen 1A 2A
❒ HUSZT (Chust) 2A
❒ IGLAU (Jihlava) Maehren 1E
❒ JABLONNE N. ORLICI (Gabel/Adler) Boehmen 1A
❒ JACHHYMOVSKE DOLY 14B
❒ JAEGERNDORF (Krnov) Maehren 1A 2B
❒ JAMNITZ (Jemnice) Maehren 2A
❒ JAROMERICE (Jaroeritz) Maehren 2B

20 Kronen, Komatau-Görkau (Aust-Hun), 1A

❒ JAUERNIG (Javornik) 1A 2B
❒ JINDRICHUV HRADEC (Neuhaus) 1A 2A
❒ JOHANNESBERG (Honsberk) Boehmen 1A
❒ JOHANNESBERG (Janovice, Janovicky) 2B
❒ KAESMARK (Kezmarok) 2B
❒ KAMMNITZ/LINDE (Ceska Kamenicenad Lipou)Boehmen 2A
❒ KARLSBAD (Karlovy Vary) Boehmen 1A
❒ KASPERSKE HORY (Bergreichenstein) Boehmen 2C
❒ KATHARINABERG Boehmen 2B
❒ KDYNE 2B
❒ KLATTAU (Klatovy) Boehmen 2A
❒ KOENIGSHOF (Kraluv Dvur) 3A 15A
❒ KOMOTAU, SEBASTIANSBERG, GOERKAU (Chomutov, Jirkov, Hora) Boehmen 1A 2A
❒ KOPRIVNICE 2
❒ KOZICHOVICE (Koziciowitz) Maehren 2A
❒ KRALUPY N. V. (Vita/Kralup/Moldau) Boehmen 1B
❒ KRASNA HORA (Schoenberg) Boehmen 1B
❒ KYSPERK (Supi Hora, Geiersberg) Boehmen 2B
❒ L'UBICE (Leibicz) 3A
❒ LANDSKRON (Lanskroun) Maehren 2A
❒ LAUN (Louny) Boehmen 1A 2B
❒ LEDEC N.S. Boehmen 2B
❒ LEITMERITZ (Litomerice) Boehmen 2A
❒ LIDMAN Boehmen 1B
❒ LOMNICE ND LUZNICI (Lomnitz/Luznitz) 1B
❒ LOSONCZ (Lucenec) 2B
❒ LOUNY (Laun) Boehmen 2A
❒ LUGOS (Stava Lubovna) Slovakia 1A
❒ LUKAVEC 1A
❒ MAEHRISCH NEUSTADT (Unicov) Maehren 1A 2C
❒ MAEHRISCH SCHOENBERG (Sumperk) Maehren 1A 2A
❒ MAEHRISCH TRUEBAU (Moravska Trebova) Maehren 2A
❒ MAERZDORF (Martinkovice) 2B
❒ MAFFERSDORF (Vratislavice nad Nis) Boehmen 2E 6A 7A
❒ MALE CHYSCE (Mala Cheska, Kleinchyschka) Boehmen 2A
❒ MARIENBAD (Marianske Lazne) 1A
❒ MEST KRALOVE (Koenigstadt) Boehmen 2C
❒ MIES Boehmen 1A
❒ MILEVSKO (Muehlhausen) Boehmen 12B
❒ MILICIN/MILITSCHIN Boehmen 2B
❒ MILOVICE 2B
❒ MLADA BOLESLAV 2B
❒ MORAVSKE BUDEJOVICE (Maehrisch Budwitz) Maehren 2A
❒ MUEGLITZ (Mohelnice) Maehren 1B
❒ MUKACEVO (Munkacs) 2A
❒ NACERADEC Boehmen 1B
❒ NADEJKOV (Nadejkau) Boehmen 2B
❒ NAGYMEGYER (Nagy-megyer, Velky Meder) Slovakia 3A
❒ NEKOR 2A

❒ NEMECKY BROD (Deutschbrod) Boehmen 2A
❒ NESSELSDORF (Koprivnice) Maehren 2B
❒ NEUBERG (Podhradi) 9A
❒ NEUERN (Nyrsko) Boehmen 2A 9A
❒ NEUHAUS Boehmen 2B
❒ NEUSTADT (Unicov) Maehren 1A
❒ NEUSTADT/METTAU Bohemia 1A
❒ NEVEKLOV Boehmen 2A
❒ NIEDEREINSIEDEL (Dolni Poustevna) 1A
❒ NIEDERULLERSDORF (Morostowice-DLN) 2A
❒ NIXDORF (Mikulasovice) 1A
❒ NEVEKLOV (Neweklau) Boehmen 2A
❒ NOVE BENATKY nad Boleslav (Neubsenatek) Boehmen 2C
❒ NOVE MESTO nad Metuji 2B
❒ NOVY BNYDZOV (Neubydzow) Boehmen 2A
❒ OBERDORF (Horni Ves) Boehmen 2B
❒ OBERGEORGENTHAL (Bruex) Boehmen 1B
❒ OELBERG (Olivetin) Boehmen 2B 9A
❒ OPOCN0 Boehmen 2A
❒ OTTENDORF (Otovice) Boehmen 2B
❒ PACOV (Pacove Patzau) Boehmen 2B
❒ PARNIK (Parnig) Boehmen 2A
❒ PECKA BOEHMEN 2A
❒ PELHRIMOV (Pilgarm) Boehmen 2A
❒ PIESTANY 2B
❒ PILSEN (Plzen) Boehmen 2A
❒ POCATKY (POCATEK) Boehm 2B
❒ PODEBRADY (Podiebrad) Boehmen 2B
❒ POLAUN (Polubny) 2A
❒ PRACHATITZ (Prachatice) 2A
❒ PRAHA (Prague) Boehmen 8A 11B 12A

Types of Emergency Money

Type	Reference #
Municipal paper	1
Private paper	2
POW paper	3
POW official metal	4
POW private metal	5
Municipal metal	6
Private metal	7
Gas tokens	8
Food; beer; konsumverein	9
Naval; military; kantine	10
Encased, unencased stamps	11
Streetcar tokens	12
Porcelain	13
World War II issues	14
Concentration, Civilian internment camps	15

Rarity grades: A, to $25; B, to $60; C, to $125; D, to $200; and E, $350

5 Kronen, Reichenburg, 1A

❒ PRERAU (Prerov) Maehren 2A
❒ PROSCHWITZ/NEISSE (Prosec nad Nisou) Boehmen 2B
❒ PROTVIN (Protiwin) Boehmen 2A
❒ REICHENBERG (Liberec) Boehmen 1A 2A 3A 4B 9B 12A
❒ ROEMERSTADT (Rymarov) Maehren 1A
❒ ROSENTHAL (Rozmital) Boehmen 2B
❒ ROZSNTO (Roznava) Boehmen 1A
❒ RUMBURG (Rumburk) Boehmen 1A
❒ RUPPERSDORF (Ruprechtice) Boehmen 2A
❒ RUZOMBEROK (Ruzomberok) 2B
❒ SAAZ (Zatec) Boehmen 1B 2B
❒ SANKT JOACHIMSTAL (Jachymov) Boehmen 1A
❒ SCHLAG/NISOU (Gablonz, Galonz-Jablonekce nad Niseu Paseky)Boehmen 2B
❒ SCHLUCKENAU (Sluknov) Boehmen 1B
❒ SCHMIEDEBERG Boehmen 2A
❒ SCHOENBACH (Krasna) 2A
❒ SCHOENBERG (Sumperk/Desse, Sumburk Maehrisch) 1A 2A
❒ SEBASTIANSBERG (Hora Sv Sebestiana) 1A
❒ SEDLCANY (Selcan) Boehmen 2C
❒ SEDLEC NA DRAZE (Sedletz) Boehm 2A
❒ SEVLUS VELKY (Szoelloes Nagyszoelloes) 2A
❒ SKALICA 2A
❒ SOBESLAV (Sobeslau) Boehmen 2A

1 Krone, Reichenberg (Czechoslovakia), 1B

❒ SOMMEREIN (Samorin, Somorja) 3A
❒ STARKSTADT (Starkov) Boehmen 2B
❒ STOSSBERG 1A
❒ SZAKOLCA (Szakolcza, Skalicz, Skalica) 12A
❒ TABOR (Tabora) Boehmen 1A 2A
❒ TELC (Teltsch) Maehren 2A
❒ TEPLITZ (Teplice) 14A
❒ TEPLICE NAD METUJI (Wekelsdorf) 2A
❒ TEPLITZ-SCHOENAU (Teplice-Sanov) Boehmen 1A 2B
❒ TESIN (Cieszyn, Teschen) 1A
❒ THERESIENSTADT (Terezin) Boehmen 3A 5A 14A
❒ TREBITSCH (Trebic) Maehren 1A
❒ TREST (Triesch) Maehren 2B
❒ TRINEC (Trzyniec) 2A
❒ TROPPAU (Opava) Maehren 2B 11B
❒ TRUEBAU (Moravska Trebova) Maehren 12A
❒ TYN NAD VLTAVOU (Moldauthein) 2C
❒ TYSSA (Tisa) Boehmen 2B
❒ UHLIRSKE JANOVICE (Kohljanowitz) Boehm 2B
❒ UNGVAR (Uzhorod) 1A
❒ UPICE 9 (Eipel) Boehmen 2A
❒ USTI NAD ORLICI (Wilderschwert/Adler) Boehm 2A
❒ USTRON 2B
❒ VAMBERK (Warnberg) Boehmen 2A
❒ VELKE HAMRY (Grosshammer) Boehm 1A
❒ VELKE MEZIRICI (Grossmeseritsch) Maehren 2A
❒ VELVARY (Welwarn) Boehmen 1A
❒ VESELI NAD LUZNICI (Weseli/Luznitz) Boehm 2B
❒ VLASIM (Wlasirn) Boehmen 1A
❒ VOTICE 9Wotitz) Boehmen 2A
❒ VYSKOV (Wischau) Maehren 2E
❒ VYSKOE VESELI (Hochwessely) Boehm 2A
❒ WARNSDORF (Varnsdorf) Boehmen 1A
❒ WECKERSDORF (Krinice) Boehmen 2A
❒ WEIDENAU 1A
❒ WEIPERT (Vejprty) Boehmen 1A
❒ WEKELSDORF (Teplice nad Metuji) Boehmen 2A
❒ WIEDENAU (Vidnava) 1A
❒ WIESEN (Viznov) Boehmen 2B

25 Øre, Dybbol, Denmark, 1B

❒ ZAHRADKA U LEDGE (Zahradka/Ledec) Boehmen 2C
❒ ZAMBERK (Senftenbergt, Stavba Kasaren) Boehmen 2B
❒ ZD'AR N. MOR (Saar) Maehren 2A
❒ ZILINA (Zilinska, Sukenna, Tovarna) 1A
❒ ZNOJMO (Znaim) Maehren 2A
❒ ZUCKMANTEL (Cukmantl, Zlate Hory) 1A
❒ ZWITTAU (Svitavy) Maehren 1A 2B 9B

DENMARK

❒ AABENRAA (Abenraa, Apenrada) 1A 2A 11A 12A
❒ AALBORG 11B 12A
❒ AARHUS 11B
❒ AUENBUELL (Aunboel) 1A
❒ AUGUSTENBURG 1A
❒ BROAGER (Broacker) 2A
❒ BRUNDE-ROTHENRUG 1A
❒ CHRISTIANSFELD 1A
❒ DALER (Dabler) 1A
❒ DYBBOEL (Dueppel, Schleswig-Holstein, Germany) 1A
❒ DYNT (Duenth) 1A
❒ ESBJERG 11B 12A
❒ ESRUM 11B
❒ FREDERICIA 11B
❒ FREDERIKSHAVN 11B
❒ FREDERIKSSUND 11B
❒ GRAMBY 1A

50 Pfennig, Gravenstein, Denmark, 1B

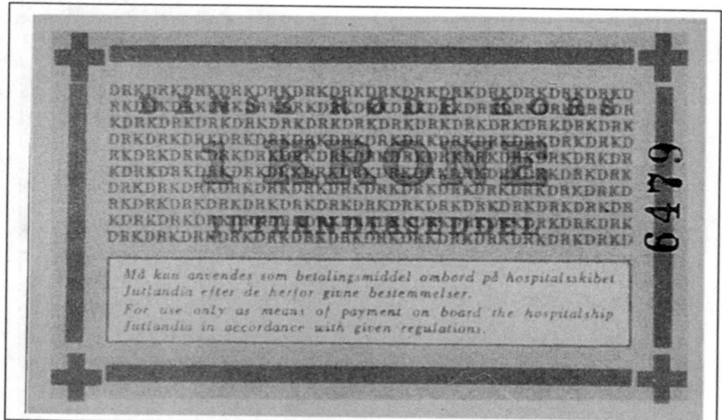

1 Krone, "Jutlandia" Denmark, 1B

❒ GRAVENSTEIN (Graasten) 1A
❒ HADERSLEBEN (Haderslev) 2A 11B 14B
❒ HARESKOV 11B
❒ HELSINGOER 11B
❒ HERNING 11B
❒ HILLEROD 12A
❒ HJERMITSLEV 11B
❒ HOEJER (Hoyer) 1A 2B
❒ HOLBAEK 11B
❒ HOLSTEBRO 11B
❒ HORSENS 12A
❒ JORD 2B
❒ JUTLANDIA 1B
❒ KOBENHAVN (Copenhagen) 11B 12A
❒ KOLDING 11B 12A
❒ KORSOER 11B
❒ KRISTIANSFELT (Christiansfeld) 1A
❒ LOEGUMKLOSTER (Luegumkloster) 1A
❒ LUNDERUP (Roeten Krug, Roede kro) 1A
❒ MOEGELTOENDER (Moegeltondern) 1A
❒ NAESTVED 11B
❒ NAKSKOV 11A
❒ NYKOEBING 11B
❒ ODENSE 12A
❒ RANDERS 12A
❒ RIBE 11B
❒ RINGKOEBING 11B
❒ RINKENAES (Rinkenis) 1A
❒ ROTHENKRUG 1B
❒ SKJERN 11B
❒ SVENDBORG 11B 14A
❒ THISTED 11B
❒ THORSHAVN Faeroeer Islands 14B

1 Krone, Copenhagen, Denmark, 1A

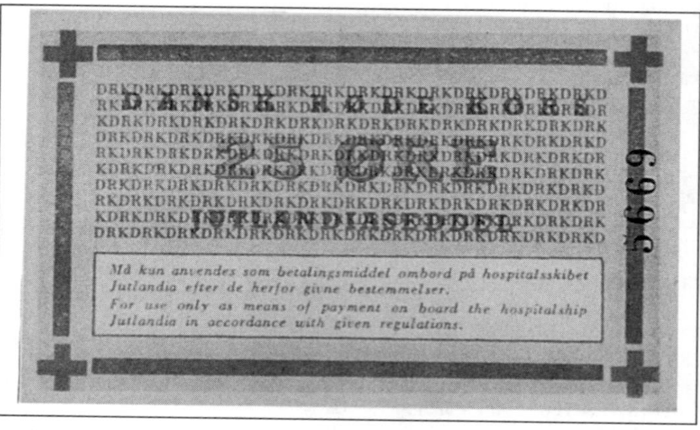

25 Øre , "Jutlandia" Denmark, 2B

❒ TINGLEV (Tingleff) 1A 2A
❒ TONDERN (Toender) 1A 11B
❒ UK (Uge) 1A
❒ VARDE 11B
❒ VARNAES (Warnitz) 2A
❒ VEJBAEK (Veibaek, Weibaek) 1A 2A
❒ VEJLE 12A
❒ VESTER SOTTRUP 11B
❒ VIBORG 11B 12A
❒ VOJENS (Woyens) 1A
❒ VORDINGBORG 11B

ESTONIA

❒ NARVA 2B
❒ PORT KUNDA 2A
❒ REVAL (Tallin, Revel) 2B
❒ ZINTENHOF BEI PERNAU Sindi 1A 2B

ETHIOPIA

❒ DIRE DAOUA (Dire Dawa) 2B

FIJI

❒ CAMP BARNES 14D

FINLAND

❒ HELSINKI (Helsingfors) Uusimaa 1C
❒ KOEYLIOE 3B
❒ OULU (Uleaborg) Oulu Prov. 2B
❒ PORVOO (Borga) Uusimaa 2B
❒ SALO Turku Ja Pori 1A

FRANCE

❒ ABANCOURT Nord 1A
❒ ABBEVILLE Somme 1A 7E
❒ ABSCON Nord 1C
❒ ACHERY Aisne 1A
❒ ACHEVILLE Pas de Calais 1A
❒ AGEN Lot et Garonne 1A 2C 3B
❒ AGEN-ALLIANCE Lot-et-Garonne 2B

25 Rubles, Port Kunda, Estonia, 2B

❒ AGEN-RUCHE Lot-et-Garonne 1B
❒ AGEN-STE L'AGENOISE Lot-et-Garonne 1B
❒ AIGES-VIVES Gard 6E
❒ AIGNES Haute Garonne 2C
❒ AIGREFEUILLE D'AUNIS Charente Inf 2C
❒ AIGUILLON Lot-et-Garonne 2C
❒ AISNE Aisne 10B
❒ AISNE-ARDENNES-MARNE 1A 2B
❒ AISNE-ET-ARDENNES 1A
❒ AISONVILLE ET BERNOVILLE 1A
❒ AIX Nord 1A 7A
❒ AIX-EN-PROVENCE Bouches du Rhone 2C 6B 7E
❒ AIX-LES-BAINS Savoie 1C
❒ AJACCIO Corse 7A
❒ AJACCIO ET BASTIA Corse 1A
❒ AJAIN Creuse 3B
❒ ALAINCOURT Aisne 1A
❒ ALAINCOURT-BERTHENICOURT Aisne 1A
❒ ALAIS (Ales) Gard 1A 2B 7B
❒ ALBERT Somme 2C 3B 7A
❒ ALBERTVILLE Savoie 3A
❒ ALBI Tarn 1A 2B 6A 7A
❒ ALCHEL 2B
❒ ALENCON Orne 1A 3B 7B
❒ ALENCON ET FLEURS Orne 1A
❒ ALENYA Pyrenees-Orientales 2B
❒ ALET LES BAINES Aude 2B
❒ ALLEMANT Aisne 1B
❒ ALLEVARD Isere 1C 2B 3A
❒ ALLIBAUDIERES (Aude) 3A
❒ ALLY (Haute Loire) 3A
❒ ALTHANN Haut-Rhin 1C 2C
❒ ALTPFIRT Haut-Rhin 1B
❒ ALZONNE Aude 2B
❒ AMBERIEU Ain 10C
❒ AMBOISE Indre et Loir 7A
❒ AMELIE-LES-BAINS Pyrennees Orientales 2B
❒ AMIENS Somme 1A 2A 3B 6A 7A 9A 10B 12B
❒ AMMERSCHWIR Haut-Rhin 1A 2B
❒ AMPLEPIUS Rhone 7A
❒ ANGERS Maine et Loire 1A 11B 14B
❒ ANGOULEME Charente 1A 2B 7B 10B 11B
❒ ANGUILCOURT-LE Aisne 1A
❒ ANHIERS Nord 1A
❒ ANIANE Herault 2B
❒ ANICHE Nord 1A 2A
❒ ANIZY-LE-CHATEAU Aisne 1A 10A

25 Centimes, Angers (France), 1A

❒ ANNECY Haute Savoie 1A 7B 10B
❒ ANNEMASSE Haute Savoie 1A 2B 7A
❒ ANNEUX Nord 1A
❒ ANNOIS Aisne 1A
❒ ANNONAY Ardeche 1A 2A 7A
❒ ANOR Nord 1A 7A
❒ ANTHIERS Nord 1A
❒ ANTONY Seine 1A
❒ ANZIN Nord 1A
❒ APPILLY Oise 1A 10B
❒ ARC-LES-GRAY Saone 11B
❒ ARCHES Vosges 2A
❒ ARCHON Ardennes 1A
❒ ARCUEIL Val de Marne 7A 11B
❒ ARCUEIL-CACHAN Seine 7A 9B
❒ ARGENTAN Orne 11B
❒ ARGENTIERE-LA-BASSEE Hautes Alps 7B
❒ ARIEGE Ariege 1A 2B
❒ ARLES (Arelate) Bouches du Rhone 2B 7B
❒ ARLES-S/TECH Pyrennees Orientales 2B
❒ ARLEUX Nord 1A
❒ ARMEE AMERICAINE EN 10A
❒ ARMEE-LES-FOYERS du Soldat 10A
❒ ARRAS Pas de Calais 1A 3A 11B
❒ ARTEMPS Aisne 1A
❒ ARVANT Haute Loire 7A
❒ ARVOINGT Nord 1A
❒ ASNIERES Seine 2B 3B
❒ ASPRES Hautes Alpes 1A
❒ ASSERVILLERS (Somme) 3B
❒ ATHIES S/LAON Aisne 1B
❒ AUBENAS Ardeche 1A 7B
❒ AUBENAS-VAL Ardeche 1A 2B
❒ AUBENCHEUL AU BAC Nord 1A
❒ AUBENCHEUL AU BOIS Aisne 1A
❒ AUBERCHICOURT Nord 1A
❒ AUBERVILLIERS (Notre Dame des Vertus) Seine 1B 2B
❒ AUBIGNY AUX KAINES Aisne 1A
❒ AUBIGNY-AU-BAC Nord 1A
❒ AUBOUE Meurthe et Moselle 1A 2B
❒ AUBY Nord 1A
❒ AUCH Gers 2A 6A 7A 10A
❒ AUCHEL Pas de Calais 1A 2B
❒ AUCHY-LES-ORCHIES Nord 1A
❒ AUDIGNY Aisne 1A
❒ AUDINCOURT Doubs 1A 7A
❒ AULNOIS/LAON Aisne 1A
❒ AULT Pas de Calais 1A
❒ AURIGNAC Haute Garonne 1A
❒ AURILLAC Cantal 1A 3B

1 Franc, D'Auxerre (France), 1A

❒ AURILLAC AND CANTAL Cantal	1A	2A	3A			
❒ AUTEUIL Hauts-de-Seine	2B	7A				
❒ AUTEUIL-LONGCHAMP Hauts-de-Seine	7B					
❒ AUTREM ENCOU RT Aisne	1A					
❒ AUTREVILLE	1B					
❒ AUVILLAR Tarn-et-Garonne	1B	2B				
❒ AUXERRE Yonne	1A					
❒ AUZAT-SUR-ALLIER Puy-de-Dome	7B					
❒ AVESNE Nord	1A	2A				
❒ AVESNE ET SOLESMES Nord	1A	2A	7A			
❒ AVESNES-LE-SEC Nord	1A					
❒ AVESNES-LES-AUBERT Nord	1A		2A			
❒ AVESNES-SUR-HELPE Nord	1A	2A				
❒ AVEYRON Aveyron	1A					
❒ AVIGNON Vaucluse	1A	3C	6B	7A	10B	12A
❒ AVIGNONNET Haute-Garonne	2B					
❒ AVION Pas-de-Calais	1A					
❒ AVIRONS Eure	2B					
❒ AVORD Cher	10B					
❒ AWOINGT Nord	1B					
❒ AX-LES THERMES Ariege	1A	2A	7A			
❒ AY Marne	1B	6A	7B			
❒ AZAY LE RIDEAU Indre-et-Loire	2B					
❒ AZILLE Aisne	1B					
❒ AZILLE Aude	2A					
❒ AZILLE Nord	2A					
❒ AZINCOURT (Agincourt) Nord	1B					
❒ BABOEUF Oise	1A	10B				
❒ BAC SAINT-MAUR Pas de Calais	2A					
❒ BACCARAT Meurthe-et-Moselle	2B					
❒ BACHANT Nord	1B					
❒ BACHY Nord	1A	2B				
❒ BADONVILLER Meurthe-et-Moselle	7A					
❒ BAGES Pyrennes Orientales	2B	7A				
❒ BAGNERES-DE-BIGORRE Haute Pyrennees	2B	11A				
❒ BAILLEUL Nord	1A	2A				
❒ BAISIEUX Nord	1A					
❒ BAIVES Nord	1A					
❒ BALAN Ardennes	1A	2B				
❒ BALBIGNY Loire	7A					
❒ BANTEUX Nord	1A					
❒ BANTOUZELLE Nord	1A					
❒ BAPAUME Pas de Calais	1A					
❒ BAR-LE-DUC Meuse	1A	7A				
❒ BARALLE Pas-de-Calais	1A					
❒ BARBAIRA Aude	1A	7A				
❒ BARBASTE Lot-et-Garonne	1A					
❒ BARBAZAN Haute-Garonne	2B					
❒ BARCELONNETTE Basses Alpes	3B					
❒ BARENTON-BUGNY Aisne	1A					
❒ BARENTON-CEL Aisne	1A					
❒ BARISIS Ain	1A					
❒ BARRAUX (Isere)	3A					
❒ BARZY Aisne	1A					
❒ BASSE-INDRE, LA Loire Inferieure	3A	7A				
❒ BASSES- ALPES	1A					
❒ BASSONES	1A					
❒ BASSOUES Gers	1B					
❒ BASTIA Corse	3A	4B				
❒ BASTIDE-DE-BESPLAS Ariege	2A					
❒ BASUEL Nord	1A					
❒ BATERE Mines	7B					
❒ BAUDRE-MOUCHARD Jura	7A					
❒ BAULE, LA Loire Inferieure	6A	7A				
❒ BAUVIN Nord	1A					
❒ BAYEUX Calvados	6A	7A				
❒ BAYONNE Basses-Pyrenees	1A	2A	6A	7B	14A	

50 Centimes, Belfort, France, 1A

❒ BAZANCOURT Marne	1B			
❒ BAZAS Gironde	2A			
❒ BAZEILLES Ardennes	1A	2A		
❒ BAZIEGE Haute Garonne	1A	2B	6A	
❒ BEAUCAIRE (Gard)	3B			
❒ BEAUCOURT Doubs	7A		9A	
❒ BEAUCOURT Territoire de Belfort	2A	9A	14B	
❒ BEAUDIGNIER Nord	1A			
❒ BEAULIEU Ardennes	1A	6A	7A	
❒ BEAULIEU Herault	1A	7A		
❒ BEAULIEU Nord	1A			
❒ BEAUMETZ - RIVIERE (Pas de Calais)	3C			
❒ BEAUMONT Haute Savoie	2A			
❒ BEAUMONT Nord	1A			
❒ BEAUMONT DE LOMAGNE Tarn et Garonne	1B	2B		
❒ BEAUMONT EN BEINE Aisne	1A			
❒ BEAUMONT ET PERSAN Val d'Oise	1A			
❒ BEAUNE Cote d'Or	2B	7A		
❒ BEAUNETZ LES CAMBRAC Pas de Calais	1A			
❒ BEAUREVOIR Aisne	1A	2A		
❒ BEAUTOR Aisne	7A			
❒ BEAUVAIS Oise	1A			
❒ BEAUVAIS Somme	6B	7A		
❒ BEAUVOIS Aisne	1A			
❒ BEAUVOIS-EN-CAMBRESIS Nord	1A			
❒ BECQUIGNY Aisne	1A	2B		
❒ BEDARIEUX Herault	2A	7A		
❒ BELFORT (Territoire de Belfort) Haute-Rhin	1A	6A	7A	
❒ BELLE-ISLE (Morbihan)	3B			
❒ BELLEGARDE Ain	7B			
❒ BELLEME Orne	2B			
❒ BELLENGLISE Aisne	1A			
❒ BELLEY Ain	2A	10B		
❒ BELLICOURT Aisne	1A			
❒ BELLONE Pas-de-Calais	1A			
❒ BELMONT-CHAVANOZ Isere	2B			
❒ BELPECH Aude	2B			
❒ BELVAL Vosges	1A			
❒ BELVES Dordogne	1A	2A		
❒ BENAY Aisne	1A			
❒ BENFELD	2A			
❒ BERAUDIERE, LA Loire	3C	5C		
❒ BERGERAC Dordogne	1A	2B	3C	7A
❒ BERGUES-SUR-SAMBRE Aisne	1A			
❒ BERLAIMONT Nord	1A	2A		
❒ BERNAY Eure	7A	11B		
❒ BERNOT Aisne	1A			
❒ BERTAUCOURT-EPOURDON Aisne	1B	2A		

10 Centimes, Besancon, France, 6A

❐ BERTHENICOURT Nord 1A
❐ BERUY Nord 1A
❐ BESANCON Doubs 1A 2B 6A 7A 11D
❐ BESSIERES Haute Garonne 1A 6A
❐ BETHENCOURT Somme 1B
❐ BETHENY Marne 1A 2B
❐ BETHUNE Pas de Calais 1A 2B 6D
❐ BEUGNIES Nord 1B
❐ BEULAY Vosges 1A
❐ BEUVRY Pas de Calais 1B
❐ BEUVY-LES-ORCHIES Nord 1A
❐ BEZIERS Herault 1A 2B 3B 6B 7B 10C
❐ BIACHE SAINT VAAST Pas de Calais 1A
❐ BIARRITZ Pyrenees Atlantiques 11B
❐ BICHANCOURT Aisne 1B
❐ BIESSARD Seine-Inferieure 3C
❐ BILLANCOURT Seine 2A 7A
❐ BILLY-MONTIGNY Pas-de-Calais 1A
❐ BITCHE Moselle 7A
❐ BITCHWEILER Ober Alsace 1B 2B
❐ BLACHE-ST. VAAST Pas del Calais 1A
❐ BLANC-MISSERON-CRESPIN Nord 1B
❐ BLANQUEFORT Lot-et-Garonne 2B
❐ BLANZY-LES-MINES Saone et Loire 7A
❐ BLAYE Gironde 3A
❐ BLENDECQUES 11B
❐ BLERANCOURT Aisne 1A
❐ BLOIS Loire et Cher 1A 6A 7A
❐ BLOIS-LA-CHAUSSEE Loire et Cher 3B
❐ BOEN Loire 3C
❐ BOHAIN Aisne 1A 2A 7A
❐ BOHAIN Nord 1A 2A
❐ BOIRY-NOTRE DAME Pas de Calais 1A
❐ BOIS BERNARD Pas de Calais 1B
❐ BOIS COLOMBES Hauts de Seine 2B 7A
❐ BOIS LES PARGNY Aisne 1B
❐ BOISSET Herault 7A
❐ BOLBEC Seine Inferieure 1A 2B
❐ BOLBEC-LILLEBONNE Seine Inferieure 2B
❐ BOLLWEILER Haut-Rhin 1B
❐ BOMPAS Pyrenees Orientales 1B 2B 7A
❐ BONDUES Nord 1B
❐ BONNEVILLE Haute Savoie 1A 2A
❐ BONY Aisne 1A
❐ BORDEAUX Gironde 1A 2B 3A 7A 10B 11B 12A
❐ BORDES-SUR-AZIZE Ariege 2A
❐ BOSMONT Aisne 1B
❐ BOSQUET-d'ORB Herault 3C
❐ BOUCHAIN Nord 1B
❐ BOUE Aisne 1A
❐ BOULE LA Loire-Atlantique 7A
❐ BOULOC Haute Garonne 2B
❐ BOULOGNE Seine 7A 12B
❐ BOULOGNE SUR GESSE Haute Garonne 2B 7A
❐ BOULOGNE SUR HELPE Nord 1A
❐ BOULOGNE-BILLANCOURT Hauts de Seine 7A 12A
❐ BOULOGNE-SUR-MER Pas de Calais 1A 7A 9A 12A
❐ BOULOU, LE Pyrenees Orientales 2B
❐ BOULT-S/SUIPPE Marne 1A
❐ BOULZICOURT Ardennes 1B
❐ BOURBON Pas de Calais 1A
❐ BOURBOULE, LA Puy-de-Dome 7A
❐ BOURG Aix 2A 10B
❐ BOURG DE SOMMEVOIRE Haute Marne 14B
❐ BOURG EN BRESSE Ain 1B 7A 10B
❐ BOURG-ARGENTAL Loire 7A
❐ BOURG-DE-PEAGE Drome 7A
❐ BOURGES Cher 1A 2B 7A
❐ BOURGET, LE Seine 1A 7 10C
❐ BOURGOIN Isaere 6A 7A
❐ BOURLEMONT Meuse 3B
❐ BOURLON Pas de Calais 1A
❐ BOURRET Tarn et Garonne 1A 2B
❐ BOUSBECQUE Nord 1A
❐ BOUSQUET-d'ORB Herault 3A
❐ BOUSIES Nord 1B 2B
❐ BOUVIGNIES Nord 1B
❐ BOUVRIE, LA 3B
❐ BOUZINCOURT Somme 3B
❐ BOVES Somme 3B
❐ BOYARDVILLE Charente Maritime 3D
❐ BRANCOURT Aisne 1B
❐ BRANCOURT LE GRAND Aisne 1A
❐ BRAUX-NOUZON Ardennes 1A
❐ BRAY ST. CHRISTOPHE 1A
❐ BRAYE EN THIERACHE Aisne 1B 2B
❐ BREBIERES Pas de Calais 1A 2A
❐ BRESSUIRE Deux-Sevres 3A
❐ BREST Finistere 3B 7B 12A
❐ BRETIGNY Oise 1B
❐ BRIANCON Hautes Alpes 7A
❐ BRIATEXTE Tarn 1B 2B
❐ BRIEULLES Ardennes 1B
❐ BRILLON Meuse 1B
❐ BRIN-SUR-SEILLE Meurthe & Moselle 7A
❐ BRISSY Aisne 1A
❐ BRISSY-CHOIGNY Aisne 2B
❐ BRIVE Correze 1A 2B 6B
❐ BRIVES-CHARENSAC Haute Loire 3B
❐ BRONS (Broons) Cotes du Nord 7A
❐ BROUCHY Somme 1A
❐ BRUAY Pas de Calais 2B
❐ BRUAY EN ARTOIS Pas de Calais 1A 2A 3B
❐ BRUILLE ST. AMAND Nord 1A
❐ BRUILLE-LEZ-MARCHIENNES Nord 1A
❐ BUISSON, LE Seine et Oise 3B
❐ BRUNEMONT Nord 1A 2A
❐ BRUNOY (Boulangerie) Bouryaillat 2B 14B
❐ BRUYERES ET MONTBERAULT Aisne 1A
❐ BUDELIERE-CHAMBUR Creuse 14B
❐ BUDOS Gironde 2A
❐ BUGNICOURT Nord 1A
❐ BUIRONFOSSE Aisne 1A
❐ BUISSON, LE Seine-et-Oise 3D
❐ BUISSY Pas de Calais 1B
❐ BUSCHWEILLER (Bischwiller) Haut Rhin 1A
❐ BUSSY Maine et Loire 1B

100 Francs, Caen, France, 14B

❒ BUZANCY Aisne 3B
❒ BUZET-S/TARN Haute Garonne 1A 6A
❒ CADILLAC Gironde 1A 2A 6A 7A
❒ CADOURS Haute-Garonne 1A 2A
❒ CAEN Calvados 3B 6A 7A 14E
❒ CAEN ET HONFLEUR Calvados 1A 3B 6A 14E
❒ CAESTRE Nord 3C
❒ CAGNAC Tarn 1A
❒ CAGNICOURT Pas de Calais 1A
❒ CAGNONCLES Nord 1A
❒ CAGNY Calvados 7B 14A
❒ CAHORS Lot 1A 6A 7B 10B
❒ CALAIS Pas de Calais 1A 2A 3B 6B 7A 12B
❒ CALAIS LA CAPELLE
Pas de Calais 6A
❒ CAMBRAI Nord 1A 2A
❒ CAMP AVIGNON 3A
❒ CAMPAGNE Ariege 2B
❒ CAMPAING-EN-PLEVE Nord 1B
❒ CANCON Lot-et-Garonne 2B
❒ CANNES Alpes Maritimes 2 B 7A
❒ CANTAING Nord 1B
❒ CANTAL 1A
❒ CAPELLE, LA Aisne 1A 6A 7A
❒ CAPELLE, LA Nord 1A 7B
❒ CARAMAN Haute Garonne 1B 2B 7A
❒ CARBONNE Haute-Garonne 1A 2B
❒ CARCASSONE Aude 1A 2A 3A 6A 7A 10B
❒ CARLA-BAYLE 2B
❒ CARMAUX Tarn 2A 7B
❒ CARPENTRAS Vaucluse 3A 7A
❒ CARPIAGNE Marseilles 3B
❒ CARTIGNIES Somme 1A
❒ CARTIGNY Somme 1A 2A
❒ CARVIN Pas de Calais 1A 2B 7A
❒ CASABIANDA Aleria Corse 3C 4A 10B
❒ CASSENUIL Lot-et-Garrone 2B
❒ CASTELJALOUX Lot-et-Garonne 1A 2B
❒ CASTELMORON Lot et Garonne 1A 2B
❒ CASTELNAU-D'AUZAN Gers 1B 6A
❒ CASTELNAU-ESSTREFONDS 1B
❒ CASTELNAU-MONTRATIER Lot 1B 6A
❒ CASTELNAUDARY Aude 2B 7B 10B
❒ CASTELSARRASIN
Tarn et Garonne 2B 7B 14B
❒ CASTERA-VERDUZAN Gers 1B 2B
❒ CASTILLON
(Castillon la Bataille) Gironde 1A 2A 7A
❒ CASTILLONES Lot-et-Garonne 1A
❒ CASTRES Aisne 2B
❒ CASTRES Tarn 3B 6B 7A 10B
❒ CASTUT, LE 3C
❒ CATEAU, LE Nord 1A 2A 9B
❒ CATELET, LE Aisne 1A
❒ CATILLON Nord 2B
❒ CATTENIERES Nord 1A
❒ CAUDEBEC-LES-ELBEUF
Seine Inferieur 1A 2B
❒ CAUDIES Pyrenees Orientales 2B
❒ CAUDRY Nord 1B 2B
❒ CAULAINCOURT Aisne 1C
❒ CAULERY Nord 1B
❒ CAUNES-MINERVOIS Aude 2B
❒ CAUROIR Nord 1A
❒ CAUSSADE Tarn et Garonne 1A 2B
❒ CAUTERETS Hautes Pyrenees 2B 7A
❒ CAUZE, LE Tarn et Garonne 1A
❒ CAYEUX-EN-SANTERRE
Somme 3C
❒ CAYLUS Tarn et Garonne 1A 2B
❒ CAZIERES Haute-Garonne 1B 7B
❒ CELLIEU Loire 7B
❒ CELLULE Puy-de-Dome 1A 3B
❒ CENTRE 1A
❒ CERIZY Aisne 1A
❒ CERNY LES BUSSY Aisne 1A
❒ CERVIONE Corse 1A 3B
❒ CESSIERES Aisne 1B
❒ CETTE (Sete) Herault 1A 6A 7B 10B
❒ CHAGNAT-EN-LIMAGNE
Puy-de-Dome 3B
❒ CHAGNY Saone et Loire 7A
❒ CHALANDRY Aisne 1A 7A
❒ CHALEASSIERE St. Etienne 2A 7B
❒ CHALETTE Loiret 3C
❒ CHAILLE-LES-MARAIS 2B
❒ CHALINDREY Haute Marne 7A
❒ CHALON SUR SAONE
Saone et Loire 7A
❒ CHALON-S/SAONE AUTIN & LOUHANS
Saone et Loire 1A
❒ CHALON-TOURNUS-CHAGNY
Saone et Loire 7A
❒ CHALONS-SUR-MARNE Marne 3A 6A 7A
❒ CHAMBERY Savoie 1A 3A 7A 14A
❒ CHAMBON LE Haute Loire 7A
❒ CHAMBON-FEUGEROLLES
Loire 7A
❒ CHAMBRY S/LAON Aisne 1C
❒ CHAMONIX Haute Savoie 1A 2B 7B
❒ CHAMPAGNOLE Jura 7A
❒ CHAMPIGNELLES Yonne 7A
❒ CHANTONNAY Vendee 3A
❒ CHARENTONNEAU 14A
❒ CHARLEVILLE Ardennes 7A 10A 12A
❒ CHARLEVILLE & SEDAN Ardennes 6A
❒ CHARLEVILLE-MEZIERES Ardennes 1A 2A
❒ CHARLEVILLE-MEZIERES-
MOHON Ardennes 1A 3A
❒ CHARLIEU Loire 3B 6A 7A
❒ CHARMES Aisne 1B
❒ CHARTRES Eure et Loire 3B 6A 10B 11B
❒ CHARVIEN Isere 2A
❒ CHASSE Isere 3B 14B
❒ CHATEAU D'ESTOUILLY-HAM Somme 1A
❒ CHATEAU-GONTIER Mayenne 3C
❒ CHATEAU-LANDON Seine-et-Marne3C
❒ CHATEAU SALINS Moselle 1B
❒ CHATEAU-REGNAULT-BOGNY Ardennes 1B
❒ CHATEAUNEUF Ille et Vilaine 4B
❒ CHATEAURENARD Bouches-du-Rhone 2A
❒ CHATEAUROUX Indre 1A 2A 3A 4C 7A 10B
❒ CHATERUROUX Indre 1B
❒ CHATEAU-THIERRY Aisne 3C
❒ CHATELLERAULT Vienne 6A 7B 11B
❒ CHATENOIS Territoire de Belfort 7A
❒ CHATILLON S/OISE Aisne 1A

20 Centimes (milk coupon), Cluses, France, 2A

❒ CHATILLON-LE-DUC Doubs 3B
❒ CHATOU Yvelines 1A 6B 7A
❒ CHAUFONTAINE Meurthe-et-Moselle 3B
❒ CHAULNES Somme 3B
❒ CHAUMONT Haute-Marne 7B 10C
❒ CHAUNY Aisne 1A 2B 3C
❒ CHAVILLE Hautes de Seine 1A
❒ CHAVANOZ 2B
❒ CHAZELLES Saone et Loire 7A
❒ CHECY-CHATEAUNEUF-SULLY-VIRTY Loire 6A
❒ CHEDDE Haute Savoie 7A
❒ CHERBOURG Loire-Atlantique 1A 3C 7B
❒ CHEROEY Charente 7A
❒ CHERY LES POUILLY 1A
❒ CHESNE, LE Ardennes 10B
❒ CHEVREGNY Aisne 2B
❒ CHEVRESIS-MONCEAU Aisne 1A 2B
❒ CHIGNY Aisne 1A
❒ CHOLET Maine et Loire 1B 2B 3B 4B 7A 10B
❒ CINQ-CANTONS-ANGLET Basses-Pyrenees 2B
❒ CINTE-GABELLE 2B
❒ CIREY Meurthe-et-Moselle 1B 6A
❒ CIREY-BLAMONT-XURES 1A
❒ CITE 7A
❒ CLAIRAC Lot-et-Garonne 2A
❒ CLASTRES Aisne 1A
❒ CLAYETTE, LA (Saone et Loire) 7A
❒ CLERMONT L'HERAULT Herault 1A
❒ CLERMONT-AULNAT Puy-de-Dome 3B
❒ CLERMONT-FERRAND & ISSOIRE Puy-de-Dome 1C
❒ CLERMONT-FERRAND Puy-de-Dome 1A 2B 3B 6A 7A 10B 12B
❒ CLICHY LA GARENNE Hautes de Seine 1B
❒ CLOS MORTIER Haute-Marne 2B
❒ CLUSES Haute-Savoie 2A

1 Franc, Colmar, France, 1A

❒ COETQUIDAN Morbihan 3C
❒ COGNAC Charente 1A 2B 7A 11B
❒ COLMAR Haut Rhin 1A 2B 6A 14A
❒ COLOGNE Gers 2B
❒ COLOMBIER 1B
❒ COLOMBIES Aveyron 2B
❒ COLONFAY Aisne 1A
❒ COMINES Nord 1A
❒ COMPIEGNE Oise 1A 3B 6B
❒ CONDOM Gers 1A 2B
❒ CONNANTRE Marne 3B 10B
❒ CONQUES Aude 2B
❒ CONTES-LES-PINS Alpes Maritimes 7B
❒ CONTESCOURT Aisne 1A
❒ CONTRES Loir et Cher 7B
❒ CORBEHEM Pas de Calais 1A
❒ CORBEIL ET ETAMPES Seine-et-Oise 1A
❒ CORBIE Somme 1A
❒ CORBIGNY Nievre 3C
❒ CORDES Tarn 1A 2A
❒ CORNIMONT Vosges 1A 2A
❒ CORRE Haute Saone 2A
❒ CORREZE Correze 1A
❒ CORSE Corse 14A
❒ CORTE Corse 3B 7C
❒ COSNE Allier 7B 14A
❒ COSNES-SUR-LOIRE Nievre 14B
❒ COTE-CHAUDE 7A
❒ COTEAU, LE Loire 2B
❒ COTES-DU-NORD Nord 14B
❒ COUCY LE CHATEAU Aisne 1A
❒ COUERON Loire Atlantique 7A
❒ COULOMMIERS Seine et Marne 11A
❒ COURCELLES-LEZ-LENS Pas de Calais 1B 3C
❒ COURCHETTES Nord 1A
❒ COURNEUVE, LA Seine-Saint Denis 1A 2A 7A 11B

Types of Emergency Money

Type	Reference #
Municipal paper	1
Private paper	2
POW paper	3
POW official metal	4
POW private metal	5
Municipal metal	6
Private metal	7
Gas tokens	8
Food; beer; konsumverein	9
Naval; military; kantine	10
Encased, unencased stamps	11
Streetcar tokens	12
Porcelain	13
World War II issues	14
Concentration, Civilian internment camps	15

Rarity grades: A, to $25; B, to $60; C, to $125; D, to $200; and E, $350

❒ COURRIERES Pas de Calais	1A	2A	
❒ COURSAN Aude	2A		
❒ COURTINE, LA Creuse	3C		
❒ COUTANCES Manche	11B		
❒ COUTICHES Nord	1A	2B	
❒ CRANSAC Aveyron	2B		
❒ CRAUX Ardennes	7A		
❒ CRECY-EN-BRIE Seine-et-Marne	6A		
❒ CRECY-SUR SERRE Aisne	1A	6A	7A
❒ CREPY-EN-LAONNOIS Aisne	1A		
❒ CRESPIN Nord	1B		
❒ CRESSY-OMENCOURT Somme	1B		
❒ CREULLY Calvados	7B		
❒ CREUSE Creuse	1A	3C	
❒ CREUSOT, LE Saone et Loire	2B	7B	10C
❒ CREVECOEUR S/ESCAUT Nord	1A		
❒ CREZY-SUR-SERRE Aisne	6A	7A	
❒ CRIGNY Aisne	1A		
❒ CRINCY Nord	1A		
❒ CROISIC, LE (Loire Inferieure) Loire Atlantique	7B		
❒ CROIX	2B		
❒ CROIX Haute-Marne	1A	2B	
❒ CROIX ET WASQUEHAL Nord	1A		
❒ CROIX-FONSOMME	1A		
❒ CROIX-MOLIGNEAUX Somme	1A		
❒ CROSNE Seine et Oise	7B		
❒ CRUPILLY Aisne	1A		
❒ CUGNY Aisne	1A		
❒ CUINCY Nord	1A		
❒ CUISEAUX Saone-et-Loire	2B		
❒ CURVILLE Haute-Marne	7B		
❒ CUTS Oise	1B		
❒ CUXAC D'AUDE Aude	7B		
❒ CYSOING Nord	1A	2A	
❒ D'URVILLE, Bateau Dumont	1A		
❒ DAIGNY Aisne	1A		
❒ DALLON Aisne	1A		
❒ DAMAZAN Lot-et-Garonne	2A		
❒ DAMIATTE Tarn	7A		
❒ DANCOURT Somme	3B		
❒ DANIZY Aisne	1A	2A	
❒ DAUPHINE Alpes-de-Haute-Provence	3B	14B	
❒ DAX Landes	6A	7A	
❒ DEAUVILLE Calvados	3A	7B	
❒ DECAZEVILLE Aveyron	2B		
❒ DECHY Nord	1A		
❒ DENAIN Nord	1B	2B	
❒ DERCY Aisne	1C		
❒ DEREY Aisne	1A		
❒ DEUTSCHRUMBACH Haut-Rhin	2B		
❒ DEUX-SEVRES	1A	6B	

1 Franc, Douai (France), 1A

❒ DIEPPE Seine Maritime	1A	3B			
❒ DIEUPENTALE Tarn-et-Garonne	1B	2B	6A		
❒ DIGOIN Saone-et-Loire	7A				
❒ DIGOIN-EST Saone-et-Loire	7A				
❒ DIJON Cote-d'Or	1A	6B	7A	11B	
❒ DINAN Cotes du Nord	3B				
❒ DINARD Ile et Vilaine	2A	7B			
❒ DISCARD	7A				
❒ DIVES Calvados	1A	7A			
❒ DIZY LE GROS Aisne	1A				
❒ DOLE Jura	7A				
❒ DOME, PUY DE Puy de Domb	1A				
❒ DOMPIERRE Nord	1A				
❒ DONCHERY Ardennes	1A				
❒ DONZERE Drome	7A				
❒ DORENGT Aisne	1B				
❒ DORTAN Ain	1A	2B	9A		
❒ DOUAI Nord	1A	2A	3A	7A	
❒ DOUAI-ET-CARVIN Nord	1A				
❒ DOUCHY Aisne	1A				
❒ DOUILLY Somme	1A				
❒ DOURGES Pas de Calais	1A				
❒ DRAGUIGNAN Tarn et Garonne	2B	3C	7B		
❒ DRIENCOURT	1A				
❒ DROCOURT Pas de Calais	1A		2B		
❒ DUNIERES Haute Loire	7A				
❒ DUNKERQUE Nord	1A	2A	6A	7A	11B
❒ DURAS Lot et Garonne	2A				
❒ DURBAN Aude	2B				
❒ DURY Aisne	1A				
❒ DURY Nord	1A				
❒ DYON Cote d'Or	1A				
❒ EAUZE Gers	1B	2B			
❒ ECOURT ST. QUENTIN Nord	1A	2A			
❒ ELBEUF Seine-Inferieure	1A	2A	6A		
❒ ELLERHOOP Als	1A				
❒ ELNE Pyrenees-Orientales	2B				
❒ ENGHIEN-LES-BAINS Val d'Oise	7A				
❒ ENGLANCOURT Aisne	1A				
❒ ENGLEFONTAINE Nord	2B				
❒ ENNEVELIN Nord	1B				
❒ EPEHY Somme	1A				
❒ EPERNAY Marne	1A	2A	7A		
❒ EPINAL Vosges	1A	7A	10B		
❒ EPINOY Pas de Calais	1A				
❒ EPPE-SAUVAGE Nord	1A				
❒ EPPEVILLE Somme	1A	2A			
❒ ERCHEU Somme	1A				
❒ ERLON Aisne	1A				
❒ ERLOY Aisne	1A				
❒ ERRE Nord	1A				
❒ ESCARMAIN Nord	1A				
❒ ESCATALENS Tarn-et-Garonne	2B				
❒ ESCAUDAIN Nord	1A	7B			
❒ ESCAUDOEUVRES Nord	1B	2A			
❒ ESCAUFORTAisne	1A	2B			
❒ ESMERY-HALLON Somme	1A	2A			
❒ ESPALOIS Tarn-et-Garonne	2B				
❒ ESQUEHERIES Aisne	1A				
❒ ESQUERCHIN Nord	1A				
❒ ESSIGNY-LE-GRAND Aisne	1A				
❒ ESSIGNY-LE-PETIT Aisne	1A				
❒ EST Banlieue	7A				
❒ ESTENOS	2B				
❒ ESTOUILLY-HAM Somme	1A				
❒ ESTREES Aisne	1A				
❒ ESTREES Nord	1A				
❒ ETAING Pas-de-Calais	1A				
❒ ETAINGS, LES Loire	3B				
❒ ETAMPES Seine et Oise	3B	4B	10B		
❒ ETAVES-ET-BOCQUIAUX Aisne	1A				
❒ ETCHEBERRYGAAY	6A				
❒ ETERPIGNY Pas-de-Calais	1B				

10 Centimes, Dunkerque (France), 6B

❒ ETRAT Loire 7B
❒ ETREAUPONT Aisne 1A
❒ ETREILLES Aisne 1A
❒ ETREUX Aisne 1A
❒ EURE ET LOIRE 1A 6A
❒ EURVILLE Haute Marne 7A
❒ EVIAN-LES-BAINS Haute Savoie 2A
❒ EVIN-MALMAISON Pas de Calais 1A
❒ EVIRES 2B
❒ EVREUX Eure 1A 3A 6A 7A 11B 14A
❒ EYMET Dordogne 1A
❒ EYSSET Dordogne 1A
❒ EYZIN-PINET Isere 1A 2B
❒ FABREZAN Aude 1A 2B
❒ FACHES-THUMESNIL Nord 1A 7A
❒ FAGNIERES Marne 3C
❒ FALAISE Calvados 7A
❒ FAMPOUX Pas de Calais 1A
❒ FARGNIERS Aisne 1B
❒ FAUCOUCOURT Aisne 1A
❒ FAULQUEMONT Lorraine 3A 14A
❒ FAUMONT Nord 1A
❒ FAVRIL Nord 1B
❒ FAYET Aisne 1A
❒ FECAMP Seine Inferieure 1A 7B 9A 11B
❒ FECAMP-FOURNEAUX Seine Inferieure 7A 9A
❒ FECHAIN Nord 1A 2A
❒ FEIGNIES Nord 1A
❒ FELLERINGEN Haut-Rhin 1B
❒ FENAIN Nord 1A
❒ FERE, LA Aisne 1A 2A
❒ FERIER Nord 1A
❒ FERIN Nord 1A
❒ FERTE-ALAIS, LA Seine et Oise 2C 7A
❒ FERTE-CHEVRESIS, LA Aisne 1A
❒ FERTE-MACE, LA Orne 2A 3C
❒ FERTE-SUR-jOUARE, lA Aisne 2B
❒ FESMY Aisne 1A
❒ FEUCHY Pas-de-Calais 1A
❒ FEUILLONEX 2B
❒ FEUQUIERES Somme 4A 7A
❒ FEURS 7A
❒ FIEULAINE Aisne 1A
❒ FILLINGES Haute Savoie 1 2B
❒ FINHAN Tarn-et-Garonne 2B
❒ FINISTERE 3A 12A
❒ FINS Tarn 1A
❒ FIRMINY Loire 2A 3C 7B
❒ FISLIS Haut-Rhin 1E
❒ FLAMENGRIE, LA Aisne 1A
❒ FLAVIGNY-LE-GRAND ET BEURAIN 1A
❒ FLAVIGNY-LE-PETIT Aisne 1A 2A
❒ FLAVY LE MELDEUX Somme 1A
❒ FLAVY-LE-MARTEL Aisne 1A 2B
❒ FLAYOSC Var 7B
❒ FLAYOX Var 7A
❒ FOLEMBRAY 2B
❒ FLERS-EN-ESCREBIEUX Nord 1A
❒ FLEURANCE 1A 2B
❒ FLINES-LES-RACHES Nord 1A
❒ FLOING Ardennes 1A
❒ FLORENSAC Herault 7A
❒ FLORY LE MELDEUX Oise 1A
❒ FLOYOX Var 7A
❒ FLUQUIERES Aisne 1A
❒ FOIX Arriege 1A 2A
❒ FOLEMBRAY Aisne 1A 2B
❒ FOLSCHVILLER Lorraine 3A 14A
❒ FONSOMME Aisne 1A
❒ FONTAINE AU PIRE Nord 1A
❒ FONTAINE NOTRE DAME Nord 1A
❒ FONTAINE-LES-CLERCS Aisne 1A
❒ FONTAINE-UTERTE Aisne 1B
❒ FONTENAY LE COMTE Vendee 7B
❒ FONTENAY-AUX-ROSES Hautes de Seine 1B
❒ FONTENELLE Aisne 1A
❒ FORBACH Moselle 1A 2A 3A 5B 14A
❒ FORENVILLE Nord 1B
❒ FOREST Nord 1B
❒ FORESTE Aisne 1A 2A
❒ FORGES DE GUEUGNON 1A
❒ FORT DE SENNECEY 3A
❒ FORT DE VAROIS 3A
❒ FORT DU MURIER Isere 3B
❒ FOS Haute-Garonne 2A
❒ FOUGERES Ille et Vilaine 3C 7B
❒ FOUILLOUZE Loire 7B
❒ FOURCHAMBAULT 14E
❒ FOURCHAMBAULT Nievre 14A
❒ FOURMIES Nord 1A 2A
❒ FOURMIES ET TRELON Nord 7B
❒ FOURQUEVAUX Haute Garonne 1B 6A
❒ FOUSSERET Haute Garonne 1B
❒ FRAISANS Jura 7A
❒ FRAISSE Loire 7B
❒ FRANCILLY-SELENCY Aisne 1A
❒ FRERENT Nord 7A
❒ FRESNES/ESCAUT Nord 2C
❒ FRESNES LES MONTAUBAN Pas de Calais 1B
❒ FRESNOY-LE-GRAND Aisne 1A
❒ FRESSAIN Nord 1A
❒ FRESSIES Nord 1A

❒ FRETOY Somme 1B
❒ FREVENT Pas-de-Calais 7A
❒ FREVENT & ENVIRONS Pas de Calais 7A
❒ FRIERES-FAILLOUEL Aisne 1A
❒ FRIGOLET Bouches du Rhone 3C 4B 10B 15B
❒ FRONCLES Haute-Marne 2B
❒ FRONTON Haut Garonne 2B
❒ FUMAY Ardennes 1A 2B
❒ FUMEL Lot et Garonne 2A 7B
❒ GACY-SUR-EURE Eure 7A
❒ GAGNY Seine et Oise 14B
❒ GAILLAC Tarn 1A 2B
❒ GAILLAC-TOULZA Haute-Garonne 1B 2B
❒ GALLICIAN Gard 7B
❒ GANGES Herault 7A
❒ GARD 6A 7A
❒ GARAISON Hautes-Pyrenees 3C
❒ GARD-HERAULT-AUDE 14A
❒ GARENNE, LA Seine 7A
❒ GAUCHY Aisne 1A
❒ GAVRELLE Pas-de-Calais 1A
❒ GEISHAUSEN Haut-Rhin 1E
❒ GENERAC Gard 2B
❒ GENERARGUES Gard 7A
❒ GENEVILLIERS Hauts-de-Seine 7A
❒ GENTILLY Seine 7B
❒ GERCY Saone et Loire 7A
❒ GERDAISES Tarn-et-Garonne 2B
❒ GERGNY Aisne 1A
❒ GERMAINE Aisne 1A 2B
❒ GERS Gers 1A
❒ GEX Ain 6A 7A
❒ GEXONNE Meurthe-et-Moselle 7A
❒ GEYRIAC MINERVOIS Aude 7A
❒ GIBERCOURT Aisne 1A
❒ GIHEL 2B
❒ GIMONT Gers 1B
❒ GIN-NICE Alpes Maritimes 7A
❒ GINOUSE Pyrenees Orientales 7A
❒ GIRAUD 7A
❒ GIVET Ardennes 2B
❒ GIVORS Rhone 1A 2B 7A
❒ GLAGEON Nord 1A 2B
❒ GOEULZIN Nord 1A
❒ GOISE LA Nord 1A
❒ GOIX-TERRON Ardennes 6A
❒ GOLANCOURT Oise 1A
❒ GOLDBACH Haut-Rhin 1A
❒ GONDRIN Gers 2B 6A 7A
❒ GONESSE Seine-Maritime 1A
❒ GONT-SUR-SEINE Aube 7A
❒ GONTAUD Lot et Garonne 1A 2B
❒ GONY Aisne 1A
❒ GONY/BELLONE Pas-de-Calais 1A
❒ GOURNAY-EN-BRAY Seine Inferieure 7A
❒ GOUY Aisne 1A
❒ GOUY-SOUS-BELLONE Pas de Calais 1A
❒ GOUZEAUCOURT Nord 1A
❒ GRADIGNAN Gironde 7B 11B
❒ GRAFENSTADEN Haut-Rhin 1A 2B
❒ GRAISSESSAC Herault 2B 3B 10B
❒ GRAMAT Lot 2A
❒ GRAND-AULNAY Seine-Inferieure 3B
❒ GRAND BOMAND Haute-Saone 2A
❒ GRAND DU ROI Gard 7A
❒ GRAND VERLY Aisne 1A
❒ GRAND-BORNAND Haute Savoie 2A
❒ GRANDE COMBE, LA Gard 3A 6A 7A 14B
❒ GRANDE-SUR-ADOUR Landes 2A
❒ GRANVILLE Manche 1A 3B 6A
❒ GRANVILLE-CHERBOURG Manche 1A
❒ GRANVILLIERS Oise 7B
❒ GRAU-DU-ROI Gard 1A 7A
❒ GRAULHET Tarn 1B 2B 7B
❒ GRAY Haute-Saone 14C
❒ GRAY ET VESOUL Haute-Saone 1A
❒ GRAY-VESOUL-LURE Haute Saone 14B
❒ GRENADE-SUR-GESSE Gard 1A
❒ GRENADE, Haute Garonne 1B 2A
❒ GRENOBLE Isere 1A 2B 7A 9A 11B
❒ GRICOURT Aisne 1A
❒ GRICOURT-NIAY-RENANSART Aisne 1A
❒ GRIEGES 2B
❒ GRIGNOLS Dordogne 1A 2B
❒ GRISOLLES Tarn-et-Garonne 2B
❒ GROISE, LA Nord 1B
❒ GROSLAY Val-d'Oise 1B
❒ GROUGIS Aisne 1A
❒ GROUPES COMMERCEAUX du Gard 7A
❒ GRUCHET LE VALASSE Seine Inferieur 1A 2B
❒ GRUGIES Aisne 1A 2A
❒ GUEBWILLER (Gebweiler) Haute-Rhin 1A
❒ GUEMAPPE Pas-de-Calais 1B
❒ GUERANDE Loire-Inferieure 3B
❒ GUERIGNY Nievre 7A
❒ GUESNAIN Nord 1A 2B
❒ GUEUGNON Saone-et-Loire 7A
❒ GUIGNIES Somme 1B
❒ GUISCARD Oise 1B 2B
❒ GUISCURE Oise 3C
❒ GUISE Aisne 1A 7B
❒ GUNY Oise 2B
❒ GUYENNE & GASCOGNE Aude 6A
❒ HAGENDINGEN Moselle 1A 2B
❒ HALLUIN Nord 1A 2A
❒ HAM Somme 1A 6A 7B
❒ HAM-NOYON-ST. SIMON Haute Saone 1B
❒ HAMBLAIN-LES-PRES Pas-de-Calais 1A
❒ HAMEGICOURT Aisne 1A 3C
❒ HAMEL Nord 1A
❒ HANCOURT Somme 1A
❒ HANNAPES Aisne 1A
❒ HANNOGNE Ariege 1B
❒ HAPPENCOURT Aisne 1A
❒ HARBY Somme 6A
❒ HARGICOURT Aisne 1A
❒ HARLY Aisne 1A
❒ HARLY PRES ST. QUENTIN Somme 7B
❒ HARNES Pas de Calais 1A
❒ HASNON Nord 1B 2A
❒ HASPRES Nord 1B 2A
❒ HAUBOURDIN Nord 11B
❒ HAUCOURT Pas-de-Calais 1A
❒ HAUTE LOIRE 3B
❒ HAUTERIVE (Hautes-Rives) Aisne 7B
❒ HAUTEVILLE Aisne 1A
❒ HAUTMONT Manche 1A
❒ HAUTMONT (Hautmond) Nord 1A 7A
❒ HAVELOY Nord 1B
❒ HAVRE, LE Seine Inferieure 1A 2B 3A 7A 10A 11B 12B
❒ HAYENCOURT Nord 1A
❒ HELCHIN Somme 1B

Location	Codes
❒ HELESMES (Hellemes) Nord	1B 7B
❒ HEM Nord	1A
❒ HEM-LENGLET Nord	1A
❒ HENIN-LIETARD Pas de Calais	1A 7B
❒ HENINEL Pas-de-Calais	1A
❒ HENNEBONT Morbihan	3C
❒ HERAULT	1A 6A 7A
❒ HERGNIES Nord	1A 2B
❒ HERIE LA VIEVILLE LA Aisne	1A
❒ HERINNES Nord	2B
❒ HERVILLY Aisne	1A 2B
❒ HEUDICOURT Somme	1A 2A
❒ HINACOURT Aisne	1A
❒ HIRSON Aisne	1A 6A 7A
❒ HIRSINGEN Oberelsass	1B
❒ HOLNON Aisne	1A
❒ HOMBLEUX Somme	1A
❒ HOMBLEY Somme	1A
❒ HOMBLIERES Aisne	1A
❒ HOMECOURT Meurthe-et-Moselle	1B 2B
❒ HONDEGEM Nord	3C
❒ HONFLEUR Calvados	11B
❒ HONNECOURT Nord	1A
❒ HORDAIN Nord	1B
❒ HORNAING Nord	1A
❒ HORME, L' Loire	3B 7B
❒ HORNAING Nord	1A
❒ HOUDAN Yvelines	1A 2B
❒ HOUILLES Yvellines	1B
❒ HOUSSAYE-BERENGER Seine-Inferieure	3B
❒ HOUSSET Aisne	1B
❒ HUESSEREN-PETIT Haut-Rhin	1A
❒ HUESSERN-WESSERLING Ober Elsass	1B
❒ IGNEY Meurthe-et-Moselle	3C
❒ ILLE Pyrenees Orientales	2B
❒ ILLE-ET-VILAINE Ille-et-Vilaine	14B
❒ ILLE-SUR-TET	2B
❒ INCHY-EN-ARTOIS Pas-de-Calais	1A
❒ INDRE	4C
❒ INDRET Loire Inferieure	7A
❒ IRON Aisne	1A
❒ ISBERGUES Pas-de-Calais	2A
❒ ISLE-ADAM	1A
❒ ISLE-EN-DODON Haute Garonne	2A
❒ ISLE-EN-JOURDAIN Gers	1A 2A
❒ ISSIGEAC Dordogne	1B
❒ ISSOIRE Puy de Dome	7A
❒ ISSOUDUN Indre	3B
❒ ISTRES Bouches du Rhone	7A 10B
❒ ITANCOURT Aisne	1A
❒ IWUY Nord	1A 2B
❒ IZEL-LES-EQUERCHIN Pas-de-Calais	1C
❒ IZIEUX Loire	7B
❒ JARNAC Charente	2B 7B
❒ JAUSIERS Basses-Alpes	3C
❒ JEANCOURT Aisne	1A
❒ JEGUN Gers	2B
❒ JEUGNY Aube	3C
❒ JOEUF Meurthe-et-Moselle	1B
❒ JOINVILLE-LE-PONT Seine	7A 10B
❒ JONCOURT Aisne	1A 2A
❒ JONZAC Charente Inferieure	7B
❒ JOUGUET Cotes-du-Nord	2B 3C
❒ JOUZIEUX Loire	7A
❒ JUVISY-SUR-ORGE Seine et Oise	7A 10A
❒ KARLINGEN Marne	2B
❒ KAYSERBERG Haut Rhin	1A 2B
❒ KERORIOU Finistere	3B
❒ KREMLIN BICETRE Val de Marne	11B
❒ KRUET Alsace	1B
❒ LABASTIDE-SAINT-PIERRE Tarn-et-Garonne	3C
❒ LACEPEDE Lot-et-Garonne	2B
❒ LAFITTE Lot et Garonne	1A
❒ LAFRANCAISE Tarn et Garonne	2B 7A
❒ LAGARDELLE Tarn-et-Garonne	2C
❒ LAGRASSE Aude	2D
❒ LAGUEPIE Tarn et Garonne	2D
❒ LAIGNEVILLE Oise	7A
❒ LALLAING Nord	1A 2C
❒ LAMBERSART Nord	2C
❒ LAMBRES Nord	1B
❒ LAMBRES-LEZ-DOUAI	2B
❒ LAMOTTE-BEUVRON Loir et Cher	7B
❒ LAMOTTE-EN-SANTERRE Somme	3B
❒ LAMOURA Jura	7A
❒ LANDAS Nord	1A
❒ LANDE, LA Dordogne	3A
❒ LANDES Nord	1A 6A 7B
❒ LANDIFAY et BERTAIGNEMONT Aisne	1A
❒ LANDRECIES Nord	1B
❒ LANGON Gironde	2C
❒ LANNEPAX Ger	1C
❒ LANNOY Nord IA	
❒ LAON Aisne	1A 4B 3B 7A 10B 14B
❒ LAPARADE Lot-et-Garonne	1B
❒ LAROCHE Yonne	3B
❒ LAROQUE D'OLMES (Laroques) Ariege	1C 6A 7A
❒ LARRAZET Tarn et Garonne	1C
❒ LARZAC Dordogne	3A 14A
❒ LASBORDES Aude 1	6A
❒ LAUWIN-PLANQUE Nord	1A
❒ LAUZERTE Tarn et Garonne	2B
❒ LAUZIERE, LA Charente Inferieure	7B
❒ LAUZUN Lot et Garonne	2A
❒ LAVAL ET MAYENNE	1A 14C
❒ LAVAQUERESSE Aisne	1A
❒ LAVARDENS Gers	2B
❒ LAVAUR Tarn	1B
❒ LAVELANET Ariege	2A
❒ LAVERGIES Aisne	1A
❒ LAVIT DE LOMAGNE Tarn et Garonne	2A
❒ LE MANS Sarthe	14A
❒ LECHERIE-VIEVILLE	1A
❒ LECLUSE Nord	1A
❒ LECTOURE Gers	1B 6A
❒ LEERS Nord	1A
❒ LEFOREST Pas de Calais	1A
❒ LEHAUCOURT Aisne	1A 3A
❒ LEME Aisne	1B
❒ LENS Pas de Calais	1A 2A 3A 6A 7B 12A 14B
❒ LENS Somme	7A 9A 12A
❒ LERIGNEAUX	7A
❒ LESCHELLE	1A
❒ LESDINS Aisne	1A
❒ LESPIGNAN Herault	7A
❒ LESQUIELLE-ST. GERMAIN Aisne	1A
❒ LESQUIELLES	1A
❒ LESTELLE Basses Pyrenees	2B
❒ LEVAL Nord	1B
❒ LEVERGIES Aisne	1A
❒ LEWARDE Nord	1A
❒ LEZAT Ariege	2B

10 Centimes, Lille, France, 1A

❒ LEZIGNAN Aude 1B
❒ LIAISON DES VOSGES 2B
❒ LIANCOURT Oise 2B 7A
❒ LIBOURNE Gironde 1A
❒ LIESSIES Nord 1B
❒ LIEVIN Pas de Calais 1A 2A 7B
❒ LIEZ Aisne 1B
❒ LILLE Nord 1A 2 3B 7A 11B
❒ LILLEBONNE Seine-Inferieure 1A 2B
❒ LIMOGES Haute Vienne 1A 6A 7A 10A 12B
❒ LIMOGES-PONT DE CHERUY Isere 2A 7A
❒ LIMOUX Aude 1A 2B
❒ LINSELLES Nord 1B
❒ LISIEUX Calvados 2A
❒ LISLE SUR TARN Tarn 1A
❒ LIVAROT ET ST. PIERRE-SUR-DIVES Calvados 7A
❒ LIZEAC Tarn et Garonne 2B
❒ LOFFRE Nord 1C
❒ LOIRE 3C
❒ LOIRET (Comtes de Checy-Chateauneuf-Sully-Vitry) 6A
❒ LONGAGES Haute Garonne 1A
❒ LONGAVESNES Somme 1A
❒ LONGCHAMPS Aisne 1A
❒ LONGUE, ILLE Finistere 3B
❒ LONGUYON Est 2A 3B
❒ LONGWY Lorraine 2A
❒ LONS-LE-SAUNIER Jura 1A 7B 14A
❒ LORIENT Morbihan 1A 7A 10A 11B
❒ LORRAINE 3B
❒ LOT 6A
❒ LOURCHES Nord 1A
❒ LOUVIERS Eure 1A
❒ LOVERVALE 1A
❒ LUCHON Huate-Garonne 1A 2A
❒ LUCHON ET CANTON Haute Garonne 1A
❒ LUCON Vendee 3C
❒ LUNEL Herault 2A 7B
❒ LUNEVILLE Meurthe et Moselle 1B
❒ LURE Haute-Saone 1A 14A
❒ LUSSAT 1A
❒ LUZENAC Ariege 2B
❒ LUZOIR Aisne 3A
❒ LYON Rhone 1A 2C 3A 6B 7B 10A 11B 12A
❒ LYON-GRANCHE-BLANCHE 3A
❒ LYS-LEZ-LANNOY Nord 1A 2B
❒ MACON Saone et Loire 1A
❒ MACON-BOURG Saone et Loire 1A
❒ MACOT Savoy 14A
❒ MACQUIGNY Ainse 1A
❒ MAGNY-LA-FOSSE Aisne 1A
❒ MAILLERAYE, LA Seine Inferieure 3A 14B
❒ MAILLY Aube 7A 10B
❒ MAISONS-LAFITTE Seine et Oise 7A
❒ MAISSENY Aisne 1A
❒ MALAKOFF Hauts-de-Seine 6A
❒ MALINCOURT Nord 1A
❒ MALMERSBACH Alsace 1A
❒ MALO-LES-BAINS Nord 7B
❒ MALZY Aisne 1A
❒ MANDE 6A
❒ MANONVILLERS Meurthe-et-Moselle 3B
❒ MANOSQUE Basses-Alpes 3C
❒ MANS, LE Sarthe 1A 2B 3B 11B 14C
❒ MANTES Seine-Maritime 1A
❒ MARAUSSAN Herault 7B
❒ MARCHIENNES Nord 1B
❒ MARCHIENNES-CAMPAGNE Nord 1A
❒ MARCIAC Gers 2B
❒ MARCILLY-LE-PAVE Loire 3D 7A
❒ MARCOING 2A
❒ MARCQ Aisne 1A
❒ MARCQ EN OSTREVENT Nord 2B
❒ MARE LE Isere 3A
❒ MARENNES1 1A
❒ MAREST Oise 1A
❒ MAREST-DAMPCOURT Oise 1A
❒ MARIGNAN E Bouches du Rhone 7A
❒ MARKIRCH (Sainte-Marie-aux-Mines) Haut Rhin 1A
❒ MARLE Aisne 1A
❒ MARLES Pas de Calais 2B
❒ MARMANDE Lot et Garonne 1B 2B 3C
❒ MARNE Marne 1A
❒ MAROILLES Nord 1A
❒ MAROIS, LE Loiret 3D
❒ MARQUION Pas-de-Calais 1A
❒ MARSEILLAN Herault 7A
❒ MARSEILLE Bouches de Rhone 1A 2B 3B 6A 7A 10A 12A
❒ MARSILLARGUES Herault 2A
❒ MARTEL Lot 2B 6A
❒ MARTEVILLE Aisne 1A
❒ MARTEVILLE-ATTILLY Aisne 1A
❒ MARTRES D'ARTIERES Puy-de-Dome 2B
❒ MARTRES-TOLOSANE Haute Garonne 1B
❒ MAS D'AGENAIS Lot et Garonne 2B
❒ MAS-ELOI, LE Haute-Vienne 3C
❒ MASNIERES Nord 1A 7A
❒ MATICHARD Loire 3C
❒ MATIGNY Somme 1A
❒ MAUBEUGE Nord 1A 2B 3C 7B
❒ MAUBEUGE & SOIRE LE CHATEAU Nord 1B 2B
❒ MAUGUIO Herault 7B 10A
❒ MAULEON Basses Pyrennees 7A
❒ MAUROIS Nord 1B
❒ MAUROY Aisne 1A
❒ MAUVEZIN Gers 1B
❒ MAYENNE Mayenne 1A 2B 6A 14A
❒ MAZAMET Tarn 2B 6A 7A
❒ MAZERES Ariege 2A
❒ MAZET, LA-ST. VOY Haute Loire 7B
❒ MEILLERAIE, LA Loire-Inferieure 3C
❒ MELUN Seine-et-Marne 1A 7B
❒ MENDE Lozere 1A
❒ MENNESSIS Aisne 1A
❒ MENNEVRET Aisne 1A
❒ MENTON Alpes Maritimes 7B
❒ MERICOURT Pas de Calais 1A
❒ MERLEBACH 3A 14A
❒ MERLEBACH Lothringen 14A
❒ MERY SUR SEINE Aube 2B

1 Franc Miramont, 1A

❒ MESBRECOURT Aisne 1A
❒ MESGRIGNY Aube 3B
❒ MESNAY Jura 6A 7B
❒ MESNIL ST. NICAISE 1A
❒ MESNIL-L'ESTRE 1A
❒ MESNIL ST. GERMAIN Calvados 1A
❒ MESNIL SAINT-LAURENT Aisne 1A
❒ METZ Moselle 1A
❒ METZ-EN-COUTURE Pas-de-Calais 1A
❒ MEULAN Pas-de-Calais 1A
❒ MEURCHIN Pas de Calais 1A
❒ MEURTHE-ET-MOSELLE-VOSGES 3B
❒ MEUSE 3C
❒ MEZIERES Ardennes 1A
❒ MEZIERES-SUR-OISE Aisne 1B
❒ MEZIN Lot et Garonne 12A
❒ MICHEVILLE Meurthe et Moselle 2B
❒ MILHAU (Millau) Aveyron 11A
❒ MINES DE BLANZY Saone et Loire 3A
❒ MINES DE LA LOIRE 3A
❒ MIRAMAS Bouches du Rhone 3B
❒ MIRAMONT Haute Garonne 2B
❒ MIRANDE Gers 2B 7B
❒ MIRAUMONT Somme 2B
❒ MITZACH 1B
❒ MODANE Savoie 3C
❒ MOHON Ardennes 7B
❒ MOISSAC Tarn et Garonne 2B
❒ MOLAIN Aisne 1A
❒ MOLIERES Tarn et Garonne 2B
❒ MOLLAU Upper Elsass 1B
❒ MONBRUN Aude 2B
❒ MONCEAU-SUR-OISE Aisne 1A
❒ MONCHECOURT Nord 1C
❒ MONCHY-LAGACHE Somme 1A
❒ MONCHY-LE-PREUX Pas-de-Calais 1A
❒ MONCLAR Tarn et Garonne 1B 2B
❒ MONDESCOURT Oise 1B
❒ MONDREPUIS Aisne 1A
❒ MONFALNQUIN Lot-et-Garonne 2C
❒ MONFORT Gers 1B
❒ MONPAZIER Dordogne 1B 2B
❒ MONS Haute-Loire 1B 3B 4B
❒ MONSEGUR Gironde 2B
❒ MONTAGNY Loire 3C
❒ MONT D'ORIGNY Aisne 1A
❒ MONT-DE-MARSAN Landes 1A 2A
❒ MONT-DORE LE Puy-de-Dome 7A
❒ MONTAGNAC Herault 7A 12A
❒ MONTAIGU Vendee 1A
❒ MONTARGIS Loiret 1B 3B
❒ MONTAUBAN Tarn et Garonne 1A 2A 3B 7A
❒ MONTAY Nord 9B
❒ MONTBELLIARD Doubs 2B
❒ MONTBREHAIN Aisne 1A
❒ MONTBRISON Loire 2B 7A 9B
❒ MONTBRUN Aude 1B 2B
❒ MONTCEAU-LES-MINES Saone 3B 7A 14C
❒ MONTCUQ Lot 2B
❒ MONTDIDIER Somme 3B 10B
❒ MONTECH Tarn-et-Garonne 2B
❒ MONTELIMAR Drome 11B
❒ MONTESCOURT-LIZEROLLES Aisne 1A
❒ MONTESQUIEU-VOLVESTRE Haute Garonne 2B
❒ MONTESQUIOU Gers 2A
❒ MONTFERRE Loire 3B
❒ MONTFORT Gers 1B
❒ MONTFORT-SUR-MEU Ile-et-Vilaine 3B
❒ MONTIGNY-EN-ARROUAISE Aisne 1B
❒ MONTIGNY-EN-GOHELLE Pas de Calais 1A
❒ MONTIGNY-SUR-CRECY 1A
❒ MONTLUCON Allier 3B 7A
❒ MONTLUCON-GANNAT Allier 1A 2B 3A 7A
❒ MONTMAGNY Seine et Oise 2B 7B
❒ MONTMEDY Meuse 1A 3B
❒ MONTMORENCE Seine et Oise 7B
❒ MONTMOROT Jura 3B
❒ MONTOIRE Loire et Cher 3A
❒ MONTOLIEU Aude 1A 7A
❒ MONTOLIEU Rhone 7A
❒ MONTPELLIER Herault 1A 7B
❒ MONTPEZAT-DE-QUERCY Tarn et Garonne 1B 6A

Types of Emergency Money

Type	Reference #
Municipal paper	1
Private paper	2
POW paper	3
POW official metal	4
POW private metal	5
Municipal metal	6
Private metal	7
Gas tokens	8
Food; beer; konsumverein	9
Naval; military; kantine	10
Encased, unencased stamps	11
Streetcar tokens	12
Porcelain	13
World War II issues	14
Concentration, Civilian internment camps	15

Rarity grades: A, to $25; B, to $60; C, to $125; D, to $200; and E, $350

1 Franc, Nancy (France), 1A

❒ MONTREAL Aude 1B 2A 6B
❒ MONTREAL-DU-GERS Gers 2B
❒ MONTREUIL-SUR-MER Pas de Calais 1A
❒ MONTREUX Meurthe-et-Moselle 3C
❒ MONTRICOUX Tarn et Garonne 1A
❒ MONTSALON Loire 3C
❒ MOOSH Alsace 1A
❒ MORBIHAN 3C
❒ MORCOURT Aisne 1A
❒ MORLAIX Finistere 11B
❒ MORTIERS Aisne 1A
❒ MOTTE-D'AVEILLANS Isere 3A 14A
❒ MOTTE-GIRON Cote-d'Or 3B
❒ MOUCHAIN Nord 1B
❒ MOUCHAN Gers 1B
❒ MOUGERES Herault 3B 10B
❒ MOULINS Allier 1A 3B
❒ MOULINS Nievre 7A
❒ MOULINS ET LAPALISSE Allier 1A 3A
❒ MOULLEAU, LE Gironde 6A 7A
❒ MOUSSOULENS Aude 2B
❒ MOUVAUX Nord 1A 9B
❒ MOUVY Oise 1A 7A
❒ MOY Aisne 1A
❒ MOYENNEVILLE Somme 3C
❒ MUILLE-VILLETTE Somme 1A
❒ MUIRACOURT Oise 1A
❒ MULHOUSE (Muelhausen) Alsace 1A 7A 10B 14A
❒ MURE, LA Isere 3B 14A
❒ MURET Haute Garonne 1B 2A
❒ MURIER, LE Isere 3B
❒ MUY, LE 7A
❒ NAMPCELLES-LA-COUR Aisne 1B
❒ NANCY Meurthe et Moselle 1A 2B 3C 7A 11B 14C
❒ NANTERRE Hauts de Seine 3B
❒ NANTES Loire Inferieure 1A 3C 7A 12A 14A
❒ NARBONNE Aude 1A 2B 6A 7A 12A
❒ NAUROY Aisne 1A
❒ NAVES Nord 1B
❒ NEGREPELISSE Tarn et Garonne 1B
❒ NEMOURS Seine et Marne 11B
❒ NERAC Lot et Garonne 1A 2B
❒ NERVIEUX Loire 7A
❒ NESLE Somme 1A
❒ NEUFCHATEAU Vosges 7A
❒ NEUILLY-SUR-SEINE Hautes de Seine 7B
❒ NEUVILLE-BOURJONVAL Pas-de-Calais 1A
❒ NEUVILLE-EN-BEINE Aisne 1A
❒ NEUVILLE-LES-DORENGT Aisne 1A
❒ NEUVILLE-LES-RAON, LA Vosges 1A 2A
❒ NEUVILLE-SAINT-AMAND Aisne 1A
❒ NEUVILLE-ST-REMY Nord 1A
❒ NEUVILETTE Somme 1A
❒ NEUVILLY Nord 2B
❒ NEUVIREUIL Pas-de-Calais 1A
❒ NEUX-LES-MINES Pas de Calais 1A 2A
❒ NEVERS Nievre 1A 3A 7A 14A
❒ NICE Alpes Maritimes 1A 2B 6A 7A 10A 11B
❒ NIEUPORT BAINS Calvados 7B
❒ NIMES Gard 1A 3B 7A 11B 12B
❒ NIZZA 6A
❒ NOEUX-LES-MINES Pas de Calais 1A
❒ NOGENT LE ROTROU Eure 11B
❒ NOGENT SUR MARNE Val de Marne 7A
❒ NOGENT-EN-BASSIGNY Haute Marne 7B
❒ NOIRMOUTIER Vendee 3C
❒ NOIRETABLE Loire 7A
❒ NOMAIN Nord 1A
❒ NORD 3B
❒ NORD-AISNE-OISE 1A
❒ NORD-PAS-DE-CALAIS 1A 3B
❒ NOUVION EN THIERACHE Aisne 1A 6A 7B
❒ NOUVION ET CATILLON Aisne 1A
❒ NOUVION-LE-COMTE Aisne 1A
❒ NOYELLES-GODAULT Pas-de-Calais 1A
❒ NOYELLES-SOUS-BELLONNE Pas-de-Calais 1A
❒ NOYON Oise 1A
❒ NOUZON Ardennes 7A
❒ NOYELLES-GODAULT
❒ Pas de Calais 1A 3A 14A
❒ NOYON Oise 1A 3B
❒ NOYON-CHAUNY-LA-FERE Oise 1A
❒ OGNOLLES Oise 1B
❒ OHAIN Nord 1A
❒ OIGNIES Nord 1A
❒ OIGNIES Pas de Calais 1A
❒ OISE 3B
❒ OISSEL Seine Inferieure 3B 10B
❒ OISY Aisne 1A
❒ OISY-LE-VERGER Pas-de-Calais 1A
❒ OLERON Charente-Inferieure 3C 10C
❒ OLLEZY Aisne 1A
❒ OLONZAC Herault 7B
❒ OLORON-STE. MARIE Basses Pyrennees 7A
❒ OMISSY Aisne 1A
❒ ORANGE Vaucluse 7A

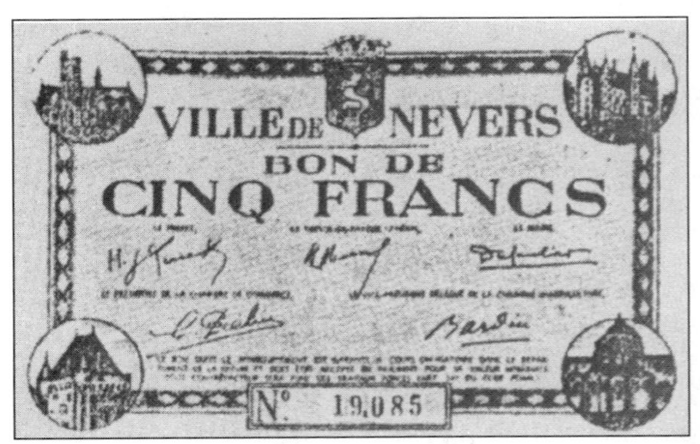

5 Francs, Nevers, France, 1A

50 Centimes (gas), Paris, France, 8B

❒ ORBEC-EN-AUGE Calvados 7A
❒ ORCHIES Nord 1A
❒ ORIGNY STE. BENOITE Aisne 1A
❒ ORLEANS Loiret 1A 3C 7A
❒ ORLEANS-ET-BLOIS Loiret 1A
❒ ORLEANS ET LOIRET Loiret 1C
❒ ORORON Basses Pyrennees 7A
❒ ORS Nord 1B
❒ ORTAFFA Pyrenees Orientales 2B
❒ OSSART 6A
❒ OULCHY-LE-CHATEAU Aisne 3B
❒ OULLINS Loiret 7B
❒ OUVEILLAN Aude 7A
❒ OYONNAX Ain 7A
❒ OYONNAX-BELLEGARDE Ain 6A 7A
❒ PACY-SUR-EURE Eure 6A 7A
❒ PAILLENCOURT Nord 1B
❒ PAIMBOEUF Loire Inferieure 1 7A
❒ PALAVAS Herault 7A
❒ PALAVAS LES FLOTS 7A
❒ PALISSE, LA Ardeche 7A
❒ PALLICE-ROCHELLE, LA Charente-Inferieure 3A
❒ PALLUEL Pas de Calais 1A
❒ PAMIERS Ariege 3B 7B
❒ PARGNY-LES-BOIS Aisne 1A
❒ PARIS Seine 1A 2A 3B 4A 6A 7A 10A 11C 12A 14A
❒ PARIS-BOULOGNE-BILLANCOURT 14A
❒ PARPEVILLE Aisne 1B
❒ PAU Basses Pyrenees 3B 6A 7A 10B
❒ PAUILLAC Gironde 7A 8A
❒ PEAGE-DE-ROUSSILLON Pyrenees-Orientales 2C
❒ PECH-LUNA Aude 2B
❒ PECQUENCOURT Nord 1A
❒ PELVES Pas-de-Calais 1A
❒ PENHOET Morbihan 7A
❒ PENNE Let et Garonne 6A
❒ PERIGUEUX Dordogne 1A 6A 7A
❒ PERONNE Somme 1A 6A 7A
❒ PERPIGNAN Pyrenees Orientales 1A 2A 6A 7B 10B
❒ PERREUX, LA Loire 3C 7A
❒ PESSAC Gironde 7A
❒ PETIT-BOURG Seine et Oise 7A
❒ PETIT-VERLY Aisne 1A
❒ PETITE-ROSELLE Kleinrosseln Moselle 3A 14A
❒ PEXONNE Meurthe et Moselle 7A
❒ PEYRIAC-MINERVOIS Aude 7B
❒ PIEGUT Dordogne 2B 6A 7A
❒ PIERREFITTE Hautes-Pyrenees 3A 14A
❒ PIERRELATTE Drome 7A
❒ PIERREMANDE Aisne 1C
❒ PIGNAN Herault 7A
❒ PINON Aisne 1A
❒ PINOUSE, MINES DE LA Pyrennes Orientales 7A
❒ PLEINE-SELVE Aisne 1B
❒ PLESSIS Oise 1A
❒ PLOUVAIN Pas-de-Calais 1A
❒ POISSY Seine et Oise 7A
❒ POITIERS Vienne 1A 3B 4C 6A 10A 11B
❒ POIX-TERRON Ardennes 1A 6A
❒ POMEROLS Herault 7A
❒ POMMEROEUL Nord 1B
❒ POMPIGNAN Tarn-et-Garonne 2B
❒ PONT AUDEMER Eure 7A
❒ PONT DE CHERUY Isere 2B 7A
❒ PONT DE CHERUY-TIGNEU Isere 2A
❒ PONT-A-MOUSSON Meurthe et Moselle 3B 7A
❒ PONT-ET-CHAUSSEES 3C
❒ PONTMAIN Mayenne 3B
❒ PONTOISE Val-d'Oise 1A
❒ PONTRU Aisne 1A
❒ PONTRUET Aisne 1A
❒ PONT-SUR-SAMBRE Nord 1A
❒ PONT-SUR-SEINE Aube 7A
❒ PONTOISON Manche 7
❒ PONTRUET 1A
❒ PORT MIOU Bouches du Rhone 1A 6A
❒ POTTE Somme 1B
❒ POUILLY Loire 7A
❒ POUILLY ET CHARLIEU Loire 7A
❒ POUILLE-SUR-SERRE Aisne 1A
❒ POULIGUEN, LE Loire-Inferieure 2A
❒ POUZAUG ES Vendee 11B
❒ PRECIGNE Sarthe 3A
❒ PREHAC Landes 2A
❒ PREMONT Aisne 1A
❒ PRESTE, LA Bazes Pyrennees 7A
❒ PREUX-AU-BOIS Nord 1B
❒ PRIN-DEYRANCON Deux-Sevres A3 14A
❒ PRISCHES Nord 1B
❒ PROISY Aisne 1B
❒ PROIVILLE Nord 1A
❒ PROIX Aisne 1A
❒ PROVENCALE 6A
❒ PROVENCE Alais 1A 6A
❒ PROVENCE Arles Gap et Toulon 1A 6A
❒ PROVENCE Avignon 1A 6A
❒ PROVENCE Marseille 1A 6A
❒ PROVENCE Nimes 1A 6A
❒ PROVILLE Nord 1A
❒ PROVIN Nord 1A
❒ PUGET S/ARGENS Var 1A
❒ PUISIEUX ET CLANLIEU Aisne 1A
❒ PUITS-GUILLELMIN Loire 3B
❒ PUSSAY Seine et Oise 7A
❒ PUY DE DOME Puy de Dome 1A
❒ PUY L'EVEQUE Lot 2B
❒ PUY, LE (Le Puy en Velay) Haute Loire 1A 3B 4B 7A
❒ PUY-DE-DOME Puy-de-Dome 1A
❒ PUYLAROQUE Tarn et Garonne 2A
❒ PUYLAURENS Tarn 1B 6A
❒ PUY-L'EVEQUE Lot 2A
❒ PYRENEES ORIENTALES Pyrenees Orientales 1A
❒ QUAROUBLE Nord 7A
❒ QUERCY 6A
❒ QUESNOY LE Nord 1A
❒ QUIBERON Morbihan 3B
❒ QUIBERON-SAINT-PIERRE Morbihan 3C
❒ QUIERY--LA-MOTTE Pas-de-Calais 1B
❒ QUILLAN Aude 1B
❒ QUIMPER Finistere 1A
❒ QUIMPER-BREST Finistere 1A
❒ QUINCY Aisne 1A
❒ QUIVIERES Somme 1A
❒ RABASTENS Tarn 1A

❒ RACHES Nord 1A 2A
❒ RACHES-THUMESNIL Nord 1B
❒ RAILLENCOURT-STE-OLLE
Nord 1A
❒ RAIMBEAUCOURT Nord 1B
❒ RAINCY, LE Seine et Oise 1A
❒ RAMBOUILLET Seine-et-Oise 10C
❒ RAMICOURT Aisne 1A
❒ RANSPACH Ober Elsass 1A
❒ RAUCOURT Ardennes 7A
❒ RAVEL Puy de Dome 7A
❒ RAVIERES Yonne 7A
❒ REALMONT Tarn 2B 7B
❒ RECKHEIM 6A
❒ REGNY Aisne 1A
❒ REIMS Marne 1A 2B 3C 7B
❒ REJET-DE-BEAULIEU Nord 1C
❒ REMAUCOURT Aisne 1A
❒ REMIGNY Aisne 1A
❒ REMIREMONT Calvados 2A
❒ REMIREMONT Vosges 1A 7B
❒ REMY Pass-de-Calais 1A
❒ RENANSART (Renausart) Aisne 1A
❒ RENNES (Roazon, Breton)
Ille et Vilaine 1A 4A 7A 10A 14A
❒ RENNES-ST. MALO Ille et Vilaine 1A 5C 7A 10A
❒ REOLE, LA Gironde 2A 6A 7A
❒ RETHEL Ardennes 1A
❒ RETHONVILLERS Somme 3B
❒ REUMONT Nord 1B
❒ REVEL Haute Garonne 1B 6A
❒ REVIGNY Meuse 4A 7B 10B
❒ REVIN Ardennes 1B
❒ REYNIES Tarn-et-Garonne 2B
❒ RIBEMONT Aisne 1A 2C 3B
❒ RIEULAY Nord 1A
❒ RIEUMES Haute Garonne 2A
❒ RIMOGNE Ardennes 1A
❒ RIOM Puy de Dome 2A 3B
❒ RIOUPEROUX Isere 3C
❒ ROANNE Loire 1A 2B 3B 6A 7A 10A
❒ ROCHE-ARNAUD
Le Puy de Dome 7A
❒ ROCHE-BIESSARD 3A
❒ ROCHE-CHALAIS, LA Dordogne 2A
❒ ROCHE-LA-MOLIERE Loire 1A 2B 3B
❒ ROCHE-MAURICE
Loire-Inferieure 3B
❒ ROCHE, LA Sur-Yon Vendee 1A 7A
❒ ROCHEFORT-SUR-MER Charente
❒ Inferieure 1A 2A 3A 4B 6A 7A 10B
❒ ROCHELLE, LA
Charente Inferieure 1A 3A 6A 7A 10A 12B
❒ RODEZ ET MILLAU (Milhau)
Aveyron 1B
❒ ROISEL Somme 1A
❒ ROMANS Drome 3B
❒ ROMILLY-SUR-SEINE Aube 1D 14A
❒ ROMORANTIN Loire et Cher 3C
❒ RONCHAMPS Haute-Saone 4B
❒ RONCHERES Aisne 3B
❒ RONCQ Nord 1B
❒ RONSSOY Somme 1A
❒ ROOST-WARENDIN Nord 1B
❒ ROSIERES Somme 3B
❒ ROUBAIX Nord 1A 7A
❒ ROUBOIX-TOURCOING Nord 1A
❒ ROUEN Seine Inferieur 1A 3B 6A 7A
10B 11B 14A
❒ ROUEN-LEVASSEUR
Seine Inferieure 3A
❒ ROUEN-QUAI DE FRANCE
Seine Inferieure 3A
❒ ROUGIERS Var 7A
❒ ROUPY Aisne 1A
❒ ROUVROY Pas-de-Calais 1A
❒ ROUY-LE-GRAND Somme 1A
❒ ROUY-LE-PETIT Somme 1B
❒ ROYAN Charente Maritime 6A 7A
❒ ROYAT LES BAINS Puy de Dome 2B 7A
❒ ROZIERES Haute Marne 2A
❒ ROZOY-SUR-SERRE Aisne 1A
❒ RUEIL Seine et Oise 2A
❒ RUFFEC Charente 7B
❒ RUGLES Eure 3C
❒ RUMAUCOURT Pas-de-Calais 1A
❒ RUMILLY Nord 1A
❒ SAARALEBEN Lorraine 7A
❒ SAARBRUCKENHEIM
Lothringen 6A
❒ SAARGEMUND (SAAREGUEMINES)
Moselle 2B
❒ SABLES D'OLONNE, LES Vendee 7A
❒ SABLETTES-LES-BAINS Var 7A
❒ SAIL-SUR-COUZAN Loire 7A
❒ SAILLY-EN-OSTREVENT
Pas-de-Calais 1A
❒ SAILLY LEZ LANNOY Nord 1A
❒ SAINS-LEZ-MARQION
Pas-de-Calais 1A
❒ SAINS-RICHAUMONT Aisne 1A
❒ SAINT AGENAU Cantal 3B
❒ SAINT-AMAND Nord 1C
❒ SAINT-AMARIN Haut-Rhin 2C 9C
❒ SAINT ANDRE DE L'EURE Eure 7A
❒ SAINT ANTOINE 2A
❒ SAINT ANTONIN Tarn et Garonne 1B
❒ SAINT-AUBIN-EPINAY
Seine-Inferieure 3A 10A
❒ SAINT AUGUSTIN
Seine-et-Marne 7A
❒ SAINT BARTHELEMY Dordogne 1B
❒ SAINT BRIEUC Cotes du Nord 1A 2A 3A 14A
❒ SAINT CERE Lot 2B
❒ SAINT CHAMOND Loire 7A
❒ SAINT-CIRQ-LAPOPIE 2B
❒ SAINT CLAR Gers 2B
❒ SAINT CLAUDE Jura 7A
❒ SAINT CLOUD Hauts de Seine 11B
❒ SAINT COME Aveyron 3B
❒ SAINT DENIS Seine 2B 7A
❒ SAINT DIDIER LA SIAUVE Loire 7A
❒ SAINT DIE Vosges 1A 3C
❒ SAINT DIZIER Haute-Marne 1A 3B 7B 10A
❒ SAINT ETIENNE Loire 1A 2B 3E 7A 11B 12B 14E
❒ SAINT ETIENNE-FIRMINY Loire 7A
❒ SAINT ETIENNE-DU ROUVRAY 3B
❒ SAINT FELIX Haute Garonne 2B
❒ SAINT FLORENTIN Yonne 3B
❒ SAINT FONS Rhone 7A
❒ SAINT GAUDENS Haute Garonne 1A 7B
❒ SAINT GENEST LERPT Loire 2A 3A
❒ SAINT GERMAINE-EN-LAYE
Yveliness 6A 7A 11B
❒ SAINT GOBAIN Aisne 1A 7A
❒ SAINT HIPPOLYTE DU FORT
Gard 7A 10B
❒ SAINT JEAN DE LUZ
Basses Pyrenees 7A
❒ SAINT JEAN DU GARD Gard 6A 7A
❒ SAINT JEAN LE COMTAL Gers 1A
❒ SAINT JEAN SOLEYMIEUX
Loire 3C
❒ SAINT JUERY Tarn 7A
❒ SAINT JUST EN CHEVALET
Loire 7A
❒ SAINT LAURENT DE CERDANS
Pyrenees Orientales 2B

❐ SAINT LAURENT DE LA L'Aude 1A
❐ SAINT LAURENT DE LA CABRERISSE L' Aude 1A 2A
❐ SAINT LAURENT-LE-MINIER Gard 3A 14A
❐ SAINT LIZAIGNE Indre 7A
❐ SAINT LO Manche 14A
❐ SAINT LOUIS DU RHONE Bouches-du-Rhone 9A
❐ SAINT MACAIRE Gironde 1A
❐ SAINT MAIXENT Deux-sevres 10A
❐ SAINT MALO Cotes du Nord 7A 12A
❐ SAINT MALO Ille-et-Vilaine 7A 12B
❐ SAINT MANDE Seine 7A
❐ SAINT MANDRIER Var 3C
❐ SAINT MARGUERITE, ILE Alpes-Maritimes 3C
❐ SAINT MARIE AUX MINES Haut Rhin 7A
❐ SAINT MARTIAL-VIVEYROL Dordogne 3A
❐ SAINT MARTIN DE CRAU Bouches du Rhone 2B
❐ SAINT MARTIN DE RE Charent-Inferieure 3A
❐ SAINT MARTIN d'ESTREAUX Loire 3C
❐ SAINT MARTIN LA LANDE Aude 1B
❐ SAINT MARTIN-VALMEROUX Aisne 2B
❐ SAINT MARTORY Haute Garonne 2B
❐ SAINT MATHIEUDE-TREVIERS Herault 7A
❐ SAINT MAURICE 14A
❐ SAINT MAXIENT L'ECOLE Deux Sevres 10B 7A
❐ SAINT MAXIMIN Var 6A 7A
❐ SAINT MEDARD EN JALLES Gironde 3A 7A 14A

Types of Emergency Money

Type	Reference #
Municipal paper	1
Private paper	2
POW paper	3
POW official metal	4
POW private metal	5
Municipal metal	6
Private metal	7
Gas tokens	8
Food; beer; konsumverein	9
Naval; military; kantine	10
Encased, unencased stamps	11
Streetcar tokens	12
Porcelain	13
World War II issues	14
Concentration, Civilian internment camps	15

Rarity grades: A, to $25; B, to $60; C, to $125; D, to $200; and E, $350

❐ SAINT MIHIEL Meuse 3A
❐ SAINT MONTANT Gard 6A
❐ SAINT NAZAIRE Haute-Loire 3C 4C 7A
❐ SAINT NIC Finistere 3D
❐ SAINT NICOLAS DE LA GRAVE Tarn-et-Garonne 2B
❐ SAINT OMER Pas de Calais 1A 7A
❐ SAINT OUEN-DU-BREUIL Seine Inferieure 3B 7A
❐ SAINT PAUL-EN-JAREZ Loire 7A
❐ SAINT PIERRE SUR/DIVES Calvados 7A
❐ SAINT PORQUIER
❐ Tarn et Garonne 2A
❐ SAINT PUY Gers 1A
❐ SAINT QUEN Seine-St. Denis 7A
❐ SAINT QUENTIN Aisne 1A 2B 3B 7A 14C
❐ SAINT QUENTIN AND Guise Aisne 1A
❐ SAINT QUENTIN-LE-PETIT Ardennes 1B
❐ SAINT QUIRC Ariege 2B
❐ SAINT RAMBERT SUR LOIRE Loire 3C 7A
❐ SAINT RAMBERT EN BUGEY Ain 2B 3A 7A
❐ SAINT-REMY Bouches du Rhone 7A
❐ SAINT RAPHAEL Var 3C
❐ SAINT REMY DE PROVENCE Bouches du Rhone 4B 7A 15C
❐ SAINT SERNIN DE DURAS Gironde 2B
❐ SAINT-SIMON Aisne 1A
❐ SAINT SULPICE Tarn 1B 7A
❐ SAINT SULPICE-SUR-LEZE Haute Garonne 1B
❐ SAINT SYMPHORIEN Indre-et-Loire 7A
❐ SAINT TROPEZ Var 3C 4B 7A 15C
❐ SAINTE CROIX Ariege 1B
❐ SAINTE DE SAINT VINCENTE DE PAUL Herault 7A
❐ SAINTE MENEHOULD Marne 7A
❐ SAINTE SIGOLENE Haute-Loire 7A
❐ SAINTES Charente Inferieure 7A
❐ SALERNE Var 7A
❐ SALIES-DU-SALAT Haute Garonne 2B
❐ SALIN-DE-PESQUIER Bouches-du-Rhone 3C
❐ SALIN DE GIRAUD Bouches du Rhone 7A
❐ SALINS LES BAINS Jura 1A 7B 10A 14A
❐ SALLANCHES Haute Savoie 1A 2A
❐ SALLANCHES-MONT BLANC Haute
❐ Savoie 2B
❐ SALLES-SUR-L'HERS Aude 2B
❐ SALON Bouches-du-Rhone 6A
❐ SALVAGNAC Tarn 1B
❐ SAMATAN ET LOMBEZ 2B
❐ SAMEON Nord 1A
❐ SAMOENS Haute Savoie 2B
❐ SANCOURT Somme 1C
❐ SANIS DU NORD Nord 1A 2A
❐ SANNOIS Seine-et-Oise 2A 7A
❐ SARAMON Gers 1B
❐ SARCELLES Val d'Oise 1B
❐ SARRE-MINES DE LA 1A
❐ SARS-POTERIES Nord 1B
❐ SARTROUVILLE Seine-Maritime 1C
❐ SASSEGNIES Nord 1B
❐ SAUCHY-LESTREES Pas-de-Calais 1A

❒ SAUDEMONT Pas-de-Calais	1A				
❒ SAULTAIN	11B				
❒ SAULZOIR Nord	7A				
❒ SAUVAIN Loire	3C				
❒ SAVERDUN Ariege	2B				
❒ SAVY Aisne	1A				
❒ SEAUVE, LA Haute Loire	7A				
❒ SEBONCOURT Aisne	1A	2B			
❒ SECLIN Nord	1A				
❒ SEDAN Ardennes	1A				
❒ SEDIERES Correze	4B				
❒ SEMPIGNY Oisne	1A				
❒ SENLIS Oise	11B				
❒ SENNECEY Cote-d'Or	3B				
❒ SENONES Vosges	6A				
❒ SENS Yonne	1A	2B	3C		
❒ SENTEIN Ariege	3A	14A			
❒ SEPTFONDS Tarn-et-Garonne	1A	7B			
❒ SEQUEHART Aisne	1A				
❒ SERAIN Aisne	1A				
❒ SERRES-CARPENTRAS Hautes-Alpes-Vaucluse	3B				
❒ SERVIAN Herault	7B				
❒ SERVIERES Correze	3B	4B			
❒ SERY-LES-MEZIERES Aisne	1B				
❒ SETE Herault	1A				
❒ SEVIGNY-WALEPPE Ardennes	1B				
❒ SEVRES Seine-et-Oise	6A				
❒ SEYCHES Lot et Garonne	1A	2A			
❒ SEZANNE Marne	7A				
❒ SIGEAN Aude	6A				
❒ SIMORRE-ET-VILLEFRANCHE Gers	1B				
❒ SIN-LE-NOBLE Nord	1B				
❒ SINCENY Aisne	1A				
❒ SIRADAN Hautes Pyrenees	2B				
❒ SIRAN Herault	7A				
❒ SISSY Aisne	1A				
❒ SISTERON Basses-Alpes	3B				
❒ SOISSONS Aisne	3C				
❒ SOLESMES Nord	1A	7A			
❒ SOLIGNAC-LE-VIGEN Haute-Vienne	3C				
❒ SOLRE-LE-CHATEAU Nord	6A				
❒ SOMAIN EN OSTREVENT Nord	1A				
❒ SOMME	3B				
❒ SOMMETTE-EAUCOURT Aisne	1B				
❒ SOMMEVOIRE Haute Marne	1B	2A	14C		
❒ SOMMIERES Gard	7A				
❒ SORGUES Vaucluse	7A				
❒ SOS Lot et Garonne	1B				
❒ SOTTEVILLE-LES-ROUEN Seine-Inferieure	3C				
❒ SOUILLAC Lot	2B				
❒ SOULAC-SUR-MER Gironde	7A				
❒ SOUS REGION Economique d'Orleans	1A				
❒ STAINS Seine	7A				
❒ STRASBOURG Bas-Rhin	1A	6B			
❒ SUD-EST	7A				
❒ SURFONTAINE Aisne	1A				
❒ SUSY Aisne	1A				
❒ TAISNIERES Nord	1A				
❒ TALAUDIERE, LA Loire	7A				
❒ TAMARIS	11B				
❒ TANINGES Haute Savoie	2B				
❒ TARARE Rhone	1A				
❒ TARARE, AMPLEPUIS, (Thizy, Lamure) Rhone	1A				
❒ TARASCON Bouches-du-Rhone	7A				
❒ TARBES Hautes Pyrenees	1A	6A	7A		
❒ TARN Tarn	1A				
❒ TAVAUX Jura	1B				
❒ TAVAUX ET PONTSERICOURT Aisne	1A				
❒ TEMPLEUVE-EN-PEVELE Nord	1B				
❒ TERGNIER Aisne	1B	7A			
❒ TERGNIER-FARGNIERS QUESSY-ET-VOUEEL Aisne	1A				
❒ TERRENOIRE Loire	3B	7A			
❒ TEUQUIERES Somme	7A				
❒ THANN Haut Rhin	1B	2C	6A		
❒ THAON-LES-VOSGES Vosges	7A				
❒ THENELLES Aisne	1A				
❒ THEZAN Aude	1B				
❒ THIAUCOURT ET ST. MIHIELI	1A				
❒ THIERACHE Aisne	7A				
❒ THILLOT LE Vosges	2B				
❒ THIOLLIERE, LA Loire	3A				
❒ THIVENCELLES-FRESNES sur Escaut	1A				
❒ THIVIERS Dordogne	7A				
❒ THONON LES BAINS Haute Savoie	11B				
❒ THUN-SAINT-MARTIN Nord	1A				
❒ TILLEUL, LE Seine-Inferieure	7A				
❒ TILLOY Nord	1C				
❒ TINCOURT-BOUCLY Nord	1B				
❒ TONNEINS Lot et Garonne	2B	11B			
❒ TORTEQUENNE Pas-de-Calais	1B				
❒ TOUFFLERS Nord	1A				
❒ TOUL Meurthe-et-Moselle	2B				
❒ TOULIS	1A				
❒ TOULON Var	1A	3C	7B	11B	12A
❒ TOULOUSE Haute Garonne	1A	2A	3B	6A	7B
	10B	11B	12A	14A	
❒ TOURCOING Nord	1B				
❒ TOURNEVILLE Eure	10B				
❒ TOURNON-D'AGENAIS Lot-et-Garonne	2A				
❒ TOURS Indre-et-Loire	1A	3B	7A		
❒ TRAIT, LE Seine Inferieure	3A	14A			
❒ TRAVECY Aisne	1B	10A			
❒ TRELON Nord	1A				
❒ TREPORT, LE Seine-Inferieure	1A				
❒ TRESSIN Nord	1B				
❒ TREZELLES Allier	7A				
❒ TRIGNAC Loire-Atlantique	7A				
❒ TRIGOLET Bouches-du-Rhone	7A				
❒ TROISSY Marne	3D				
❒ TROISVILLES Nord	1B				
❒ TROMPELOUP Gironde	3B				
❒ TROUVILLE-DEAUVILLE Calvados	3D				
❒ TROUVILLE-SUR-MER Calvados	2A	7A	11A	14B	
❒ TROYES Aube	1A	7A			
❒ TUGNY-ET-PONT Aisne	1A				
❒ TULLE Correze	1A	3A	14A		
❒ TULLE ET USSEL Correze	1A				
❒ TUPIGNY Aisne	1A				
❒ UGINE Savoie	7A				
❒ UGNY-L'EQUIPEE Somme	1B				
❒ UNIEUX Loire	7A				
❒ URVILLERS Aisne	1A				
❒ URVILLE Bateau Dumont	1A				
❒ UZES Gard	3B				
❒ VACQUIRES Haute Garonne	1B				
❒ VALDOIE Territoire de Belfort	7A				
❒ VALENCE AND DROME Drome	1A	3A	7A	14A	
❒ VALENCE-D'AGEN Tarn-et-Garonne	2B				
❒ VALENCIENNES Nord	1A	2A	3A	11B	14A
❒ VALENTIGNEY Doubs	2A	7A			
❒ VALLEE-MULATRE LA Aisne	1A				
❒ VANDIERES Meurthe-et-Moselle	3C				

25 Centimes, Vienne, France, 2A

❒ VANNES Morbihan 6A
❒ VANVES Hautes de Seine 1A 9A
❒ VARENNE, LA Seine 7A
❒ VAROIS Cote d'Or 3B
❒ VAUCIENNES Oise 7A
❒ VAUXAILLON Aisne 1B
❒ VAUX-ANDIGNY Aisne 1A
❒ VAYRAC Lot 2B
❒ VENDELLES Aisne 1A
❒ VENDEUIL Aisne 1B
❒ VENDHUILE Aisne 1A
❒ VENEROLLE Aisne 1A
❒ VENNISSIEUX Rhone 3A 14A
❒ VERDUN Meuse 3B 14C
❒ VERFEIL Haute-Garonne 2B
❒ VERGUIER, LE Aisne 1A
❒ VERMAND Aisne 1A
❒ VERMANDOVILLERS Somme 3B
❒ VERNER-D'ARIEGE Ariege 3A 14A
❒ VERNEUL-SUR-SERRE 1A
❒ VERSAILLES Seine-et-Oise 7A 10B
❒ VERTUS Marne 1A
❒ VERVINS Aisne 1A 7A
❒ VESOUL Haute Saone 7A 14A
❒ VESOUL-GRAY ET LURE Haute Saone 14B
❒ VIANNE Lot et Garonne 1B
❒ VIC-FEZENSAC Gers 1B
❒ VICHY Allier 7A 11B
❒ VICOGNE ET NOEUX Pas-de-Calais 2C
❒ VIENNE Isere 1A 2B 7A
❒ VIERZON Cher 3B 10A
❒ VIEUX-CONDE Nord 2B
❒ VIGAN Gard 7A
❒ VILLARET Loire 3A 14A
❒ VILLARS Loire 7A
❒ VILLEBRUMIER Tarn et Gar 1B
❒ VILLECOURT Somme 1B
❒ VILLEFRANCHE S/SAONE Rhone 1A
❒ VILLEFRANCHE-LAURAGEAIS Haute Garonne 1A
❒ VILLEGUSIEN Haute-Marne 3C
❒ VILLEMOMBLE Seine et Oise 14C
❒ VILLEMUR Haute Garonne 1A 7B
❒ VILLENAUXE Aube 3B
❒ VILLENEUVE-LES-BOULOC Haute Garonne 2A
❒ VILLENEUVE-ST. GEORGES Seine 7A
❒ VILLENEUVE-SUR-LOT Lot et Garonne 1B 2A
❒ VILLENEUVOIS Lot-et-Garonne 2B
❒ VILLEQUIER-AUMONT Aisne 1A
❒ VILLERET 1A
❒ VILLERS Aisne 1A
❒ VILLERS-CAMPEAU Nord 1A
❒ VILLERS-FAUCON Somme 1B
❒ VILLERS-GUISLAIN Nord 1A
❒ VILLERS-LE-SEC Aisne 1A
❒ VILLERS-LES-GUISE Aisne 1A 3A
❒ VILLERS-LEZ-CAGNICOURT Pas de Calais 1A
❒ VILLERS-OUTREAUX Nord 1B 2A
❒ VILLERS-PLOUICH Nord 1B
❒ VILLERS-SAINT CHRISTOPHE Nord 1A
❒ VILLESELVE Oise 1B
❒ VILLEUBRANNE Rhone 7A
❒ VILOSNES-SUR-MEUSE Meuse 3B
❒ VIMOUTIERS Orne 2C 7A
❒ VINCENNES Seine 7A
❒ VIRE Calvados 2 3B
❒ VIRY-NOUREUIL Aisne 1B
❒ VIS-EN-ARTOIS Pas-de-Calais 1A
❒ VITRY-EN-ATROIS Pas de Calais 1B
❒ VITRY Seine 7A
❒ VIUZ-EN-SACCAZ (Viuz-en-Sallaz) Haute Savoie 1B 2A
❒ VIVIERS Ardeche 1B 2B 3B 7A
❒ VOSGES Vosges 2A
❒ VOUZIERS Ardennes 3C
❒ VOYENNE Aisne 1A
❒ VOYENNES Somme 1A
❒ VRAIGNES-ROISEL Somme 1A
❒ VRED Nord 1A
❒ WALINCOURT Nord 1A
❒ WALLERS-TRELON Nord 1A
❒ WALLERS Nord 7A
❒ WANDIGNIES-HAMAGE Nord 1A
❒ WANNEHAIN Nord 1B
❒ WARLAING Nord 1A
❒ WASSIGNY Aisne 1B
❒ WASSY Haute Marne 1A 14E
❒ WATTRELOS Nord 1A
❒ WAVRECHAIN-SOUS-DENAIN Nord 1B
❒ WAZIERS Nord 1A
❒ WIGNEHIES Nord 1A
❒ WILLEMS Nord 1A
❒ WIMY Aisne 1A
❒ WISSIGNICOURT Aisne 1A
❒ WITRY-LES-REIMS Marne 3B

FRENCH EQUATORIAL AFRICA

❒ HAUT-CONGO 7B

FRENCH INDO-CHINA

❒ HAIPHONG 7B
❒ HANOI 7B
❒ TRANG-DA 7B

FRENCH OCEANIA

❒ FRENCH OCEANIA 1B

FRENCH SOMALILAND

❒ DJIBOUTI (Afars, Issas) 1B 6C

FRENCH WEST AFRICA

❒ DAHOMEN (Dahomey, Benin) 1A

GABON

❒ GABON 6B

GERMAN EAST AFRICA

❒ DAR-ES-SALAAM (Mzizima) 1A 6A
❒ TABORA 1A 6A 14A

50 Centimes, Djibouti, Fr. W. Africa, 6B

GERMAN SAMOA

- ❒ SAMOA — 2B

GERMAN NEW GUINEA

- ❒ RABAUL — 1E

GERMAN SOUTHWEST AFRICA

- ❒ GIBEON — 1B
- ❒ GROOTFONTEIN — 2C
- ❒ KARIBIB — 2C
- ❒ KARIBIB AND OMARURU — 2C
- ❒ KLEIN-WINDHUK — 2B
- ❒ LUEDERITZBUCH — 2B
- ❒ NEUHEUSIS — 2C
- ❒ OKAHANDA — 2C
- ❒ POMONAHUEGEL — 2B
- ❒ SWAKOPMUND — 2C
- ❒ TSUMEB — 2B
- ❒ WINDHUK — 1C 2B

GERMANY

- ❒ AACHEN Rheinland — 1B 3D 4D 6A 7A 11B 12A 14A
- ❒ AALEN-BOPFINGEN/EGER Baden-Wuerttemberg — 14A
- ❒ AALEN/KOCHER Wuerttemberg — 1A 2A 6A
- ❒ ABBACH/DONAU (Bad Abbach) Bayern — 7A
- ❒ ABELBECK (Hannover) — 3A
- ❒ ABENSBERG/ABENS Bayern — 1A 6A
- ❒ ACHERN Baden — 1B 2D 6B 7D 10A
- ❒ ACHIM Hannover — 1A
- ❒ ACHTERBERG (Hannover) — 3A
- ❒ ADELNAU (Odolanow) Posen — 1A 2B
- ❒ ADELSHAUSEN Hessen 1B
- ❒ ADELSHEIM Baden — 1A 6A
- ❒ ADENAU Rheinland — 1A
- ❒ ADLDORF Bayern — 2C
- ❒ ADLER (See Kupferdreh)
- ❒ ADOLFSHUETTE (See Niedersscheld) Hessen-Nassau
- ❒ ADORF/VOGTLAND Sachsen — 1A 2A 14B
- ❒ AGATHARIED Bayern — 6A
- ❒ AGNETENDORF/RIESENGEBIRGE (Jagniatkow) Schlesien — 1B
- ❒ AHAUS Westfalen — 1A 2B
- ❒ AHLBECK Pommern — 1E 8B
- ❒ AHLEN/WERSE Westfalen — 1A 2E 3A 5A 6A 7A
- ❒ AHLHORN (Oldenburg) — 3A
- ❒ AHRENSBOEK Oldenburg-Eutin — 1A
- ❒ AHRWEILER & ADENAU Rheinland — 1B
- ❒ AHRWEILER/AHR Rheinland — 1A 7A
- ❒ AIBLING/BAD Bayern — 2A 6A
- ❒ AICHACH/PAAR Bayern — 2C
- ❒ AIDENBACH Bayern — 1A 2B 6E
- ❒ AISTAIG/OBERNDORF Wuerttemberg — 7B 9A
- ❒ AKEN/ELBE (Acken) Provinz Sachsen — 1A
- ❒ ALBERSDORF, BAD Schleswig-Holstein — 1A
- ❒ ALBERSWEILER Pfalz — 2A 7A
- ❒ ALDEKERK Rheinland — 1A
- ❒ ALEXISBAD Anhalt — 2E
- ❒ ALFELD/LEINE Hannover — 1A 2A 7A 11B
- ❒ ALGRINGEN (Algrange) Lothringen — 6A
- ❒ ALLENDORF-SOODEN/WERRA Hessen Nassau — 2A
- ❒ ALLENDORF/WERRA Hessen-Nassau — 1A
- ❒ ALLENSTEIN/ALLE (Olsztyn) Ostpreussen — 1A 2B 7B 10A 12A
- ❒ ALLERINGHAUSEN Waldeck — 2E
- ❒ ALLERSBERG Bayern — 7A
- ❒ ALLSTEDT (Allstaedt) Sachsen-Wei-Eisen — 1A 2B 6A
- ❒ ALMSICK Westfalen — 3C 4A 5B
- ❒ ALPERBECK — 2A
- ❒ ALPIRSBACH/KINZIG Wuerttemberg — 2B
- ❒ ALSDORF Rheinland — 1A 2B 3B 5B 7A
- ❒ ALSENBORN Pfalz — 2A
- ❒ ALSFELD/SCHWALM Hessen — 1A 6A
- ❒ ALT-GAARZ (Alt-Garz) Mecklenburg-Schwerin — 2A
- ❒ ALT-NEISSBACH/GLATZ Schlesien — 2B
- ❒ ALT-PFIRT (Vieux Ferrette) Elsass — 1A
- ❒ ALT-STRELITZ Mecklenburg-Strelitz — 5E
- ❒ ALTDAMM/PLOENE (Szczecin Dabie) Pommern — 1A 4B 5A
- ❒ ALTDORF/SCHWARZACH Bayern — 1B 6A 7A
- ❒ ALTEN Sachsen — 7A
- ❒ ALTEN-GRABOW Provinz Sachsen — 3B
- ❒ ALTEN-UND FRAUEN-BREITUNGEN Sachsen-Meiningen — 1A
- ❒ ALTENA Westfalen — 1A 2A 7B 11B
- ❒ ALTENA-OLPE Westfalen — 7A
- ❒ ALTENAU/HARZ Hannover — 1A 3B
- ❒ ALTENBACH Elsass — 1A
- ❒ ALTENBERG/ERZGEBIRGE Sachsen — 1A
- ❒ ALTENBURG Sachsen-Altenburg — 1A 2B 6A 8B 10A 12A 13A
- ❒ ALTENBURG-KOTTERITZ Thueringen — 2B

50 Pfennig, Achim, 1A

25 Pfennig, Ahaus, 1A

50 Pfennig, Aken, 1A

10 Pfennig, Allenstein, 1A

25 Pfennig, Allstedt, Germany, 1A

Gut für 25 Pfg.

Westf. Eisen-u. Drahtwerke A.G.
Abteilung Aplerbeck.

Nur zur Verwendung für Gefangene
in dem Werks-Unterkunftshaus.

Aplerbeck, März 1916.

25 Pfennig, Aplerbeck, 1A

10 Pfennig, Altgaarz, Germany, 1A

50 Pfennig, Altdamm, 4A

50 Pfennig, Altenburg, 1A

10 Pfennig, Altusried, Germany, 9A

❒ ALTENDERNE Westfalen 4B 5B
❒ ALTENDORF/RUHR Westfalen 3C
❒ ALTENESSEN Rheinland 1E 3B
❒ ALTENFELD Thueringia 2A 9A
❒ ALTENGLAN Pfalz 2A
❒ ALTENKIRCHEN & WALDBROEL Rheinland 1A
❒ ALTENKIRCHEN/WIED Rheinland 1A
❒ ALTENKUNDSTADT Bayern 2D
❒ ALTENSTEIG/NAGOLD (Alltenstaig) Wuerttemberg 1A 2A
❒ ALTENVOERDE (Ennepetal) Westfalen 2C
❒ ALTENWAHLINGEN (Hannover) 3A
❒ ALTENWERDER U. FINKENWAERDER Hamburg 1A
❒ ALTENWIED Rheinland 2C
❒ ALTFELDE (Stare Pole) Westpreussen 2B
❒ ALTHAIN/DITTERSBACH Schlesien 2C
❒ ALTHEIDE, BAD (Polanica-Zdroj) Schlesien 1A 2C
❒ ALTKIRCH Elsass 2B
❒ ALTKLOSTER/ESTE (Buxtehude) Hannover 1A 2A
❒ ALTMITTWEIDA Sachsen 1B
❒ ALTMORSCHEN Hessen-Nassau 2A
❒ ALTOETTING Bayern 1A 2B
❒ ALTONA/ELBE Schleswig-Holstein 1A 2A 3 7A 8B 14B
❒ ALTONA-BAHRENFELD Schleswig-Holstein 2B
❒ ALTRAHLSTEDT Schleswig-Holstein 2C
❒ ALTROGGENRAHMEDE Westfalen 2C
❒ ALTTHANN (Vieuz Thann) Elsass 1A 2A
❒ ALTUSRIED Bayern 1B 2A 14A
❒ ALTWASSER (Szczawnica Zdroj) Schlesien 2B 3C 5B
❒ ALZENAU/UNTERFRANKEN Bayern 1B
❒ ALZEY/SELZ Hessen 1C 6A 8A 11C
❒ AMBERG/VILS Bayern 1A 2B 3A 5A 6A 7A 8A 9A 10A 13A
❒ AMBERG-VILSECK Bayern 2E
❒ AMELINGHAUSEN Niedersachsen 14B
❒ AMERIKA/MULDE Sachsen 2A
❒ AMMENDORF Provinz Sachsen 2A
❒ AMMERSCHWEIGER Elsass 1A 2A
❒ AMOENEBURG Hessen-Nassau 2A
❒ AMORBACH/MUDAU Bayern 1A 2A
❒ ANDERBECK Provinz Sachsen 2B
❒ ANDERNACH Rheinland 1A 2A 11B
❒ ANDERNACH & MAYEN Rheinland 1B
❒ ANDERSDORF (Przysieczna) Schlesien 7B
❒ ANDREASBERG Westfalen 2B
❒ ANGELRODA Sachsen-Weimar 9B
❒ ANGERBURG/ANGERAP (Wegorzewo) Ostpreussen 1A
❒ ANGERMUENDE Brandenburg 1A 2A 10A
❒ ANGERMUND Rheinland 1A
❒ ANHALT Anhalt 1A 6A
❒ ANKLAM/PEENE (Anclam) Pommern 1B 2A 7A
❒ ANNABERG & MARIENBERG Sachsen 1A
❒ ANNABERG/ERZGEBIRGE Sachsen 1A 2A 7A 8A
❒ ANNAHUETTE N.L. Brandenburg 2B 5A 7A
❒ ANNEN Westfalen 2A 7A
❒ ANNWEILER/QUEICH Pfalz 1A 6A 7A 9A
❒ ANRATH Rheinland 1A 2B
❒ ANSBACH Bayern 1A 2A 7A 9A 10A
❒ ANSPACH Hessen-Nassau 7B
❒ ANSPRUNG Sachsen 2A
❒ ANTFELD Westfalen 2A
❒ ANTONIENHUETTE (Huta Antonia; Wirek) Schlesien 1C 2B

50 Pfennig, Alzey, 1A

25 Pfennig, Angerburg, 1A

❒ APENRADE (Abenraa, Denmark) Schleswig-Holstein 1A 2B 7B
❒ APLERBECK/DORTMUND Westfalen 2A 5A
❒ APOLDA Sachsen-Weimar-Eisenach 1A 2A 6A
❒ APPEL Hannover 1A
❒ APPEN Schleswig-Holstein 1A
❒ ARCHSUM/SYLT Schleswig-Holstein 1A
❒ ARENDSEE Mecklenburg-Schwerin 2A
❒ ARFELD Westfalen 2E
❒ ARLEN Baden 2E 7E 9B
❒ ARNSBERG (Podgorze) Schlesien 2B
❒ ARNSBERG (Arensberg) Westfalen 1A 2A 6A
❒ ARNSTADT/GERA Thueringen 1A 2A 6A 8A 11C
❒ ARNSTORF Bayern 2B
❒ ARNSWALDE Brandenburg 1A 2E
❒ AROLSEN Waldeck 1A 2A 6A
❒ ARTERN Provinz Sachsen 1A 2A 6A
❒ ARYS (Orzysz) Ostpreussen 1A 3A 8B
❒ ARZBERG Bayern 1C 2A 6A 9A
❒ ASCHAFFENBURG/MAIN Bayern 1A 2A 3A 6A 7A 8B 10A
❒ ASCHENDORF (Hannover) 3A
❒ ASCHERSLEBEN/EINE Provinz Sachsen 1A 2B 8B 9B 11B
❒ ASPERG (Asberg) Wuerttenberg 15C
❒ ASSELN (Dortmund) Westfalen 2A 3B 4B 5A
❒ ASSELN UND BRAKEL (Dortmund) Westfalen 2A
❒ ASSINGHAUSEN Westfalen 2A
❒ ATTENDORN Westfalen 1A 2A 6A
❒ AUBING Bayern 1A

5 Pfennig, Annaberg, Germany, 1A

❒ AUE/ERZEBIRGE Sachsen 1A 2B 9B
❒ AUENBUELL (Avenoel, Demark) Schleswig-Holstein 1A
❒ AUERBACH Bayern 2A 7A
❒ AUERBACH/VOGTLAND Sachsen 1A 2A 8A
❒ AUERSWALDE Sachsen 1E
❒ AUGSBURG Bayern 1A 2B 7A 8B 9B 10A 11B 12B 14B
❒ AUGUSTENBURG (Augustenborg, Denmark) Schleswig-Holstein 2A
❒ AUGUSTENTHAL Westfalen 2C
❒ AUGUSTFEHN Oldenburg 7A
❒ AUGUSTUSBURG/ERZGEBIRGE Sachsen 2B
❒ AUMA/ORLA Sachsen-Weimar-Eisenach 1A 2A
❒ AUMUND-VEGESACK Hannover 7A
❒ AURA/SAALE Bayern 14B
❒ AURAS/ODER (Uraz) Schlesien 1E
❒ AURICH/OSTFRIESLAND Hannover 1A 2A
❒ AUSSERNZELL Bayern 2B
❒ AVENTOFT Schleswig-Holstein 2A
❒ BABENHAUSEN Bayern 1A
❒ BACHEM Rheinland 2A 7B
❒ BACKNANG Wuerttemberg 1A 2A 6A
❒ BADBERGEN Hannover 1A 2C
❒ BADEN-BADEN Baden 1A 2A 6A 7C 8B 9A
❒ BADEN-ETELSER MOOR (Hannover) 3A
❒ BADENWEILER Baden 7E 11C
❒ BADERSLEBEN Provinz Sachsen 1A
❒ BADETZ/ ZERBST Anhalt 1A
❒ BAERENSTEIN/CHEMNITZ 2B
❒ BAERENSTEIN/DRESDEN 2B
❒ BAERENWALDE (Barwice; Bincze) Westpreussen 7B
❒ BAERNAU Bayern 1D
❒ BAERWALDE (Barwice) Pommern 1A 6B
❒ BAERWALDE (Mieszkowice) Brandenburg 1A 6B
❒ BAERWALDE Sachsen 8A
❒ BAEUMENHEIM Bayern 7B 9B
❒ BAIENFURT Wuerttemberg 2A
❒ BAIERSBRONN Wuerttemberg 1A
❒ BALDENBURG (Bialy Dwor) Westpreussen 1B
❒ BALINGEN Wuerttemberg 1A 2B 6A
❒ BALLENSTEDT/HARZ Anhalt 1A 2B 11E
❒ BALVE Westfalen 2E

50 Pfennig, Apolda, 1A

❒ BAMBERG Bayern 1A 2A 4B 6A 7A 9B 10B 12A
❒ BAMBERG-GAUSTADT Bayern 2A
❒ BANSIN, SEEBAD Pommern 2D
❒ BARAKU Pommern 3D
❒ BARBY/ELBE Provinz Sachsen 1A 2B
❒ BARCHFELD/WERRA Hessen-Nassau 2D
❒ BARGTEHEIDE Schleswig-Holstein 2A
❒ BARMEN-HATZFELD Rheinland 3B
❒ BARMEN-LANGERFELD Rheinland 7A
❒ BARMEN-RITTERSHAUSEN Rheinlarid 2B
❒ BARMEN-UNTER ESCHBACH Rheinland 2A
❒ BARMEN-WICHLINGHAUSEN Rheinland 2B

Types of Emergency Money

Type	Reference #
Municipal paper	1
Private paper	2
POW paper	3
POW official metal	4
POW private metal	5
Municipal metal	6
Private metal	7
Gas tokens	8
Food; beer; konsumverein	9
Naval; military; kantine	10
Encased, unencased stamps	11
Streetcar tokens	12
Porcelain	13
World War II issues	14
Concentration, Civilian internment camps	15

Rarity grades: A, to $25; B, to $60; C, to $125; D, to $200; and E, $350

❒ BARMEN/WUPPER Rheinland 1A 2B 5B 6A 7B 8A 9B 11B
❒ BARMSTEDT Schleswig-Holstein 2B
❒ BARNTRUP Lippe 2D
❒ BARSINGHAUSEN Hannover 2A 3B
❒ BARTENSTEIN/ALLE (Bartoszyce O.L.) Ostpreussen 1A
❒ BARTH (Bardt) Pommern 1A 2B
❒ BARUM Hannover 3B
❒ BARUTH Brandenburg 1A 2B
❒ BASSUM Hannover 2E
❒ BAU (Bov, Denmark) Schleswig-Holstein 2B
❒ BAUERWITZ/ZINNA (Baborow) Schlesien 1C
❒ BAUMHOLDER Rheinland 2A
❒ BAUSTETTEN Wuerttemberg 2B
❒ BAUTZEN/SPREE (Budissin) Sachsen 1A 2A 3A 4A 7A 8B 9A 10A 11C
❒ BAYERHOF/Gaedheim Bayern 7B
❒ BAYREUTH/RED MAIN (Bai Reuth) Bayern 1A 2A 3A 4B 7A 8A 9B 10C 11B
❒ BECKUM/BALVE Westfalen 1A 6A
❒ BEDERKESA Hannover 3A
❒ BEDERUNGEN 1B
❒ BEDESBACH Pfalz 2A
❒ BEELITZ Brandenburg 1A
❒ BEEDENBOSTEL Hannover 3B
❒ BEENDORF Provinz Sachsen 2A 9A
❒ BEENDORF/HALDENSLEBEN Braunschweig 2B 9B
❒ BEESKOW/SPREE Brandenburg 2B 3A
❒ BEETZENDORF Provinz Sachsen 1A
❒ BEIERFELD Sachsen 2A
❒ BEIERSDORF Sachsen 2B
❒ BEILNGRIES/ALTMUEHL Bayern 1A 2B 6A 14B
❒ BELGARD/PERSANTE (Bialogard) Pommern 1A
❒ BELGERN/ELBE Provinz Sachsen 1A 6A
❒ BELLEBEN Provinz Sachsen 2B
❒ BELLENBERG Bayern 2B 14B
❒ BELLHEIM/SPIEGELBACH Pfalz 1A
❒ BELZIG Brandenburg 2A 9A
❒ BENDLEWO Posen 9A
❒ BENDORF Rheinland 2B
❒ BENDSIN (Bedzina; Bendzin) Schlesien 1A 2B 14A
❒ BENEDIKTBEUREN (Benedictbeuren) Bayern 3B

2 Mark, Archsum, 1A

❐ BENFELD Elsass 2B
❐ BENNECKENSTEIN/HARZ Provinz Sachsen 1A 2E
❐ BENNINGHAUSEN Westfalen 4B
❐ BENNUNGEN/SANGERHAUSEN Provinz Sachsen 1B
❐ BENRATH Rheinland 1 2A 5B 7A
❐ BENSBERG Rheinland 1E 2A
❐ BENSHEIM Hessen 1A 4B 6A
❐ BENTHEIM Westfalen 1A
❐ BENTSCHEN (Zbaszyn) Posen 1A
❐ BENRATH Rheinland 3B 5A
❐ BERBISDORF Sachsen (today Einsiedel) 1A
❐ BERCHING/OBERPFALZ Bayern 1A 6A 7A
❐ BERCHTESGADEN Bayern 1A
❐ BERENT/FERSE (Behrend, Koscierzyna) Westpreussen 1A 2B
❐ BERGA/ELSTER Thueringia 1A 2B
❐ BERGEDORF Hamburg 1A 2A 6A 7B
❐ BERGEN/DUMME Hannover 1A 8B
❐ BERGEN/RUEGEN Pommern 1A
❐ BERGER DAMM/NAUEN Brandenburg 3C
❐ BERGERHOF Rheinland 2B
❐ BERGHEIM/ERFT Rheinland 2A 4A 5A
❐ BERGISCH-GLADBACH Rheinland 1A 2A 14B
❐ BERGNEUSTADT Rheinland 2C
❐ BERGNEUSTADT & VOLLMERSHAUSEN Rheinland 2B
❐ BERGZABERN BAD/ERLBACH Pfalz 1A 6A
❐ BERKA, BAD/WERRE Sachsen-Weimar-Eisenach 1A
❐ BERLEBURG, BAD Westfalen 1A 2C 6A
❐ BERLIN/SPREE 1A 2A 6B 7A 8A 11B 12B 13B
❐ BERLIN UND NOWAWES (Babelsberg) 2B
❐ BERLIN-BRITZ Brandenburg 2A 5B 7B
❐ BERLIN-CHARLOTTENBURG Brandenburg 2B 3A 7A 9A 11B 12A 13C
❐ BERLIN-COEPENICK (Koepenick) 1B 9A
❐ BERLIN-DESSAU Brandenburg 2B
❐ BERLIN-FRIEDENAU Brandenburg 11B
❐ BERLIN-FRIEDRICHSHAGEN Brandenburg 2D
❐ BERLIN-GARTENFELD Brandenbrg 7A
❐ BERLIN-HASENHEIDE Brandenburg 7A
❐ BERLIN-JOHANNISTHAL Brandenburg 1B
❐ BERLIN-LICHTENBERG Brandenburg 2A 7B
❐ BERLIN-LUDWIGSHAVEN (See Wuerttemberg)
❐ BERLIN-NEUKOELLN Brandenburg 2A 8A
❐ BERLIN-NIEDER-SCHOENHAUSEN Brandenburg 2D
❐ BERLIN-NIEDERSCHOENWEIDE Brandenburg 1C 2B
❐ BERLIN-NEWEIDE Brandenburg 2A
❐ BERLIN-OBERSCHOENWEIDE Brandenburg 2A
❐ BERLIN-PANKOW Brandenburg 7A
❐ BERLIN-RAUXEL Westfalen 2B
❐ BERLIN-SCHOENEBERG Brandenburg 2D
❐ BERLIN-SIEMENSSTADT Brandenburg 2B
❐ BERLIN-SPANDAU Brandenburg 2C 7B 8A 12A
❐ BERLIN-TEGEL Brandenburg 2A 3B 7A 9A 11B
❐ BERLIN-TEMPELHOF Brandenburg 2E 7B
❐ BERLIN-TREPTOW Brandenburg 1B 2B
❐ BERLIN-WEISSENSEE Brandenburg 7B
❐ BERLIN-WEDDING Brandenburg 7B
❐ BERLIN-WILMERSDORF Brandenburg 2D 7A 11E
❐ BERLIN-WITTENAU Brandenburg 3C 8B
❐ BERLIN-ZEHLENDORF Brandenburg 7B
❐ BERLINCHEN (Barlinek) Brandenburg 1D
❐ BERNAU Brandenburg 1D
❐ BERNBURG/SAALE Anhalt 1A 2C 7B 12A
❐ BERNCASTEL-CUES/MOSELLE (Bernkastel) Rheinland 1A 2B 11C
❐ BERNE Oldenburg 2C
❐ BERNECK/FICHTELGEBIRGE AM WHITE MAIN Bayern 1A 14B
❐ BERNSBACH Sachsen 1A
❐ BERNSTADT Sachsen 1A 2A
❐ BERNSTADT (Bierutow) Schlesien 1A
❐ BEROLZHEIM Bayern 2A 7A
❐ BERSENBRUECK Hannover 2E

10 Pfennig, Artern, 1A

1 CBM Gas, Arys, 8A

25 Pfennig, Aschaffenburg, 1A

1 Reichsmark, POW, Asperg, Germany, 3B

50 Pfennig, Auenbuell, 1A

5 Pfennig, Auma, 1A

50 Pfennig, Aurich, 1A

50 Pfennig, Badbergen, 1A

50 Pfennig, Baden-Baden, 1A

❒ BERTRICH, BAD Rheinland 1A 6B 7C
❒ BERXEN Hannover 3B 4A
❒ BERZDORF/EIGEN Schlesien
(today Schoenau-Berzdorf) 2B
❒ BESIGHEIM/NECKAR-ENZ
Wuerttemberg 2A 11B
❒ BESTWIG Westfalen 1A 2A
❒ BETHEL/BIELEFELD Westfalen 1B
❒ BETTRUM Hannover 3A
❒ BEUCHEN Bayern 1A
❒ BEUEL Rheinland 1A 2A
❒ BEULWITZ Thueringen 1E
❒ BEUTHEN-CARLSHOF Schlesien 2E 5A 7C 8A
❒ BEUTHEN-FREUDENSHUETTE
Schlesien 2B
❒ BEUTHEN-HINDENBURG (Bytom)
Schlesien 2C 8A
❒ BEUTHEN/ODER (Bytom Odrzanski)
Schlesien 1A 2A 3C 5B
6B 7B 8A 14A
❒ BEUTSCHEN (Zbaszyn) Posen 1A
❒ BEVENSEN Hannover 2A
❒ BEVERN Schleswig-Holstein 1A
❒ BEVERSTEDT Hannover 1A
❒ BEVERUNGEN/WESER
Westfalen 1A
❒ BEXBACH Pfalz 2A 7B
❒ BEXTEN Oldenburg 3B
❒ BEXTEN-LISTRUP Oldenburg 3B
❒ BEYENBURG Rheinland 2A
❒ BEYERNAUMBURG
Provinz Sachsen 2E

❒ BIALLA (Biala Piska) Ostpreussen 1B 2A
❒ BIBERACH Baden 6C
❒ BIBERACH/RISS Wuerttemberg 1A 2B
❒ BIBRA, BAD Provinz Sachsen 1Z 2B
❒ BIEBRICH/RHEIN (Bieberich; Biberich)
Hessen-Nassau 1A 2A 7A 8B
❒ BIEDENKOPF/LAHN
Hessen-Nassau 1A 2D 14A
❒ BIEDRUSK 2B 3B
❒ BIELEFELD Westfalen 1A 2A 6A 7A 8A 11B
❒ BIELITZ/BIALA (Bielsk Podlaski;
Bielsko; Sielice)Schlesien 1A 2A 7B 14A 15E
❒ BIELSCHOWITZ (Bielszowice)
Schlesien 1B 4A 5B 7B
❒ BIELSTEIN Rheinland 1A 2B 14A
❒ BIERE Provinz Sachsen 7A 9B
❒ BIERSTADT Hessen-Nassau 1B
❒ BIETIGHEIM Wuerttemberg 1A 2B 8B
❒ BIGGE Westfalen 1C
❒ BILSEN Schleswig-Holstein 1A
❒ BINGEN/RHEIN Hessen 1A 6A
❒ BINGERBRUECK Rheinland 1A 2B
❒ BIRKENFELD Rheinland 1A 2A
❒ BIRKENHAIN (Brzezina) Schlesien 1A 5B
❒ BIRKENWERDER Brandenburg 2D
❒ BIRNBACH Bayern 2A
❒ BIRNBAUM/WARTA
(Miedzychod) Posen 1B
❒ BIRRESBORN Rheinprovinz 11B
❒ BIRSTEIN Hessen-Nassau 1A
❒ BISCHOFFERODE
Provinz Sachsen 2C

5 Pfennig, Baden, Germany, 14B

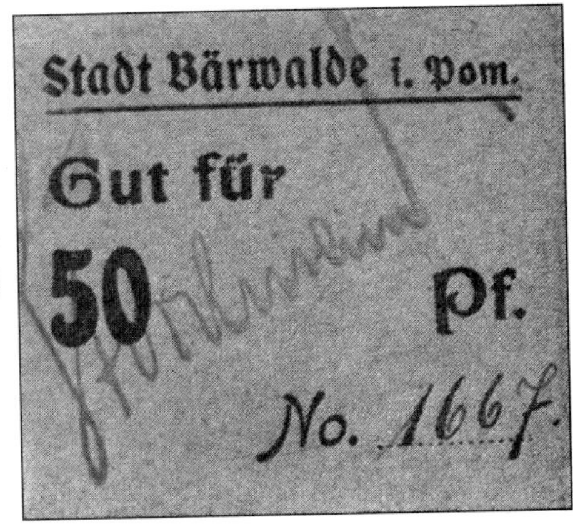

50 Pfennig, Baer-walde/Pommerania, Germany, 1B

Mark, Baerwalde, 6A

❒ BISCHOFSBURG/DIMMER (Biskupiec) Ostpreussen 1A 6C
❒ BISCHOFSGRUEN Bayern 1A 9A
❒ BISCHOFSHEIM/RHOEN Bayern 1A
❒ BISCHOFSTEIN (Bisztynek, Poland) Ostpreussen 1A
❒ BISCHOFSWERDA Sachsen 1A 2A 3A
❒ BISCHWALDE/LOEBAU Westpreussen 2B
❒ BISKUPITZ Oberrschlesien 1A
❒ BISMARCKHUETTE (Hajduki Wielkie; Hajducka) Schlesien 1A 4B
❒ BISMARK Provinz Sachsen 1A
❒ BISPINGEN Hannover 2A
❒ BISSINGEN/ENZ Wuerttenberg 2D 7C
❒ BITBURG/EIFEL Rheinland 1A 6A
❒ BITSCH (Bitche) Lothringen 5A 10B
❒ BITSCHWEILER (Bitschwiller) Elsass 1B 2B
❒ BITTERFELD/MULDE Provinz Sachsen 1A 2A 6A 7A 8B 13A
❒ BLAICHACH Bayern 2A 7A
❒ BLANKENBURG/HARZ (Bad Blankenburg) Provinz Sachsen 1A 2E 3A 6A
❒ BLANKENESE Schleswig-Holstein 1A 2A
❒ BLANKENHAIN (Blankenhayn) Thueringen 1A 2A
❒ BLANKENSTEIN/RUHR Westfalen 1A 2A 7A
❒ BLANKENSTEIN/SAALE Thueringen 1A 6A
❒ BLAUBEUREN/BLAU Wuerttemberg 1A
❒ BLASEWITZ Sachsen 2C
❒ BLECKEDE/ELBE Hannover 1A
❒ BLEICHERODE/BUDE-HARZ Provinz Sachsen 1A 2A
❒ BLENHORST, BAD Hannover 4A 9A
❒ BLEXEN Oldenburg 1C 2B
❒ BLITZENROD Hessen 2B
❒ BLOMBERG/DISTEL Lippe 1A 2A
❒ BLUMBERG/DOELITZ Pommern 2A
❒ BLUMENTHAL Hannover 1A 2B
❒ BLUMENTHAL-ROENNEBECK Hannover 2A
❒ BNIN (Bninska) Posen 1B 6B
❒ BOBINGEN Bayern 2B
❒ BOBISCHAU/MITTELWALDE Schlesien 2A
❒ BOBREK Oberschlesien 1C 3A 5B
❒ BOCHOLT/ (Bochold) Westfalen 1A 2A 7A 14A
❒ BOCHUM Westfalen 1A 2A 3A 5B 6B 7A 9B 11B 12A
❒ BOCHUM-HARPEN Westfalen 2B
❒ BOCHUM, GELSENKIRCHEN, HATTINGEN ETC. Westfalen 1B 6A 14B
❒ BOCKENEM Hannover 2A
❒ BOCKHORN 2E
❒ BOCKSWIESE-HAHNENKLEE Hannover 1A
❒ BOCKWITZ N.L. Brandenberg 2A
❒ BODENBURG Niedersachsen 14B
❒ BODENFELDE Hannover 2A
❒ BODENMAIS Bayern 2A 7A
❒ BODENWERDER/WESER Hannover 1A 2A
❒ BOEBLINGEN Wuerttemberg 1A
❒ BOEBLINGEN UND SINDELFINGEN Wuerttemberg 1A 6A
❒ BOECKINGEN Wuerttemberg 1A
❒ BOEDEFELD Westfalen 2A
❒ BOEEL Schleswig-Holstein 1A 2A
❒ BOEHL Pfalz 2A
❒ BOEHLEN Sachsen 2B 9B 15E
❒ BOEHLITZ-EHRENBERG Sachsen 1E 2B
❒ BOEHRINGEN Baden 1B 6C
❒ BOELE Westfalen 1A
❒ BOENNINGHEIM Wuerttemberg 2B
❒ BOENNINGSTEDT Schleswig-Holstein 1A
❒ BOESDORF/ELSTER Sachsen 1A 2A
❒ BOESEL Hannover 3B
❒ BOGEN/STRAUBING Bayern 2A 6A
❒ BOHMTE Hannover 3B
❒ BOIZENBURG/ELBE (Boitzenburg) Mecklenburg-Schwerin 1A 2A
❒ BOKEL Schleswig-Holstein 1A
❒ BOKELAH Hannover X A.K. 3B
❒ BOKELSESS Schleswig-Holstein 1A
❒ BOKERN Oldenburg 3B
❒ BOLDIXUM Schleswig-Holstein 13A
❒ BOLKENHAIN/NEISSE (Bolkow) 1A 2A
❒ BOLLWEILER (Bollwiller) Elsass 1A
❒ BOLTENHAGEN (Ostseebad) Mecklenburg-Schwerin 2A
❒ BOMMELSEN Hannover 3B
❒ BOMMERN Westfalen 2A 3E 9A
❒ BOMST (Babimost) Posen 1A
❒ BONIKOW Posen 7B 9A
❒ BONN Rheinland 1A 2A 6A 7B 8B 9B 11B 13D
❒ BOPFINGEN/EGER Baden-Wuerttemberg 1A 7A
❒ BOPPARD (Boppart) Rheinland 1A 6A
❒ BORBECK Rheinland 3B 8B 9A
❒ BORCHEL Oldenburg 3B
❒ BORDELUM Schleswig-Holstein 1A
❒ BORDESHOLM Schleswig-Holstein 1A

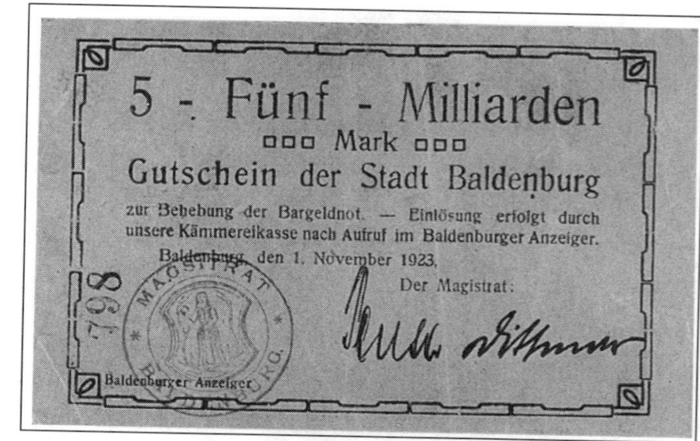

5 Milliarden Mark, Baldenburg, 1A

50 Pfennig, Bargteheide, 1A

❒ BOREK (Borken) Posen 1D
❒ BORGENTREICH Westfalen 2A
❒ BORGHORST Westfalen 2D 14B
❒ BORK Westfalen 2A 7A
❒ BORKEN Hessen 1A
❒ BORKEN Westfalen 1A 14A
❒ BORKUM Hannover 1A 8A
❒ BORNA Sachsen 1A 2A 9A 10B
❒ BORNHEIM Hessen-Nassau 7B 9A
❒ BORNSTEDT Provinz Sachsen 2B
❒ BORSIGWERK (Zaklady Borsiga) Schlesien 1B 5B 7B 9B
❒ BORSTEL Schleswig-Holstein 1A
❒ BORSTENDORF/ERZGEBIRGE Sachsen 1B 2B
❒ BORY (Borysa) 2A
❒ BOSAU Schleswig-Holstein 2A 9A
❒ BOSENBACH Hessen 1A
❒ BOSSE Hannover 3B
❒ BOSLER Wuerttemberg 2E
❒ BOTTORF Hannover 3B
❒ BOTTROP Westfalen 1B 2A 6A
❒ BOTTROP, GLADBECK UND OSTERFELD Westfalen 1A
❒ BRACHT Rheinland 1A
❒ BRACKEL Westfalen 5B
❒ BRACKENHEIM/LABER Wuerttemberg 1B
❒ BRAENDSTRUP Schleswig-Holstein 2A
❒ BRAEUNLINGEN Baden 1A 7B
❒ BRAKE (Braake) Oldenburg 1A 2A 10A
❒ BRAKEL/HOEXTER Westfalen 1A 2C
❒ BRAMBACH, BAD Vogtland Sachsen 1A 2A
❒ BRAMBAUER/DORTMUND Westfalen 3D 5B
❒ BRAMFELD Schleswig-Holstein 1A
❒ BRAMSTEDT, BAD/BRAMAUE Schleswig-Holstein 1A
❒ BRAND-ERBISDORF Sachsen 1A 2A
❒ BRAND/AACHEN Rheinland 2A 7A
❒ BRANDE-HOERNERKIRCHEN Schleswig-Holstein 1A
❒ BRANDENBURG/HAVEL Brandenburg 1A 2C 3A 7A 8B 9A 10A 12A
❒ BRANDIS Sachsen 1B 2B
❒ BRANNENBURG/INN Bayern 2B
❒ BRAUBACH/RHEIN Hessen-Nassau 2A 7A
❒ BRAUNLAGE/HARZ Braunschweig 1A 7B
❒ BRAUNSBERG/PASSARGE (Braniewo) Ostpreussen 1B
❒ BRAUNSCHWEIG Braunschweig 1A 2A 6A 7A 8A 9A 11C 12A
❒ BREBACH Pfalz 9A
❒ BRECKERFELD Westfalen 2C 3B
❒ BREDENSCHEID Westfalen 3B
❒ BREDSTEDT Scheswig-Holstein 1A
❒ BREESEN Mecklenburg 3B
❒ BREHME Provinz Sachsen 2B
❒ BREHNA Provinz Sachsen 1A
❒ BREISACH/RHEIN Baden 1A 6A
❒ BREITENBACH/HERZBERG Hessen-Nassau 2A
❒ BREMEN/WESER 1A 2A 5B 6B 7A 8A 9B 10A 11B 12A

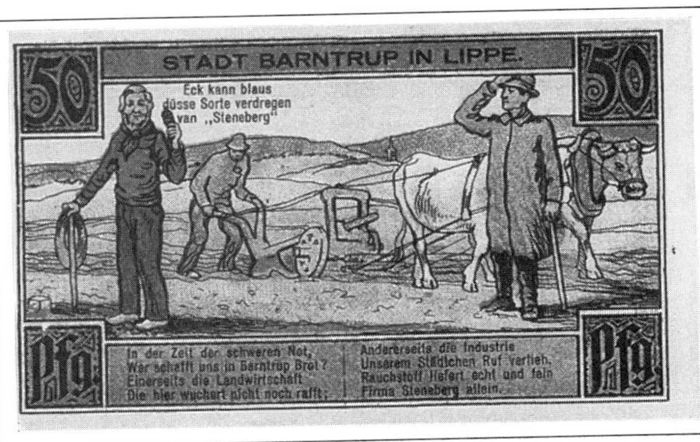

50 Pfennig, Barntrup, 1A

1 Mark, Beckum, 1B

❒ BREMERHAVEN/WESER Bremen — 1C 2A 5B 7C 8A 9B 10B 11B
❒ BREMERHAVEN, GEESTEMUENDE, LEHE Bremen — 1A 2C
❒ BREMERVOERDE/OSTE Hannover — 1A
❒ BRESLAU/ODER (Wroclaw) Schlesien — 1A 2A 5B 7A 8A 10A 11B 12A 13A
❒ BRETEL Hannover — 3B
❒ BRETLEBEN/ARTERN Provinz Sachsen — 2A
❒ BRETNIG Sachsen — 1A 2A
❒ BRETTEN Baden — 2C 7E
❒ BREYELL Rheinland — 1A
❒ BRIEG/ODER (Brzeg) Schlesien — 1A 2B 7A
❒ BRIESEN/GRAN (Bries; Wabrzezno) Westpreussen — 1B 6A
❒ BRIESNITZ/Sachsen — 11B
❒ BRIEST/Brandenburg — 10A
❒ BRILON Westfalen — 1A 2B
❒ BRITZ Brandenburg — 5B 7B
❒ BROACKER (Broager, Denmark) Schleswig Holstein — 1A 2C
❒ BROCKAU (Brochow; Brockow) Schlesien — 1A 2B 7B
❒ BROCKESWALDE/CUXHAVEN Hamburg — 2B
❒ BROCKHAGEN Westfalen — 5B
❒ BROCKHOEFE Hannover — 3B
❒ BROCKWITZ Sachsen — 2B 7B
❒ BROMBACH Baden — 1A 6A
❒ BROMBERG/BRAHE (Bydgoszcz) Posen — 1A 2A 6A 7A 9B 10B 12A
❒ BRONAU (Bronow) Schlesien — 7B
❒ BROTTERODE Thueringia (See Steinbach-Hallenberg)
❒ BRUCHHAUSEN/HUESTEN Westfalen — 1A 2A
❒ BRUCHSAL/SALZBACH Baden — 1A 6A 8B
❒ BRUDERSDORF/NABBURG Bayern — 2B
❒ BRUDERZECHE Kriebitzsch — 5B
❒ BRUECKEN/BIRKENFELD Pfalz — 2C
❒ BRUECKENAU Bayern — 1A 2B
❒ BRUEEL Mecklenburg-Schwerin — 1A
❒ BRUEGGEN Rheinland — 1A 2E 7B
❒ BRUEHL/KOELN Rheinland — 1A 2E
❒ BRUNDE-ROTHENKRUG Schleswig-Holstein — 1A
❒ BRUNNDOEBRA Sachsen — 2A
❒ BRUNSBUETTELKOOG Schleswig-Holstein — 2A
❒ BRUNSHAUPTEN Mecklenburg-Schwerin — 1A
❒ BRZEZOWITZ (Brzozowice) Schlesien — 1A 3A
❒ BUBLITZ (Bobolice) Pommern — 1D 6A
❒ BUCHA/KOENITZ Sachsen-Weimar-Eisenach — 2A
❒ BUCHAU-FEDERSEE Wuerttemberg — 2A
❒ BUCHBRUNN Bayern — 14B
❒ BUCHENAU Hessen-Nassau — 1A
❒ BUCHENWALD/WEIMAR Sachsen — 15B
❒ BUCHHOLZ Hannover — 3B

50 Pfennig, Beendorf, Germany, 2B

25 Pfennig, Belgard, 1A

5 Pfennig, Benneckenstein, 1A

50 Pfennig, Bensheim, 1A

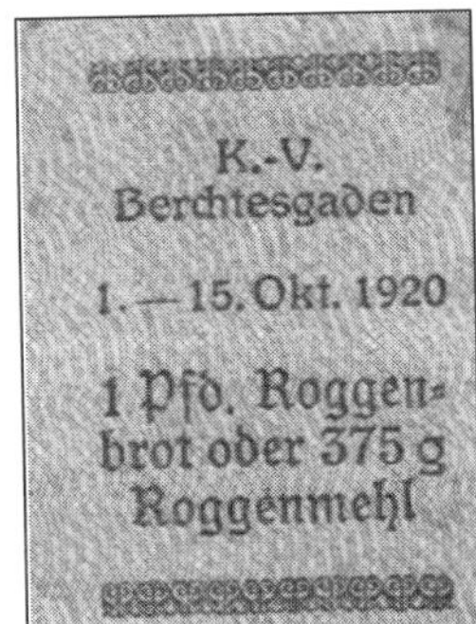

1 Pfund ryebread, Berchtesgaden, Germany, 9B

50 Pfennig, Berchtesgaden, 1A

75 Pfennig, Berga, 1A

1 Mark, Berleburg, 1A

5 Millionen Mark, Berlin, 2A

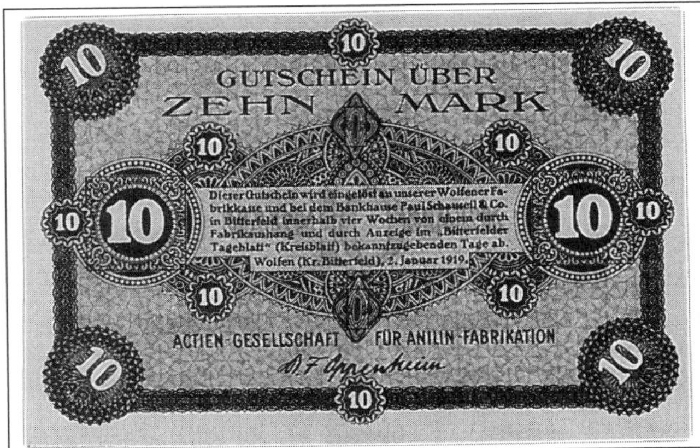

10 Mark, Berlin-Treptow, 2A

❐ BUCHHOLZ Sachsen 1A 2A
❐ BUCHSWEILER (Bouxwiller; Bouxviller; Buchswiller) Elsass 1B 6B
❐ BUDZIN (Budsin) Posen 1C 8A
❐ BUECHEN-BAHNHOF Hannover 1A
❐ BUECKEBURG Schaumburg-Lippe 2A 6A 8B
❐ BUEDELSDORF Schleswig-Holstein 1A 9B
❐ BUEDERICH Nordrhein-Westfalen 14A
❐ BUEDERICH-MEERBUSCH Westfalen 14A
❐ BUEDINGEN Hessen 1A 6A 8B
❐ BUEHL Baden 1A 2B 6A 7C
❐ BUENDE Westfalen 1A
❐ BUER (now Gelsenkirchen) Westfalen 1A 2A 3E 4B 5E 6A
❐ BUEREN Westfalen 1A 2C 3D 5E
❐ BUEREN BEI COESFELD Westfalen 5B 7B
❐ BUERGEL Sachsen-Weimar-Eisenach 1A 2A 9A
❐ BUESUM Schleswig-Holstein 1A 2B
❐ BUETOW (Bytow) Pommern 2A 3E 4A
❐ BUETTGEN Rheinland 1A
❐ BUETZOW Mecklenburg-Schwerin 1A 6B
❐ BULLENKUHLEN Schleswig-Holstein 1A
❐ BUNZLAU (Boleslawiec) Schlesien 1A 2A 8B 9B 11B 13A
❐ BURG Provinz Sachsen 1A 2B 3B 4A
❐ BURG Schleswig-Holstein 1A 6A
❐ BURG-MAGDEBURG/IHLE Provinz Sachsen 1A 4A 9B
❐ BURG/FEHMARN Schleswig-Holstein 1A 6A
❐ BURG/SUEDERDITHMARSCHEN Schleswig-Holstein 2A
❐ BURG/WUPPER (Wipper) Rheinland 1A
❐ BURGAU Bayern 2C 6B
❐ BURGBROHL Rheinland 7B
❐ BURGDAMM Hannover 11B
❐ BURGDORF/AA Hannover 2A

25 Pfennig, Berncastel Cues, 2A

10 Pfennig, Bethel, 2A

❒ BURGHASLACH Bayern	6B	7B				
❒ BURGHAUSEN/SALZACH Bayern	1A	2B	6A	7A		
❒ BURGKUNDSTADT/MAIN Bayern	2B					
❒ BURGLENGENFELD/NAAB Bayern	1A	2B	6B			
❒ BURGRIEDEN/LAUPHEIM Wuerttemberg	2B	7B				
❒ BURGSTAEDT Sachsen	2A					
❒ BURGSTEINFURT Westfalen	1A	2A	3C	4B	6A	14A
❒ BURHAVE Oldenburg	1D					
❒ BURKERSDORF/ERZGEBIRGE Sachsen	2A					
❒ BURKHARDTSDORF Sachsen	1B					
❒ BURKHARDTSDORF & TALHEIM Sachsen lA						
❒ BURSCHEID (Borcette; Burtscheid) Rheinland	1A					
❒ BUSENDORF (Bouzonville) Lothringen	7A					
❒ BUSS Saar	2B					
❒ BUTTENWIESEN Bayern	14B					
❒ BUTTLAR Hessen	2B					
❒ BUTTSTAEDT (Buttstadt) Thueringen	1A	2B				
❒ BUTZBACH (Boutschbach) Hessen	1A	2A				
❒ BUXTEHUDE/ESTE Hannover	1A	7B	9A			
❒ CAEMMERSWALDE Sachsen	2B					
❒ CALAU N.L. Brandenburg	1A	2A				

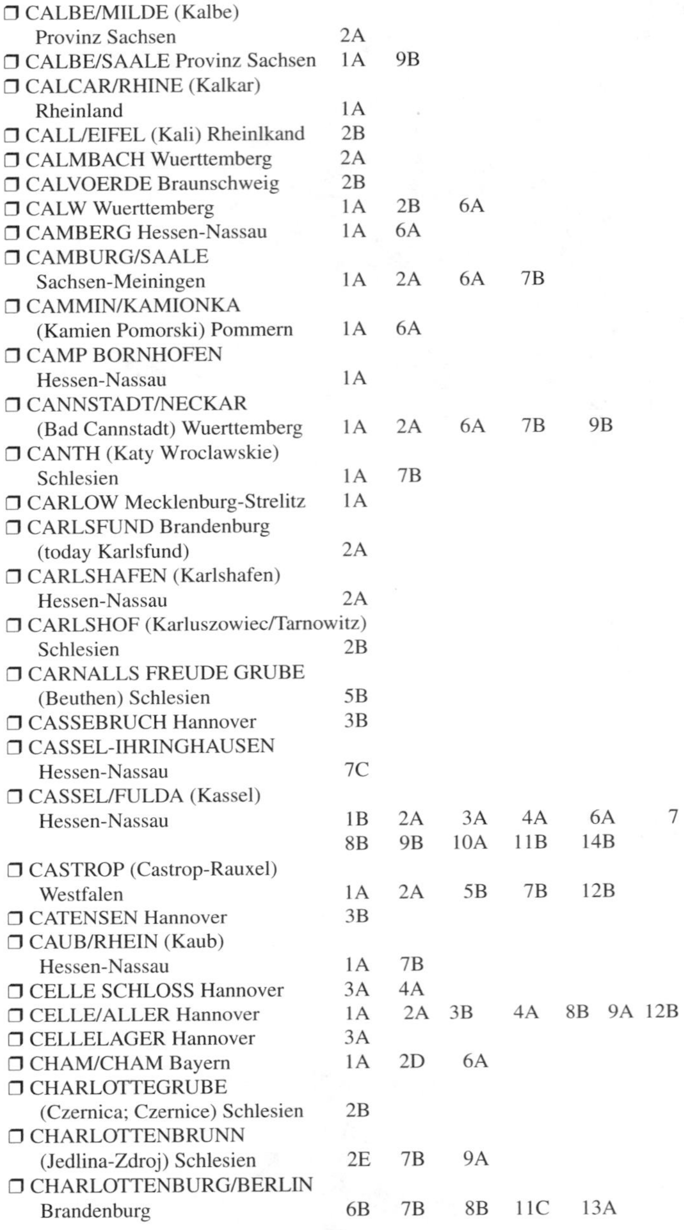

❒ CALBE/MILDE (Kalbe) Provinz Sachsen	2A						
❒ CALBE/SAALE Provinz Sachsen	1A	9B					
❒ CALCAR/RHINE (Kalkar) Rheinland	1A						
❒ CALL/EIFEL (Kali) Rheinlkand	2B						
❒ CALMBACH Wuerttemberg	2A						
❒ CALVOERDE Braunschweig	2B						
❒ CALW Wuerttemberg	1A	2B	6A				
❒ CAMBERG Hessen-Nassau	1A	6A					
❒ CAMBURG/SAALE Sachsen-Meiningen	1A	2A	6A	7B			
❒ CAMMIN/KAMIONKA (Kamien Pomorski) Pommern	1A	6A					
❒ CAMP BORNHOFEN Hessen-Nassau	1A						
❒ CANNSTADT/NECKAR (Bad Cannstadt) Wuerttemberg	1A	2A	6A	7B	9B		
❒ CANTH (Katy Wroclawskie) Schlesien	1A	7B					
❒ CARLOW Mecklenburg-Strelitz	1A						
❒ CARLSFUND Brandenburg (today Karlsfund)	2A						
❒ CARLSHAFEN (Karlshafen) Hessen-Nassau	2A						
❒ CARLSHOF (Karluszowiec/Tarnowitz) Schlesien	2B						
❒ CARNALLS FREUDE GRUBE (Beuthen) Schlesien	5B						
❒ CASSEBRUCH Hannover	3B						
❒ CASSEL-IHRINGHAUSEN Hessen-Nassau	7C						
❒ CASSEL/FULDA (Kassel) Hessen-Nassau	1B	2A	3A	4A	6A	7	
	8B	9B	10A	11B	14B		
❒ CASTROP (Castrop-Rauxel) Westfalen	1A	2A	5B	7B	12B		
❒ CATENSEN Hannover	3B						
❒ CAUB/RHEIN (Kaub) Hessen-Nassau	1A	7B					
❒ CELLE SCHLOSS Hannover	3A	4A					
❒ CELLE/ALLER Hannover	1A	2A	3B	4A	8B	9A	12B
❒ CELLELAGER Hannover	3A						
❒ CHAM/CHAM Bayern	1A	2D	6A				
❒ CHARLOTTEGRUBE (Czernica; Czernice) Schlesien	2B						
❒ CHARLOTTENBRUNN (Jedlina-Zdroj) Schlesien	2E	7B	9A				
❒ CHARLOTTENBURG/BERLIN Brandenburg	6B	7B	8B	11C	13A		

50 Pfennig, Beuthen/O, 1A

25 Pfennig, Bevern, 1A

Location	Ratings
❒ CHATEAU-SALINS Elsass	2B
❒ CHEMNITZ-FURTH Sachsen	2B
❒ CHEMNITZ-GABLENZ Sachsen	2B
❒ CHEMNITZ-HILBERSDORF Sachsen	2B
❒ CHEMNITZ-KAPPEL Sachsen	2A
❒ CHEMNITZ-SCHOENAU Sachsen	2A
❒ CHEMNITZ (Karl Marx Stadt) Sachsen	1A 2A 3A 5B 7B 8A 11B 12B 14A
❒ CHEMNITZ-FURTH Sachsen	2A
❒ CHEMNITZ-HILBERSDORF Sachsen	2A
❒ CHEMNITZ-KAPEL Sachsen	2A
❒ CHEMNIT-SCHOENAU Sachsen	2A
❒ CHLUDOWO Posen	2B
❒ CHODZIEZ Posen	2A
❒ CHORZOW (Chorzowska) Schlesien	1C 5C
❒ CHRISTBURG/SORGE (Dziezgan) Westpreussen	1C 2B
❒ CHRISTIANSFELD (Kristiansfelt, Denmark) Schleswig-Holstein	1A
❒ CHRISTIANSTADT/BOBER (Krzystkowice) Brandenburg	2B
❒ CHROSCZUETZ (Chroscice) Schiesien	1B 2B
❒ CHURSDORF Sachsen	2A
❒ CHWALLOWITZ (Chwalowice; Chwalkowska) Schlesien	2B 5B
❒ CLAUSSNITZ Sachsen	1A
❒ CLAUSTHAL/HARZ Hannover	1A 3A
❒ CLETTENBERG Provinz Sachsen	2A
❒ CLEVE (Kleve) Rheinland	1A 2B
❒ CLOETZE (Kloetze) Provinz Sachsen	9B
❒ CLOPPENBURG Oldenburg	1A
❒ COBLENZ (Koblenz) Rheinland	1A 2E 3A 6A 7A 9B 10B 11B
❒ COBLENZ-LUETZEL Rheinland	2A 7A 11B
❒ COBLENZ-NEUENDORF Rheinland	2A
❒ COBURG/(Sachsen-Coburg) Bayern	1A 2A 6A 7B 8B 9B
❒ COCHEM-SIMMERN-ZELL Rheinland	1A
❒ COCHEM/MOSEL (Kochem) Rheinland	1A
❒ COENNERN (Koennern) Provinz Sachsen	9B
❒ COESFELD Westfalen	1A 2E 5E
❒ COETHEN (Koethen) Anhalt	1E 2A 9B
❒ COLBERG, BAD (Sachsen-Meiningen)	1A 3A
❒ COLDITZ/MULDE (Kolditz) Sachsen	1A 2A
❒ COLMAR/LAUCH Elsass	1C 7B 9B
❒ COLNRADE Hannover	3B
❒ COLONNOWSKA Schlesien	2D
❒ CONSTMETTINGEN Wuerttemberg	1A
❒ COPITZ/ELBE Sachsen (today Pirna)	2A
❒ CORBACH/ITTER (Korbach) Waldeck	1A 2A
❒ CORDINGEN Hannover	2A 3B
❒ COSEL (Kozle) Schlesien	1A 2B 5B 7B
❒ COSSMANNSDORF Sachsen	2A
❒ COSWIG Anhalt	2A
❒ COSWIG/ELBE (Koswigk) Provinz Sachsen	1A 2A 7B
❒ COTTBUS/SPREE (Kottbus Brandenburg	1A 2A 3A 6A 12B 14A

75 Pfennig, Beverstedt, 1A

10,000 Mark, Bielefeld, Germany, 1B

10 Reichspfennig, Bielstein, 14B

50 Pfennig, Bielschowitz, 1A

10 Mark, Bingen, 1A

50 Pfennig, Birkenfeld, 1A

50 Pfennig, Bischofsburg, 6C

❒ CRAILSHEIM/JAXT (Krailsheim) Wuerttemberg 1A 6A 7B 9A
❒ CRANENBURG (Kranenburg) Rheinland 1A
❒ CRANZAHL Sachsen 1B 2A
❒ CREFELD Rheinland 1A 2D 3C 4B 5B 6A 7B 11B 12A
❒ CREFELD-GLADBACH-GREVENBROICH-KEMPEN-NEUSS Rheinland 1A
❒ CREFELD-UERDINGEN Rheinland 1A 2A
❒ CREFELD-DUISBURG 2A
❒ CRENGELDANZ Westfalen 5C 7B
❒ CREUSSEN/OBERFRANKEN Bayern 1B
❒ CRIMMITSCHAU/PLEISSE (Crimmitzschau) Sachsen 1A 2A 8B 11B
❒ CRIVITZ (Krivitz) Mecklenburg-Schwerin 1A
❒ CROEBERN/LEIPZIG Thueringen (today Kroebern) 1A 2A
❒ CRONE/BRAHE (Koronowo) Posen 1D
❒ CRONENBERG Rheinland 1A 2B 8B
❒ CROSSEN/ODER & BOBER (Krosno; Krossen) Brandenburg 1A 3A 6A
❒ CROSSEN Sachsen 3A 7A
❒ CROSTA-ADOLFSHUETTE Sachsen 2A
❒ CROTTENDORF/ERZGEBIRGE (Krottendorf) Sachsen 1E
❒ CUESTRIN (Kostrzyn; Kostrzynska) Brandenburg 1A 2B 3A 6A 8B 12A 13D
❒ CUKROWNIA/ZNIN Posen 2A
❒ CULM (Kulm; Chelmno, Chelmska) Westpreussen 1B
❒ CULMSEE (Kulmsee; Chelmza; Chelmska) Westpreussen 1E
❒ CUNEWALDE Sachsen 1A 2B
❒ CURSDORF Thueringen 1A
❒ CUXHAVEN Hamburg 1A 2B 8B 9A
❒ CZARNKOW (Czarnikau) Posen 1B
❒ CZELADZ (Tcheliadz, Tscheliads) Silesia 2B
❒ CZEMPIN Posen 1A 2D
❒ CZERNITZ (Czernica) Schlesien 1B 2A 5A
❒ CZERSK (Marienwalde) Westpreussen 1E 2D 3A
❒ CZERWIONKA Schlesien 2E
❒ CZESTOCHOWA (Tchenstokov; Chenstokhov; Czenstochau) Schlesien 2B
❒ DABER (Dobra) Pommern 1A
❒ DABIE (Dombe, Altdamm) Galicia 1A 4B 9A
❒ DABROWA GORNICZA (Dombrau; Dombrova) Schlesien 1A 2B 6A
❒ DACHAU/AMMER Bayern 7A 15C
❒ DAENISCHBURG Luebeck 2B
❒ DAHLBRUCH Westfalen 3B
❒ DAHLE Westfalen 2B
❒ DAHLEN Sachsen 1B 2B
❒ DAHLENBURG Hannover 1A 2A 3B 14B
❒ DAHLERAU Rheinland 7B
❒ DAHLERBRUECK/Hagen/ Westfalen 3B
❒ DAHLHAUSEN/WUPPER Rheinland 1A 2D 7A
❒ DAHME/DAHME Brandenburg 1A
❒ DALER Schleswig-Holstein 1A
❒ DALHAUSEN/HOEXTER Westfalen 1A 2B 7B
❒ DALSHEIM Hessen 7A
❒ DAMME Oldenburg 2C
❒ DANNEFELD/ALTMARK Provinz Sachsen 2A
❒ DANNENBERG/JEETZE Hannover 2A
❒ DANSTEDT Provinz Sachsen 3C
❒ DANZIG-KRAJOWY (Gdansk-Krajowy) 2D
❒ DANZIG-LANGFUHR (Gdansk-Wrzeszcz) Westpreussen 2B
❒ DANZIG-OLIVIA (Gdansk-Oliwa) 2D

50 Pfennig, Bismarckhuette, 1A

50 Pfennig, Berchtesgaden, 1A

25 Pfennig, Bitburg, 1A

10 Pfennig, Bielefeld, 1A

10 Pfennig, Blankenburg/H, 1A

50 Pfennig, Blankenese, 1A

25 Pfennig, Blankenstein/S, 1A

50 Pfennig, Blenhorst, Bad, POW, 3B

1 Mark, Blomberg/L, 1A

25 Pfennig, Blumenthal/H, 1A

❒ DANZIG-TROYL
(Gdansk Przerobka) Westpreussen 4A 5A
❒ DANZIG/VISTULA(Gdansk)
Westpreussen 1B 2A 4A 6B 7B 9A 10B 12A 13C
❒ DANZIG-ZOPPOT (Sopot)
Westpreussen 1A 2B 9B
❒ DARFELD Westfalen 2C 5C 14C
❒ DARGUN/KLOSTERSEE
Mecklenburg-Schwerin 1A
❒ DARKEHMEN/ANGERAPP
(Oziersk) Ostpreussen 1C 10B
❒ DARLINGERODE
Provinz Sachsen 1A
❒ DARMSTADT /Hessen 1A 2A 3E 6A 7A 8B 9B
❒ DECK (Swierklaniec) Schlesien 1B
❒ DASSEL Hannover 2A 3B
❒ DASSOW Mecklenburg-Schwerin 1A
❒ DATTELN Westfalen 1A 2A 3C 11E
❒ DAUN Rheinland 1A 6A 7B
❒ DEERSHEIM Sachsen 7A
❒ DEESBACH U. LICHTENHAIN
Thueringen 1A
❒ DEGGENDORF/DANUBE
(Deckendorf) Bayern 1A 2A 6A 7A 15A
❒ DEIFELD Westfalen 2A
❒ DELBRUECK Westfalen 1A 2A 9B
❒ DELITZSCH/LOBER
Provinz Sachsen 1A 2A
❒ DELMENHORST/DELME
Oldenburg 1A 2A 8A
❒ DEMITZ-THUMITZ Sachsen 1A
❒ DEMMIN/TOLLENSE & TREBEL
Pommern 1B 2B
❒ DENKLINGEN Rheinland 1B
❒ DERENBURG/HARZ
Provinz Sachsen 1A
❒ DERFELD Westfalen 1A
❒ DERMBACH/RHOEM
Sachsen-Wei-Eisen 1A 2A 7A
❒ DERNE Westfalen 4B 5B
❒ DERSCHLAG Rheinland 2B
❒ DESSAU/MULDE
(Dessaw) Anhalt 1A 2A 6A 7B 10B 12B
❒ DETMOLD/WERRA Lippe 1A 2D 9B
❒ DETTINGEN/ERMS
Wuerttemberg 7A
❒ DETTINGEN/MAIN Bayern 2B 7B
❒ DEUTSCH PIEKAR
(Piekary Wielkie) Schlesien 1B
❒ DEUTSCH-EYLAU (Elk Ilawa)
Westpreussen 1D 6B
❒ DEUTSCH-KRONE (Walcz)
Westpreussen 1B 7B
❒ DEUTSCHNEUDORF/Olbernhau
Sachsen 2E
❒ DEUTSCH-RUMBACH Elsass 2B
❒ DEUTSCHENBORA Sachsen 1A
❒ DIEBAN (Dziewin) Schlesien 7B
❒ DIEBURG/GERSPRENZ Hessen 6A
❒ DIEDENHOFEN Lothringen 1A 2B 3A 6B 7A 9B 10B 12A
❒ DIEDENHOFEN-NIEDERJEUTZ
Lothringen 3A 7A
❒ DIEKHOLZEN Hannover 5B
❒ DIEPHOLZ/HUNTE Hannover 1A 3B
❒ DIERINGHAUSEN Rheinland 2B 7A
❒ DIESSEN-ST. GEORGEN Bayern 2A
❒ DIESSEN/AMMERSEE Bayern 1A 2B
❒ DIETESHEIM Hessen 7B 9B
❒ DIETFURT Bayern 7A
❒ DIETFURT/ALTMUEHL Bayern 2B
❒ DIEZ/LAHN (Dietz)
Hessen-Nassau 1A
❒ DILLENBURG/DILLE
Hessen-Nassau 1A
❒ DILLINGEN/DONAU Bayern 1A 2A 4A 5A 6A 10A
❒ DILLINGEN/SAAR Rheinland 4A 5B
❒ DILLKREIS Hessen-Nassau 1B 6A
❒ DINGELSTAEDT/UNSTRUT
Provinz Sachsen 1A 2A 6A
❒ DINGOLFING/ISAR Bayern 1B 2A 6A
❒ DINKELSBUEHL/WERNITZ
Bayern 1B 6A
❒ DINSLAKEN Rheinland 1A 3B 6A
❒ DIPPOLDISWALDE/WEISSERITZ
Sachsen 1A 2A
❒ DIRLEWANG Bayern 1A
❒ DIRSCHAU/VISTULA (Tczew)
Westpreussen 1A 2A 7B
❒ DITFURT Provinz Sachsen 1A
❒ DITTERSBACH (Walbrzych; Starsow)
Schlesien 1A

50 Pfennig, Bnin, 6D

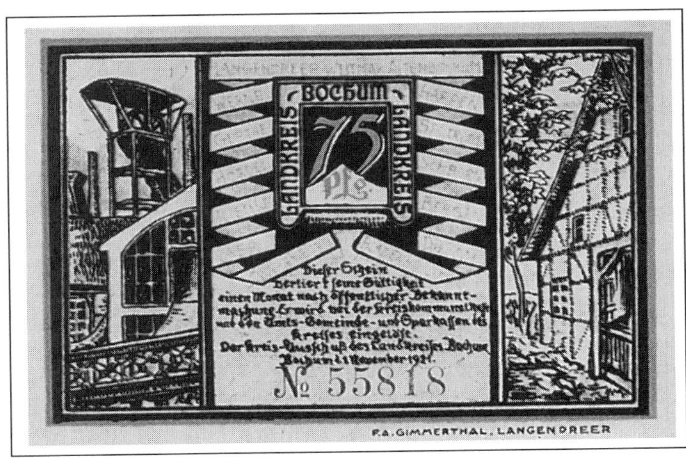

75 Pfennig, Bochum, 1A

❒ DITTERSDORF/ERZGEBIRGE Sachsen 2B
❒ DITTMANNSDORF Sachsen 2B
❒ DOBERAN (Bad Doberan) Mecklenburg-Schwerin 1A
❒ DOEBELN Sachsen 1A 2B 3A 4A 6A 8B 12A
❒ DOEBERITZ Brandenburg 2E 3A 10A
❒ DOEBERN N.L. Brandenburg 1A 2A 6B
❒ DOEMITZ Mecklenburg-Schwerin 1A 2B 7B
❒ DOERFEL/Annaberg Sachsen 2E
❒ DOERVERDEN Hannover 10A
❒ DOLLBERGEN Hannover 2A
❒ DOLSTHAIDA Provinz Sachsen 1A
❒ DOMB (Dab) Schlesien 1E 5B
❒ DOMBROWO (Dabrowo; Dabrowki) Posen 2C
❒ DOMMELSTADL/PASSAU Bayern 2B
❒ DOMMITZSCH/ELBE (Dommitsh) Provinz Sachsen 1A
❒ DOMNAU (Domnowo) Ostpreussen 1A
❒ DONAUESCHINGEN/ Baden 1B2 6B 7D 9B
❒ DONAUWOERTH/Bayern 1A 2A
❒ DONAUWOERTH/WERNITZ & DANUBE Bayern 1A 2B
❒ DONNDORF Provinz Sachsen 2A
❒ DONNERHORST Hannover 3B
❒ DOPIEWO (Wanenfeld) Posen 2B
❒ DORDORF/DORNBURG Thueringen 14A
❒ DORFBACH Bayern 1A
❒ DORFCHEMNITZ Sachsen 2E
❒ DORFEN/Bayern 2B
❒ DORMAGEN Rheinland 2B
❒ DORNAP Rheinland 2A 3B 5B
❒ DORNBURG/SAALE Sachsen-Weimar-Eisenach 1A
❒ DORNDORF/RHOEN Thueringen 2A
❒ DORNSTETTEN Wuerttemberg 1A
❒ DORSTEN/LIPPE Westfalen 1A 2C
❒ DORSTFELD Westfalen 5B
❒ DORTMUND Westfalen 2A 5B 6A 7A 8A 9B 11B 14C
❒ DORTMUND UND HOERDE Westfalen 1A
❒ DORUM Hannover 2A
❒ DOTTERNHAUSEN Baden-Wuerttember 14B
❒ DRABENDERHOEHE Nord Rhein-Westfalen 14B
❒ DRACHSELSRIED Bayern 2B
❒ DRAHOMISCHL Schlesien 2B

75 Pfennig, Bodenwerder/W, 1A

10 Pfennig, Boizenburg, 1A

❒ DRAMBURG/DRAGE
(Drawsko Pomorskie) Pommern 1A
❒ DRASCHWITZ Sachsen 9B
❒ DREBACH Sachsen 1B 2A
❒ DREIWERDEN Sachsen 2A
❒ DRENKE/HOEXTER Westfalen 1A
❒ DRESDEN & RADEBERG Sachsen 2A
❒ DRESDEN-ALTSTADT Sachsen 1A 7A 11B 12A
❒ DRESDEN-HEIDENAU Sachsen 2E
❒ DRESDEN-LAUBEGAST Sachsen 2B
❒ DRESDEN-LEUBEN Sachsen 2B
❒ DRESDEN-LOCKWITZGRUND
Sachsen 2E
❒ DRESDEN-NEUSTADT Sachsen 1A 9A
❒ DRESDEN-NEUSTADT-ALTSTADT
Sachsen 1A
❒ DRESDEN-RADEBEUL Sachsen 7B
❒ DRESDEN-STETZSCH 14A
❒ DRESDEN-TRACHAU Sachsen 2B
❒ DRESDEN-ZITTAU Sachsen 1A
❒ DRESDEN/ELBE Sachsen 1A 2A 6A 7B 9A 11B 12A 13A
❒ DRESOW Pommern 7B
❒ DREWER Brandenburg 2B
❒ DREWER MARK Westfalen 3B
❒ DRIBURG, BAD Westfalen 1A 2A 7A
❒ DRIESEN/NETZE (Drezdenko)
Brandenburg 1B 6A
❒ DROLSHAGEN Westfalen 1E 2E
❒ DROSSEN (Osno Lubuskie)
Brandenburg 2A
❒ DROYSSIG Provinz Sachsen 2C
❒ DUBENSKO GRUBE Schlesien 1E 5B
❒ DUDERSTADT/HAHLE
Provinz Sachsen 1A 2A
❒ DUEBEN Provinz Sachsen 1A
❒ DUELKEN Rheinland 1A 2A
❒ DUELMEN Westfalen 1A 2E 3C 4A
❒ DUEMMLINGHAUSEN
Rheinland 2C
❒ DUENEBERG Hamburg 7A
❒ DUENSEN Hannover 3B
❒ DUENTH (Dynt, Denmark)
Schleswig-Holstein 1A
❒ DUEPPEL (Dybboel, Denmark)
Schleswig-Holstein 1A
❒ DUEREN Rheinland 1A 2B 6A 7B 8B 9B 12A
❒ DUERKHEIM, BAD Pfalz 1A
❒ DUERREN Wuerttemberg 2A
❒ DUERRKUNZENDORF Rheinland 7A
❒ DUESSELDORF Rheinland 1B 2D 3A 5A 6B
7A 9A 11B 12A 14B
❒ DUESSELDORF-DERENDORF
Rheinprovinz 2B 7E
❒ DUESSELDORF-GERRESHEIM
Rheinprovinz 2A 5C 7A
❒ DUESSELDORF-GRAFENBERG
Rheinland 2B
❒ DUESSELDORF-HEERDT
Rheinland 2B
❒ DUESSELDORF-OBERKASSEL
Rheinland 2A
❒ DUESSELDORF-RATH Rheinland 2B
❒ DUESSELDORF-RATINGEN
Rheinland 2A
❒ DUISBURG Rheinland 1A 2A 4A 5B 7A
8B 11B 12A 14A
❒ DUISBURG-BEEK Rheinland 11B
❒ DUISBURG-HOCHFELD
Rheinland 2A
❒ DUISBURG-MEIDERICH
Rheinland 2A 5C
❒ DUISBURG-MUELHEIM
Rheinland 2A
❒ DUISBURG-RUHRORT

Types of Emergency Money

Type	Reference #
Municipal paper	1
Private paper	2
POW paper	3
POW official metal	4
POW private metal	5
Municipal metal	6
Private metal	7
Gas tokens	8
Food; beer; konsumverein	9
Naval; military; kantine	10
Encased, unencased stamps	11
Streetcar tokens	12
Porcelain	13
World War II issues	14
Concentration, Civilian internment camps	15

Rarity grades: A, to $25; B, to $60; C, to $125; D, to $200; and E, $350

50 Pfennig, Bolkenhain, 1A

Rheinland	2A	5A				
❒ DUISBURG-WANHEIM Rheinland	2A					
❒ DUISDORF Rheinland	7A					
❒ DURLACH/PFINZ Baden	1A	6A				
❒ DYROTZ Brandenburg	3A					
❒ DZIEDZICE Schlesien 1B						
❒ EBENHAUSEN Bayern	7B					
❒ EBERBACH/NECKAR Baden	1A	6A	7E	8B		
❒ EBERNBURG Rheinland	2A					
❒ EBERSBACH Sachsen	1A	2A	8B			
❒ EBERSBERG Bayern	1A	2B				
❒ EBERSDORF Thueringen	1A					
❒ EBERSDORF/HABELSCHWERDT (Bystrzyca Klodzka) Glatz	2B					
❒ EBERSWALDE Brandenburg	1A	2A	7A	9A	12B	14B
❒ EBINGEN/SCHMIECHA Wuerttemberg	1B	2A	6A	9B		
❒ EBSTORF Hannover	2B					
❒ ECKARTSBERGA Provinz Sachsen	1A					
❒ ECKENHAGEN Rheinland	1A					
❒ ECKERNFOERDE Schleswig-Holstein	1A	2A	8B	10A		
❒ ECKKAMP Rheinland	1E					
❒ EDENKOBEN Pfalz	1A	2A				
❒ EDLING Bayern	1C					
❒ EGELN/BODE Provinz Sachsen	14A					
❒ EGENBUETTEL Schleswig-Holstein	1A					
❒ EGGE/VOLMARSTEIN Westfalen	2B					
❒ EGGENFELDEN/ROTT Bayern	1A	2A	6A			
❒ EGGOLSHEIM Bayern	7A					
❒ EGING/VILSHOFEN Bayern	2B					
❒ EGLOSHEIM Wuerttemberg	3A					
❒ EHINGEN/DONAU Wuerttemberg	1A	2A	6A			
❒ EHMEN/FALLERSLEBEN (Wolfsberg, Niedersachsen) Hannover	2A					
❒ EHRANG/KYLL & MOSEL Rheinland	2A					
❒ EHRENBREITSTEIN/RHINE Rheinland	1A	8B				
❒ EHRENFRIEDERSDORF Sachsen	1A	2A				
❒ EIBAU/RUMBURGE (Eybau) Sachsen	1A	2A	11B			
❒ EIBELSHAUSEN Hesse-Nassau	7A					
❒ EIBENBERG Sachsen	1A					
❒ EIBENSTOCK Sachsen	1A	2A	9A			
❒ EICHENDORF Bayern	2A					
❒ EICHRODT-WUTHA Sachsen-Weimar-Eisenach	1A					
❒ EICHSTAETT/ALTMUEHL (Aichstadt) Bayern	1A	4A	10B	14A		
❒ EICKEL (Wanne-Eickel) Westfalen	1A	2B	9A			
❒ EICKELBORN Westfalen	9A					
❒ EIDELSTEDT Schleswig-Holstein	2A					
❒ EILENBURG/MULDE Provinz Sachsen	1A	2B	6A	7A	8A	9A
❒ EILSEN, BAD/AU Schaumburg-Lippe	7B	8A	9A	12A	13C	
❒ EILSLEBEN Provinz Sachsen	1A					
❒ EINBECK Hannover	1A	2A				
❒ EINBRUCH/RUHR Westfalen	1A					
❒ EINOELLEN Pfalz	1A					
❒ EINSIEDEL/GOLNITZ Sachsen	2B					
❒ EINSWARDEN Oldenburg	2B					
❒ EISBERGEN Westfalen	1A	2A				

50 Pfennig, Bonn, 1A

75 Pfennig, Bordesholm, 1A

50 Pfennig, Borstel, 1A

50 Pfennig, Braunlage/H, 1A

10 Pfennig, Braunschweig, 1A

50 Pfennig, Brehna, 1A

75 Pfennig, Bremen, 1A

50 Pfennig, Bremen, 1A

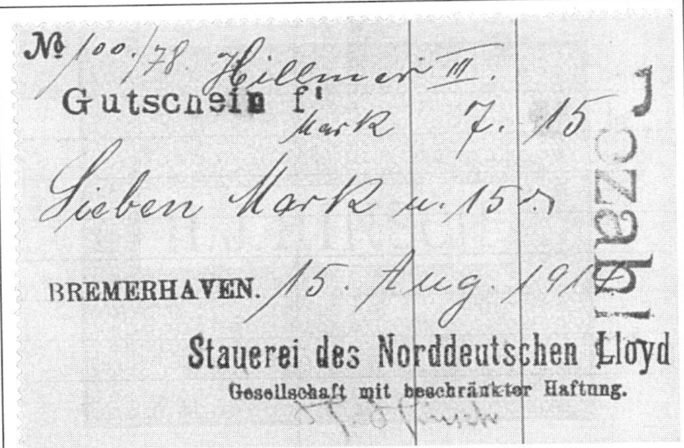

7.15 Mark, Bremerhaven, 1B

50 Pfennig, Bremrhaven, Lehe, Ges, 1A

1 Mark, Breslau, POW, 3B

1 Mark, Broacker, 1A

50 Pfennig, Bromberg, 1A

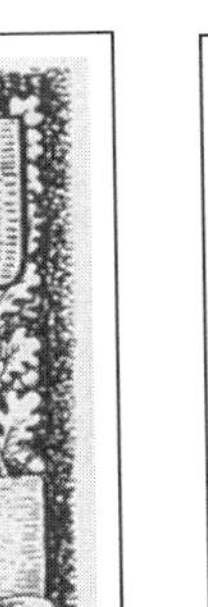

1 Mark, Bruchhausen, 1A

❒ EISDORF/HARZ Provinz Sachsen 2A
❒ EISENACH Sachsen-Weimar-Eisenach 1A 2A 6A 7A 9B 11B 12A 13A
❒ EISENBACH/HOERSEL Baden 2A 7E
❒ EISENBERG (Sachsen-Altenburg) 1A 2A
❒ EISENBERG-MORITZBURG (after 1934 Moritzburg) 2B
❒ EISERFELD Westfalen 2E
❒ EISSENBERG Waldeck 1A
❒ EISENBERG Sachsen-Altenburg 1A 2A 9B
❒ EISENSTEIN Bayern 7B
❒ EISERFELD Westfalen 7B
❒ EISFELD Sachsen-Meiningen 1A 2A 6A 7B
❒ EISLEBEN Provinz Sachsen 1A 2A 7A 12A 13D
❒ EITORF Rheinland 1A 2B 7A 14A
❒ ELBERFELD-BARMEN Rheinland 11B 12B
❒ ELBERFELD/WUPPER Rheinland 1A 2D 3B 4C6A7A8B9A 11B 12B
❒ ELBING/ELBING (Elblag) Westpreussen 1B 6A 8B
❒ ELBINGERODE (Provinz Sachsen) Hannover 2B 7A
❒ ELDAGSEN Hannover 1A 6A
❒ ELDINGEN Hannover 2E
❒ ELGERSBURG Sachsen-Coburg-Gotha 2A 7A 9A
❒ ELISENFELS/ARZBERT Bayern 2B
❒ ELLEFELD/VOGTLAND Sachsen 1A
❒ ELLERBEK Schleswig-Holstein 1A 12B
❒ ELLERHOOP Schleswig-Holstein 1A
❒ ELLGUTH-STEINAU (Ligota-Scienawska) Schlesien 2B
❒ ELLINGEN Bayern 2B
❒ ELLRICH/HARZ Provinz Sachsen 1A 2B
❒ ELLWANGEN/JAGST Wuerttemberg 1A 2B 3B 6A
❒ ELMSCHENHAGEN Schleswig-Holstein 1A 2A 13A
❒ ELMSHORN/ELBE Schleswig-Holstein 1A 2D 7A
❒ ELPE Westfalen 2A
❒ ELSEN Rheinland 2A
❒ ELSENAU (Domaslawek) Posen 1B
❒ ELSENBORN/MALMEDY Rheinland 10B
❒ ELSENTHAL Bayern 7B
❒ ELSNIGK Sachsen 7B
❒ ELSTER, BAD/LITTLE ELSTER Sachsen 1A 2A 7B
❒ ELSTERBERG/WHITE ELSTER Sachsen 1A
❒ ELTERLEIN Sachsen 2A
❒ ELTMANN/MAIN Bayern 1A 7B
❒ ELTVILLE/RHEIN (Elfeld) Rheinland 1A 7A
❒ ELVERDISSEN Westfalen 2B
❒ ELVERLINGSEN/ALTENA Westfalen 2D 5B
❒ ELZACH Baden 1A 6B
❒ ELZE Hannover 1A
❒ EMANUELSSEGEN Schlesien 5B 9A
❒ EMDEN (Embden) Hannover 1A 2B 8B 14A
❒ EMMAGRUBE (Kopalina Emma) Schlesien 2E 5B
❒ EMMENDINGEN/ELTZ Baden 1A 6A 7B 8B 9B

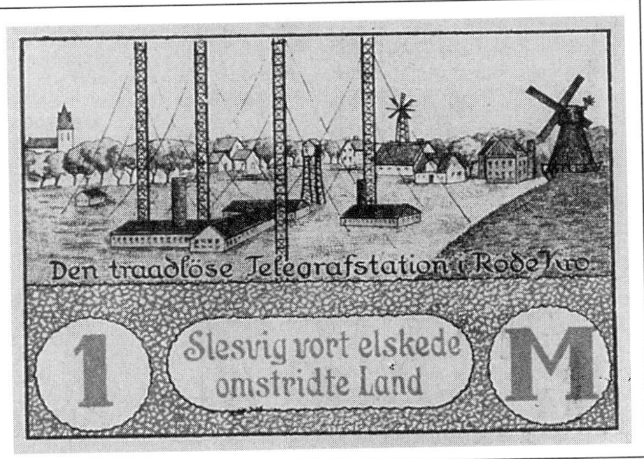

1 Mark, Brunde, 1A

25 Pfennig, Brunsbuettlekoog, 1A

❒ EMMERICH/RHEIN (Emrich) Rheinland 1A 6A 8B
❒ EMMERTHAL Hannover 2A
❒ EMS, BAD/LAHN Hessen-Nassau 1A 8B 9A 11B
❒ EMSDETTEN Westfalen 2A 11B 14A
❒ ENDINGEN/K Baden 6E
❒ ENDORF/SAUERLAND Westfalen 7B
❒ ENGELSDORF Sachsen 1B 2B
❒ ENGELSKIRCHEN Rheinland 1B
❒ ENGEN Baden 1 6B 7C
❒ ENKENBACH Pfalz 2A
❒ ENNEPE Westfalen 1C
❒ ENNIGERLOH Westfalen 1A
❒ ENSEN/KOELN Rheinland 2A
❒ EPE (Eep) Westfalen 7A
❒ EPPELBORN-DIRMINGEN Rheinland 1A
❒ EPPENDORF (Eppindorf) Sachsen 1A 2A
❒ EPPINGHOVEN Rheinland 3C
❒ ERBACH-REISKIRCHEN Pfalz 1E
❒ ERBACH/DONAU Wuerttemberg 1A
❒ ERBACH/ODENWALD Hessen 1A
❒ ERBENDORF/WAALDNAAB Bayern 2A 6A
❒ ERBLAND Nordhein-Westfalen 14B
❒ ERDING Bayern 2B
❒ ERDMANNSDORF Sachsen 1B 2B
❒ ERFDE Schleswig-Holstein 1A
❒ ERFENSCHLAG Sachsen 2A
❒ ERFURT Provinz Sachsen 1A 2A 3A 7A 9A 10B 11B 12B 13B
❒ ERGOLDSBACH Bayern 1A
❒ ERING Bayern 1B
❒ ERKELENZ Rheinland 1A 2A
❒ ERKHEIM/Bayern 1C
❒ ERKRATH Rheinland 1B
❒ ERLA Sachsen 2B
❒ ERLANGEN Bayern 1A 2A 7A 8B 9B 10A 11B
❒ ERLAU/EGER Sachsen 2A
❒ ERLBACH/VOGTLAND Sachsen 1A
❒ ERLENBACH/MAIN Bayern 1B 2A
❒ ERMANNSDORF Sachsen 1A 2B 9A
❒ ERMSLEBEN/HARZ Provinz Sachsen 1A
❒ ERNDTEBRUECK Westfalen 2E
❒ ERSTEIN Elsass 6B
❒ ERWITTE-ANROECHTE Westfalen 2A
❒ ESCHERFELD/BORNA Sachsen 2A
❒ ESCHERSHAUSEN/LENNE Braunschweig 1A 2A
❒ ESCHWEGE/WERRA Hessen-Nassau 1A 3A 4A 6A 10A 14B
❒ ESCHWEILER Rheinland 1A 5B 6A 7A 9A
❒ ESCHWEILER & STOLBERG Rheinland 1A 2B
❒ ESENS Hannover 1A
❒ ESENSHAM Hannover 1E
❒ ESINGEN Schleswig-Holstein 1A
❒ ESLARN Bayern 7A
❒ ESLOHE Westfalen 1C
❒ ESPERSTEDT/KYFFHAEUSER Thueringen 2C
❒ ESSEN Rheinland 1B 2A 3C 4B 5B 6A 7A 8B 11B 12B 14A
❒ ESSEN-ALTENESSEN Rheinland 2A
❒ ESSEN-BORBECK Rheinland 5C
❒ ESSEN-BERGEBORBECK Rheinland 2A 5C

75 Pfennig, Brushaupten, 1A

50 Pfennig, Buergel, 1A

10 Pfennig, Bunzlau, 13B

75 Pfennig, Burg/Fehmarn, 1A

50 Pfennig, Burghausen, 1A

25 Pfennig, Butzbach, 1A

25 Pfennig, Buxtehude, 1A

10 Pfennig, Calbe/Milde, Germany, 2B

50 Pfennig, Calbe/S, 1A

- ❒ ESSEN-FRILLENDORF Rheinland 2B 5C
- ❒ ESSEN-KARNAP Rheinland 5B
- ❒ ESSEN-RUETTENSCHEID Rheinland 2A
- ❒ ESSINGEN Bayern 7B
- ❒ ESSLINGEN Wuerttemberg 1A 2B 8B 9B
- ❒ ESSWEILER Pfalz 1A
- ❒ ESTERN Westfalen 3E
- ❒ ETELSEN Hannover 3B
- ❒ ETTAL Bayern 2A
- ❒ ETTENHEIM Baden 1A 6A 10B
- ❒ ETTLINGEN/ALB Baden 1A 6B 7E 8A 9A 10A
- ❒ ETZDORF Sachsen-Altenburg 7B
- ❒ EULAU-WILHELMSHUETTE Schlesien 2A
- ❒ EUPEN/VESDRE Rheinland 1A 6B 7B 9B
- ❒ EUSKIRCHEN Rheinland 1A 7B
- ❒ EUTIN Schleswig-Holstein 1A 2A 3B
- ❒ EVENKAMP Westfalen 7B 9A
- ❒ EVERSBERG Westfalen 1B
- ❒ EVINGSEN Westfalen 2B
- ❒ EYSTRUP Hannover 3B
- ❒ EXIN (Kcynia) Posen 1C
- ❒ EYDTKUHNEN (Kybartai, Lithuanian USSR) Ostpreussen 7B
- ❒ FAHR Rheinland 2B
- ❒ FAHRNAU Baden 7E
- ❒ FAEHRBRUECKE Sachsen 11D
- ❒ FALKEN beiHohenstein=Ernstthal Sachsen 1E 2E
- ❒ FALKENAU Sachsen 2B
- ❒ FALKENBERG Provinz Sachsen 2A
- ❒ FALKENBERG (Niemodlin) Schlesien 1A 2C
- ❒ FALKENBURG (Zlocieniec) Pommern 1A 2B
- ❒ FALKENSTEIN/VOGTLAND Sachsen 1A 2A 6A 7C 8B
- ❒ FALLERSLEBEN Hannover 1A
- ❒ FALLINGBOSTEL Hannover 1A 2A
- ❒ FALLINGBOSTEL & WALSRODE Hannover 2A
- ❒ FARNRODA Sachsen-Gotha 2A
- ❒ FEHRENBACH Thueringia 2B
- ❒ FELDBERG Mecklenburg-Strelitz 1A
- ❒ FELDBERGEN 9E
- ❒ FELDBERGER/SCHWARZWALD Baden 1B 7B
- ❒ FELLBACH Wuerttemberg 1A
- ❒ FELLERINGEN Elsass 1A
- ❒ FELLHAMMER (Boguszow) Schiesien 1B
- ❒ FERDINANDSGRUBE (Kopalnia Ferdynand) Schlesien 5B
- ❒ FESTENBERG (Twardagora) Schlesien 2B
- ❒ FEUCHT Bayern 6B
- ❒ FEUCHTWANGEN/SULZ (Feuchtwang) Bayern 6A
- ❒ FEUDINGEN Westfalen 2E
- ❒ FEUERBACH Wuerttemberg 1A 6A 9A 10B
- ❒ FILEHNE/NETZE (Wielen, Wulen) Posen 1B 2B

25 Pfennig, Camp/Rhein, 1A

75 Pfennig, Carlow, 1A

❒ FINKENWALDE/SZCZECIN
Pommern 2A
❒ FINNENTROP Westfalen 2E
❒ FINSTERBERGEN Thueringen 9B
❒ FINSTERWALDE N L Brandenburg 1A 2A 6B 8A
❒ FISCHELN/KREFELD Rheinland 1A 5C
❒ FISLIS Elsass 1E
❒ FLADUNGEN Bayern 2B
❒ FLATOW (Zlotow, Zlotowo, Czlotowo)
Westpreussen 1B
❒ FLENSBURG (Flensborg)
Schleswig-Holstein 1A 2A 6A 7A 8A
9A 10A 12B 14A
❒ FLOEHA Sachsen 1A 2A 11B
❒ FLOERSHEIM/MAIN
Hessen-Nassau 1A
❒ FLOSS Bayern 1A 2A
❒ FLOSSENBURG Bayern 15D
❒ FLOSSMUEHLE/BORSTENDORF
Sachsen 2B
❒ FOCKBEK (Fokbek)
Schleswig-Holstein 2A
❒ FOCKENDORF Thueringen 2A 7A
❒ FORBACH Lothringen 1A 2B 6A 14A
❒ FORBACH/MURG Baden 1A 6A
❒ FORCHHEIM Sachsen 1B
❒ FORCHHEIM/REGNITZ Bayern 1B 2C 7B 9A
❒ FORDON Posen 1A
❒ FORST Pfalz 2A
❒ FORST/LAUSITZ Brandenburg 1A 2A 6A 11B 12A
❒ FRAENKISCH-CRUMBACH
Hessen 2A
❒ FRANKENBERG/EDER
Hessen-Nassau 1A
❒ FRANKENBERG/ZSCHOPAU
Sachsen 1A 2B 8B
❒ FRANKENHAUSEN/KYFFHAEUSER
(Bad Frankenhausen) Thueringen 1A 2A 6A 9A
❒ FRANKENSTEIN (Zabkowice)
Schlesien 1A 2A 5B 6A 7B 8B 9A
❒ FRANKENTHAL Pfalz 1A 2A 6A 7B 8B 9B
❒ FRANKENTHAL/GERA
Thueringen 2A
❒ FRANKFURT-HEDDERNHEIM
Hessen-Nassau 7B 8A
❒ FRANKFURT/MAIN
Hessen-Nassau 1A 2A 3A 4A 6A 7B8A
9A 10A 11B 12B
❒ FRANKFURT/MAIN-GRIESHEIM
Hessen-Nassau 8A
❒ FRANKFURT/MAIN-NIEDERRAD
Hessen-Nassau 2D

2 Mark, Castrop, 1A

75 Pfennig, Chrosczuetz, 1A

75 Pfennig, Cleve, 1A

10 Pfennig, Coblenz, Germany, 6A

50 Pfennig, Coesfeld, 1A

1 Mark, Colberg, Bad, 1B

50 Pfennig, Colditz, 1A

50 Pfennig, Cosel, Silesia, Germany, 1A

❒ FRANKFURT/MAIN-ROEDELHEIM Hessen-Nassau 7A
❒ FRANKFURT/MAIN-WEST Hessen-Nassau 7B
❒ FRANKFURT/ODER (Sublice) Brandenburg 1A 2B 3A 8A 10A 12B
❒ FRANZBURG Pommern 1A 2A
❒ FRAUENAU Bayern 2A 7A
❒ FRAUENDORF (Wroblin) Schlesien 7A
❒ FRAUENSTEIN/ERZGEBIRGE Sachsen 1A 2A
❒ FRAUENWALDAU/TREBNITZ Schlesien 2B
❒ FRAUENZELL Bayern 2A 14B
❒ FRAUREUTH Thueringen 2B
❒ FRAUSTADT (Wschowa) Schlesien 1A 2B
❒ FRAUWALDAU/TREBNITZ Schlesien 2A
❒ FRECHEN Rheinland 1B 3C 7A
❒ FREDEBURG Westfalen 1B
❒ FREDEN/LEINE Hannover 2B 7A
❒ FREIBERG Sachsen 1A 2A 7A 8A 10A 11E 12B 13A
❒ FREIBURG/Breisgau Baden 1A 2B 3B 6A 7A 8B 11C
❒ FREIBURG (Swiebodzice) Schlesien 1A 2B
❒ FREIBURG/BREISGAU Baden 1A
❒ FREIBURG, SCHOPFHEIM und VILLIGEN Baden 2A
❒ FREIBURG/ELBE Hannover 2A
❒ FREIBURG/TREISAM-BREISGAU Baden 1A 2B 6A 7C 8A 9B 11B 13A
❒ FREIENOHL Westfalen 1A
❒ FREIENWALDE/ODER (Oberbarnim, Moorbad; Bad Freienwalde) Brandenburg 1A 2A
❒ FREIENWALDE/ODER (Chociwel) Pommern 1A
❒ FREILASSING Bayern 2B
❒ FREILINGEN Rheinland 2D
❒ FREISING/ISAR Bayern 1A 2A 7A
❒ FREISTATT Hannover 3B
❒ FREITAL Sachsen 1A 2B
❒ FREMDISWALDE Sachsen 2A
❒ FREREN Hannover 1A
❒ FREUDENBERG Westfalen 2E
❒ FREUDENSTADT UND BAIERSBRONN Wuerttemberg 1A 2A
❒ FREUDENSTADT/MURG Wuerttemberg 1A 6A
❒ FREUDENTHAL/WANDERSLEBEN Provinz Sachsen 1A
❒ FREYBURG/UNSTRUT Provinz Sachsen 1A
❒ FREYENSTEIN/OSTPRIGNITZ Brandenburg 1B
❒ FREYSTADT (Kozuchow) Schlesien 1A 2A 6A
❒ FREYSTADT (Freistadt) Westpreussen 1A
❒ FREYUNG/WALD Bayern 2A 6A 7A
❒ FRICKENHAUSEN/MAIN Wuerttemberg 2A
❒ FRIEDBERG Bayern 1A 2B
❒ FRIEDBERG Hessen 1A 3A 4A 9A
❒ FRIEDEBERG Bayern 1A 2B
❒ FRIEDEBERG/PEZA-NEUMARK (Strzelce Kraienskie, Poland) Brandenburg 1A 2B
❒ FRIEDEBERG/QUEIS (Mirsk) Schlesien 1A 2B
❒ FRIEDENFELS Bayern 6B
❒ FRIEDENSAU Provinz Sachsen 7B
❒ FRIEDENSGRUBE (Kopalnia Pokoj) Schlesien 4A 5A
❒ FRIEDENSHUETTE (Huta Pokoj) Schlesien 1A 2B 3A 4B 5C 7B
❒ FRIEDLAND Mecklenburg-Strelitz 1A 2B
❒ FRIEDLAND MAERKISCH (Prawdinsk; Pravdinsk) Ostpreussen 1B 8B

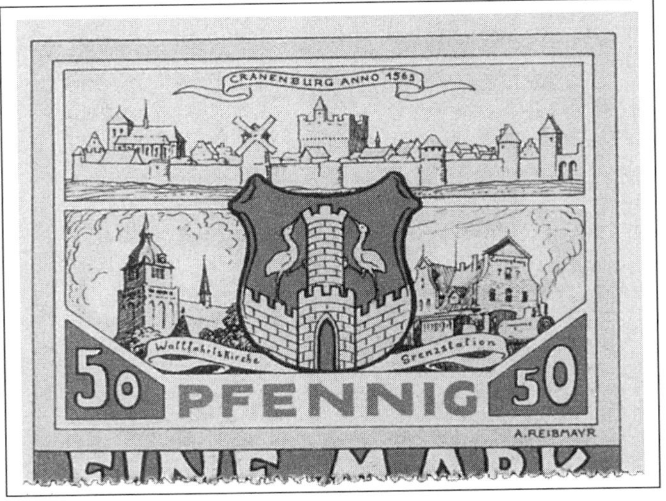

50 Pfennig, Cranenburg, 1A

50 Pfennig, Crivitz, 1A

❒ FRIEDLAND/STEINAU (Korfantow) Schlesien 1A 2B 4B 7B
❒ FRIEDRICH-AUGUSTHUETTE Oldenburg 2A
❒ FRIEDRICHRODA Sachsen-Gotha 1A 2A
❒ FRIEDRICHSBRUNN/HARZ Provinz Sachsen 1A
❒ FRIEDRICHSDORF (Bykowina) Schlesien 1E 4A
❒ FRIEDRICHSDORF/TAUNUS Hessen-Nassau 2B 7B
❒ FRIEDRICHSFELD/WESEL Rheinland 1A 3A
❒ FRIEDRICHSHAFEN/BUCHHORN Wuerttemberg 1A 2A 6A 8B 11C
❒ FRIEDRICHSHAIDE Ruess j. Linie 7B
❒ FRIEDRICHSHAIN Brandenburg 7B 9B
❒ FRIEDRICHSHALL Hannover 3A
❒ FRIEDRICHSHUETTE Westfalen 2C
❒ FRIEDRICHSORT Schleswig-Holstein 10A
❒ FRIEDRICHSRODA Thueringen 1A 2B
❒ FRIEDRICHSTADT Schleswig-Holstein 1A 2A 8B
❒ FRIEDRICHSTHAL-SAAR Rheinland 1E 4B
❒ FRIEDRICHSUETTE-LAASPHE Westfalen 2B
❒ FRIEDRICHSWERTH Sachsen-Gotha 2A 7A
❒ FRIELENDORF Hessen 5B
❒ FRIESACK Brandenburg 1A 8B
❒ FRIESOYTHE/SOESTE Oldenburg 2A
❒ FRITZLAR Hessen 1A 2B 14A
❒ FROENDENBERG/RUHR Westfalen 1A 2C
❒ FROHBURG Sachsen 1B 2A
❒ FROHNAU/ERZGEBIRGE Sachsen 2B
❒ FROHSE/ELBE Provinz Sachsen 1A
❒ FRONTENHAUSEN/VILS Bayern 2A
❒ FROSE Anhalt 1A
❒ FRUECHT/EMS Hessen-Nassau 1A
❒ FUCHSBERG Hannover 3B
❒ FUERSTENAU Hannover 1A
❒ FUERSTENBERG Mecklenburg-Strelitz 1A
❒ FUERSTENBERG/ODER (Stalinstadt, Eisenhuettenstadt) Brandenburg 2A 3A
❒ FUERSTENBERG/WESER Westphalia 1A 3C
❒ FUERSTENFELDBRUCK Bayern 2A 10A

50 Pfennig, Crossen/Oder, 6A

1 Pfennig, Cuestrin, POW, 1A

50 Pfennig, Cuxhaven, 1A

❒ FUERSTENFELDE N M (Boleszkowice) Brandenburg	6B					
❒ FUERSTENGRUBE	5A					
❒ FUERSTENHAUSEN/SAAR Rheinland	3C	7B				
❒ FUERSTENWALDE/SPREE Brandenburg	1A	2A	6A	9B		
❒ FUERSTENZELL Bayern	2D	14A				
❒ FUERTH Bayern	1A	2A	4B	6A	7B	
	8A	9A	10A	11B	13E	
❒ FUESSEN Bayern	1A	2A	4A	5A	7A	9A
❒ FULDA Hessen-Nassau	1A	2A	6A	8B	9A	
❒ FURTH/WALDE Bayern	1A	2A	6A			
❒ FURTWANGEN Baden	1A	6A	7E	9B		
❒ GAANSAGER (Gaansager, Denmark) Schleswig-Holstein		2A				
❒ GADEBUSCH Mecklenburg-Schwerin	1A					

Types of Emergency Money

Type	Reference #
Municipal paper	1
Private paper	2
POW paper	3
POW official metal	4
POW private metal	5
Municipal metal	6
Private metal	7
Gas tokens	8
Food; beer; konsumverein	9
Naval; military; kantine	10
Encased, unencased stamps	11
Streetcar tokens	12
Porcelain	13
World War II issues	14
Concentration, Civilian internment camps	15

Rarity grades: A, to $25; B, to $60; C, to $125; D, to $200; and E, $350

❒ GAGGENAU/MURG Baden	1A	2A	6A	7E	9B
❒ GAHLEN Westfalen	5B				
❒ GAILDORF/KOCHER Wuerttemberg	2B	6A	13A		
❒ GAMSEN-KAESTORF Hannover	3B				
❒ GAIMERSHEIM Bavaria	10B				
❒ GANDERKESEE Oldenburg	2B				
❒ GANDERSHEIM/GANDE Braunschweig	2B	14B			
❒ GANGELT Rheinland	1A				
❒ GANGKOFEN Bayern 1B					
❒ GARBUS Thueringia	2A				
❒ GARDELEGEN Provinz Sachsen	2A	3A	6A	9B	
❒ GARMISCH/LOISACH Bayern	1A	2B	6A	7B	
❒ GARSTEDT Schleswig-Holstein	1A				
❒ GATERSLEBEN Provinz Sachsen	1A	7B			
❒ GAUTING Bayern	2D				
❒ GAUTZSCH/LEIPZIG Sachsen	2B	9A			
❒ GDYNIA/DANZIG (Gdingen) Westpreussen	2B				
❒ GEBESEE/GERA Provinz Sachsen	1A				
❒ GEBWEILER Guebwiller) Elsass	1A				
❒ GEESTEMUENDE (Bremerhaven) Hannover	1B	2A			
❒ GEFREES Bayern	2C	9B			
❒ GEHOFEN Provinz Sachsen	1E				
❒ GEHREN Schwarzburg-Sonderhausen	2B	9A			
❒ GEILENKIRCHEN & HEINSBERG Rheinland	1A				

Pfund meat, Czempin, Germany 9B

10 Pfennig, Daber, 1A

Location	Grades
❒ GEILENKIRCHEN/WURM Rheinland	1A
❒ GEISA/RHOEN Thueringen	1A 2A
❒ GEISELHOERING/KLEIN LABER Bayern	6B
❒ GEISENFELD Bayern	2C
❒ GEISENHAUSEN Bayern	2D
❒ GEISENHEIM/RHEIN Hessen-Nassau	7B 8B 9B
❒ GEISHAUSEN Elsass	1A
❒ GEISING Sachsen	1A
❒ GEISLINGEN/STEIG Wuerttemberg	1A 2A 9B
❒ GEISSFOERTH Hessen-Nassau	2E
❒ GEISWEID Westfalen	2E 9B
❒ GEITHAIN (Geiten) Sachsen	2B
❒ GEITLING Bayern	2B
❒ GELDERN Rheinland	1A 2A
❒ GELENAU Sachsen	2B
❒ GELNHAUSEN/KINZIG Hessen-Nassau	1A 2C 8B
❒ GELSENKIRCHEN Westfalen	1A 2A 3B 5B 6A 8B 9B 11B
❒ GELSENKIRCHEN-BISMARCK Westfalen	2A
❒ GELSENKIRCHEN UND ROTTHAUSEN Westfalen	1A 6A
❒ GELSENKIRCHEN-SCHALKE Westfalen	2B
❒ GELTING Schleswig-Holstein	2A
❒ GEMBITZ (Gebice) Posen	1B
❒ GEMUENDEN/MAIN Bayern	1A 6A
❒ GENGENBACH/KINZIG Baden	1B 2D 6B 7C
❒ GENSUNGEN Hessen-Nassau	1E
❒ GENTHIN Provinz Sachsen	1A
❒ GEORGENSGMUEND Bayern	7A
❒ GEORGESHUETTE Schlesien	1A
❒ GEORGESWALDE Sachsen (Today Jirikov, Czech Rep.)	2B
❒ GEORGSMARIENHUETTE Hannover	3B 9B
❒ GERA Reuss j.L	1A 2A 7A 8A 11B 12A 14A
❒ GERA-DEBSCHWITZ Thueringen	2A
❒ GERA-ZWOETZEN Thueringen	2A
❒ GERA/ELGERSBURG Sachsen-Gotha	9A
❒ GERABERG/ELGERSBURG Thueringen	2A
❒ GERABRONN Wuerttemberg	2A
❒ GERBSTEDT Provinz Sachsen	2A
❒ GERINGSWALDE Sachsen	2B
❒ GERLEVE Westfalen	3E
❒ GERMERSHEIM/RHEIN Pfalz	1A 3A 6A 7B 10A
❒ GERNRODE/HARZ Anhalt	1A 2E
❒ GERNSBACH/MURG Baden	1A 2E 6A 7E
❒ GEROLDSGRUEN Bayern	1B
❒ GEROLSTEIN Rheinland	2A 9A
❒ GEROLZHOFEN Bayern	6A
❒ GERRESHEIM/DUESSELDORF Rheinland	7A
❒ GERSDORF/Chemnitz Sachsen	2A
❒ GERSFELD Hessen	1A 14A
❒ GERSTETTEN Wuerttemberg	1A
❒ GERTHE (Bochum) Westfalen	2A 3C 5D 7B 9B 12A
❒ GERWERMINGHOFF Grube Schlesien	3A
❒ GESCHER Westfalen	2B
❒ GESCHWENDAThueringen	2A
❒ GESEKE Westfalen	1C 2C
❒ GEVELSBERG Westfalen	1B 2A 8B 11B
❒ GEVELSBERG-NORD Westfalen	2E
❒ GEYER Sachsen	1A 2A
❒ GEYERSDORF Sachsen	2B
❒ GIENGEN/BRENZ Wuerttemberg	1A 2A
❒ GIERSDORF (Grottkau; Galaszczyce) Schlesien	2A
❒ GIESENKIRCHEN/RHEYDT Rheinland	1E
❒ GIESSEN/LAHN Hessen-Nassau	1B 2A 6A 8B 12B
❒ GIESUEBEL Thueringen	2A
❒ GIFHORN/ALLER Hannover	1A 2A
❒ GILDENHALL/FREILAND SIEDLUNG Brandenburg	2B
❒ GILENKIRCHEN & HEINSBERG Rheinland	1A
❒ GILGENBURG (Dabrowno) Ostpreussen	1B 6A
❒ GINGEN/FILS Wuerttemberg	2B
❒ GISPERSLEBEN Sachsen	7B
❒ GITTELDE Braunschweig	5B 7C
❒ GLADBACH (See Bergisch Gladbach) Rheinland	
❒ GLADBECK Westfalen	1A 3B 4B
❒ GLADENBACH Hessen-Nassau	1A
❒ GLAESENDORF/FRANKENSTEIN (Szklary) Schlesien	5A 7B
❒ GLASHUETTE Sachsen	1A 2A
❒ GLATZ/NEISSE (Kladsko; Klodzko) Schlesien	1A 2B 6A 11B
❒ GLAUCHAU/MULDE Sachsen	1A 2A 8B 11B 14B
❒ GLAUCHAU-WEST/MULDE Sachsen	14B
❒ GLEHN Rheinland	1A
❒ GLEIDINGEN/INNERSTE Hannover	2A

5 Pfennig, Dannenberg, Germany, 1A

50 Pfennig, Dannefeld, 2A

50 Pfennig, Danzig, 1A

15 Pfennig, Danzig, 6B

5 Goldpfennig, Danzig, 2B

25 Pfennig, Dassow/M, 1A

25 Pfennig, Daun, Germany, 1A

1 Mark, Dermbach, 1A

50 Pfennig, Detmold, 1A

(Gültig bis zum 30. September 1914)

895 Gutschein

über 1 Mark.

Deutsch Piekar, den 6. August 1914.

Der Gemeindevorsteher.

1 Mark, Deutsch Piekar, 1B

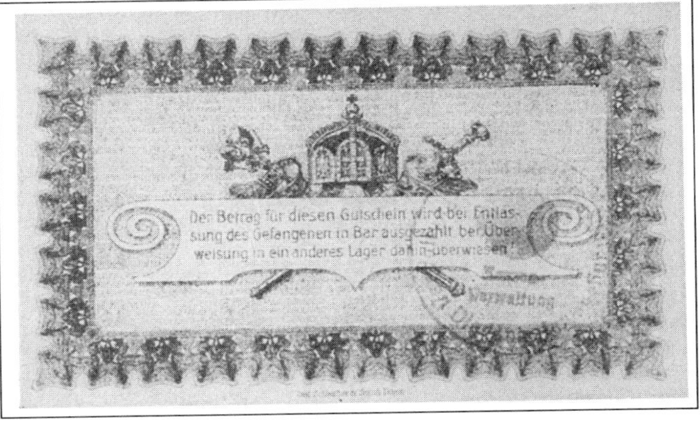

5 Mark, Diedenhofen, POW, 3B

75 Pfennig, Diepholz, 1A

❒ GLEIWITZ/KLODNITZ
(Gilwice; Gliwicka) Schlesien 1A 2A 5B 7B 11E
❒ GLINDE Schleswig-Holstein 2A
❒ GLOESA Sachsen 2B
❒ GLOETHE/FOERDERSTEDT
Provinz Sachsen 2B 7B
❒ GLOGAU/HOTZENPLOTZ
(Glogow; Zielona Gora) Schlesien 1A 2A 7A 9A 10A
❒ GLUECKFRIED 5A
❒ GLUECKSBURG
Schleswig-Holstein 1A
❒ GLUECKSTADT/ELBE
Schleswig-Holstein 1A 2A
❒ GNADENFREI (Pilawa Gorna)
Schlesien 1A 2B 3B 4A 7A
❒ GNARRENBURG Hannover 1A 3B
❒ GNESEN (Gniezno) Posen 1B 2A 5A 6B 10A 14A
❒ GNOIEN Mecklenburg-Schwerin 1A
❒ GOCH/NIERS Rheinland 1A 7B 8A
❒ GODELHEIM/HOEXTER
Westfalen 1A
❒ GODESBERG/BAD/RHEIN
Rheinland 1A 2E 8B 11B
❒ GODULLASCHACHT Schlesien 5A
❒ GOEGGINGEN Bayern 2A 8B 11B
❒ GOELTZSCH Thueringen 2A
❒ GOEPPERSDORF Sachsen 2A
❒ GOEPPINGEN/FILS
Wuerttemberg 1A 2A 6A 7A 8B 14A
❒ GOERCHEN (Miejska Gorka)
Posen 1A 7B
❒ GOERGENSGMUEND Bayern 7A
❒ GOERLITZ/NEISSE
(Zgorzelec) Schlesien 1A 2A 4B 5B 7B
8B 9A 12B 14A
❒ GOERNE Brandenburg 7B
❒ GOERSDORF Sachsen 2B
❒ GOERZKE 13D
❒ GOESLOH Hannover 3B
❒ GOESSNITZ/PLEISSE Thueringen 1B 2A 6A 8B 11B
❒ GOETTINGEN/LEINE Hannover 1A 2A 3A 8A
❒ GOHFELD Westfalen 1A
❒ GOHLIS Sachsen 7B
❒ GOLDAP Ostpreussen 1D
❒ GOLDBACH Elsass 1A
❒ GOLDBACH Sachsen 2A
❒ GOLDBERG
Mecklenburg-Schwerin 1A
❒ GOLDBERG/KATZBACH
(Zlotoryja) Schlesien 1B
❒ GOLDLAUTER Provinz Sachsen 7B
❒ GOLDSCHMIEDEN
(Wroclaw Zlotniki) Schlesien 5C
❒ GOLENCIN Posen 2A
❒ GOLINA 2B
❒ GOLLANTSCH (Golancz) Posen 1A 2E
❒ GOLLESCHAU Sschlesien 2B
❒ GOLLNOW (Goleniow) Pommern 1A 13A
❒ GOLPA Provinz Sachsen 2A 7B
❒ GOLZERN/MULDE Sachsen 3A
❒ GOLZWARDEN Oldenburg 2B
❒ GOMPERSDORF Schlesien 9B
❒ GONSAWA (Gasawa) Posen 1A
❒ GONSENHEIM Hessen 1A
❒ GORA Posen 2A
❒ GORASDZE (Gorazdze) Schlesien 2A
❒ GORGAST Brandenburg 10B
❒ GORLICE (Reszow, Reichshof) 1A 2B
❒ GORNOSLASKI OKREG
(Przemyslowy) Schlesien 1A
❒ GORNSDORF/ERZGEBIRGE
Sachsen 2A
❒ GORZEWO/GROSS GOLLE
Posen 2B
❒ GORZNO (Gohren) Westpreussen 1A
❒ GOSLAR-LANGELSHEIM
Hannover 2A
❒ GOSLAR/OCKER (Hannover) 1A 2A 9B 14A
❒ GOSSLERSHAUSEN (Sadlinek)
Westpreussen 1A 7B
❒ GOSSWITZ Sachsen-Altenburg 9A
❒ GOSTYN (Gostingen) Posen 1C 2A 5B 6A
❒ GOTHA Sachsen-Gotha 1A 2A 4A 6A 7B 8B
9B 10B 12B 13A 14A
❒ GOTHMUND-LUEBECK
Schleswig-Holstein 2A
❒ GOTSCHDORF Schlesien 2A
❒ GOTT MIT UNS GRUBE
(Lazisk) Schlesien 5A

Gutschein über 5 Pfg. / Notgeld
der Fa. Jos. C. Huber, Diessen vor München
Der Betrag dieses Notgeldes ist bei dem Bankhause A. Unterauers Nachf. Carl Högg, Diessen, deponiert und wird jederzeit an dessen Kassa oder meiner Hauptgeschäftskassa in Diessen im Betrag von nicht unter 5 Mk. in bar zurückbezahlt.
Jos. C. Huber
Graph. Kunstanstalt Diessen / Georgenwerk

5 Pfennig, Diessen, Germany, 2A

25 Pfennig, Diez, 1A

❒ GOTTESBERG (Boguszow; Boguslawskiego) Schlesien 1A 2B 5A 7B
❒ GOTTESZELL Bayern 1A
❒ GOTTLEUBA Sachsen 2B
❒ GOTTMADINGEN Baden 2D 7D
❒ GOTTSCHALP/PLESSEN Westpreussen 2B
❒ GRAACH/MOSEL Rheinland 2A
❒ GRAAL (Graal-Mueritz) Mecklenburg-Schwerin 2A
❒ GRABOW Mecklenburg-Schwerin 1A 2B
❒ GRABSTEDE Oldenburg 5B
❒ GRAEFELFING Bayern 7B
❒ GRAFENASCHAU Bayern 5C
❒ GRAEFENHAIN Sachsen-Coburg-Gotha 1A 9B
❒ GRAEFENHAINICHEN Provinz Sachsen 1A
❒ GRAEFENRODA Sachsen-Gotha 1A 2A 9B
❒ GRAEFENTHAL Sachsen-Meiningen 1A 9B
❒ GRAEFRATH (Solingen) Rheinland 1A 6A
❒ GRAETZ (Grodzisk) Posen 1B
❒ GRAF VON BALLESTRANISCHE Werke Schlesien 5A
❒ GRAFENAU Bayern 1B 2A 7A
❒ GRAFENSTADEN Elsass 2B
❒ GRAFENWOEHR Bayern 3A 4B 7B 10B
❒ GRAFING Bayern 6A
❒ GRAINET Bayern 1B
❒ GRAMBY (Denmark) Schleswig-Holstein 1A
❒ GRANSEE Brandenburg 2A
❒ GRASSAU Bayern 1B
❒ GRAUDENZ/VISTULA (Grudziadz) Westpreussen 1A 3A 7B 8B 10B 12B
❒ GRAVENSTEIN (Graasten, Denmark) Schleswig-Holstein 1A
❒ GREFRATH/CREFELD Rheinland 1A 2A
❒ GREIFENBERG/REGA (Gryfice; Gryfow) Pommern 1A 2A 4A 9A
❒ GREIFENHAGEN (Gryfino) Pommern 1A 2A 6A
❒ GREIFENSTEIN/BLANKENBURG Thueringen 2A
❒ GREIFFENBERG (Gryfow Slask) Schlesien 1A 2B 6A
❒ GREIFSWALD/RYCK (Gripeswold) Pommern 1B 2D 6A 9A 12A
❒ GREIZ UND ZEULENRODA Thueringen 1A
❒ GREIZ/WHITE ELSTER Thueringen 1A 2A 8A 11E
❒ GREIZ-DOELAU Thueringen 2A
❒ GRENZACH Baden 7E
❒ GRENZENDORF (Graniczna, Glatz) Schlesien 2B
❒ GREPPIN Sachsen 7A
❒ GRETHEM-BUECHTEN Hannover 5B
❒ GREUSSEN Schwarzburg-Sondershausen 1A
❒ GREVEN/EMS Westfalen 9A 11B
❒ GREVENBROICH Rheinland 1A 2A
❒ GREVENBROICH-JUECHEN NORD Westfalen 14A

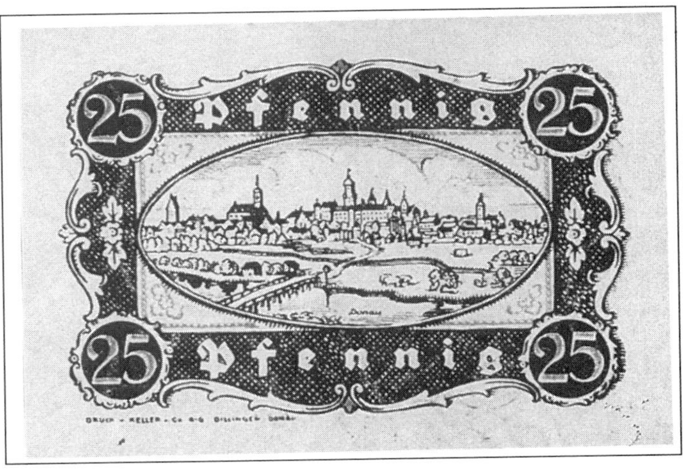

25 Pfennig, Dillingen, 1A

10 Pfennig, Dirschau, Germany, 2B

❒ GREVESMUEHLEN Mecklenburg-Schwerin 1A
❒ GRIESBACH/ROTTAL Bayern 2A
❒ GRIESHEIM/DARMSTADT Hessen 1B
❒ GRIESHEIM/MAIN Hessan-Nassau 2A 5A 7B
❒ GRIESSBACH/ZSCHOPAUTAL Sachsen 2A
❒ GRIETHAUSEN/KLEVE Rheinland 3A 4B
❒ GRIMMA/MULDE Sachsen 1A 2A 9A
❒ GRIMMEN/TREBEL (Grimme) Pommern 12A
❒ GRODZISK: (Grodzisk Mazowiecki) Posen 2B
❒ GROEBA/ELBE Sachsen 1A 2A
❒ GROEDEN Provinz Sachsen 1E
❒ GROEDITZ/RIESA Sachsen 2B
❒ GROEMITZ Schleswig-Holstein 1A
❒ GROENINGEN Wuerttemberg 2D
❒ GROHN-VEGESACK Hannover (today Bremen) 2A
❒ GROHN/BREMEN Hannover 2A 10B
❒ GROITZSCH Sachsen 1A 2A
❒ GRONAU/LEINE Westfalen 1A 2A 6A
❒ GROSCHOWITZ (Groszowice) Schlesien 2B 3A 5B
❒ GROSSAUHEIM Hessen-Nassau 7A
❒ GROSSBOTHEN Sachsen 2A
❒ GROSS DOMBROWSKA (Dabrowo) Schlesien 1B
❒ GROSS OTTERSLEBEN Sachsen 8B
❒ GROSS PORITSCH Sachsen 3A 10A
❒ GROSS SOLSCHEN (Gross Solchen) Hannover 9B
❒ GROSS STREHLITZ (Strzelce) Schlesien 1B 2B 5A 7B 8B
❒ GROSS ZIEGENORT (Trzebiez) Pommern 2E
❒ GROSS-APENBURG (today Apenburg) Provinz Sachsen 2A
❒ GROSS-AUHEIM Hessen-Nassau 2A 7A 9B
❒ GROSS-BORN (Borne; Gross-Boernecke, Jencow) 3E
❒ GROSS-DUENGEN Hannover 2A 5B
❒ GROSS-EULAU/SPROTTAU (Ilawa) Schlesien 1A 2D
❒ GROSS-FLOTTBEK Schleswig-Holstein 1A 2A
❒ GROSS-GERAU Hessen 1A
❒ GROSS-GRABEN (Grabowno Wielkie) Schlesien 2A
❒ GROSS-HEINS Hannover 3B
❒ GROSS-ILSEDE Hannover 2A
❒ GROSS-IPPENER Hannover 3B
❒ GROSS-KALDENBERG Rheinland 11B
❒ GROSS-KAYNA Sachsen 2B
❒ GROSS-KOSCHEN Brandenburg 7B
❒ GROSS-LUCKOW/BLUMENHAGEN Brandenburg 2A
❒ GROSS-NENNDORF Hannover 2B
❒ GROSS-NORDENDE Schleswig-Holstein 1A
❒ GROSS-OSTHEIM Bayern 2B
❒ GROSS-PANIOW Schlesien 2A
❒ GROSS-RAUDEN (Rudy) Schlesien 1A
❒ GROSS-REKEN Westfalen 1A
❒ GROSS-ROSEN (Rogozinski; Strzelce) Schlesien 15E
❒ GROSS-ROSENBURG Provinz Sachsen 2A 7B
❒ GROSS-SALZA (Bad Saizelmen) Provinz Sachsen 1A 6A
❒ GROSS-SCHLIEWITZ (Sliwice) Westpreussen 2A
❒ GROSS-SCHWEIDNITZ Sachsen 2E
❒ GROSS-STECHAU-NOEBDENITZ Provinz Sachsen 5C
❒ GROSS-UMSTADT Hessen 1A
❒ GROSS-WARTENBERG (Sycow) Schlesien 1A 6A 13C
❒ GROSS-WIRSCHLEBEN Provinz Sachsen 1A
❒ GROSS-ZIMMERN Hessen 1A
❒ GROSSALMERODE Hessen-Nassau 2A 7B
❒ GROSSBOI'HEN Sachsen 2A
❒ GROSSBREITENBACH Thueringen 1A 2A 9B
❒ GROSSBRUDESTEDT Thueringen 1A

20 Mark, Dirschag, 1B

50 Pfennig, Ditfurt, 1A

50 Pfennig, Doebeln, 1A

50 Pfennig, Doemitz, 1A

25 Pfennig, Domnau/Pomm., 1B

10 Pfennig, Dornburg, Germany, 1A

❐ GROSSDEUBEN Sachsen 1B
❐ GROSSENBAUM/DUISBURG Rheinland 2B 11D
❐ GROSSENHAIN/ROEDER (Groszenhain) Sachsen 1A 2E 8B
❐ GROSSHARTMANNSDORF Sachsen 2B
❐ GROSSHENNERSDORF Sachsen 2B
❐ GROSSKAMSDORF Provinz Sachsen 1A
❐ GROSSKOENIGSDORF Rheinland 2B
❐ GROSSLUGA Sachsen 7B
❐ GROSSROEHRSDORF/ROEDER Sachsen 1A 2A
❐ GROSS-ROSENBURG Provinz Sachsen 7B
❐ GROSSRUDESTEDTSachsen-Weimar-Eisenach1A
❐ GROSSRUECKERSWALDE/ERZGEBIRGE Sachsen 2A
❐ GROSS-STREHLITZ (Strzelce Opolskie) Schlesien 5B 7B
❐ GROSSSCHOENAU Sachsen 1A 2A 8B
❐ GROSS-WARTENBERG (Sycow) Schilesien 6A 13A
❐ GROSSWERDER Hannover 3B
❐ GROSSWEIL/KOCHEL Bayern 2A
❐ GROSSZOESSEN Sachsen 2B
❐ GROSSZSCHOCHER Sachsen 2A
❐ GROTTKAU (Grodkow) Schlesien 1A
❐ GRUBE ILSE N.L. Brandenburg 2A
❐ GUBEN Brandenburg (today Gubin, Poland) 1A 3A
❐ GRUENA Sachsen 1A 2A 9A
❐ GRUENBACH/VOGTLAND Sachsen 1A
❐ GRUENBERG Hessen 1A
❐ GRUENBERG (Zielona Gora) Schlesien 1A 2A 6A 9B 13A
❐ GRUENHAIN Sachsen 1A 2A 6A
❐ GRUENHAINICHEN/FLOEHA Sachsen 2B
❐ GRUENSTADT Pfalz 1A 2A 8B
❐ GRUENTHAL Bayern 2E 7A 9B
❐ GRUENTHAL Sachsen 7B
❐ GRUESSOW Pommern 9A
❐ GRUMBACH Sachsen 2B
❐ GRUND, BAD Hannover 1A 2B
❐ GRUNDHOF/ANGELN Schleswig-Holstein 1A
❐ GUBEN (Gubin, Zielonogorskie) Brandenburg 1B 3A 6A 8B 10A 12B
❐ GUECKELSBERG-FLOEHA Sachsen 2A
❐ GUENTHERSFIELD Sachsen-Meiningen 2A
❐ GUENZBURG/DONAU Bayern 1A 2A 6A
❐ GUESTEN Anhalt 1A
❐ GUESTROW/NEBEL Mecklenburg-Schwerin 1A 2B 3A 4A 9A
❐ GUETERSLOH Westfalen 1A 3B 4B 9A
❐ GUETZKOW Pommern 1B 2E
❐ GUETZOW Mecklenburg-Schwerin 1B 6A
❐ GUHRAU (Gora Slask) Schlesien 1A 2B 12B
❐ GUIDOTT Huette Schlesien 5A
❐ GUMBINNEN (Gusiew USSR) Ostpreussen 1B 8B
❐ GUMMERSBACH Rheinland 1B 2B 6A 14B
❐ GUNNERSDORF Sachsen 2B
❐ GUNZENHAUSEN Bayern 1A 2A 6A
❐ GUSTAVSBURG Hessen 2A 7B 9B 14B
❐ GUTACH/Breisgau Baden 7E
❐ GUTACH/Kinzigtal Baden 2A 6C
❐ GUTOW/PLESCHEN (Pleszew) Posen 1A 2B
❐ GUTTENTAG (Dobrodzien) Schlesien 1A 12B
❐ GUTTSTADT (Dobre Miasto) Ostpreussen 1A
❐ HAAG Bayern 1A 2A
❐ HAAN Rheinland 1A 2B 3E 6A
❐ HAAR/MUENCHEN Bayern 1A 2D 10B
❐ HAARBRUECK Westfalen 1A
❐ HAASSEL Hannover 3B
❐ HABELSCHWERDT (Bystrzyca Klodzka) Schlesien 1B 2A 6A 7A
❐ HABIGHORST Westfalen 2E
❐ HACHENBURG Hessen-Nassau 1A 7A
❐ HADAMAR Hessen 14A
❐ HADELN/OTTENDORF Hannover 2A
❐ HADEMARSCHEN Schleswig-Holstein 2E
❐ HADERSLEBEN (Haderslev, Denmark)

Types of Emergency Money

Type	**Reference #**
Municipal paper	1
Private paper	2
POW paper	3
POW official metal	4
POW private metal	5
Municipal metal	6
Private metal	7
Gas tokens	8
Food; beer; konsumverein	9
Naval; military; kantine	10
Encased, unencased stamps	11
Streetcar tokens	12
Porcelain	13
World War II issues	14
Concentration, Civilian internment camps	15

Rarity grades: A, to $25; B, to $60; C, to $125; D, to $200; and E, $350

50 Pfennig, Dramburg, 1A

Schleswig-Holstein 1C 2A
❒ HAEMMERN Rheinland 7A
❒ HAENIGSEN Hannover 2E
❒ HAGEN Westfalen 1A 2A 3C 5B 6A 7A 9A 11B 12A 14A
❒ HAGEN & BERLIN Brandenburg 11B
❒ HAGEN-ECKESEY Westfalen 2C
❒ HAGEN-GRUENTHALER Westfalen 1A
❒ HAGEN/BREMEN Bremen 1A
❒ HAGENAU Elsass 6A 7B 9A 10A
❒ HAGENAUerin 1A
❒ HAGENDINGEN Lothringen 2E
❒ HAGENOW Mecklenburg-Schwerin 1A
❒ HAHNEMUEHLE Hannover 2B
❒ HAHNENKLEE Hannover 2A
❒ HAHNENMOOR Hannover 3B
❒ HAIDEMUEHLE Provinz Sachsen 2A
❒ HAIDHOF Bayern 7A
❒ HAIGER Hessen-Nassau 1B 5B 7A
❒ HAIN Schlesien 2D
❒ HAINEWALDE Sachsen 2B
❒ HAINHOLZ Schleswig-Holstein 1A
❒ HAINICHEN Sachsen 1A 2A 8B
❒ HAINITZ Sachsen 7A
❒ HAINSBERG Sachsen 2A
❒ HAINSTADT Baden 7B
❒ HAINSTADT Hessen 7B
❒ HAKENMOOR Hannover 3B
❒ HALBAU Schlesien 2A
❒ HALBERG GRUBE (Lohmar) Rheinland 7B
❒ HALBERSTADTProvinz Sachsen 1A 2A 6B 7B 8B 10A 11B 12B
❒ HALDEN Westfalen 2E
❒ HALDERN Rheinland 1B
❒ HALEBUELL Schleswig-Holstein 1B
❒ HALL, SCHWAEBISCH Wuerttemberg 6A 7A 8B 9A 10B
❒ HALLBACH Sachsen 1B
❒ HALLE Westfalen 1C
❒ HALLE-CROELLWITZ Provinz Sachsen 2A
❒ HALLE-MERSEBURG Provinz Sachsen 1D
❒ HALLE-TROTHA Provinz Sachsen 12B
❒ HALLE/SAALE Provinz Sachsen 1A 2A 3A 4A 5C 6A 7A 8B 9A 12B
❒ HALLENBERG Westfalen 1A 2B
❒ HALLIGEN Schleswig-Holstein 1A
❒ HALSTENBEK Schleswig-Holstein 1A
❒ HALTERN Westfalen 1A 2B 6A 14D
❒ HALVER Westfalen 1B 2B
❒ HAMBERGEN Hannover 3B
❒ HAMBORN Rheinland 1A 2B 5C 6A 7B 11B
❒ HAMBOSTEL Hannover 3A
❒ HAMBRUNN Bayern 1A
❒ HAMBURG Hamburg 1A 2A 3A 5B 6A 7A 8A 11B 12A 13A 14A
❒ HAMBURG-HARBURG Hamburg 2A 14B
❒ HAMBURG-HARVESTEHUDE Hamburg 2A 14A
❒ HAMBURGER HALLIG Schleswig-Holstein 2A
❒ HAMELN Hannover 1A 2A 3B 5B 12A 14A
❒ HAMFELDE Schleswig-Holstein 2A
❒ HAMM Westfalen 1A 2A 5B 6A 7A 9A 10B 11B 12A 14A
❒ HAMMELBURG Bayern 1A 3A 4A 6A 10B
❒ HAMMERAU Bayern 7B
❒ HAMMERSTEIN Rheinland 3A 6A 14A
❒ HAMMERSTEIN (Czarne) Westpreussen 3A 6A
❒ HAMMERTHAL Westfalen 3C
❒ HANAU/MAIN Hessen-Nassau 1A 2A 7A 8A 9A
❒ HANGEN Hannover 3B
❒ HANKENSBUETTEL Hannover 1A
❒ HANNOVER Hannover 1B 2A 3A 5B 7B 8A 9A 10B 11B 12A 13A 14A
❒ HANNOVER & HILDESHEIM Hannover 1A
❒ HANNOVER-BRINK Hannover 2A
❒ HANNOVER-DOEHREN Hannover 1A 3A
❒ HANNOVER-HAINHOLZ Hannover 2B

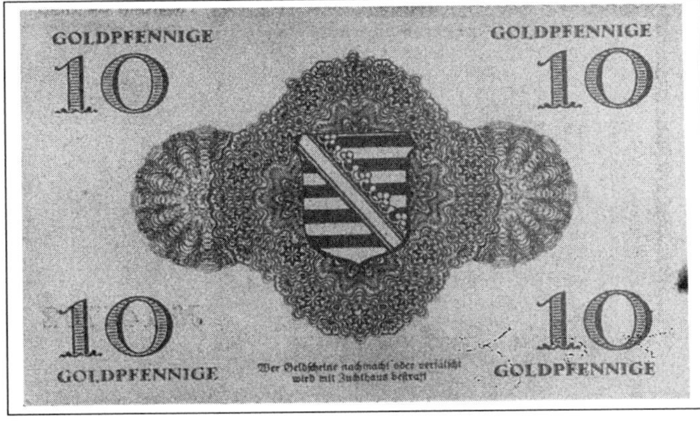

10 Goldpfennig, Dresden, 1A

10 Pfennig, Droyssig, 1A

❒ HANNOVER-HERRENHAUSEN Hannover 2A 3A
❒ HANNOVER-LAATZEN Hannover 2A 3A
❒ HANNOVER-LANGENHAGEN Hannover 2A 3A
❒ HANNOVER-LIMMER Hannover 2A 3A
❒ HANNOVER-LINDEN Hannover 2A 5B 7A
❒ HANNOVER-WALDHAUSEN Hannover 2A 3A
❒ HANNOVER-WUELFEL Hannover 2B 3A . 9B
❒ HANNOVERISCHE-MUENDEN Hannover (today Muenden) 1A 2A 3A 4A 11B 14A
❒ HANSDORF/PAKOSCH (Piechocin) Posen 2A
❒ HARBKE Provinz Sachsen 5A 7A
❒ HARBURG/ELBE Schleswig-Holstein 1A 2A 7A 9A 13C
❒ HARDENBERG-NEVIGES Rheinland 1A
❒ HARKORTEN (Haspe) Westfalen 2B
❒ HARPEN Westfalen 1A 2A
❒ HARTENSTEIN Sachsen 1B
❒ HARTHA/CHEMNITZ Sachsen 1B 2A 8B
❒ HARTHAU Sachsen 2A
❒ HARTKIRCHEN (Pocking) Bayern 6B 7A
❒ HARTMANNSDORF Sachsen 1A 2B 9A
❒ HARZBURG BAD Braunschweig 1A 9A
❒ HARZGERODE Anhalt 1A
❒ HASELDORF Schleswig-Holstein 2B
❒ HASELHORST-NORD Hannover 15E
❒ HASELUENNE Hannover 1A 2A
❒ HASLACH/KINZIGTAL Baden 1A 6A 7D
❒ HASLACH, HAUSACH, SCHILTACH U. WOLFACH Baden 1A 6A
❒ HASLACH, HAUSACH, SCHILTACH, WOLFACH, GENGENBACHBaden 1A 6A
❒ HASLOH Schleswig-Holstein 1A
❒ HASPE (Hagen) Westfalen 1A 2B 5B 8B 9A
❒ HASSENBERG Sachsen-Coburg 4A
❒ HASSERODE Provinz Sachsen 11B
❒ HASSFURT Bayern 1A 6A
❒ HASSLINGHAUSEN (Sprockhoevel) Westfalen 1A 2B 9A
❒ HASSLOCH Pfalz 1A 2A
❒ HATTINGEN/RUHR Westfalen 1A 2A 5C 6A 11C
❒ HATTORF/OSTERODE Hannover 2A
❒ HAUNERSDORF Bayern 1B
❒ HAUS/GRAFENAU Bayern 1B
❒ HAUSACH Baden 1A 6A
❒ HAUSBERGE/WESER Westfalen 2A
❒ HAUSEN-REITBACH Baden 2A 7E
❒ HAUSHAM Lothringen 2B 7B
❒ HAUSHAM/OBERBAYERN Bayern 2A 7B 9B
❒ HAUS KLYE (Coesfeld) 3A
❒ HAUSEN-RAITBACH Baden 2E
❒ HAUZENBERG Bayern 2A 6A
❒ HAVELBERG Brandenburg 2A 3A 6A
❒ HAYINGEN (Hayange) Lothringen 6A 7B
❒ HAYNAU (Chojnow) Schlesien 1C 2C 6A 7A
❒ HEBER Hannover 3B
❒ HEBERTSFELDEN Bayern 7B
❒ HECHINGEN Hohenzollern 1A 6A
❒ HECHINGEN U. HAIGERLOCH Hohenzollern Wuerttemberg 1B

100 Pfennig, Duelken, 1A

10 Pfennig, Dueren, 1A

❒ HECKLINGEN Anhalt 1B
❒ HEDDERNHEIM/FRANKFURT/M Hessen-Nassau 7A
❒ HEEDE Schleswig-Holstein 1A
❒ HEEREN (Kamen-Heeren-Werve) Westfalen 5B
❒ HEESSEN, BAD/Eilsen Lippe 1A
❒ HEESTENMOOR Hannover 3B
❒ HEHLEN Hannover 3A
❒ HEIDE Schleswig-Holstein 1A 2E 8B
❒ HEIDELBERG Baden 1A 6A 7B 8B 9A 13A
❒ HEIDENAU Sachsen 2B 7B 8B 9A
❒ HEIDENAU-NORD Sachsen 2E
❒ HEIDENAU-SUED Sachsen 2B
❒ HEIDENHEIM/BRENZ Wuerttemberg 1B 2A 7A 9A 14A
❒ HEIDERSDORF/Erzgebirge Sachsen 2A
❒ HEIDGRABEN Schleswig-Holstein 1A
❒ HEIDHAUSEN/RUHR Rheinland 2B
❒ HEIDINGSFELD Bayern 1A
❒ HEIERSDORF/ERZGEBIRGE Sachsen 2E
❒ HEILBRONN Wuerttemberg 1A 2A 6A 7A 12B
❒ HEILIGENDAMM (Bad Doberan) Mecklenburg-Schwerin 2A
❒ HEILIGENFELDE Hannover 2B
❒ HEILIGENHAFEN Schleswig-Holstein 1A 2A 6B
❒ HEILIGENHAUS Rheinland 1E 8B
❒ HEILIGENSTADT Thueringen 1A
❒ HEILIGENSTADT U. WORBIS Provinz Sachsen 1A 6A
❒ HEILSBERG (Lidzbark Warminski) Ostpreussen 1A
❒ HEIMINGHAUSEN Westfalen 2E
❒ HEINRICHAU/MUENSTERBERG (Glinno) Schlesien 2E
❒ HEINRICHSDORF/RAMSBECK Westfalen 2A
❒ HEINRICHSHALL (Koestritz) Thueringen 2A
❒ HEINSBERG Rheinland 1A
❒ HEINUM Hannover 2A
❒ HEISFELDE 2B
❒ HEISTERBACH Rheinland 2A
❒ HELDBURG Bayern 2A
❒ HELDBURG Sachsen-Meiningen 1A 2A
❒ HELDRITT Sachsen-Coburg 7C
❒ HELDRUNGEN Provinz Sachsen 2A 6A 7A
❒ HELENE & AMALIA (Essen) Rheinland 5A
❒ HELLFENBERG Sachsen 2C
❒ HELGOLAND Schleswig-Holstein 1B 2A 8B 11B
❒ HELMARSHAUSEN Hessen-Nassau 1A
❒ HELMBRECHTS Bayern 1A 2B
❒ HELMSDORF Baden 7A
❒ HELMSDORF Provinz Sachsen 2B 7C
❒ HELMSTEDT, BAD Braunschweig 2A 3A 9B 11B
❒ HEMAU Bayern 2A
❒ HEMDINGEN Schleswig-Holstein 1A
❒ HEMELINGEN (Bremen) Hannover 2A 7B
❒ HEMER Westfalen 1A 2E
❒ HENGERSBERG Bayern 2B 7A
❒ HENNEF/SIEG Rheinland 1A 8B
❒ HENRIETTENHUETTE (Opalanki; Przemkow) Schlesien 2C 7A
❒ HEPPENHEIM/BERGSTEIN Hessen 1A 6A
❒ HEPPENSEN (Wilhelmshaven) Hannover 2A
❒ HERBERGER ZUSCHLAG Hannover 3B
❒ HERBOLZHEIM/BREISGAU Baden 2B 7B
❒ HERBRECHTINGEN Wuerttemberg 1A
❒ HERDECKE Westfalen 1A 2B
❒ HERFORD Westfalen 1A 2C 9A 11B
❒ HERINGEN W. Hessen-Nassau 2C
❒ HERMSDORF Sachsen 1A 2D 9A
❒ HERMSDORF-KLOSTERLAUSNITZ Thueringen 2D
❒ HERMSDORF/KYNAST (Sobieszow) Schlesien 1B
❒ HERMUELHEIM Rheinland 5B 7B

1 Mark, Eggenfelden, 1A

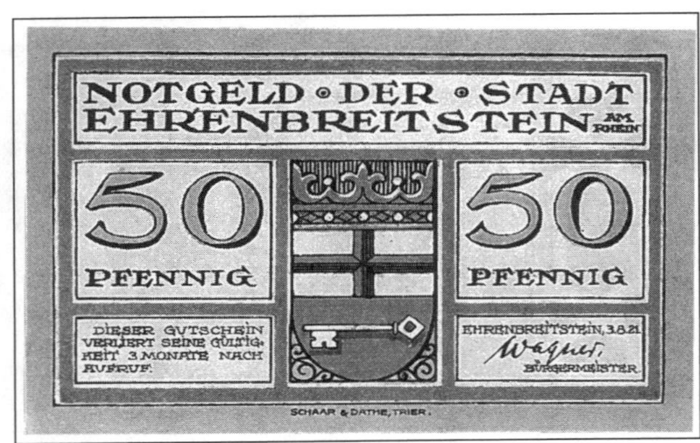

50 Pfennig, Ehrenbreitsteim, 1A

❒ HERNE Westfalen 1A 2A 3A 5B 9A 11B
❒ HEROLD Sachsen 1A
❒ HEROLDSBERG Bayern 2A
❒ HERRENBERG Wuerttemberg 1A 6A
❒ HERRENWYK Luebeck 1A
❒ HERRNHUT Sachsen 1A
❒ HERRNSTADT (Wasosz) Schlesien 1A
❒ HERSBRUCK Bayern 1A 2B 6B
❒ HERSCHBACH/UNTERWESTER-WALDKREIS Hessen-Nassau 1C
❒ HERSFELD (Bad Hersfeld) Hessen-Nassau 1A 2A 6A 9B 10A
❒ HERSTELLE/HOEXTER Westfalen 1A
❒ HERTEN Westfalen 1A 2A 3B 5C
❒ HERTWIGSWALDAU (Snowizda/Jawor, Chotkow/Zagan,Doboszoice/Zabkowice) Schlesien 2A
❒ HERVEST-DORSTEN (Dorsten) Westfalen 3C 5C
❒ HERWIGSDORF Sachsen 2A
❒ HERZBERG/ELSTER Provinz Sachsen 1A 2A
❒ HERZBERG/HARZ Hannover 2A
❒ HERZEBROCK Westfalen 1E 2E
❒ HERZHORN Schleswig-Holstein 1A
❒ HERZLAKE Hannover 2A
❒ HERZOG-JULIUSHUETTE Braunschweig 2A
❒ HERZOGENAURACH Bayern 1A
❒ HERZOGENRATH Rheinland 2A 9A
❒ HERZOGSWALDE/GLATZ (Nagodzice) Schlesien 2A
❒ HESEPE Hannover 3A
❒ HESSISCH-OLDENDORF Hessen-Nassau 1A 2E
❒ HETTENLEIDELSHEIM Pfalz 1A
❒ HETTSTEDT Provinz Sachsen 1E
❒ HEUBACH (Gross-Umstadt) Hessen-Nassau 7C
❒ HEUBERG Baden 7B 10B
❒ HEYDEKRUG/MEMELGEBIET (Silute, Luthuanian SSR) Ostpreussen 1A
❒ HIESFELD Rheinland 9E
❒ HILDBURGHAUSEN Sachsen-Meiningen 1A 2A
❒ HILDBURGHAUSEN, EISFELD, THEMAR, ETC 1A
❒ HILDEN Rheinland 1A 2A 5C 8B
❒ HILDESHEIM Hannover 1A 2B 5B 6A 7B 8A 9A 12A 14A
❒ HILDESHEIM Sachsen-Meiningen 1A
❒ HILPOLTSTEIN/MITTELFRANKEN Bayern 7A
❒ HINDENBURG (Zabrze) Schlesien 1B 2B 5C 6B 7A 8A
❒ HINTERNAH Sachsen-Coburg 7B 9A
❒ HIRSCHBERG (Eberfing) Bayern 3A 4A
❒ HIRSCHBERG (Herborn) Hessen-Nassau 7B
❒ HIRSCHBERG (Jelenia) Schlesien 1A 2A 4A 7B 9A
❒ HIRSCHBERG JELENIA GORA LOEWNBERG U. S. Schlesien 1A 7C 9A
❒ HIRSCHBERG (Handelskammer) LOEWENBERG, SCHMIEDEBERG,SCHOENAU, FRIEDEBERG/Q, GREIFFENBERG, LAEHN 1A
❒ HIRSCHBERG/SAALE Thueringen 1A 2A 3A 7B 9B
❒ HIRSCHBERG, SCHLOSS Bayern 3A 4A 7A
❒ HIRSCHFELD Sachsen 2B 7B 9A
❒ HIRSCHFELDE Sachsen 1A 2A 7A
❒ HIRSIGEN Ober Elsass 1A
❒ HITDORF Rheinland 2B
❒ HOCHEMMERICH (Diergardt) 4A 5C
❒ HOCHEMMERICH (Duisburg) 3A 5B 11E
❒ HOCHHEIM/MAIN Hessen-Nassau 1B
❒ HOCHNEUKIRCH Rheinland 1B 2A
❒ HOCHSTEIN Pfalz 2B
❒ HOCKENSBUELL Schleswig-Holstein 1A
❒ HOECHST/MAIN Hessen-Nassau 1A 2A 7C 9A
❒ HOECHSTADT/AISCH Bayern 2C 6A 7A
❒ HOECHSTAEDT/DONAU Bayern 1A 2C 6A
❒ HOEHN Hessen-Nassau 5B 7A
❒ HOEHR Rheinland 13A
❒ HOEHSCHEID/SOLINGEN Rheinland 1A 6A
❒ HOELLRIEGELSKREUTH Bayern 7B
❒ HOELLSTEIN Baden 7E
❒ HOENNETHAL Westfalen 2B 3C 5B
❒ HOENTROP/BOCHUM Westfalen 6A
❒ HOERDE (Dortmund) Westfalen 1A 2A 5B 6A 7A 8A 12A
❒ HOERDT Pfalz 1A
❒ HOERNERKIRCHEN Schleswig-Holstein 1A
❒ HOERSTE Westfalen 5C
❒ HOEXTER Westfalen 1A 2B
❒ HOF Bayern 1A 2B 6A 7A 8A 12B
❒ HOFFNUNGSTHAL Rheinland 1A 2B
❒ HOFGEISMAR/WESER (Horengeismar) Hessen-Nassau 2A
❒ HOFHEIM/TAUNUS Hessen 1A
❒ HOFHEIM/UNTERFRANKEN Bayern 2A
❒ HOHEN NEUENDORF Brandenburg 1B 2A
❒ HOHENASPERG Wuerttemberg 3E
❒ HOHENBERG/EGER Bayeren 2D
❒ HOHENBUDBERG Rheinland 5B

1 Mark, Eickel, 1A

50 Pfennig, Eilenburg, 1A

25 Pfennig, Einbeck, 1A

50 Pfennig, Elbingerode, 1A

50 Pfennig, Eisfeld, 1A

1 Mark, Elberfeld, 1A

75 Pfennig, Ellrich, 1A

2 Mark, Elmshorn, 1A

50 Pfennig, Ennigerloh, 1A

1 Mark, Erfde, 1A

50 Pfennig, Erfurt, 1A

50 Pfennig, Erkelenz, 1A

❐ HOHENERXLEBEN Anhalt 2E
❐ HOHENERXLEBEN Provinz Sachsen 2D
❐ HOHENFELS/STOCKACH Baden 14A
❐ HOHENFICHTE Sachsen 2A
❐ HOHENFRIEDEBERG (Dobromierz) Schlesien 1A
❐ HOHENLEIPISCH Provinz Sachsen 1A
❐ HOHENLIMBURG Westfalen 1C 2A
❐ HOHENLINDE (Lagiewniki) Schlesien 1E 2E
❐ HOHENLOHEHUETTE (Katowice) Schlesien 5A
❐ HOHENMOELSEN Provinz Sachsen 1A 7A 9A
❐ HOHENOELLEN Pfalz 1B
❐ HOHENSALZA (Inowroclaw) Posen 1A 6B 11B 12B
❐ HOHENSCHAMBACH (Hemau) Bayern 2A 7C
❐ HOHENSTEIN Provinz Sachsen (See Nordhausen)
❐ HOHENSTEIN-ERNSTTHAL Sachsen 1A 2B 7A 8A
❐ HOHENWESTEDT Schleswig-Holstein 1A 6B
❐ HOHENZOLLERISCH-SIGMARINGEN
❐ Hohenzollern 1A
❐ HOHENZOLLERN Hohenzollern 1E
❐ HOHENZOLLERNBRUECKE Hohenzollern 1A
❐ HOHNDORF/CHEMNITZ Sachsen 1A 2A
❐ HOHNSTEIN Sachsen 2B
❐ HOLENBRUNN/WUNSIEDEL Bayern 7B
❐ HOLNIS Schleswig-Holstein 1A
❐ HOLSTERHAUSEN-DORSTEN Westfalen 2E
❐ HOLTE Westfalen 3C
❐ HOLTENAU (Kiel-Holtenau) Schleswig-Holstein 2B 10B
❐ HOLTHAUSEN/PLETTENBERG Westfalen 2E 9A
❐ HOLTWICK Westfalen 3E
❐ HOLZHAUSEN Nordhein-Westfalen 2D 6A 14C
❐ HOLZHAUSEN/LEIPZIG Sachsen 2B
❐ HOLZHEIM-GREFRATH Rheinland 1B
❐ HOLZKIRCHEN Bayern 6A
❐ HOLZMINDEN Braunschweig 1A 2A 3B
❐ HOLZWICKEDE Westfalen 2C 5B
❐ HOMBERG/DUISBURG Rheinland 1A 5C 14B
❐ HOMBERG/KASSEL Hessen 1B
❐ HOMBURG/SAAR Pfalz 1A
❐ HOMBURG, BAD V.D. HOEHE Hessen-Nassau 1A 5C 6A 8B 9A 11C 14A
❐ HOMECOURT Lothringen 1A 3A
❐ HONNEF/RHEIN (Bad Honnef) Rheinland 2A 9A

50 Pfennig, Eschershausen, 1A

10 Pfennig, Eulau-Wilhelmshütte, 1A

❒ HOPE Hannover 3B
❒ HOPPECKE Westfalen 2E
❒ HOPPSTAEDTEN Oldenburg 11C
❒ HORB/NECKAR Wuerttemberg 1A 2B 6A
❒ HORDEL Westfalen 2C 5B
❒ HORDORF Hannover 3B
❒ HORGEN/ROTTWEIL Wuerttemberg 1A
❒ HORMERSDORF/ERZGEBIRGE
❒ Sachsen 2B
❒ HORN/WESTFALEN Lippe 1A 4A
❒ HORNBERG Baden 2A 6A 7E
❒ HORNBOSTEL Hannover 2A
❒ HORNEBURG/UNTER ELBE Hannover 2A
❒ HORREM/BOCHUM Rheinland 1A 5B
❒ HORST-EMSCHER (Gelsenkirchen) Westfalen 1A 2A 6A 11B
❒ HORST/LEGDEN Westfalen 3C
❒ HORSTMAR Westfalen 2D
❒ HOYER (Hoejer, Denmark) Schleswig-Holstein 1A 2A
❒ HOYERSWERDA Schiesien 1A
❒ HOYM Anhalt 1A
❒ HOYMGRUBE Schlesien 2C
❒ HUCKINGEN/DUISBURG
❒ Rheinland 2B 5B
❒ HUDE Niedersachsen 14B
❒ HUDDESTORF Hannover 3B
❒ HUECKELHOVEN Rheinland 2A
❒ HUECKESWAGEN Rheinland 1B 2B 5A 9A
❒ HUEFINGEN Baden 1B 2B 6A 7B
❒ HUELS Rheinland 2A 5C
❒ HUELSEBERG Hannover 3B
❒ HUELSEN Hannover 3B
❒ HUELSENBUSCH Rheinland 1B
❒ HUELZWEILER Rheinland 1D
❒ HUENFELD Hessen-Nassau 2A 6A
❒ HUEPSTEDT Provinz Sachsen 7A
❒ HUERTH/KOELN Rheinland 11B
❒ HUESSEREN-WESSERLING (Hunsseren-Weiserling) Elsass 1A 2B
❒ HUESTEN (Neheim-Huesten) Westfalen 1C 2A 11B
❒ HUETTENHAUSEN Rheinland 2C
❒ HUETTENSTEINACH Sachsen-Meiningen 13E
❒ HUFEN Ostpreussen 2B
❒ HUGH ZWANG GRUBE Schiesien 5A
❒ HUNDSHUEBEL/ERZGEBIRGE Sachsen 1E
❒ HUSBY Schleswig-Holstein 1A
❒ HUSBYHOLZ Schleswig-Holstein 1A
❒ HUSUM Schleswig-Holstein 1A 2A 9A 14B
❒ IBBENBUEREN Westfalen 2C 9A
❒ ICHENHAUSEN Bayern 6A
❒ ICHSTEDT Schwarzburg-Rudolstadt 7A
❒ ICHTERSHAUSEN Thueringen 2A 9A
❒ IDAR Oldenburg-Birkenfeld 1A 2A
❒ IDAR-MUENSTER Rheinland 2E
❒ IDAR-OBERSTEIN Rheinland 2A
❒ IDSTEIN Hessen-Nassau 1A 2B 6A
❒ IGELSHIEB Sachsen-Meiningen 1A
❒ ILFELD (today Ilfeld-Weigersdorf)

50 Pfennig, Eutin, 1A

10 Pfennig, Exin, Germany, 1B

Hannover 1E 3B
❒ ILSEDER HUETTE Hannover 5B
❒ ILLERTISSEN Bayern 1A
❒ ILLKIRCH Elsass 2B
❒ ILLSCHWANG Bayern 2B
❒ ILMENAU Sachsen-Weimar-Eisenach 1A 2A 9A
❒ ILSE, GRUBE Brandenburg 2A
❒ ILSEDER HUETTE Hannover 5B
❒ ILSENBURG Provinz Sachsen 1A 2A 9A
❒ ILSENHAGEN Hannover 2A
❒ ILSHOFEN Wuerttemberg 2B
❒ ILSTER Hannover 3B
❒ IMMENSTADT/ALLGAEU Bayern 1A 2A 6A 9A
❒ IMMIGRATH Rheinland 2B
❒ INGOLSTADT Bayern 1A 2A 4A 7A 10A
❒ INSTERBURG (Czerniachowsk) Ostpreussen 1A 2B 8A 10A
❒ IRGERSDORF Sachsen 2B
❒ ISEN Bayern 2E
❒ ISENHAGEN/WITTINGEN Hannover 2B
❒ ISERLOHN Westfalen 1A 2C 6A 8A 11B
❒ ISNY/ALLGAEU Wuerttemberg 1A 6A
❒ ISSELBURG Rheinland 2E
❒ ITTENBACH Rheinland 1E
❒ ITTENBEUREN-RAVENSBURG Wuerttemberg 2A
❒ ITZEHOE Schleswig-Holstein 1A 2D 6C 8A 9B 10A 14A
❒ IUNCEWO (Lwonicka,) Posen 1B
❒ JACOBSHAGEN (Dobrzany) Pommern 1A
❒ JAEGERNDORF Schlesien 1A 2B
❒ JAHNSBACH Sachsen 2E
❒ JAKOBSBERG Westfalen 1A
❒ JAKOBSDORF Brandenburg 2A
❒ JAKOBSHAGEN (Dobrzany) Ostpreussen 1A
❒ JANOW Schlesien 1A
❒ JANOWITZ (Janowiec) Posen 1B 2B
❒ JARATSCHEWO (Jaraczewo) Posen 1B
❒ JARMEN Pommern 1A
❒ JAROTSCHIN (Jarocin) Posen 1C
❒ JASCHINE (Jasienie) Schlesien 2E
❒ JASTROW (Jastrowie) Westpreussen 1A
❒ JAUER (Jawor) Schlesien 1A
❒ JAUERNIG/FREIWALDAU Schlesien 1A
❒ JENA Sachsen-Weimar-Eisenach 1A 2A 7A 9A 11A 12B
❒ JERICHOW (Jericho) Provinz Sachsen 1A 7B
❒ JESCHUETZ (Jezyce) Schlesien 2B 7B
❒ JESSEN Provinz Sachsen 1A
❒ JESSENITZ Mecklenburg-Schwerin 1A 7A
❒ JESSNITZ Anhalt 1A 2B 7B
❒ JESTERBURG Hannover 3B
❒ JESTETTEN Baden 1A 2E 6B 7E
❒ JEVER Oldenburg 1A 2A
❒ JEZIORKI (Seeheim) Posen 2B
❒ JOCKGRIM Pfalz 1A 2A
❒ JOEHSTADT Sachsen 1E 2B
❒ JOHANNGEORGENSTADT Sachsen 2A
❒ JOHANNISBURG (Jansborg; Pisz) Ostpreussen 1B
❒ JORK Hannover 2A
❒ JUDENBACH Sachsen-Meiningen 7A 9A
❒ JUECHEN Rheinland 1A 9A 14B
❒ JUELICH Rheinland 1A
❒ JUETERBOG Brandenburg 1A 10A 12B
❒ JUETERBOG-LUCKENWALDE Brandenburg 1A
❒ JUIST Hannover 1A
❒ JULIUSBURG (Radzijow)
❒ Schlesien 2A
❒ JUNCEWO (Junkers) Posen 2B
❒ JUNGENTHAL Rheinland 2B
❒ JUNKERSDORF Bayern 2B 14B
❒ JUTROSCHIN (Jutrosin) Posen 1A
❒ KABEL (Hagen-Kabel) Westfalen 2A
❒ KAENDLER Sachsen 1B
❒ KAHLA Sachsen-Altenburg 1A 2A
❒ KAHLA-LEUCHTENBURG Thueringen 2A
❒ KAISERODA Sachsen-Weimar-Eisenach 2A 7A
❒ KAISERSLAUTERN Pfalz 1B2A 6A 8B 11B 12B
❒ KAISERSWERTH (Duesseldorf-Kaiserswerth) Rheinland 1A
❒ KALBSRIETH/GOLDENEN AUE Provinz Sachsen 2A

50 Pfennig, Flensburg, Germany, 1A

30 Pfennig, Flensburg, 2A

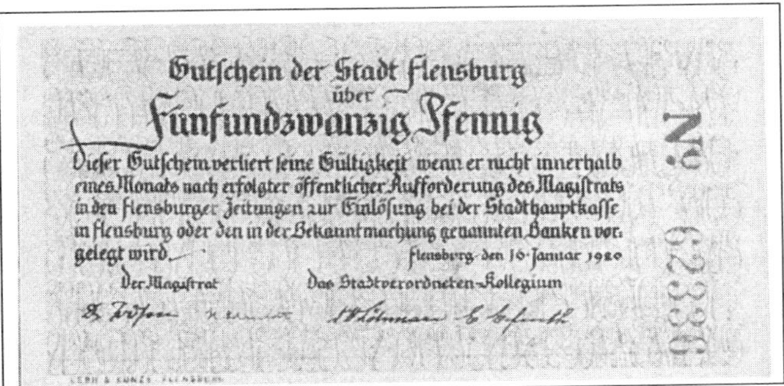

25 Pfennig, Flensburg, 1A

50 Pfennig, Fockbek, 1A

10 Pfennig, Frankfurt/O, 7B

20 Pfennig stamp, Frankfurt/Main, Germany, 11B

25 Pfennig, Frankfurt/O, 1A

❒ KALDENKIRCHEN Rheinland 2A
❒ KALLIES (Kalisz/Pomorski) Pommern 1A
❒ KALLMUENZ Bayern 2C
❒ KALMIERSCHUETZ Posen 3A
❒ KALTENNORDHEIM Thueringen 1A 2A
❒ KAMEN Westfalen 1A
❒ KAMENZ Sachsen 1A 2A 10A
❒ KAMIN (Kamien; Kamienna) Schlesien 1C
❒ KAMIN (Kamien) Westpreussen 1B
❒ KEMMLITZ Sachsen 2B
❒ KAMPEN/SYLT Schleswig-Holstein 2A 3B
❒ KAMSTIGALL/PILLAU (Kaukehmen) Ostpreussen 1B 3A
❒ KANDEL Pfalz 1A 2B
❒ KANDERN Baden 1A 6A
❒ KANDRZIN-POGORZELLETZ (Kedzierzyn-Pogorzelec) Schlesien 1A
❒ KAPPEL Sachsen 7A
❒ KAPPELEN Rheinland 1A 2A
❒ KAPPELN Schleswig-Holstein 1A 2A
❒ KARBY Schleswig-Holstein 2A
❒ KARF (Karb) Schlesien 1B
❒ KARKEN Rheinland 2A 14B
❒ KARLINGEN Carlinge) Lothringen 2B
❒ KARLSMARKT (Karlowice)
❒ Schlesien 1A 7B
❒ KARLSRUHE Baden 1D 2A 3A 6A 7A 9A 11B 12A
❒ KARLSTADT/MAIN Bayern 1A 2A 6A 7A 8A 9A
❒ KARLSTADT-ARNSTEIN Bayern 2A
❒ KARNAP (Essen) Rheinland 2A 5B
❒ KARTHAUS (Kartuzy) Westpreussen 1A
❒ KASSEL Hessen 1A 2D 14A
❒ KASSEL-WILHELMSHOEHE Hessen 14A
❒ KASTL Bayern 2B
❒ KATERNBERG Rheinland 2A 5A
❒ KATSCHER (Kietrz) Schlesien 1A
❒ KATTOWITZ (Katowice) Posen 1A 2E 4B 5C 7A 9A
❒ KATZENSTEIN Provinz Sachsen 1C
❒ KATZENSTEIN/OSTERODE Hannover 2A
❒ KATZHUETTE Schwarzburg-Rudolstadt 1A 2A 7B 9A
❒ KAUFBEUREN Bayern 1A 2A 6A 7B
❒ KAUFFUNG/KATZBACK (Wojcieszow) Schlesien 1A 7B
❒ KAUKEHMEN Ostpreussen 1A 12A
❒ KAWALLEN (Kowale) Schlesien 7B
❒ KAYNA Provinz Sachsen 9B
❒ KAYSERSBERG Elsass 1A 2B
❒ KEHL/RHEIN Baden 1A 2A 6A 7B 10A
❒ KEILHAU Schwarzburg-Rudolstadt 1A
❒ KEITUM/SYLT Schleswig-Holstein 1A 2A
❒ KELBRA/KYFFHAEUSER Provinz Sachsen 1A 6B
❒ KELHEIM/DONAU Bayern 1A 6A 7B
❒ KELLENGHUSEN, BAD Schlesig-Holstein 1A 6A 8A
❒ KELLINGHUSEN Schleswig-Holstein 1A
❒ KEMBERG Provinz Sachsen 1A
❒ KEMNATH Bayern 1A 2B 6A
❒ KEMPEN (Kepno) Posen 1A 6A
❒ KEMPEN/RHEIN Rheinland 1A 2B 6A 8B
❒ KEMPTEN/ALLGAEU Bayern 1A 2A 6A 7A 9B
❒ KENZINGEN Baden 1A
❒ KETTWIG Rheinland 1A 2A 7B
❒ KEVELAER Rheinland 1A
❒ KIEL Schleswig-Holstein 1A 2A 6A 7A 9B 10A 11B 12B 14B
❒ KIEL-EIGENTHEIM-PRITSFRIEDRICHSORT Schleswig-Holstein 1A
❒ KIEL-ELMSHENHAGEN Schleswig-Holstein 1A
❒ KIEL-GAARDEN Schleswig-Holstein 2B
❒ KIEL-HOLTENAU Schleswig-Holstein 2B
❒ KIEL-NEUMUEHLEN-DIETRICHSDORF Schleswig-Holstein 1A
❒ KIEL-WELLINGDORF

10 Pfennig, Freiberg/Sachsen, Germany, 1A

50 Pfennig, Freiburg/Br., 1A

Schleswig-Holstein	2B			
❒ KIELCZYGLOW (Keltsey) Posen	2B			
❒ KIERSPE Westfalen	2E			
❒ KIMRATHSHOFEN Bayern	14B			
❒ KINDELBRUECK Provinz Sachsen	1A	2A		
❒ KIPFENBERG Bayern	2B			
❒ KIRCHBERG Sachsen	1A			
❒ KIRCHENDEMENREUTH Bayern	7B			
❒ KIRCHENLAMITZ Bayern	6B			
❒ KIRCHENPOPOWO (Popowo Koscielne) Posen	1A			
❒ KIRCHHAIN Bayern	1A			
❒ KIRCHHAIN Brandenburg	1A			
❒ KIRCHHAIN Hessen-Nassau	1B			
❒ KIRCHHEIM Bayern	2A	7B		
❒ KIRCHHEIM/TECK Wuerttemberg	1A	2A	6A	
❒ KIRCHHEIMBOLANDEN Pfalz	1A	7B		
❒ KIRCHHELLEN Westfalen	1E			
❒ KIRCHRARBACH Westfalen	2E			
❒ KIRCHWEYHE Hannover	3A			
❒ KIRCHZARTEN Baden	1A			
❒ KIRCHZELL Bayern	1A			
❒ KIRN/NAHE Rheinland	1A	6A		
❒ KIRSCHAU Sachsen	2B	7A		
❒ KISSINGEN (Bad Kissingen) Bayern	1A	2A	6A	
❒ KISSINGEN-MUENNERSTADT Bayern	1A			
❒ KISSLEGG/ALLGAEU				
❒ Wuerttemberg	2B	6A		
❒ KITZINGEN Bayern	1A	2A	6A	13A
❒ KLAEDEN Provinz Sachsen	2A			
❒ KLAFFENBACH/CHEMNITZ Sachsen	1A			
❒ KLANXBUELL Schleswig-Holstein	1A			
❒ KLAUSDORF Schleswig-Holstein	1A			
❒ KLEIN WANZLEBEN Provinz Sachsen	2B	7A		
❒ KLEIN-AUHEIM Hessen-Nassau	9B			
❒ KLEIN-NORDENDE-LIETH Schleswig-Holstein	1A			
❒ KLEIN-PODLESS/GROSS-KLINSCH Westpreussen	2B			
❒ KLEINEN BAD Mecklenburg-Schwerin	1A			
❒ KLEINHEUBACH/MAIN Bayern	1A	2B		
❒ KLEINLAUFENBURG Baden	1A			
❒ KLEINNEUSCHOENBERG Sachsen	2B			
❒ KLEINSAUBERNITZ Sachsen	2B	7A		
❒ KLEINSCHMALKALDEN Thueringen	1A			
❒ KLEINSORGE Ostpreussen	7B			
❒ KLEINSTEINBERG Sachsen	2B			
❒ KLENKA (Kleka) Posen	1A	2A		
❒ KLEPZIG Anhalt	7B			
❒ KLESCHKAU (Kleszczewo) Westpreussen	2A			
❒ KLETTENDORF (Klecina) Schlesien	1A	2A	3C	
❒ KLETZKO				

50 Pfennig, Freiberg, 1A

25 Pfennig, Freienwalde, 1A

(Kloetzen; Klecko) Posen 1A
❒ KLEVE (Cleve) Rheinland 4B 5B 7B
❒ KLEY/DORTMUND Westfalen 3E 14B
❒ KLINGENBERG/MAIN Bayern 1A
❒ KLINGENTHAL Sachsen 1A 2B 11B
❒ KLODNITZ-ODERHAFEN (Klodnica) Schlesien 1A
❒ KLOSTER ZINNA Brandenburg 1A
❒ KLOSTERMANSFELD Provinz Sachsen 2B
❒ KLOTZSCHE Sachsen 9A
❒ KLUETZ Mecklenburg-Schwerin 1A
❒ KNAPPSACK Rheinland 2B
❒ KNEITLINGEN Braunschweig 1A
❒ KNIVSBERG (Knivsbjerg, Denmark) Schleswig-Holstein 1B
❒ KNUROW Schlesien 1B 2B 3A 7B
❒ KOBERG Schleswig-Holstein 1A
❒ KOCHEL Bayern 2B
❒ KOCHLOWITZ (Kochlowice) Schlesien 1A 2B
❒ KOEBEN/ODER (Chobienia) Schlesien 1A
❒ KOEBLITZ Sachsen 2B
❒ KOELLN-REISIEK Schleswig-Holstein 1A
❒ KOELN Rheinland 1A 2B 3A 5B 7B 8B 9A 11B 12A 13A
❒ KOELN-BAYENTHAL Rheinland 2B 7B
❒ KOELN-BRAUNSFELD Rheinland 11B
❒ KOELN-BRUEHL Rheinland 1A
❒ KOELN-DELLBRUECK Rheinland 2A 11B
❒ KOELN-DUETZ Rheinland 2B

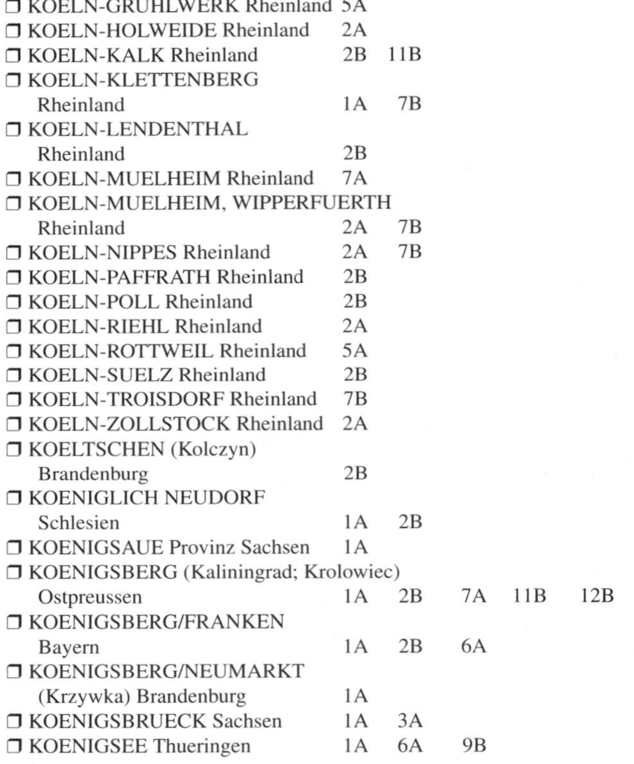

❒ KOELN-EHRENFELD Rheinland 2A 3A
❒ KOELN-GRUBE FORTUNA Rheinland 5A
❒ KOELN-GRUHLWERK Rheinland 5A
❒ KOELN-HOLWEIDE Rheinland 2A
❒ KOELN-KALK Rheinland 2B 11B
❒ KOELN-KLETTENBERG Rheinland 1A 7B
❒ KOELN-LENDENTHAL Rheinland 2B
❒ KOELN-MUELHEIM Rheinland 7A
❒ KOELN-MUELHEIM, WIPPERFUERTH Rheinland 2A 7B
❒ KOELN-NIPPES Rheinland 2A 7B
❒ KOELN-PAFFRATH Rheinland 2B
❒ KOELN-POLL Rheinland 2B
❒ KOELN-RIEHL Rheinland 2A
❒ KOELN-ROTTWEIL Rheinland 5A
❒ KOELN-SUELZ Rheinland 2B
❒ KOELN-TROISDORF Rheinland 7B
❒ KOELN-ZOLLSTOCK Rheinland 2A
❒ KOELTSCHEN (Kolczyn) Brandenburg 2B
❒ KOENIGLICH NEUDORF Schlesien 1A 2B
❒ KOENIGSAUE Provinz Sachsen 1A
❒ KOENIGSBERG (Kaliningrad; Krolowiec) Ostpreussen 1A 2B 7A 11B 12B
❒ KOENIGSBERG/FRANKEN Bayern 1A 2B 6A
❒ KOENIGSBERG/NEUMARKT (Krzywka) Brandenburg 1A
❒ KOENIGSBRUECK Sachsen 1A 3A
❒ KOENIGSEE Thueringen 1A 6A 9B

75 Pfennig, Friedrichsbrunn, 1A

50 Pfennig, Friedrichroda, 1A

75 Pfennig, Friesack, 1A

10 Pfennig, Frose/Anhalt, Germany, 1A

25 Pfennig, Gatersleben, 1A

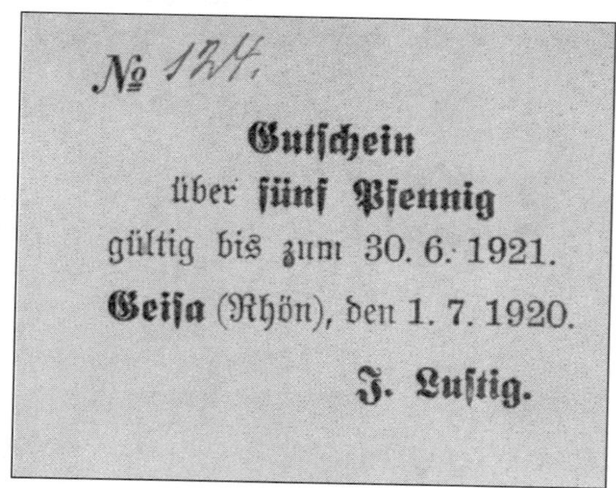

№ 124.

Gutschein
über fünf Pfennig
gültig bis zum 30. 6. 1921.
Geisa (Rhön), den 1. 7. 1920.
J. Lustig.

5 Pfennig, Geisa/Rhoen, Germany, 2B

❒ KOENIGSHOFEN/GRABFELD Bayern 1A
❒ KOENIGSHUETTE (Krolewska Huta) Schlesien 1A 2B 3B 5B 8A
❒ KOENIGSMOOR Hannover 3A
❒ KOENIGSSEE Bayern 1A
❒ KOENIGSSTEELE-HORST Westfalen 2B
❒ KOENIGSSTEELE/ESSEN Westfalen1A 2A 6A 7B 8B
❒ KOENIGSTEIN/ELBE Sachsen 1A 2C 3A 6A
❒ KOENIGSTEIN/TAUNUS Hesse-Nassau 1A
❒ KOENIGSTHOR (Neuruppin) Brandenburg 9B
❒ KOENIGSWALDE Schlesien 1A 3C
❒ KOENIGSWARTHA Sachsen 2A
❒ KOENIGSWINTER & HONNEF Rheinland 2A
❒ KOENIGSWINTER/RHEIN Rheinland 1A
❒ KOENIGSWUSTERHAUSEN Brandenburg 1A
❒ KOENNERN Provinz Sachsen 1A
❒ KOEPPELSDORF Sachsen-Meiningen 7B
❒ KOERLIN/PERSANTE (Karlino) Pommern 1B
❒ KOERNER Sachsen-Gotha 1A 7B
❒ KOESCHING Bayern 6A
❒ KOESEN, BAD Provinz Sachsen 1A 2B
❒ KOESLIN (Koszalin) Pommern 1A 6A 12B
❒ KOESTRITZ (Bad Koestritz) Reuss 1A 7B
❒ KOETHENSDORF-REITZENHAIN Sachsen 1B
❒ KOETITZ/COSWIG Sachsen 2A 7A
❒ KOETSCHENBRODA (Radebeul) Sachsen 1A 2B 8A
❒ KOETTWITZ Sachsen 2B
❒ KOETZTING/WALD Bayern 1A 2B 6A
❒ KOHLENBACH Hannover 1A
❒ KOHLSCHEID Rheinland 2B
❒ KOHREN Sachsen 1A
❒ KOLBERG, BAD (Sachsen-Meiningen) 4A
❒ KOLBERG (Colberg; Kolobrzeg) Pommern 1A 2A 4A 6A 7B 11B
❒ KOLBERMOOR Bayern 2B
❒ KOLLNAU/BREISGAU Baden 2B
❒ KOLMAR (Chodziez) Posen 1A 2B 6B
❒ KOLO Posen 1A
❒ KONARZEWO Posen 6B
❒ KONITZ (Chojnice) Westpreussen 1B 6B 9A 14B
❒ KONSTADT (Wolczyn) Schlesien 1A 7B
❒ KONSTANZ Baden 1A 2A 6A 7B 8B
❒ KOPPELSDORF Sachsen-Meiningen 7B
❒ KOPPITZ Schlesien 1A 2A
❒ KORNER Sachsen-Gotha 7A
❒ KORNTAL Wuerttemberg 1A
❒ KORNWESTHEIM/STUTTGART Wuerttemberg 1A 2B
❒ KORSCHENBROICH Rheinland 1A
❒ KOSCHMIN (Kozmin) Posen 1A 6A
❒ KOSLIN (Koszalin) Pommern 1A 6A 12B
❒ KOSLOWAGORA (Kozlowagora) Schlesien 1A
❒ KOSTEN (Koscian) Posen 1A
❒ KOSTSCHIN (Kostrzyn) Posen 1A
❒ KOTTERN (Kempten) Bayern 2B 7B
❒ KOTTHAUSEN Rheinland 1A
❒ KOWNO (Kaunas) Posen 1A
❒ KRAIBURG/INN Bayern 1B
❒ KRAKOW Mecklenburg-Schwerin 1A
❒ KRANICHFELD Sachsen-Meiningen 1A
❒ KRAPPAMUEHLE (Krupskimlyn) Schlesien 7B
❒ KRAPPITZ (Krapkowice) Schlesien 1A 2B 7A
❒ KRAUSCHWITZ Schlesien 7B
❒ KREISCHA Sachsen 1A
❒ KREMPE Schleswig-Holstein 1A
❒ KREUZBERG/WALD Bayern 7B
❒ KREUZBURG (Kluczbork) Schlesien 1A 2C 7B

1 Mark Geldern, 1A

30 Pfennig, Gerbstedt, Germany, 9A

❒ KREUZNACH (Bad Kreuznach) Rheinland	1A	2B	6A	8B	
❒ KREUZTAL Westfalen	1E				
❒ KREUZWALD (Creutzwald) Lothringen	9B				
❒ KRIEBENAU (Kriebethal) Sachsen	9B				
❒ KRIEBITSCH Sachsen	2B				
❒ KRIEBSTEIN/WALDWHEIM Sachsen	2A	9B			
❒ KRIEWALD (Knurow) Schlesien	6A				
❒ KRIEWEN (Krzywin) Posen	1A				
❒ KRIPP/RHEIN (Remagan) Rheinland	7B				
❒ KRIPPEN Sachsen	6A				
❒ KROEBEN (Krobia) Posen	1A				
❒ KROELPA Provinz Sachsen	1A				
❒ KROEPELIN Mecklinburg-Schwerin	1A				
❒ KRONACH Baden	1A	6A			
❒ KRONACH Bayern	1A	2A	6A		
❒ KROPP Schleswig-Holstein	10A				
❒ KROTOSCHIN (Krotoszyn) Posen	1A	6B			
❒ KRUEMMEL (Geesthacht) Schleswig-Holstein	2A	3A	7A		
❒ KRUET Elsass	1A				
❒ KRUMBACH Bayern	1A	6A			
❒ KRUMHERMERSDORF/ERZGEBIRGE Sachsen	12A				
❒ KRUPPAMUEHLE Schlesien	7B				
❒ KRUSCHIN/NAYMOWO (Kruszyna) Westpreussen	2B	6A			
❒ KRUSCHWITZ (Kruszwica) Posen	1A				
❒ KUCHEN Wuerttemberg	2A				
❒ KUDOWA, BAD (Kudowa-Zdroj) Schlesien	1A				
❒ KUEHNHAIDE/ZWOENITZ Sachsen	1A	2B			
❒ KUELLENHAIN/ELBERFELD Rheinland	2B				
❒ KRUEMMEL Schleswig-Holstein	5D				
❒ KUENZELSAU Wuerttemberg	1A	2B	6A		
❒ KUEPPERSTEG Rheinland	2B				
❒ KUEPPSTEG Rheinland	2B				
❒ KUEPS Bayern	7A	9A			
❒ KULKWITZ Rheinland	2B				
❒ KULMBACH Bayern	1A	2B	6A	7A	11B
❒ KUMMERFELD Schleswig-Holstein	1A				
❒ KUNZENDORF (Konczyce) Schlesien	1A	3A			
❒ KUPFERDREH (Essen) Rheinland	1A	2B	5B	7B	
❒ KUPFERHAMMER-GRUENTHAL Sachsen	2B				
❒ KUPFERMUEHLE Schleswig-Holstein	2B				
❒ KURL (Courl) Westfalen	2E				
❒ KURNIK (Kornik) Posen	1B				
❒ KURZENMOOR Schleswig-Holstein	1A				
❒ KUSEL Pfalz	1A	14B			
❒ KUSEY/ALT MARK Provinz Sachsen	2A	7B			
❒ KUTTLAU (Kotla) Schlesien	2A	7B			
❒ KUZLE/LUBESIN Posen	2A				
❒ KYLLBURG/EIFEL Rheinland	2A				
❒ KYRITZ Brandenburg	1B	2A			
❒ LAAGE Mecklenburg-Schwerin	1A				
❒ LAASPHE Westfalen	2E				
❒ LAATZEN Hannover	9C				
❒ LABAND (Labady) Schlesien	5B				
❒ LABES (Lobez) Pommern	1A	2B	6A		
❒ LABIAU (Polessk) Ostpreussen	1A				

10 Pfennig, Germersheim (POW) 3A

Types of Emergency Money

Type	Reference #
Municipal paper	1
Private paper	2
POW paper	3
POW official metal	4
POW private metal	5
Municipal metal	6
Private metal	7
Gas tokens	8
Food; beer; konsumverein	9
Naval; military; kantine	10
Encased, unencased stamps	11
Streetcar tokens	12
Porcelain	13
World War II issues	14
Concentration, Civilian internment camps	15

Rarity grades: A, to $25; B, to $60; C, to $125; D, to $200; and E, $350

50 Pfennig, Trier, 1A

❒ LABISCHIN (Labiszyn) Posen 1A
❒ LABOE Schleswig-Holstein 1A 7B
❒ LADENBURG Baden 1A 2B
❒ LAEGERDORF
Schleswig-Holstein 1A 2B
❒ LAEHN (Wlen) Schlesien 1A 2B
❒ LAER Westfalen 2B
❒ LAGE Lippe 1A 2B
❒ LAHR Baden 1A 2B 3B 7B 8A
❒ LAINECK/BAYREUTH Bayern 2B
❒ LAMBRECHT Pfalz 1A 6A 8A
❒ LAMPERTHEIM Hessen 1A
❒ LAMPERTSMUEHLE Pfalz 1A 7B
❒ LAMSDORF Oberschlesien 3B 4A
❒ LAMSPRINGE Hannover 1A
❒ LAMSTEDT Hannover 3A
❒ LANDAU Pfalz 1A 3A 6A 8B
❒ LANDAU/ISAR Bayern 1A 2B
❒ LANDECK, BAD
(Ladek-Zdroj) Schlesien 1A 2B 6A 8B
❒ LANDESHUT
(Kamienna Gora) Schlesien 1A 2B 6A 7B
❒ LANDKIRCHEN/FEHMARN
Schleswig-Holstein 1A
❒ LANDSBERG (Koszalin; Ledyczek;
Gorzow Slask) Schlesien 1A 2B 6A 8B
❒ LANDSBERG/LECH Bayern 1A 2A 3B 6A 9B
❒ LANDSHUT Bayern 1A 2B 3B 4A 7A 11B
❒ LANDSTUHL Pfalz 2B
❒ LANGAU (Oberviechtach) Bayern 7B
❒ LANGBURKERSDORF Sachsen 1A
❒ LANGELN Schleswig-Holstein 1A
❒ LANGELOHE Schleswig-Holstein 1A
❒ LANGELSHEIM Braunschweig 2B
❒ LANGEMOOR Westfalen 3B
❒ LANGENALTHEIM Bayern 1A
❒ LANGENAU Sachsen 1A
❒ LANGENBERG Rheinland 1A 2B 7A
❒ LANGENBERG-REUSS (Gera)
Thueringen 2A 8B
❒ LANGENBIELAU Schlesien 2A
❒ LANGENBRUCK Bayern 7A 8A
❒ LANGENBURG Wuerttemberg 7B
❒ LANGENDREER (Bochum)
Westfalen 1B 2A 3B 5B 9A 11B
❒ LANGENESS-NORDMARSCH
Schleswig-Holstein 1A
❒ LANGENHAGEN Hannover 2A
❒ LANGENHORN/HUSUM
Schleswig-Holstein 1A
❒ LANGENLEUBA Sachsen 2A
❒ LANGENOELS
(Olszyna) Schlesien 1A 2B 7A
❒ LANGENSALZA Provinz Sachsen 1A 2A 3B
❒ LANGENSCHWALBACH
Hessen-Nassau 1A 6A
❒ LANGENZENN Bayern 14B
❒ LANGERFELD/BARMEN
(Wuppertal) Westfalen 7A
❒ LANGEWIESEN
Schwarzburg-Sondershausen 1A
❒ LANGGUHLE
(Golina Wielka) Posen 2A
❒ LANGQUAID Bayern 1A
❒ LANGWEDEL Hannover 3B
❒ LANK (Meerbusch) Rheinland 1A 6A

25 Pfennig, Gifhorn, 1A

10 Pfennig, Gifhorn, Germany, 2B

❒ LANNSCHWALD Hannover 3A
❒ LASSAN Pommern 1A 2A 7A
❒ LAUBAN (Luban) Schlesien 1A 2B 4A 6A 8B
❒ LAUBAU Schlesien 6A
❒ LAUCHA Provinz Sachsen 1A
❒ LAUCHERTHAL Hohenzollern 1A
❒ LAUCHHAMMER Provinz Sachsen 2A
❒ LAUCHSTEDT BAD Provinz Sachsen 1A 13E
❒ LAUENBRUECK Altmark 11C
❒ LAUENBURG (Lebork) Pommern 1A 2B 4A 6A
❒ LAUENBURG/ELBE Schleswig-Holstein 1A 2A 6B
❒ LAUENSTEIN Bayern 1A
❒ LAUF/PEGNITZ Bayern 1A 2A 6A
❒ LAUFEN Bayern 1A 6A
❒ LAUFEN-TITTMONING Bayern 1A
❒ LAUFFEN/NECKAR Wuerttemberg 1A
❒ LAUINGEN/DONAU Bayern 1A 2B 6A
❒ LAUPHEIM Wuerttemberg 1A 2B
❒ LAURAHUETTE (Huta Laura) Schlesien 1A 2A 3A 6A
❒ LAUSCHA Sachsen-Meiningen 1A 7B
❒ LAUSICK, BAD Sachsen 1A
❒ LAUTA Brandenburg 1A 7B
❒ LAUTAWERK Brandenburg 2B
❒ LAUTENBACH Elsass 2A
❒ LAUTENBURG (Lidzbark) Westpreussen 1A
❒ LAUTENTHAL/HARZ Hannover 1A
❒ LAUTER Sachsen 2A 6B
❒ LAUTERBACH Hessen 1A 6A
❒ LAUTERBACH Wuerttemberg 2A

1 Mark, Gladbeck/W, POW, 1B

❒ LAUTERBACH/GLATZ Schlesien 2A
❒ LAUTERBERG/HARZ (Bad Lauterberg/Harz) Hannover 1A 2B
❒ LAUTERECKEN Pfalz 1A
❒ LAUTERN Ostpreussen 2A
❒ LAZISK Schlesien 5B
❒ LEBA Pommern 4A
❒ LEBUS Brandenburg 1A
❒ LECHENICH Nordrhein-Westfalen 14B
❒ LECHFELD Bayern 3A 9B
❒ LECK Schleswig-Holstein 1A
❒ LEER Hannover 2A 6A 8B 14E
❒ LEHE Hannover 1A 8A 10B
❒ LEHESTEN Sachsen-Meiningen 1A 2A 6A 7A 9B
❒ LEHRTE Hannover 1A 2C 9A
❒ LEICHLINGEN Rheinland 1A 6A
❒ LEIPHEIM Bayern 6A
❒ LEIPZIG Sachsen 1A 2A 7A 8B 9A 11B 12A 13A 14B
❒ LEIPZIG-BOEHLITZ-EHRENBERG Sachsen 2B
❒ LEIPZIG-CONNEWITZ Sachsen 2B
❒ LEIPZIG-DOELITZ Sachsen 2A
❒ LEIPZIG-EUTRITZSCH Sachsen 2A
❒ LEIPZIG-GAUTZSCH Sachsen 2B
❒ LEIPZIG-GOHLIS Sachsen 2B 7B
❒ LEIPZIG-GROSSZSCHOCHER Sachsen 2B
❒ LEIPZIG-HEITERBLICK Sachsen 2A 7B
❒ LEIPZIG-LEUTZSCH Sachsen 2A
❒ LEIPZIG-LIEBERTWOLKWITZ Sachsen 2A
❒ LEIPZIG-LINDENAU Sachsen 2A

1 Mark, Glashuette, 1A

10 Pfennig, Glatz, 6A

❒ LEIPZIG-MOELKAU Sachsen 2A 7B
❒ LEIPZIG-OETZSCH-MARKKLEEBERG Sachsen 2B
❒ LEIPZIG-PAUNSDORF Sachsen 2A
❒ LEIPZIG-PLAGWITZ Sachsen 2A 7B
❒ LEIPZIG-REUDNITZ Sachsen 2B
❒ LEIPZIG-SCHOENAU Sachsen 2A
❒ LEIPZIG-SELLERHAUSEN Sachsen 2A
❒ LEIPZIG-STOETTERITZ Sachsen 2B
❒ LEIPZIG-THONBERG Sachsen 2B
❒ LEIPZIG-VO Sachsen 2A
❒ LEIPZIG-WAHREN Sachsen 2B
❒ LEITHE Westfalen 2E
❒ LEKNO Posen 1B
❒ LEMBECK (Dorsten) Westfalen 1B 6A
❒ LEMBEK-ALTSCHERMBECK Westfalen 1B
❒ LEMGO Westfalen 1A 2B
❒ LENDRINGSEN (Soest) Westfalen 5A
❒ LENGEFELD/ERZGEBIRGE-VOGTLAND Sachsen 1A 2B 8A 13A
❒ LENGERICH Westfalen 1B 2E 7B
❒ LENGENERMOOR Hannover 3B
❒ LENGFURT/MAIN (Triefenstein) Bayern 7B
❒ LENGGRIES Bayern 1A 6B
❒ LENNEP (Remscheid) Rheinland 1A 2B 6A 7A 8B
❒ LENZEN/ELBE Brandenburg 1A
❒ LEOBSCHUETZ (Glubczyce) Schlesien 1A 2B 6A 8B
❒ LEONBERG Wuerttemberg 1A 7B
❒ LEOPOLDSHALL Anhalt 1A 3B
❒ LERBACH Hannover 1A
❒ LESSEN Westpreussen 6C
❒ LESUM Hannover 2A
❒ LETMATHE Westfalen 1A 2B 4B 5B 6A 7B
❒ LETTE/MUENSTER (Oelde) Westfalen 3C 7A
❒ LETTENREUTH (Michelau) Bayern 7A
❒ LEUBNITZ Sachsen 1A
❒ LEUBSDORF Sachsen 1A
❒ LEUKERSDORF Erzgebeit Sachsen 1A
❒ LEUNA WERKE (Leuna Werke "Walter Ulbricht") Provinz Sachsen 2B
❒ LEUTENBERG Schwarzburg-Rudolstadt 1A 6A 7B
❒ LEUTERSDORF O.L. Sachsen 1A 9A
❒ LEUTKIRCH/ALLGAEU Wuerttemberg 1A 6A 7B
❒ LEUTZSCH/LEIPZIG Sachsen 2A 7A
❒ LEVERKUSEN Rheinland 2A 3B 4B 5B 8B 14B
❒ LEVERKUSEN-WIESDORF Rheinland 2B
❒ LEWIN (Lewin Klodzki) Schlesien 1A
❒ LIBLAR (Erftstadt) Rheinland 4B 5B
❒ LICH Hessen 1A
❒ LICHTENAU (Loreba) Schlesien 2B 7A
❒ LICHTENBERG/ERZGEBIRGE Sachsen 7A
❒ LICHTENBURG/TORGAU Sachsen 3D 15B
❒ LICHTENFELS/MAIN Bayern 1A 2B 6A 8A 14B
❒ LICHTENHAIN (Schwarzburg-Rudolstadt) 7B
❒ LICHTENHORST Hannover 2A 3A 9A
❒ LICHTENSEE Sachsen 2A
❒ LICHTENSTEIN-CALLNBERG Sachsen 1A 2B
❒ LICHTENTAL Baden 7B
❒ LICHTENTANNE Sachsen 1A
❒ LICHTENWALDE/GLATZ Schlesien 2A
❒ LIEBAU (Lubawka) Schlesien 1A 2B 6A 7B
❒ LIEBENSTEIN BAD Sachsen-Meiningen 1A
❒ LIEBENWERDA (Bad Liebenwerda) Provinz Sachsen 1A 7B
❒ LIEBEROSE Brandenburg 1A
❒ LIEBERTWOLKWITZ Sachsen 1A 14B
❒ LIEBSTADT (Milakowo, Poland) Ostpreussen 1A 2B
❒ LIEGNITZ (Legnica) Schlesien 1A 2B 8A 11B 12A
❒ LIEPGARTEN Pommern 1A
❒ LIESEN Westfalen 2A
❒ LILIENTHAL Hannover 1A
❒ LIMBACH (Limbach-Oberfrohna) Sachsen 1A 2B 7B

50 Pfennig, Glauchau, 1A

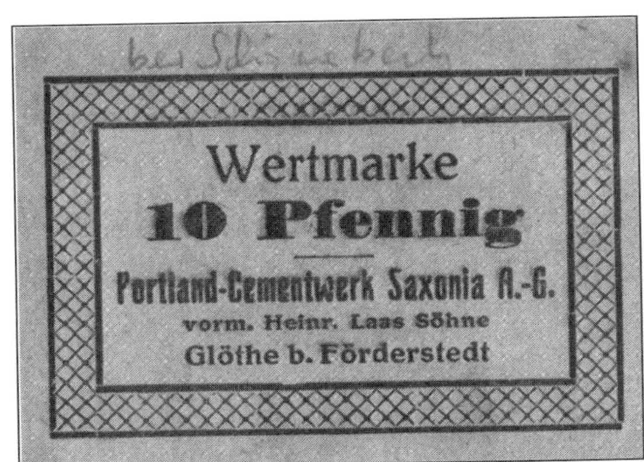

10 Pfennig, Gloethe, Germany, 2B

❒ LIMBURG/LAHN Hessen-Nassau 1A 7B 11B
❒ LINDAU UND WEILER Bayern 1A
❒ LINDAU/BODENSEE Bayern 1A 2A 11E 14B
❒ LINDAU/HARZ Hannover 1A 7B
❒ LINDEN-DAHLHAUSEN (Bochum) Westfalen 3B
❒ LINDEN/HANNOVER Hannover 2A
❒ LINDENAU (Leipzig) Sachsen 7B
❒ LINDENBERG/ALLGAEU Bayern 1A 2A 14B
❒ LINDENTHAL/LEIPZIG Sachsen 1A
❒ LINDERODE N-L (Lipinki; Luzyskie) Brandenburg 2A
❒ LINGEN Hannover 1A
❒ LINNICH Rheinland 1A
❒ LINTFORT (Kamp-Lintfort) Rheinland 2A 4B 5C
❒ LINTORF Rheinland 2B
❒ LINZ/RHEIN Rheinland 1A 2A 6A
❒ LIPINE (Lipiny) Schlesien 1A 2A 3C
❒ LIPPE Lippe 1A 6A
❒ LIPPEHNE (Lipiany) Brandenburg 1A 6A
❒ LIPPSPRINGE BAD Westfalen 1A
❒ LIPPSTADT Westfalen 1A 2C 6A 11B 13A
❒ LISDORF (Saarlouis) Rheinland 7B
❒ LISSA (Leszno) Posen 1A 6A
❒ LIST/SYLT Schleswig-Holstein 1A
❒ LOBBERICH Rheinland 1A 2B
❒ LOBEDA Sachsen-Weimar-Eisenach 1A
❒ LOBENSTEIN Thueringen 1A 2B
❒ LOBSDORF Sachsen 2B
❒ LOBSENS (Lobzenica) Posen 1A
❒ LOBSTAEDT Sachsen 1A
❒ LOCKSTEDT LAGER Schleswig-Holstein 1A 2A 10B
❒ LOEBAU Sachsen 1A 2B
❒ LOEBAU (Lubawa) Westpreussen 1A
❒ LOEBEJUEN Provinz Sachsen 1A
❒ LOEBERITZ/BITTERFELD Provinz Sachsen 2B
❒ LOECKNITZ Pommern 2B
❒ LOEFFINGEN Baden 1A
❒ LOENINGEN Oldenburg 3B
❒ LOERRACH Baden 1A 2A 6A 8A 9B
❒ LOESENBACH (Post Bruegge) Westfalen 2C
❒ LOESSE Hannover 3B
❒ LOESSNITZ/ERZGEBIRGE Sachsen 1A 2B
❒ LOETZEN (Lec; Gizycko) Ostpreussen 1A 3E
❒ LOEWEN (Lewin Brzeski) Schlesien 1B
❒ LOEWENBERG (Lwowek Slask) Schlesien 1A 2B 6A
❒ LOHMEN Sachsen 1B
❒ LOHNE Weser-Ems 3B
❒ LOHR/MAIN Bayern 1A 2A 6A 7B
❒ LOITZ Pommern 1A 8B
❒ LOLLAR Hessen 9B
❒ LOMMATZSCH Sachsen 1A 7A
❒ LOPISCHEWO (Lopiszewo/Ritschenwalde) Posen 1A 2B
❒ LORCH Hessen-Nassau 1A
❒ LORCH Wuerttemberg 2A 7B
❒ LORENZDORF (Lawszowa) Schlesien 7A
❒ LOSCHWITZ (Dresden) Sachsen 7B
❒ LOSLAU (Wodzislawska) Schlesien 1A 6A
❒ LOSSEN (Losina; Losiow) Schlesien 7A
❒ LOTHRINGEN Lothringen 1A
❒ LUBAN (Lubau) Posen 1A 2A 5B
❒ LUBICHOW (Lubiechowo) Westpreussen 1A
❒ LUBLIN (Lueben; Lioublin) Schlesien 1A 2A
❒ LUBLINITZ (Lubliniec) Schlesien 1A
❒ LUCKA Sachsen-Altenburg 1A
❒ LUCKAU Brandenburg 1A 13A
❒ LUCKENWALDE Brandenburg 1A 2A 7B
❒ LUDENDORF Rheinland 1A
❒ LUDWIGSBURG Wuerttemberg 1A 3B 6A 8B
❒ LUDWIGSDORF Schlesien 3D
❒ LUDWIGSHAFEN/RHEIN Pfalz 1A 2B 3E 6A 7A 8A
❒ LUDWIGSHUETTE/BIEDENKOPF Hessen-Nassau 2B
❒ LUDWIGSLUST Mecklenburg-Schwerin 1A
❒ LUDWIGSSTADT Bayern 1A
❒ LUDWIGSTEIN Hessen-Nassau 1A
❒ LUDWIGSTAL Wuerttemberg 3C
❒ LUEBBECKE Westfalen 1A 2D
❒ LUEBBEN/SPREE Brandenburg 1A 14B
❒ LUEBCHEN (Lubow; Lubin) Schiesien 7B 10B
❒ LUEBECK Schleswig-Holstein 1A 2A 3B 7A 10A 12B 14B
❒ LUEBEN (Lubin) Schlesien 1A 2A 7A
❒ LUEBBERSTEDT Hannover 3B
❒ LUEBTHEEN Mecklenburg-Schwerin 1A
❒ LUEBZ Mecklenburg-Schwerin 1A
❒ LUECHOW Hannover 1A
❒ LUECHTRINGEN Westfalen 1A

10 Pfennig, Gnoien, Germany, 1A

50 Pfennig, Goch, 1A

❒ LUEDENSCHEID Westfalen 1A 2B 6A 8A
❒ LUEDERSDORF Brandenburg 2A
❒ LUEDINGHAUSEN Westfalen 1A 5B 7A
❒ LUEGDE Westfalen 1A 2C 3C 7B
❒ LUEGUMKLOSTER (Loegumkloster, Denmark) Schleswig-Holstein 1A
❒ LUENEBURG Hannover 1A 2A 3B 5B 6A 10A 14B
❒ LUENEN Westfalen 1A 2A 4B 7B
❒ LUENOW/ANGERMUENDE Brandenburg 2B
❒ LUETGENDORTMUND (Dortmund) Westfalen 1A 2B 5B 11B
❒ LUETJENBURG Schleswig-Holstein 1A 2B
❒ LUETTRINGHAUSEN Rheinland 1A 2B
❒ LUETZELHAUSEN Elsass 1A
❒ LUETZEN Sachsen 6A 13D
❒ LUETZSCHENA Sachsen 7A
❒ LUGA Sachsen 7A
❒ LUGAU Sachsen 1A 7B
❒ LUGAU Schiesien 5A
❒ LUND-SCHOBUELL Schleswig-Holstein 1A
❒ LUNDEN Schleswig-Holstein 1A
❒ LUNDERUP (Roten Krug; Roede Kro, Denmark) Schleswig-Holstein 1A
❒ LUNOW/ANGERMUENDE Brandenburg 2A
❒ LUNZENAU/MULDE Sachsen 1A
❒ LUTTER/BARENBERGE Braunschweig 1A 2A

25 Pfennig, Goerlitz, Germany, 2B

❒ LUTTERBACH Elsass 1A
❒ LUTZHOEFT Schleswig-Holstein 1A
❒ LUXEMBURG-HOLLERICH Ruhr 7A
❒ LYCHEN Brandenburg 2A 7B
❒ LYCK Ostpreussen 1A
❒ MACZEIKOWITZ (Maciejkowice) Schiesien 1A
❒ MADEBACH Sachsen-Gotha 1A
❒ MADUESEE (Miedwie) Pommern 2A
❒ MAGDEBURG Provinz Sachsen 1A 2A 3A 4B 5D 6A 7A 9A 11B 12C
❒ MAGDEBURG UND HALBERSTADT Provinz Sachsen 1A 2B
❒ MAGDEBURG-BUCKAU Provinz Sachsen 2A 7A
❒ MAGDEBURG-SUEDOST Provinz Sachsen 7A
❒ MAGDEBURG/NEUSTADT Provinz Sachsen 2A 3A
❒ MAIKAMMER Pfalz 1A
❒ MAINBERNHEIM Bayern 1A
❒ MAINBURG Bayern 2A 6A
❒ MAINZ Hessen 1A 2A 3A 4A 5B 6A 7B 8B 9B 10A 11B
❒ MAINZ-WIESBADEN Hessen 11B
❒ MAISACH Bayern 4A
❒ MALAPANE (Ozimek) Schlesien 3C 9B
❒ MALBERG/KYLLBURG Rheinland 2C
❒ MALCHIN Mecklenburg-Schwerin 1A
❒ MALCHOW Mecklenburg-Schwerin 1A
❒ MALENTE-GREMSMUEHLEN Schleswig-Holstein 1A
❒ MALLMITZ (Malomice) Schiesien 1A 2B
❒ MALMERSPACH Elsass 1A
❒ MALTSCHAWE (Malazow) Schlesien 1A 7B
❒ MAMMING Bayern 1A
❒ MANEBACH Sachsen-Gotha 1A 9B
❒ MANNHEIM Baden 1A 2B 3E 6A 7A 11A 12B 14A
❒ MANNHEIM-WALDHOF Baden 2B
❒ MANSFELD-LANGENDREER Zeche Westfalen 5B
❒ MANSFELD/SEEKREIS Sachsen 1A
❒ MARBACH/FLOEHATAL Sachsen 1A
❒ MARBACH/NECKAR Wuerttemberg 1A 2B 6A 13B
❒ MARBURG/LAHN Hessen-Nassau 1A 6A 10A 11C 12A

1 Pfennig, Goerlitz, 1A

❒ MARCARDSMOOR Hannover 3B
❒ MARGGRABOWA (Marggrabowo, Treuburg, Olecko, Oletzko) Ostpreusse 1A
❒ MARIENBERG Hessen-Nassau 1A 7B
❒ MARIENBERG Sachsen 1B
❒ MARIENBERG/WUERZBURG Bayern 3B
❒ MARIENBERGHAUSEN Rheinland 1A
❒ MARIENBORN Westfalen 2E
❒ MARIENBURG (Maiborg) Westpreussen 1A 2B
❒ MARIENHAGEN Hannover 2A 7B
❒ MARIENHEIDE Rheinland 1A
❒ MARIENHOEHE/SCHWETZ Posen 2B
❒ MARIENHUETTE Schlesien 1A
❒ MARIENSTEIN Bayern 1A 3C 7B
❒ MARIENTHAL Bayern 2A
❒ MARIENTHAL Schiesien 2B
❒ MARIENWERDER/LITTLE NOGAT (Kwidzyn) Westpreussen 1A 2A 6A
❒ MARKDORF Baden 1A
❒ MARKERSDORF/LEIPZIG Sachsen 1A 2A 7A
❒ MARKIRCH (Sainte-Marie-aux-Mines) Elsass 1A 2B
❒ MARKLISSA/QUEISS (Lesna, Nowe Hajduki) Schlesien 2B 7A
❒ MARKNEUKIRCHEN Sachsen 1A
❒ MARKRANSTAEDT Sachsen 1A 2A
❒ MARKSTAEDT (Miescisko) Posen 1A 6B
❒ MARKTBIBART/EHE Bayern 6B
❒ MARKTHEIDENFELD Bayern 1A 6A
❒ MARKTLEUTHEN Bayern 2A 6B
❒ MARKTREDWITZ Bayern 1A 2A 6A
❒ MARKTSCHORGAST Bayern 1A 6A
❒ MARL Westfalen 1A 2B 3C 5C
❒ MARLOW (Mecklenburg-Schwerin) 1A
❒ MARNE Schleswig-Holstein 1A 2A
❒ MARSBERG Westfalen 2A
❒ MARTEN Westfalen 1A 2C
❒ MARTERBUESCHEL Sachsen 2A
❒ MARTINRODA Sachsen-Gotha 7A
❒ MASMUENSTER Elsass 1A 2A
❒ MASSEN/UNNA Westfalen 2A 5B 7A
❒ MASSING/ROTT Bayern 1A
❒ MASSOW (Maszewo, Mascewo) Pommern 1A
❒ MAUDACH Pfalz 7B
❒ MAULBRONN Wuerttemberg 1A 6A
❒ MAULBURG Baden 1A
❒ MAUTH Niederbayern 1A
❒ MAXIMILIANSAU Pfalz 1A
❒ MAYEN Rheinland 1A 2A 6E 7B 8B 11B
❒ MAYEN UND ANDERNACH Rheinland 1A
❒ MECHERNICH Rheinland 1B 2B
❒ MECKENHEIM Rheinland 1B
❒ MECKLENBURG-SCHWERIN 1A
❒ MECKLENBURG-STRELITZ (Neustrelitz) 1A
❒ MECKLINGEN Hannover 3B
❒ MEDEBACH (Medebeke) Westfalen 1A 2B 7A
❒ MEERANE Sachsen 1A 7B 8B
❒ MEERANE & MUELSEN-ST. JAKOB Sachsen 2A
❒ MEHLEM/RHEIN Rheinland 2A 5B
❒ MEHLIS (Zella-Mehlis, Melis) Sachsen-Gotha 1A 7B
❒ MEHLSACH (Olsztyn, Pienieznc) Ostpreussen 2A 7B
❒ MEIDERICH (Duisburg) Rheinland 7B
❒ MEINERSDORF/ERZGEBIRGE Sachsen 1A
❒ MEINERSEN Hannover 2A
❒ MEINERZHAGEN Westfalen 1A 2A
❒ MEININGEN Sachsen-Meiningen 1A 2A 7B
❒ MEISENHEIM/GLAN Rheinland 1A
❒ MEISSEN/ELBE Sachsen 1A 2C 7A 8B 12A 13A
❒ MEISSEN/MINDEN Westfalen 2A
❒ MELDORF Schleswig-Holstein 2A
❒ MELLE/ELSE Hannover 1A
❒ MELLENBACH Schwarzburg-Rudolstadt 1A 2B
❒ MELLRICHSTADT/SAALE Bayern 1A

10 Pfennig, Goerlitz, POW, 6A

50 Pfennig, Goettingen, 1A

❒ MELSUNGEN/FULDA Hessen-Nassau 1A 6A
❒ MEMEL/DAMGE NEMAN, NEMUNAS NIEMAN (Klaipeda) Ostpreussen 2A
❒ MEMEL/DAMGE NEMAN, NEUMUNAS NIEMEN(Memelburg) Ostpreussen 1A
❒ MEMMINGEN Bayern 1A 14B
❒ MENDEN Westfalen 1A 2C 6A 7B
❒ MENGEDE Westfalen 1A
❒ MENGEN/DANUBE Wuerttemberg 1A 2B 6A
❒ MENTERODA Provinz Sachsen 1A 2A 7A
❒ MEPPEN/EMS Hannover 1A 2C 7A 14B
❒ MERGELSTETTEN Wuerttemberg 2A
❒ MERGENTHEIM, BAD/TAUBER (Marienthal) Wuerttemberg 1A 6A
❒ MERLENBACH Lothringen 6B
❒ MERSEBURG/SAALE Sachsen 1A 2A 3A 7A 9B 13B
❒ MERZDORF (Marcinkowice, Zagan) Schiesien 5B 7B
❒ MERZIG-WADERN/SAAR Rheinland 2A
❒ MERZIG/SAAR Rheinland 1A 3B
❒ MESCHEDE/RUHR Westfalen 1A 2D 9A
❒ MESERITZ/OBRA (Miedzyrzecs) Posen 1A 6A
❒ MESSEL Hessen 7A
❒ MESSINGHAUSEN BEI BRILON Westfalen 2D
❒ METTENDORF Rheinland 2B
❒ METTERNICH (Rheinprovinz) 11B
❒ METTLACH Rheinland 1A 2A
❒ METTMANN/DUESSEL Rheinland 1A 2A 6A 7A 11B
❒ METZ/MOSELLE-SEILLE Lothringen 1A 3B 5C
❒ METZERAL Elsass 2A
❒ METZINGEN Wuerttemberg 1A
❒ MEURA Thueringen 1A
❒ MEUSELBACH Thueringen 1B 6A
❒ MEUSELWITZ Thueringen 1A 2A 6A 7A 11B
❒ MEWE/VISTULA (Gniew nad Wisla) Westpreussen 1A 3E 4A
❒ MEYENBURG/PRIGNITZ Brandenburg 1A 3B
❒ MICHAELSTHAL/GLATZ Schlesien 1A 2B
❒ MICHALKOWITZ (Michalkowice, Michalowskiego Piotra) Schlesien 1A
❒ MICHELAU Bayern 1A
❒ MICHELBACH/ODENWALD Hessen 1A
❒ MICHELSTADT Hessen-Nassau 4B 7C
❒ MICHENDORF Brandenburg 2A
❒ MIDDOGE Weser-Ems 1D
❒ MIECHOWITZ (Miechowice, Miechowska) Schlessien 1A 5B
❒ MIESBACH Bayern 1A 2A 6A 7B 9A
❒ MIETINGEN Wuerttemberg 1A
❒ MIKOLOW Schlesien 1A
❒ MIKULTSCHUETZ (Mikulskiego) Schiesien 1A 5B
❒ MILBERTSHOFEN Bayern 2A
❒ MILDENAU/ERZGEBIRGE Sachsen 1A
❒ MILITSCH (Milicz, Milicka) Schiesien 1A
❒ MILLINGEN Rheinland 1A
❒ MILOSLAW (Miloslau) Posen 1A
❒ MILSPE Westfalen 1A 2A
❒ MILTENBERG/MAIN Bayern 1A 2A 14B
❒ MILTITZ Sachsen 2A
❒ MINDELHEIM/MINDE Bayern 1A 4A 7A 8B
❒ MINDEN Westfalen 1A 2E 3B 4A 7B 8A
❒ MINISTER ACHENBACH 5A
❒ MIROW Mecklenburg-Strelitz 1A 2A
❒ MISBURG Hannover 2A
❒ MISDROY (Miedzyzdroje) Pommern 2B
❒ MISTELBACH/LAYA Bayern 1A
❒ MITTEL-LAZISK Schlesien 1A
❒ MITTELBACH/CHEMNITZ Sachsen 2A
❒ MITTELFROHNA Sachsen 1A
❒ MITTELSTEINE Schiesien 2A
❒ MITTELWALDE (Miedzylesie) Schiesien 1A 2B 7A
❒ MITTENWALD/ISAR Bayern 1A
❒ MITTERTEICH Bayern 1A 2A 7B 9A
❒ MITTWEIDA/ZSCHOPPAU Sachsen 1A 2A 7B 8B
❒ MITZACH Elsass 1A 7B 8B
❒ MONCHEHOF Bayern 3C
❒ MOCHENWANGEN Wuerttemberg 2B
❒ MOEGELTONDERN (Moegeltoender, Denmark) Schleswig-Holstein 1B

1 Pfennig, Goldbach, Germany, 7B

1 Pfg.
Centralmolkerei
Goldbach

25 Pfennig, Goldberg/Schl, 1A

❐ MOELKAU-LEIPZIG Sachsen 1A
❐ MOELKE (Milko, Silkowska) Schlesien 2A 4A 5B 7A
❐ MOELKE-LUDWIGSDORF Schiesien 5A
❐ MOELLENBECK Hessen-Nassau 1A
❐ MOELLENBECK Schaumburg 1A
❐ MOELLN Schleswig-Holstein 1A 2B
❐ MOERS Rheinland 1A 2A
❐ MOGILNO (Gembitz, Gebice) Posen 1A 6B 14B
❐ MOHLSDORF/GREIZ Reuss J.L. 2A 7B
❐ MOHRKIRCH Schleswig-Holstein 14B
❐ MOHRUNGEN (Morag) Ostpreussen 1A
❐ MOLLAU Elsass 1A
❐ MOMBACH Hessen 7B
❐ MONHEIM Rheinland 2A
❐ MONSCHAU Rheinland 1A
❐ MONTABAUR Hessen-Nassau 1A 4A 5E 6A 7A
❐ MOOS Bayern 1A

Types of Emergency Money

Type	Reference #
Municipal paper	1
Private paper	2
POW paper	3
POW official metal	4
POW private metal	5
Municipal metal	6
Private metal	7
Gas tokens	8
Food; beer; konsumverein	9
Naval; military; kantine	10
Encased, unencased stamps	11
Streetcar tokens	12
Porcelain	13
World War II issues	14
Concentration, Civilian internment camps	15

Rarity grades: A, to $25; B, to $60; C, to $125; D, to $200; and E, $350

❐ MOOSBURG/ISAR Bayern 1A 3A 7A
❐ MOOSCH Elsass 1A 7B
❐ MORGENROTH Kreis Beuthen Schiesien 5A
❐ MORINGEN Hannover 2A
❐ MORSBACH Rheinland 1A
❐ MORSUM/SYLT Schleswig-Holstein 1A
❐ MOSBACH Baden 1A 2A 6A
❐ MOYS Schlesien 1A 2A
❐ MROTSCHEN (Mrocza) Posen 1A
❐ MUCH Rheinland 1A
❐ MUCHENITZ (Mechnice) Schlesien 1B
❐ MUECHELN/GEISSELBACH Provinz Sachsen 1A 2A 7B
❐ MUECKENBERG Provinz Sachsen 1A
❐ MUEDEN/Oertze Hannover 3B
❐ MUEGELN Sachsen 1A
❐ MUEGGENBUURGER MOOR Hannover 3B
❐ MUEHLACKER Wuerttemberg 7B
❐ MUEHLAU/CHEMNITZ Sachsen 1A 2A
❐ MUEHLBERG/ELBE Provinz Sachsen 1A 6A 14B
❐ MUEHLDORF-NEUMARKT/ROTT Bayern 6A
❐ MUEHLDORF/INN Bayern 1A 2A
❐ MUEHLEN Rheinland 2A
❐ MUEHLENRAHMEDE Westfalen 2B
❐ MUEHLHAUSEN (Thomas Muentzer-Stadt Muehlhausen) Provinz Sachsen 1A 2A 6A 7A 8B 12B
❐ MUEHLRAUSEN, WORBIS & HEILIGENSTADT Provinz Sachsen 2A
❐ MUEHLHEIM/MAIN Hessen-Nassau 1A 6A 7A
❐ MUEHLWAND/VOGTLAND Sachsen 2A
❐ MUELHAUSEN/ILL (Mulhouse) Elsass 1A 7B 10A 12B 14B
❐ MUELHEIM Elsass 7B
❐ MUELHEIM/RUHR Rheinland 1A 2A 3A 5B 6A 7B 10B 11B 12A
❐ MUELLHEIM Baden 1A 6A
❐ MUELSEN-ST. JAKOB Sachsen 1A
❐ MUELSEN-ST. MICHELN Sachsen 1A
❐ MUENCHBERG/PULSNITZ Bayern 1A 2A 6A
❐ MUENCHEBERG Brandenberg 3A 6A
❐ MUENCHEHAGEN Hannover 2C

10 Pfennig, Gorzno/Westpreussen, Germany, 1B

2 Mark, Gostyn, Germany, 2B

Types of Emergency Money

Type	Reference #
Municipal paper	1
Private paper	2
POW paper	3
POW official metal	4
POW private metal	5
Municipal metal	6
Private metal	7
Gas tokens	8
Food; beer; konsumverein	9
Naval; military; kantine	10
Encased, unencased stamps	11
Streetcar tokens	12
Porcelain	13
World War II issues	14
Concentration, Civilian internment camps	15

Rarity grades: A, to $25; B, to $60; C, to $125; D, to $200; and E, $350

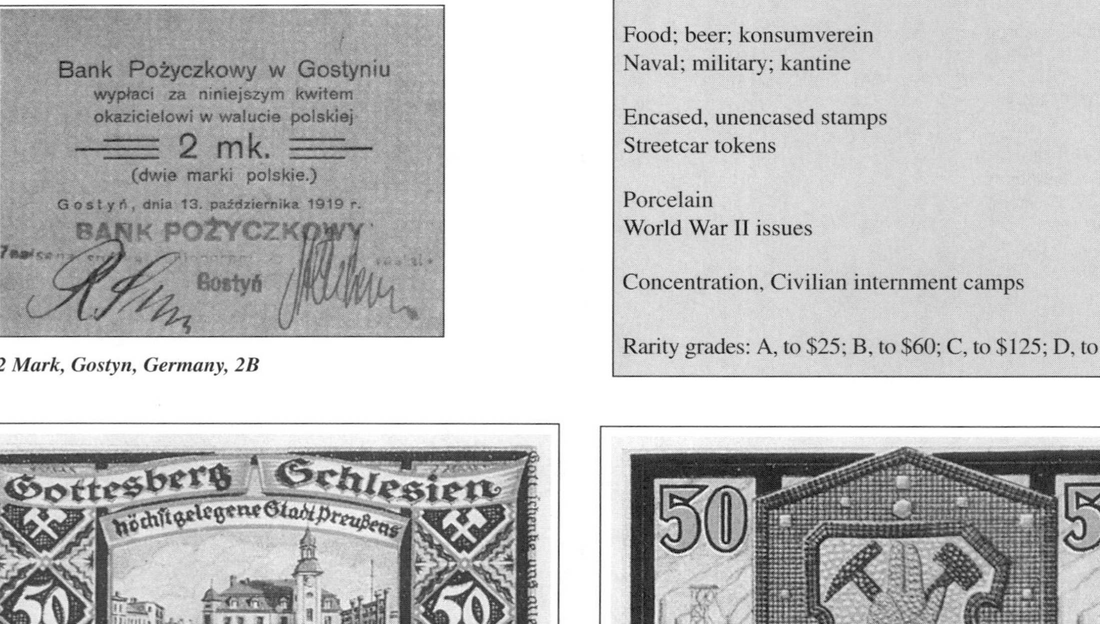

50 Pfennig, Gottesberg, 1A

50 Pfennig, Graefenthal, 1A

50 Pfennig, Grafenstaeden, 1A

1 Mark, Gramby, 1A

50 Pfennig, Graudenz, Germany, 1B

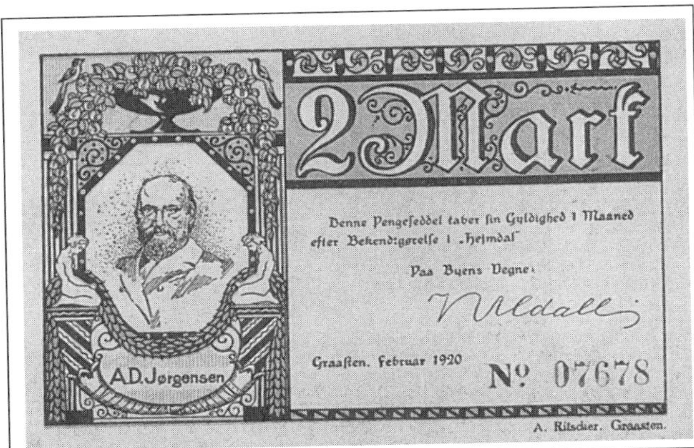

2 Mark, Graasten, 1A

50 Pfennig, Greiz, 1A

25 Pfennig, Greussen, 1A

50 Pfennig, Grevesmuehlen/M, 1A

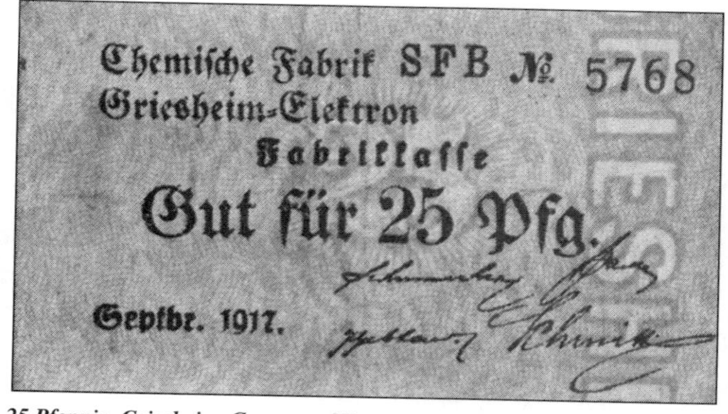

25 Pfennig, Griesheim, Germany, 2B

75 Pfennig, Groemitz, 1A

20 Pfennig, Groitzsch/S, Germany, 2A

❒ MUENCHEN-FREISING Bayern 7A
❒ MUENCHEN-GIESING Bayern 7A
❒ MUENCHEN-GLADBACH (Moenchen Gladbach) Rheinland 1A 2E 7B 8A
❒ MUENCHEN-GLADBACH & RHEYDT Rheinland 1A 2A 8B
❒ MUENCHEN-MOOSACH Bayern 7B
❒ MUENCHEN-NEUAUBINGBayern2A
❒ MUENCHEN-NYMPHENBURG Bayern 2A
❒ MUENCHEN-PASING Bayern 1A
❒ MUENCHEN-PERLACH Bayern 2A
❒ MUENCHEN-SOLLN Bayern 2A
❒ MUENCHEN-SUED Bayern 7A
❒ MUENCHEN/ISARBayern 1A 2A 5E 6A 7A 8A 9A 10B 11B 12B 14B
❒ MUENCHENBERNSDORF Thueringen 1A 2A
❒ MUENDEN (Hannoverisch-Muenden) Hannover 4A 6B 11B
❒ MUENDER/DEISTER (Bad Muender) Hannover 2C
❒ MUENNERSTADT Bayern 1A
❒ MUENSINGEN Wuerttemberg 3A 4A 6A
❒ MUENSTER Elsass 1A
❒ MUENSTER Westfalen 1A 2A 3A 4A 6A 11B 14B
❒ MUENSTER/NECKAR Wuerttemberg 4A 6A 7C
❒ MUENSTERBERG/OHLAU (Ziebice) Schiesien 1A 6A 7B 13C
❒ MUENSTEREIFEL/ERFT Rheinland 1A
❒ MUENSTERMAIFELD (Muenster-Mayfeld) Rheinland 1A
❒ MUERITZ/OSTSEEBAD (Graal-Mueritz)
❒ MUERWIK Schleswig-Holstein 2A 10B
❒ MUESCHEDE (Arnsberg) Westfalen 7B
❒ MULDA Sachsen 1A
❒ MULDENSTEIN Provinz Sachsen 7A
❒ MUMSDORF Provinz Sachsen 2A 7B
❒ MUNDERKINGEN/DANUBE Wuerttemberg 1A 6A
❒ MUNSTER/Oertze Hannover 5B
❒ MUNSTERLAGER/Oertze Hannover 2A 3B 10B
❒ MURG Baden 1A 2A
❒ MURNAU Bayern 1A 2A 3C 5C 14B
❒ MURRHARDT/MURR Wuerttemberg 1A 2A 6A
❒ MUSKAU/NEISSE (Bad Muskau) Schiesien 1A 2B 11C
❒ MUTZSCHEN (Mutzchen) Sachsen 1A
❒ MYLAU/Vogtland Sachsen 1A 2A 7A
❒ MYSLOWITZ (Myslowice) Schiesien 1B

❒ NABBURG/NAAB Bayern 1A 2A
❒ NACHOD/METTAU Westfalen 7A
❒ NACHRODT Westfalen 2B 5B
❒ NACHTERSTADT Provinz Sachsen 1A
❒ NAGOLD-ALTENSTEIG Wuerttemberg 2A
❒ NAGOLD/ NAGOLD Wuerttemberg 1A 2A 6A
❒ NAILA Bayern 1A 2A 6A
❒ NAKEL/NETZKE (Naklo, Nackel) Posen 1A
❒ NAMSLAU/WEIDA (Namyslow) Schiesien 1A 2B
❒ NANDLSTADT Bayern 2A
❒ NANSEN Hannover 3B
❒ NASSAU/LAHN Hessen-Nassau 1A
❒ NASTAETTEN/MUEHLBACK Hessen-Nassau 1A 8B
❒ NATTHEIM Wuerttemberg 1A
❒ NAUEN/OSTHAVELLAND Brandenburg 7B
❒ NAUGARD (Nowogard) Pommern 2A
❒ NAUHEIM BAD Hessen 1A 2A 8B
❒ NAUMBURG/QUEISS Schlesien 2B
❒ NAUMBURG/SAALE Provinz Sachsen 1A 2D 6A 8A 9A 10B
❒ NAUNDORF/KOETZSCHENBRODA Sachsen 12B
❒ NAUNHOF/PAARDE Sachsen 1A 2A 7B 13B
❒ NEBRA/UNSTRUT Provinz Sachsen 1A
❒ NECKARGEMUEND/ELSENZ & NECKAR Baden 1A
❒ NECKARSULM/SULM & NECKAR Wuerttemberg 1A 2A 6A
❒ NECKENDORF (Lutherstadt Eisleben) Provinz Sachsen 7A
❒ NEHEIM/RUHR Westfalen 1A 2E 6A
❒ NEHEIM-HUESTEN Westfalen 14A
❒ NEIDENBURG (Nidzica, Nidborg) Ostpreussen 1A 6A
❒ NEIDENFELS Pfalz 1A
❒ NEINBERG Bremen 14B
❒ NEINDORF/HEDWIGSBURG Braunschweig 2A
❒ NEINSTEDT/HARZ Provinz Sachsen 1A 7B
❒ NEISSE-NEULAND Schlesien 1A 3B
❒ NEISSE/NEISSE (Nysa, Nyska, Schlesien) 1A 2B 3A 4A 6A 8B 9A 10A
❒ NERCHAU/MULDE Sachsen 1A 2A
❒ NERESHEIM Wuerttemberg 1A 2A
❒ NERKEWITZ/JENA Thueringen 5C 14B
❒ NESSELWANG Bayern 1A 8B
❒ NETZEKREIS (Schoenlanke, Trzcianka) Pommern1A

10 Pfennig, Gronau/H, Germany, 1A

50 Pfennig, Gross-Poritsch, 1A

❐ NETZSCHKAU/VOGTLAND Sachsen 1A 2A 9B
❐ NEU ASTENBERG Westfalen 1A
❐ NEU EIBENBERG Sachsen 2A
❐ NEU ROETHENBACH Bayern 7A
❐ NEU ULM Bayern 1A 6A
❐ NEU WEISSTEIN (Kamionek) Schiesien 2B
❐ NEUBAMBERG Hessen 1A
❐ NEUBECKUM Westfalen 1E 2D 5D
❐ NEUBERUN (Nowy Bierun) Schlesien 7B
❐ NEUBRANDENBURG Mecklenburg-Strelitz 1A 2A 3C 14B
❐ NEUBUKOW Mecklenburg-Schwerin 1A 2A
❐ NEUBURG/DONAU Bayern 1A 2A 3C 6A
❐ NEUBURG/INN Bayern 2E
❐ NEUBURG/KAMMEL Bayern 3B
❐ NEUDAMM (Debno) Brandenburg 1A 6A
❐ NEUDAMM/FRANKFURT/MAIN Hessen-Nassau 6A
❐ NEUDECK (Swierklaniec) Schiesien 2B
❐ NEUDORF (Nowa Wies) Schlesien 1A 2B
❐ NEUDORF/ERZGEBIRGE Sachsen 1A
❐ NEUEIBAU Sachsen 2A
❐ NEUENAHR, BAD Rheinland 1A 2A 7A
❐ NEUENBEKEN Westfalen 3D
❐ NEUENBUERG/ERZ Wuerttemberg 2A 6A
❐ NEUENGAMME/HAMBURG Hamburg 3E 15B
❐ NEUENHAUS/HILGEN Rheinland 2D
❐ NEUENKIRCHEN Westfalen 1E 3B 4B 14D
❐ NEUENMARKT Bayern 1A 4B
❐ NEUENRADE Westfalen 1A 2C 3B
❐ NEUENSCHWAND (Bodenwoehr) 9B

5 Pfennig, Grossdeuben, Germany, 1B

50 Pfennig, Grosswartenburg, 13B

❐ NEUENSTADT/KOCHER Wuerttemberg 2A
❐ NEUENWERK Hannover 3B
❐ NEUERBURG Rheinland 2A
❐ NEUFFEN Wuerttemberg 1A
❐ NEUGERSDORF Sachsen 1A 2A
❐ NEUGRABEN-HAUSBRUCH (Hamburg) Schleswig-Holstein 1A
❐ NEUHALDENSLEBEN Sachsen 1A 2D
❐ NEUHAMMER Schlesien 3A
❐ NEUHAUS Sachsen-Meiningen 2A 6A
❐ NEUHAUS Thueringen 2A 6A
❐ NEUHAUS/ELBE Hannover 1A 2A 3D
❐ NEUHAUS/INN Bayern 2A
❐ NEUHAUS/OSTE Hannover 1A
❐ NEUHAUS/OSTSEE Mecklenburg-Schwerin 2A
❐ NEUHAUS/RENNWEG Schwarzburg-Rudolstadt 1A 6A
❐ NEUHAUS Westfalen 1A 2A 3C
❐ NEUHAUS/AVIGNON Westfalen 4A
❐ NEUHAUSEN/ERZGEBIRGE Sachsen 1A 2A
❐ NEUHEIDUK (Nowe Hajduki, Hajducka) Schlesien 1B
❐ NEUHOF Hessen-Nassau 1A
❐ NEUKALEN Mecklenburg-Schwerin 1A
❐ NEUKIRCH Luebeck Swindle issue 2A
❐ NEUKIRCH (Nowa Cerkwia, Kerekwie) Schlesien 2B 7A
❐ NEUKIRCHEN/HEIL BLUT Bayern 1A 6A
❐ NEUKIRCHEN/PLEISSE Sachsen 2A
❐ NEUKIRCHEN/VOGTLAND Sachsen 1A

1.50 Mark, Hahnenklee/Harz, Germany, 2A

75 Pfennig, Altona, 1A

50 Pfennig, Apolda, 1A

2 Mark, Archsum/Sylt, 1A

50 Pfennig, Berchtesgaden, 1A

1 Mark, Berleburg, 1A

10 Gold Mark, Bielefeld, 1B

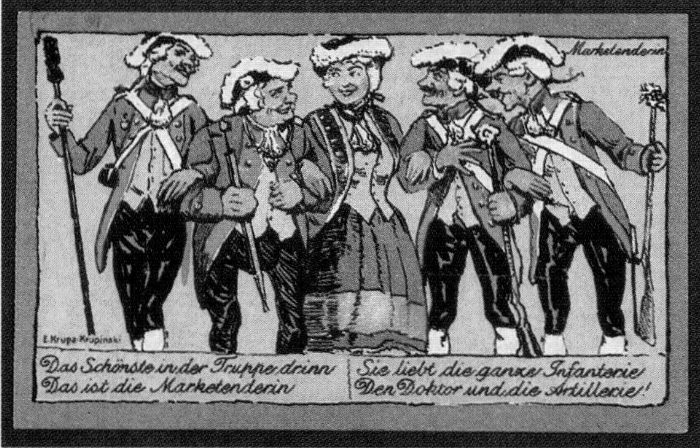

50 Pfennig, Bonn, 1A

75 Pfennig, Bordesholm, 1A

50 Pfennig, Borstel, 1A

80 Heller, Brandenberg/Tirol, 1A

50 Pfennig, Braunlage, 1A

10 Pfennig, Braunschweig, 1A

50 Pfennig, Brehna, 1A

75 Pfennig, Bremen, 1A

10 Mark, Breslau, 1B

1 Mark, Broacker, 1A

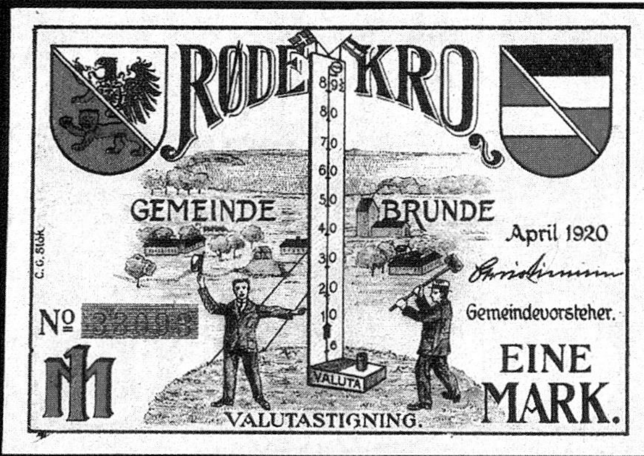

1 Mark, Brunde, 1A

25 Pfennig, Brunsbüttelkoog, 1A

1 Mark, Bruchhausen, 1A

50 Pfennig, Calbe, 1A

75 Pfennig, Chrosczütz O/S, 1A

50 Pfennig, Crivitz, 1A

50 Pfennig, Cuxhafen, 1A

10 Pfennig, Eferding, 1A

1 Mark, Eickel, 1A

1 Mark, Eisbergen, 1A

2 Mark, Elmshorn, 1A

1 Mark, Erfde, 1A

50 Pfennig, Erfurt, 1A

50 Pfennig, Flensburg, 1A

50 Pfennig, Friedrichroda, 1A

1 Mark, Glücksburg, 1A

25 Pfennig, Gatersleben, 1A

25 Pfennig, Gräfenroda, 1A

10 Heller, Hadersfeld, 1A

30 Heller, Hall/Tyrol, 1A

50 Pfennig, Harburg, 1A

10 Heller, Hausmening, 1A

90 Heller, Irdning, 1A

50 Pfennig, Kahla, 1A

50 Pfennig, Karlstadt, 1A

50 Pfennig, Kampen/Sylt, 1A

25 Pfennig, Kiel, 1A

50 Pfennig, Kirn, 1A

50 Pfennig, Köln, 1A

50 Pfennig, Königsberg/Pr., 1A

50 Pfennig, Königswinter, 1A

25 Pfennig, Kudowa, Bad, 1A

50 Pfennig, Lausa, 1A

75 Pfennig, Lippspringe, 1A

50 Pfennig, Lichtenhorst, 1A

25 Pfennig, Lübtheen, 1A

1 Mark, Lund, 1A

50 Pfennig, Namslav, 1A

50 Pfennig, Marktschornest, 1A

50 Pfennig, Mögeltondern, 1A

2 Mark, Neheim, 1A

10 Pfennig, Netzschau, 1A

3 Mark, Neuhaus, 1A

50 Pfennig, Neuruppin, 1A

75 Pfennig, Nimptscht/Schlesien, 1A

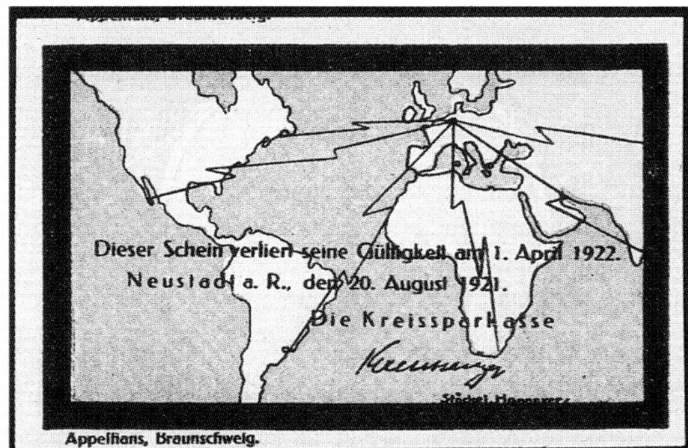

50 Pfennig, Neustadt, 1A

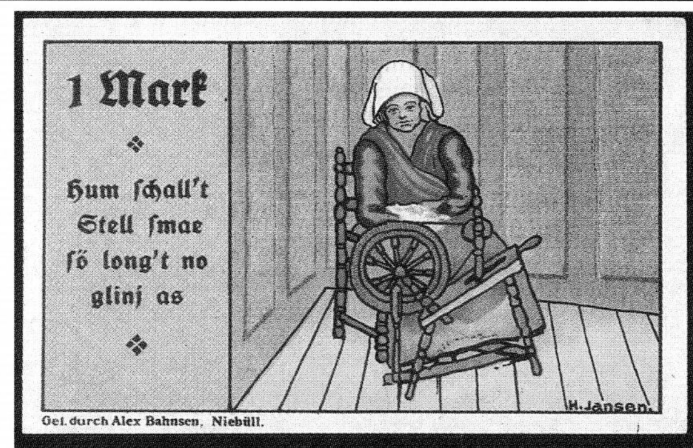

1 Mark, Niebüll, 1A

25 Pfennig, Nordenhausen, 1A

25 Pfennig, Nortorf, 1A

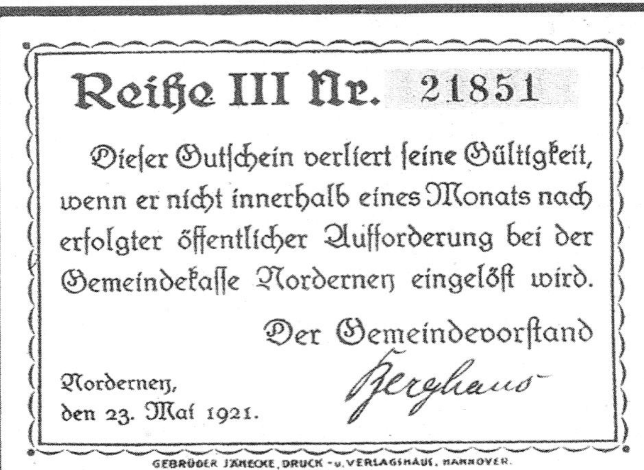

25 Pfennig, Norderney, 1A

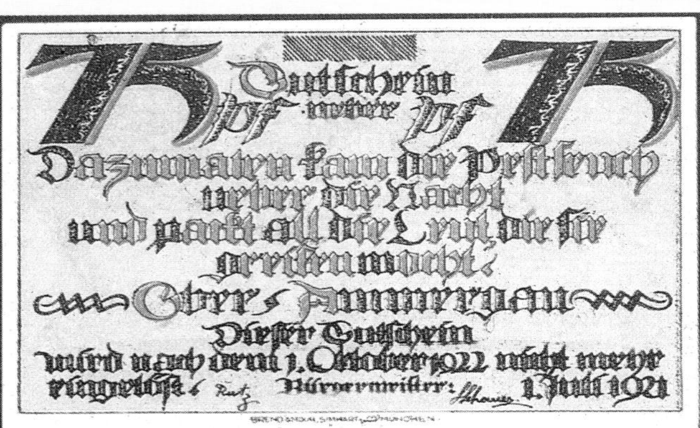

75 Pfennig, Oberammergau, 1A

50 Pfennig, Oberheldrungen, 1A

50 Heller, Obernberg, 1A

100 Pfennig, Oels, 1A

50 Pfennig, Ohlau, 1A

50 Pfennig, Oldenburg/Olden, 1A

40 Heller, Ostermiething, 1A

75 Pfennig, Pössneck, 1A

25 Pfennig, Plathe, 1A

100 Pfennig, Rüdolstadt, 1A

50 Pfennig, Bad Salzbrunn, 1A

10 Kronen, Sälzburg, 1A

50 Pfennig, Schierke, 1A

50 Pfennig, Schroeich, 1A

25 Pfennig, Segeberg, 1A

75 Pfennig, Seeth, 1A

75 Pfennig, Soltau, 1A

60 Pfennig, Soltau, 1A

50 Pfennig, Steinfeld, 1A

1 Mark, Sörup, 1A

50 Pfennig, Strelitz, 1A

1 Mark, Stuttgart, 1A

50 Pfennig, Suchsdorf, 1A

50 Pfennig, Süderbarup, 1A

25 Pfennig, Thale Walpurgis, 1A

1 Mark, Tilsit, 1A

50 Pfennig, Traunstein, 1A

50 Pfennig, Treuchtlingen, 1A

100 Pfennig, Ulm, 1A

50 Heller, Unterwald, 1A

75 Pfennig, Vacha, 1A

50 Pfennig, Vaethen-Tangerhuette, 1A

25 Pfennig, Vlotho, 1A

75 Pfennig, Warin, 1A

25 Pfennig, Weinheim, 1A

2 Mark, Wenningstedt, 1A

25 Pfennig, Wernigerode, 1A

10 Pfennig, Wetzlar, 1A

25 Pfennig, Winsen, 1A

299 Pfennig, Wittenburg, 1A

1 Mark, Winterberg, 1A

25 Pfennig, Wismar, 1A

1 Mark, Wittdun, 1A

2 Mark, Wittmund, 1A

5 Mark, Wyk/Fehmarn, 1A

50 Pfennig, Zella-Mehlis, 1A

50 Pfennig, Hamburg, 1A

❐ NEUKIRCHEN/WYHRA Sachsen	2A					
❐ NEUKIRCHHOF Fantasy City	1A					
❐ NEUKLOSTER Mecklenburg-Schwerin	1A					
❐ NEUMARK Sachsen	2A					
❐ NEUMARK-BEDRA Provinz Sachsen	2A					
❐ NEUMARK/DREWENZ (Nowe Miasto, Lubawskie) Westpreussen	2A	7B				
❐ NEU MARKT (Sroda Slask) Schlesien	2A	6A	7A			
❐ NEUMARKT/ ROTT (Neumarkt-St. Veit, Meumarkt-St. Veit) Bayern	2A	7A				
❐ NEUMARKT/SULZ Bayern	1A	6A	7B			
❐ NEUMUEHLE/MIESBACH Bayern	2A					
❐ NEUMUEHLEN-DIETRICHSDORF Schleswig-Holstein	2A					
❐ NEUMUENSTER Schleswig-Holstein	1A	2B	7A	14B		
❐ NEUNBURG/WALD Bayern	1A					
❐ NEUNDORF Anhalt	1A					
❐ NEUNDORF/GLATZ Schlesien	1A	2B				
❐ NEUNHOFEN Sachsen-Weimar-Eisenach	1A					
❐ NEUNKIRCHEN Rheinland	1A	2E	3B	9B		
❐ NEUOETTING Bayern	1A	2A				
❐ NEUOETTING/ALTOETTING Bayern	2A					
❐ NEUOFFSTEIN Pfalz	7B					
❐ NEUPETERSHAIN N. L. Brandenburg	2A					
❐ NEURATH Rheinland	7A					
❐ NEURODE/EULENGEBIRGE (Nowa Ruda) Schiesien	1A	2A	4B	5A	6A	
❐ NEURUPPIN Brandenburg	2A	6A	8B			
❐ NEUSALZ/ODER (Nowa Sol) Schiesien	1A	2B	6A	7A	11C	
❐ NEUSALZA-SPREMBERG Sachsen	1A	2A				
❐ NEUSS/ERFT Rheinland	1A	2A	3C	7B	8B	14B
❐ NEUSSAU/BUCHEN Schleswig-Holstein	7B					
❐ NEUSTADT Baden	1A	2A	6A	7B		
❐ NEUSTADT Sachsen	1A	2A	8B			
❐ NEUSTADT (Prudnik) Schiesien	1A	2A	6A	7A	8B	
❐ NEUSTADT Schleswig-Holstein	1A	8B	14B			
❐ NEUSTADT/AISCH Bayern	1A	6A				
❐ NEUSTADT/COBURG	1A					
❐ NEUSTADT/DONAU Bayern	1A	6A				
❐ NEUSTADT/ELBE Mecklenburg-Schwerin	1A					
❐ NEUSTADT/HAARDT Pfalz	1A	6A	8A			
❐ NEUSTADT/KULM Bayern	1A					
❐ NEUSTADT/ORLA Thueringen	1A	7B				
❐ NEUSTADT/PINNE (Lwowek) Posen	1A					
❐ NEUSTADT/REHDE (Weihersfrei, Wejherowo) Westpreussen	1B					
❐ NEUSTADT/RUEBENBERG Hannover	1A	2A	7A			
❐ NEUSTADT/SAALE Bayern	1B	2B	6A			
❐ NEUSTADT/WALDNABB Bayern	1A	7A				
❐ NEUSTADT/WARTHE (Nowe Miasto, Pomorze) Posen	1A					
❐ NEUSTAEDTEL (Nowe Miasteczke) Schlesien	1B					
❐ NEUSTETTIN (Szczecinek) Pommern	1A	2B	6A	7B		
❐ NEUSTRELITZ Mecklenburg-Strelitz	1A					
❐ NEUTEICH (Nytych, Nowy Staw) Danzig Westpreussen	1A	2B				
❐ NEUTOMISCHEL (Nowy Tomsyl) Posen	1A	2B				
❐ NEUWEDELL (Drawno) Brandenburg	1A	7A				
❐ NEUWERK/OELZE Thueringen	2A					
❐ NEUWIED-RASSELSTEIN Rheinland	1A	2A				
❐ NEUWIED/RHEIN Rheinland	1A	2A	6A	8A	11C	12A
❐ NEUWIESE Sachsen	1A					
❐ NEVIGES Rheinland	2A	8A				
❐ NIEBUELL Schleswig-Holstein	1A					
❐ NIED/MAIN Hessen-Nassau	1A	2A	9A			
❐ NIEDER HERMSDORF/WALDENBURG Schlesien	1B					

Gas, Haynau, 8A

25 Reichspfennig, Hildsheim, 14B

❒ NIEDER INGELHEIM/RHEIN
(Ingelheim) Hessen 1A
❒ NIEDER MARSBERG Sachsen 1A
❒ NIEDER MARSBERG Westfalen 1A 2B
❒ NIEDER RYDULTAU
(Rydultowy Dolne) Schlesien 1B
❒ NIEDER ULLERSDORF
(Mirostowice) Brandenburg 2A
❒ NIEDER ZWOENITZ Sachsen 1A
❒ NIEDERCUNNERSDORF
Sachsen 1A
❒ NIEDERDORF/ERZGEBIRGE
Sachsen 2A
❒ NIEDERFRIEDERSDORF
Sachsen 2A
❒ NIEDERHADAMAR Hessen 14B
❒ NIEDERHARTMANNSDORF/SAGAN
Schlesien 1B
❒ NIEDERKAUFUNGEN
Hessen-Nassau 1A
❒ NIEDERKRUECHTEN Rheinland 2A
❒ NIEDERLAHNSTEIN
Hessen-Nassau 1A
❒ NIEDERLAHNSTEIN-OBERLAHNSTEIN
Rheinland 2A
❒ NIEDERLAUSITZ Sachsen 7B
❒ NIEDERLUNGWITZ Sachsen 1A
❒ NIEDERMENDIG Rheinland 1A
❒ NIEDERODERWITZ Sachsen 1A 2B 7A
❒ NIEDERRAMSTADT Hessen 7A
❒ NIEDERSACHSWERFEN
Sachsen 2A
❒ NIEDERSALZBRUNN Schlesien 1A 2B
❒ NIEDERSCHELD (Dillenburg)
Hessen-Nassau 1A 7A
❒ NIEDERSCHELDEN Westfalen 2C 5B
❒ NIEDERSCHLEMA Sachsen 2A 7B
❒ NIEDERSEDLITZ Sachsen 2A

Gas, Hindenburg, 8A

❒ NIEDERSEIFFENBACH Sachsen 1A 2A
❒ NIEDERSFELD Westfalen 2A
❒ NIEDER-OHE Hannover 3B
❒ NIEDER-STUETER Westfalen 2C 5C
❒ NIEDERWIESA Sachsen 1A
❒ NIEDERWUERSCHNITZ Sachsen 1A
❒ NIEDOBSCHUETZ Schlesien 5B
❒ NIEHEIM Westfalen 2A
❒ NIENBURG/SAALE Sachsen 2A 9A
❒ NIENBURG/WESER Hannover 1A 2B
❒ NIENDORF (Hamburg) Hamburg 2A
❒ NIENDORF/OSTSEEBAD
Schleswig-Holstein 1A
❒ NIENHAGEN
Mecklenburg-Schwerin 2A
❒ NIENSTEDTEN
Schleswig-Holstein 2A 9A
❒ NIEPOLOMICE Galicia 2B
❒ NIESKY O.L. Schlesien 2B
❒ NIEVERN Hessen-Nassau 1A
❒ NIEZYCHOWO/SEEHEIM Posen 2B
❒ NIKOLAI (Mikolow) Schlesien 1A 2A
❒ NIMPTSCH (Niemcza) Schlesien 1A 2B
❒ NININO/RITSCHENWALDE
Posen 2B
❒ NITTENAU/REGEN Bayern 6B
❒ NOERDLINGEN/GOLDBACH
Bayern 1A 6A
❒ NOERENBERG (Insko) Pommern 1A
❒ NOESCHENRODE
Provinz Sachsen 1A
❒ NORDDORF/AMRUM
Schleswig-Holstein 2A
❒ NORDEN Hannover 1A 11B 14B
❒ NORDENHAM Hannover 1A 2A 6A
❒ NORDENHAM-EINSWARDEN
Hannover 2B
❒ NORDER-UND SUEDERDITHMARSCHEN
Schleswig-Holstein 1A
❒ NORDERNEY Hannover 1A 2A 7B
❒ NORDHALBEN-RODACH Bayern 2A 6A
❒ NORDHAUSEN/ZORGE
Provinz Sachsen 1A 2E 5B 6A
❒ NORDHORN/VECHTE Hannover 1E 2A 8B 14A
❒ NORTHEIM Hannover 1A 2A 6A
❒ NORTORF Schleswig-Holstein 1A
❒ NOSSEN/MULDE Sachsen 1A 2A
❒ NOWAWES
(Babelsberg) Brandenburg 2A 7B 9A
❒ NUEMBRECHT Rheinland 1B
❒ NUENCHWITZ Sachsen 1B
❒ NUERNBERG REICHELSDORF
Bayern 1B
❒ NUERNBERG UND FUERTH
Bayern 1B
❒ NUERNBERG-FUERTH Bayern 2A 12A
❒ NUERNBERG-REICHELSDORF U.
SCHWABACH Bayern 2A
❒ NUERNBERG/PEGNITZ Bayern 1A 2D 3C 4A 6A
7A 8B 9A 10A 11B
❒ NUERTINGEN/NECKAR
Wuerttemberg 1A 2A 6A 9A 14A
❒ NUTTELN Oldenburg 6B 7B
❒ OBER DITTMANNSDORF
Sachsen 2A
❒ OBER ELSASS Elsass 1A
❒ OBER EULA Sachsen 2A
❒ OBER LESCHEN
(Lezno Gorne) Schlesien 2A
❒ OBER NIEWIADOM
(Niewiadom) Schlesien 4B 5B
❒ OBER SALZBRUNN
(Szczawno-zdrot) Schlesien 1A

50 Pfennig, Hockensbuell, 1A

❒ OBER UND UNTER-GRAINAU (Grainau) Bayern 6A
❒ OBER-SALZBRUNN (Szczawno-zdrot) Schlesien 2B
❒ OBERAMMERGAU/AMMER Bayern 1A 6A
❒ OBERBACH-RHOEN Bayern 1A 2A
❒ OBERBARNIM Brandenburg 2A
❒ OBERBERGISCHER Nordrhein-Westfalen 14A
❒ OBERBRUCH/HEINSBERG Rheinland 2A
❒ OBERCASSEL Rheinland 1A
❒ OBERCUNNERSDORF Sachsen 1A
❒ OBERDORF, MARKT Bayern 1A 2A
❒ OBERDORLA Provinz Sachsen 1A
❒ OBERELSBACH Bayern 7A
❒ OBERESSLINGEN Wuerttemberg 2A
❒ OBERFRIEDERSDORF Sachsen 1A
❒ OBERFROHNA Sachsen 1A 2A
❒ OBERGEBRA Provinz Sachsen 2A
❒ OBERGELERA Sachsen 1A
❒ OBERGLOGAU (Glogowek, Glozowek) Schlesien 1A 6A 8B
❒ OBERGUENZBURG Bayern 2A
❒ OBERHAGEN Westfalen 3D 7B
❒ OBERHAUSEN Rheinland 1A 2A 3B 4B 5A 6A 7A 8B 9A
❒ OBERHEIM Wuerttemberg 1A
❒ OBERHELDRUNGEN Sachsen 2A
❒ OBERHESSEN Hessen 1A
❒ OBERHODE Hannover 3A
❒ OBERHOF Sachsen-Gotha 1A
❒ OBERHOFEN Elsass 1A 3B 7B 10A
❒ OBERHOHNDORF Sachsen 1A
❒ OBERKIRCH Baden 1A
❒ OBERKIRCH, OPPENAU U. BAD PETERSTAL Baden 1A
❒ OBERKIRCHEN Westfalen 2C 4A 5B
❒ OBERLAHNKREIS (Weilburg) Hessen-Nassau 1A
❒ OBERLAHNSTEIN Hessen-Nassau 1A 2D 7A
❒ OBERLANGENBIELAU (Bielawa) Schlesien 1A 2A
❒ OBERLENNINGEN Wuerttenlberg 2A
❒ OBERLICHTENAU Sachsen 1A
❒ OBERLIND (Sonneberg) Sachsen-Meiningen 1A 7A
❒ OBERLOEDLA-LOSSEN Thueringen 10B
❒ OBERLUNGWITZ Sachsen 1A 2B
❒ OBERLUSTADT Pfalz 1A
❒ OBERNBURG/MAIN Bayern 1A 2A
❒ OBERNDORF/NECKAR Wuerttemberg 1A 2A 6A 7B
❒ OBERNEUHUETTENDORF 7A
❒ OBERNEUKIRCH Sachsen 1A 2A
❒ OBERNEUSCHOENEBERG/ERZGEBIRGE Sachsen 1A
❒ OBERNHEIM Wuerttemberg 2A
❒ OBERNIEWIADOM (Niewiadom) Schlesien 2A
❒ OBERNKIRCHEN Hessen-Nassau 1A 2B
❒ OBERNZELL/DONAU Bayern 6B
❒ OBERODERWITZ Sachsen 1A 2A
❒ OBERRAD/MAIN Hessen-Nassau 7B
❒ OBERRARBACH Westfalen 7A
❒ OBERRENGERSDORF O.L. Schlesien 2A
❒ OBERROEBLINGEN/SEE Provinz Sachsen 2A
❒ OBERROT-RENDORF Sachsen 2A

Types of Emergency Money

Type	Reference #
Municipal paper	1
Private paper	2
POW paper	3
POW official metal	4
POW private metal	5
Municipal metal	6
Private metal	7
Gas tokens	8
Food; beer; konsumverein	9
Naval; military; kantine	10
Encased, unencased stamps	11
Streetcar tokens	12
Porcelain	13
World War II issues	14
Concentration, Civilian internment camps	15

Rarity grades: A, to $25; B, to $60; C, to $125; D, to $200; and E, $350

50 Pfennig, Hoexter, 1A

❒ OBERSACHSENBERG/VOGTLAND Sachsen 1A
❒ OIBERSDORF Westfalen 2E
❒ OBERSITZKO (Obrzycko, Obesrsitsko, Obersycko, Oberzyko) Schlesien 1B
❒ OBERSTDORF Bayern 2A
❒ OBERSTEIN Rheinland 1A 2A 6A
❒ OBERSTEIN UND IDAR Rheinland 1A
❒ OBERSTUETZENGRUEN Sachsen 1A
❒ OBERURSEL/TAUNUS Hessen-Nassau 1A
❒ OBERVIECHTACH Bayern 7A
❒ OBERWEILER-TIEFENBACH Pfalz 1A
❒ OBERWEISSBACH Thueringen 1A
❒ OBERWEISSBACH, CURSDORF DEESBACH Thueringen 1A
❒ OBERWESEL Rheinland 1A 2A 6A
❒ OBERWESTERWALDKREIS Hessen-Nassau 1A
❒ OBERWIESENTHAL Sachsen 1A
❒ OBERWOLFACH Baden 2A
❒ OBERWUERSCHNITZ Sachsen 1A
❒ OBERZWIESELAU (Lindberg) Bayern 7B
❒ OBORNIK/WARTA (Oborniki) Posen 1A 6B
❒ OBRIGHOVEN-LACKHAUSEN Rheinland 1A
❒ OCHSENFURT/MAIN Bayern 1A 2A 6B
❒ OCHSENHAUSEN Wuerttemberg 1A
❒ OCHTRUP/VECHTE Westfalen 2B 14D
❒ ODENKIRCHEN/NIERS Rheinland 1A
❒ ODERBERG/ODER Brandenburg 1A
❒ ODERN Elsass 1A
❒ OEBISFELDE-KALTENDORF Provinz Sachsen 1A
❒ OEDERAN Sachsen 1A 2A 8A 9A
❒ OEDESSE Hannover 2A
❒ OEDT-ST. HUBERT Rheinland 2A 7A
❒ OEDT/NIERS (Grafrath) Rheinland 7A
❒ OEHRINGEN/OHR Wuerttemberg 1A 2A 6A
❒ OELDE Westfalen 1A 2E 6A
❒ OELKINGHAUSEN (Schwelm) 5A 7B
❒ OELS/OELS (Olesnica, Olesnicka) Schlesien 1A 2A 6A 7A 8B 10A
❒ OELSNITZ/ELSTER Sachsen 1A 2A 8B
❒ OELZE Thueringen 2A
❒ OERLINGHAUSEN Lippe 1A 7B
❒ OERREL Hannover 3B
❒ OESE Westfalen 2B
❒ OETTINGEN/WERNITZ Bayern 6A
❒ OETZSACH-MARKKLEEBERG Sachsen 1A
❒ OEVENTROP Westfalen 2E
❒ OEYNHAUSEN, BAD Westfalen 2A 7A
❒ OFFENBACH/MAIN Hessen-Nassau 1A 6A 7A 8B 9A 11B 12B
❒ OFFENBURG/KINZIG Baden 1A 2A 6A 7B
❒ OFFLEBEN Provinz Sachsen 1A
❒ OGGERSHEIM Pfalz 1A
❒ OHEIMGRUBE/KATTOWITZ (Kopalnia Wujek) Schlesien 5B
❒ OHLAU/ODER (Olawa) Schlesien 1A 2B 7B 8B
❒ OHLE (Altena) Westfalen 2E
❒ OHLEN/ALTENA (Ahlen) Westfalen 5A
❒ OHLIGS Rheinland 1A 2A 3B 4B 6A 11B
❒ OHRDRUF Sachsen-Coburg-Gotha 1A 2A 3A 4A 6A
❒ OKER/OKER (Ocker) Braunschweig 2A
❒ OLAND (Hallig) Schleswig-Holstein 1A 3A
❒ OLBERNHAU Sachsen 1A
❒ OLBERSDORF Sachsen 2A
❒ OLDAU Hannover 2A
❒ OLDENBURG Oldenburg 1A 2A 6A 7A 10B 11E
❒ OLDENBURG/HUNTE Oldenburg 1A 2B
❒ OLDENBURG Schleswig-Holstein 1A 2A
❒ OLDESLOE, BAD/TRAVE Schleswig-Holstein 1A 2A 7E

5 Pfennig, Hohenbudberg, 1A

10 Pfennig, Hohenleipisch, Germany, 1A

❒ OLDISLEBEN/UNSTRUT Sachsen-Weimar-Eisenach 1A 6A
❒ OLETZKO (Olecko) Ostpreussen 1A
❒ OLIVIA/DANZIG (Oliwska) Westpreussen 2A
❒ OLKUSZ (Olkouch, Olkuska, Kopalnia, Wujek) Silesia 2A
❒ OLPE Westfalen 1A 2E 6A
❒ OLSBERG Westfalen 2A
❒ OLTINGEN Elsass 1A
❒ OMULLE/STEPHANSDORF Westpreussen 2A
❒ ONSTMETTINGEN Wuerttemberg 1A
❒ OOS Baden 2A
❒ OPALENITZA (Opalenica) Schlesien 1A 2A 3C
❒ OPLADEN/WIPPER Rheinland 1A
❒ OPPACH Sachsen 11A
❒ OPPAU Schlesien 1A
❒ OPPELN/ODER (Opole) Schlesien 1A 2B 7B 8B
❒ OPPENAU Baden 6A
❒ OPPENHEIM/RHEIN Hessen 1A
❒ OPPURG Sachsen Weimar Eisenach 1A
❒ ORANIENBAUM Anhalt 1A 2A
❒ ORANIENBURG Brandenburg 1A 2A 3E 7B 9A
❒ ORB BAD/ORB Hessen-Nassau 2A 7B
❒ ORLAMUENDE/SAALE Sachsen-Altenburg 1A
❒ ORSOY/RHEIN Rheinland 1A
❒ ORTELSBURG (Szczytno) Ostpreussen 1A 10B
❒ ORTENBURG Bayern 1A 2A
❒ ORTRAND Provinz Sachsen 6B
❒ ORZEGOW Schlesien 1A 5B 7A
❒ OSBERGHAUSEN Rheinland 2A 14B
❒ OSCHATZ Sachsen 1A 2A 7A 9A
❒ OSCHERSLEBEN/BODE Provinz Sachsen 1A 2A 6A 7B
❒ OSNABRUCK Hannover 1A 2A 3C 5B 7B 8B 11C 12B
❒ OSTENWALDE-HUEMMLING Hannover 3B
❒ OST-STERNBERG (Zielenzig) Brandenburg 1A
❒ OSTERBURG Provinz Sachsen 1A
❒ OSTERFELD Westfalen 1A 6A 7A
❒ OSTERHOFEN Bayern 1A 2A
❒ OSTERHOLZ Hannover 1A
❒ OSTERHORN Schleswig-Holstein 1A
❒ OSTERNIENBURG Anhalt 2A
❒ OSTERODE (Ostroda) Ostpreussen 1A 2A 6A
❒ OSTERODE/HARZ Brandenburg 1A 2A
❒ OSTERRATH Rheinland 1A
❒ OSTERWALD-MEYENFELD Hannover 3B
❒ OSTERWIECK Westfalen 4A 5E
❒ OSTERWIEK/HARZ Provinz Sachsen 1A 5A 14B
❒ OSTHEIM/RHOEN Bayern 1A 2B
❒ OSTPREUSSEN 1A 2B
❒ OSTPRIGNITZ/KYRITZ Brandenburg 1A
❒ OSTRAU Sachsen 2A
❒ OSTRITZ/NEISSE Sachsen 1A 2A
❒ OSTROG/GORIN Russ. Poland 1B
❒ OSTROWO (Ostrow) Posen 1A 2B 6A 7B
❒ OTTENDORF (Ocice) Schlesien 2A 6A
❒ OTTENDORF-OKRILLA Sachsen 1A 2A
❒ OTTER Hannover 3B
❒ OTTERBERG Pfalz 1A
❒ OTTERNDORF/ELBE Hannover 1A 8B
❒ OTTERSEN Hannover 3B
❒ OTTMACHAU/NEISSE (Otmuchow) Schlesien 1A 2A 6A
❒ OTTOBEUREN Bayern 7A
❒ OTTWEILER Rheinland 1A
❒ OUTSCHEID/EIFEL Rheinland 2A
❒ OVER Hannover 3B
❒ OVERRATH Rheinland 1A
❒ OYBIN Sachsen 2A
❒ PADERBORN/PADER Westfalen 1A 2A 4A 6A 7A 10A
❒ PAKOSCH (Pakosc) Posen 1A
❒ PALENBERG Rheinland 2A
❒ PALS Pommern 1B
❒ PALSCHAU (Palczewo) Westpreussen 1B
❒ PAPENBURG Hannover 1A 2C 11E
❒ PAPPENHEIM/ALTMUEHL Bayern 6A
❒ PARCHIM/ELBE (Parchen) Mecklenburg-Schwerin 1A 7B 11B
❒ PAREY/ELBE Provinz Sachsen 1A 2A
❒ PARTENKIRCHEN (Garmisch-Partenkirchen) Bayern 1A 6A
❒ PARUSCHOWITZ (Paruszowiec) Schlesien 2A 5B
❒ PASEWALK/UCKER (Passewalk) Pommern 1A 2A
❒ PASING Bayern 1A 2A
❒ PASSAU/INN, DANUBE Bayern 1A 2A 7A
❒ PATSCHKAU/NEISSE (Paczkow) Schlesien 1A
❒ PAULINZELLA Schwarzburg-Rudolstadt 1A
❒ PAULSBORN Bayern 7B
❒ PAULSDORF (Pawlow) Schlesien 1A
❒ PAUNSDORF Sachsen 1A
❒ PECHBRUNN Bayern 7B
❒ PEGAU/WHITE ELSTER Sachsen 1A 2A
❒ PEGNITZ/PEGNITZ Bayern 6A
❒ PEINE Hannover 1A 2A 5B 6A 7B 11C 13A
❒ PEISERN/WARTA (Pyzdry) Schlesien 1B
❒ PEISSENBERG Bayern 1A 7A
❒ PENIG/MULDE Sachsen 1A 2A 7A
❒ PENKUN Pommern 1A
❒ PENZBERG Bayern 1A 2A 7B
❒ PENZIG O.L. (Piensk) Schlesien 1A 2A 7A
❒ PENZLIN Mecklenburg-Schwerin 1A
❒ PERLEBERG/STEPNITZ Brandenburg 1A 8B
❒ PETERSDORF Schleswig-Holstein 14B
❒ PETERSDORF/ZACKEN (Piechowice) Schlesien 1A 2A
❒ PETERSHAGEN/WESER Brandenburg 2A

50 Pfennig, Hohenmoelsen, 1A

10 Pfennig, Hohensalza, 1A

1 Mark, Holnis, 1A

50 Pfennig, Homburg/Pfalz, Germany, 1A

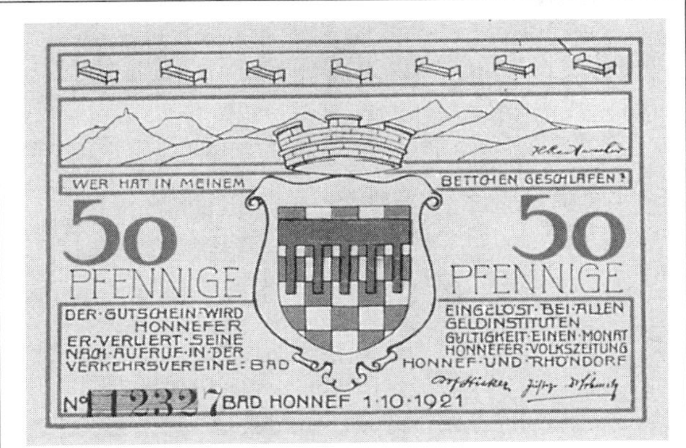

50 Pfennig, Honnef, Bad, 1A

1 Mark, Horn/Lippe, 1A

50 Pfennig, Hoyer, 1A

50 Pfennig, Husby/A, 1A

50 Pfennig, Ilmenau, 1A

25 Pfennig, Ilsenburg, 1A

50 Pfennig, Immenstadt, 1A

1 Mark, Iserlohn, Germany, 1A

1 Mark, Iserlohn, 1A

❐ PETERSTAL Baden 1A
❐ PETERSWEILER Lothringen 3B
❐ PETROWITZ (Piotrowice, Piotrkowska) Schlesien 1A
❐ PFAFFENDORF Rheinland 1A
❐ PFAFFENHAUSEN Bayern 2A
❐ PFEDDERSHEIM Hessen 1A
❐ PFOERRING/DONAU Bayern 1A 2A 6B
❐ PFOERTEN N.L. Brandenburg 1A
❐ PFORZHEIM/ENZ, NAGOLD Baden 1A 2A 3A 6A 7A 8A 11B
❐ PFULLENDORF Baden 1A
❐ PFULLINGEN Wuerttemberg 1A 2A
❐ PHILIPPSTHAL Hessen-Nassau 1A
❐ PHILLIPPSBURG Baden 1A
❐ PIESTERITZ/HALLE Provinz Sachsen 2A
❐ PILLAU (Baltijsk, USSR) Ostpreussen 1A 6A 10B
❐ PILLKALLEN (Dobrowolsk, USSR) Ostpreussen 1A 2A
❐ PINNE (Pniewy) Posen 1A
❐ PINNEBERG Schleswig-Holstein 1A 2A 6A 8B
❐ PIRMASENS Pfalz 1A 2E 6A 7A 11B
❐ PIRNA/ ELBE Sachsen 1A 2A 5B 7A 8A
❐ PITSCHEN (Byczyna) Schlesien 1A 2B
❐ PLANEGG/MUENCHEN Bayern 2B
❐ PLASSENBURG (Kulmbach) Bayern 3A 4A
❐ PLATHE (Ploty) Pommern 1A
❐ PLATTING/ISAR Bayern 1A 2A
❐ PLAU Mecklenburg-Schwerin 1A
❐ PLAUE-BERNSDORF Sachsen 1A
❐ PLAUE-THÜR 1A
❐ PLAUE/HAVEL Sachsen 1A 2A 7A
❐ PLAUEN/WHITE ELSTER Sachsen 1A 2A 7B 8A 12B
❐ PLEISSA Sachsen 1A 2B
❐ PLESCHEN (Pleszew) Posen 1A 2B
❐ PLESS (Pszczyna) Schlesien 1A 5A
❐ PLESSA Provinz Sachsen 1A
❐ PLETTENBERG Westfalen 5C
❐ PLESSER GRUBE Schlesien 4A
❐ PLETTENBERG/ELSE Westfalen 1A 2A 7D
❐ PLOCHINGEN/NECKAR Wuerttemberg 2A
❐ PLOEN Schleswig-Holstein 1A 2A
❐ PLOETZ Provinz Sachsen 2A

50 Pfennig, Jena, 1A

50 Pfennig, Johannisburg, 1A

❒ PNIOWITZ Schlesien 5C
❒ PNIOWITZ (Pniowiec) Schlesien 2A 3A
❒ POBERSHAU Sachsen 1A
❒ POCKAU/FLOEHATAL Sachsen 1A
❒ POCKING Bayern 2A
❒ PODEJUCH (Podjuchy) Pommern 2A
❒ PODOLIN/WAPNO Posen 2B
❒ POELITZ (Police) Pommern 1B
❒ POELZIG Sachsen-Altenburg 1A
❒ POESSNECK Sachsen-Meiningen 1A 2B 6A 7A
❒ POETTMES Bayern 1A 6A
❒ POGGENMOOR Hannover 3B
❒ POGHAUSEN/GROSS OLDENDORF Weser-Ems 2B
❒ POGORZELA (Pogoschella, Pogorzela) Posen 1B
❒ POHLSDORF (Pazdziorno) Schlesien 7C
❒ POLENZ Sachsen 2A
❒ POLEY Brandenburg 5A
❒ POLLNOW (Polanow) Pommern 1A
❒ POLZIN, BAD (Polczyn Zdroj) Pommern 1A 6A
❒ POMORZE (Pomorska) Pommern 3A
❒ PONHOLZ (Oberpfalz) Bayern 2A
❒ POPPENBUETTEL Schleswig-Holstein 1A
❒ POREBA Posen 2A 3A
❒ PORTA WESTPHALICA Westfalen 1B 2E
❒ PORZ-URBACH Rheinland 2A
❒ PORZ/RHEIN Rheinland 2A 7B
❒ POSADOWO Posen 1A 2B
❒ POSEN-OST (Poznan) Posen 1A
❒ POSEN-WEST (Poznan, Zachod) Posen 1A 2B 3A

10 Pfennig, Jüterbog, Germany, 1A

❒ POSEN/WARTA (Poznan) Posen 1A 2B 6A 7A 8A 10A
❒ POSSENDORF Sachsen 2A
❒ POTARZYCE Posen 1A
❒ POTSDAM/ Brandenburg 1A 2A 7B 11C
❒ POTTENDORF 1E
❒ POTULICE/NAKEN (Potulitz) Posen 1A
❒ POUCH Provinz Sachsen 1A 9A
❒ PRAUST/DANZIG (Prause, Pruszcz Gdanski) Westpreussen 2A
❒ PREETZ/PORETZ Schleswig-Holstein 1A 2A 6B
❒ PREMNITZ Brandenburg 2A
❒ PRENZLAU/UCKER (Prenzlow) Brandenburg 1A 2A 3A 6A 13A
❒ PRESSATH Bayern 6A 7A
❒ PRESSECK Bayern 7B
❒ PRESSIG Bayern 7B
❒ PRETZSCH Provinz Sachsen 1A
❒ PREUSSISCH HOLLAND (Paslek) Ostpreussen 1A 3A
❒ PREUSSISCH-EYLAU (Bagrationowsk) Ostpreussen 1A
❒ PREUSSISCH-STARGARD (Stargard Gdanski, Starogard) Westpreussen 1B
❒ PRICHSENSTADT Bayern 7B
❒ PRIEBUS/NEISSE (Prezewoz) Schlesien 1A 2B
❒ PRIEN Bayern 1A 2C
❒ PRIES-FRIEDRICHSORT Schleswig-Holstein 2A
❒ PRIESTERATH Nordrhein-Westfalen 14B

75 Pfennig, Kahla/Saale, Germany, 2A

50 Pfennig, Kahla, 1A

❒ PRIESTERITZ-HALLE/SAALE Sachsen 2A
❒ PRISDORF Schleswig-Holstein 1A
❒ PRITZWALK/DOMNITZ Brandenburg 1A 7B
❒ PROBSTZELLA Sachsen-Meiningen 1A
❒ PROESSDORF Sachsen-Altenburg 1A 2B
❒ PROFEN Provinz Sachsen 2A
❒ PRORA Pommern 7A
❒ PRÜM Rheinland 1A 2A 6A
❒ PRZYSCHETZ (Przyrzecz) Schlesien 1A
❒ PSCHOW/RYBNIK Schlesien 5B
❒ PUCHHEIM Bayern 3C 4B 7B
❒ PUECHERSREUTH Bayern 2A
❒ PUELZHEIM Pfalz 1A
❒ PUETTLINGEN Rheinland 8B
❒ PULSNITZ (Pulssnitz) Sachsen 1A 2A
❒ PUNITZ (Poniec) Posen 1B
❒ PUTBUS (Ruegen) Pommern 1A
❒ PUTLITZ Brandenburg 2A 7A
❒ PUTZIG (Puck) Westpreussen 1A 7C
❒ PYRITZ (Pyrzyce) Pommern 1A 2A
❒ PYRMONT, BAD Waldeck 1A 2B 7B 14B
❒ PYZDRY Posen 1B
❒ QUADRATH Rheinland 2B
❒ QUAKENBRUECK Hannover 1A 6A
❒ QUASNITZ Sachsen 1A
❒ QUEDLINBURG/BODE Provinz Sachsen 1A 2A 3A 7A 8B 9A 13A
❒ QUERFURT/QUERN (Quernfurt) Provinz Sachsen 1A 2A 6A
❒ QUERN Schleswig-Holstein 1A
❒ QUICKBORN Schleswig-Holstein 7B
❒ QUIERSCHIED Rheinland 1A 2A
❒ RAA-BESENBECK Schleswig-Holstein 1A
❒ RABENSTEIN (Karl-Marx-Stadt) Sachsen 2A 8B
❒ RACHTIG/MOSEL Rheinland 2A
❒ RACOT (Rakoly, Rakoty) Posen 1A
❒ RADEBERG Sachsen 1A 2A 7A
❒ RADEBEUL Sachsen 2A 7A 9A
❒ RADEVORMWALD Rheinland 1A 2A 3D
❒ RADLIN Wodzislaw Slaski Schlesien 5B
❒ RADOLFZELL Baden 1A 2A 6A
❒ RADZIONKAU (Radzionkow) Schlesien 1A 2A 3A 5B
❒ RAGNIT/NIEMAN Ostpreussen 1B
❒ RAGUHN/MULDE Anhalt 1A 2A
❒ RAISTING Bayern 2A
❒ RAKWITZ (Rakoniewice) Posen 1B
❒ RAMMELSBACH Pfalz 1A
❒ RAMSBECK Westfalen 2A
❒ RAMSDORF/AS (Velen) Westfalen 7A
❒ RAMSLOH Oldenburg 3B
❒ RANDOW Pommern 1A
❒ RANIS Provinz Sachsen 1A
❒ RANSPACH Elsass 1A
❒ RAPPOLTSWEILER Elsass 1A
❒ RASCHAU/ERZGEBIRGE Sachsen 1A
❒ RASCHEWITZ (Raszowice, Zmigrod) Schlesien 7B
❒ RASCHKOW (Raschkau, Raszkow) Posen 1B

50 Pfennig, Kahla, 1A

15 Pfennig, Kaiserslautern, 1A

Location						
❒ RASTATT Baden	1A	2A	3C	6A	8A	
❒ RASTENBERG, BAD Sachsen-Weimar-Eisenach	1A	2A				
❒ RASTENBURG (Ketrzyn) Ostpreussen	1B					
❒ RATHEIM Rheinland	2A					
❒ RATHENOW/HARD (Rathenau) Brandenburg	1A	2D	7A	11B		
❒ RATIBOR/ODER (Raciborz) Schlesien	1A	2A	4A	5B	6A	7A
❒ RATINGEN Rheinland	1A	2A				
❒ RATINGEN-DUESSELDORF Rheinland	2A					
❒ RATZEBUHR (Okonek) Pommern	1B					
❒ RATZEBURG (Racisburg) Schleswig-Holstein	1A	2A				
❒ RALINHEIM Hessen	1A					
❒ RAUENSTEIN Sachsen-Meiningen	1A	2A	7B			
❒ RAUSCHA O.L. (Ruszuw) Schlesien	1A	2B				
❒ RAUSCHEN (Ryn, Svetlogorsk, USSR) Ostpreussen	1A					
❒ RAUXEL Westfalen	1A	2A	5B	6A		
❒ RAVENSBRUECK Brandenburg	3E	5E	15B			
❒ RAVENSBURG Wuerttemberg	1A	6A	13B			
❒ RAWITSCH (Rawicz) Posen	1A	2B				
❒ REBBELROTH Rheinland	2A					
❒ RECHENBERG Sachsen	1A					
❒ RECKE Westfalen	2E					
❒ RECKLINGHAUSEN Westfalen	1A	2B	3B	5C	8A	
❒ RECKLINGHAUSEN-SUED Westfalen	2A	3A				
❒ REDDINGEN Hannover	3B					
❒ REES Rheinland	1A	2A	3B			
❒ REES-ESSERDEN Rheinland	2A	3B				
❒ REETZ/IHNA (Recz, Poland) Brandenburg	1A					
❒ REGEN ZWIESEL, OSTERHOFEN Bayern	7A					
❒ REGEN/REGEN Bayern	2A	7A				
❒ REGENHUETTE Bayern	2A					
❒ REGENSBURG/DANUBE (Ratisbon) Bayern	1A	2A	3C	4B	11B	12A
❒ REGENSTAUF Bayern	1A					
❒ REGENWALDE/REGA (Resko) Pommern	1A	6A				
❒ REGIS/PLEISSE (Regis-Breitingen) Sachsen	1A					
❒ REHAU/GRUENEBACH (Rechau) Bayern	1A	2A	6A			
❒ REHBURG, BAD Hannover	2A					
❒ REHMEN Sachsen-Meiningen	1A					
❒ REHNA Mecklenburg-Schwerin	1A					
❒ REICHENAU Sachsen	1A	2A	11C			
❒ REICHENBACH (Dzierzoninow) Ostpreussen	1B					
❒ REICHENBACH Sachsen	1A	2A	7A	8B	9A	
❒ REICHENBACH (Dzierzoniow) Schlesien	1A	2B	7B	8B		
❒ REICHENBACH/REGEN Bayern	1A	2B	7B			
❒ REICHENBRAND Sachsen	2A					
❒ REICHENFELS Reuss juengere Linie	2A					
❒ REICHENHAIN Sachsen	2A					
❒ REICHENHALL Bad/Saal	1A	2B	6A	8A		
❒ REICHENHALL/FILS Wuerttemberg	2A					
❒ REICHENSTEIN (Zloty stok) Schlesien	7B					
❒ REICHENWEIER (Riquewihr) Elsass	1A	2B				
❒ REICHMANNSDORF/WITTENBERG Sachsen-Meiningen	9B					
❒ REINERZ, BAD/WEISTRITZ (Duszniki-Zdroj) Schlesien	1A	2B				
❒ REINFELD Schlesien	1B					
❒ REINFELD Schleswig-Holstein	2E					
❒ REINSDORF Provinz Sachsen	2A	7B				
❒ REIPOLTSKIRCHEN Pfalz	1A					
❒ REISEN (Rydzyna, Leszno) Posen	4A					
❒ REISHOLZ/DUESSELDORF Rheinland	2A	5A	7A			
❒ REITZENHAIN Sachsen	1A					
❒ REKUM Hannover	7B					
❒ RELLINGEN Schleswig-Holstein	1A					
❒ REMAGEN/RHEIN (Rheinmagen) Rheinland	1A	2D	7A	9B	11B	14B
❒ REMDA/RINNEThueringen	1A	2B				
❒ REMPTENDORF Reuss Altere Linie	7B					

50 Pfennig, Kampen/Sylt, 1A

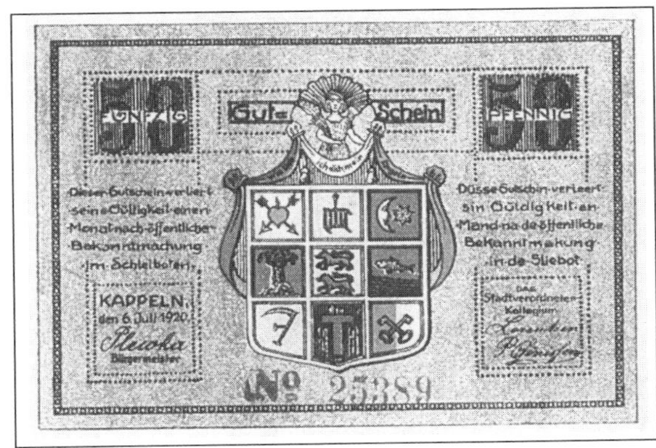

50 Pfennig, Kappeln, 1A

❒ REMSCHEID Rheinland 1A 2A 3C 5A 11B 14B
❒ REMSCHEID-BLOMBACHT Rheinland 2B
❒ REMSCHEID-HASTEN Rheinland 2A 5C
❒ REMSCHEID-VIERINGHAUSEN Rheinland 2A
❒ RENCHEN/RENCH Baden 1A
❒ RENDSBURG/EYDER Schleswig-Holstein 1A 2B 8A
❒ RENGERSDORF (Krosnowice) Schlesien 2B
❒ REPPEN Brandenburg 1A 2A
❒ RETHEM Hannover 3B
❒ RETTGENSTEDT/COELLEDA Provinz Sachsen 2A
❒ REULBACH/RHOEN Hessen-Nassau 2A
❒ REUTH Sachsen 2A
❒ REUTLINGEN/ESCHATZ Wuerttemberg 1A 2B 6A 7B 8A
❒ REYERSHAUSEN Hannover 2B
❒ RHEDA/EMS Westfalen 1C
❒ RHEIN Ostpreussen 1B
❒ RHEINBACH Rheinland 1A
❒ RHEINE Westfalen 1B 2A 6A 11A 14B
❒ RHEINFELDEN Baden 1A 2B
❒ RHEINGAUKREIS (Ruedesheim) Hessen-Nassau 1A
❒ RHEINHAUSEN Rheinland 1A 2C 5A
❒ RHEINISCH Westfalen 5B
❒ RHEINPROVINZ Rheinland 1A
❒ RHEINSBERG Brandenburg 1A 11C

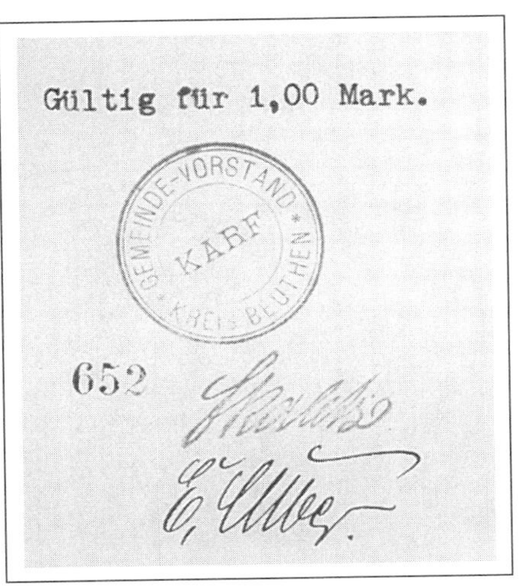

1 Mark, Karf, 1A

❒ RHEINZABERN/ERLBACH Pfalz 1A
❒ RHEURDT-SCHAEPHUYSEN Rheinland 1A
❒ RHEYDT/NIERS (Rheidt, Rheid, Rheyd) Rheinland 1A 2A 7A 14B
❒ RHINOW (Rhin) Brandenburg 2A
❒ RHODT Pfalz 1A
❒ RIBNITZ/RECKNITZ Mecklenburg-Schwerin 1A
❒ RICHTORSCHÄCHTE 3A
❒ RICKELSHAUSEN Baden 2A
❒ RIEDENBURG Bayern 1A 2B 3A
❒ RIEDER/OSTHARZ Anhalt 1A
❒ RIEDLINGEN/DANUBE Wuerttemberg 1A 2A
❒ RIEGEL Baden 11B
❒ RIESE/ELBE (Riesa) Sachsen 1A 2A 12A
❒ RIESENBURG (Prabuty, Poland) Westpreussen 1A 5E 6A
❒ RIETBERG/EMS Westfalen 1A 2B

Types of Emergency Money

Type	Reference #
Municipal paper	1
Private paper	2
POW paper	3
POW official metal	4
POW private metal	5
Municipal metal	6
Private metal	7
Gas tokens	8
Food; beer; konsumverein	9
Naval; military; kantine	10
Encased, unencased stamps	11
Streetcar tokens	12
Porcelain	13
World War II issues	14
Concentration, Civilian internment camps	15

Rarity grades: A, to $25; B, to $60; C, to $125; D, to $200; and E, $350

50 Pfennig, Karstadt, 1A

❐ RIETSCHEN Schlesien 1A 2A
❐ RIMBERG Westfalen 1A
❐ RINGENBERG Rheinland 2A
❐ RINKENIS (Rinkenaes, Denmark) Schleswig-Holstein 1A
❐ RINTELN/WESER Hessen-Nassau 1A 2B 7B
❐ RITSCHENWALDE (Ryczlow) Posen 2B
❐ RITTERHUDE Hannover 1A
❐ RIXHEIM (Rexen) Elsass 1B
❐ ROCHLITZ/MULDE Sachsen 1A 2A 7B
❐ ROCHSBURG Sachsen 2B
❐ RODA Sachsen-Altenburg 1A 2A 7B
❐ RODACH/RODACH Coburg-Bayern 1A 2A 6A 7A
❐ RODENBERG und GROSS NENNDORF Hannover 2C
❐ RODEWISCH Sachsen 1A 2A 7B 8A
❐ RODIGKAU Provinz Sachsen 2A
❐ RODING/REGEN Bayern 1D
❐ RODLEBEN Anhalt 2A
❐ ROEBEL Mecklenburg-Schwerin 1A
❐ ROEBELN Mecklenburg-Schwerin 1A
❐ ROEDDING (Roedding, Denmark) Schleswig-Holstein 1A 2A
❐ ROEDELNSTEIN Westfalen 2A
❐ ROEHLINGSHAUSEN Westfalen 2B 11B
❐ RÖHRIGSHÖFE/WERRA Hessen-Nassau 1A
❐ ROEHRSDORF Sachsen 1A
❐ ROELLFELD Bayern 1A
❐ ROEMHILD Sachsen-Meiningen 1A 2B
❐ ROENNEBECK Hannover 2A
❐ ROESA Provinz Sachsen 9B
❐ ROESRATH Rheinland 2A
❐ ROESSEL (Reszel) Ostpreussen 1A 2B
❐ ROETHA/PLEISSE Sachsen 1A 2A
❐ ROETHENBACH/PEGNITZ Bayern 2A 7C
❐ ROGASEN/WETNA (Rogozno. Rogozinska) Posen 1B
❐ ROGOWO Posen 1B
❐ ROHR Bayern 1A 2B
❐ ROHRBACH/HEIDELBERG Baden 1A 2B 7A
❐ ROISDORF Rheinland 2B
❐ ROITZSCH/BITTERFELD Provinz Sachsen 1A 2B 7B 9A
❐ ROKIETNICE (Rokietnicka) Posen 2B
❐ ROKITTNITZ (Rokitnica) Sileslen 1A
❐ ROLLSHAUSEN Hannover 1A 2A
❐ ROMBACH Lothringen 2A 5C
❐ ROMBURG/HOHENSALZA Posen 2B
❐ RONDORF/RODENKIRCHEN Rheinland 1A
❐ RONHOFEN Lothringen 5C
❐ RONNEBERG Hannover 3B
❐ RONNEBURG Sachsen-Altenburg 1A 2A 7B
❐ RONSDORF Rheinland 1A 2A 3E 11B
❐ ROPPENZWEILER Elsass 1A
❐ ROSBACH/SIEG Rheinland 1A
❐ ROSCHKOW (Roszkow) Posen 1B
❐ ROSDZIN (Rozdzien) Schlesien 1B
❐ ROSENAU-ISARMOOS Bayern 1A
❐ ROSENBERG-KRONACH Bayern 4B
❐ ROSENBERG/OBERPFALZ Bayern 2A 4B 7B 9A
❐ ROSENBERG/STOBER (Olesno, Olesnicka) Schlesien 1B
❐ ROSENBURG (Susz) Westpreussen 1A
❐ ROSENHEIM Westpreussen 1A
❐ ROSENHEIM/INN Bayern 1A 2A 6A 7B
❐ ROSENTHAL-REUSS Thueringen 2B

75 Pfennig, Katscher, 1A

1 Mark, Keitum, 1A

50 Pfennig, Kelbra, 1A

25 Pfennig, Kellenhusen, 1A

5 Pfennig, Kempen/P, 6B

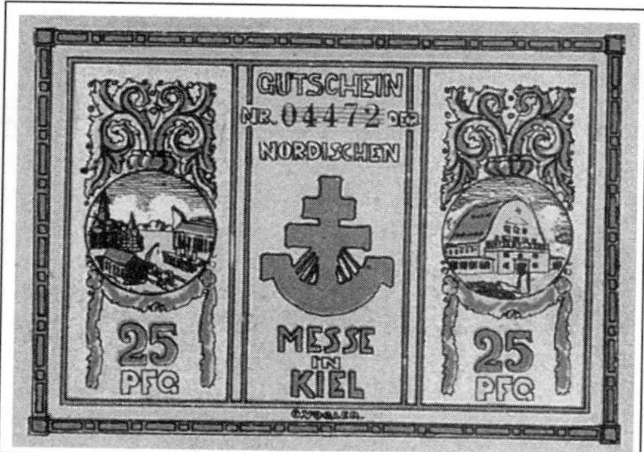

25 Pfennig, Kiel, 1A

59 Pfennig, Kirn, 1A

50 Pfennig, Kissingen, Bad, 1A

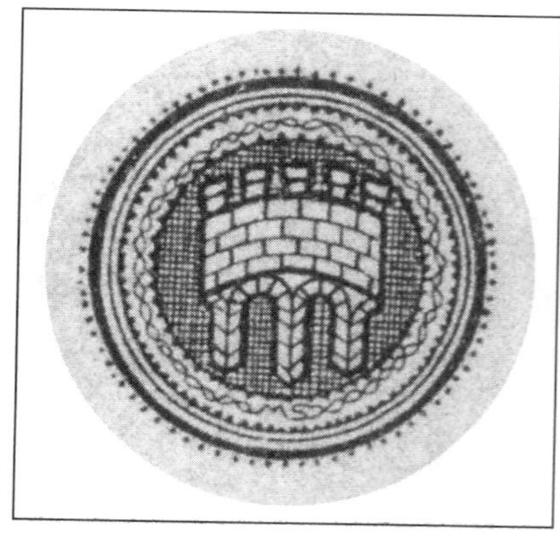

1 Pfennig, Kitzingen/M, 1A

50 Pfennig, Kitzingen/M, 1A

50 Pfennig, Kluetz, 1A

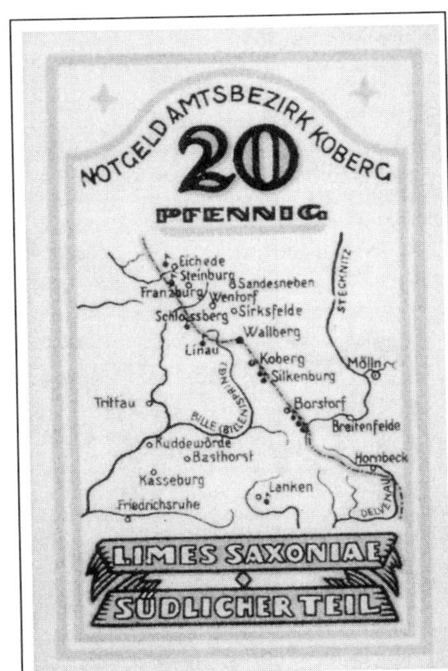

20 Pfennig, Koberg, 1A

50 fennig, Koeln, 1A

❒ ROSENTHAL/GLATZ Schlesien 2A
❒ ROSITZ Sachsen-Altenburg 2A 7A
❒ ROSSBACH Pfalz 1A 7B
❒ ROSSBACH Provinz Sachsen 1A 7B
❒ ROSSBACH/ROSSBACH Hessen-Nassau 7B
❒ ROSSBERG Wuerttemberg 5A
❒ ROSSLA Provinz Sachsen 1A 7B
❒ ROSSLAU/ELBE Anhalt 1A 2A
❒ ROSSLEBEN/UNSTRUT Provinz Sachsen 2B
❒ ROSSWEIN/MULDE Sachsen 1A 2A
❒ ROSTOCK/WARNOW Mecklenburg-Schwerin 1A 2A 7A 12B
❒ ROSWADZE (Rozwada) Schlesien 2A 5C
❒ ROTENBURG Hannover 1A 2A 3A 6A
❒ ROTENBURG/FULDA Hessen-Nassau 1A
❒ ROTH/REDNITZ Bayern 2B 6A 7A
❒ ROTHAUS Baden 4A
❒ ROTHENBACH/LANDESHUT Schlesien 1A 2B 7A
❒ ROTHENBURG/NEISSE Schlesien 2A 7B
❒ ROTHENBURG/TAUBER Bayern 1A 2A 6A
❒ ROTHENKIRCHEN/VOGTLAND Sachsen 1A 7A
❒ ROTHSELBERG Pfalz 1A
❒ ROTHWASSER O.L. Schlesien 1A 6B
❒ ROTTENBACH/THUERINGEN Saxe-Coburg 7B
❒ ROTTENBURG/LAABER Bayern 1A 6A
❒ ROTTENBURG/NECKAR Wuerttemberg 1A 2A 6A
❒ ROTTHALMUENSTER Bayern 1A 2B
❒ ROTTHAUSEN Rheinland 1A 7B 8B
❒ ROTTHAUSEN Westfalen 1E 2A
❒ ROT-TLUFF Sachsen 1A

❒ ROTTWEIL/NECKAR Wuerttemberg 1A 5B 6B 7A
❒ RUDA Schlesien 1A 5B 7B
❒ RUDELSBURG/BAD KOESEN Provinz Sachsen 2A 7B
❒ RÜDOLSTADT/SAALE Thueringen 1A 2B 6A 8A
❒ RUEBELAND/BODE Braunschweig 2A
❒ RUEDESHEIM/RHEIN Rheinland 1A 8A 11B
❒ RUEGEN Pommern 2A
❒ RUEGENWALDE (Darlowo) Pommern 1A 2B 6B
❒ RUEGENWALDERMUEND (Darlowko, Ruegenwalde) Pommern 1A
❒ RUELZHEIM Pfalz 1A
❒ RUENDEROTH Rheinland 1A 2B 14B
❒ RUESSELSHEIM/MAIN Hessen-Nassau 1A 7B 8B 11B
❒ RUESTRINGEN (Wilhelmshaven) Oldenburg 1A 2B
❒ RUETHEN/MOEHNE Westfalen 1A
❒ RUFACH Elsass 1A
❒ RUHLA/RUHE Sachsen-Gotha 1A 7A
❒ RUHLAND/ELSTER Schlesien 7B
❒ RUHLSDORF Brandenburg 7B
❒ RUHMANNSFELDEN Bayern 2A
❒ RUHNOW Pommern 2B
❒ RUHPOLDING Bayern 1A
❒ RUHR & RHEINE Westfalen 7A
❒ RUMMELSBURG (Miastko) Pommern 1A 7A
❒ RUMMENOHL Westfalen 2C
❒ RUPPERSDORF (Wyszonowice) Schlesien 1A 7A
❒ RUSS/NIEMEN Ostpreussen 1B
❒ RUSSDORF Sachsen 1A
❒ RUSSDORF/ROTTAL Bayern 1A 2B
❒ RUTSWEILER/LAUTER Pfalz 1A

75 Pfennig, Königsaue, 1A

50 Pfennig, Koenigsberg, 1A

❒ RYBNIK/RUDKA
(Rynsk) Schlesien 1A 2A 7A
❒ RYMANOW (Rzeszow) Galicia 2B
❒ SAALBURG Reuss juengere Linie 1A
❒ SAALFELD (Zalewo) Ostpreussen 1A 6B
❒ SAALFELD UND RUDOLSTADT
Thueringen 1A
❒ SAALFELD/SAALE Thueringen 1A 2B 6A 7B 11B
❒ SAAR-BUCKENHEIM Lothringen 6A
❒ SAARALBEN Lothringen 7A
❒ SAARAU (Zarow) Schlesien 1A 9B
❒ SAARBRUECKEN Rheinland 1A 2B 3A 7A 8A 12B
❒ SAARBRUECKEN-BURBACH
Rheinland 2A
❒ SAARBURG/LOTHRINGEN 6A
❒ SAARBURG/TRIER Rheinland 1A 2A 3C 6A
❒ SAARGEMUEND Lothringen 1A 2A 6A
❒ SAARLAUTERN (Saarlouis)
Rheinland 1A 3A
❒ SAATZIG (Szadko) Pommern 1B
❒ SABORWITZ
(Zaborowice) Schlesien 6B 7B
❒ SACHSA, BAD Hannover 1A
❒ SACHSEN (Freistaat) 6A
❒ SACHSENBURG Sachsen 1A 2A
❒ SACHSENHAUSEN Brandenburg 3E 5E
❒ SACHSENHAUSEN
Hessen-Nassau 7B
❒ SAECKINGEN Baden 1A
❒ SAERCHEN N. L.
(Annahuette) Brandenburg 7A
❒ SAGAN (Zagan) Schlesien 1A 3A 4A 6A 7A 8A 14B
❒ SALEM Baden 7A
❒ SALZBRUNN, BAD
(Szczawno-Zdroj) Schlesien 1A 2A
❒ SALZBURGHOFEN Bayern 1A
❒ SALZDETFURTH, BAD
Hannover 2A 9B 14B
❒ SALZGITTER Hannover 2A 9B
❒ SALZIG BAD Rheinland 1A
❒ SALZUFLEN, BAD
Lippe-Detmold 1A 10B
❒ SALZUNGEN
(Bad Salzungen) Thueringen 1A 6A
❒ SALZWEDEL Provinz Sachsen 1B 2A 5A 11D
❒ SAMOSTRZEL Posen 1A 2B
❒ SAMOTSCHIN (Szamocin) Posen 1A 2B
❒ SAMTER
(Szamotulska, Szamotuly) Posen 1A
❒ SANDAU/ELBE Sachsen 6A
❒ SANDBERG (Piaski) Posen 1A
❒ SANDBOSTEL Bremen 14B
❒ SANDE Schleswig-Holstein 1A 2A
❒ SANDOW (Cottbus) Pommern 7A
❒ SANGERHAUSEN
Provinz Sachsen 1A 2A 6A
❒ SANKT AMARIN Elsass 1A 2B
❒ SANKT ANDREASBERG
Hannover 1A 2A
❒ SANKT ANDREASBERG-SILBERHUETTE
Hannover 2A
❒ SANKT ANDREASBERG-WALDHAUS
Hannover 2A
❒ SANKT AVOLD Lothringen 6A
❒ SANKT BLASIEN Baden 1A 2A
❒ SANKT EGIDIEN Sachsen 1A 7B
❒ SANKT GEORGEN/SCHWARZWALD
Baden 1A 6A 7B
❒ SANKT GOAR Rheinland 1A

50 Pfennig, Königsee 1A

2 Mark, Koenigswalde, POW, 3C

❒ SANKT GOARSHAUSEN Hessen 1A
❒ SANKT GOARSHEIM Hessen 1A
❒ SANKT HUBERT Rheinland 1A
❒ SANKT INGBERT Pfalz 1A 9B
❒ SANKT MAGNUS/BREMEN Hannover 1A
❒ SANKT TÖNIS Rheinland 1A
❒ SANKT WENDEL Rheinland 1A
❒ SANNUM Oldenburg 3B
❒ SANTOMISCHEL (Zaniemysl) Posen 1A 2B
❒ SARNINGHAUSEN Hannover 3B
❒ SARSTEDT Hannover 2C
❒ SATRUP (Sottrup, Denmark) Schleswig-Holstein 1A
❒ SATZUNG Sachsen 1A
❒ SAULGAU Wuerttemberg 1A 2A 6A
❒ SAUPERSDORF Sachsen 1A 2A
❒ SAYDA Sachsen 1A
❒ SCHAALA Schwarzburg-Rudolstadt 1A
❒ SCHAEDLITZ/PLESS Schlesien 2B
❒ SCHAFSTAEDT Provinz Sachsen 1A 2A
❒ SCHALKAU Sachsen-Meiningen 1A
❒ SCHALKSMUEHLE Westfalen 2C 7B
❒ SCHANDAU BAD Sachsen 1A
❒ SCHAPEN Hannover 3B
❒ SCHARFENORT (Ostrorog) Posen 1A
❒ SCHARLEY (Szarlej) Schlesien 1A 2B 7B 9B
❒ SCHARMBECK (Osterholz-Scharmbeck) Hannover 1A 2B 7B
❒ SCHARNHORST/DORTMAND Westfalen 4A
❒ SCHAUBERG Bayern 2A
❒ SCHAUENSTEIN Schaumburg 1A 2A 7A
❒ SCHAUMBURG Hessen-Nassau 1A
❒ SCHAUMBURG Lippe 1A
❒ SCHAUMBURG-LIPPE 1A
❒ SCHEESSEL Hannover 1A
❒ SCHEIBENBERG Sachsen 1A
❒ SCHEIDEGG/ALLGAUE Bayern 14B
❒ SCHELEJEWO (Szelejewo) Posen 1B
❒ SCHELLENBERG Sachsen 1A
❒ SCHELSEN Rheinland 1A
❒ SCHERMBECK Rheinland 1A
❒ SCHERREBECK (Skaerbaek, Denmark) Scheswig-Holstein 1A
❒ SCHERSINGEN Elsass 3C
❒ SCHIEFBAHN Rheinland 1A
❒ SCHIERAU/DOMBROWKA Posen 2B
❒ SCHIERKE Provinz Sachsen 1A 2A
❒ SCHIFFBEK (Hamburg) Scheswig-Holstein 2A 13B
❒ SCHIFFERSTADT Pfalz 1A
❒ SCHIFFWEILER/SAAR Rheinland 1A
❒ SCHILDBERG (Ostrzeszow) Posen 1B
❒ SCHILDHORST/FREDEN Hannover 1A 2A
❒ SCHILTACH Baden 1A 2A
❒ SCHIRGISWALDA Sachsen 1A 2A
❒ SCHIRMECK/MOLSHEIM Elsass 1A
❒ SCHIRNDING Bayern 2A
❒ SCHIRRHEIN BEI HAGENAU Elsass 1A
❒ SCHIVELBEIN (Slawno, Swidwin) Pommern 1A
❒ SCHKEUDITZ Provinz Sachsen 1A
❒ SCHLAWE (Slawno) Pommern 1A 6B
❒ SCHLEBUSCH Rheinland 1A 2A 5C
❒ SCHLEBUSCH-MONTFORT (Schlebusch-Manfort) Rheinland 2B
❒ SCHLEID Rheinland 2B
❒ SCHLEIDEN Rheinland 1A
❒ SCHLEIZ Reuss J.L. 1A 2B 7B 13A
❒ SCHLESIENGRUBE (Chropaczow) 1A 2B 3A 5B
❒ SCHLESIENGRUBE (Kopalnia Slask) Schlesien 1A 2A 3B 5A
❒ SCHLESWIG Schleswig-Holstein 1A 2B 3A 7B 10B 12B
❒ SCHLETTAU Sachsen 1A
❒ SCHLETTSTADT (Selestat) Elsass 1A 6A
❒ SCHLEUSINGEN Thueringen 1A 2B 7B
❒ SCHLICHT Bayern 2B
❒ SCHLICHT Oberpfalz 2A
❒ SCHILDBERG Posen 3D
❒ SCHLIERBACH (Brachttal) Hessen-Nassau 1A 7A 13B
❒ SCHLIERSEE Bayern 1A
❒ SCHLITZ Hessen-Nassau 7A
❒ SCHLOCHAU (Schochau, Czluchow) Westpreussen 1A
❒ SCHLOSS hOLTE Westfalen 3B

50 Pfennig, Koenigswinter, 1A

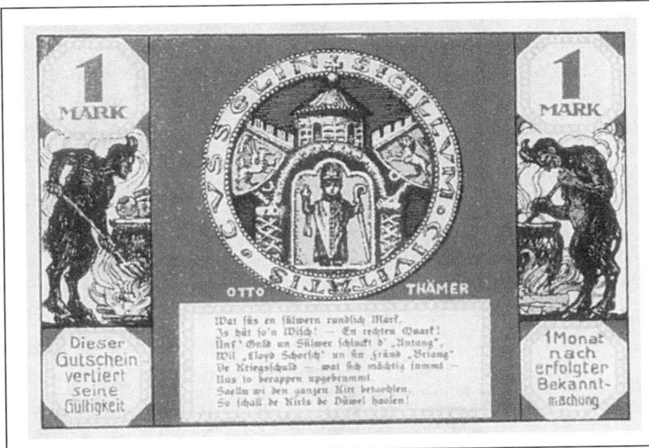

1 Mark, Koestin, 1A

❒ SCHLOSSVIPPACH
Sachsen-Weimar-Eilsenach 1A
❒ SCHLOTHEIM Thueringen 1A 2B
❒ SCHLUECHTERN Hessen-Nassau 1A
❒ SCHMALKALDEN
Hessen-Nassau 1A 2A 7A
❒ SCHMALLENBERG Wastfalen 1A 2B
❒ SCHMIEDEBERG/RIESENGBIRGE
(Bad Schmiedeberg, Kowary) Schlesien 1A 2A
❒ SCHMIEDEBERG, BAD
(Eisenmoorbad) Provinz Sachsen 1A 2B 6A
❒ SCHMIEDEFELD Provinz Sachsen 1A 2B 6B 7B 9B
❒ SCHMIEGEL
(Szmigiel, Smigiel) Posen 1A 2A 6A
❒ SCHMOELZ (Kueps) Bayern 6A 9A
❒ SCHNEEBERG Bayern 1A
❒ SCHNEEBERG-NEUSTAEDTEL
Sachsen 1A 2B
❒ SCHNEEBERG/ERZGEBIRGE
Sachsen 1A 8B
❒ SCHNEEHEIDE 3B
❒ SCHNEIDEMUEHL (Pila) Posen 1A 2A 3A 4A 6A
❒ SCHNELSEN Schleswig-Holstein 1A
❒ SCHNEVERDINGEN Hannover 1A 2A
❒ SCHNUFENHOFEN Bayern 6A
❒ SCHOBUELL Schleswig-Holstein 1A
❒ SCHOLVEN-GLADBECK
Westfalen 3A 4A
❒ SCHOEMBERG
(Szombierki, Szymrych) Schlesien 1A 2B 5A
❒ SCHOENAICH/STUTTGART
Wuerttemberg 7A

Gut für eine Mark.

Einzulösen bei der Stadthauptkasse spätestens am 1. Oktober 1914, widrigenfalls der Gutschein verfällt.

Kolmar i. P., den 3. August 1914.

Der Magistrat.

1 Mark, Kolmar/Posen, Germany, 1B

❒ SCHOENAU/CHEMNITZ
Sachsen 2B
❒ SCHOENAU/KATZBACH
(Swierzawa, Glatz) Schlesien 1A 2B
❒ SCHOENAU/WIESEN Baden 1A 2B
❒ SCHOENBACH Sachsen 1A 2B
❒ SCHOENBERG
Mecklinburg-Strelitz 1A 7B
❒ SCHOENBERG O.L.
(Sulikow) Schlesien 1A 2B
❒ SCHOENBERG/GRAFENAU Bayern 6B 7A
❒ SCHOENBERG/LANDSHUT
(Schoemberg, Szombierki, Szymbork, Szymrych, Sulikow) Schlesien 1A 2B 5B
❒ SCHOENEBECK & GROSS-SALZA
Provinz Sachsen 1A
❒ SCHOENEBECK/ELBE
Provinz Sachsen 1A 2B 12B
❒ SCHOENEBERG-FRIEDENAU
Brandenburg 2D
❒ SCHOENECK (Skarzcewy, Skarszewy)
Westpreussen 1A 7B
❒ SCHOENECK/VOGTLAND
Sachsen 1A 6A 7A
❒ SCHOENECKEN-WETTELDORF
Rheinland 2A
❒ SCHOENENBERG
Nordhein-Westfalen 14A
❒ SCHOENENBUCHEN Baden 1A
❒ SCHOENENTHAL Rheinland 2A
❒ SCHOENFELD/GLATZ
(Klodzka) Schlesien 1A 2B 7A
❒ SCHOENFELD/ZSCHOPAUTAL
Sachsen 1A 2A 7A
❒ SCHOENFLIESS
(Trzeinsko-Zdroj) Brandenburg 6A
❒ SCHOENHAGEN Hannover 2A 7A
❒ SCHOENHEIDE Sachsen 1A 2A
❒ SCHOENINGEN Braunschweig 7B
❒ SCHOENINGSDORF Hannover 2C
❒ SCHOENLANKE
(Trzcianka) Posen 1A 6B 7B
❒ SCHOENTHAL Schlesien 2B
❒ SCHOENWALD Bayern 1A 2A 6A
❒ SCHOEPPENSTAEDT
Braunschweig 1A
❒ SCHOETMAR Lippe 1A
❒ SCHOKKEN (Skoki) Posen 1B
❒ SCHOLVEN Westfalen 3A
❒ SCHONAICH/STUTTGART
Baden 7B
❒ SCHONDORF Ammersee 14B

50 Pfennig, Konstedt/O.S., 1A

50 Pfennig, Kreises Lebus in Seelow, 1A

25 Pfennig, Kreuzburg, 1A

2 Mark, Krotoschin, 1B

5 Pfennig, Krotoschin, 6B

25 Pfennig, Kudowa, Bad, 1A

2 Mark, Kunzendorf, 1A

40 Pfennig, Kurzenmoor, 1A

2 Mark, Labes/Pomm, 1A

25 Pfennig, Lage/Lippe, 1A

10 Pfennig, Landeck/Schl, 6A

50 Pfennig, Landeck, Bob, 1A

100 Pfennig, Landsberg/Os, 1A

75 Pfennig, Langeln, 1A

50 Pfennig, Langelohe, 1A

❐ SCHONDORF Bayern 14A
❐ SCHONFLIESS/ODER Brandenburg 6A
❐ SCHONGAU Bayern 1A 7B
❐ SCHONINGEN Braunschweig 7A
❐ SCHOPFHEIM Baden 1A 2A 7B
❐ SCHOPPNITZ (Szopienice) Schlesien 2B
❐ SCHORNDORF Wuerttemberg 1A 2A 7A
❐ SCHOTTEN Hessen 1A
❐ SCHRAMBERG Wuerttemberg 1A 2A 6A 7B 8A 9A 13C
❐ SCHREIBERHAU (Szklarska Poreba) Schlesien 1A 7B
❐ SCHRETZHEIM Bayern 7B
❐ SCHRIESHEIM Baden 1B
❐ SCHRIMM (Srem) Posen 1B
❐ SCHROBENHAUSEN Bayern 1A 2A 6A
❐ SCHRODA (Sroda) Posen 1A 2A 6A
❐ SCHROEICH/M 1A
❐ SCHUBIN (Szubin) Posen 1B
❐ SCHUEREN/HOERDE Westfalen 5C
❐ SCHUETTORF Hannover 1A
❐ SCHUETZENDORF (Wilemowice, Strzawa) Schlesien 7B
❐ SCHULITZ (Solec) Posen 1A
❐ SCHUSSENRIED Wuerttemberg 2A
❐ SCHWAAN Mecklenburg-Schwerin 1A
❐ SCHWABACH Bayern 1A 2B 7A
❐ SCHWABEN UND NEUBURG Bayern 1A
❐ SCHWABEN/ERDING Bayern 2A
❐ SCHWABMUENCHEN Bayern 1A
❐ SCHWABSTEDT Schleswig-Holstein 2D
❐ SCHWAEBISCH GMUEND Wuerttemberg 1A 2A 7B
❐ SCHWAEBISCH HALL Wuerttemberg 1A 2A 6A
❐ SCHWALINGEN Hannover 3B
❐ SCHWANDORF-WACKERSDORF Bayern 2A
❐ SCHWANDORF/OBERPFALZ Bayern 1A 2A 7A 9A
❐ SCHWANEBECK Provinz Sachsen 1A 2A
❐ SCHWARMSTEDT Hannover 3A 4A
❐ SCHWARZA/SAALE Schwarzburg-Rudolstadt 1A
❐ SCHWARZBURG Schwarzburg-Rudolstadt 1A 7A
❐ SCHWARZBURG Schwarzburg-Sonderhausen 6A
❐ SCHWARZENBACH/SAALE Bayern 1A 2A 6A
❐ SCHWARZENBECK Schleswig-Holstein 2B
❐ SCHWARZENBERG Sachsen 1A 2A 7A 14B
❐ SCHWARZENFELD Bayern 2A
❐ SCHWARZENHAMMER Bayern 2A
❐ SCHWARZFELD Niedersachsen 14A
❐ SCHWARZHOFEN Bayern 1A
❐ SCHWARZWALDAU Schlesien 2B
❐ SCHWEDT/ODER Brandenburg 1A 2B
❐ SCHWEGENHEIM Pfalz 1A
❐ SCHWEGER MOOR Hannover 3B
❐ SCHWEICH/MOSEL Rheinland 2A
❐ SCHWEIDNITZ (Swidnica) Schlesien 1A 2B 3B 4A
❐ SCHWEINA Thueringen 1A

75 Pfennig, Langeness, Nordmarsch, 1A

50 Pfennig, Langensalza, 1A

❒ SCHWEINFURT Bayern 1A 2A 6A 7A 11C 12B
❒ SCHWEINITZ Provinz Sachsen 1A
❒ SCHWEIZERTAL Sachsen 2A
❒ SCHWELM Westfalen 1A 2B
❒ SCHWENNINGEN/NECKAR Wuerttemberg 1A 2A 7A
❒ SCHWEPNITZ Sachsen 1A
❒ SCHWERIN Mecklinburg-Schwerin 1A 2E 6A 12A
❒ SCHWERIN/WARTHE (Kierszkowo, Skwierzyna) Posen 1A 2B 6A 7B
❒ SCHWERSENZ (Swarzedz) Posen 1B
❒ SCHWERTE Westfalen 2B 5C 7B 11E 15A
❒ SCHWETZ (Swiecie) Westpreussen 1B
❒ SCHWETZINGEN Baden 1A 8B
❒ SCHWIEBUS (Swiebodzin, Poland) Brandenburg 1A 2A
❒ SCHWIECHELDT/PEINE Hannover 2A
❒ SCHWIENTOCHLOWITZ (Swietochlowice) Schlesien 1A 2B 3B 5B
❒ SEBALDSBRUECK Bremen 3B
❒ SEBNITZ Sachsen 1A 2A 8B 13A
❒ SEEBACH Sachsen-Weimar-Eisenach 7B
❒ SEEBERGEN Sachsen-Coburg-Gotha 7B
❒ SEEBURG (Jeziorany) Ostpreussen 1A
❒ SEEFELD Weser-Ems 1D
❒ SEEGEFELD (Falkensee) Brandenburg 7B
❒ SEEHAUSEN/ALTMARK Provinz Sachsen 1A
❒ SEEHEIM (Jeziorki) Posen 2B

❒ SEELHORST Hannover 3B
❒ SEELINGSTAEDT/GRIMMA Sachsen 2A
❒ SEELOW Lebus 1A
❒ SEELZE Hannover 7B
❒ SENNE Westfalen 3A
❒ SEPPENRADE Westfalen 5D
❒ SEESEN Braunschweig 2A 8A
❒ SEETH Schleswig-Holstein 1A
❒ SEETH-ECKHOLT Schleswig-Holstein 1A
❒ SEFFERN/EIFEL Rheinland 2A
❒ SEGEBERG, BAD Schleswig-Holstein 1A 2A 6A 8B
❒ SEHMA Sachsen 1A 7B
❒ SEHNDE Hannover 2E
❒ SEIDENBERG O.L. (Zawidow) Schlesien 1A 2A
❒ SEIFERSDORF/RADEBERG Sachsen 2A
❒ SEIFFEN Sachsen 1A
❒ SEIFHENNERSDORF Sachsen 1A 2A
❒ SEITENBERG/GLATZ (Stronie Slaskie) Schlesien 1A 6A
❒ SEITENDORF/DRESDEN Sachsen 2A
❒ SEITENDORF/GLATZ Schlesien 2A
❒ SELB Bayern 1A 2A 6A 13B
❒ SELBITZ Bayern 2A
❒ SELIGENSTADT Hessen 1A 7B
❒ SELLIN/RUEGEN Pommern 1A
❒ SELM Westfalen 5B 7A
❒ SELSINGEN Hannover 1A
❒ SELTERS Rheinland 14A

1 Mark, Langenschwalbech, Bad, 1A

5 Pfennig, Langewiesen/Thür., Germany, 1A

❒ SENDEN Bayern 2A
❒ SENFTENBERG Brandenburg 1A 2B
❒ SENNE Westfalen 3A 4A
❒ SENNHEIM Elsass 1A 2A
❒ SENSBURG (Mragowo O.L.) Ostpreussen 2D 6A
❒ SEPPENRADE Westfalen 5B
❒ SETTRUP (Hoexter) Westfalen 11B
❒ SEVERINSBERG Rheinprovinz 1A 2B
❒ SIEBENLEHN Sachsen 2B
❒ SIEBIGERODE Provinz Sachsen 2B
❒ SIEBLEBEN Sachsen-Gotha 1A
❒ SIEDENBURG Hannover 2A
❒ SIEDENHOLZ Hannover 3B
❒ SIEDLINGHAUSEN Westfalen 2A
❒ SIEGBURG Rheinland 1A 8B 14B
❒ SIEGEN Westfalen 1A 2E 6A 8A
❒ SIEGERSLEBEN Provinz Sachsen 2A
❒ SIEGKREIS Rheinland 1A 2A
❒ SIEGMAR Sachsen 1A 2A 8B
❒ SIEMIANOWITZ (Siemianowice) Schlesien 1A 2B 3C
❒ SIEMIANOWITZ-GEORGSHUETTE (Siemianowice-Huta Jerzy)Schlesien 2B
❒ SIEMIANOWITZ-LAURAHUETTA (Siemianowice-Huta Laura)Schlesien 2B
❒ SIERSLEBEN Provinz Sachsen 2C 6B 11B
❒ SIERSZA (Sierszy) Schlesien 2B
❒ SIGMARINGEN Hohenzollern 1A 6A
❒ SIGOLSHEIM Elsass 1A
❒ SILBACH Westfalen 1A
❒ SILBERBERG (Srebrna) Schlesien 1A
❒ SILBERHUETTE Anhalt 2A 7B
❒ SILSCHEDE Westfalen 2A
❒ SIMBACH/INN Bayern 1A 2A 6A
❒ SIMMERN Rheinland 1A 5C
❒ SINGEN Baden 1A 7B
❒ SINGEN-HOHENTWIEL Baden 1A 2A
❒ SINGHOFEN Hessen-Nassau 7B
❒ SINSHEIM/ELSENZ Baden 2A 6A
❒ SINZIG Rheinland 1D 2A 6A
❒ SITZENDORF Thueringen 2A
❒ SKALMIERSCHUETZ (Skalmierzyce) Posen 1A 3E 4A
❒ SKURZ (Skorcz, Skurcz) Westpreussen 1A 2A
❒ SLOMOWO Posen 7B
❒ SLUPCA (Slouptsy) Posen 2A
❒ SOBERNHEIM Rheinland 1A
❒ SODENTORF (Bad Soden) Hessen-Nassau 7B
❒ SODINGEN (Herne) Westfalen 1A 2A 3A 5A
❒ SOEHLINGEN Hannover 3B
❒ SOELDE (Dortmund) Westfalen 2E 5B
❒ SOEMMERDA Provinz Sachsen 1A 6A 7A
❒ SOERNEWITZ/MEISSEN (Coswig) Sachsen 7B
❒ SOERUP Schleswig-Holstein 1A 14B
❒ SOEST Westfalen 1A 2A 5C 6A 7B
❒ SOHLAND/SPREE Sachsen 1A 2A 7B
❒ SOHRAU (Zory) Schlesien 1A
❒ SOHREN Rheinland 7A 14A
❒ SOLDAU (Dzialdowo) Ostpreussen 6A 10A
❒ SOLDEN (Mysliborz, Poland) Brandenburg 1A
❒ SOLDIN N.M. (Mysliborz) Brandenburg 1A 6A
❒ SOLEC (Schulitz, Solecka) Posen 1B
❒ SOLINGEN Rheinland 1A 2A 6A 7B 11B 12A 14B
❒ SOLINGEN-WEYER Rheinland 2A
❒ SOLNHOFEN Bayern 1A
❒ SOLTAU Hannover 1A 2A 3B 7B
❒ SOMMERFELD (Lubsko, Poland) Brandenburg 1A
❒ SOMMERHAUSEN Bayern 6B
❒ SONDERBURG (Soenderborg, Denmark) Schleswig-Holstein 1A
❒ SONDERNACH Elsass 1A
❒ SONDERNHEIM Pfalz 1A
❒ SONDERSHAUSEN Schwarzburg-Sondershausen 1A 2B 7B
❒ SONNEBERG Thueringen 1A 2B 6A 7A
❒ SONNEBURG/NEUMARK Sachsen 2B
❒ SONSBECK Rheinland 2A
❒ SONTHEIN/N Wuerttemberg 1A 2A
❒ SONTHOFEN Bayern 2D 6A
❒ SONTHOFEN-IMMENSTADT Bayern 1A

25 Pfennig, Lauban/Schl, 1A

10 Pfennig, Lauchstedt, Bad, 1A

1 Mark, Lauenburg/Elbe, 1A

10 Pfennig, Lechfeld, POW, 3B

25 Pfennig, Leck, 1A

75 Pfennig, Leer, 1A

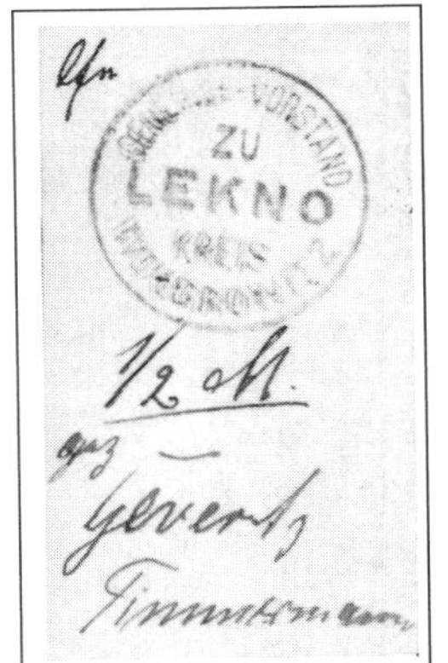

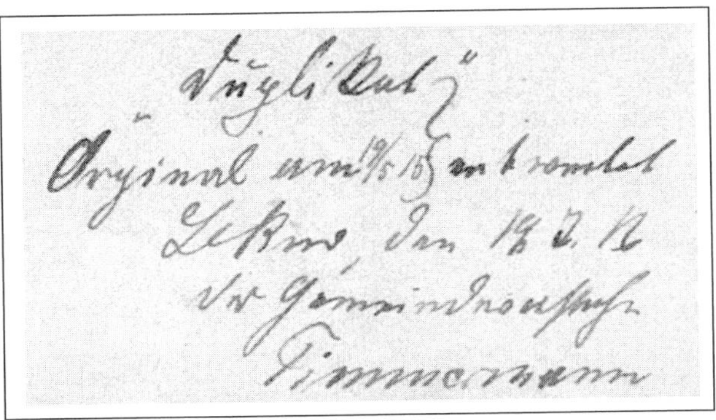

Mark, Lekno, 1A

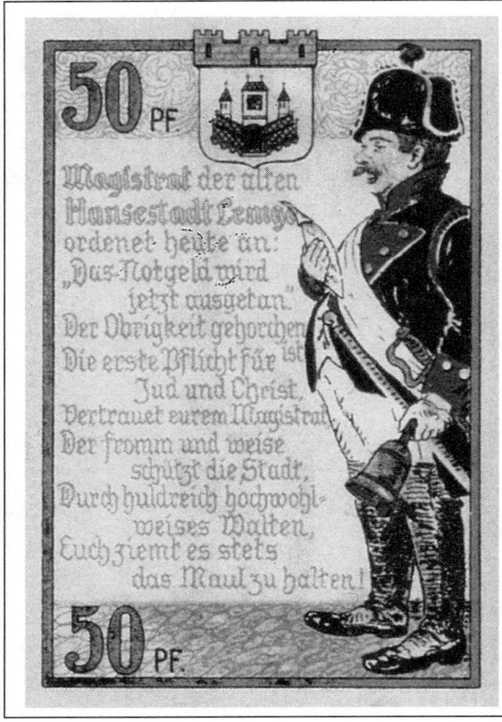

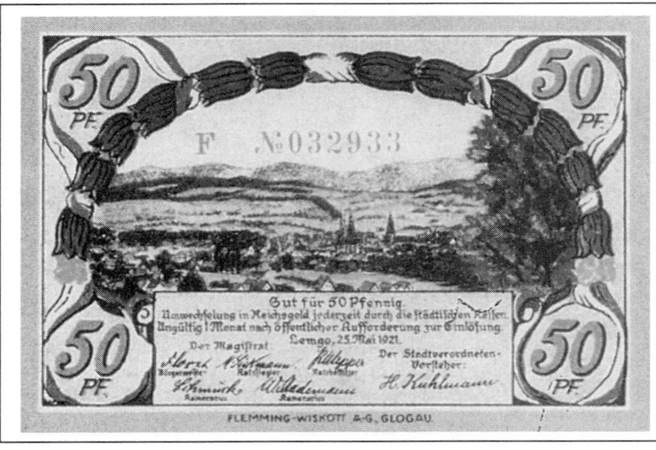

50 Pfennig, Lemgo, 1A

❒ SONTRA Hessen 1A
❒ SOODEN/WERRA
(Bad) Hessen-Nassau 1A
❒ SORAU N.L. (Zary, Poland)
Brandenburg 1A 11B
❒ SOSNOWIEC
(Sosnowice, Sosnovitsy) Schlesien 2B
❒ SOTTORF Niedersachsen 3B 14B
❒ SPAICHINGEN Wuerttemberg 1A 8A

Types of Emergency Money

Type	Reference #
Municipal paper	1
Private paper	2
POW paper	3
POW official metal	4
POW private metal	5
Municipal metal	6
Private metal	7
Gas tokens	8
Food; beer; konsumverein	9
Naval; military; kantine	10
Encased, unencased stamps	11
Streetcar tokens	12
Porcelain	13
World War II issues	14
Concentration, Civilian internment camps	15

Rarity grades: A, to $25; B, to $60; C, to $125; D, to $200; and E, $350

❒ SPANDAU Brandenburg 1A 7B 8B 12B 14B
❒ SPANGDAHLEM Rheinland 10B
❒ SPANGENBERG Hessen-Nassau 14B
❒ SPARNECK Bayern 1A
❒ SPEICHER/EIFEL Rheinland 1A 2A
❒ SPETZERFEHN/OSTFR.
Hannover 2B
❒ SPEYER/ RHEIN Pfalz 1A 6A 7A 8B 14B
❒ SPIEGELAU Bayern 7A
❒ SPIEKEROOG Weser-Ems 2B
❒ SPINNMUEHLE-REICHENBACH/
❒ Vogtland Sachsen 2A
❒ SPITZKUNNERSDORF Sachsen 2A
❒ SPLITTER (Tilsit-Splitter)
Ostpreussen 1B
❒ SPOHLE Oldenburg 3B
❒ SPORA Provinz Sachsen 5C
❒ SPRAKENSEHL Hannover 3B
❒ SPREMBERG/LAUSITZ
Brandenburg 1A 2A 6A 7B
❒ SPRENDLINGEN
(Dreieich) Hessen-Nassau 7A 9A
❒ SPRINGE Hannover 1B 2B
❒ SPROCKHOEVEL Westfalen 5A
❒ SPROTTAU
(Szprotawa) Schlesien 1A 2A 3B 4A 5B 6A 7B
❒ STAAKEN Brandenburg 7B
❒ STADE Hannover 1A 8A 14B
❒ STADTAMHOF Bayern 2A 7A
❒ STADTHAGEN Lippe 2A 9A
❒ STADTILM
Schwarzburg-Rudolstadt 1A 7B
❒ STADTKYLL Rheinland 2A
❒ STADTLENGSFELD
Sachsen-Weimar-Eisenach 1A 2A 7B 13A
❒ STADTLOHN Westfalen 2C 7B
❒ STADTOLDENDORF
Braunschweig 1B 2C 7B
❒ STAFFELSTEIN Bayern 1A
❒ STAHLHEIM (Amneville)
Lothringen 7B
❒ STAHLMARK (Wengern)
Rheinland 2A

50 Pfennig, Lenzen/Elbe, 1A

- ❐ STALLUPOENEN (Niesterow) Ostpreussen — 1A
- ❐ STAMMBACH Bayern — 1A
- ❐ STARBACH Sachsen — 2A
- ❐ STARGARD Mecklenburg-Strelitz — 1A 2A 3A
- ❐ STARGARD (Starogard, Starndworska, Szezecinski) Westpreussen — 1A 2A 3A 4A 14B
- ❐ STASSFURT Provinz Sachsen — 1A 2A 5C
- ❐ STAUCHITZ Sachsen — 2A
- ❐ STAUFEN/BREISGAU Baden — 1A
- ❐ STAVENHAGEN Mecklenburg-Schwerin — 1A 6A
- ❐ STECHAU/HERZBERG AM ELSTER Provinz Sachsen — 2A
- ❐ STECKLENBERG/HARZ Provinz Sachsen — 1A
- ❐ STEDESAND Schleswig-Holstein — 1A
- ❐ STEELE Rheinland — 3A 5A 8B
- ❐ STEIN Bayern — 2A 6A 7A
- ❐ STEINACH Sachsen-Meiningen — 1A 6A
- ❐ STEINAU Hannover — 3B
- ❐ STEINAU/ODER (Scinawa) Schlesien — 1A
- ❐ STEINBACH Sachsen-Meiningen — 1A
- ❐ STEINBACH-HALLENBERG Hessen-Nassau — 1A 2A
- ❐ STEINBACH/GLATZ Schlesien — 1A 2A
- ❐ STEINBACH/WALD Bayern — 2A
- ❐ STEINBRUECKEN Hessen-Nassau — 7A
- ❐ STEINBURG Schleswig-Holstein — 1A
- ❐ STEINEN Baden — 1A 2A
- ❐ STEINFELD Schleswig-Holstein — 1A
- ❐ STEINFELS (Parkstein) Bayern — 7A
- ❐ STEINFOERDE Hannover — 2A
- ❐ STEINFOERDE-WIETZ Hannover — 1A
- ❐ STEINFURT Westfalen — 1A
- ❐ STEINHEID Sachsen-Meiningen — 1A
- ❐ STEINHEIM Westfalen — 1A 2E
- ❐ STEINHORST Hannover — 3B
- ❐ STEINIGTWOHNSDORF O.L. Sachsen — 1A
- ❐ STEINWIESEN Bayern — 6A 7A
- ❐ STELLAU Schleswig-Holstein — 2A
- ❐ STELLINGEN (Hamburg) Schleswig-Holstein — 1A 7B 8B
- ❐ STELLINGEN-LANGENFELDE Schleswig-Holstein — 2E
- ❐ STENDAL Provinz Sachsen — 1A 2A 3A 5A 6A 7A 8B 12A
- ❐ STENDSITZ Westpreussen — 2B
- ❐ STENSCHEWO (Steszew) Posen — 1A
- ❐ STEPENITZ/CAMMIN (Stepnica) Pommern — 2A
- ❐ STERKRADE Rheinland — 1A 5C 6A
- ❐ STERNBERG Mecklenburg-Schwerin — 1A
- ❐ STESZEWO (Steszewska) Posen — 1B
- ❐ STETTIN (Szececin) Pommern — 1A 2A 5B 6A 7B 11B 12B
- ❐ STEUDNITZ/DORNBURG Thueringen — 2A 7B

50 Pfennig, Leopoldshall, 1A

50 Pfennig, Lessen/Wpr, 2C

❒ STEYERBERG Hannover 3B
❒ STINNES ZECHE (Essen-Karnap) Rheinland 3A 4A
❒ STOCKACH Baden 1A
❒ STOCKELSDORF Schleswig-Holstein 2A
❒ STOCKHAUSEN/LAHN Hessen-Nassau 11B
❒ STOCKHEIM Bayern 7A
❒ STOECKHEIM Hannover 1A 7B
❒ STOERMEDE (Geseke) Westfalen 3D
❒ STOESSEN Provinz Sachsen 1A
❒ STOLBERG Rheinland 1A
❒ STOLBERG/HARZ Provinz Sachsen 1A
❒ STOLLBERG/ERZGEBIRGE Sachsen 1A 2B 14B
❒ STOLP (Slupsk) Pommern 2A
❒ STOLPEN Sachsen 1A 2A
❒ STOLZENAU/WESER Hannover 1A 2A
❒ STOLZENBURG Pommern 7A
❒ STOLZENHAGEN Brandenburg 7A
❒ STORCHNEST (Osieczna) Posen 1A 2B
❒ STORKENSAUSEN/OBERELSASS Elsass 1A
❒ STORKOW Brandenburg 1A
❒ STORMARN Schleswig-Holstein 1A
❒ STORMEDE Westfalen 5C
❒ STOSSWEIER Elsass 1A
❒ STOTEL Hannover 1A
❒ STRAELEN Rheinland 1A 2A
❒ STRAHWALDE-HERRNHUT Sachsen 2A 11C
❒ STRALKOWO (Strahlau, Strzalkowo) Posen 3A 10B
❒ STRALSUND Pommern 1A 2B 4B 6A 7B 8A 10B 12A
❒ STRALSUND-DAENHOLM Pommern 3B 4B
❒ STRASBURG (Brodnice, Brodnica) Westpreussen 1A 2A 3A 6B 7B
❒ STRASBURG/UCKERMARK Brandenburg 1A 2A 6A
❒ STRASSBURG (Strasbourg) Elsass 1A 3A 6A 7B 10B
❒ STRASSEBERSBACH (Dietzhoelztal) Hessen-Nassau 6B
❒ STRAUBING Bayern 1A 2A 7A 10A
❒ STRAUSBERG Brandenburg 1A 2B 7B
❒ STREEK Oldenburg 3B
❒ STREHLEN (Strzelin) Schlesien 1A 2A 6A 7B
❒ STREHLITZ (Strzelce) Schlesien 7B
❒ STRELA/ELBE Sachsen 1A 2A
❒ STRELITZ (Altstrelitz) Mecklenburg-Strelitz 1A 2A 3A 7B
❒ STRELNO (Strzelno) Posen 1B
❒ STRICHE (Stryschek, Stryszek) Posen 1B
❒ STRIEGAU (Strzegom) Schlesien 1A 2B 4A 5B 7B
❒ STROEBECK Provinz Sachsen 1A
❒ STROEHEN Hannover 3A
❒ STUEHLINGEN Baden 1A
❒ STUER, BAD IX Armeekorps 3C 10B
❒ STÜTZERBACH Provinz Sachsen 1A 2A 7B 9B
❒ STUHM (Sztum) Westpreussen 1B
❒ STUTTGART Wuerttemberg 1A 2A 3A 6A 7A 8B 9A 10A 11B 13A 14A
❒ STUTTGART-OBERTUERKHEIM Wuerttemberg 2A
❒ STUTTHOF (Sztutowo, Koebyly) Westpreussen 15B
❒ SUCHSDORF Schleswig-Holstein 1A
❒ SUDER-DITHMARSCHEN Schleswig-Holstein 1A
❒ SUDERODE, BAD Provinz Sachsen 1A
❒ SUECHTELN Rheinland 1A 8B
❒ SUEDERBRARUP Schleswig-Holstein 1A 2A
❒ SUEDERHOLZ (Soenderskov, Denmark) Schleswig-Holstein 1A
❒ SUEDEWECHT Oldenburg 3B
❒ SUELZE Mecklenburg-Schwerin 1A
❒ SUEPPLINGENBURG Braunschweig 2A
❒ SUERTH/KOELN Rheinland 2A
❒ SUESEL Schleswig-Holstein 1A 2A
❒ SUHL Provinz Sachsen 1A 2A 6A 7A 8B
❒ SULMIRSCHUETZ (Sulmierzyce) Posen 1B
❒ SULZ Elsass 1A
❒ SULZA, BAD Sachsen-Weimar-Eisenach 1A 3A

50 Pfennig, Lichtenfels, 1A

50 Pfennig, Lichenhorst, 1A

❒ SULZBACH-SAAR Rheinland	1A		
❒ SULZBACH/OBERPFALZ Bayern	1A		
❒ SULZERN Elsass	1A		
❒ SULZMATT Elsass	1A		
❒ SUNDERN Westfalen	2E		
❒ SUNDREMDA Thueringen	2A		
❒ SUNDWIG Westfalen	2C		
❒ SUTTHOF (Elbing) Westpreussen	15B		
❒ SUTTROP Nordhein-Westfalen	14D		
❒ SWARZEDZ Schlesien	1B		
❒ SWIERKLANIEC (Neudeck) Schlesien	2B		
❒ SWIETOCHLOWICE (Schwientochlowitz) Schlesien	1B		
❒ SWINEMUENDE (Swinoujscie) Pommern	2A	6A	8B
❒ SWINESNUTEN Scherzscheine	2E		
❒ SYLT Schleswig-Holstein	10B		
❒ TAILFINGEN (Albstadt) Wuerttemberg	1A	2A	6A
❒ TAMBACH-DIETHARZ Sachsen-Gotha	1A		
❒ TANGERHUETTE Provinz Sachsen	2C	6A	
❒ TANGERMUENDE Provinz Sachsen	1A	2A	6A
❒ TANGSTEDT Schleswig-Holstein	1A		
❒ TANNA Reuss j. L.	1A		
❒ TANNENBERG/ERZGEBIRGE Sachsen	1A		

❒ TANNENBERGSTHAL/VOGTLAND Sachsen	1A				
❒ TANNHAUSEN Schlesien	1A	2A	7A	13A	
❒ TANNHAUSEN-WUESTEIGERSDORF Schlesien	2B				
❒ TANNRODA Sachsen-Weimar-Eisenach	1A				
❒ TARNOWITZ (Tarnowskie Gory) Schlesien	1A	2A	7C	9A	11C
❒ TAUBENHEIM/SPREE Sachsen	1A				
❒ TAUBERBISCHOFSHEIM Baden	1A	6A			
❒ TAURA Sachsen	1A	2A			
❒ TECKLENBURG Westfalen	1C	2E			
❒ TEGERNSEE Bayern	1A				
❒ TEICHHUETTE/HARZ (Gittelde) Braunschweig	2A				
❒ TEISENDORF Bayern	1A	2A			
❒ TEISNACH Bayern	1A	2A	7A		
❒ TEMPELBURG (Dzarlinek, Czaplinek) Pommern	1A	2A	6A		
❒ TEMPLIN Brandenburg	1A	2A			
❒ TENINGEN Baden	1A	2A			
❒ TENNSTEDT Provinz Sachsen	1A				
❒ TESSIN Mecklenburg-Schwerin	1A				
❒ TETEROW Mecklenburg-Schwerin	1A	6A	7B		
❒ TETTAU (Mainleus) Bayern	2A	13B			
❒ TETTENBORN Provinz Sachsen	2A				
❒ TETTNANG Wuerttemberg	1A	2A	6A		
❒ TEUCHERN Provinz Sachsen	1A	2A	7B		
❒ TEUDITZ (Grosskorbetha) Provinz Sachsen	7B				
❒ TEUFELSMOOR Hannover	3A				

50 Pfennig, Liebenwerda, 1A

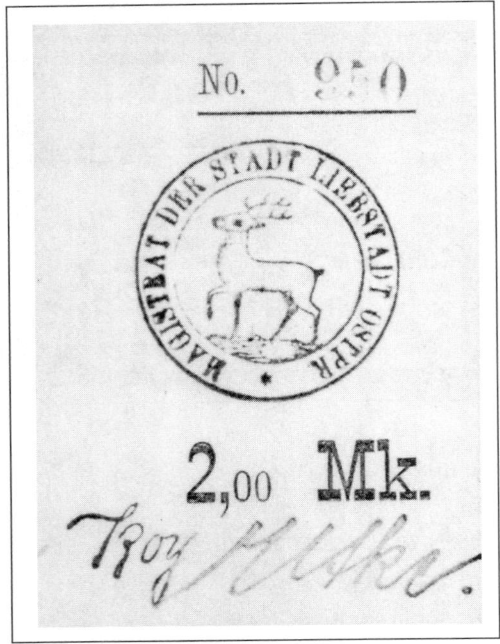

2 Mark, Liebstadt, 1B

❒ TEUSCHNITZ Bayern 1A 7B
❒ TEUTSCHENTHAL Sachsen 7A
❒ TEVEREN Nordrhein-Westfalen 14B
❒ THALE/ HARZ Provinz Sachsen 1A 2A 6A
❒ THALHEIM Provinz Sachsen 2A
❒ THALHEIM Sachsen 1A 2A
❒ THANN Elsass 1A 2A 6A
❒ THANNDORF/GLATZ Schlesien 1A 2A
❒ THANNHAUSEN Bayern 1A
❒ THEISBERGSTEGEN Pfalz 1A
❒ THEISSEN Provinz Sachsen 7B
❒ THEMAR Thueringen 2A
❒ THESDORF Schelswig-Holstein 1A
❒ THIERSHEIM/OBERFRANKEN Bayern 2A
❒ THONBERG Sachsen 2A
❒ THORN (Torun) Westpreussen 1A 6A 12B 14B
❒ THRAEHNA S.-A. Thueringen 2A
❒ THUELEN Westfalen 1E
❒ THUM/ERZGEBIRGE Sachsen 1A 2B
❒ TICHAU (Tichy) Schlesien 2A
❒ TIEFENFURT (Parowa) Schlesien 2A 7B
❒ TIEFURT/WEIMAR Sachsen 1A
❒ TIEGENDORF/DANZIG Westpreussen 1A
❒ TIEGENHOF/DANZIG (Nowy Dwor, Dworska) Westpreussen 1A
❒ TIENGEN Baden 1A 2A
❒ TILSIT (Sovetsk, Sowietsk, Sowjetsk, USSR) Ostpreussen 2A 6A 7B 8B 12B
❒ TINGLEFF (Tinglev, Denmark) Schleswig-Holstein 1A 2A
❒ TINNUM/SYLT Schleswig-Holstein 1A
❒ TIRSCHENREUTH Bayern 1A 2B 7B
❒ TIRSCHTIEGEL (Trziel) Posen 1B
❒ TITTMONING Bayern 1A 2A
❒ TOCKENDORF Sachsen-Altenburg 7B
❒ TODTNAU Baden 1A 2A
❒ TOELZ BAD Bayern 1A 6A 8B
❒ TOENNING Schleswig-Holstein 2 A 6A
❒ TOEPINGEN Hannover 3B
❒ TONDERN (Toender, Denmark) Schleswig-Holstein 1A 7B
❒ TONNDORF-LOHE Scheswig-Holstein 1A
❒ TORGAU Provinz Sachsen 1A 2B 3B 6A 8B 10B 13B
❒ TORGELOW Pommern 1A 6A
❒ TOST (Toszek) Schlesien 1A 2B
❒ TOSTEDT Hannover 1A
❒ TRAAR Rheinland 1A
❒ TRABEN-TRARBACH Rheinland 2C
❒ TRACHENBERG (Zmigrod) Schlesien 1A 2B
❒ TRAPPSTADT Bayern 1A
❒ TRAUNSTEIN Bayern 1A 2A 3C 4A 6A
❒ TRAUTZSCHE Sachsen 2A
❒ TRAVEMUENDE Schleswig-Holstein 2A
❒ TREBNITZ (Trzebinia) Schlesien 1A 2B 8B 11B
❒ TREBSEN/MULDE Sachsen 1A 2A
❒ TREFFURT Provinz Sachsen 1A 2D
❒ TREMESSEN (Trzemeszno, Trzemeszenska) Posen 1A 6A
❒ TRENNFURT/MAIN Bayern 1A 2A
❒ TREPTOW/REGA (Trzebiatow) Pommern 1A 2B
❒ TREPTOW/TOLLENSEE (Altentreptow) Pommern 1A 2B
❒ TREUCHTLINGEN Bayern 1A 2A 6A
❒ TREUCHTLINGEN-WEISSENBURG Bayern 1A 2A
❒ TREUEN Sachsen 1A 2A
❒ TREUENBRIETZEN Brandenburg 1A
❒ TREYSA Hessen-Nassau 2A
❒ TRIBERG Baden 1A 6A 14B
❒ TRIBSEES Pommern 1A 2A
❒ TRIEBEL N.L. Brandenburg 2A
❒ TRIEBES Thueringen 1A 2A
❒ TRIER Rheinland 2B 3E 6A 7A 11C
❒ TRIFTERN Bayern 1A
❒ TRIPTIS Thueringen 1A 2A
❒ TRITTAU Schleswig-Holstein 1A
❒ TROISCHEN/ROSSWEIN Sachsen 2A
❒ TROISDORF Rheinland 1A 2A 7A
❒ TROSSINGEN Wuerttemberg 1A 2A 6A 7A
❒ TROSTBERG Bayern 1A 2A 7A

3 Mark, Liebstadt/Ostpreussen, Germany, 1B

75 Pfennig, Lippspringe, 1A

50 Pfennig, Lobeda, 1A

10 Pfennig, Masuren, 1A

50 Pfennig, Lorch, 1A

50 Pfennig, Lorch/Rheingau, Germany, 1A

50 Pfennig, Lucka/S. A., 1A

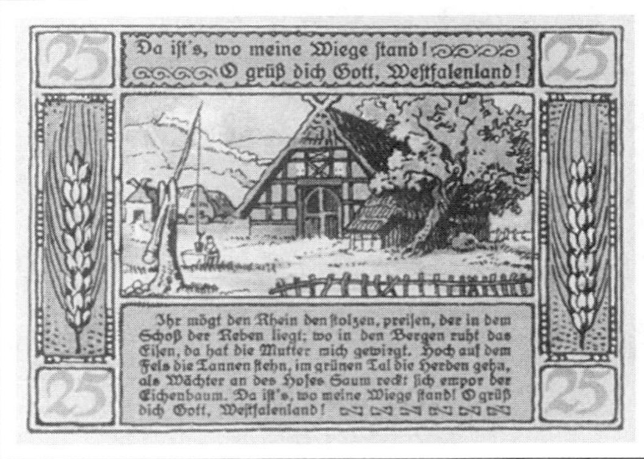

25 Pfennig, Lübbecke/W, 1A

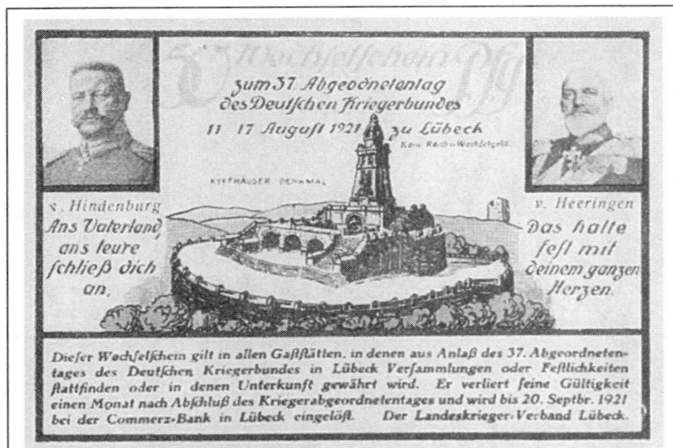

50 Pfennig, Luebeck, 1A

25 Pfennig, Lübtheen/M, 1A

❒ TSCHERBENEY/GLATZ Schlesien	2B						
❒ TUCHEL (Tuchola) Westpreussen	1A	4A					
❒ TUEBINGEN Wuerttemberg	1A	2A	6A	14B			
❒ TUERKHEIM Bayern	1A	2A					
❒ TUNGENDORF Schleswig-Holstein	1A						
❒ TUNTSCHENDORF (Tlumaczow) Schlesien	4A						
❒ TUREW (Turwia) Posen	1A	2B					
❒ TUTTLINGEN Wuerttemberg	1A	6A	7A				
❒ TWISTRINGEN Hannover	2A						
❒ UEBERLINGEN Baden	1A	2A	6A	7B			
❒ UEBERRUHR Rheinland	2A						
❒ UEBIGAU Provinz Sachsen	1A						
❒ UECKERMUENDE Pommern	1A	7A					
❒ UEDEM-KEPPELN Rheinland	1A						
❒ UELZEN Hannover	1A	2A	7A	11C			
❒ UERDINGEN Rheinland	1A	2A	4A	5A	6A	8B	
❒ UETERSEN Schleswig-Holstein	1A	2A					
❒ UETZE Hannover	3B						
❒ UFFENHEIM Bayern	1A	2A	6A				
❒ UFFHOLZ Elsass	1A						
❒ UHYST/TAUCHER Sachsen	2A						
❒ UJEST (Ujazd) Schlesien	1A						
❒ UK (Uge, Denmark) Schleswig-Holstein	1A						
❒ ULLERSRICHT Bayern	2A						
❒ ULM-EINSINGEN Wuerttemberg	2A						
❒ ULM/DONAU Wuerttemberg	1A	2A	4A	7A	8B	12B	13B
❒ UNKEL Pfalz	14B						
❒ UNKEL-SCHEUREN Rheinland	2A						
❒ UNNA Westfalen	1B	5B	6A	11B			
❒ UNNA-KAMEN Westfalen	1A						
❒ UNNA-KOENIGSBORN Westfalen	2B						

❒ UNRUHSTADT (Kargowa) Posen	1A	
❒ UNTER ELSASS Elsass	1A	
❒ UNTER PEISSENBERG Bayern	6A	
❒ UNTERBARMEN Rheinland	2A	
❒ UNTERBREIZBACH/RHOEN Sachsen-Meiningen	2A	
❒ UNTERESCHBACH Rheinland	2A	
❒ UNTERGRIESBACH Bayern	2A	
❒ UNTERHACHING/MUENCHEN Bayern	2A	
❒ UNTERHAUSEN Wuerttemberg	1A	
❒ UNTERKOCHEN Wuerttemberg	2A	7B
❒ UNTERKREUZBERG VOR WALD Bayern	7A	
❒ UNTERLUESS Hannover	3B	
❒ UNTERNEUBRUNN Thueringen	2A	
❒ UNTERPOERLITZ Sachsen-Meiningen	2A	9B
❒ UNTERSACHSENBERG Sachsen	1A	
❒ UNTERTAUNUSKREIS Hessen-Nassau	1A	
❒ UNTERTEUTSCHENTHAL Provinz Sachsen	1A	
❒ UNTERTUERKHEIM Bayern	7B	14B
❒ UNTERWEISSBACH Schwarzburg-Rudolstadt	1A	
❒ UNTERWELLENBORN Thueringen	2A	
❒ UNTERWESERSTAEDTE (Bremerhaven) Bremen	2A	6A
❒ UNTERWESTERWALDKREIS Hessen-Nassau	1A	
❒ URACH Wuerttemberg	1A	
❒ URBIS Elsass	1A	
❒ URMATT Elsass	1A	2A

1 Mark, Luechtringen, 1A

50 Pfennig, Luetjenburg, 1A

Location				
❐ USCH (Ujscie) Posen	1A	6B		
❐ USEDOM Pommern	1A	7B		
❐ USEDOM-WOLLIN Pommern	1A			
❐ USINGEN Hessen-Nassau	1A	6A		
❐ USLAR Hannover	1A	2A		
❐ USTRON Schlesien	2A			
❐ UTZENFELD Baden	1A			
❐ VACHA Thueringen	1A	2A		
❐ VAETHEN-TANGERHUETTE Provinz Sachsen	2A	7B		
❐ VAIHINGEN/ENZ Wuerttemberg	1A	5C	14B	
❐ VALBERT Westfalen	1B			
❐ VALLENDAR Rheinland	1A			
❐ VANDSBURG (Wiecbork) Westpreussen	1A			
❐ VAREL Oldenburg	2C	7B		
❐ VECHTA Oldenburg	1A	2A		
❐ VEGESACK Bremen	1A	2A	5B	8A
❐ VEHNEMOOR Hannover	3B			
❐ VEILSDORF Sachsen-Meiningen	7B			
❐ VELBERT Rheinland	1A	2A	6A	
❐ VELEN-RAMSDORF Westfalen	3E			
❐ VELPE Westfalen	2B			
❐ VELSEN Rheinland	5A			
❐ VELTEN Brandenburg	1A	2A	7B	
❐ VENUSBERG Sachsen	2A			
❐ VERDEN/ALLER Hannover	1A	3B	11E	
❐ VETSCHAU/SPREEWALD Brandenburg	1A			
❐ VIECHTACH Bayern	1A	2A	6A	7B
❐ VIENENBURG/HARZ Hannover	1A	2A		
❐ VIERSEN Rheinland	1A	2A	3B	
❐ VILLINGEN Baden	1A	2A	3B	9B

Location				
❐ VILSBIBURG Bayern	1A	6A	7B	
❐ VILSECK Bayern	2A			
❐ VILSHOFEN/DONAU Bayern	1A	2A		
❐ VINSEBEK Westfalen	1A			
❐ VISSELHOEVEDE Hannover	1A	2A		
❐ VLOTHO/WESER Westfalen	1A	2A		
❐ VOEHRENBACH Baden	1A	3B		
❐ VOELKLINGEN Rheinland	2A	7B		
❐ VOELPKE Hannover	3B			
❐ VOERDE Rheinland	1B	3E		
❐ VOERDE Westfalen	1A	2A		
❐ VOERDEN Nordrhein-Westfalen	14D			
❐ VOGELBECK Hannover	2A			
❐ VOGELKOJE/SYLT Schleswig-Holstein	1A			
❐ VOGELSANG/HAGEN Westfalen	2C	11B		
❐ VOHWINKEL Rheinland	1A	2E	6A	11B
❐ VOIGTSDORF/ERZGEBIRGE Sachsen	2A			
❐ VOIGTSTEDT Sachsen	1A			
❐ VOITHENBERG Bayern	2A			
❐ VOLKACH Bayern	6A			
❐ VOLKSTEDT Schwarzburg-Rudolstadt	1A			
❐ VOLLERUP Schleswig-Holstein	2A			
❐ VOLMARSTEIN Westfalen	1B	2E		
❐ VOLLMERHAUSEN Rheinland	2A	14B		
❐ VOLMERSWERTH (Duesseldorf) Rheinland	5B			
❐ VOLPRIEHAUSEN Hannover	2A			
❐ VORHALLE Westfalen	1B			
❐ VORST Rheinland	1A			
❐ VREDEN Westfalen	1A	2B	14D	

1 Mark, Lund, 1A

50 Pfennig, Lunderup, 1A

❒ WACHTENDONK Rheinland 1A
❒ WAECHTERSBACH Hessen-Nassau 1A 7B
❒ WAGENFELDER MOOR Hannover 3B
❒ WAHMBECK Hessen-Nassau 3A
❒ WAHN Rheinland 3A
❒ WAHREN (Leipzig) Sachsen 7B
❒ WAIBLINGEN Wuerttemberg 1A 2A 6A 9A 13B 14B
❒ WALBACH (Guensbach) Elsass 1A
❒ WALBECK Provinz Sachsen 1A 2A 7B
❒ WALD/SOLINGEN Rheinland 1A 2A 6A
❒ WALDBROEHL Rheinland 1A
❒ WALDDORF Sachsen 1A
❒ WALDECK Waldeck 1A
❒ WALDENBURG Sachsen 1A 2A 13B
❒ WALDENBURG (Walbrzych) Schlesien 1A 2B 4A 5B 6A 7B 13A
❒ WALDENBURG-ALTWASSER (Walbrzych) Schlesien 2B
❒ WALDFISCHBACH Pfalz 1A
❒ WALDHEIM Sachsen 1A 2A
❒ WALDHOF/PFARRKIRCHEN Bayern 7A
❒ WALDKIRCH Baden 1A 2A 7A
❒ WALDKIRCHEN Bayern 1A 2A 7A
❒ WALDKIRCHEN/ZSCHOPAUTAL Sachsen 1A
❒ WALDMOHR Pfalz 1A 9A
❒ WALDMUENCHEN Bayern 1A
❒ WALDNIEL Rheinland 1A
❒ WALDSASSEN Bayern 1A 2A
❒ WALDSEE (Bad Waldsee) Wuerttemberg 1A 2A 6A
❒ WALDSHUT (Waldshut-Tiengen) Baden 1A 2A 5B 6A 7B 14A
❒ WALLDORF Baden 1A
❒ WALLDORF Hessen-Nassau 1A 7B
❒ WALLDUERN Baden 6A
❒ WALLENDORF Sachsen-Meiningen 7A
❒ WALLENSEN (Salzhemmendorf) Hannover 7A
❒ WALLERSDORF Bayern 1A
❒ WALLERSTEIN Bayern 7B
❒ WALLERTHEIM Hessen 1A 7A
❒ WALLHAUSEN-HELME Provinz Sachsen 2A
❒ WALSRODE Hannover 1A 2A 3B 5B 7A
❒ WALSTATT-LIEGNITZ (Legnica) Schlesien 14B
❒ WALSUM (Duisburg) Rheinland 7B
❒ WALTERSDORF Sachsen 1A 2A
❒ WALTERSHAUSEN Thueringen 1A 2C
❒ WALTROP Westfalen 1A 5B
❒ WANDERSLEBEN Provinz Sachsen 7B
❒ WANDSBEK (Wandsbeck) Schleswig-Holstein 1A 2B 7B 8B
❒ WANFRIED Hessen-Nassau 1A
❒ WANGEN/ALLGAEU Wuerttemberg 1A 2A 6A

1 Mark, Lutzhoetz, 1A

3 Mark, Malchow/Mecklenburg, Germany, 1A

Location						
❐ WANGEROOG (Wangerooge) Oldenburg	2A	7B				
❐ WANNE (Herne) Westfalen	1A	5B	7B			
❐ WANNE-EICKEL Westfalen	1A	14B				
❐ WANSEN (Wiazow) Schlesien	1A	6C	7A			
❐ WANZLEBEN Provinz Sachsen	1A					
❐ WAPIENNO (Kalkbruch, Wielichowo) Posen	7B					
❐ WAPPINGEN Lothringen	3B					
❐ WARBURG Westfalen	1A	6A				
❐ WARDBOEHMEN Hannover	3B					
❐ WARDENBURG Oldenburg	2E					
❐ WAREN Mecklenburg-Schwerin	1A					
❐ WARENDORF Westfalen	1A	6A	14B			
❐ WARIN Mecklenburg-Schwerin	1A					
❐ WARMBRUNN, BAD (Cieplice-Zdroj) Schlesien	2B	7A				
❐ WARNEMUENDE Mecklenburg-Schwerin	2A	7A	10B			
❐ WARNITZ (Vaernaes, Denmark) Schleswig-Holstein	1B					
❐ WARSTEIN Westfalen	1A	14B				
❐ WARTENBURG (Barczewo) Ostpreussen	1A	6A				
❐ WARTHA (Bardo) Schlesien	1A					
❐ WARTHELAGER (Biedrus) Posen	1A	2A	3A	4A	10A	
❐ WARTIN Pommern	7B					
❐ WASSELNHEIM Elsass	1A					
❐ WASSENBERG Rheinland	2B					
❐ WASSERALFINGEN Wuerttemberg	1A	2A	6A	7B		
❐ WASSERBURG/INN Bayern	1A	2A	6A			
❐ WASSERLEBEN Provinz Sachsen	1A					
❐ WASSERMUNGENAU Bayen	7A					
❐ WASUNGEN Thueringen	1A	2A				
❐ WATHLINGEN/CELLE Hannover	2A					
❐ WATTENSCHEID Westfalen	1A	2A	5B	6A		
❐ WATTWEILER Elsass	1A					
❐ WEBERSTEDT Provinz Sachsen	2A					
❐ WECHSELBURG Sachsen	1A	2A				
❐ WEDAU Rheinland	1A					
❐ WEDDERSLEBEN Provinz Sachsen	1A					
❐ WEDEL Schleswig-Holstein	1A	2A				
❐ WEENER/EMS Hannover	1A	2A	6A			
❐ WEEZE Rheinland	1A	3C				
❐ WEFERLINGEN Provinz Sachsen	1A	2B				
❐ WEGELEBEN Provinz Sachsen	7B					
❐ WEGSCHEID Bayern	2A	15B				
❐ WEHLEN/MOSEL Rheinland	2B					
❐ WEHR Baden	1A					
❐ WEHRSDORF Sachsen	2A					
❐ WEHRSTADT Niedersachsen	14C					
❐ WEIBEK (Vejbaek) Schleswig-Holstein	2A					
❐ WEIDA Thueringen	1A	2D	6A			
❐ WEIDEN/OBERPFALZ Bayern	1A	2A	3A	6A		
❐ WEIDENAU/SIEG Westfalen	2E					
❐ WEIDENBACH-TRIESDORF Bayern	7A					
❐ WEIGMANNSDORF Sachsen	1A					
❐ WEIHERHAMMER Bayern	2A					
❐ WEIKERSHEIM Wuerttemberg	2A					
❐ WEIL-FRIEDLINGEN Baden	2A					
❐ WEILBACH Bayern	1A					
❐ WEILBURG/LAHN Hessen-Nassau	2D	4A	6A	10A		
❐ WEILER/ALLGAEU Bayern	2A	6A				
❐ WEILER/THANN (Willer) Elsass	1A	2A	3C			
❐ WEILHEIM/AMPER Bayern	1A	2A	6A			
❐ WEIMAR Thueringen	1A	2A	6A	7B	8B	12B
❐ WEINBOEHLA Sachsen	1A					
❐ WEINGARTEN Pfalz	1A					
❐ WEINGARTEN Wuerttemberg	1A	2A				
❐ WEINHEIM Baden	2A					
❐ WEINHEIM/BADISCHE Bergstrasse Baden	1A	7A	8A			
❐ WEINSBERG Wuerttemberg	1A	3A				

50 Pfennig, Magdeburg, 1A

10 Pfennig, Mainz, 1A

50 Pfennig, Malchin, 1A

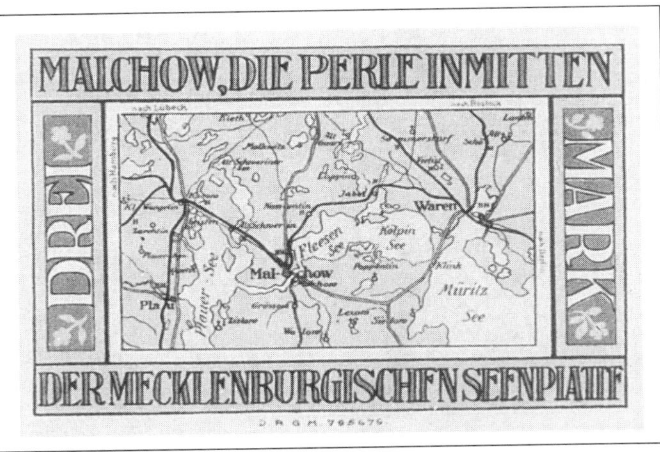

3 Mark, Malchow/M, 1A

10 Pfennig, Mallmitz/B, 1A

3 Mark, Marienstein, POW, 3B

50 Pfennig, Marienwerder, 6A

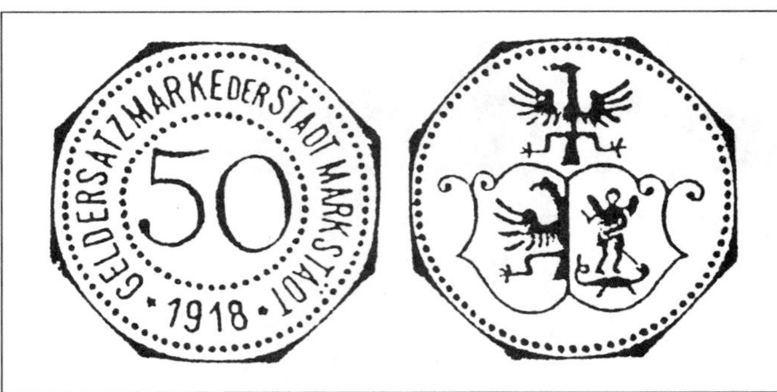

50 Pfennig, Markstadt, 6B

70 Pfennig, Marktbibart, 6E

50 Pfennig, Marktschorgast, 1A

2 Mark, Marne, 1A

50 Pfennig, Mayen, 1A

1 Mark, Medebach, 1A

50 Pfennig, Meiningen, 1A

❐ WEISSBACH Sachsen 1A
❐ WEISSENBERG Sachsen 1A
❐ WEISSENBORN Sachsen 7A
❐ WEISSENBURG Bayern 1A 2A 6A 7A
❐ WEISSENBURG (Wissembourg) Elsass 6A
❐ WEISSENFELS Provinz Sachsen 1A 2A 6A
❐ WEISSENFELS-NAUMBURG Provinz Sachsen 9A
❐ WEISSENHORN Bayern 1A
❐ WEISSENSEE Provinz Sachsen 1A 6A
❐ WEISSENSTADT Bayern 1A 6A
❐ WEISSENSTEIN Bayern 2A
❐ WEISSWASSER O.L. (Biala Woda, Weiszwasser) Schlesien 1A 2A
❐ WEISWEIL Baden 1A
❐ WEIXDORF/LAUSA Sachsen 6A 13A
❐ WELLENDORF Hannover 2A
❐ WELSEN Rheinland 5B
❐ WELZHEIM Wuerttemberg 1A 2A 6A
❐ WELZOW N.L. Brandenburg 2A
❐ WEMDING Bayern 6A
❐ WENDELSTEIN Bayern 2A 9B
❐ WENDESSEN Hannover 5B
❐ WENDEWISCH Hannover 3B
❐ WENDISHAIN/LEISNIG Sachsen 2A
❐ WENDTHOHE Schaumburg-Lippe 2B
❐ WENGERN/HAGEN (Wetter) Westfalen 5B
❐ WENNINGSTEDT/SYLT Schleswig-Holstein 2A
❐ WERDAU Sachsen 1A 2A 6A 7A 8A
❐ WERDEN/RUHR Rheinland 1A 2A 3C 6A 7B 8B
❐ WERDOHL Westfalen 2A 7A
❐ WERL Westfalen 1A 3B 4B
❐ WERMELSKIRCHEN Rheinland 2A
❐ WERMINGHOFF Grube Schlesien 5C
❐ WERMSDORF Sachsen 1A 2B
❐ WERNBERG Bayern 2A
❐ WERNE Westfalen 1E 2B 5A 6A 7B
❐ WERNIGERODE Provinz Sachsen 1A 2A 11B
❐ WERNSDORF I E. Sachsen 2A
❐ WERSTE Westfalen 1E
❐ WERTHEIM/MAIN Baden 1A 6A
❐ WERTHER Westfalen 1B
❐ WERTINGEN Bayern 1A 7A
❐ WESEL Rheinland 1A 2A 5B 7B 8A
❐ WESENBERG Mecklenburg-Strelitz 1A
❐ WESSELBUREN/DITHMARSCHEN Schleswig-Holstein 1A
❐ WESSELING Rheinland 1A 2A
❐ WESSERLING (Huesseren-Wesserling) Elsass 1A
❐ WEST STERNBERG (Zielona Gora, Poland) 1A
❐ WESTERBOEDEFELD Westfalen 2A
❐ WESTERBURG Hessen-Nassau 1A
❐ WESTEREGELN Provinz Sachsen 2A
❐ WESTERFILDE Westfalen 2D
❐ WESTERHOLT (Herten) Westfalen 1A 6A
❐ WESTERHORN Schleswig-Holstein 1A
❐ WESTERKAPPELN Westfalen 2A
❐ WESTERLAND/SYLT Schleswig-Holstein 1A 2A
❐ WESTERNBOEDEFELD Westfalen 2A
❐ WESTERSTEDE Oldenburg 2A
❐ WESTFALEN (Provinz Westfalen) 1A 6A
❐ WESTHAUSEN Elsass 1A 2A
❐ WESTHEIM Pfalz 1A
❐ WESTHOFEN Hessen-Nassau 7A
❐ WETTER/RUHR Westfalen 1A 2A 3A 5D 6A
❐ WETTIN Provinz Sachsen 1A
❐ WETZLAR/LAHN Rheinland 1B 2A 4B 7A
8BWEYHAUSEN Hannover 3B
❐ WICKEDE-ASSELN Westfalen 1E
❐ WICKRATH Rheinland 1A 2A
❐ WIEBELSKIRCHEN Rheinland 1A
❐ WIEDENBACH-TRIESDORF Bayern 7A
❐ WIEDENBRUECK Westfalen 1A 3C

10 Pfennig, Melle, Germany, 1A

50 Pfennig, Melle, 1A

❐ WIEDENEST Rheinland	1A				
❐ WIEDENSAHL Hannover	1A				
❐ WIEDERAU Sachsen	1A	2A			
❐ WIEDEREST Rheinland	1A				
❐ WIEHE Provinz Sachsen	1A	2A	7B		
❐ WIEHL Rheinland	1A	2A			
❐ WIELICHOWO (Wiesenstadt) Posen	1B				
❐ WIERSEN Hannover	3B				
❐ WIESA/ANNABERG (Zschopautal) Sachsen	1A	3A			
❐ WIESAU/SAGAN Bayern	2A	7A			
❐ WIESBADEN Hessen-Nassau	1A	2A	6A	7A	
	8A	10A	11B	14B	
❐ WIESCHOWA (Wieszowa) Schlesien	1A	2B			
❐ WIESDORF Rheinland	1A				
❐ WIESENBAD/ERZGEBIRGE Sachsen	2A				
❐ WIESLOCH Baden	1A				
❐ WIESMOOR Hannover	3B				
❐ WIESSENSTADT Bayern	1A	6A			
❐ WIETZE Hannover	2A				
❐ WIGGENSBACH Bayern	14B				
❐ WILDBAD Wuerttemberg	1A	2A	3A	13B	
❐ WILDBERG Wuerttemberg	1A				
❐ WILDEMANN Hannover	3A				
❐ WILDENFELS Sachsen	1A	2A			
❐ WILDENSTEIN (Dietfurt) Bayern	7B				
❐ WILDESHAUSEN Oldenburg	1A	2D			
❐ WILDUNGEN, BAD Waldeck	2A				
❐ WILHELMSBURG (Hamburg) Hannover	1A	2A	7B		
❐ WILHELMSHAVEN Hannover	1A	2B	3B	7B	12B
❐ WILHELMSHAVEN-RUESTRINGEN Hannover	1A	2D			
❐ WILHELMSHORST (Kleszczewo) Posen	2B				
❐ WILHERMSDORF Bayern	14B				
❐ WILISCHTHAL Sachsen	2A				
❐ WILKAU Sachsen	1A	2A	3A		
❐ WILLEMOOR Oldenburg	3B				
❐ WILLERSHAUSEN Hannover	2A				
❐ WILLICH Rheinland	1A	2A	5B	14B	
❐ WILLINGEN Waldeck	1A	3A			
❐ WILSDRUFF Sachsen	1A				
❐ WILSNACK Brandenburg	1A	2D			
❐ WILSTER Schleswig-Holstein	1A				
❐ WILTHEN Sachsen	1A	2A			
❐ WIMPFEN/NECKAR Wuerttemberg	1A				

10 Pfennig, Mellrichstadt, 1A

Types of Emergency Money

Type	**Reference #**
Municipal paper	1
Private paper	2
POW paper	3
POW official metal	4
POW private metal	5
Municipal metal	6
Private metal	7
Gas tokens	8
Food; beer; konsumverein	9
Naval; military; kantine	10
Encased, unencased stamps	11
Streetcar tokens	12
Porcelain	13
World War II issues	14
Concentration, Civilian internment camps	15

Rarity grades: A, to $25; B, to $60; C, to $125; D, to $200; and E, $350

50 Pfennig, Memmingen, 1A

❒ WINDISCH-ESCHENBACH (Windischeschenbach) Bayern 1A 2A 7A
❒ WINDSHEIM (Bad Windsheim) Bayern 1A 2A 7A
❒ WINGENDORF/FRANKENSTEIN Sachsen 2A
❒ WINNAGORA (Winenberg) Posen 1A 2A 7B
❒ WINNENDEN Wuerttemberg 1A
❒ WINNWEILER Pfalz 2A
❒ WINSEN/LUHE Hannover 1A
❒ WINTERBERG Westfalen 1A 2B
❒ WINTERBORN Rheinland 2A
❒ WINTERLINGEN Wuerttemberg 1A
❒ WINTERSDORF Sachsen-Altenburg 2A 7B
❒ WINZELDORF Schleswig-Holstein 1A
❒ WINZIG (Winsko) Schlesien 2B
❒ WIPPERFUERTH Rheinland 1A 2A
❒ WIREK (Antonienhuette) Schlesien 2A
❒ WIRSITZ Posen 1A
❒ WISMAR Mecklenburg-Schwerin 1A 2A 5D 8B
❒ WISSEK (Wysoka) Posen 1B
❒ WISSEN/SIEG Rheinland 1A 7B
❒ WISSING (Seubersdorf) Bayern 6A
❒ WITKOWO (Wittkowo, Witkowska) Posen 1A 2A 7B
❒ WITTDUEN/AMRUM Schleswig-Holstein 1A
❒ WITTEN Westfalen 1A 2A 6A 7B 11B
❒ WITTENBERG (Wittenberg Lutherstadt) Provinz Sachsen 1A 2A 3A 6A 7B
❒ WITTENBERGE Brandenburg 1A 2A 6A 7B 8A
❒ WITTENBURG Mecklenburg-Schwerin 1A
❒ WITTENHEIM Elsass 1A
❒ WITTERSCHLICK (Alfter-Witterschlick) Rheinland 5B
❒ WITTGENSDORF/CHEMNITZ Sachsen 1A 2A
❒ WITTGENSTEIN Westfalen 1B
❒ WITTICHENAU O.L. Schlesien 1A
❒ WITTINGEN Hannover 1A
❒ WITTLICH Rheinland 1A 6A
❒ WITTMUND Hannover 2A
❒ WITTSTOCK/DOSSE Brandenburg 1A 7B
❒ WITZENHAUSEN Hessen-Nassau 2A
❒ WITZNITZ Sachsen 2A
❒ WOELFERSHEIM Hessen-Nassau 1A
❒ WOERISHOFEN, BAD Bayern 1A
❒ WOERLITZ Anhalt 1A
❒ WOERTH/DONAU Bayern 1A 7A
❒ WOERTH/MAIN Bayern 1A 7A
❒ WOHLAU (Wolow) Schlesien 1A 2E 4B 6A 7B
❒ WOHLDORF Schleswig-Holstein 1A
❒ WOLDEGK Mecklenburg-Strelitz 1A
❒ WOLDENBERG (Neumark; Dobiegniew) Brandenburg 1A 6A 14B
❒ WOLFACH Baden 1A 2A 6A
❒ WOLFEN Provinz Sachsen 2A 14B
❒ WOLFENBUETTEL Braunschweig 1A 2A 7B 8A
❒ WOLFHAGEN Hessen-Nassau 1A
❒ WOLFMANNSHAUSEN Sachsen-Meiningen 1A
❒ WOLFRATSHAUSEN Bayern 1A 2A
❒ WOLFSBERG Bayern 14B
❒ WOLFSTEIN Pfalz 1A
❒ WOLGAST Pommern 1A 7B

25 Pfennig, Menteroda, 1A

1 Pfennig, Merseburg, Germany, 2A

❒ WOLKENBURG Sachsen 2A
❒ WOLKENSTEIN Sachsen 1A 2A
❒ WOLLENTHAL (Wolenthal) Posen 2A
❒ WOLLIN (Wolin) Pommern 1A 6B
❒ WOLLMATINGEN (Konstanz) Baden 1A
❒ WOLLSTEIN (Wolsztyn) Posen 1B
❒ WOLMIRSTEDT Provinz Sachsen 1A
❒ WOLNZACH Bayern 6A
❒ WOLTWIESCHE Hannover 3B
❒ WONGROWITZ (Wagrowiec, Wagrowska) Posen 1A 2B
❒ WONSAWA (Wonsowo, Wasawa) Posen 7B
❒ WORBIS Provinz Sachsen 1A
❒ WORMDITT (Orneta) Ostpreussen 1A
❒ WORMS Hessen 1A 3A 4B 5B 6A 7A 8A 11C 12B
❒ WORPSWEDE Hannover 1A
❒ WOYENS (Vojens, Denmark) Schleswig-Holstein 1A
❒ WRESCHEN (Wrzesnia) Posen 1B
❒ WRIEZEN Brandenburg 1A 2A
❒ WROBLE/STRELNO Posen 2B
❒ WRONKE (Wronki) Posen 1A 2B
❒ WSZEMBORZ/BORZYKOWO Posen 2B
❒ WUELFEL Hannover 2B 7B 9B
❒ WUELFRATH Rheinland 1A 2A 5C 8B
❒ WUELZBURG (Weissenburg) Bayern 3E 4B
❒ WUENSCHENDORF/ELSTER Sachsen-Weimar-Eisenach 1A
❒ WUENSCHENDORF Schlesien 1A 2B
❒ WUENSDORF Brandenburg 2A
❒ WUERTTEMBERG-HOHENZOLLERN Wuerttemberg 14B
❒ WUERZBURG Bayern 1A 2A 3A 7A 12B
❒ WUESTEGIERSDORF (Gluszyca) Schlesien 2A
❒ WUESTEWALTERSDORF (Walim) Schlesien 1A 2A 7A
❒ WULFEN Westfalen 1A
❒ WUNSIEDEL Bayern 1A 2A 6A 7B
❒ WUNSTORF Hannover 1A 2A 7B
❒ WURZACH, BAD Wuerttemberg 1A 6A
❒ WURZBACH Thueringen 1A 2A 6A
❒ WURZEN Sachsen 1A 2A 8A
❒ WUSTERHAUSEN/DOSSE Brandenburg 1A
❒ WUSTROW Mecklenburg-Schwerin 2A
❒ WYHLEN (Grenzach-Wyhlen) Baden 1A 6A
❒ WYK/FOEHR Schleswig-Holstein 1A 2A 6A
❒ XANTEN Rheinland 1A 2A 3C
❒ XIONS (Ksiaz) Posen 1B
❒ ZABERN (Saverne) Elsass 6A 7B 10B
❒ ZABKOWICE (Zombkovitsi; Frankenstein Schlesien 2B
❒ ZABORZE Schlesien 1A 3C 6A
❒ ZABRZE (Hindenburg) Schlesien 1A 6A 7B 8A
❒ ZAGLEBIE DABROWSKIE (Dombrowskie Kop.) 2B
❒ ZAGOROW Posen 2B
❒ ZAHNA Provinz Sachsen 1A
❒ ZALENZE (Zaleze) Schlesien 1A
❒ ZANIEMYSL (Santomischel) Posen 1A 2B
❒ ZARRENTIN Mecklenburg-Schwerin 1A
❒ ZAUCH-BELZIG Brandenburg 1A
❒ ZAWADZKI (Zawadzkie) Schlesien 5B
❒ ZDUNY (Freihaus, Zerkow) Posen 1A
❒ ZECHE HOLLAND 3B
❒ ZEHDENICK Brandenburg 2A
❒ ZEISKAM Pfalz 1A
❒ ZEISSHOLZ/LIEGNITZ Schlesien 5B
❒ ZEITHAIN Sachsen 1A 2A
❒ ZEITZ Provinz Sachsen 1A 2A 6A 7A 8A
❒ ZELENIN/BERENT Westpreussen 2B
❒ ZELL-HARMERSBACH Baden 2A
❒ ZELL/HARMERSBACH (UNTERHARMERSBACH NORDRACH BIERACH) Baden 1A 7A
❒ ZELL/WIESENTHAL Baden 1A 2A 6A 7A
❒ ZELLA (Zella-Mehlis) Sachsen-Coburg-Gotha 1A 7B 9A
❒ ZELLA ST. BLASII UND MEHLIS Sachsen 1A
❒ ZELLA-ST. BLASII Sachsen 1A
❒ ZELTINGEN/MOSEL Rheinland 2A
❒ ZEMPELBURG (Sepolno) Westpreussen 1A
❒ ZERBST Anhalt 1A 2A 3E 12B
❒ ZERKOW (Zlotowski) Posen 1B
❒ ZERNICKOW (Seelow) Brandenburg 7B
❒ ZERNSDORF Brandenburg 2A
❒ ZETHAU Sachsen 1A
❒ ZEULENRODA Thueringen 1A 2A 7A 8B
❒ ZEVEN Hannover 1A
❒ ZEVEN, WILSTEDT UND SITTENSEN Hannover 2A
❒ ZIEGENHAIN Hessen-Nassau 1A 3A
❒ ZIEGENHALS (Glucholazy) Schlesien 1A 2A 6A 7A 8B
❒ ZIEGENRUECK Provinz Sachsen 1A 2A 6A
❒ ZIELENZIG (Sulecin, Poland) Brandenburg 1A
❒ ZIELENZIG/OST-STERNBERG Brandenburg 1A
❒ ZIESAR Provinz Sachsen 1A 2A

50 Pfennig, Meseritz, 6C

50 Pfennig, Meura, 1A

50 Pfennig, Miesbach, 1A

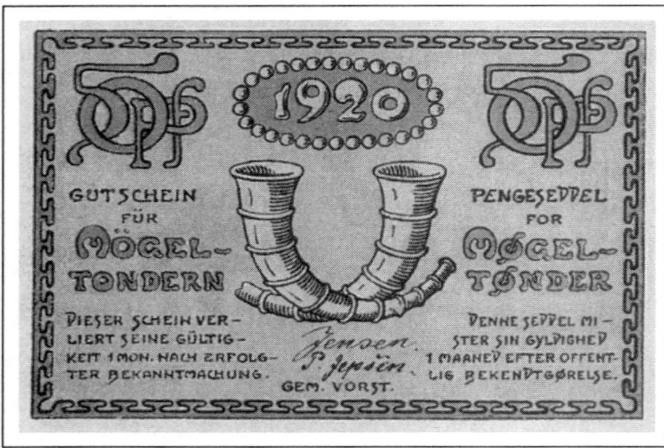

50 Pfennig, Moegeltondern, 1A

50 Pfennig, Monschau, 1A

2 Mark, Moosch/Elsass, Germany, 1B

1 Pfennig, Muehldorf, Germany, 1A

1 Pfennig, Mühldorf, 1A

5 Mark, Muelhausen/Elsass, Germany, 1B

10 Pfennig, Muelheim/Ruhr, 1B

50 Pfennig, Muelsen-St. Jakob, 1A

50 Pfennig, Mylau/V, Germany, 1A

40 Pfennig, Nabburg, 2B

50 Pfennig, Namslav, 1A

3 Mark, Naugard/Pomm, 1A

50 Pfennig, Naumburg/S, 1A

5 Mark, Neheim/Ruhr, 1A

50 Reichspfennig, Neheim-Huesten, Germany, 2B

2 Mark, Neheim/Ruhr, 1A

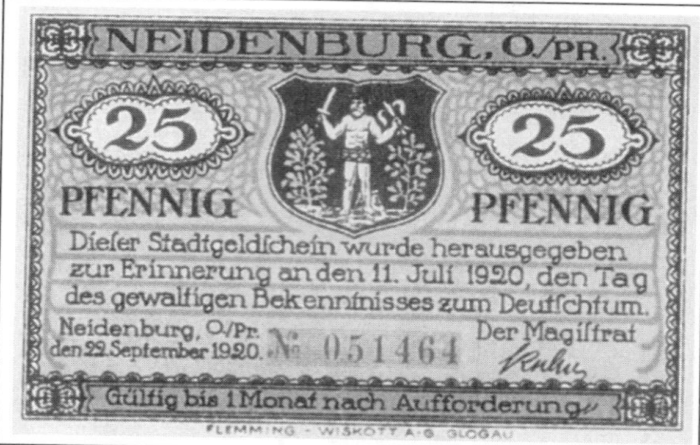

25 Pfennig, Neidenburg/O/PR, 1A

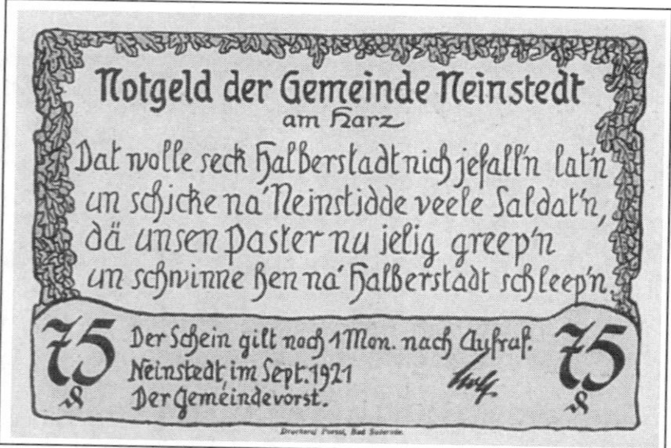

75 Pfennig, Neinstedt/H, 1A

10 Pfennig, Neisse, POW, 3A

50 Pfennig, Neu-Astenburg, 1A

25 Pfennig, Neubrandenburg, 1A

50 Pfennig, Neuburg/D, 1A

1 Mark, Neuenahr, Bad, 1A

75 Pfennig, Neugraben-Hausbruch, 1A

60 Pfennig, Neugraben-Hausbruch, 1A

5 Pfennig, Neuhammer, POW, 3B

25 Pfennig, Neuhaus/Rwg, 1A

3 Mark, Neuhaus/Westfalen, 1A

10 Pfennig, Neukloster, Germany, 1A

1 Pfennig, Neumuehlen-Dietrichsdorf, Germany, 1A

50 Pfennig, Neumuenster, Germany, 2B

25 Pfennig, Neuruppin, 1A

50 Pfennig, Neusalz/Oder, 6A

25 Pfennig, Neustadt O/S, 6A

10 Pfennig, Neustadt/Coburg, Germany, 1A

50 Pfennig, Neustadt/Coburg, 1A

75 Pfennig, Neustadt/M, 1A

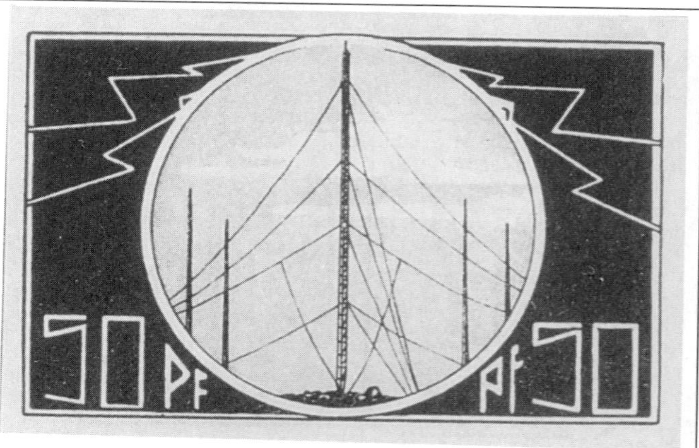

50 Pfennig, Neustadt/R, 1A

50 Pfennig, Neustettin, 1A

10 Pfennig, Neustettin, 6A

5 Pfennig, Neuteich/Danzig, Germany, 1A

50 Pfennig, Niebuell, 1A

1 Mark, Nieder-Marsberg, 1A

20 Mark, Niederlahnstein, 1A

2 Mark, Nieheim/W, 1A

1 Mark, Nikolai, 1A

75 Pfennig, Nimptsch/Schl., 1A

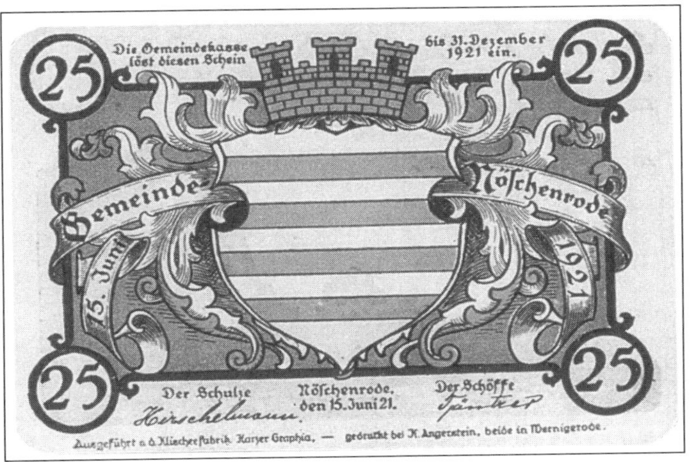

25 Pfennig, Noeschenrode, 1A

25 Pfennig, Norddorf/A, 1A

25 Pfennig, Nordenham, 1A

10 Pfennig, Norderney, 1A

25 Pfennig, Norderney, 1A

25 Pfennig, Nortorf, 1A

2 Pfennig, Nuernberg, Germany, 2A

25 Pfennig, Oberdorla/Vogtei, Germany, 1A

50 Pfennig, Obërglogau, 1A

1,000 Mark, Oberlödla, Germany, 9A

5 Pfennig, Oberndorf/Wuerttemberg, Germany, 6A

10 Pfennig, Oberndorf/Wuerttemberg, Germany, 6A

50 Pfennig, Oberndorf/Wuerttemberg, Germany, 6A

25 Pfennig, Oberwesel/Rh., 1A

25 Pfennig, Oebisfelde-Kaltendorf, 1A

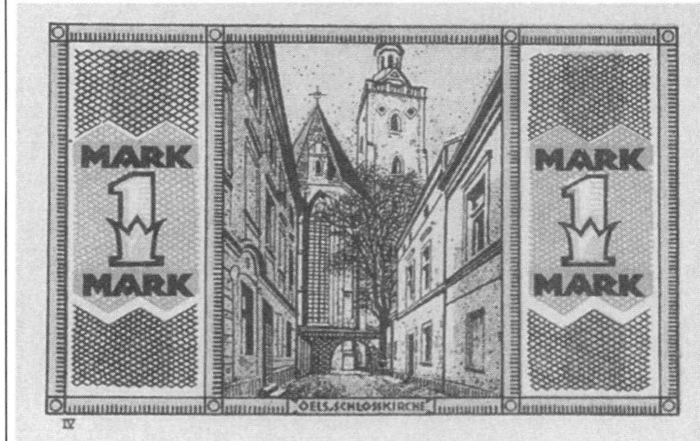

1 Mark, Oels/Schl., 1A

50 Pfennig, Oelsnitz/V, Germany, 1A

50 Pfennig, Ohlau, 1A

50 Pfennig, Oland, 1A

3 Mark, Oldenburg/O, 1A

50 Pfennig, Oldenburg/O, 1A

50 Pfennig, Oldesloe, Bad, 1A

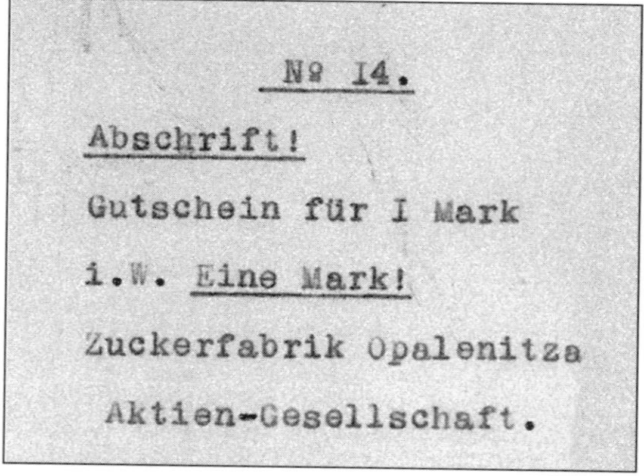

№ 14.

Abschrift!

Gutschein für I Mark

i.W. Eine Mark!

Zuckerfabrik Opalenitza

Aktien-Gesellschaft.

1 Mark, Opalenitza, 1B

Gas, Oppeln, 8B

25 Pfennig, Oranienbaum, 1A

50 Pfennig, Orsoy, 1A

25 Pfennig, Osnabrueck, 2A

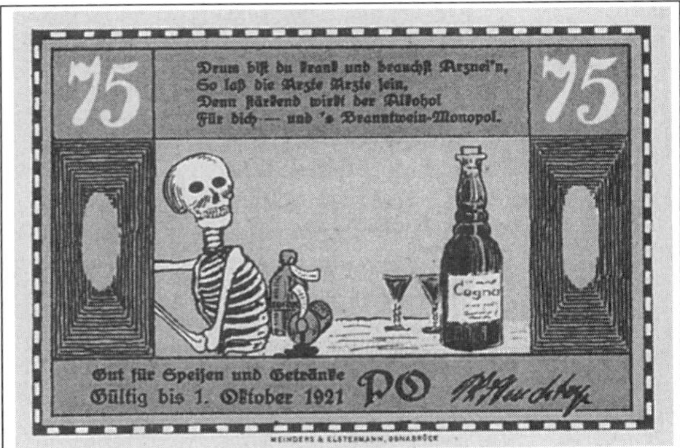

75 Pfennig, Osnabrueck, 2A

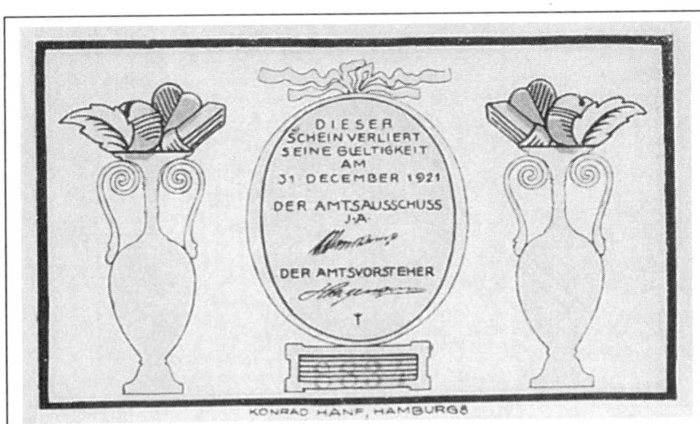

40 Pfennig, Osterhorn, 1A

10 Pfennig, Ostrowo, 6A

50 Pfennig, Otterndorf, 1A

10 Pfennig, Ottmachau, 6A

50 Pfennig, Pakosch, Germany, 1A

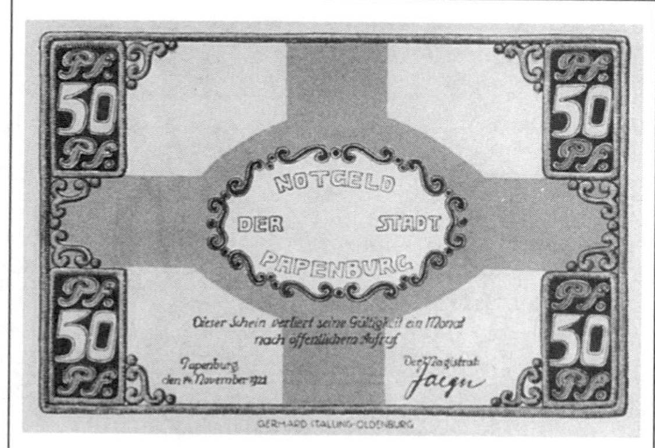

50 Pfennig, Papenburg, 1A

Fünfzig Pfennig zahlt die Spar- und Creditbank zu Parey a. Elbe gegen Einlösung dieses Scheines bis zum 30. Juni 1921.

Föftig Penn gift all Parey
för Bismarcken sin Konterfei.
Bunt ist dat papierne Geld;
bunt geit's her hier up de Welt.
Föftig Penn het nich vel Wert
kost up stunns en Heringsstert.

Ausgabe B. Nr. 1211

50 Pfennig, Parey/E, 1A

Wenn mir weg'n der Steuer
Mei' „Kurze" wird pfändt,
Dös macht nichts, da tanz i
Halt oafach im Hemd.—
20 Notgeld. 20
Pfg. Partenkirchen. Pfg.

20 Pfennig, Partenkirchen, 1A

2 Pfennig, Pasing, Germany, 1A

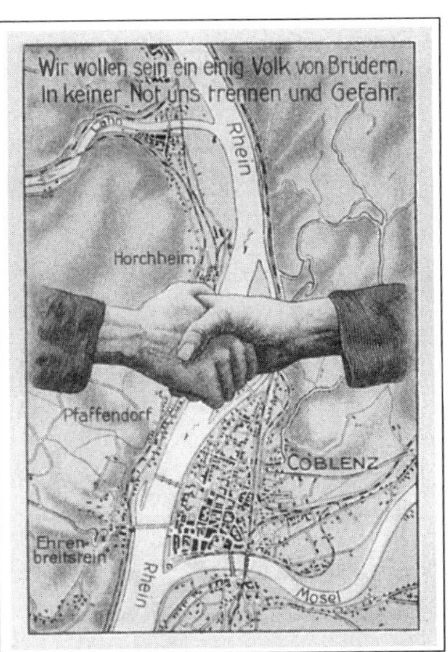

75 Pfennig, Pfaffendorf, 1A

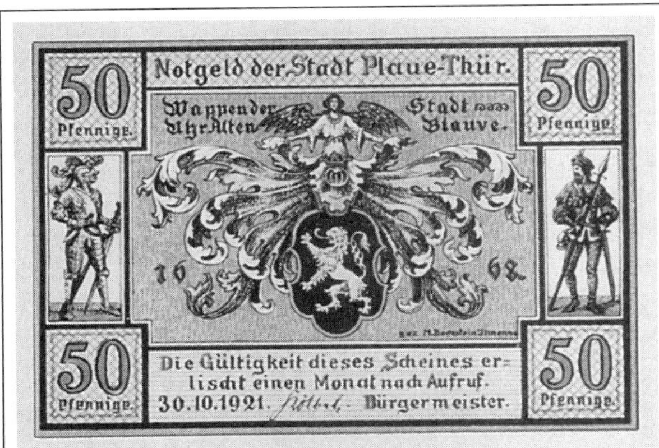

50 Pfennig, Plaue/Thür, 1A

10 Pfennig, Plauen/V, Germany, 1A

50 Pfennig, Poessneck, 1A

50 Pfennig, Potsdam, 1A

25 Pfennig, Prien/Chiemsee, Germany, 1A

50 Pfennig, Prisdorf, 1A

25 Pfennig, Prüm, 1A

50 Pfennig, Pyritz/Pomm, 1A

10 Pfennig, Quedlinburg, Germany, 1A

1 Mark, Quedlinburg, 3A

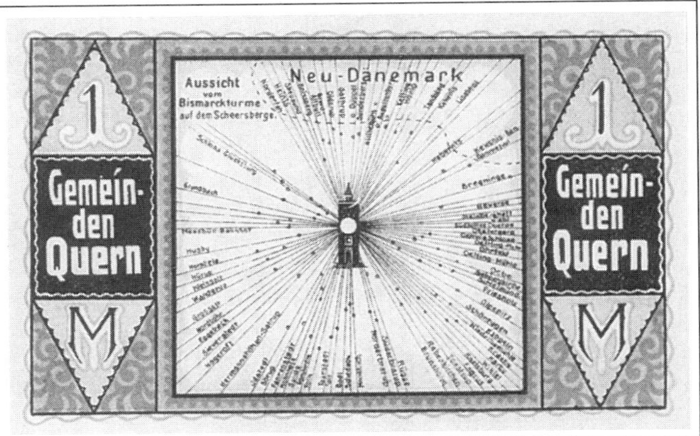

1 Mark, Quern, 1A

25 Pfennig, Racot, 1A

50 Pfennig, Raguhn, 1A

10 Pfennig, Raschkow, Germany, 1B

50 Pfennig, Regensburg, 1A

25 Pfennig, Reinerz, 1A

5 Pfennig, Reichenbach/V, Germany, 1A

20 Pfennig, Reichenweier/Elsass, Germany, 1A

50 Pfennig, Ranis, Bad, 1A

1000 Pfennig, Reisen/Pos, POW, 4B

5 Milliarden (MK), Renchen, 1B

50 Pfennig, Reutlingen, Germany, 6A

5 Pfennig, Richterschächte, POW, 3B

50 Pfennig, Riesenburg W/Pr, 6A

25 Pfennig, Rietberg/W, 1A

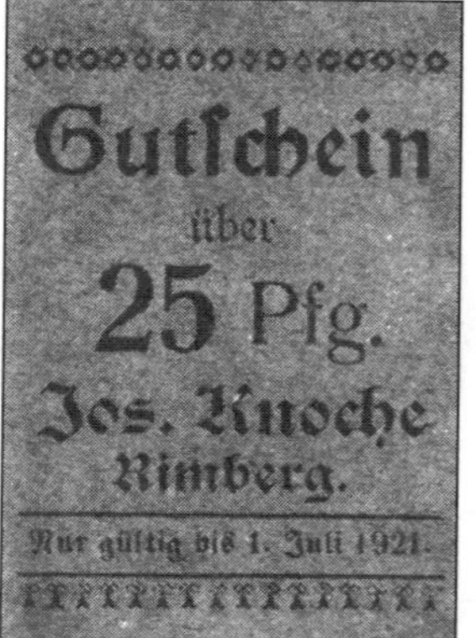

25 Pfennig, Rimberg, Germany, 2B

50 Pfennig, Roda, 1A

50 Pfennig, Regensburg, 1A

10 Pfennig, Rodach, Germany, 1A

50 Pfennig, Röhrigshöfe/W, 1A

500 Mark, Roethenbach, Germany, 7C

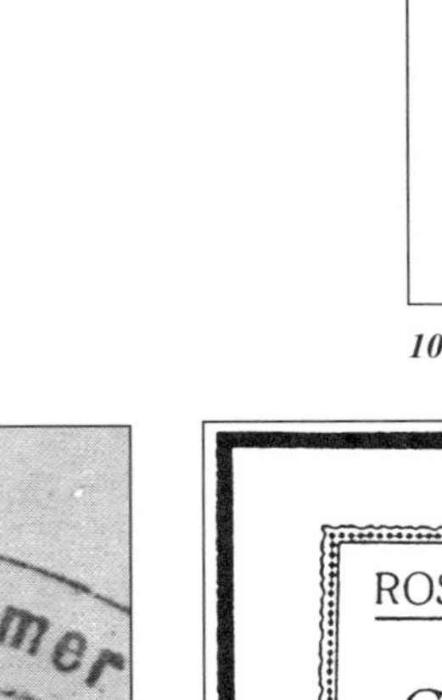

100 Mark, Roethenbach, Germany, 7C

10 Pfennig, Roitzsch, Germany, 2B

50 Pfennig, Roschkow/Posen, 1B

50 Pfennig, Rosenheim/B, 1A

50 Pfennig, Rossbach, 1A

50 Pfennig, Rothenburg/T, 1A

Mark, Ruda/Schlesien, Germany, 1B

100 Pfennig, Rüdolstadt, 1A

50 Pfennig, Rüdolstadt, 1A

50 Pfennig, Ruedelsburg, 1A

50 Pfennig, Ruhla, 1A

10 Pfennig, Saalburg/Schlesien, Germany, 1A

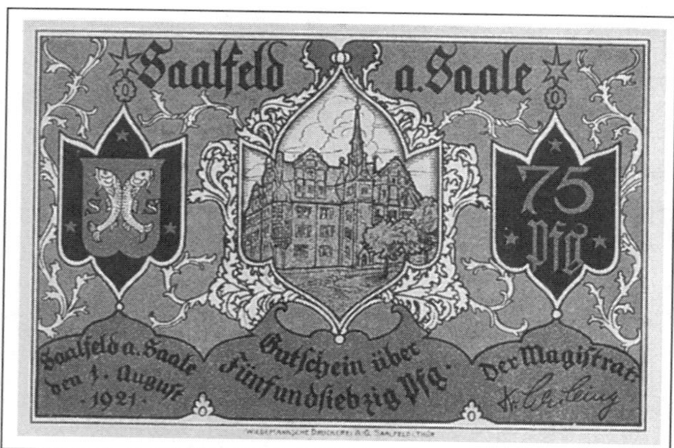

75 Pfennig, Saalfield/S, 1A

50 Pfennig, Saarburg, 1A

10 Pfennig, Sagan, POW, 4A

50 Pfennig, Ober Salzbrunn, 1A

10 Pfennig, Salzburghofen, Germany, 1A

25 Pfennig, Salzig/Bad (Rh) 1A

1/6 Mark, Salzuflen, Germany, 10A

1 Mark, Salzwedel, 1A

50 Pfennig, St. Andreasbrg, 1A

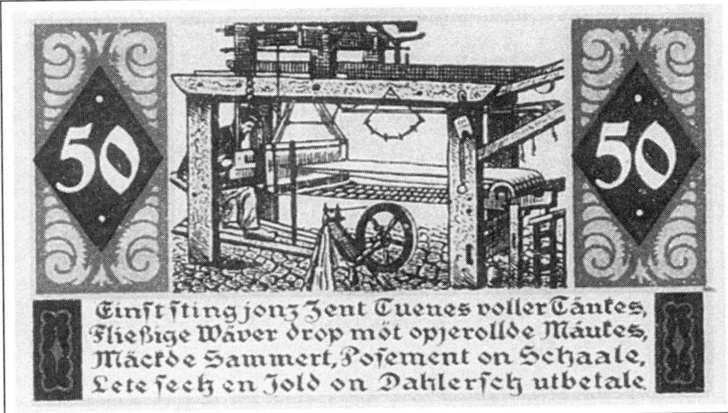

50 Pfennig, St. Tönis, 1A

50 Pfennig, Scheessel, 1A

50 Pfennig, Schierke, 1A

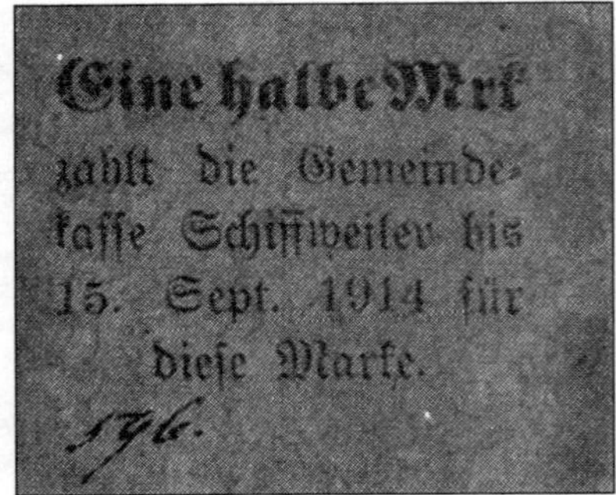

Mark, Schiffweiler, Germany, 1B

50 Pfennig, Schlawe/Pommern, Germany, 1A

50 pfennig, Schlawe, 6A

50 Pfennig, Schleisien, Germany, 2B

10 Pfennig, Schleswig, Gemany, 1A

20 Pfennig, Schleusingen, 1A

10 Pfennig, Schliersee, 1A

50 Pfennig, Schmiedefeld, 1A

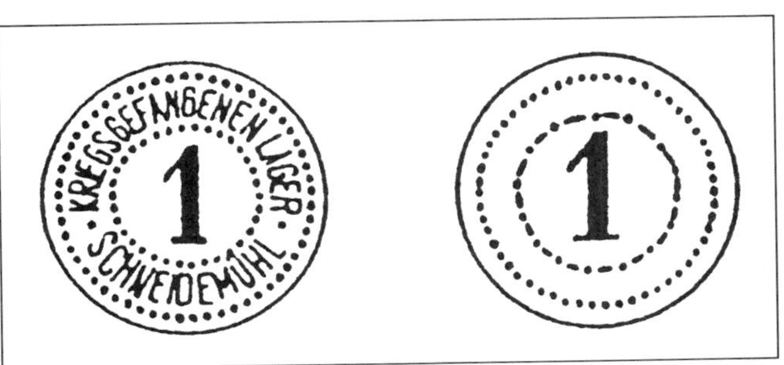

1 Pfennig, Schneidemuehl, POW, 4A

25 Pfennig, Schoenlanke, Germany, 1A

Mark, Schroda, Germany, 1B

50 Pfennig, Schroda, 6B

10 Pfennig, Schroeich, 1A

50 Pfennig, Schroeich, 1A

10 Pfennig, Schwarza, Germany, 1A

50 Pfennig, Schwarzburg, 1A

10 Pfennig, Schwarzenberg, Germany, 1A

10 Pfennig, Schweich, 1A

50 Pfennig, Schweinitz, 1A

50 Pfennig, Schwersenz, Germany, 1A

50 Pfennig, Seelow, 1A

25 Pfennig, Segeberg, 1A

5 Pfennig, Seitenberg, Germany, 1A

75 Pfennig, Siedenburg, 1A

50 Pfennig, Siedlinghausen, 1A

25 Pfennig, Siegburg, 1A

10 Pfennig, Sinzig, Germany, 2B

5 Pfennig, Skalmierschütz, POW, 4A

2 Mark, Sodingen, Germany, 1B

50 Pfennig, Soemmerda, 1A

1 Mark, Soerup/A, 1A

25 Pfennig, Soest, Germany, 1B

75 Pfennig, Soltau, 1A

50 Pfennig, Sonderburg, 1A

50 Pfennig, Sondershausen, 1A

25 Pfennig, Sonneberg, 1A

50 Pfennig, Sooden, Bad/Werra, 1A

10 Pfennig, Sorau, 1A

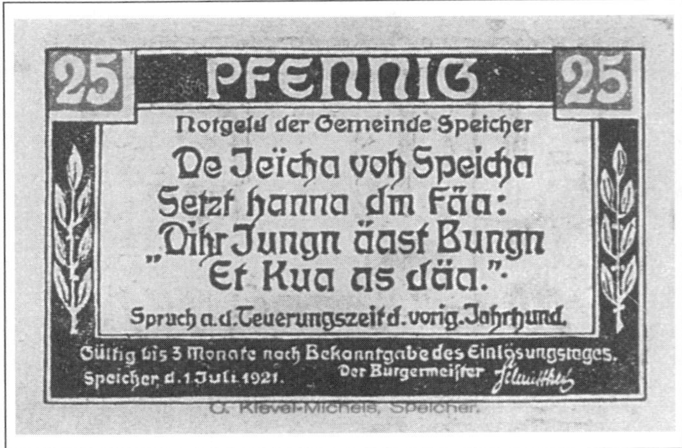

25 Pfennig, Speicher, 1A

5 Pfennig, Sprottau, 1A

50 pfennig, Stadtlengsfeld, 1A

50 Pfennig, Stassfurt, 1A

50 Pfennig, Staufen/B, 1A

25 Pfennig, Stavenhagen, 1A

75 Pfennig, Stecklenberg, 1A

60 Pfennig, Stedesand, 1A

50 Pfennig, Steinau, 1A

50 Pfennig, Steinbach, 1A

50 Pfennig, Steinfeld, Germany, 1A

50 Pfennig, Steinheim (Germany), 1A

200 Pfennig, Stettin, 9B

50 Pfennig, Stettin, 1A

50 Pfennig, Stettin, 1A

50 Pfennig, Stolberg, 1A

50 Pfennig, Stolp, 1A

5 Pfennig, Straslund, Germany, 6A

10 Pfennig, Straslund, Germany, 6A

500 Mark, Stralsund, 1B

50 Pfennig, Straubing, 1A

1 Mark, Strausberg, 1A

50 Pfennig, Strehlen, 6A

75 Pfennig, Stroebeck, 1A

50 Pfennig, Stützerbach, 1A

1 Mark, Stuttgart, 1A

75 Pfennig, Sulza, Bad, 1A

15 Pfennig, Tarnowitz, 1A

40 Pfennig, Tegernsee, 1A

75 Pfennig, Thale, 1A

1 Mark, Tingleff, 1A

25 Pfinnig, Tondern, 1A

25 Pfennig, Traben-Trarbach, 1A

50 Pfennig, Treffurt, 1A

50 Pfennig, Treysa, 1A

1 Pfennig, Triebes, Germany, 1A

50 Pfennig, Trier, Germany, 1A

50 Pfennig, Trier, 1A

50 Pfennig, Triptis, 1A

50 Pfennig, Triptis, Germany, 1A

50 Pfennig, Trostberg, 1A

50 Pfennig, Twistringen, 1A

50 Pfennig, Uelzen, Germany, 2A

5 Mark, Uerdingen, 1A

10 Pfennig, Unterweissbach, Germany, 1A

25 Pfennig, Verden, Germany, 1A

50 Pfennig, Verden/Aller, 1A

5 Mark, Villingen, 1A

50 Pfennig, Visselhoevede, 1A

5 Pfennig, Vollmerhausen/Koeln, Germany, 2B

1 Mark, Walsrode, 1A

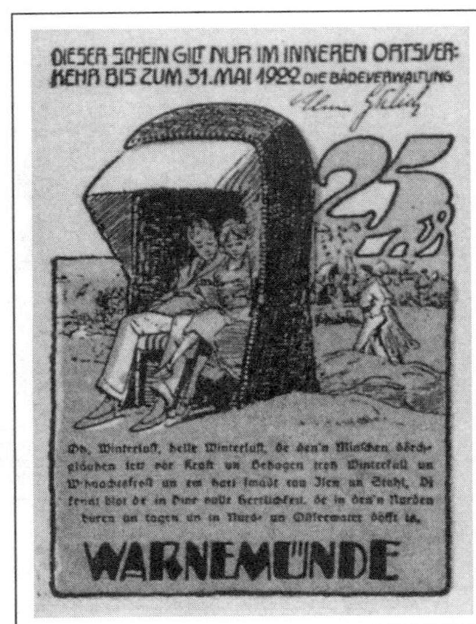

25 Pfennig, Warnemuende, 1A

5 Reichspfennig, Warstein, Germany, 14B

50 Pfennig, Wasserburg/Inn, 1A

1 Mark, Wedel, 1A

50 Pfennig, Weimar, 1A

Notgeldschein der Stadt Weißenburg i. B.
ausgegeben mit Genehmigung des Reichsministers der Finanzen
über
1 Mk. Gold 07843
1 Mark Gold
Diese wertbeständigen Notgeldscheine sind durch Hinterlegung von wertbeständiger Anleihe des Deutschen Reiches gedeckt. Der Aufruf der Scheine zur Einlösung wird seinerzeit bekannt gegeben. Weißenburg i. B., 1. Dezember 1923
Stadtrat:
Der 1. rechtskundige Bürgermeister: Der Kassier:

1 Gold Mark, Weissenburg/V, 1A

50 Pfennig, Weissenfels/Saale, 1A

20 Goldpfennige, Werdau, Germany, 1A

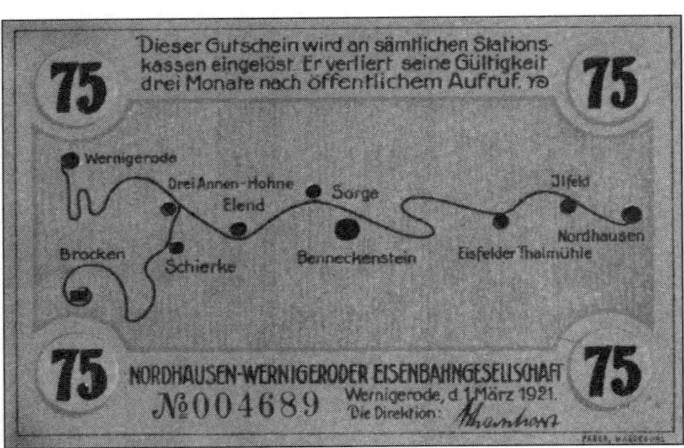

75 Pfennig, Wernigerode, Germany, 2A

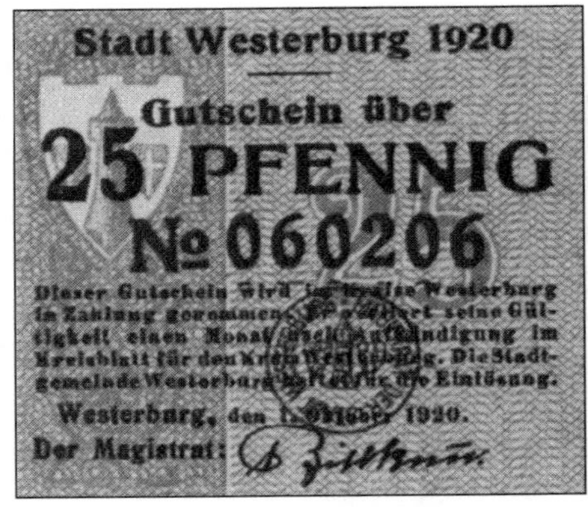

25 Pfennig, Westerburg, Germany, 1A

80 Pfennig, Westerhorn, 1A

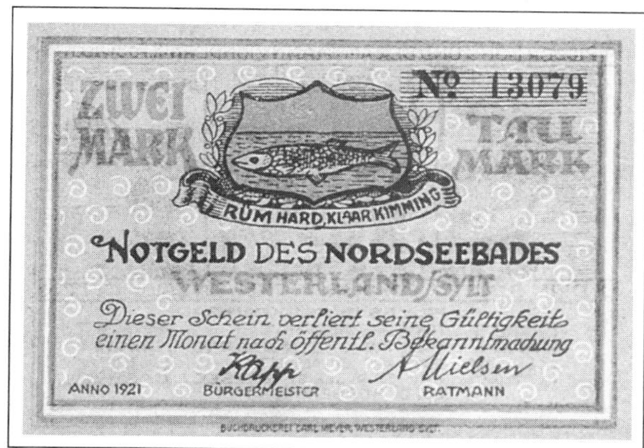

2 Mark, Westerland/Sylt, 1A

1 Billion Mark, Westfalen, Germany, 7C

10 Pfennig, Wetzlar, Germany, 1A

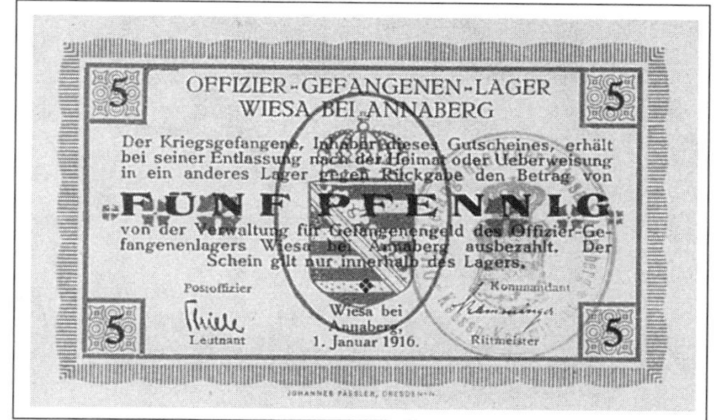

5 Pfennig, Wiesa bei Annaberg, POW, 3B

10 Pfennig, Wiggensbach, Germany, 2B

1 Pfennig, POW, Wildemann, Germany, 3B

10 Pfennig, Wirsitz, Germany, 2B

3 Pfennig, Witten, Germany, 1A

50 Pfennig, Wollin, 1A

10 Pfennig, Wreschen, Germany, 1B

25 Pfennig, Wriezen, 1A

75 Pfennig, Wuenschendorf, 1A

50 Pfennig, Neuenbuerg, Wuerttemburg, Germany, 6A

1.50 Mark Xanten/Rhein, Germany, 1A

50 Pfennig, Xions, Germany, 1A

1 Pfennig, Zeulenroda, Germany, 1A

25 Pfennig, Ziesar, 1A

50 Pfennig, Zitttau, Germany, 1A

50 Pfennig, Zoerbig, 1A

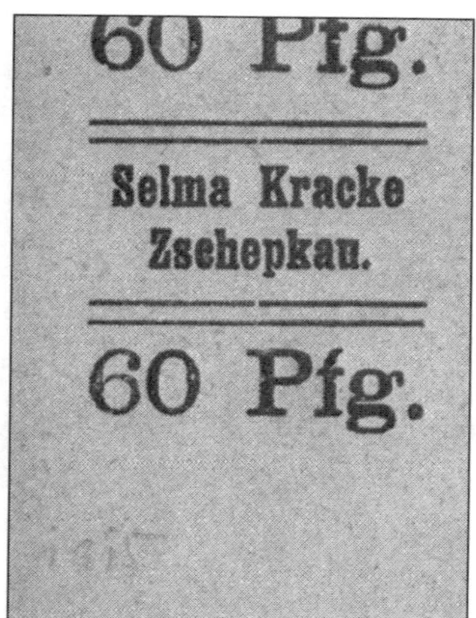

60 Pfennig, Zschepkau, Germany, 2B

5 Pfennig, Zuellichau, 6A

50 Pfennig, Zwickau, Germany, 1A

❒ ZILLERTHAL (Myslakowice) Schlesien 7B
❒ ZILLY Provinz Sachsen 1A 7A 12B
❒ ZINNA Sachsen 1A
❒ ZINNOWITZ Pommern 1A 7B
❒ ZINTEN (Korniewo, Karszewo) Ostpreussen 1A
❒ ZIPSENDORF Provinz Sachsen 2A
❒ ZIRNDORF Bayern 1A 2A 6A 8B
❒ ZITTAU UND BAUTZEN Sachsen 1A
❒ ZITTAU/MAUDAU (Svitavy) Sachsen 1A 2E 7A 8B 12A
❒ ZNIN Posen 1A 2A 6B
❒ ZOBTEN/BERGE (Sobotka) Schlesien 1A 2B
❒ ZOEBLITZ Sachsen 1A
❒ ZOERBIG Provinz Sachsen 1A 2A
❒ ZOESCHLINGSWEILER/DILLINGEN Bayern 2A
❒ ZONS/RHEIN Rheinland 1A
❒ ZOPPOT/DANZIG (Sopot) Westpreussen 1A 8A 13B
❒ ZOSSEN Brandenburg 3A
❒ ZOSSEN-HALBMONDLAGER Brandenburg 1A 3A
❒ ZOSSEN-WEINBERGE Brandenburg 3A
❒ ZSCHEPKAU Sachsen 2A
❒ ZSCHIPKAU (Schipkau) Sachsen 7B
❒ ZSCHOPAU Sachsen 1A 2A
❒ ZUELLICHAU (Sulechow) Brandenburg 1A 2A 6A
❒ ZUELZ O.S. (Biala Prudnicka) Schlesien 1A
❒ ZUESCHEN Westfalen 2A 9A
❒ ZUETTLINGEN Wuerttemberg 1A
❒ ZUFFENHAUSEN/STUTTGART Wuerttemberg 1A 6A 8B 9B
❒ ZWEIBRUECKEN Pfalz 1A 2A 6A 7A
❒ ZWEINAUNDORF Sachsen 1A
❒ ZWENKAU Sachsen 1A
❒ ZWICKAU Sachsen 1A 3A 4A 6A 7A 8B 11B 12B
❒ ZWIESEL Bayern 1A 2A 6A 7A
❒ ZWINGENBERG Hessen 1A
❒ ZWISCHENAHN (Bad Zwischenahn) Oldenburg 2A 7B
❒ ZWOENITZ Sachsen 1A 2A 7A
❒ ZWOTA/VOGTLAND Sachsen 1A

GIBRALTAR

❒ LAGUNA CAMP 3D 14B

GRAND COMORO

❒ GRANDE COMORE 7C

GREAT BRITAIN

❒ SANDHILL PARK 3E

GREECE

❒ CALAMATA 14C
❒ CEFALONIA 14C
❒ GREECE 11C
❒ ITHAK 14C
❒ NAUPLIA 14C
❒ PATRAS 14C
❒ ZANTE 14C

GREENLAND

❒ EGEDESMINDE 14D

HONG KONG

❒ HONG KONG 14C

HUNGARY

❒ ADAMOS (Adamov) Siebenbuergen 1A
❒ ALMASFUEZITOE 2B
❒ ANTALDES 1A
❒ ANTALOCZ 3A
❒ ARAD 1A
❒ BALF (Wolfs) 1A
❒ BARCS 1A
❒ BEKESCSABA 1A
❒ BEREGSRASZ 1B
❒ BOLDOGASSZONY 3A
❒ BRODE 1B
❒ BUDAPEST 1A 2A 14B
❒ BUDAPEST-KOEBANYA 2A
❒ CSOT 3A
❒ CZEGLED (Cegled) 1B
❒ CZERNOWITZ (Chernovtsy, Chernovitsy, Cernauti, Romania, Cernovoy, USSR) 1A 3A
❒ DIOSGYOER 1B
❒ DUNASZERDAHELY 3B
❒ ENYING 3B
❒ ERZSBETFALA (Pestszenterzsebet, Erzsebetfalva, Leninvaros, Pesterzsebe 2B
❒ ESZTERGOM 1B
❒ FELED 1B
❒ FELSOSAG 3B
❒ FERTOEBOZ (Holing) 1A
❒ FERTOERAKOS (Kroisbach) 1B
❒ FUENFKIRCHEN (Pecs) 2A
❒ GOEDOELLOE 14B
❒ GROSZ-SCHOENAU 1B
❒ GURAHUMORA (Provinz Bukowinia, Gura Humorului, Rumania) 3B
❒ GYOER (Raab) 1A 2B
❒ HAID 14B
❒ HAJMASKER 1A 3A
❒ HARKA (Harkau) 1A
❒ HAZTARTAS 2A
❒ HOMOKSZIL 2A 3A
❒ HOREPNIKU 3A
❒ KALOCSA 14B
❒ KAPOSVAR 1A 14B
❒ KARANSEBES 1B
❒ KATY 2A
❒ KECSKEMET 1A
❒ KENYERMEZOE 3A 4B
❒ KESZTHELY 14B
❒ KISKUNHALAS 14B
❒ KOLOZSVAR 1A
❒ KOMAROM (Komorn, Komaromujvaros) 3A

50 Filler, Hajmasker, Hungary, 3A

❒ KOPHAZA (Kohlnhof) 1A
❒ KOZICHOVICE 1A
❒ KUEKOELLODOMBO 1A
❒ LABATLAN 1A
❒ LEIBICZ 3A
❒ MAADI Zemplin 14B
❒ MALE CHYSCE 2A
❒ MEZOETUR 14B
❒ MISKOLCZ (Miskolc, Borsod-Abauj-Zemplen) 1A
❒ MOHACS 14B
❒ MOSON (Mosony, Wieselburg) 1A
❒ MUNKACS (Mukachevo USSR) 1A
❒ NAGYBANYA (Baia Mare, Rumania) 1A
❒ NAGYCZENK (Grosszinkendorf) 1A
❒ NAGYKAROLYFALVA (Velke Karlovice) 1A
❒ NAGYMEGYER 3B
❒ NAGYSZALONTA (Nagy-Szalatna, Salonta, Rumania) 1A
❒ NAGYSZOELLOES (Nagy-Szollos, Vinogradov, USSR) 1B
❒ NEPSZAVA UTALVANY 1A
❒ NEZSIDER 3B
❒ NYIREGYHAZA 1A
❒ OEDENBURG (Sopron) 1A
❒ OHRA 9A
❒ ORSOVA 1A
❒ OSTFFYASSZONFYA (Ost-Asszonyfa) 3A
❒ PACOVE 1B
❒ PAPA 1B
❒ PECS 1A 14B
❒ PESTIHIRLAP 2B
❒ PUTNOK 1A 2B
❒ RAKOSFALVA 1B
❒ REIFENSTEIN 1A
❒ ROZSNYO (Rosenau, Roznava, Czechoslovakia) 1B
❒ SAROSPATAK 1A
❒ SATORALJAUJIHELY (Gruenhut) 1A
❒ SCHLAG/GABLONZ (Gablonz-Jablonec nad Nisou, Czechoslovakia) 9B
❒ SKALOLCZA (Slowakel, Skalicz, Hungary, Skalica, Czechoslovakia) Hungary 2B
❒ SKERKSENY 1B
❒ SOMORJA 3A
❒ SOPRONNYEK (Sopron, Oldenburg, Germany) 3A
❒ SZABAD NEP UTALVANY 1A
❒ SZAKOLCZA (Slowakei) 1A
❒ SZCERCU (Szcerecz) 1A
❒ SZECZENY 1A
❒ SZEFESHERVAR 1A
❒ SZEGED 1A
❒ SZENT MARGITSZIGET 1B
❒ SZENTGOTTHARD 1A

10 & 25 Aurar, 1 krona, Camp Knox, Iceland, U.S. Navy, 3B

❒ SZERENCS 1A
❒ SZERSZARD 14B
❒ SZIGETVAR 14B
❒ SZOMBATHELY (Steinamanger) 1A
❒ TABOR Pont 14B
❒ TORDA (Turda, Rumania) 1C
❒ TREBITSCH (Trebic) 1A
❒ VAROSSZALONAK 3B
❒ VAS (Eisenburg) 1B
❒ VASMEGYE 1A
❒ VERSECZ 2A
❒ VESZPREM 1B
❒ ZALACSANY 3B
❒ ZALAEGERSZEG-TABOR 3B

ICELAND

❒ CAMP KNOX 14D

INDIA

❒ AHMEDNAGAR Maharashtra 15B
❒ BANGALORE 3B
❒ BHOPAL 3B
❒ BIKANER 3A
❒ CLEMENT TOWN 3B
❒ DEOLI 3B
❒ NOVA GOA Goa 1C
❒ PREMNAGAR AT DEHRA DUN 15B
❒ RAMGARH 15B

IRELAND

❒ BALLYKINDAR 15B
❒ CURRAGH 15B

ISLE OF MAN

❒ DOUGLAS (CAMP) 15B
❒ GRANVILLE (Douglas) 15B
❒ HUTCHISON CAMP (Douglas) 15B
❒ ONCHAN 15B
❒ P CAMP 15C
❒ PEVERIL (Peel) 15B
❒ QUARMBY 14C

ITALY

❒ ACQUAVIVA DELLE FONTI Bari, Puglia 3A
❒ ACQUI (Ovada, Alessandria, Piemonte) 3A
❒ ADERNO (Catania) 3A
❒ ADERNO Sicilia 3A
❒ AGNANO-TERME Napoli 3B
❒ AIX LA PROVENCE 14B
❒ ALDI FREDDO 3B
❒ ALESSANDRIA Piemonte 3B

2 Shillings, 6 pence, Peveril POW camp, Isle of Man, 3B

❒ AMALFI 3C
❒ AMELIA 3B
❒ AQUILA Abruzzo 3C
❒ ARBE 3A 14B
❒ AREZZO 3B 14B
❒ ARQUATA-SCRIVIA Alessandria Genova 3A 14B
❒ ASCOLI PICENO 14B
❒ ASINARA Sardinia 3B
❒ ASSISI 3B
❒ ASTI Piedmonte (BASSO ASTIGIANO) 14D
❒ AVERSA 15C
❒ AVEZZANO Abruzzo 3B
❒ AVEZZANO Aquila 3B
❒ AVIETO 3B
❒ AZINO 3B
❒ BAGNARIA D'ARSA 3B
❒ BAIA 14B
❒ BALESTRATE 3B
❒ BARDI 14B
❒ BARILE 3B
❒ BARONISSI Campania 3B
❒ BARONISSI Salerno 3B
❒ BELLUNO (NATIONALE BEFREIUNGSFRONT) 14D
❒ BENEVENTO Campania 3B
❒ BERCHIDDA Sardegna 3B
❒ BERCHIDDA Sassari 3B
❒ BIBBIANO Arezzo 3B
❒ BIBBIANO Toscana 3B
❒ BITETTO Bari 3B
❒ BITETTO Puglia 3C
❒ BOGLIACO 14B
❒ BOLOGNA Mantova Lombardia 3B 14B
❒ BOLZANO 15D
❒ BONAVENTO SIENA 3B
❒ BONORVA Sardegna 3B
❒ BORDIGHERE English 3B
❒ BORDONECCHIA English 3B
❒ BORGO D'ALE Novara 3B
❒ BORGO D'ALE Piemonte 3B
❒ BORGO DI S. DONNINO Emilia 3B
❒ BORGO DI S. DONNINO Parma 3B
❒ BORGO FORTE Lombardia 3B
❒ BORGO FORTE Mantova 3B
❒ BOZEN 1A 14B
❒ BRESCIA Castello/Lombardia 3B 14B
❒ BUIA 1B
❒ BUONO CONVENTO (Toscana) 3B
❒ CAGLIARI Sardegna 3B
❒ CALCE Bari 3B
❒ CALCE Puglia 3B
❒ CALCE Sicilia 3B
❒ CALCI Pisa 3B
❒ CALCI Toscana 3B
❒ CAMAIORE Lucca Toscana 3B
❒ CAMALDOLI Genova 3C
❒ CAMPAGNA Compania 3B
❒ CAMPAGNA Salerno 3B
❒ CAMPLI Abruzzi 3B
❒ CAMPLI Terrano 3C
❒ CAMPO BASSO 3B
❒ CAMPO FELICE 3C
❒ CANORS 15C
❒ CAPRAIAL Genova 3B
❒ CAPRAIAL Isola 3C
❒ CAPRAIAL Liguria 3B
❒ CAPUA-CASERTA 14B
❒ CARINI Palermo 3B
❒ CARINI Sicilia 3C
❒ CARPI (Modena) 14B
❒ CASAGIOVE Napoli 3B
❒ CASAL Cremona 3C
❒ CASAL Lombardia 3B
❒ CASAL Maggiore 3B
❒ CASAL D'ALTAMURA 3B
❒ CASALE Alessandria 3B
❒ CASALE Monferrato 3A
❒ CASALE Piemonte 3A
❒ CASERTA Aldifreddo 3B
❒ CASERTA Campania 3C
❒ CASERTA Caserma 3A
❒ CASERTA CASERMA Padiglione 3A
❒ CASINO Colli d'Asti 3A
❒ CASSANO Avellino 3A
❒ CASSINO Campania 3C
❒ CASSINO Caserta 3A
❒ CASSINO Molini Villa 3B
❒ CASTEL Franco 3B
❒ CASTEL ROCCHERE Alessandria 3A
❒ CASTEL ROCCHERE Piemonte 3A
❒ CASTEL URSINO Catania 3B
❒ CASTEL URSINO Sicilia 3A
❒ CASTELLANA Bari 3C
❒ CASTELLANA Puglia 3C
❒ CASTELLO Allessandria Piemonte 3B
❒ CASTELLO DEL TREBBIO Firenza Toscana 3A
❒ CATANIA Sicilia 3A
❒ CAVA Hospital 3B
❒ CAVI Alessandria Piemonte 3B
❒ CAVI Castello 3B
❒ CEFALU Palermo 3B
❒ CEFALU Sicilia 3C
❒ CENTO Emilia 3B
❒ CENTO Ferrara 3B
❒ CERIGNOLA Abruzzo 3A
❒ CERTOSA 3B
❒ CERTOSA DI PADULA 3B
❒ CESENA Forli 3B
❒ CESENA Marche 3C

Types of Emergency Money

Type	**Reference #**
Municipal paper	1
Private paper	2
POW paper	3
POW official metal	4
POW private metal	5
Municipal metal	6
Private metal	7
Gas tokens	8
Food; beer; konsumverein	9
Naval; military; kantine	10
Encased, unencased stamps	11
Streetcar tokens	12
Porcelain	13
World War II issues	14
Concentration, Civilian internment camps	15

Rarity grades: A, to $25; B, to $60; C, to $125; D, to $200; and E, $350

❒ CHIAVARI 14B
❒ CICAGNA 3A
❒ CITTA'DUCALE Abruzzo 3A
❒ CITTA'DUCALE Aquila 3B
❒ CIVIDALE 3B
❒ CIVITA CASTELLANA Lazio 3A
❒ CIVITA CASTELLANA Roma 3A
❒ COCCONATE D'ASTI Alessandia Piemonte 3A
❒ COLLE DI TENDA Cunei 3A
❒ COLLE DI TENDA Liguria 3B
❒ COLLIO 14B
❒ COMO 3A
❒ CONCA D'ORO Sicilia 3A
❒ CONVERSANO Bari Puglia 3A
❒ COPUA-CASERTA 14A
❒ CORMONS 3B
❒ CORONATO Genova 3B
❒ CORONATO Hospital 3C
❒ CORTE Maggiore 3B
❒ CORTE Piacenza 3A
❒ CREMONA 15B
❒ CUNEO Piemonte 3A
❒ DANTON (BRIGADEN PASUBIO) 14D
❒ DOLCEDO Liguria 3A
❒ DOLCEDO Porto Maurizio 3B
❒ EDOLO Brescia 3B
❒ EDOLO Lombardia 3B
❒ EMILIA 14B
❒ EST-TAGLIAMENTO 14B
❒ FANNA 14B
❒ FENESTRELE Piemonte 3B
❒ FIESOLE Hospital 3C
❒ FINALMARINA Castelfranco 3B
❒ FINALMARINA Forte 3B
❒ FINALMARINA Genova 3B
❒ FINALMARINA Liguria 3B
❒ FIRENZE (FLORENCE) 3A
❒ FIUME (Rieka, Rijeka, Yugoslavia) 1A 14B
❒ FONTE D'AMORE DI SYLMONA 3B 14C
❒ FORLI Marche 3B
❒ FORNELLI Sardegna 3B
❒ FOSSANO Cueno 3B
❒ FOSSANO Piemonte 3B
❒ FOSSOMBRONE 3B
❒ FRATTAMAGGIORE 11B
❒ FRIAUL (Friuli) Venice 14C
❒ FROSINONE 14B
❒ GARIBALDI Genova 3B
❒ GARIBALDI Hospital 3B
❒ GAVI Ligure 3B
❒ GAVI CASTELLO Alessandria Piemonte 3B
❒ GENOVA (GENOA) 3A 4B
❒ GHILARZA Sardegna 3A
❒ GHINAGLIA 14B
❒ GIMINAGNO Siena 3B
❒ GIONIURAGGIO Sardegna 3B
❒ GONARS (Camp #89) 14C 15C
❒ GOVORRANO Piemonte 3B
❒ GRIGNASCO 3A
❒ GRUMELLO 14B
❒ GRUPPLGNANO 3C
❒ IMOLA 3B
❒ INGUTOSU Bau 3B
❒ INGUTOSU Sardegna 3B
❒ ISEO Brescia 3B
❒ ISEO Lombardia 3B
❒ ISERNIA Campo Basso 3B
❒ ISOLA di Ponsa 3B
❒ ITS SULMONA AQUILA AGRUZZO 3B
❒ KRAS 14B
❒ LACCONI Cagliari 3B
❒ LACCONI Sardegna 3C
❒ LA FRASCHETTE DI ALTARI 14B
❒ LATERNIA 14C
❒ LATISANA 3B
❒ LAVORO 14B
❒ LECCE 3C
❒ LIGURIA 14B
❒ LIVORNO CASERMA Cavalleria Toscana 3B
❒ LOMBARDA 14B
❒ LUCCA 14B
❒ LUSERNA S. Giovanni 3B
❒ LUSERNA Torino Piemonte 3B
❒ MACERADA 14C
❒ MADDALON Campania 3B
❒ MADDALON Caserta 3B
❒ MANDAS Sicilia 3B
❒ MANTOVA Lombardia 3B 14C
❒ MANTUA 14C
❒ MAREMMA Sardegna 3B
❒ MARSALA Sicilia 3B
❒ MARSALA Trapani 3B
❒ MATERA Bari 3B
❒ MATERA Puglia 3B
❒ MATTEOTTI (Rino de Mono) BRIGADEN PASUBIO 14D
❒ MELEDA 14C
❒ MELFI FOTENZA Balilicata 3B
❒ MENDRISIO Sicilia 3B
❒ MERGO 3B
❒ MESTRE 14B
❒ MILANO 11A 14A
❒ MILAZZO 3A 14B
❒ MILETTO Catania 3B
❒ MILETTO Sicilia 3B
❒ MILOWITZ 3B
❒ MODENA 3A 14B
❒ MOLINO 3B
❒ MOMBRACELLI D'ASTI Piemonte 3A
❒ MONASTIR Cagliari 3A
❒ MONASTIR Sardegna 3B
❒ MONCENISIO Piemonte 3A
❒ MONCENISIO Torino 3B
❒ MONIGO (Treviso) 14C
❒ MONOPOLI 3A
❒ MONREALE Palermo 3B
❒ MONREALE Sicilia 3B
❒ MONTE NARBA Sardegna 3B
❒ MONTEMALE Genua 14C
❒ MONTI Sardegna 3B
❒ MONZA Lombardia 3B

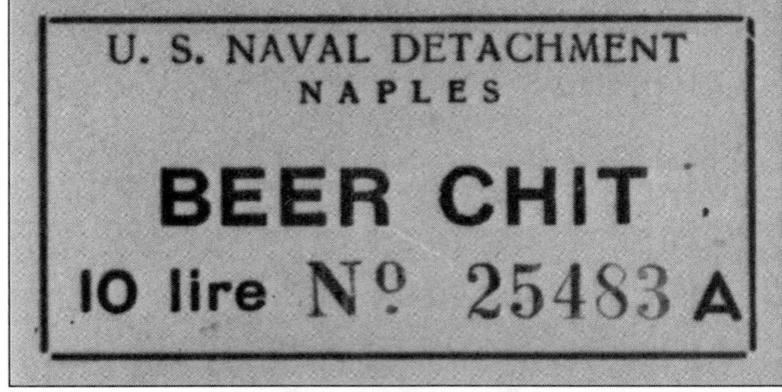

10 Lire, Naples, Italy, U.S. Naval Detachment, 10B

❒ MONZA Milano 3B
❒ MURO LUCANO Basilicata 3A
❒ MURO LUCANO Potenza 3C
❒ NAPOLI Castel 3B
❒ NAPOLI S. Elmo 3B
❒ NARNI Perugia 3B
❒ NARNI Umbria 3B
❒ NISIDA Isole 3A
❒ NOCERA 3A
❒ NOCERA UMBRA BAGNI Sardegna 3B
❒ NOLA CASERTA Campania 3B
❒ NOTO PALAZZOLO Syrakus Sicilia 3A 14B
❒ NOUVO SARDEGNA Sardegna 3A
❒ NOVI Ligure 3A
❒ NUGHEDU, SAN NICOLO Sardegna 3B
❒ NUGHEDU, SAN NICOLO Sasari 3B
❒ OLEGGIO Navara 3B
❒ OLEGGIO Piemonte 3B
❒ ONEGLIA3B
❒ ORVIETO Perugia 3B
❒ ORVIETO Umbria 3B
❒ OSOPPO-FRIAUL 14B
❒ OSSOLA BRIGADE OSSOLA-TAL 14D
❒ OSTUNI Di LECCE 3B
❒ OVADA 3B
❒ PADOVA (BRIGATA GARIBALDI) 2D
❒ PADOVA (CHIESANUOVA) 3B 14C
❒ PADULA Campania 3B
❒ PADULA Salerno 3C
❒ PALMA Nova 3B
❒ PARMA 14B
❒ PAVIA 3B 14B
❒ PELAGO Toscana 3B
❒ PELAGO Villa Paterno 3B
❒ PERUGIA 14C
❒ PESCANTINA Veneto 3B
❒ PESCANTINA Verona 3B
❒ PETROIO 3B
❒ PIACENZA 3B 14D
❒ PIANOSA Isole 3B
❒ PIAVE (BRIGATA BANDIERA) 14D
❒ PIAZZA ARMERINA Caltanisetta 3B
❒ PIAZZA ARMERINA Sicilia 3B
❒ PICCHETTA 3B
❒ PIETRA Ligure 3B
❒ PINEROLO 3B 14B
❒ PISA Toscana 3B
❒ PIZZIGHETTONE Cremona 3B
❒ PIZZIGHETTONE Lombardia 3B
❒ POLA 3A 14B
❒ POMAROLO Torino Piemonte 3A
❒ PORTO ERCOLE Grosseto Liguria 3B
❒ PORTO FERRAIO Isola d'Elba 3B
❒ PORTO TORRES Sardegna 3B
❒ PORTO TORRES Sassari 3B
❒ POTENZA Basilicata 3B
❒ POZZOLO 3B
❒ PRESIDIO Di TRAPANI Sicilia 3A
❒ QUERCIA Roma Latina 3C
❒ REGGIA 14C
❒ REGGIO EMILIA 3B 14B
❒ RENICCI Arezzo (POW CAMP K#97) 3B 14C
❒ RIBOLLA Grosseto Toscana 3B
❒ RICTORIA 3B
❒ RIETI 14B
❒ RIGOROSO Sciura 3B
❒ RODI Sicilia 3B
❒ ROME 11A 14C
❒ SALA CONSILINA 3C
❒ SALUSSOLE Piemonte 3B
❒ SAMBUCA Zabut 3B
❒ SAN FELICE (Verona) 3B 14B
❒ SAN FELICE Caserma 3B 14C
❒ SAN FELICE Veneta 3B 14C
❒ SAN GIMIGNANO Siena 3B
❒ SAN GIMIGNANO Toscana 3B
❒ SAN GIOVANNI LA PUNTA Sicilia 3B
❒ SAN GIOVANNI VALDARNO Avezzano Piemonte 3B
❒ SAN LAZARO Parmense 3B
❒ SAN PIETRO 3C
❒ SAN REMO Hospital 3A
❒ SAN REMO Liguria 3A
❒ SAN SEVERINO Macerata Marche 3A
❒ SAN VITO Cagliari Sardegna 3B
❒ SANTA MARIA Capua 3B
❒ SANTA MARIA Caserta 3B
❒ SANTA MARIA Compania 3B
❒ SANTA MARIA Vetere 3B
❒ SANTULUSORGIO Cagliari 3B
❒ SANTULUSORGIO Sardegna 3B
❒ SAPRAIA Isola 3C
❒ SARDARA Cagliari 3B
❒ SARDARA Sardegna 3B
❒ SASSARI Sardegna 3B
❒ SAVIGLIANO Hospital 3B
❒ SAVONA Genova 3A
❒ SAVONA Liguria 3B
❒ SCANDIANO Emilia 3B
❒ SCANDIANO Reggio Emilia 3C
❒ SCARPANTO Isola 3B
❒ SCIACCA 3B
❒ SCORDEVOLE Novara 3B
❒ SCORDEVOLE Piamonte 3A
❒ SCORZE Carelle 3B
❒ SEMINARIO SAN GIOVANNI 3B
❒ SERVIGLIANO Ascoli 3A
❒ SINNAI Sardegna 3C
❒ SPINETO DI CASTELLAMIENTE 14B
❒ SPOLETA 3B
❒ STAZZANO Alessandria 3B
❒ STAZZANO Piemonte 3B
❒ STRETTI Sardegna 3C
❒ SUBIACO 3B
❒ SULMONE Aquila Abruzzo 3B
❒ SURIGEDHO Asinara 3B
❒ TABANELLO English 3B
❒ TAGGIA Liguria 3B
❒ TAGGIA San Remo 3C
❒ TARRANA SARENA 14B
❒ TAVERNELLO 14B
❒ TERNI 14B
❒ TERRASSINI Palermo 3B
❒ TERRASSINI Sicilia 3B
❒ THIESI 3B
❒ TOMBARINI Sardegna 3B
❒ TORINI 3A 11A
❒ TORTONA Alessandria Piemonte 3B
❒ TOSCANO 14B
❒ TRENTINO 14C
❒ TREVISO 3A 14B
❒ TREVISO English 3B 14B
❒ TRIESTE 14B
❒ TRINO NOVARA Piemonte 3A
❒ TULA Sardegna 3B
❒ TURA 14B
❒ TURIN (Turino) VI. ALPINENDIVISION DES CANAVESE 14D

❐ UDINE 3B 14B
❐ URBANIA Pesaro 3B
❐ VAL CHIAMPO (BRIGADEN PASUBIO) 14D
❐ VARZI 14B
❐ VENETO (BRIGATA PIAVE) 14D
❐ VENICE 14B
❐ VENOSA Potenza 3B
❐ VERONA (Camp #28 Fantasy?) 14B
❐ VETRALLA-VITERBO 14B
❐ VIAREGGIO Toscana 3B
❐ VICENZA (BRIGADEN PASUBIO) 3B 14D
❐ VIGEVANO Lombardia 3B
❐ VIGEVANO Pavio 3B
❐ VILLA CIDRO Sardegna 3B
❐ VILLABATE 3B
❐ VILLANOVA-MONTELEONE 3C
❐ VINADIO Cunco 3A
❐ VINADIO Piemonte 3B
❐ VISCO 14B
❐ VITERBO 3B
❐ VITTORIA Trapani Sicilia 3A
❐ VOGHERA Lombardia 3B
❐ VOGHERA Pavia 3C
❐ VOLTAGGIO Alessandria 3B
❐ VOLTAGGIO Piemonte 3B
❐ VOLTERRA Pisa 3B
❐ VOLTERRA Toscana 3B
❐ YOL 14A
❐ ZAMBO (BRIGADEN PASUBIO) 14D

JAPAN

❐ BANDO/SHIKOKU 3E

KENYA

❐ NAIVASKA 14B

LATVIA

❐ MITAU (Yelgava, Jelgava) 1A 11B
❐ RIGA 1A

LIECHTENSTEIN

❐ LIECHTENSTEIN 1A

LITHUANIA

❐ KOWNO (Kaunas) 1A
❐ SEDA (SIADY) 1B

LUXEMBURG

❐ BETTEMBOURG 1B
❐ DIFFERDINGEN (Differdange) 7B
❐ EICH 1A 2B
❐ ESCH-SUR-ALZETTE 1A 2A
❐ LAROCHETTE/FELS 1B

3 Rubles, Riga, Latvia, 1A

20 Heller, Liechenstein, 1A

❐ LUXEMBURG 1A 11B
❐ RUMELINGEN 7B
❐ TROIS VIERGES 7A
❐ ULFLINGEN 7B

MACAO

❐ CARDIGOS 1B
❐ LISBOA 1B
❐ MACAO 1B 2C

MADAGASCAR

❐ MADAGASCAR 2A 7B 11B

MADEIRA

❐ FUNCHAL Madeira 2B

MARTINIQUE

❐ MARTINIQUE 1B

MONACO

❐ MONACO 1B 11B

MONTENEGRO

❐ CETINJE (Cettinje) 2B
❐ IPEK (Pec) 1B
❐ KOLASIN 1B
❐ MONTENEGRO 1B
❐ NIKSIC 1B
❐ PLJEVUA 1B
❐ PODGORICA (Titograd) 1B
❐ STARI BAR 1A

MOROCCO

❐ CASABLANCA (Dar el Beida) 7C
❐ KOUIF 7B
❐ MAROC 6A
❐ MARRAKECH 9B

1 Centavo, Macao, 1B

25 Centimes, Casablanca, Morocco, 1B

MOZAMBIQUE

❒ BEIRA 1A
❒ INHAMBANE 2B
❒ LOURENCO MARQUES 1A 12B
❒ QUELIMANE 1A 2B
❒ TETE 1B

NETHERLANDS

❒ ALBLASSERDAM South Holland 14C
❒ ALKMAAR North Holland 8B
❒ ALMKERK North Brabant 14B
❒ ALPHEN/RIJN South Holland 8B
❒ AMERSFOORT Utrecht 15B
❒ AMSTENRADE Limburg 14B
❒ AMSTERDAM North Holland 1A 2B 8B
❒ ANNA PAULOWNA North Holland 14B
❒ APELDOORN Gelderland 1A 14B
❒ ARNHEIM Gelderland 8A
❒ ASSEN Drenthe 1B
❒ BAARN Utrecht 8A
❒ BEEK Limburg 14B
❒ BERGEN OP ZOOM North Brabant 1A 14B
❒ BERGHAREN Gelderland 14B
❒ BERGHEM North Brabant 14B
❒ BEVERWIJK North Holland 8A 14B
❒ BODEGRAAF 8A
❒ BOLSWARD Friesdland 2B
❒ BORCULO Gelderland 14B
❒ BORGER Drenthe 1A 14B
❒ BORNE 8A
❒ BRAKEL Gelderland 14B
❒ BREDE North Brabant 8A
❒ BRUNSSUM Limburg 14B
❒ BUNDE Limburg 14B
❒ BUSSOM North Holland 8A
❒ CAPELLE A/D IJSSEL South Holland 14B
❒ COEVRDEN Drenthe 1A 14B
❒ CULEMBORG Gelderland 1A

50 Centimes, Marrakech, Morocco, 4th Legionaires, 10B

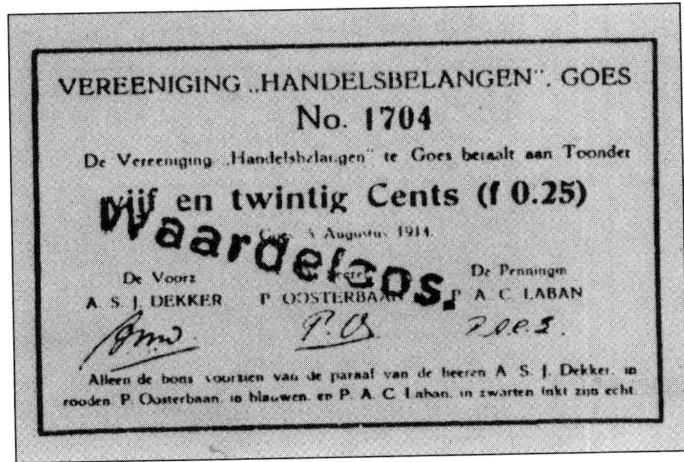

25 Cents, Goes, Netherlands, 1B

❒ DANTUMADEEL 1A
❒ DELDEN Overijssel 2B
❒ DELFT South Holland 8A
❒ DENEKAMP Overijssel 14B
❒ DEURNE North Brabant 14B
❒ DEVENTER Overijssel 8A 14B
❒ DINTERLOORD North Brabant 1A
❒ DINXPERLO Gelderland 14B
❒ DOETINCHEM Gelderland 14B
❒ DOKKUM Friesland 8A
❒ DONGE North Brabant 1A
❒ DORDRECHT South Holland 8A
❒ DREISCHOR Zeeland 1A
❒ DRENTE 14B
❒ DRIEL Gelderland 14B
❒ DRUTEN Gelderland 14B
❒ DUSSEN North Brabant 14B
❒ EDE Gelderland 8A
❒ EERBEEK N.V. Gelderland 14B
❒ EINDHOVEN North Brabant 8A
❒ ELSLOO Limburg 14B
❒ ELST Gelderland 14B
❒ EMMEN Drenthe 14B
❒ ENKHUIZEN North Holland 8A
❒ ENSCHEDE Overijssel 1A 14B
❒ ERMELO Gelderland 14B
❒ ETTEN EN LEUR North Brabant 14B
❒ FRIESLAND 14B
❒ GELEEN Limberg 14B
❒ GEULLE Limburg 14B
❒ GIESSEN North Brabant 14B
❒ GOES Zeeland 1A 8A
❒ GORINCHEM South Holland 8A
❒ GRAVE North Brabant 14B
❒ GRAVENHAGE South Holland 1A 8A
❒ GRIENDTSVEEN Limburg 2B
❒ GRONINGEN 14B
❒ HAARLEM North Holland 14B
❒ HAARLEMMERMEER North Holland 14B
❒ HARDEWIJK Gelderland 14B
❒ HATTEM Gelderland 14B
❒ HAVELTE Drenthe 14B
❒ HEDEL Gelderland 14B
❒ HEEMSTEDT North Holland 1A 8A 14B
❒ HEER Limburg 14B
❒ HEERENVEEN Friesland 14B
❒ HEERLEN Limburg 1A 14B
❒ HELDER, DEN North Holland 14B
❒ HELMOND North Brabant 8A 14B
❒ HENDRIK-IDO-AMBRACHT South Holland 14B

50 Cents, Krimpen/Lek, Netherlands, 1A

- ❒ HENGELO Overijssel 14B
- ❒ HERPEN North Brabant 14B
- ❒ HERTOGENBOSCH South Holland 8B
- ❒ HETEREN Gelderland 14B
- ❒ HEUSDEN Brabant 8A
- ❒ HILLEGOM South Holland 14B
- ❒ HILVERSUM North Holland 8A
- ❒ HOENSBROCK Limburg 14B
- ❒ HOORN North Holland 14B
- ❒ HORST Limburg 1B
- ❒ HUISSEN Gelderland 14B
- ❒ HUIZEN North Holland 14B
- ❒ HURWENEN Gelderland 14B
- ❒ IJSSELMONDE South Holland 14B
- ❒ IJSSELSTEIN South Holland 2A
- ❒ KAMPEN Overijssel 14B
- ❒ KLUNDERT North Brabant 1A
- ❒ KOLLUMERLAND Friesland 14B
- ❒ KRIMPEN/IJSSEL South Holland 1A 2B 14B
- ❒ KRIMPEN/LEK South Holland 1A 14B
- ❒ LAREN North Holland 14B
- ❒ LEEUWARDEN Friesland 8A
- ❒ LEIDSCHENDAM South Holland 14B
- ❒ LEKKERKERK South Holland 1A
- ❒ LISSE South Holland 14B
- ❒ LOON OP ZAND North Brabant 14B
- ❒ MADE North Brabant 14B
- ❒ MEERLO Limburg 14B
- ❒ MEERSSEN Limburg 14B
- ❒ MIDDELBURG Zeeland 2A
- ❒ MIDWOUD North Holland 14B
- ❒ NIEUWERKERK/IJSSEL South Holland 14B
- ❒ NIJMEGEN Gelderland 14B
- ❒ NOORDGOUWE Zeeland 1B
- ❒ NUTH 14B
- ❒ OISTERWIJK Brabant 8A
- ❒ OLDENZAAL Overijssel 14B
- ❒ OLST Overijssel 14B
- ❒ OOSTERHOUT North Brabant 1A 14B
- ❒ OSS North Brabant 1A 14B
- ❒ OUDERKERK/IJSSEL South Holland 14B
- ❒ OVERIJSSEL 14B
- ❒ OVERSCHIE South Holland 14B
- ❒ PEIZE Drenthe 14B
- ❒ POEDEROIJN Gelderland 14B
- ❒ POORTUGAAL South Holland 14B
- ❒ POSTERHOLT 1A
- ❒ PROVIEND 1A
- ❒ PURMEREND North Holland 14A
- ❒ RAAMSDONK North Brabant 14B
- ❒ RAVENSTEIN North Brabant 14B
- ❒ RHEDEN Gelderland 8A
- ❒ RHENEN Gelderland 1A
- ❒ RIJSWIJK South Holland 1B 8A 14B
- ❒ ROERMOND Limburg 8A
- ❒ ROSMALEN North Brabant 14B
- ❒ ROSSUM Gelderland 14B
- ❒ ROTTERDAM South Holland 1A 8A 14B
- ❒ SASSENHEIM South Holland 14B
- ❒ SCHAESBERG Limburg 1A
- ❒ SCHIEDAM South Holland 8A 14B
- ❒ SIMPELVELD Limburg 14B
- ❒ SLIEDRECHT South Holland 14B
- ❒ SLIKKERVEER 14B
- ❒ SOEST Utrecht 14B
- ❒ STEENBERGEN North Brabant 1A
- ❒ STEENWIJK Overijssel 1A
- ❒ STEIN Limburg 14B
- ❒ TERNEUZEN 14B
- ❒ TERSCHELLING 14B
- ❒ TILBURG North Brabant 8B
- ❒ UBACH/WORMS Limburg 14B
- ❒ UDEN North Brabant 1A
- ❒ URK North Holland 14B
- ❒ UTRECHT Utrecht 8A 14B
- ❒ VAALS Limburg 1A 14B
- ❒ VALKENSWAARD North Brabant 8A 14B
- ❒ VEEN North Brabant 14B
- ❒ VEENDAM Groningen 1B
- ❒ VELP North Brabant 14B
- ❒ VELSEN North Holland 8A
- ❒ VENDRAY (Venray) Limburg 14B
- ❒ VENLO Limburg 1A 8B
- ❒ VLAARDINGEN South Holland 8B 14B
- ❒ VLAGTWEDDE Groningen 14B
- ❒ VLIELAND North Holland 14B
- ❒ VLISSINGEN North Brabant 1B
- ❒ VOORBURG South Holland 8A
- ❒ VUGHT (s-Hertogenbosch) North Brabant 15B
- ❒ WAALWIJK North Brabant 14B
- ❒ WADDINXVEEN South Holland 8A

1.50 Gulden, Venlo, Netherlands, 1B

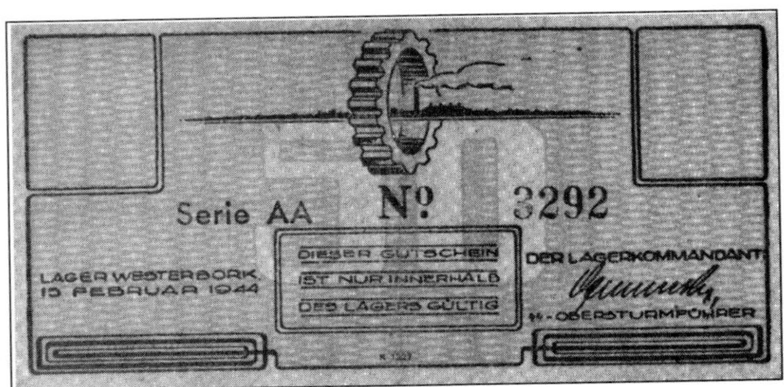

50 Cents, Westerbork, Netherlands, 15B

❒ WAGEMINGEN 1A
❒ WAPENVELD Gelderland 14B
❒ WASPIK North Brabant 14B
❒ WASSENAAR South Holland 8B
❒ WEHL Gelderland 14B
❒ WESTERBORK Drenthe 15C
❒ WESTZAAN North Holland 14B
❒ WIERINGEN North Holland 14B
❒ WIJCHEN (Wychen) Gelderland 14B
❒ WIJK/AALBURG North Brabant 14B
❒ WILDERVANK Groningen 1A
❒ WILLEMSTAD North Brabant 14B
❒ WINTERSWIJK Gelderland 8A
❒ WOERDEN South Holland 8B
❒ WOLPHAARTSDIJK Zeeland 1A
❒ WOUDRICHEM North Brabant 14B
❒ ZAANDAM North Holland 8A
❒ ZAANSTREEK 8B
❒ ZALTBOMMEL Gelderland 14B
❒ ZANDVOORT North Holland 14B
❒ ZEELAND 14B
❒ ZEVENBERGEN North Brabant 14B
❒ ZIERIKZEE Zeeland 8A
❒ ZWIJNDRECHT South Holland 14B

NETHERLANDS EAST INDIES

❒ ALASVALLLELI/Sumatra 15C
❒ KOETATJANE/Sumatra 15C
❒ TJIDENG/DHAJARTA 15C

NEW CALEDONIA

❒ NOUVELLE-CALEDONIE 1B 11C

NEW ZEALAND

❒ FEATHERSTON 4B

NORWAY

❒ ABELVAER 14C
❒ AFJORD 14C
❒ ALESUND 14C
❒ ALGARD 14C
❒ ASKIM 14C
❒ BANGSUND 14C
❒ BERGEN 14C
❒ BREKKVASSEL 14C
❒ BREVIK 14C
❒ BRUSAND 14C
❒ BUVIK 14C
❒ DALANE 14C
❒ DRAMMEN 14C
❒ DRANGEDAL 14C
❒ EGERSUND 14C
❒ EIDSHAUG 14C
❒ EITRHEIM 14C
❒ FANNREM 14C
❒ FARSUND 14C
❒ FEDA 14C
❒ FLA 14C
❒ FLATVALSUNDET 14C
❒ FLEKKEFJORD 14C
❒ FLISA 14C
❒ FOLLAFOSS 14C
❒ FOSSLANDSOSEN 14C
❒ FRESVIK 14C
❒ FROSTA 14C
❒ GANDDAL 14C
❒ GJEMLESTAD 14C
❒ GJERPEN 14C
❒ GLOMFJORD 14C
❒ GRESSVIK 14C
❒ GRIMSTAD 14C
❒ GRINE 3E
❒ GULSKOGEN 14C
❒ GYLAND 14C
❒ HARRAN 14C
❒ HAUGE 14C
❒ HEIMDAL 14C
❒ HELLELAND 14D
❒ HESKESTAD 14D
❒ HIDRASUNDET 14C
❒ HOELONDA 14C
❒ HOEYANGER 14C
❒ HOEYHEIMSVIK 14C
❒ HOEYLAND 14C
❒ HOMMELVIK 14C
❒ HOVIN 14C
❒ HOYANGER 14C
❒ KIRKEHAVN 14D
❒ KIRKNESVA 14C
❒ KNABEN 14C
❒ KONGSBERG 14C
❒ KOPERVIK 14C
❒ KOPPERA 14C
❒ KRAGEROE 14C
❒ KRAKEROEY 14C
❒ KRISTIANIA 11C
❒ KRISTIANSUND 14C
❒ KVAL 14C
❒ KVINESDAL 14C
❒ KYRKJEBOE 14C
❒ KYRKSAETEROERA 14C
❒ LAERDAL 14C
❒ LAKESVAG 14D
❒ LANGANGEN 14C
❒ LANGESUND 14C
❒ LEVANGER 14C
❒ LIKNES 14D
❒ LINDAS 14C
❒ LUNDAMO 14C
❒ LUNDE 14C
❒ MAELOEY 14C
❒ MAERE 14C
❒ MALM 14C

Nº 03252 NARVIK SPAREBANK 5 KR. 00 ØRE

NARVIK SPAREBANK — NARVIK

betaler mot denne anvisning til Narvik kommune eller ihendehaveren

— Kroner fem. —

Narvik, den 15. mai 1940.

NARVIK SPAREBANK

Kun gyldig med anvisningens beløp i rødt bankstempel. —

5 Kroner, Narvik, Norway, 2C

❒ MELHUS	14C
❒ MERAKER	14C
❒ MERKEBEKK	14C
❒ MOI	14C
❒ MOLDE	14C
❒ MOSS	14C
❒ MOSTER	14C
❒ MOSVIK	14C
❒ MYRA	14C
❒ NAERBOE	14D
❒ NARVIK	14C
❒ NESLANDSVATN	14C
❒ NOTODDEN	14C
❒ ODDA	14C
❒ OEIE	14C
❒ OESTFOLD	14C
❒ ORKANGER	14C
❒ OSLO	14C
❒ OVERHALLA	14C
❒ PORSGRUNN	14C
❒ RAKKESTAD	14C
❒ RANHEIM	14C
❒ ROERA	14D
❒ ROEROS	14C
❒ ROMMETVEIT	14C
❒ RYGGE	14C
❒ SAKSHAUG	14C
❒ SANDEFJORD	14C
❒ SANDNES	14C
❒ SARPSBORG	14C
❒ SAUDA	14C
❒ SCHILDBERG	14C
❒ SELBU	14C
❒ SELSBAK	14C
❒ SILJAN	14C
❒ SIRDALSVATNET	14C
❒ SIREVAG	14C
❒ SIRNES	14C
❒ SKATVAL	14C
❒ SKIEN	14C
❒ SKJEBERG	14C
❒ SKOGN	14C
❒ SKUDENESHAMN	14C
❒ SOERGJAESLINGAN	14C
❒ SPARBU	14C
❒ SPILLUM/NAMDALEN	14C
❒ STAMNAN	14C
❒ STATHELLE	14D
❒ STAVANGER	14C
❒ STEINKJER	14C
❒ STJOERDAL	14C
❒ STOEREN	14C
❒ STOKKOEY	14C
❒ STOKSUND	14C
❒ STORAS	14C
❒ STORD	14C
❒ SULITJELMA	14D
❒ SVELGEN	14C
❒ SVORKMO	14C
❒ TOENSBERG	14C
❒ TRONDHEIM	14C
❒ TUNE	14C
❒ TYNSET	14C
❒ TYSSEDAL	14C
❒ UALAND	14C
❒ ULEFOSS	14C
❒ VADHEIM	14D
❒ VAFOSS	14C
❒ VARHAUG	14C
❒ VENNESHAMN	14C
❒ VERDAL	14C
❒ VERRASTRANDA	14C
❒ VIGRESTAD	14C
❒ VIKEDAL	14C
❒ VOLLEN	14C
❒ VOSS	14C
❒ YRETTINJE	14C
❒ YTTEROEY	14C

PHILIPPINES

❒ MANILA	15C

PORTUGAL

❒ ABRANTES Santarem	1B	2A	14B
❒ AGUIAR DA BEIRA Guarda	1B	2A	
❒ ALANDROAL Evora	1A	2A	
❒ ALBERGARIA	2C		
❒ ALBUFEIRA Faro	1B	2E	
❒ ALCACER DO SAL Setubal	1B	2C	
❒ ALCANENA Santarem	2C		
❒ ALCOBACA Leiria	1A	2C	
❒ ALCOCHETE Setubal	1C		
❒ ALCOUTIM Faro	2C		
❒ ALDEGALEGA Setubal	1A		
❒ ALENQUER Lisboa	2D		
❒ ALFANDEGA DA FE Braganca	1A		
❒ ALIJO Vila Real	2A		
❒ ALJEZUR Faro	1A		
❒ ALJUSTREL Beja	1A	2E	
❒ ALMADA Setubal	1A	2C	
❒ ALMEIDA Guarda	1B		
❒ ALMEIRIM Santarem	1A		
❒ ALMODOVAR Beja	1A		
❒ ALPAIRCA Santarem	1B		
❒ ALTER DO CHAO Portalegre	1A		
❒ ALVAIAZERE Leiria	1B		
❒ ALVITO Beja	1A	2B	
❒ AMARANTE Porto	2D		
❒ ANADIA Aveiro	1B		
❒ ARCOS DE VALDEVEZ Viana do Castelo	1B	2B	
❒ ARMAMAR Viseu	2C		
❒ AROUCA Aveiro	1A	2E	
❒ ARRAIOLOS Evora	1A	2C	
❒ ARRONCHES Portalegre	1B	2C	
❒ ARRUDA DOS VINHOS Lisboa	2C		
❒ AVEIRO Aveiro	1A		
❒ AVIZ Portalegre	2C		
❒ AZAMBUJA Lisboa	1B		
❒ BARCELLOS (Barcelos) Braga	1C	2A	
❒ BARRANCOS Beja	1B		
❒ BARREIRO Setubal	1C	2C	
❒ BEJA Beja	1A	2D	
❒ BENAVENTE Santarem	1C	2E	
❒ BOMBARRAL Leiria	1B	2C	
❒ BORBA Evora	1C		
❒ BRAGA Braga	1A	2A	
❒ BRAGANCA Braganca	1B	2C	
❒ CADAVAL Lisboa	1C		
❒ CALDAS DA RAINHA Leiria	1A	2B	
❒ CAMINHA Viana do Castelo	1B	2C	
❒ CAMPO MAIOR Portalegre	1B		
❒ CANTANHEDE Coimbra	2D		
❒ CASCAIS Lisboa	2D		
❒ CASTELO BRANCO Castelo Branco	1B	2D	
❒ CASTELO DE PAIVA Aveiro	1A	2C	
❒ CASTELO DE VIDE Portalegre	1B		
❒ CEARA	1B		
❒ COVILHA Castelo Branco	1A		
❒ CRATO Portalegre	1B	2B	
❒ CUBA Beja	1A	2C	
❒ ELVAS Portalegre	2A		
❒ ESPINHO Aveiro	2A		
❒ ESPOZENDE (Esposende) Braga	2A		
❒ ESTARREJA Aveiro	2C		

❒ ESTREMOZ Evora 1A 2D
❒ EVORA Evora 2A
❒ FARO Faro 1B 2B
❒ FEIRA Aveiro 1A 2D
❒ FELGUEIRAS Porto 1A
❒ FERREIRA DO ALENTEJO Beja 2C
❒ FERREIRA DO ZEZERE Santarem 1B 2C
❒ FIGUEIRA DA FOZ Coimbra 1A 2A
❒ FIGUEIRA DE CASTELO RODRIGO Guarda 1B
❒ FIGUEIRO DOS VINHOS Leiria 1B 2B
❒ FORNOS DE ALGODRES Guarda 2C
❒ FREIXO DE ESPADA A CINTA Braganca 1B 2D
❒ FRONTEIRA Portalegre 1B 2C
❒ FUNDAO Castelo Branco 1A 2D
❒ GAIA 6A 13A
❒ GAVIAO Portalegre 1B 2C
❒ GOLEGA Santarem 2C
❒ GONDOMAR Porto 1A
❒ GOUVEIA Guarda 2D
❒ GRANDOLA Setubal 1B
❒ GUARDA Guarda 1A 2C
❒ GUIMARAES Braga 1A 2B
❒ IDANHA A NOVA Castelo Branco 2B
❒ ILHAVO Aveiro 1B 2D
❒ LAGOA Faro 1A
❒ LAGOS Faro 1A 2D
❒ LAMEGO Viseu 1A
❒ LAPA 1B
❒ LEIRIA Leiria 1C 2A
❒ LISBOA (Lisbon) Lisboa 2B
❒ LOULE Faro 1A 2D
❒ LOURES Lisboa 1B
❒ LOURINHA Lisboa 1B 2B
❒ LOUZA Coimbra 1A
❒ LOUZADA Porto 1A 2B
❒ MAFRA Lisboa 1A 2D
❒ MANGUALDE Viseu 1B
❒ MANTEIGAS Guarda 1B
❒ MARCO DE CANAVEZES Porto 2C
❒ MARINHA GRANDE Leiria 1A
❒ MARVAO Portalegre 1B
❒ MATOSINHOS Porto 1A
❒ MEALHADA Aveiro 1A
❒ MEDA Guarda 1A 2C
❒ MELGACO Viana do Castelo 2B
❒ MERTOLA Beja 1B 2D
❒ MIRANDA DO CORVO Cormbra 1A
❒ MIRANDELA Braganca 1A
❒ MOGADOURO Breganca 1B
❒ MOIMENTA DA BEIRA Viseu 1A
❒ MOITA Setubal 1A

1 Centavo, Miranda do Corvo, Portugal, 1A

❒ MONCAO Viana do Castelo 1B 2C
❒ MONCHIQUE Faro 1A
❒ MONFORTE Portalegre 1A 2C
❒ MONTEMOR O NOVA Evora 1B 2C
❒ MONTEMOR-O-VELHO Coimbra 1A 2A
❒ MORA Evora 2C
❒ MOURA Beja 1B 2C
❒ MOURAO Evora 1B 2C
❒ MURCA Vila Real 1A
❒ NAZARE Leiria 1B 2E
❒ NELAS Viseu 1A 2D
❒ NISA (Niza) Portalegre 1B 2C
❒ OBIDOS (Leiria) 1B
❒ ODEMIRA Beja 1A
❒ OEIRAS Lisboa 2E
❒ OLHAO Faro 1A 2D
❒ OLIVEIRA DE AZEMEIS Aveiro 1A 2E
❒ OLIVEIRA DE FRADES Viseu 2D
❒ OLIVEIRA DE HOSPITAL Coimbra 1A
❒ OVAR Aveiro 1A
❒ PACOS DE FERREIRA Porto 2C
❒ PAREDES Porto 1A 2E
❒ PAREDES DE COURA Viana do Castelo 2C
❒ PELOTAS 1B
❒ PENAFIEL Porto 1A 2D
❒ PENALVA DO CASTELO Viseu 1A 2D
❒ PENELA Coimbra 1A
❒ PENICHE Leiria 1B 2C
❒ PESO DA REGUA Vila Real 1A 2C
❒ PINHEL Guarda 1A
❒ POMBAL Leiria 2A
❒ PONTE DA BARCA Viana do Castelo 2B
❒ PONTE DE LIMA Viana do Castelo 2A
❒ PONTE DO SOR Portalegre 2B
❒ PORTALEGRE Portalegre 1A 2D

Types of Emergency Money

Type	Reference #
Municipal paper	1
Private paper	2
POW paper	3
POW official metal	4
POW private metal	5
Municipal metal	6
Private metal	7
Gas tokens	8
Food; beer; konsumverein	9
Naval; military; kantine	10
Encased, unencased stamps	11
Streetcar tokens	12
Porcelain	13
World War II issues	14
Concentration, Civilian internment camps	15

Rarity grades: A, to $25; B, to $60; C, to $125; D, to $200; and E, $350

❒ PORTEL Evora 1B 2C
❒ PORTIMAO Faro 1A 2B
❒ PORTO Porto 2A
❒ PORTO DE MOZ Leiria 2C
❒ POVOA DE LANHOSO Braga 2B
❒ POVOA DE VARZIM Porto 1A 2B
❒ PROENCA A NOVA
Castelo Branco 2D
❒ REDONDO Evora 1B 2B
❒ REGUENGOS DE MONSARAZ
Evora 1A
❒ REZENDE Viseu 1A
❒ RIO MAIOR Santarem 1B
❒ SABROSA Vila Real 1A
❒ SABUGAL Guarda 1A
❒ SALVATERRA DE MAGOS
Santarem 1B
❒ SANTA COM BA DAO Viseu 1A
❒ SANTAREM Santarem 1A 2C
❒ SANTIAGO DE CACEM Setubal 1B 2C
❒ SANTO TIRSO Porto 1A 2A
❒ SAO BRAS DE ALPORTEL Faro 1C 2D
❒ SAO JOSE DO MONTE Negro 1B
❒ SAO PEDRO DO SUL Viseu 2C
❒ SARDOAL Santarem 1B 2B
❒ SEIXAL Setubal 1B
❒ SERNANCELHE Viseu 1B
❒ SERPA Beja 1C 2B
❒ SETUBAL Setubal 1A 2C
❒ SEVER DO VOUGA Aveiro 2C
❒ SILVES Faro 1B 2D
❒ SINES Setubal 1B
❒ SINTRA Lisboa 1A
❒ SOURE Coimbra 1C 2D
❒ SOUZEL Portalegre 1A
❒ TAROUCA Viseu 1B
❒ TAVIRA Faro 2C
❒ TOMAR (Thomar) Santarem 1A 2A
❒ TONADELA Viseu 1C 2D
❒ TORRE DE MONCORVO Braganca1A
❒ TORRES NOVAS Santarem 2B
❒ TORRES VEDRAS Lisboa 1B 2D
❒ TRANCOSO (Trancozo) Guarda 1A 2C
❒ VAGOS Aveiro 1B
❒ VALENCA Viana do Castelo 1A 2D
❒ VALONGO Porto 2C
❒ VALPACOS Vila Real 1A
❒ VIANA DO ALENTEJO Evora 1C 2B
❒ VIANA DO CASTELO
Viana do Castelo 1A 2C
❒ VIDIGUEIRA Beja 1B 2D
❒ VIEIRA DO MINHO Braga 2C
❒ VILA DE REI Castelo Branco 1E
❒ VILA DO CONDE Porto 1B 2A
❒ VILA FRANCA DE XI RA Lisboa 1B 2B
❒ VILA NOVA DA BARQUINHA
Santarem 1A 2C
❒ VILA NOVA DE CERVEIRA
Viana do Castelo 1A
❒ VILA NOVA DE FAMALICAO
Braga 1A 2B
❒ VILA NOVA DE FOZCOA
Guarda 1A
❒ VILA NOVA DE GAIA Porto 1D
❒ VILA NOVA DE OUREM
Santarem 1B
❒ VILA NOVA DE PAIVA Viseu 1C
❒ VILA POUCA DE AGUIAR
Vila Real 2D
❒ VILA REAL Vila Real 1C 2B
❒ VILA REAL DE SANTO ANTONIO
Faro 1A 2B
❒ VILA VERDE Braga 2C
❒ VILA VICOSA Evora 1A 2B
❒ VISEU (Vizeu) Viseu 1B 2B
❒ VOUZELA Viseu 1A

PORTUGUESE GUINEA

❒ BOLAMO Portuguese Guinea 1B
❒ REUNION 2C
❒ ST DENIS 1B

RHODESIA

❒ SALISBURY 14B

ROMANIA

❒ ARAD 1A 2A 14B
❒ BAIA MARE 1A 2B 14B
❒ BAIA SPRIE 1B 14B
❒ BUCURESTI (Bucharest) 1A 2A 12A 14B
❒ CAMPINA 1A
❒ CAREI 14B
❒ CLUJ (Klausenburg) 2B
❒ CZERNOWITZ 2C
❒ ELISABETHSTADT
(lbasfalau, Dumbraveni) 1A
❒ GALATI 12A
❒ HERMANNSTADT/ZIBIN
(Nagy Szeben,
❒ Sibiu) 2A 12A
❒ KARLOVAC (Karlstadt) 1A
❒ MARAMURES 2B
❒ MEDIAS 14B
❒ RADAUTZ (Radauit) 2B
❒ SCHAESSBURG (Sighisoara) 2B
❒ SEPSISZENTGYOERGYOEN
(Sfintu Gheorghe) Transylvania 1A
❒ SIGHETUL MARMATIEI 2A
❒ SUCZAWA (Suceava) 1A
❒ TEMESVAR (Timisoara) 1A 2A

RUSSIAN POLAND

❒ ANDREEV Jedrzejow 1A 2A
❒ ANDRYCHOW Galicia 2B
❒ ANTONIOW 2B
❒ BEDZIN (Bendin, Bendzin) 2C 3A 14B
❒ BELCHATOW
(Piotrkow Trybunalski) 2A
❒ BENIAMINOW 2B 3B
❒ BIALA 2A
❒ BIALYSTOK (Belostok) 1E 2B 9A 15B
❒ BITKOW 2B
❒ BOCHNIA Galicia 1C 2D
❒ BOLECHOW (Stanislawow Ukraine,
Bolekhov, USSR, Ivano Frankovsk)Galicia 2C
❒ BOLESLAW 2B 3A 9A
❒ BORY 2B
❒ BORYSLAW 2B
❒ BRANICE 1A
❒ BRODY Ukraine 1D 9A
❒ BRUDZEW (Broudzew) 1A 2B 3A
❒ BRZESKO Galicia 2B
❒ BRZESZCZE 2C
❒ BRZEZANY (Berezhany) Galicia 2B
❒ BUKOWSKO Galicia 2A
❒ BYTOM 14A
❒ CHABIELICE 2B
❒ CHODECZ (Khodetch, Kodetch) 2C
❒ CHODOROW (Chodorov) Galicia 1A
❒ CHOJNICE 14B
❒ CHRZANOW (Krenau) Galicia 1A 2B 14B
❒ CHTCHERTSOV Szczercow 1A 2B
❒ CIECHOCINEK (Tcheckhotsinek,
Hermannsbad, Wloclawek) 2C
❒ CIELCE 2A
❒ CIEZKOWICE (Cieskowice)
Galicia 2B

10 Fen., Jaworznie, 2C

❒ CZELADZ (Tcheliadz) 2A
❒ CZESTOCHOWA (Tchenstokov) 1A 2A
❒ CZYZYNY (Czyzynska) 2A
❒ DABIE (Dombe, Altdamm) Galicia 1D
❒ DABROWA 1B 2B
❒ DANDOWKA 2A
❒ DOBRA/LIMANOWA Galicia 2B
❒ DOBRE 2B
❒ DOBRZELIN/PLOCK 2A
❒ DROHOBYCZ (Drogobyc) Galicia 2A
❒ DUBNO (Doubno,) Galicia 1B 2A
❒ DZIALOSZYCE (Dzialochitzi) 2D
❒ DZIEDZICE (Dziedzicka) 2A
❒ DZIKOW (Dzikownowy, Tarnobrzeg) Galicia 2C
❒ FIREJOW (Ferlejuv) 2C
❒ GLINK MARIAMPOLSKI 2E
❒ GNIEZNO 14B
❒ GOLINA 2A
❒ GOMBIN 2D
❒ GORZKOWICE 2B
❒ GRODEK JAGIELLONSKI (Gorodok, Lvov Oblask) Galicia 2B
❒ GRODNO (Gardinas, Belorussiya USSR) 2A
❒ GRODZETZ Grodziec 2A
❒ GRODZISK 2A
❒ GRYBOW Galicia 2B
❒ HOSZCZA (Hoszca) 2A
❒ JABLONOW/LUCZKA (Gesslershausen) 1A
❒ JASLO (Jessel) Galicia 2B
❒ JAWORZNIE (Javorzno, Jaworzno) 2B
❒ JEDLICZE (Jedlice) 2A
❒ JEDRZEJOW 1C 2D
❒ KALISZ (Kalich, Kalisz Pomorski, Kallies) 1A 2B
❒ KAMINSK 1A
❒ KARTUZY 1A
❒ KAZIMIERZ (Kazimerj) 1A
❒ KAZIMIERZA WIELKA 2B
❒ KETY 2B
❒ KHODETCH Chodecz 2A
❒ KIELCZYGLOW 2B
❒ KLECZEW (Kletchev) 1A
❒ KLEMENSOW (Szczebrzeszyn) 2A
❒ KLIMINTOW (Klimontow) 2B
❒ KOLO 1C
❒ KONIECPOL 2B
❒ KONIN 1A
❒ KONSKIE (Konsk, Konski) 2A
❒ KOPRZYWNICA 2A
❒ KORZEC (Korec, Koretz) 1A
❒ KOWAL 2E
❒ KRAKOW (Krakau, Crakow) Galicia 2A
❒ KROSCIENKO (Dunajcem/Chyrov) Galicia 2B
❒ KROSNIEWICE (Krosnevitsi) 2A
❒ KROSNO Galicia 2A
❒ KROTOSZYN 14A
❒ KRYNICA-ZDROJ Galicia 1B
❒ KRZEMIENIEC (Kremenetz, Kremenets) 1A 2A
❒ KRZESZOWICE (Kressendorf) Galicia 1B
❒ KUTNO (Koutno) 2E
❒ LAGISZA 2A
❒ LECZYCA (Lentichitsa, Lentschuetz) Galicia 2A
❒ LEMBERG (Lwow, L'vov, L'viv) Galicia 1A 2A 3A
❒ LIDA Beloussiya 2B
❒ LIMANOWA (Ilmenau) Galicia 1B 2A
❒ LIPNO (Leipe) 1C
❒ LITZMANNSTADT (Lodz) 2A 9A 14B 15B
❒ LOWICZ (Lovitch) 1A
❒ LUBLIN (Lioublin) 1A 2B
❒ LUBRANIEC 1E
❒ LUCK (Loutsk) 1A
❒ MANIOWY 2B
❒ MIELEC Galicia 2A
❒ MIERZYN 2A
❒ MIJACZOW (Mijaczow et Myszkow, Miatchev et Michkov) 2B
❒ MIKOLAJOW/BRODY (Mikhaylouka, Mikhaylovka, Mikhalpol) Galicia 2B
❒ MLAWA (Mielau) 2C
❒ MOGILNO 14B
❒ MOSINA 2A
❒ MYSLENICE Galicia 1B

20 Mark, Litzmannstadt, Russ/Poland, 15B

1 Krone, Teschen, Russ/Poland, 1B

❒ NEUMARKT/WALD
(Nowry Targ) Galicia 1A
❒ NIECHCICE 2E
❒ NIEPOLOMICH 2B
❒ NOWA SACZ
(Neu-Sandec, Neu-Sandez) 2A
❒ NOWOGRODEK (Novogrovkok) 1A
❒ NOWORADOMSK (Radomsko) 2D
❒ OGRODZIENIEC 2D
❒ OKOCIM 2B
❒ OLKUSZ 2D
❒ OSIECINY (Osentsiny) 2E
❒ OSJAKOW 2D
❒ OSTROG 1C
❒ OSTROWIEC (Ostrowiecka) 2A
❒ OSWIECIM (Oswiecin, Auschwitz) 2A 14A
❒ OZORKOW 2D
❒ PAJECZNO 2B
❒ PETROKOV Piotrkow) 1A
❒ PETROKOV Piotrkow Kojawski) 2A
❒ PIECHCIN 2A
❒ PILIAV (Pilawa) 2A
❒ PILICA (Pilitsa) 2A
❒ PINCZOW 1B
❒ PIOTRKOW (Pitrokov, Belorussiya) 2C
❒ PLESZEW (Pleschen) 1A 2A 14C
❒ PLOCK
(Plozk, Plotsk, Schroettersburg) 1B 2A 14B
❒ PLONSK (Ploehnen) 2A
❒ PODGORZE Galicia 2A
❒ PLONSK 2B
❒ POLESIE/KRAKOW 1A
❒ POREBA 2B
❒ PRZEDBORZ (Przedborska) 2A
❒ PRZEMYSL (Peremyshl, Deutsch Przemysl)
Galicia 2B
❒ PRZYROW 2A
❒ PYZDRY 1E
❒ RABKA 2C
❒ RADOM 2A
❒ RADZIEJOW (Radzeieov) 1B
❒ RAKOW (Rakowska) 2C
❒ RASZKOW 1A
❒ ROWNE/DUKLA (Wolyn, Rovno,
Ukraine, Reichenstein, Zloty Stok) 1A 2B 14A
❒ ROZPRZA 2A
❒ RYMANOW 2B
❒ RYPIN (Rippin) 2B
❒ RZESZOW 2A
❒ SAMBOR/DNIESTER
(Sambora) Galicia 2B
❒ SANDOMIERZ/SAN AND VISTULA
(Sandomier, Sandomir) 1B
❒ SANNIKI 2C
❒ SANOK Galicia 2A

❒ SEPOLNO (Krainski, Zempelburg) 1A
❒ SIEDLCE (Sedletz) 1C
❒ SIEMIANOWICE 14B
❒ SIERADZ/WARTA
(Sieraje, Seradz, Schieratz) 1B 2B
❒ SIERPC (Sichelberg) 2A
❒ SIERSZA 2A
❒ SLAWKOW 2C
❒ SLAWSK 2A
❒ SLOUPTSY (Slupca) 1A
❒ SMIGIEL 1A
❒ SOKAL/BUG Galicia 2A
❒ SOSNOVITSY (Sosnowice) 2A
❒ SPORYSZ/ZYWCA 2B
❒ SREM 1A
❒ STANISLAWOW (Stanislav, Stanislau,
Ivano-Frankovsk) Galicia 2A
❒ STARACHOWICE 2B
❒ STAROGARD 14B
❒ STAWISZYN 2A
❒ STOPNICA 2A
❒ SZAKOLCZA 2A
❒ SZCERCU/LEMBERG Galicia 3A
❒ SZCZAKOWA 2A
❒ SZCZERCOW (Chtchertsov) 2A
❒ SZCZERZEC
(Shchirets, Scirec) Galicia 2A
❒ SZELEJEWO 1A
❒ SZYMANOWICE (Chimanowitsy) 2C
❒ TARNOBRZEG Galicia 1B
❒ TARNOPOL/SERED
(Ternopol) Galicia 1A 2B
❒ TARNOW/BIALA Galacia 2B
❒ TEMESVAR/ALT-BEGA
(Timisoara) Galacia 2A
❒ TEMESVAR/ALT-BEGA (Temeswar,
Temeschwar, Temesar Banat) Gali 2B
❒ TESCHEN/OLSA
(Cieszyn, Cesky Tesin) Galicia 1A
❒ TORUN (Thorn) 14B
❒ TOMASZOW RAWSKI/PILICA
(Tomachov-Ravsky) 2B
❒ TRZEBINIA 2A
❒ TULISZKOW (Toulichkov) 1B
❒ TUREK (Tourek) 1E
❒ TUSTANOWICE 1B
❒ UNIEJOW/WARTA 10A
❒ USCILUG 2A
❒ WADOWICE/SKAWA
(Wadertz, Wadowyce, Frauenstadt) 1A 2B
❒ WARSAW/VISTULA
(Warszawa, Varsovie) 2A 14B
❒ WARTA 1A
❒ WIDAWA/WIDAWKA (Widawka) 2A
❒ WIELICZKA 2A

❒ WIELUN (Welun, Welungen, Welioun) 2A
❒ WILCZAGORA (Viltchagora) 1B
❒ WINDAU/VINDAU (Vindau, Vindava) 1A
❒ WLADYSLAWOW (Osada) 1C
❒ WLOCLAWEK/VISTULA (Vlotslawsk, Leslau) 2C
❒ WOLHYNIE/VOLHYNIA (Wotyn) 2A
❒ WRZOSOWA 2D
❒ WYPICHOW 2A
❒ WYRZYSKA (Wirsitz) 1A
❒ WYSOKA 2A
❒ ZABKOWICE 2B
❒ ZAGLEBIE 2C
❒ ZAGOROW 2C
❒ ZAKOPANE (Zakopuno) 2A
❒ ZAMOSC 1A 14C
❒ ZAWIERCIE (Warthenau, Zavertse) 2C
❒ ZBARAZ 2A
❒ ZDUNSKA WOLA 1C 2A
❒ ZLOCZEW/SIERADZ (Zlotchev, Zloczow) Galicia 2C
❒ ZOMBKOVITSI (Zabkowice) 2A
❒ ZURAWNO (Zurawna, Zhuravno, Zuravno) 2A
❒ ZYDACZOW (Zhidachov, Zidaccov) 2B
❒ ZYRARDOW 2B
❒ ZYTYN (Zytin, Jitin) 2A
❒ ZYWIEC/SOLA (Savbusch) 2B

RUSSIA

❒ ABAKAN (Abakanskij, Ust-Abanskoye) 1A
❒ ABRAU-DYURSA 1A
❒ ACHINSK (Atchinsk) 1A 3A
❒ ACHTARSKAJA (Akhtari, Axtarskaja, Primorske-Akhtarsk) 1B
❒ AKMOLINSK 1A
❒ AKUTIKHA 1A
❒ ALEXANDRIA (Alexandrija) 1A 14A
❒ ALEXANDROPOL (Leninaken) 2A
❒ ALEXANDROV-KUJAWSKI 1A
❒ ALEXANDROVSK (Central Russia) 1A
❒ ALEXANDROVSK (Olexandrivsk) 2A
❒ ALEXANDROVSK (Ukraine) 2A
❒ ALEXANDROVSK-GRUSHEVSKI (Shachty, Shakhty) Don 2A
❒ ALEXANDROVSK-SAKHALINSKI 2A
❒ ALEXANDROVSKOI 1A
❒ ALEXEEVSK Siberia 2A
❒ ALEXEJEWSKOJE (Alexeevsk) 1A
❒ ALM-ATA (Vyerny) 1A
❒ ALTAI 1B
❒ ALTAS 1A
❒ ALUPKA (Aloupka) Crimea 2A
❒ ALYATY 1A
❒ ANANIEV (Ananyev, Ananiev, Ananjew) 1A
❒ ANAPA Caucaus 2A
❒ ANDIJAN 1B
❒ ANDISHAN (Andizhan) 1A
❒ ANGARA 1A
❒ ANGERE Siberia 2B
❒ ANTONINI 1A
❒ ANUCHINO (Anoutchino, Anutchino) Siberia 1B
❒ ANZHERO-SUDZHENSK (Anzhersky, Anscher Grube) 1A
❒ ARCHANGEL (Arckangel) 2B
❒ ARMAVIR Caucaus 1A 2A
❒ ARTEMOVSK 1A
❒ ARTEMOVSK-RUDNIK (Bachmut Artemovsk, Bakhmout) 1A
❒ ARZAMAS 2A
❒ ASHKHABAD (Askhabad, Aschabad, Poltoratsk) 2B
❒ ASTRAKHAN 1A
❒ ATCHINSK Siberia 2A
❒ AVDOTINO Siberia 1B
❒ BAJENOVO Ural 2B
❒ BAKHMOUT 2A
❒ BAKU (Bakou) 1A 2B
❒ BALACLAVA (Balaklava) Crimea 1A 2B
❒ BALAKLEYA (Balakleia) 10A
❒ BALTA Ukraine 1A
❒ BALTALPASHINSK (Batalpachinsk) 1A
❒ BAR Ukraine 1A
❒ BARGUZIN (Bargousin) Siberia 1B
❒ BARNAUL (Barnaoul) Siberia 1A 3B
❒ BARNOVKA Ukraine 2B
❒ BATALACHINSK 2A
❒ BASCHENOVO (Bazhenovo) 1A
❒ BATAREINAIA (Batarejnaja) Ukraine 3C
❒ BATUM (Batoum) 1A
❒ BAZHENOVO 1A
❒ BEDNO-DEMYANSK (Spask) 1A
❒ BEDZIN 1A
❒ BEHRING ISLAND 1A
❒ BELAYA GLINA 1A
❒ BELCHATOW (Belkhatov) 1A
❒ BELORETZ (Beloretsk) 1A
❒ BERDICHEZ (Berditchev) 1A
❒ BERDYANSK 1A
❒ BEREZNIK 1A
❒ BEREZOVKA 3A
❒ BERGUSIN (Barguzin) 1A
❒ BERIKAI 1A
❒ BERIKUL (Berikulski) 1A
❒ BEZHETSK 1A
❒ BIELSK 15A
❒ BIISK (Bijsk, Bisk, Biysk) Siberia 1B 3A
❒ BJELORETZKIJE ZAVOD (Beloretz) 1A
❒ BLAGODARNOYE 1A
❒ BLAGOVESCHENSK 1A
❒ BLASHKI (Blaszki) 1A
❒ BOBRUISK (Bobrouisk) 1A
❒ BOGOSLOVSK (Bogoslov) 1A
❒ BOGUTCHAR 1A
❒ BOLSHOI TOKMAK (Bol Choi) 1A
❒ BONDIOUJSK (Bondyuzhski, Bondjuschskij) 2B
❒ BORISOGLEBSK 1A
❒ BOROVITCHY (Borovitchi) 2A
❒ BORYSLAW (Borisov, Borislav, Galicia) 2A
❒ BOUGLAI 2B
❒ BRAZLAV (Bratslav) 2A
❒ BRODY 1A
❒ BUDENNOVSK (Svyatoi Krest) 1A
❒ BUGURUSLAN 1A
❒ BUKHARA 1B
❒ BUTURLINOVKA 1A
❒ BUZULUK (Busuluk) 1A
❒ CAUCASE DU NORD 10B
❒ CHARDZHUI 1A
❒ CHELIABNISK (Chelyabinsk, Tscheljabinsk) 1A
❒ CHENKOURSK 2B
❒ CHEPETOVKA Ukraine 2A
❒ CHERDYN (Tscherdyn) 1A
❒ CHEREMKHOVO (Tcheremkhovo) 1A

❒ CHEREPOVETZ (Tscernevitz) 1A
❒ CHERKASSKOE (Tchersasskoe) 1A
❒ CHERKASSY 1A
❒ CHERNIS ANOUI S (Tchernij Anou) 1A
❒ CHERNOISTOCHINSK 1A
❒ CHERNOVETZ (Tchernevetz) 1A
❒ CHEZLADZ (Czeladz) 1A
❒ CHIMANOWITSY Szymanowice 1A
❒ CHISTOPOLTChistopol 1A
❒ CHITA Tchita 1A 3A
❒ CHTCHERBINOVKA 2B
❒ CIECHOCINEK 1A
❒ CIELCE (Kielce) 1A
❒ CRONSTADT 1B
❒ CZESTOCHOWA (Chenstokhov, Tchenstovok) 1A
❒ DABIE (Dombe) 1A
❒ DABROWA GORNICZA 1A
❒ DABROWSKIE ZAGLEBIE 1A
❒ DAURIA 1A
❒ DEBRA 1A
❒ DERBENT Georgia 2B
❒ DJALMAN-KIL-BOUROUN 2A
❒ DJANKOI 2B
❒ DMITRIEV-CONSTANTINOFF (Dmitriev-Poselok) 1A
❒ DMITRIEVSK (Dmitriyevsk) Ukraine 2B
❒ DNEPROPETROVSK (Ekaterinoslav) 1A
❒ DOBRA (Poland) 1A
❒ DRUZHKOVKA (Droujkovka) 2B
❒ DUNAJEVZY (Dunayevtzi, Dunayeuzy) 1A
❒ DZIALOSZYCE (Dzialochitzi, Dzyaloshitse) 1A
❒ EISK 1A 2B 9A
❒ EKATERINBURG Ural 2B 9A
❒ EKATERINODAR 1A 2B
❒ EKATERINOSLAV 2A 12A
❒ ELABUGA (Elabouga, Yelabuga) 2A
❒ ELETS (Eletz, Yelets) 2A
❒ ENAKIEVO Don 2B
❒ ELINIKI (Eininsk) 1A 2A
❒ ELISAVETGRAD (Elizabethgrad, Lisavethad,Jelisavetgrad) 1A 2A
❒ ELIZABETHPOL 2A
❒ ENAKIYEVO (Yenakyevo, Enakievo, Yevo, Yenaki) 1A
❒ ENISEI Siberia 1B
❒ ERIVAN 1A 2A
❒ EUPATORIA Crimea 2A
❒ FEDOSIA (Foudziadian, Fudziadian) 1A
❒ FERGANA 2A
❒ FOUDZIADIAN Siberia 2B
❒ FRAUENKOPF 1A
❒ GABIN (Gombin) 2D
❒ GAGRI (Gagry) 1B 2B
❒ GAISIN Ukraine 2A
❒ GALZOV 1A
❒ GATCHINA (Trotzk) 1A
❒ GEORGIYEVSK 1A
❒ GLASOV (Glazov) 1A
❒ GLUCHOV (Glukhov, Gloukov) 2B
❒ GLUTVIN (Goloutvin) 2A
❒ GOMEL 1A
❒ GORKI (Nizhne Novgorod) 1A
❒ GORLUVKA 2A
❒ GORODOK 1A
❒ GORZKOWICE 2A
❒ GOURZOUF (Gurzuf) 1A
❒ GRODNO (Gardinas) 1A
❒ GRODZTEZ (Grodziec, Grodzetz) 1A
❒ GROSNYJ (Grozny) 2A
❒ GRUSHEVSKI (Alexandrovsk-Grushevski) 1A
❒ GUDAUTI (Goudaouty) 1A
❒ GURIEV (Guriev) 1A
❒ HAI-SHEN-WEI (Vladivostok) 1A
❒ HANGDAO-KHETSZY 1A
❒ HARBIN (Charbin, Kharbin) 1A 2A
❒ HOSZCA (Hoszcza, Goskcha) 1A
❒ IACHKINO Siberia 1A
❒ IAKOVLEVSKAIA Don 2B
❒ IGUMEN (Igoumen, Cherven) 1A
❒ IMAN 1A
❒ IRKUTSK (Irkoutsk) 1A 2A
❒ IRYTSH 1A
❒ ISHIM (Ichim) 1A
❒ ISJUM (Izium, Isyoum) 1A
❒ IVANOVO-VEZNESSENSK 1A
❒ IVANOVSKOE 1A
❒ JITOMIR Ukraine 1A 2A
❒ KADOM 2A
❒ KALICH (Kalisz) 1B 2A
❒ KAMCHATKA 1C
❒ KAMENETZ-PODILSK (Kamenetz-Podolsk) 1A
❒ KANSK Siberia 2A 3C
❒ KAPUSTJANY (Kapustin) 1A
❒ KARA-KILIS 1A 2A
❒ KARAKUS 1A
❒ KARGOPOL 1A
❒ KARPINSKI (Bogoslovsk, Bogoslov) 1A
❒ KARS 1A 2A
❒ KARSUN 1A
❒ KASAN (Kazan) 2A
❒ KASIMOV 1C
❒ KATARSKI ZAVOD 1A
❒ KATERINOSLAV (Ekaterinoslav, Yekaterinoslav) 1A
❒ KAUKAZKAYA (Kavkazskaya) 1A
❒ KAZALINSK (Kasalinsk, Kasli) 1A
❒ KCHBANSKI SOYUZ 1A
❒ KEDABEK 1A
❒ KELABERDA 1A
❒ KELTSY (Kielce) 1A
❒ KERB Siberia 2C
❒ KERTCH-YENIKALE (Kerch) Crimea 1B
❒ KHAILAR Siberia 2A
❒ KHABAROVSK Siberia 2A 9A
❒ KHAN-DAO-KHE-DZY Siberia 2A
❒ KHARBINE Siberia 1A 2A
❒ KHARKIV (Kharkov, Charkov) Ukraine 2A
❒ KHERSON Siberia 2A
❒ KHOJENT (Khodzhent) 1A
❒ KIAKHTA (Kjachta) 1A
❒ KICHTIM Ural 2A
❒ KIEV (Kiiv, Kiyev) Ukraine 2A
❒ KIM (Santo) 1A
❒ KISEL (Kizel) 2A
❒ KISLAR (Kizlyar) 2A
❒ KISLOVODSK 2A
❒ KIZYL-KIIA 2A
❒ KLINTSKY (Klintzy) Ukraine 2A
❒ KNIZHKA 1A
❒ KOKAND 2B
❒ KOKCHANSK (Kokshaisk Zavod, Kokschajski Zavod) 1A 2A
❒ KOLCHUGINO (Leninsk-Kuznetski) Siberia 1B

❒ KOLUSZKI (Kolyschki, Kolyushki) 1A
❒ KORBECK 1A
❒ KOSTROMA 2A
❒ KOTELNICH (Kotelnitsch) 1A
❒ KOULEBAKI 2A
❒ KOUPIANSK Ukraine 2A
❒ KOURGAN (Kurgan) Siberia 2A
❒ KOUTAIS (Kutais) 2A
❒ KOUZMINSK ROUNDNIK (Kuzminsk Rudnik) 2A
❒ KOVNO (Kaunas) 1A
❒ KOVROV 1A
❒ KOZLOV (Michurinsk, Eupatoria, Evaptoriya) 1A
❒ KRAMATORSKAIA (Kramatovskaya, Kramatoirskaia) 2A
❒ KRASINIEC 1A
❒ KRASNAIA RETSKA (Krasnaya Rechka, Krasnaja Rjetschka) Siberia 3E
❒ KRASNODAR (Ekaterinodar, Ekaterinburg, Jekaterinodar, Kouban) 2A
❒ KRASNOE SELO 2A
❒ KRASNOOUFIMSK Ural 2A
❒ KRASNOYARSK (Krasnoiarsk) Siberia 2A
❒ KREMENCHUG (Kreminchuk, Krementchoug)Siberia 1A 2A
❒ KRIM 1A
❒ KRIVI RIH (Krivoy Rog) 1A
❒ KRONSTADT (Cronstadt) 1A
❒ KROSNEVETSK (Krosniewice, Krosnevitsi, Xenievka) 2B
❒ KRYUKOV (Krioukovo) 2A
❒ KRZEMIENIEC 1A
❒ KSENYEVKA (Ksenievskaya) 1A
❒ KULIBAK (Koulebaki) 1A
❒ KUPIANSK (Koupiansk) 1A
❒ KURMISH (Kurmysh) 1A
❒ KUSCHVA (Kushva, Kursk) 1A
❒ KUSMINSKOJE (Kuzminskoye) 1A
❒ KUSNETZK (Kuznetsk) 1A
❒ KYAKHTA (Troitskosavsk) 1A
❒ KYSCHTYMSKIJ (Kyshtym) 1A
❒ L'GOV 1B
❒ LABINSK (Labinskaya) 1A
❒ LADIJIN (Ladyschin) 2A
❒ LAGISZA 1A
❒ LAPYSCHTA 1A
❒ LECZYCA (Lenchitsa, Lentchitsa) 2A
❒ LEMBERG (Lvov, Lviv, Lwow) 1A
❒ LENINGRAD 2A
❒ LEPSINSK 11B
❒ LETICHEV (Letitchev) 1A
❒ LEVASHOVO 1A
❒ LIBAU (Libava, Liepaja) 1A
❒ LIDA 1A
❒ LIOUBERTZ 2A
❒ LIOUSTDORF 2A
❒ LIPECK (Lipetsk, Lipetzk) 2A
❒ LIPNO 1A
❒ LISVA (Lysva, Lysvensk) 2A
❒ LIVADIA 1A
❒ LODZ 1A
❒ LOGOISK (Logoysk, Lohojsk) 1A
❒ LOVITCH (Lowicz) 1A
❒ LUBLIN (Lioublin, Lyublin) 1A
❒ LYSVENSK Ural 2A
❒ LYUBERTZY (Lioubertz) 1A
❒ MADJANY 1A
❒ MAIKOP 1A 2A
❒ MAKEYEVKA (Dmitrievsk) 1A
❒ MAKINSK KHUTORA (Makinskie Khoutora) 1A
❒ MALIN (Ukraine) 2A
❒ MANCHURCIA STATION (Mantchjouria) 2A
❒ MARIUPOL (Marioupol, Mariiupil) 2A
❒ MEDJANY 2A
❒ MEDJIBOJ 2A
❒ MEDVEZHYE (Molotovskoye, Yevdokimovskoye) 1A
❒ MELEKESS 1A
❒ MERV 1A 2A
❒ MGHLIN (Mglin) 1A
❒ MIATCHEV ET MICHKOW (Mijaczow et Myazkow) 2A
❒ MIERZYN 1A
❒ MINERALNIYE VODI (Mineralni Vodi) 1A
❒ MINKOVCY (Minkovtsy) 1A
❒ MINSK 2A
❒ MITAU (Mitava, Jelgava, Yelgava) 1A
❒ MITITCHTCHI (Mytischi) 2A
❒ M LAVA (M lawa) 1A
❒ MOGILEV (Moghilev) 1A
❒ MOGILEV-PODOLSK (Moghilev-Podolsk) Ukraine1A 2A
❒ MOLOCHANSK (Molotchansk) Crimea 2A
❒ MONASTYREK 1A
❒ MORSHANSK 1A
❒ MOSCOW (Moskova) 2A
❒ MOSDOK (Mozdok) 2A
❒ MOSYR (Mozyr) 1A
❒ MOTOVILIKHA 2A
❒ MURMANSK (Mourmansk) 1A
❒ MUROM (Mourom) 2A
❒ NADESCHDINSKY (Nadezhdinsky, Nadejdinsk) Ural 2A
❒ NALCHIK (Naltchik) 1A
❒ NERCHINSK (Nertchinsk) Siberia 2A
❒ NESVETEVKHEVO (Nesvetevitchi) 2A
❒ NICOLAEVSK-SUR-AMOUR Siberia 2A

5 Marka, Odessa, Russia, 1A

❒ NIECHCICE 1A
❒ NIKITOVKA 2A
❒ NIKOLAEV/AMUR (Mikolaiv) 1C
❒ NIKOLSK-USSURIISKY (Nicolsk-Oussourisky) Siberia 2A 3B
❒ NIKOPIL (Nikopol) Siberia 2A
❒ NIZHNE NOVGOROD 1A
❒ NOVAYA USHITSA (Novo-Utchitsa, Nowa Uszyca, Nowes Uszyey, Novo-Ouchitsa) 1A
❒ NOVGOROD 2A
❒ NOVO-VORONIKOVSK 1A
❒ NOVOCHERKASSK (Novotcherkassk) 1A
❒ NOVOGRAD VOLYINSK (Novograd Volynsi, Volinsk) Ukraine 1A
❒ NOVOGROD VELIKI 1A
❒ NOVOROSSISK (Novorossijsk) 2A
❒ NOVOSYBKOV (Novozybkov) 1B
❒ NOVO-VORONIKOVSK 2A
❒ NOVOZYBKOV 1A
❒ NOVY MARGELAN (Fergana) 1A
❒ OCHEMCHIRI (Otchemtchiri) 1A
❒ ODESSA (Jelisawetgrad) 1A 2B 14B
❒ ODONOV 1A
❒ OKULOVKA (Okoulovka) 2A
❒ OMSK 1A
❒ OPOCHNO (Opoczno) 1A
❒ ORDZHONIKIDZE (Yenakyevo, Vladikavkaz) 1A
❒ ORENBURG Ural 2A
❒ OSIPENKO (Berdyansk) 1A
❒ OSTROGOZHSK 1A
❒ OTCHEMTCHIRI 1E
❒ OUFA Ural 2A
❒ OUMAN Ukraine 2A
❒ OURALSK Ural 2A
❒ OUSOLE 2A
❒ PACHIA (Pashiya) 2A
❒ PANEVEZHIS (Panevezys) 1A
❒ PAVLOHRAD (Pavlograd) 1A
❒ PAVLOVO 2A
❒ PAVLOVSK 1A
❒ PENSA (Penza) 2A
❒ PERESLAV (Pereslavl-Zalesski) 1A
❒ PERM (Motovilika) Ural 1B 2A
❒ PESTCHANKA Siberia 3B
❒ PETR-ALEXANDROVSK (Turtkul) 2A
❒ PETRIKAU (Piotrkow) 1A
❒ PETROGRAD (Leningrad) 1A 2B
❒ PETROPAVLOSK (Petropavlosk-S. Kamtchatke) Siberia 2A 3B
❒ PETROVSK (Petrovskoye, Petroskaya) 1B
❒ PETROZAVODSK 1A 2A
❒ PIATIGORSK 1A 2A
❒ PILENKOVA (Pilenkovo) 2A
❒ PINCHOV (Pinczow) 1A
❒ PIOTRKOW TRYBUNALSKI (Piotrkow) 1A
❒ PIROGOVSK (Pirogovskoe) 2A
❒ PJATIGORSK (Pyatigorsk, Piatigorsk) 1A
❒ PJ ESTSCHAN KA (Pestchanka) 1A
❒ POLTAVA Ukraine 2A
❒ POLTORADSK (Poltoratsk, Askhabad) 2A
❒ PONEVEJ (Panevezys, Ponevezh) 2A
❒ PRIKUMSK (Svyatoi Krest) 1A
❒ PRILUKI 1A
❒ PROSKURIV (Proskurov, Proskourov) Ukraine 1A 2A
❒ PSKOV (Pskow, Pieskau) 1A 2A
❒ PYATIGORSK 1A
❒ RADOMYSL Ukraine 2B
❒ REVDA (Siberia) 2A
❒ REZEKNE (Rositten, Rezhitsa) 1A
❒ RIAZAN 1A 2A
❒ RIBINSK 1A
❒ RIDDER (Leninogorsk) 1A
❒ RIGA 1A
❒ RIVNE (Rowne) 1A
❒ ROGACHEV (Rogatchev, Rogarschev) 1B
❒ ROSTOKINO 2A
❒ ROSTOV/DON (Rostow) 2A 12A
❒ RYATIGORSK 1A
❒ RYAZAN (Rjazan) 1A
❒ RYKOVO (Yenakyevo) 1A
❒ SAD 2A
❒ SAKI (Crimea) 2A
❒ SAKHALIN 2E
❒ SALDINSKY (Nizhne Saldinsky) 1A
❒ SAMARA 2A
❒ SAMARKAND 1A
❒ SARDAR ABAD 1B
❒ SELESNEVKA 1A
❒ SEMIPALATINSK (Siberia) 2A 11B
❒ SENGHILEI (Sengilei) 2A
❒ SERGINSKI ZAVOD 1A
❒ SERGUINSK-OUFALEISK Ural 2A
❒ SEVASTOPIL (Sevastopol, Sebastopol) 2A 10A 11B
❒ SHALYGINO (Schalygina) 1A
❒ SHCHERBINOVKA (Dzerzhinsk, Chtcherbinovka) 1A
❒ SHCHERKOV (Shchertovsov, Szczercow, Chtchertsov) 1A
❒ SHENKURSK (Chenkoursk, Chenkursk) 1A
❒ SHEPETOVKA (Schepetovka, Chepetovka) 1A
❒ SHUYA (Schuja) 1A
❒ SIADI (Siady) 2A
❒ SIERADZ (Seradz) 1A
❒ SIMBURSK (Simbirsk) 2A
❒ SIMFEROPOL (Crimea) 2A
❒ SIMSK (Sim, Simski Zavod) (Ural) 2A
❒ SKALA PODALSKAYA (Skala nad Zbruczem) 1A
❒ SKOBELEV (Fergana, Skobelef) 3B
❒ SLOUTSK 2A
❒ SLAVUSCHA 1A
❒ SLAVYANSK (Slaviansk) (Ukraine) 1A 2A
❒ SMELA (Ukraine) 1A
❒ SMOLENSK 2A
❒ SNEJNY 2A
❒ SOCHI (Stochi) 1A
❒ SOLIKAMSK 1A
❒ SOMPOLNO 1A
❒ SOUDJENKA (Sudzhenka) 1A
❒ SOUTCHAN (Sutchan) 1A
❒ SRETENSK Siberia 3B
❒ STARI OSKOL (Stary Oskol) 1A
❒ STARO-KONSTANTINOV (Volhynie) 1A
❒ STAVNITSA 1A
❒ STAVROPOL 1A
❒ STERLITAMAK 1A
❒ STOPNICA 1A
❒ SUCHUM (Sukhum) 1A
❒ SUKHONA (Soukhona) 1A
❒ SULIN (Sulinovskoye, Krasny Sulin) 1A
❒ SUMY 1A
❒ SVERDLOVSK (Ekaterinburg) 1A
❒ SYSERT (Sysertski Zavod) 1A

1 Ruble, Tiflis, Russia, 1B

❒ TAGANROG (Don) 1A 2A
❒ TAGUIL (Nizhne Taguil) 1A
❒ TAHANRIH (Taganrog) 1A
❒ TAMAN 2A
❒ TAMBOV 1A
❒ TANNUTUVA 1A
❒ TARASOVKA 1A
❒ TASHKENT (Taschkent, Tachkent) 1A
❒ TATARSKAYA 1A
❒ TCHARDJOUl 2A
❒ TCHERDYN (Tcherdin) Ural 2A
❒ TCHEREMKHOVO Siberia 2A
❒ TCHERNIJ ANOUI 2A
❒ TCHISTIAKOVO 2A
❒ TCHISTIAKOVO 2A
❒ TCHISTOPOL 2A
❒ TCHITA Siberia 2A 3B
❒ TEREK 1A
❒ THEODOSIE Crimea 2A
❒ TIFLIS Georgia 2A 12A
❒ TIUMEN (Tioumen) Siberia 2A
❒ TKIBULI (Tkvibuli, Tkvibouli) Georgia 2A
❒ TOBOLSK Siberia 2A
❒ TOKMAK (Bolshoi Tokmak) 1A
❒ TOMACHPOL Ukraine 2A
❒ TOMSK Siberia 2A
❒ TOUAPSE 2A
❒ TOULA 1A 2A
❒ TOULTCHIN Ukraine 1A
❒ TREBOUKHOVETZ 2A
❒ TROITSK (Troizk) 1A
❒ TROIZKOSSAWSK (Troitskosavsk) 1A
❒ TSARITSIN (Tsaritsyn) 1A 2A
❒ TSCHEREMCHOVO (Cheremkhovo) 1A
❒ TSCHEREPOVEZ (Cherepovetz) 1A
❒ TSCHERNO-ISTOTSCHINSKIJ (Chernoistochinsk) 1A
❒ TSEKHOTSINEK (Ciechocinek) 1A
❒ TUAPSE (Touapse) 1A
❒ TULA (Toula) 1A
❒ TULCHIN (Toultchin) 1A
❒ TULISHKOV (Tuliszkow, Toulichkov) 1A
❒ TURINSKI RUDNIK (Turjinskie) 1A
❒ TVER 1A
❒ UFA (Oufa) 1A
❒ UGOLNY (Bogoslovsk) 1A
❒ ULAN-UDE (Verkhneudinsk) 1A
❒ ULYANOVSK (Ulyanovka, Sablino, Simbursk) 1A
❒ UMAN (Ouman) 1A
❒ UMANSKAYA (Leningradskaya) 1A
❒ URALSK (Ouralsk) 1B
❒ USHITSA (Uszycy, Novo-Utichitsa) 1A
❒ USOLYE (Ousole, Bereznik) 1A
❒ UST-KATAVSKI ZAVOD (Ust-Katay) 1B
❒ USTILUG (Uscilug) 1A
❒ VAGARSHAPAD 1A
❒ VARCHAVA Ukraine 1A
❒ VASILKOV 1A
❒ VELIKI (Novgorod Veliki) 1A
❒ VENTSPILS (Vindava, Windau, Vindau) 1A
❒ VERCHNYATSK (Verchnjatschka) 1A
❒ VERKHNE SALDINSKI ZAVOD (Verkhne-Saldin, Verkhnyaya Saida) Ural 2A
❒ VERKHNE-ISSETSK Ural 2A
❒ VERKHNEDNIEPROVSK (Verchnednjeprovsk, Verhne-Dnyeprovsk) Ukraine 2A
❒ VEZNESSENSK (Ivanovo-Veznessensk) 1A
❒ VIATKA (Vjatka) 2A
❒ VIAZEMSK (Vyazemski) 1A
❒ VIAZMA (Vyazma) 2A
❒ VINNITZA Ukraine 2A
❒ VISIMO SHAITANSKI (Visim) 1A
❒ VISIMO UTKINSK 1A
❒ VLADIKAVKAZ (Vladicaucase, Dzaudzhikua) 2A
❒ VLADIVOSTOCK Siberia 2A
❒ VLADIMIR 1A
❒ VLASOV/Don 2A
❒ VOLOGDA 2A
❒ VORONEZH 1A
❒ VORONIKOVSK (Novo-Voronikovsk) 1A
❒ VORONTSOVO-ALEXANDOVSKOYE 1A
❒ VOROSHILOV (Nikolsk-Ussuriisky) 1A
❒ VOSNESENSK (Voznesensk) 1A
❒ VOTCHINO 1A
❒ VOTKINSK (Votkin, Votkinski Zavod) 2A
❒ WALDGHEIM (Valdeheim) Crimea 2A
❒ WELSK (Velsk) 2A
❒ WENDEN (Venden, Cesis) 1A
❒ WLADIWOST6K 1A
❒ WRZOSOWA (Yrsozova) 1A
❒ WYPICHOW 1A
❒ YAKOVLEVKOYE Don 2A
❒ YALTA (lalta) Ukraine 2A
❒ YAMPOL (Iampol, Jampol) Ukraine 2A
❒ YANOVKA (Ianovka, Janovka) Ukraine 2A
❒ YAROSLAV (Iaroslav, Iaroslovl, Jaroslav) 2A
❒ YASHKINO (Yaskino, Iachkino, Jaschkino) 1A
❒ YAKUTIA 1E
❒ YELNIKI (Elninsk) 1A
❒ YENISELISK (Yenakyevo, Enisel, Jenisejsk) 1A 2B
❒ YESSENTUKI (Essentuki) 1A
❒ YEVPATORIYA (Eupatoria) 1A
❒ YUCHNOV (Juchnov) 1A
❒ YURIEV-POLSKI (Yuryev-Polski) 1A
❒ YUSOVKA (Yuzovka, Stalino, Hughesovka, Donetsk) Ukraine 2A
❒ YOUSOVO 2A
❒ ZAGLEBIE DABROWSKIE (Dabrowskie Zaglebie) 1A

❒ ZAGUROV (Zagorow) 1A
❒ ZAIRKUTNY GORODOK 1A 3A
❒ ZALESSKI (Pereslav) 1A
❒ ZAPORIZHIA (Alexandrovsk, Zaporzhye) 1A
❒ ZARIZYN (Tsaritsin) 1A
❒ ZAVERTSE (Zawiercie, Warthenau) 1A
❒ ZAWIERCIE (Zavertse) 1A
❒ ZBARAZ (Zbarazh) 1A
❒ ZDUNSKAYA VOLYA (Zdunska Wola) 1A
❒ ZEA (Zeia, Seja) 2A
❒ ZEMLYANSK 1A
❒ ZENKOV (Sinkov) Ukraine 2A
❒ ZGERZH (Zgierz) 1A
❒ ZHIRARDOV (Zyrardow) 1A
❒ ZHITNY 1A
❒ ZHITOMIR (Schitomir, Jitomir) 1A
❒ ZLATOUST (Slatoust) 1A
❒ ZLYNKA 1A
❒ ZOMBKOVITSI (Zabkowice) 1A
❒ ZVENIGOROD 2A

SAINT THOMAS & PRINCE

❒ SAO TOME Sao Tome e Principe 1B

SENEGAL

❒ DAKAR 6B 7B
❒ KAYES 6B
❒ RUFISQUE 6B
❒ SENEGAL 1B 6B
❒ ZIGUINCHOR 6C

SERBIA

❒ CACAK 1B
❒ KRAGUJEVAC 1A
❒ KRUSEVAC 1A
❒ SABAC 1A
❒ SMEDEREVO 1A
❒ UZICE (Titovo Uzice) 1A
❒ VALJEVO 1A

SPAIN

❒ ABABUJ Teruel 1D
❒ ABANILLA Murcia 1A
❒ ABARAN Murcia 1A
❒ ABENOJAR Ciudad Real 1A
❒ ABLA Almeria 1A
❒ ABRERA Barcelona 1A
❒ ADAMUZ Cordoba 1A 2A
❒ ADEMUZ Valencia 1A
❒ ADRA Almeria 1A
❒ ADZANETA Castellon 1E
❒ AGER Lerida 1A
❒ AGRAMON Albacete 2C
❒ AGRAMUNT Lerida 1A
❒ AGRES Alicante 1A
❒ AGUAVIVA Teruel 2E
❒ AGUDO Ciudad Real 1A
❒ AGUILAR DE SEGARRA Barcelona 1A
❒ AGUILAR DEL ALFAMBRA Teruel 1C
❒ AGUILAS Murcia 1A 2A
❒ AGULLANA Gerona 1A
❒ AGULLENT Valencia 1A
❒ AIGUAMURCIA Tarragona 1B
❒ AIGUES TOSSES DEL LLOBREGAT (Sant Andreu de la Barca) Barcelona 1B
❒ AIGUESBONES (Sant Quinten de Mediona) Barcelona 1A
❒ AIGUESBONES DE MONTBUI (Santa Margarida de Montbui) Barcelona 1B
❒ AIGUFREDA Barcelona 1A
❒ AIGUMURCIA Tarragona 1A
❒ AIGUESBONES (Sant Quintin de Mediona) Barcelona 1B
❒ AIGUESBONES DE MONTBUI (Santa Margrida de Montbui) Barcelona 1B
❒ AIGUES TOSSES DEL LLOBREGAT (Sant Andreu de la Barca) Barcelona 1A
❒ AINSA Huesca 2A
❒ AITONA Lerida 1A
❒ AJOFRIN Toledo 1A
❒ ALACON Teruel 1A
❒ ALAMILLO Ciudad Real 1A
❒ ALARCON Cuenca 1A
❒ ALBA DEL VALLES (Sant Fost de Campsentelles) Barcelona 1A
❒ ALBACETE Albacete 1A 2A 12A
❒ ALBADALEJO Ciudad Real 1A
❒ ALBAGES Lerida 1A
❒ ALBAIDA Valencia 1A
❒ ALBALAT DE LA RIBERA Valencia 1A
❒ ALBALAT DE TARONCHERS Valencia 1B
❒ ALBALATE DE CINCA Huesca 1C
❒ ALBALATE LUCHADOR Teruel 1B
❒ ALBALATILLO Huesca 2C
❒ ALBANCHEZ Almeria 1A
❒ ALBATARRECH Lerida 1A
❒ ALBATERA Alicante 1A
❒ ALBELDA Huesca 1A
❒ ALBENTOSA Teruel 1B
❒ ALBERIQUE Valencia 2A
❒ ALBESA Lerida 1B
❒ ALBI, L' Lerida 1A
❒ ALBIOL, L'Tarragona 1A
❒ ALBOCACER Castellon 1B
❒ ALBOLODUY Almeria 1B
❒ ALBONDON Granada 1B
❒ ALBONS Gerona 1A
❒ ALBOX Almeria 1B
❒ ALBUDEITE Murcia 1A 2C
❒ ALBUNOL Granada 1B
❒ ALCALA DE CHIVERT Castellon 1A
❒ ALCALA DE LA SELVA Teruel 2A
❒ ALCALA DEL JUCAR Albacete 1A
❒ ALCALHALI Alicante 1C
❒ ALCAMPEL Huesca 1A 2B
❒ ALCANAR Tarragona 1A
❒ ALCANIZ Teruel 1A
❒ ALCANO Lerida 1A
❒ ALCANTARA DEL JUCAR Valencia 1B
❒ ALCARACEJOS Cordoba 1A
❒ ALCARRAS Lerida 1A
❒ ALCAUDETE Jaen 1A 2B

25 Centimos, Alcaniz, Spain, 1A

❒ ALCAZARES, LOS Murcia 1B
❒ ALCIRA Valencia 1A
❒ ALCOBA Ciudad Real 1A
❒ ALCOLEA Almeria 1A
❒ ALCOLEA DE CINCA Huesca 1A 2B
❒ ALCOLECHA Alicante 1B
❒ ALCOLETGE Lerida 1A
❒ ALCONTAR Almeria 1C
❒ ALCORIZA Teruel 2A
❒ ALCOVER Tarragona 1A
❒ ALCOY Alicante 1A
❒ ALCUBIERE Huesca 2A
❒ ALCUBLAS Valencia 1A
❒ ALCUDIA DE CARLET Valencia 1A
❒ ALCUDIA DE CRESPINS Valencia 1A
❒ ALDAYA Valencia 1A
❒ ALDEA DE SAN BENITO Cuidad Real 1A
❒ ALDEA DEL REY (Cuidad Real) 1A
❒ ALDEANUEVA DE BARRARROYA Toledo 1A
❒ ALDEIRE Granada 1C
❒ ALDOVER Tarragona 1A
❒ ALELLA Barcelona 1A
❒ ALFAFARA Alicante 1C
❒ ALFAMBRA Teruel 2C
❒ ALFARA Tarragona 1A
❒ ALFARRAS Lerida 1A
❒ ALFAZ DEL PI Alicante 1B
❒ ALFES Lerida 1A
❒ ALFONDEGUILLA Castellon 1B
❒ ALFORJA Tarragona 1A
❒ ALGAR DE PALANCIA Valencia 1C
❒ ALGEMESI Valencia 1A
❒ ALGINET Valencia 2A
❒ ALGUAIRE Lerida 1A
❒ ALGUENA Alicante 1A
❒ ALHABIA Almeria 1A
❒ ALHAMA DE MURCIA Murcia 1A
❒ ALHAMA DE SALMERON Almeria 1A
❒ ALHAMBRA Ciudad Real 1B
❒ ALIAGA Teruel 1E
❒ ALICANTE Alicante 1A
❒ ALIO Tarragona 1A
❒ ALLEPUZ Teruel 1C
❒ ALLOZA Teruel 1C 2B
❒ ALMACELLES Lerida 1A
❒ ALMADEN Ciudad Real 1A 2C
❒ ALMADENEJOS Ciudad Real 1A
❒ ALMAGRO Ciudad Real 1A
❒ ALMANSA Albacete 1A
❒ ALMATRET Lerida 1A
❒ ALMEDINA Ciudad Real 1A
❒ ALMENAR Lerida 1A
❒ ALMERIA Almeria 1A 2B
❒ ALMODOVER DEL CAMPO Ciudad Real 2B
❒ ALMOLDA, LA Zaragoza 1B
❒ ALMONACID Toledo 1C
❒ ALMONACID DE LA CUBA Zaragoza 2A
❒ ALMORADI Alicante 1A
❒ ALMOSTER Tarragona 1A
❒ ALMUNIA DE CINCA Zaragoza 2A
❒ ALMURADIEL Ciudad Real 1B
❒ ALMUSAFES Valencia 1A
❒ ALORA Malaga 2B
❒ ALP Gerona 1A
❒ ALPERA Albacete 1A
❒ ALSODUX Almeria 1C
❒ ALTAFULLA Tarragona 1A
❒ ALTORRICON Huesca 1A 2D
❒ AMER Gerona 1A
❒ AMETLLA DE MAR Tarragona 1A
❒ AMETLLA DE MEROLA Barcelona 1A
❒ AMETLLA DEL VALLES Barcelona 6D
❒ AMPOLLA Tarragona 1B
❒ AMPOSTA Tarragona 1A
❒ ANDORRA Teruel 2B
❒ ANDUJAR Jaen 2A
❒ ANGLES Gerona 1A
❒ ANNA Valencia 1A
❒ ANTAS Almeria 1A
❒ ARAHAL Sevilla 6D
❒ ARBECA Lerida 1A
❒ ARBOC Tarragona 1A
❒ ARBUCIES Gerona 1B
❒ ARCHENA Murcia 1A
❒ ARCHS Lerida 1A
❒ AREN Huesca 1B
❒ ARENAS DE SAN JUAN Ciudad Real 1B
❒ ARENS DE LLEDO Teruel 1B
❒ ARENYS DE MAR Barcelona 1B 6E
❒ ARENYS DE MUNT Barcelona 1A
❒ ARGAMASILLA DE ALBA Ciudad Real 1A
❒ ARGAMASILLA DE CALATRAVA Ciudad Read 1A
❒ ARGELAGUER Gerona 1A
❒ ARGENSOLA Barcelona 1B
❒ ARGENTERA Tarragona 1A
❒ ARGENTONA Barcelona 1B
❒ ARJONA Jaen 2B
❒ ARJONILLA Jaen 1B
❒ ARNES Tarragona 1A
❒ ARSEGUEL Lerida 1A
❒ ARTES Barcelona 1A
❒ ARTESA DE LLEIDA Lerida 1A
❒ ARTESA DE SERGE Lerida 1A
❒ ASCO Tarragona 1A
❒ ASPA Lerida 1A
❒ ASPE Alicante 1A
❒ ASTURIAS Y LEON 6D
❒ AURORA DE LLUCANES (Sant Boi de Llucanes) Barcelona 1A
❒ AVIA Barcelona 1A
❒ AVILES Asturias 2E 2 B 12E
❒ AVINYO Barcelona 1B
❒ AYELO Valencia 2C
❒ AYODAR Castellon 1B
❒ AYORA Valencia 1B
❒ AZANUY Huesca 1B 2C
❒ AZUARA Zaragoza 1A
❒ BACARES Almeria 1B

25 Centimos, Asturias y Leon, 1A

❒ BACELLA Lerida 1A
❒ BADAJOZ 1A
❒ BADALONA Barcelona 2B
❒ BAELLS Huesca 1C
❒ BAEZA Jaen 1A
❒ BAGA Barcelona 1B
❒ BAGES D'EN SELVES
(Sant Mateu de Bages) Barcelona 1A
❒ BAILEN Jaen 1A 2C
❒ BAIX MONTSENY
(Sant Celoni) Barcelona 1A
❒ BALAGUER Lerida 1A
❒ BALENYA Barcelona 1A
❒ BALLESTAR Castellon 1A
❒ BALLESTEROS DE CALATRAVA
Ciudad Real 1B
❒ BALONES Alicante 1C
❒ BALSARENY Barcelona 1A
❒ BANERES Alicante 1A
❒ BANOS Jaen 1A
❒ BANYERES Tarragona 1A
❒ BANYOLES Gerona 1A
❒ BARBASTRO Huesca 1A
❒ BARBENS Lerida 1A
❒ BARBERA DE LA CONCA
Barcelona 1D
❒ BARBERA DEL VALLES
Barcelona 1B
❒ BARCELONA Barcelona 1A 2B 8B 9B 11B 12B
❒ BARCHETA Valencia 1B
❒ BARIG Valencia 1B
❒ BARONIA DE RIALB Lerida 1C
❒ BARRAX Albacete 1E
❒ BARRIO DE ABAJO Ciudad Real 2D
❒ BATEA Tarragona 1B
❒ BAYARQUE Almeria 1C
❒ BAZA Granada 1A
❒ BEAS DE SEGURA Jaen 1A
❒ BECEITE Teruel 1B

Types of Emergency Money

Type	Reference #
Municipal paper	1
Private paper	2
POW paper	3
POW official metal	4
POW private metal	5
Municipal metal	6
Private metal	7
Gas tokens	8
Food; beer; konsumverein	9
Naval; military; kantine	10
Encased, unencased stamps	11
Streetcar tokens	12
Porcelain	13
World War II issues	14
Concentration, Civilian internment camps	15

Rarity grades: A, to $25; B, to $60; C, to $125; D, to $200; and E, $350

❒ BECHI Castellon 1A
❒ BEDAR Almeria 1A
❒ BEDMAR Jaen 1A
❒ BEGET Gerona 1A
❒ BEGIJAR Jaen 1C
❒ BEGUDA Gerona 1A
❒ BEGUDA ALTA Barcelona 1A
❒ BEGUES Barcelona 1A
❒ BEGUR Gerona 1B
❒ BELALCAZAR Cordoba 1A
❒ BELIANES Lerida 1B
❒ BELILLA DE CINCA Huesca 2C
❒ BELL-LLOC D'URGELL Lerida 1B
❒ BELLAGUARDA (La Pobleta de la Granadella)
Lerida 1B
❒ BELLCAIRE D'URGELL Lerida 1A
❒ BELLICAIRE D'EMPORDA Gerona1B
❒ BELL-LLOC D'URGELL Lerida 1B
❒ BELLMUNT D'URGELL Lerida 1A
❒ BELLPUIG D'URGELL Lerida 1A
❒ BELLREGUART Valencia 1A
❒ BELLSERRAT
(Sant Pere de Torello) Barcelona 1B
❒ BELLTALL Tarragona 1A
❒ BELLVEI Tarragona 1A
❒ BELLVERDECERDANYA Lerida 1A
❒ BELLVIS Lerida 1B
❒ BELMEZ Cordoba 2D
❒ BELMONTE Cuenca 1C
❒ BELVIS DE LA JARA Toledo 1A
❒ BENABARRE Huesca 2B
❒ BENAHADUX Almeria 1B
❒ BENAJAMA Alicante 1A
❒ BENALUA DE GUADIX Granada 1A 2A
❒ BENALUA DE LAS VILLAS
Granada 1A
❒ BENAMAUREL Granada 2C
❒ BENASAL Castellon 1A
❒ BENASQUE Huesca 1A
❒ BENATAE Jaen 2C
❒ BENAVENT DE SEGRIA Lerida 1A
❒ BENAVITES Valencia 1C
❒ BENEJAMA Alicante 1A
❒ BENEJUZAR Alicante 1A
❒ BENETUSER Valencia 1B
❒ BENIARBEIG Alicante 1B
❒ BENIARDA Alicante 1A
❒ BENIARJO Valencia 1A
❒ BENIARRES Alicante 1A
❒ BENIATJAR Valencia 1C
❒ BENICARLO Castellon 1A
❒ BENICASIM Castellon 1C
❒ BENIDORM Alicante 1A
❒ BENIEL Murcia 1A
❒ BENIFAIRO DE VALLDIGNA
Valencia 2A
❒ BENIFALLET Tarragona 1A
❒ BENIFALLIM Alicante 1C
❒ BENIFATO Alicante 1C
❒ BENIFAYO Valencia 1B
❒ BENIGANIM Valencia 1A
❒ BENILLOBA Alicante 1B
❒ BENIMANTELL Alicante 1B
❒ BENIMASOT Alicante 1D
❒ BENINAR Almeria 1B
❒ BENIPEIXCAR Valencia 2B
❒ BENISA Alicante 2B
❒ BENISSANET Tarragona 1A
❒ BENLLOCH Castellon 1A
❒ BENQUERENCIA Caceres 1C
❒ BENTARIQUE Almeria 2C
❒ BERGA Barcelona 1A
❒ BERJA Almeria 1A 2C

❒ BESALU Gerona 1B
❒ BESCANO Gerona 1B
❒ BESORA Gerona 1B
❒ BETERA Valencia 1A
❒ BIAR Alicante 1A
❒ BIENSERVIDA Albacete 1A
❒ BIGUES Barcelona 1A
❒ BINACED Huesca 1A
❒ BINEFAR Huesca 1A 2B
❒ BIOSCA Lerida 1A
❒ BISAURA DE TER (Sant Quirze de Besora) 1A
❒ BISBAL DE FALSET Tarragona 1C
❒ BISBAL DEL PENEDES, LA Tarragona 1A
❒ BISBAL, LA Gerona 1A
❒ BLANCA Murcia 2A
❒ BLANCAFORT Tarragona 1D
❒ BLANES Gerona 1A
❒ BLESA Teruel 1B
❒ BOBERA Lerida 1A
❒ BOCAIRENTE Valencia 1A
❒ BOIX DE NOGUERA (Trago de Noguera) Lerida 1A
❒ BOLANOS Ciudad Real 1A
❒ BOLBAITE Valencia 1A
❒ BOLTANA Huesca 1A
❒ BONASTRE Tarragona 1A
❒ BONETE Albacete 1A
❒ BORDES, LES Lerida 1C
❒ BORDILS Gerona 1B
❒ BORGES BLANQUES, LES Lerida 1A
❒ BORGES DEL CAMP Tarragona 1A
❒ BORRASSA Gerona 1A
❒ BORREDA Barcelona 1A
❒ BOSOST Lerida 1A
❒ BOT Tarragona 1A
❒ BOTARELL Tarragona 1A
❒ BRAFIM Tarragona 1A
❒ BRAZATORTAS Ciudad Real 1A
❒ BREDA Gerona 1A
❒ BRONCHALES Teruel 1C
❒ BROTO Huesca 1B
❒ BRUCH, EL Barcelona 1A
❒ BRULL Barcelona 1D
❒ BUJALANCE Cordoba 2A
❒ BULLAS Murcia 1A
❒ BUNOL Valencia 1A
❒ BURGOS Burgos 1A 6B
❒ BURJASOT Valencia 1A
❒ BURRIANA Castellon 1A
❒ BUSAURA DE TER (Sant Quirze de Besora) 1B
❒ BUSQUISTAR Granada 1B
❒ CABANABONA Lerida 1C
❒ CABANES Castellon 1A
❒ CABASSERS Tarragona 1C
❒ CABEZA DE BUEY Badajoz 2A
❒ CABEZARADOS Cuidad Real 1A
❒ CABEZARRUBIAS DEL PUERTO Cuidad Real 1B
❒ CABRA (Cabra del Santo Cristo) Jaen 2A
❒ CABRA D'ANOIA Barcelona 1B
❒ CABRA DEL CAMP Tarragona 1A 2C
❒ CABRA D'ANOIA Barcelona 1A
❒ CABRERA DE MATARO Barcelona 1D
❒ CABRILS. Barcelona 1A
❒ CADAQUES Gerona 1A
❒ CADIAR Granada 1B
❒ CALACEITE Teruel 1A 2C
❒ CALAF Barcelona 1A
❒ CALAFELL Tarragona 1A
❒ CALANDA Teruel 1A 2B
❒ CALANDA DE DIA Teruel 1A
❒ CALASPARRA Murcia 1A
❒ CALDERS Barcelona 1A
❒ CALDES D'ESTRAC Barcelona 1A
❒ CALDES DE MALAVELLA Gerona 1A
❒ CALDES DE MONTBUI Barcelona 1A
❒ CALELLA Barcelona 1A
❒ CALIG Castellon 1A
❒ CALLDETENES Barcelona 1A
❒ CALLOSA DE ENSARRIA Alicante 1A
❒ CALLOSA DE SEGURA Alicante 2A
❒ CALLUS Barcelona 1A
❒ CALONGE DE LA COSTA BRAVA Gerona 1A
❒ CALONGE DE SEGARRA Barcelona 1A
❒ CALPE Alicante 1A
❒ CALZADA DE CALATRAVA Cuidad Real 1A
❒ CAMARASA Lerida 1A
❒ CAMARENA Teruel 1C
❒ CAMARILLAS Teruel 1C
❒ CAMARLES Tarragona 1B
❒ CAMBIL Jaen 1A
❒ CAMBRILS DE MAR Tarragona 1A
❒ CAMPANARIO Badajoz 1A
❒ CAMPANETA, LA Alicante 2B
❒ CAMPDEVANOI Gerona 1B
❒ CAMPELLO Alicante 1A
❒ CAMPILLO Cuenca 1B
❒ CAMPILLO DE ALTOBUEY Cuenca 1B
❒ CAMPILLO DE ARENAS Jaen 1A 2C
❒ CAMPILLO DE LA JARA, EL Toledo 1B
❒ CAMPO Huesca 2C
❒ CAMPO RUS Cuenca 1E
❒ CAMPORROBLES Valencia 1A
❒ CAMPOS DEL RIO Murcia 1A
❒ CAMPOTEJAR Granada 1A
❒ CAMPREDO Tarragona 1D
❒ CAMPRODON Gerona 1D
❒ CAMUNAS Toledo 1A
❒ CANADA Alicante 1B
❒ CANALS Valencia 1A 2C
❒ CANDASNOS Huesca 1A 2B
❒ CANENA Jaen 1A
❒ CANET DE MAR Barcelona 1A
❒ CANET LO ROIG Castellon 1A
❒ CANETE DE LAS TORRES Cordoba 2A
❒ CANILES Granada 2B
❒ CANJAYAR Almeria 1A 2A
❒ CANONJA, LA Tarragona 1A
❒ CANTALLOPS Gerona 1A
❒ CANTAVIEJA Teruel 2B
❒ CANYA, LA Gerona 1D
❒ CAPAFONTS Tarragona 1A
❒ CAPCANES Tarragona 1A
❒ CAPELLADES Barcelona 1A
❒ CAPILLA Badajoz 2C
❒ CAPSECH Gerona 2D
❒ CARAVACA Murcia 1A
❒ CARBONERAS Almeria 1A
❒ CARCAGENTE Valencia 1A
❒ CARCER Valencia 1A
❒ CARCHELEJO Jaen 2B

❒ CARDEDEU Barcelona 1A
❒ CARDENA Cordoba 2A
❒ CARDONA Barcelona 1A
❒ CARLET Valencia 1A
❒ CARME Barcelona 1A
❒ CAROLINA, LA Jaen 1A 2B
❒ CARRION DE CALATRAVA Ciudad Real 1A
❒ CARRIZOSA Ciudad Real 1A
❒ CARTEGENA Murcia 1A 2C
❒ CASAS BAJAS Valencia 1C
❒ CASAS DE HARO Cuenca 1D
❒ CASAS DE JUAN NUNEZ Albacete 1A
❒ CASAS IBANEZ Albacete 1A 2C
❒ CASERES Tarragona 1C
❒ CASPE Zaragoza 1A
❒ CASSA DE LA SELVA Gerona 1A
❒ CASTALLA Alicante 1A
❒ CASTANESA Huesca 1C
❒ CASTEJON DE SOS Huesca 1A 2B
❒ CASTEL DE CABRA Teruel 1B
❒ CASTELL DE FERRO Granada 1C
❒ CASTELLAR Jaen 1A
❒ CASTELLAR DE N'HUG Barcelona 1A
❒ CASTELLAR DE SANTIAGO Ciudad Real 1A
❒ CASTELLAR DEL VALLES Barcelona 1A
❒ CASTELLBELL I EL VILAR Barcelona 1A
❒ CASTELLBO, VALL DE Lerida 1D
❒ CASTELLCIUTAT Lerida 1A
❒ CASTELLDANS Lerida 1A
❒ CASTELLDEFELS Barcelona 1A
❒ CASTELLET DE LLOBREGAT (Sant Vicent de Castellet) Barcelona 1A
❒ CASTELLFOLLIT DE LA ROCA Gerona 1A
❒ CASTELLFULLIT DE RIUBREGOS Barcelona 1D
❒ CASTELLFULLIT DEL BOIX Barcelona 1D
❒ CASTELLIGALI Barcelona 1A
❒ CASTELLNOU DE BAGES Barcelona 1E
❒ CASTELLNOU DE SEANA Lerida 1A
❒ CASTELLO D'EMPURIES Gerona 1A
❒ CASTELLO DE FARFANYA Lerida 1A
❒ CASTELLOLI Barcelona 1A
❒ CASTELLON DE LA PLANA 1A
❒ CASTELLOTE Teruel 1A
❒ CASTELLSARROCA (Sant Marti Sarroca) Barcelona 1A
❒ CASTELLSERA Lerida 1C
❒ CASTELLTERSOL Barcelona 1A
❒ CASTELLVELL Tarragona 1A
❒ CASTELLVI DE LA MARCA Barcelona 1A
❒ CASTELNOU Teruel 1C
❒ CASTELSERAS Teruel 1A
❒ CASTIGALEU Huesca 1A
❒ CASTILLO DE LOCUBIN Jaen 1A
❒ CASTRIL Granada 1A
❒ CASTRO-URDIALES Santander 1E
❒ CASTUERA Badajoz 1A
❒ CATLLAR EL Tarragona 1C
❒ CATRAL Alicante 1A
❒ CAUDETE Albacete 1A
❒ CAUDETE DE LAS FUENTES Valencia 1C
❒ CAVA, LA (Tarragona) 1A
❒ CAZALLA DE LA SIERRA Sevilla 6E
❒ CAZORLA Jaen 2A
❒ CECILIA DE VOLTREGA Barcelona 1C
❒ CEHEGIN Murcia 1A
❒ CELLERA DE TER, LA Gerona 1A
❒ CELRA Gerona 1A
❒ CENTELLES Barcelona 1A
❒ CERVELLO Barcelona 1A
❒ CERVERA Lerida 1D 2D
❒ CERVERA DE LLANO Cuenca 1C
❒ CERVERA DEL MAESTRO Castellon 1B
❒ CERVIA Lerida 1A
❒ CERVIA DE TER Gerona 1A
❒ CEUTI Murcia 1E
❒ CHERT Castellon 2B
❒ CHESTE Valencia 1A
❒ CHILLON Ciudad Real 1A
❒ CHINCHILLA Albacete 1A
❒ CHIRIVEL Almeria 1A
❒ CHIVA Valencia 1A
❒ CHIVA DE MORELLA Castellon 1C
❒ CHULILLA Valencia 1A 2C
❒ CIEZA Murcia 1A 2D
❒ CINCO OLIVAS Zaragoza 2D
❒ CINCTORRES Castellon 2C
❒ CIRERER DE LLOBREGAT, EL (Sant Climent de Llobregat) Barcelona 1A
❒ CIUDAD REAL Ciudad Real 1A 2C
❒ CIUTADILLA Lerida 1A
❒ CLARVALLS Lerida 1D
❒ COBDAR Almeria 1C
❒ COCENTAINA Alicante 1A
❒ CODINES DE VALLES (Sant Feliu de Codines) Barcelona 1A
❒ COFRENTES Valencia 1A
❒ COGUL Lerida 1C
❒ COLL DE NARGO Lerida 1A
❒ COLLBATO Barcelona 1A
❒ COLLDEJOU Tarragona 1D
❒ COLL DE NARGO Lerida 1A
❒ COLLSESPINA (Collsuspina) Barcelona 1A
❒ COLOMERA Granada 1A
❒ CONFRIDES Alicante 1B 2C
❒ CONQUISTA Cordoba 1A
❒ CONSTANTI Tarragona 1A 2E
❒ CONSUEGRA Toledo 1A
❒ COPONS Barcelona 1A
❒ CORBERA DE LLOBREGAT Barcelona 1A
❒ CORBERA DE TERRA ALTA Tarragona 1A 2E
❒ CORBINS Lerida 1A
❒ CORNELLA DE LLOBREGAT Barcelona 1A
❒ CORNUDELLA Tarragona 1A
❒ CORNUDELLA DE MONTSANT Tarragona 1A
❒ CORONADA, LA Badajoz 1A
❒ CORRAL DE ALMAGUER Toledo 1A
❒ CORRAL DEL CALATRAVA Ciudad Real 1A
❒ CORRAL-RUBIO Albacete 1B
❒ CORTES DA PALLAS Valencia 1D
❒ CORTIJO ALTO Ciudad Leal 2C
❒ COX Alicante 1A

❒ CREIXELL DE MAR Tarragona 1A
❒ CRETAS Teruel 2A
❒ CREVILLENTE Alicante 2A
❒ CRIPTANA Ciudad Real 1A
❒ CUATRETONDETA Alicante 1C
❒ CUBELLS Lerida 1A
❒ CUEVAS DE ALMONZORA Almeria 1A
❒ CUEVAS DE CANART Teruel 1C
❒ CUEVAS DE VINROMA Castellon 1A 2C
❒ CULLAR-BAZA Granada 1A 2C
❒ CULLERA Valencia 1A 2A
❒ DAGANZO Madrid 2C
❒ DAIMIEL Ciudad Real 1A 2C
❒ DALIAS Almeria 1A 2A
❒ DARMOS Tarragona 1A
❒ DARRO Granada 1C
❒ DEHESA DE GUADIX Granada 1B
❒ DENIA Alicante 1A 2B
❒ DEZMA Granada 2C
❒ DOLAR Granada 1A
❒ DOLORES Alicante 1A
❒ DOMENYS DEL PENEDES Tarragona 1A
❒ DON BENITO Badajoz 1A 2C
❒ DONA MARIA OCANA Almeria 1B
❒ DONZELL D'URGELL Lerida 1A
❒ DOS TORRES Cordoba 1A 2C
❒ DOSRIUS Barcelona 1A
❒ DUESAIGUES Tarragona 1A
❒ ELCHE Alicante 2A
❒ ELCHE DE LA SIERRA Albacete 1A
❒ ELDA Alicante 1A
❒ ELLAR Jaen 2B
❒ EMPORI, LA VILA D' (Sant Pere Pescador) Gerona 1E
❒ ENGUERA Valencia 1A
❒ ENIX Almeria 2C
❒ ESCALE, L' Gerona 1A
❒ ESCANUELA Jaen 1A
❒ ESCATRON Zaragoza 1A
❒ ESCORIAL DE LA SIERRA (San Lorenzo del Escorial) Madrid 1A
❒ ESCUCHA Teruel 1A
❒ ESPARRAGOSA DE LARES Badajoz 2A
❒ ESPARREGUERA (Esparraguera) Barcelona 1A 2C
❒ ESPELUY Jaen 1B
❒ ESPINELVES Gerona 1B
❒ ESPLUGA CALVI Lerida 1A
❒ ESPLUGA DE FRANCOLI Tarragona 1A
❒ ESPLUGUES Barcelona 1B
❒ ESPLUS Huesca 1A
❒ ESPOLLA Gerona 1A
❒ ESTADA Huesca 1C
❒ ESTADILLA Huesca 1B 2C
❒ ESTANY L'Barcelona 1B
❒ ESTERCUELTeruel 1B 2C
❒ ESTERRI D'ANEU Lerida 1A
❒ ESTICHE DE CINCA Huesca 2C
❒ ESTIVELLA Valencia 1A
❒ ESTOPINAN Huesca 1A
❒ EUZKADI Vizcaya 6B
❒ FABARA Zaragoza 1A 2B
❒ FACHECA Alicante 1C
❒ FALSET Tarragona 1A
❒ FAMORCA Alicante 1D
❒ FARNERS DE LA SELVA (Santa Coloma de Farners) Gerona 1A
❒ FATARELLA, LA Tarragona 1A
❒ FAURA Valencia 1C
❒ FAYON Zaragoza 1A
❒ FEBRO, LA Tarragona 1C
❒ FELGUERA, LA Asturias 2E
❒ FELIX Almeria 1A
❒ FERNANCABALLERO Ciudad Real 1A
❒ FERREIRA Granada 1C
❒ FIGOLS DE SEGRE Lerida 1A
❒ FIGUERES Gerona 1A 2C
❒ FIGUEROLA D'ORCAU Lerida 1C
❒ FINANA Almeria 1A
❒ FINESTRAT Alicante 1A
❒ FINESTRES Gerona 1D
❒ FLACA Gerona 1A
❒ FLIX Tarragona 1A
❒ FLOREAL DEL RASPEIG Alicante 1A
❒ FLORESTA, LA Lerida 1A
❒ FOIXA Gerona 1A
❒ FOLGUEROLES Barcelona 1C
❒ FONDON Almeria 1A
❒ FONELAS Granada 1A
❒ FONOLLOSA Barcelona 2B
❒ FONTANARES Valencia 1A
❒ FONTS DE SACALM (Sant Hilari Sacalm) Gerona 1A
❒ FONZ Huesca 1A
❒ FORCA, LA Barcelona 1A
❒ FORCALL Castellon 2A
❒ FORES Tarragona 1E
❒ FORMENTERA DEL SEGURA Alicante 1A
❒ FORNELLES DE LA SELVA Gerona 1A
❒ FORTANETE Teruel 1D
❒ FORTUNA Murcia 1A
❒ FOYOS Valencia 1C
❒ FOZ-CALANDA Teruel 1C
❒ FRAGA Huesca 1A 2B
❒ FRAILES Jaen 1A
❒ FRANQUESES, LES Barcelona 1A
❒ FREGINALS Tarragona 1C
❒ FREIXANET (Sant Guim Estacio) Lerida 1A
❒ FRESNEDA, LA Teruel 1A
❒ FRUITERS (Castellbisbal) Barcelona 1A
❒ FUENLABRADA DE LOS MONTES Badajoz 1B
❒ FUENTE Cuenca 2A
❒ FUENTE DEL FRESNO Ciudad Real 2C
❒ FUENTE LA HUGUERA Valencia 1A
❒ FUENTE LA LANCHA Cordoba 1C
❒ FUENTE-ENCARROZ Valencia 1A
❒ FUENTEALAMO Albacete 1A
❒ FUENTEALBILLA Albacete 1B
❒ FUENTESPALDA Teruel 1C
❒ FULIOLA, LA Lerida 1A
❒ FULLEDA Lerida 1A
❒ GADOR Almeria 1A
❒ GALAGUER Lerida 1B
❒ GALERA Granada 1A
❒ GALERA DEL PLA, LA Tarragona 1B
❒ GALLARDOS, LOS Almeria 1A
❒ GALVEZ Toledo 1A
❒ GANDESA Tarragona 1A
❒ GANDIA Valencia 1A
❒ GARBAYUELA Badajoz 1A
❒ GARCIA Tarragona 1B 2A
❒ GARGALLO Teruel 1C

❒ GARGANTA, LA Ciudad Real 2C
❒ GARRIGA, LA Barcelona 1B 2D
❒ GARRIGUELLA Gerona 1B
❒ GARRUCHA Almeria 1A
❒ GATA DE GORGOS Alicante 1A 2B
❒ GAVA Barcelona 1A 2A
❒ GAYANES Alicante 2C
❒ GELIDA Barcelona 1A
❒ GELSA Zaragoza 1A
❒ GERGAL Almeria 1A
❒ GERRI DE LA SAL Lerida 1B
❒ GIJON Asturias 2E
❒ GINESTAR D'ERBE Tarragona 1B
❒ GIRONA Gerona 1A 2D
❒ GIRONELLA Barcelona 1A
❒ GISCLARENY Barcelona 1B
❒ GLEVINYOL DE TER (Les Masies de Sant Hipolit) Barcelona 1B
❒ GODALL Tarragona 1D
❒ GOLMES Lerida 1B 2A
❒ GOR Granada 1A
❒ GORAFE Granada 1B
❒ GORGA Alicante 1D
❒ GOSOL Lerida 1B
❒ GRAMENET DEL BESOS Barcelona 1A
❒ GRANADA DEL PENEDES Barcelona 1B
❒ GRANADA, LA Barcelona 1A
❒ GRANADELLA, LA Lerida 1A
❒ GRANATULA Ciudad Real 1A
❒ GRANJUEL, LA Cordoba 1B
❒ GRANEN Huesca 1A
❒ GRANER DE BAGES (Santpedor) Barcelona 2B
❒ GRANJA DE ESCARPE (Grania D'ESCARP) Lerida 1C 2C
❒ GRANJUELA, LA Cordoba 1B
❒ GRANOLLERS Barcelona 1A
❒ GRANYENA DE LES GARRIGUES Lerida 1B
❒ GRANYENA DE SEGARRA Lerida 1C
❒ GRATALLOPS Barcelona 6B
❒ GRAUS Huesca 1A 2D
❒ GUADAHORTUNA Granada 1A
❒ GUADALAJARA Guadalajara 1A
❒ GUADAMUR Toledo 1A
❒ GUADASUAR Valencia 1C
❒ GUADIX Granada 1C 2A
❒ GUALBA Barcelona 1A
❒ GUALCHOS Granada 2C
❒ GUARDAMAR DEL SEGURA Alicante 1A
❒ GUARDIA DE NOGUERA Lerida 1D
❒ GUARDIA, LA Jaen 1A
❒ GUARDIOLA DE BAGES (Sant Salvador de Guardiola) Barcelona 1A
❒ GUARDIOLA DE BERGA Barcelona 1A
❒ GUARDIOLA DEL PENEDES (Font-Rubi) Barcelona 2D
❒ GUARROMAN Jaen 1A
❒ GUIAMETS, LES Tarragona 1B
❒ GUIJO, EL Cordoba 1B
❒ GUILLS DEL CANTO Lerida 1D
❒ GUIMERA Lerida 1B
❒ GUISSONA Lerida 1B
❒ GUIXOLS Gerona 1A 2B
❒ HELECHAL Badajoz 2C
❒ HELLIN Albacete 11B
❒ HERENCIA Ciudad Real 1A
❒ HERRERA DE LOS NAVARROS Zaragoza 1A 2C
❒ HIGUERUELA Albacete 1A
❒ HIJAR Teruel 2A
❒ HINAJOSA DEL DUQUE Cordoba 1A
❒ HORCAJO Cuenca 1A
❒ HORNOS DE SEGURA Jaen 1D
❒ HORTA DE TERRA ALTA (Horta de Sant Joan) Tarragona 1A
❒ HORTS DEL LLOBREGAT (Sant Vincenc dels Horts) Barcelona 1A
❒ HOSTALETS DE PIEROLA Barcelona 1A
❒ HOSTALRIC Gerona 1A
❒ HOSTOLES (Sant Feliu de Pallarols) Gerona 1A
❒ HUERCAL-OVERA Almeria 1A
❒ HUERTEZUELAS Ciudad Real 1A
❒ HUESA Jaen 1A
❒ HUESCAR Granada 1A
❒ HUETE Cuenca 1A 2A
❒ IBARS DE NOGUERA Lerida 1A
❒ IBI Alicante 6C
❒ IBIECA Huesca 2D
❒ IBORRA (Misspelling of Ivorra) Lerida 1A
❒ IBROS Jaen 1A
❒ IGLESUELA DEL CID Teruel 2A
❒ IGUALDA Barcelona 1A 2A
❒ INFANTES Ciudad Real 1C
❒ INSTINCION Almeria 1A
❒ ISONA Lerida 1B
❒ IVARS D'URGELL Lerida 1B
❒ IVORRA Lerida 1B
❒ IZNALLOZ Granada 1B 2C
❒ JAEN Jaen 2B
❒ JALANCE Valencia 1C
❒ JALON Alicante 1B
❒ JATIEL Teruel 1D
❒ JATIVA Valencia 1A
❒ JAVEA Alicante 1A 2A
❒ JERESA Valencia 1B
❒ JEREZ DEL MARQUESADO Granada 1A
❒ JERICA Castellon 1A
❒ JIJONA Alicante 2C
❒ JIMENA Jaen 1A
❒ JODAR Jaen 2A
❒ JONQUERA, LA Gerona 1A
❒ JORBA Barcelona 1B
❒ JORQUERA Albacete 1B
❒ JUIA Gerona 1A
❒ JUMILLA Murcia 1A
❒ JUNCOSA DE LES GARRIGUES (Juncosa) Lerida 1D 2D
❒ JUNEDA Lerida 1A
❒ JUST DESVERN Barcelona 1A
❒ LABUERDA Huesca 1C
❒ LAGATA Zaragoza 2D
❒ LAGUARRES Huesca 1B
❒ LALUEZA Huesca 1A
❒ LASCUARRE Huesca 1A
❒ LASPAULES Huesca 1C
❒ LASPUNA Huesca 1C
❒ LAUJAR Almeria 1A 2B
❒ LAYOS Toledo 1C
❒ LECERA Zaragoza 2A
❒ LECINA DE CINCA Huesca 1B
❒ LES Lerida 1B
❒ LETUR Albacete 1A
❒ LIBRILLA Murcia 1A
❒ LIETOR Albacete 1B
❒ LIJAR Almeria 1C
❒ LILLA Tarragona 1B

❒ LILLO Toledo 1A
❒ LINARES Jaen 1A
❒ LINYOLA Lerida 1A
❒ LLACUNA Barcelona 1A 2C
❒ LLADO Gerona 1B
❒ LLAGOSTA, LA Barcelona 1B
❒ LLAGOSTERA, Gerona 1A
❒ LLANES Asturias 1E
❒ LLARDECANS Lerida 1A
❒ LLAVANERES Barcelona 1A
❒ LLAVANERES DE MONTAL (Sant Vicent de Montal) Barcelona 1A
❒ LLAVORSI Lerida 1A
❒ LLEIDA Lerida 1A 2C
❒ LLEVANTI DE MAR (Sant Antoni de Mar) Gerona 1A
❒ LLIBER Alicante 2C
❒ LLICA DE MUNT Barcelona 1A
❒ LLINARS Barcelona 1A
❒ LLIVIA Gerona 2C
❒ LLOA Tarragona 1A
❒ LLOMBAY Valencia 1A 2C
❒ LLORENC DE MORUNYS Lerida 1D
❒ LLORENS D'HORTONS Barcelona 1A
❒ LLORENS DEL PANADES Tarragona 1A
❒ LLORET DE MAR Gerona 1B
❒ LLORIANA DE TER (Sant Vicenc de Torello) Barcelona 1B
❒ LLUCA Barcelona 1B
❒ LOPERA Jaen 2A
❒ LORA DEL RIO Sevilla 6E
❒ LORCA Murcia 1A
❒ LOSA DEL OBISPO Valencia 1C
❒ LUBRIN Almeria 2A
❒ LUCAINENA DE LAS TORRES Almeria 1B
❒ LUCENA DEL CID Castellon 1A
❒ LUGROS Granada 1B
❒ LUJAR Granada 1A
❒ LUPION Jaen 1A
❒ MACAEL Almeria 2C
❒ MACANET DE LA SELVA Gerona 1A
❒ MADRID Madrid 1A 2A 6B 12A
❒ MADRIDEJOS Toledo 1A
❒ MADRIGUERAS Albacete 1A
❒ MAELLA Zaragoza 1A
❒ MAHORA Albacete 1A
❒ MAIA DE MONTCAL Gerona 1A
❒ MAIALS Lerida 1A
❒ MALAGON Ciudad Real 1A
❒ MALDA Lerida 1B
❒ MALGRAT Barcelona 1A
❒ MALLA I MIRAMBERC Barcelona 1A
❒ MALPARTIDA DE LA SERENA Badajoz 1B
❒ MALPICA DE TAJO Toledo 1B
❒ MAMOLA, LA Granada 2C
❒ MANCHA REAL Jaen 1A
❒ MANISES Valencia 1A
❒ MANJIBAR Jaen 1B
❒ MANLLEU Barcelona 1A 2D
❒ MANRESA Barcelona 1A 2D
❒ MANRESANA, LA Barcelona 1A
❒ MANUEL Valencia 1A
❒ MANZANARES Ciudad Real 1A
❒ MARCA Tarragona 1A 2D
❒ MARCHENA Sevilla 6E
❒ MARGALEF DE MONTSANT Tarragona 1B
❒ MARGANELL Barcelona 2A
❒ MARIA Almeria 1A
❒ MARJALIZA Toledo 1C
❒ MARMOLEJO Jaen 1A
❒ MARTORELL Barcelona 1A
❒ MARTORELLES DE BAIX Barcelona 1B
❒ MARTOS Jaen 1A
❒ MAS DE BARBERANS Tarragona 1A
❒ MAS DE LAS MATAS Teruel 2C
❒ MASDENVERGE Tarragona 1B
❒ MASNOU, EL Barcelona 1A
❒ MASO Tarragona 2B
❒ MASPUJOLS Tarragona 1A
❒ MASQUEFA Barcelona 1C
❒ MASROIG Tarragona 1A
❒ MASSALCOREIG Lerida 1C
❒ MASSANES Gerona 1A
❒ MATARO Barcelona 1A 2A
❒ MATEO DE LAS FUENTES (San Mateo) Castellon 1A
❒ MAZARRON Murcia 1A 2C
❒ MECINA BOMBARON Granada 1A 2C
❒ MEDIONA Barcelona 1A
❒ MELIANA Valencia 1A
❒ MELILLA (Riff) Spanish Morocco 1C
❒ MENAGUENS Lerida 1B
❒ MENASALBAS Toledo 1A
❒ MENJIBAR Jaen 1A
❒ MENORCA 6B
❒ MEQUINENZA Zaragoza 1A
❒ MEZQUITA DE JARQUE Teruel 1C
❒ MIGUEL ESTEBAN Toledo 1A
❒ MIGUELTURRA Ciudad Real 1A
❒ MILA, EL Tarragona 1D
❒ MILERES Asturias 2E
❒ MINAS DEL HORCAJO Ciudad Real 1A
❒ MINGLANILLA Cuenca 1A
❒ MIRAFLOR Alicante 1D
❒ MIRAMAR Valencia 1C
❒ MIRAVET Tarragona 1B
❒ MISLATA Valencia 1A
❒ MOGENTE Valencia 1A
❒ MOIA Barcelona 1A
❒ MOJACAR Almeria 1A
❒ MOLINS DE LLORBREGAT (Molins de Rei) Barcelona 1A
❒ MOLLERUSSA Lerida 1B
❒ MONFORTE Alicante 1C
❒ MONFORTE Teruel 2C
❒ MONISTROL (Monistrol de Calders) Barcelona 1A
❒ MONISTROL DE BAGES Barcelona 1A
❒ MONJOS DEL PENEDES (Santa Margariday Els Monjos) Barcelona 1A
❒ MONOVAR Alicante 1A
❒ MONT-RAL Tarragona 1B
❒ MONT-ROIG Tarragona 1A 2B
❒ MONTAGUT DE FLUVIA Gerona 1A
❒ MONTALBAN Teruel 1A
❒ MONTANANA Huesca 1A
❒ MONTBLANC Tarragona 1A 2D
❒ MONTBRIO DEL CAMP Tarragona 1A
❒ MONTCADA I REIXAC Barcelona 1A
❒ MONTCLAR Barcelona 1D
❒ MONTCORTES Lerida 1B
❒ MONTEALEGRE DEL CASTILLO Albacete 1A

❒ MONTELLA I MARTINET Lerida	1A		
❒ MONTERRUBIO DE LA SERENA Badajoz	1A		
❒ MONTESA Valencia	1A		
❒ MONTFERRI Tarragona	1A		
❒ MONTGAT Barcelona	1A		
❒ MONTIEL Ciudad Real	1A		
❒ MONTILLANA Granada	1C		
❒ MONTMANEU Barcelona	1C		
❒ MONTMANY FIGARO Barcelona	1A		
❒ MONTMELO Barcelona	1A		
❒ MONTORNES Lerida	1A		
❒ MONTORO Cordoba	2D		
❒ MONTROS Lerida	1A		
❒ MONTSENY Barcelona	1B		
❒ MONZON Huesca	1A		
❒ MORA D'EBRE (Mora de Ebro) Tarragona	1C		
❒ MORA DE RUBIELOS Teruel	1A		
❒ MORA LA NOVA Tarragona	1A		
❒ MORAL DE CALATRAVA Ciudad Real	1A		
❒ MORATALLA Murcia	1A		
❒ MOREDA Granada	1A		
❒ MORELL, EL Tarragona	1A		
❒ MORELLA Castellon	1A	2B	
❒ MORUNYS Lerida	1B		
❒ MOSQUERUELA Teruel	1A		
❒ MOTILLEJA	1E		
❒ MOTRIL Granada	2A		
❒ MOYUELA Zaragoza	2C		
❒ MULA Murcia	1A		
❒ MUNIESA Teruel	2C		
❒ MURA Barcelona	1A		
❒ MURCIA Murcia	1A	2A	
❒ MURES-ALCALA LA REAL Jaen	2C		
❒ MURLA Alicante	1A		
❒ MURO DEL ALCOY Alicante	2A		
❒ MURTAS, COJAYAR Y MECINA TEDEL Granada	1A		

Types of Emergency Money

Type	Reference #
Municipal paper	1
Private paper	2
POW paper	3
POW official metal	4
POW private metal	5
Municipal metal	6
Private metal	7
Gas tokens	8
Food; beer; konsumverein	9
Naval; military; kantine	10
Encased, unencased stamps	11
Streetcar tokens	12
Porcelain	13
World War II issues	14
Concentration, Civilian internment camps	15

Rarity grades: A, to $25; B, to $60; C, to $125; D, to $200; and E, $350

❒ NACHA Huesca	1C		
❒ NACIMIENTO Almeria	1B		
❒ NALEC (also spelled Nalech) Lerida	1A		
❒ NAQUERA Valencia	1C		
❒ NAVAHERMOSA Toledo	1C		
❒ NAVAL Huesca	2A		
❒ NAVALMORALES Toledo	1A		
❒ NAVALUCILLOS Toledo	1B		
❒ NAVARCLES Barcelona	1A		
❒ NAVAS (Castelladral) Barcelona	1A		
❒ NAVAS DE SAN JUAN Jaen	1A		
❒ NAVATA Gerona	1A		
❒ NERPIO Albacete	1A		
❒ NIJAR Almeria	1A		
❒ NOALEJO Jaen	1A	2C	
❒ NOBLEJAS Toledo	1A		
❒ NOGUERONES DE ALCAUDETE Jaen	1A		
❒ NONASPE Zaragoza	1A		
❒ NOVELDA Alicante	1A		
❒ NOVES DE SEGRE Lerida	1B		
❒ NUCIA Alicante	2C		
❒ NULES Castellon	1A		
❒ NULLES Tarragona	1A	2D	6E
❒ OCANA Toledo	1A		
❒ ODENA Barcelona	1A		
❒ OGASSA Gerona	1B		
❒ OHANES Almeria	2B		
❒ OIX Gerona	1B		
❒ OJOS Murcia	1A	2B	
❒ OLBA	1A		
❒ OLESA DE MONTSERRAT Barcelona	1A		
❒ OLESTRIA (Sidamon) Lerida	1B		
❒ OLIANA Lerida	1A		
❒ OLIVA Valencia	1A		
❒ OLLEIRA Valencia	1A		
❒ OLO Bages Barcelona	1A		
❒ OLOST DE LLUCANES Barcelona	1A		
❒ OLOT Gerona	1A	2D	6E
❒ OLUGES Lerida	1B		
❒ OLVAN Barcelona	1A		
❒ OLVENA Huesca	1D		
❒ OMELLONS, ELS Lerida	1B		
❒ OMELLS DE NA GAIA, ELS Lerida	1C		
❒ ONDA Castellon	1A		
❒ ONDARA Alicante	1A		
❒ ONIL Alicante	1A		
❒ ONTENIENTE Valencia	2A		
❒ ONTINENA Huesca	1A		
❒ ORBA Alicante	1A		
❒ ORCE Granada	1A		
❒ ORCERA Jaen	1C		
❒ ORELLANA LA VIEJA Badajoz	1C		
❒ ORGANYA Lerida	1A		
❒ ORIA Almeria	1B		
❒ ORIHUELA Alicante	1A		
❒ ORISTA Barcelona	1A		
❒ OS DE BALAGUER Lerida	1A		
❒ OSOR Gerona	1A		
❒ OSSO DE CINCA Huesca	1B		
❒ OTOS Valencia	1C		
❒ PACHECO Murcia	1A		
❒ PADUELES Almeria	1B		
❒ PAIPORTA Valencia	2B		
❒ PALAFOLLS Barcelona	1A		
❒ PALAFRUGELL Gerona	1A		
❒ PALAMOS Gerona	1A		
❒ PALAU D'ANGLESOLA Lerida	1A		

10 Centims, Parets del Valles, Spain, 2B

- ❒ PALAU SACOSTA Gerona 1A
- ❒ PALAU-SABARDERA Gerona 1D 2D
- ❒ PALAU-SOLITA (also Pallau-Solitar) Barcelona 1A
- ❒ PALAUTORDERA Barcelona 1A
- ❒ PALLARUELO DE MONEGROS Huesca 1C
- ❒ PALLEJA Barcelona 1A
- ❒ PALMA D'EBRE Tarragona 1D
- ❒ PALMA DE CERVELLO, LA Barcelona 1A
- ❒ PALMERA Valencia 1C
- ❒ PALS Gerona 1A
- ❒ PANTANO DEL CIJARES Caceres 1B
- ❒ PAPIOL Barcelona 1A
- ❒ PARDINES Gerona 1B
- ❒ PARDO, EL Madrid 1C
- ❒ PARETS DEL VALLES Barcelona 2A
- ❒ PARRAS DE CASTELLOTE Teruel 1B
- ❒ PARTALOA Almeria 1B
- ❒ PASSANANT Tarragona 1B
- ❒ PAU Gerona 1B
- ❒ PAU DE SERT (Santa Pau) Gerona 1A
- ❒ PAULS Tarragona 1B
- ❒ PEAL DE BECERRO Jaen 2A
- ❒ PECHINA Almeria 1A
- ❒ PEDERNOSO, EL Cuenca 1A
- ❒ PEDREGUER Alicante 2A
- ❒ PEDRO MARTINEZ Granada 1A
- ❒ PEDRO MUNOZ Ciudad Real 1A
- ❒ PEDROCHE Cordoba 1A
- ❒ PEDRONERAS Cuenca 1A
- ❒ PEGO Alicante 1A
- ❒ PENAGUILLA Alicante 1C
- ❒ PENALBA Huesca 1A
- ❒ PENALSORDO Badajoz 1A
- ❒ PENARROYA DE TASTAVINS Teruel 1B
- ❒ PENELLES Lerida 1C
- ❒ PENSICOLA Castellon 1A
- ❒ PERA, LA Gerona 1A
- ❒ PERAFITA Barcelona 1A
- ❒ PERAFORT Tarragona 1B
- ❒ PERAMOLA Lerida 1A
- ❒ PERELLO Tarragona 1A
- ❒ PERPETUA DE MOGUDA 1A
- ❒ PETREL Alicante 1A
- ❒ PETROLA Albacete 1A
- ❒ PI DE LLOBREGAT Barcelona 1A
- ❒ PICANA Valencia 1A
- ❒ PIEDRABUENA Ciudad Real 1A
- ❒ PIERA Barcelona 1A
- ❒ PILAR DE LA HONRADADA Alicante 2D
- ❒ PILES Valencia 1B
- ❒ PINAR Granada 1A
- ❒ PINATAR Murcia 1B 2A
- ❒ PINEDA Barcelona 1A 2D
- ❒ PINEDA DE SEGARRA (Freixenet de Segarra) Lerida 1A
- ❒ PINEDES DE LLOBREGAT (Santa Coloma de Cervello) Barcelona 1B
- ❒ PINELL Lerida 1B
- ❒ PINELL DE BRAI Tarragona 1A
- ❒ PINOSO Alicante 1A
- ❒ PINS DEL VALLES Barcelona 1A
- ❒ PIRA Tarragona 1C
- ❒ PLA DE CABRA, EL Tarragona 1A 2D
- ❒ PLA DE CADI Lerida 1A
- ❒ PLA DE TER (Santa Eugenia de Ter) Gerona 1A
- ❒ PLA DEL PENEDES, EL Barcelona 1C
- ❒ PLANA DE RIUCORP (Sant Marti de Malda) Lerida 1A
- ❒ PLANES D'HOSTOLES, LES Gerona 1A
- ❒ PLANES DE MONTSIA (Santa Barbera) Tarragona 1A
- ❒ PLANOLES Gerona 1A
- ❒ PLIEGO Murcia 1A
- ❒ PLOU Teruel 2C
- ❒ POAL Lerida 1B
- ❒ POBLA DE CIERVOLES Lerida 1A
- ❒ POBLA DE CLARAMUNT Barcelona 1A
- ❒ POBLA DE LILLET, LA Barcelona 1A
- ❒ POBLA DE MASSALUCA Tarragona 1B
- ❒ POBLA DE MONTORNES Tarragona 1A 2C
- ❒ POBLA DE MUFAMET Tarragona 1A
- ❒ POBLA DE SEGUR Lerida 1A
- ❒ POBLE DE CEDO Lerida 1D
- ❒ POBLE DEL LLIERCA (Sant Jaume de Llierca) Gerona 1A
- ❒ POBOLEDA Tarragona 2A
- ❒ POLAN Toledo 1A
- ❒ POLENINO Huesca 1A
- ❒ POLICAR Granada 1C
- ❒ POLINYA Barcelona 1A
- ❒ POLOPOS Granada 2A
- ❒ PONT D'ARMENTERA Tarragona 1B
- ❒ PONT DE SUERT Lerida 1B
- ❒ PONT DE VILOMARA, EL Barcelona 1D
- ❒ PONTONS Barcelona 1D
- ❒ PONTS Lerida 1A
- ❒ PORCUNA Jaen 2A
- ❒ PORRERA Tarragona 1A
- ❒ PORT BOU Gerona 1A
- ❒ PORT DE LA SELVA Gerona 1A
- ❒ PORTELL DE MORELLA Castellon 1B
- ❒ PORTELLA, LA Lerida 1A
- ❒ PORTELLADA, LA Teruel 1C 2C
- ❒ PORZUNA Ciudad Real 1A 2D
- ❒ POTRIES Valencia 1C
- ❒ POZO RUBIO DE SANTIAGO Cuenca 1A
- ❒ POZO-ALCON Jaen 2C
- ❒ POZO-ESTRECHO Murcia 2A
- ❒ POZOBLANCO Cordoba 1A 2A

❒ POZUELO DE CALATRAVA Ciudad Real 1A
❒ PRADELL Tarragona 1A
❒ PRADES Tarragona 1A
❒ PRAT DE COMPTE Tarragona 1B
❒ PRAT DE LLOBREGAT Barcelona 1A
❒ PRATDIP Tarragona 1B
❒ PRATS D'ANOIA (Els Prats de Rei) Barcelona 1A
❒ PRATS DE LLUCANES Barcelona 1A
❒ PREIXANA Lerida 1C
❒ PREIXENTS (A Freixens) Lerida 1A
❒ PREMIA Barcelona 1A
❒ PREMIA DE MAR Barcelona 1A
❒ PRESES, LES Gerona 1A
❒ PRIEGO Cuenca 1A
❒ PROVENCIO, EL Cuenca 1A
❒ PUEBLA DE ALMORADIEL Toledo 1A
❒ PUEBLA DE CASTRO Huesca 2B
❒ PUEBLA DE CAZALLA Sevilla 6E
❒ PUEBLA DE D. FADRIQUE Granada 1A
❒ PUEBLA DE RODA, LA Huesca 1A
❒ PUEBLA DEL DUC Valencia 1A
❒ PUEBLA LARGA Valencia 1A
❒ PUEBLA NUEVA Toledo 1C
❒ PUEBLA TORNESA Castellon 1C
❒ PUENTE DE GENAVE Jaen 1A
❒ PUERTA DE SEGURA, LA Jaen 1A
❒ PUERTO HURRACO Badajoz 1D
❒ PUERTO LAPICE Ciudad Real 1A
❒ PUERTOLAS Huesca 1B
❒ PUERTOLLANO Ciudad Real 1A
❒ PUIG (Sant Mori) Gerona 1A
❒ PUIG Valencia 1A
❒ PUIG-ALT DE TER Gerona 1A 2D
❒ PUIGCERDA Gerona 1A
❒ PUIGPELAT Tarragona 1A
❒ PUIGREIG Barcelona 1A
❒ PUIGVERD Lerida 1B
❒ PUIGVERD D'AGRAMUNT Lerida 1B
❒ PULPI Almeria 1A 2B
❒ PURCHENA Almeria 1A 2C
❒ PUZOL Valencia 1A
❒ QUERALBS Gerona 1A
❒ QUEROL Tarragona 2C
❒ QUINTANA DE LA SERENA Badajoz 1A
❒ QUINTANAR Cuenca 1A
❒ QUINTANAR DE LA ORDEN Toledo 2A
❒ RAFAL Alicante 1B
❒ RAFELBUNOL Valencia 1C
❒ RAFELCOFER Valencia 1C
❒ RAFELGUARAF Valencia 1A
❒ RAFOL DE SALEM Valencia 1C
❒ RAGOL Almeria 1C
❒ RAJADELL Barcelona 1B
❒ RAPITA DELS ALFACS, LA (Sant Carles de La Rapita) Tarragona 1A
❒ RASPAY Murcia 2C
❒ RASQUERA Tarragona 1A
❒ RAYMOT Lerida 2D
❒ REAL DE GANDIA Valencia 1A
❒ REAL DE MONTROY Valencia 1A
❒ REINOSA Santander 1D
❒ RELLINARS Barcelona 1A
❒ REQUEJO Santander 2D
❒ REQUENA Valencia 2B
❒ REUS Tarragona 1A 2D
❒ RIALP Lerida 1A
❒ RIBA, LA Tarragona 1A
❒ RIBADESELLA Asturias 1D
❒ RIBARROJA Valencia 1A
❒ RIBARROJA D'EBRE Tarragona 1A 2E
❒ RIBERA DE CARDOS Lerida 1A
❒ RIBES DE FRESER Gerona 1A
❒ RIBES DEL PENEDES (Sant pere de Ribes) Barcelona 1A
❒ RICOTE Murcia 1A
❒ RIDAURA Gerona 1A
❒ RIELLS DE MONTSENY Gerona 1C
❒ RIELLS DEL FAI Barcelona 1C
❒ RIERA DE GAIA, LA Barcelona 1B
❒ RIODEVA Teruel 1B
❒ RIOJA Almeria 2B
❒ RIONANSA Santander 1D
❒ RIPOLL Gerona 1A
❒ RIPOLL DEL VALLES (Sant Lorenc Savall) Barcelona 1A
❒ RIPOLLET Barcelona 1A
❒ RIUDARENES Gerona 1A
❒ RIUDECANYES Tarragona 1A
❒ RIUDECOLS Tarragona 1D
❒ RIUDIBITLLES Barcelona 1A
❒ RIUDOMS Tarragona 1B
❒ RIUDOR DE BAGES (Sant Fruitos de Bages) Barcelona 1A
❒ ROBRES Huesca 1B
❒ ROCA DEL VALLES Barcelona 1A
❒ ROCAFORT DE BAGES Barcelona 2D
❒ ROCAFORT DE QUERALT Tarragona 1A
❒ ROCAFORT DE VALLBONA Lerida 1A
❒ ROCALLAURA Lerida 1C
❒ RODA DE BARA Tarragona 1B
❒ RODA DE ISABENA Huesca 1C
❒ RODA DE TER Barcelona 1A
❒ RODA, LA Albacete 1A
❒ RODONYA Tarragona 1A
❒ ROJALES Alicante 1A
❒ ROMANA, LA Alicante 1A
❒ RONDA Malaga 2E
❒ ROQUES D'OSONA (Sant Marti de Sobremunt) Barcelona 1A
❒ ROQUETAS DE MAR Almeria 1A
❒ ROQUETES (Roquetas) Tarragona 1B
❒ ROSELL Castellon 1A
❒ ROSES Gerona 1A
❒ ROSES DE LLOBREGAT (Sant Feliu de Llobregat) Barcelona 1A
❒ ROSSELLO Lerida 1B
❒ ROURELL, EL Tarragona 1C
❒ RUBI Barcelona 1A 2A
❒ RUBIELOS DE MORA Teruel 1A
❒ RUBITE Granada 1B
❒ RUPIA Gerona 1C
❒ RUPIT Barcelona 1A
❒ RUS Jaen 1A
❒ SABADELL Barcelona 1A 2C
❒ SADURNI D'ANOIA Barcelona 1A
❒ SAGRA Alicante 1C
❒ SAGUNTO Valencia 1A 2A
❒ SALARDU Lerida 1C
❒ SALAS ALTAS Huesca 2B
❒ SALAS DE PALLARS Lerida 1B
❒ SALEM Valencia 1C
❒ SALINAS Alicante 2A
❒ SAL-LAVINERA D'ANOIA Barcelona 1B
❒ SALLENT Barcelona 1A

❒ SALOMO Tarragona 1B
❒ SALSADELLA Castellon 1A
❒ SALTOS DE FLIX Tarragona 1C
❒ SAMPER DE CALANDA Teruel 1A
❒ SAN CARLOS DEL VALLE Ciudad Real 1A
❒ SAN CLEMENTE Cuenca 1A
❒ SAN JAVIER Murcia 1A 2C
❒ SAN LORENZO DE CALATRAVA Ciudad Real 1A
❒ SAN MIGUEL DEL SALINAS Alicante 1A
❒ SAN RAFAEL DEL RIO Castellon 1B
❒ SANAHUJA Lerida 1A
❒ SANET Y NEGRALS Alicante 1C
❒ SANT GUIM ESTACIO (See Freixanet) Lerida
❒ SANT MARTI DEL BAS Barcelona 1C
❒ SANT POL DE MAR Barcelona 1A
❒ SANTA CREU DE XUTGLAR Barcelona 1C
❒ SANTA CRUZ Almeria 1C
❒ SANTA CRUZ DE LA ZARZA Toledo 1A
❒ SANTA CRUZ DE LOS CANAMOS Ciudad Libre 1B
❒ SANTA CRUZ DE MUDELA Ciudad Real 1A
❒ SANTA ELENA Jaen 1C
❒ SANTA EUFEMIA Cordoba 1A
❒ SANTA FE Almeria 1A
❒ SANTA LECINA Huesca 1C
❒ SANTA POLA Alicante 1A
❒ SANTANDER, PALENCIA Y BURGOS Santander 6B
❒ SANTES CREUS Tarragona 2C
❒ SANTIAGO DE LA ESPADA Jaen 1A
❒ SANTISTEBAN DEL PUERTO Jaen 1A 2B
❒ SANTORENS Huesca 1C
❒ SARDANOLA-RIPOLLET Barcelona 2A
❒ SARIENA Huesca 1A
❒ SARRAL Tarragona 1A
❒ SARRIA DE TER Gerona 1B
❒ SARRION Teruel 1A 2C
❒ SARROCA DE SEGRE Lerida 2D 6A
❒ SASSERRA Barcelona 1B
❒ SASTIGO Zaragoza 1A
❒ SAX Alicante 1A
❒ SEDAVI Valencia 1A
❒ SEGARRA DE GAIA (Santa Coloma de Queralt) Tarragona 1A 6C
❒ SEGURIES DE TER Gerona 1A
❒ SEIRA Huesca 1C
❒ SELGUA Huesca 1A
❒ SELVA DE MAR Gerona 1C
❒ SELVA DEL CAMP, LA Tarragona 1A
❒ SENA Huesca 1B
❒ SENDALAMULA-CARACOLLERA Ciudad Real 2C
❒ SENIA, LA Tarragona 1A
❒ SENTERADA Lerida 1A
❒ SENTIU, LA Lerida 1A
❒ SENTMENAT Barcelona 1A
❒ SERON Almeria 1A
❒ SEROS Lerida 1A 2D
❒ SERRA D'ALMOS Tarragona 1A
❒ SESGARRIGUES DEL PENEDES (Sant Cugat Sesgarrigues) Barcelona 2B
❒ SESGUEIOLES Barcelona 2B
❒ SESROVIRES Barcelona 1A
❒ SETLA Y MIRARROSA Alicante 1C
❒ SEU D'URGELL, LA (Seo de Urgel) Lerida 1A 2D
❒ SEVA Barcelona 1B
❒ SEVILLEJA DE LA JARA Toledo 1B
❒ SIERRO Almeria 2C
❒ SILES Jaen 2A
❒ SILS Gerona 1A
❒ SIMAT DE VALLDIGNA Valencia 1A
❒ SISANTE Cuenca 1A 2C
❒ SITGES Barcelona 1A 2E
❒ SOCOVOS Albacete 1A
❒ SOCUELLAMOS Ciudad Libre 1A
❒ SOLANA, LA Ciudad Real 1A
❒ SOLERA Jaen 1B
❒ SOLERAS, EL Lerida 1B
❒ SOLIVELLA Tarragona 2A
❒ SOLLANA Valencia 1A
❒ SOLSONA Lerida 1A
❒ SOMONTIN Almeria 1A 2C
❒ SONSECA CON CASALGORDO Toledo 1A
❒ SORBAS Almeria 1A
❒ SORT Lerida 1A
❒ SOSES Lerida 1A
❒ SUBIRATS Barcelona 1A
❒ SUDANELL Lerida 1A
❒ SUECA Valencia 1A
❒ SUNYER Lerida 1A
❒ SURIA Barcelona 1A
❒ SUSQUEDA Gerona 1B
❒ TABAL Almeria 2B
❒ TABERNAS Almeria 1A
❒ TABERNES DE VALLDIGNA Valencia 1A
❒ TAGAMANENT Barcelona 1A
❒ TALAMANCA Barcelona 2D
❒ TALARRUBIAS Badajoz 1A
❒ TAMARITE Huesca 1A 2C
❒ TARADELL Barcelona 1A
❒ TARANCON Cuenca 1E
❒ TARAZONA Albacete 2E
❒ TARRAGONA Tarragona 1A
❒ TARREGA Lerida 1A 2D
❒ TARROS Lerida 1A
❒ TEIA Barcelona 1A
❒ TERESA DE COFRENTES Valencia 1B
❒ TERMENS Lerida 1A
❒ TERRASOLA I LAVIT Barcelona 1A
❒ TERRASSA Barcelona 1A
❒ TERRASOLA I LAVIT Barcelona 1A
❒ TERRINCHES Ciudad Real 1A
❒ TEVAR Cuenca 1A
❒ TIANA Barcelona 1A
❒ TIJOLA Almeria 1A 2C
❒ TIRIG Castellon 2C
❒ TIRVIA Lerida 1B
❒ TIURANA Lerida 1C
❒ TIVENYS Tarragona 1B
❒ TIVISSA Tarragona 1A
❒ TOBARRA Albacete 1A
❒ TOBOSO, EL Toledo 1A
❒ TOMELLOSO Ciudad Real 1A
❒ TONA Barcelona 1A
❒ TORA Lerida 1A
❒ TORA DE RIUBREGOS Lerida 1A
❒ TORDERA Barcelona 1A
❒ TORELLO Barcelona 1A 2C
❒ TORLA Huesca 1C
❒ TORMS, ELS Lerida 1C

❒ TORNABOUS Lerida 1B
❒ TORRALBA DE ARAGON Huesca 1C
❒ TORRALBA DE CALATRAVA Ciudad Real 1A
❒ TORRE CARDELA Granada 1A
❒ TORRE DE CABDELLA Lerida 1E
❒ TORRE DE CLARAMUNT Barcelona 2E
❒ TORRE DE L'ESPANYOL Tarragona 1C 2D
❒ TORREBESSES Lerida 1B
❒ TORREBLANCA Castellon 1A
❒ TORREBLASCOPEDRO Jaen 1A
❒ TORRECAMPO Cordoba 1A
❒ TORRECILLA DE ALCANIZ 2C
❒ TORREDELCAMPO Jaen 2B
❒ TORREDEMBARA Tarragona 1A
❒ TORREDONJIMENO Jaen 1A
❒ TORREFARRERA Lerida 2A
❒ TORREGROSSA Lerida 1A
❒ TORRELAMEU Lerida 1A
❒ TORRELLES DE FOIX Barcelona 1A
❒ TORRELLES DE LLOBREGAT Barcelona 1A
❒ TORREMANZANAS Alicante 1C
❒ TORRENTE DE CINCA Huesca 2C
❒ TORRENUEVA Ciudad Real 1A
❒ TORREPERROGIL Jaen 1A
❒ TORRES DE ALBANCHEZ Jaen 1A
❒ TORRES DE SEGRE Lerida 1C
❒ TORRES DEL OBISPO Huesca 1C
❒ TORREVELILLA Teruel 2D
❒ TORREVIEJA Alicante 2A
❒ TORROELLA DE FLUVIA Gerona 1B
❒ TORROELLA DE MONTGRI Gerona 1B
❒ TORROJA Tarragona 1B
❒ TORTELLA Gerona 1A
❒ TORTOSA Tarragona 1A 2C
❒ TORVIZCON Granada 1A
❒ TOSES DE LA MONTANYA Gerona 1B
❒ TOSSA Gerona 1A
❒ TOTANA Murcia 1A
❒ TOUS D'ANOIA Barcelona 1A
❒ TRAGO DE NOGUERA Lerida 1A
❒ TREMP Lerida 1A
❒ TURON Guadalajara 1B
❒ TURRE Almeria 1A
❒ UBEDA Jaen 1A
❒ UGIJAR Granada 1B
❒ ULEA Murcia 1A
❒ ULEILA DEL CAMPO Almeria 1C
❒ ULLASTRELL Barcelona 1A
❒ ULLDECONA Tarragona 1A 2D
❒ ULLDEMOLINS Tarragona 1A
❒ ULTRAMORT Gerona 1B
❒ UNION, LA Murcia 1A
❒ URDA Toledo 1A
❒ URRACEL Almeria 1B
❒ URREA DE GAEN Teruel 1B
❒ URTG Gerona 1C
❒ UTIEL Valencia 1A
❒ UTRILLAS Teruel 1A
❒ VACARISSES (Vaquerisses) Barcelona 1A
❒ VALDEALGORFA Teruel 1A
❒ VALDELTORMO Teruel 1C
❒ VALDEPENAS Ciudad Real 1A 2C
❒ VALDEPENAS DE JAEN Jaen 1A
❒ VALDERROBLES Teruel 1A 2C
❒ VALENCIA Valencia 2A
❒ VALENZUELA Cordoba 2A
❒ VALENZUELA DE CALATRAVA Ciudad Real 1A
❒ VALJUNQUERA Teruel 1C
❒ VALL DE GALLINERA Alicante 1A
❒ VALL DE UXO Castellon 1A
❒ VALLALTA DEL MARESME Barcelona 1B
❒ VALLBONA D'ANOIA Barcelona 1A
❒ VALLBONA DE LOS MONGES Lerida 1B
❒ VALLCEBRE Barcelona 1A
❒ VALLCLARA Tarragona 1D
❒ VALLE DE LA SERENA Badajoz 1B
❒ VALLFLORIDA (Sant Esteve de Palautordera) Barcelona 1A
❒ VALLFOGONA DE BALAGUER Lerida 1A
❒ VALLFOGONA DE RIUCORP Tarragona 1A 2D
❒ VALLGORGUINA Barcelona 1A
❒ VALLIBONA Castellon 1A
❒ VALLMOLL Tarragona 1A
❒ VALLS Tarragona 1A
❒ VALLVERT D'URGELL (Vallvert) Lerida 1A
❒ VALOR Granada 1B
❒ VALSEQUILLO Cordoba 1B
❒ VALVERDE DEL JUCAR Cuenca 1A
❒ VANDELLOS Tarragona 1B
❒ VARA DE REY Cuenca 1B
❒ VELEFIQUE Almeria 1C
❒ VELEZ-BLANCO Almeria 1A
❒ VELEZ-RUBIO Almeria 1A
❒ VELILLA DE EBRO Zaragoza 1C
❒ VENDRELL, EL Tarragona 1A
❒ VERA Almeria 1A
❒ VERGEL Alicante 1A
❒ VERGES Gerona 1A
❒ VIATOR Almeria 1A
❒ VIC Barcelona 1A 2C
❒ VIDRERES Gerona 1A
❒ VIELLA Lerida 1A
❒ VILA DE TOLO (Sant Salvador de Tolo) Lerida 1C
❒ VILA-RODONA Tarragona 1A
❒ VILA-SANA Lerida 1A
❒ VILA-SECA DE SOLCINA Tarragona 1A
❒ VILABOI (Sant Boi de Llobregat) Barcelona 1A 2D
❒ VILADA Barcelona 1A
❒ VILADECANS Barcelona 1A 2A
❒ VILADECAVALLS Barcelona 1A
❒ VILADEMAT Gerona 1A
❒ VILADRAU Gerona 1A
❒ VILAFANT Gerona 1A
❒ VILAFRANCA DEL PENEDES Barcelona 1A 2C
❒ VILAJUIGA Gerona 1C
❒ VILALBA DELS ARCS Tarragona 1D 2D
❒ VILALLER Lerida 1B
❒ VILALLONGA DE TER Gerona 1A
❒ VILALLONGA DEL CAMP Tarragona 1A
❒ VILAMAJOR Barcelona 1A
❒ VILANANT Gerona 1A
❒ VILANOVA D'ALPIGAT Lerida 2A
❒ VILANOVA D'ESCORNALBOU Tarragona 1A
❒ VILANOVA D'ESPOIA Barcelona 2C
❒ VILANOVA DE BELLPUIG

Lerida 1A
❒ VILANOVA DE LA AGUDA Lerida 1C
❒ VILANOVA DE LA BARCA Lerida 1A 2D
❒ VILANOVA DE LA MUGA Gerona 2D
❒ VILANOVA DE MEIA Lerida 1A
❒ VILANOVA DE PRADES Tarragona 1A
❒ VILANOVA DE SAU Barcelona 1A
❒ VILANOVA DE SEGRIA Lerida 1A
❒ VILANOVA DEL VALLES Barcelona 1A
❒ VILANOVA I LA GELTRU Barcelona 1A
❒ VILAPLANA DEL CAMP Tarragona 1A
❒ VILASSAR DE DALT Barcelona 1A
❒ VILASSAR DE MAR Barcelona 1A
❒ VILATORTA Barcelona 1A
❒ VILLA DE DON FADRIQUE Toledo 1A
❒ VILLA DEL RIO Cordoba 2A
❒ VILLACANAS Toledo 1A
❒ VILLACARRILLO Jaen 1A
❒ VILLADOMPARDO Jaen 1B 2C
❒ VILLAFRANCA DE LOS CABALLEROS Toledo 1A
❒ VILLAFRANCA DEL CID Castellon 1A
❒ VILLAGARCIA DEL LLANO Cuenca 1A
❒ VILLAHERMOSA Ciudad Real 1A
❒ VILLAJOYOSA Alicante 1A
❒ VILLALBA BAJA Teruel 1C
❒ VILLALGORDO DEL JUCAR Albacete 1B
❒ VI LLALONGA Valencia 1A
❒ VILLAMANRIQUE Ciudad Real 1A
❒ VILLAMARCHANTE Valencia 1A
❒ VILLAMAYOR DE CALATRAVA Ciudad Real 1A
❒ VILLAMAYOR DE SANTIAGO Cuenca 1A
❒ VILLANUEVA Murcia 1A
❒ VILLANUEVA DE ALCAUDETE Toledo 1A
❒ VILLANUEVA DE ALCOLEA Castellon 1A
❒ VILLANUEVA DE CASTELLON Valencia 2B
❒ VILLANUEVA DE CORDOBA Cordoba 1A
❒ VILLANUEVA DE LA JARA Cuenca 1A
❒ VILLANUEVA DE LA SERENA Badajoz 1A
❒ VILLANUEVA DEL ARZOBISPO Jaen 2A
❒ VILLANUEVA DEL DUQUE Cordoba 1A
❒ VILLANUEVA LA ROJA 1D
❒ VILLAR DE LA LIBERTAD (Villar del Arzobispo) Valencia 1C
❒ VILLAR DE LOS NAVARROS Zaragoza 2C
❒ VILLAR DE OLALLA Cuenca 1C
❒ VILLARALTO Cordoba 1A
❒ VILLARGORDO Jaen 1A
❒ VILLARLUENGO Teruel 2C
❒ VILLARREAL Castellon 2B
❒ VILLARROBLEDO Albacete 1A
❒ VILLARRODRIGO Jaen 1C
❒ VILLARROYA DE LOS PINARES Teruel 1D
❒ VILLARRUBIA DE LOS OJOS Ciudad Real 1A
❒ VILLARTA Ciudad Real 1A
❒ VILLATOBAS Toledo 1A
❒ VILLAVERDE DE GUADALIMAR Albacete 1C
❒ VILLENA Alicante 2A
❒ VILLORES Castellon 1C
❒ VILOSELL Lerida 1C
❒ VILOVI D'ONYAR Gerona 1A
❒ VIMBODI Lerida 1A 2C
❒ VINAIXA Lerida 1A
❒ VINALESA Valencia 2B
❒ VINAROZ Castellon 1A
❒ VINEBRE Tarragona 1A
❒ VISO DE LOS PEDROCHES Cordoba 1A
❒ VISO DEL MARQUES Ciudad Real 1A
❒ VIVEROS Albacete 1C
❒ VOLTREGA Barcelona 1A
❒ XERTA Tarragona 1C
❒ YEBENES Toledo 1A
❒ YECLA Murcia 1A 2B
❒ YEGEN Granada 1C
❒ YEPES Toledo 1A
❒ YESTE Albacete 1A
❒ ZAIDA, LA Zaragoza 1C
❒ ZALAMEA DE LA SERENA Badajoz 1A
❒ ZARRA Valencia 2C
❒ ZARZA-CAPILLA Badajoz 1C
❒ ZORITA Castellon 2C
❒ ZURGENA Almeria 1D
❒ ZURGENA DEL RIO Almeria 2B

Types of Emergency Money

Type	Reference #
Municipal paper	1
Private paper	2
POW paper	3
POW official metal	4
POW private metal	5
Municipal metal	6
Private metal	7
Gas tokens	8
Food; beer; konsumverein	9
Naval; military; kantine	10
Encased, unencased stamps	11
Streetcar tokens	12
Porcelain	13
World War II issues	14
Concentration, Civilian internment camps	15

Rarity grades: A, to $25; B, to $60; C, to $125; D, to $200; and E, $350

SUDAN BAMAKO

❒ SUDAN BAMAKO 1B

SWEDEN GOTEBORG

❒ SWEDEN GOTEBORG 2C

SWITZERLAND

❒ HOFSTETTEN BRIENZ 1B

SYRIA

❒ SYRIA SYRIA 7B

TUNISIA GAFSA

❒ TUNISIA GAFSA 2C
❒ TUNIS 1B 2B 7B

URUGUAY

❒ URUGUAY URUGUAY 11B

YUGOSLAVIA

❒ YUGOSLAVIA BASKO 1B
❒ BEOGRAD (Belgrad) 1A
❒ BJELOVAR 14A
❒ BROA 1A
❒ CACAK 14C
❒ DUBROVNIK 8B
❒ FIUME (Rijeka) 1C
❒ GORIZIA 14B
❒ HOMOLJSKOG 1A
❒ IDRIA (Idrija) 1B
❒ ISTRIA (Pola) 1A
❒ JASENICKOG 1B
❒ KANAL 1B
❒ KARLOVAC (Karlstadt) 1A
❒ KRAS 1A
❒ LAIBACH (Ljubljana) 1B 14B
❒ LUZNICKOG 1A
❒ MARIBOR (Marburg/Drau) 1A 3B
❒ MONFALCONE 14B
❒ MORAVSKOG (Moravskog-Nis, Morava) 1B
❒ NIS (Nish) Serbia 1B
❒ OSIJEK 1A
❒ POZAREVACKOG (Pozarevac) 1B
❒ POZEGA 14A
❒ PULA 14E
❒ RAB (Rabu, Arbe) 15C
❒ SAREJEVO (Serajevo) 1A 2B
❒ SPLIT (Spalto, Spljet) 1B
❒ STAJERSKA 14A
❒ UETNKE-CETINJE Montenegro 14A
❒ VAROSKI-BEOGRAD (Varoski-Belgrade) 1A
❒ VIPAVSKO 14B
❒ ZAGREB (Agram) 1A 14A
❒ ZARA Dalmai 1B

Alphabetical Listing of Issuing Cities

A

❒ AABENRAA (Abenraa, Apenrada) Den 1 2 11 12
❒ AABYHOEJ Den 11
❒ AACHEN Rheinland Ger 1 2 3 4 5 6 7 9 11 12 14
❒ AALBORG Den 11 12
❒ AALEN-BOPFINGEN/ EGER Baden-Wuerttemberg Ger 14
❒ AALEN/ KOCHER Wuerttemberg Ger 1 2 6 7 14
❒ AALST (Alost) East Flanders Bel 1
❒ AALST-HERZELE East Flanders Bel 1
❒ AARHUS Den 12
❒ ABABUJ Teruel Spa 1
❒ ABAKAN (Abakanskij, Ust-Abanskoye) Rus 1
❒ ABANCOURT Nord Fan 1
❒ ABANILLA Murcia Spa 1
❒ ABARAN Murcia Spa 1
❒ ABBACH/ DONAU (Bad Abbach) Bayern Ger 7
❒ ABBEVILLE Somme Fan 1
❒ ABEE Liege Bel 1
❒ ABELVAER Nor 14
❒ ABENOJAR Ciudad Real Spa 1
❒ ABENSBERG/ ABENS Bayern Ger 1 6
❒ ABETZBERG NO Aus 1
❒ ABLA Almeria Spa 1
❒ ABRANTES Santarem Por 1 2 14
❒ ABRAU-DYURSA Rus 1
❒ ABRERA Barcelona Spa 1
❒ ABSCON Nord Fan 1
❒ ABSTETTEN NO Aus 1
❒ ABTENAU Salzburg Aus 1
❒ ACH OO Aus 2
❒ ACHERN/ ACHERN Baden Ger 1 2
❒ ACHERY Aisne Fan 1
❒ ACHEVILLE Pas de Calais Fan 1
❒ ACHIM Hannover Ger 1
❒ ACHINSK (Atchinsk) Rus 1 3
❒ ACHTARSKAJA (Akhtari, Axtarskaja, Primorske-Akhtarsk) Rus 1
❒ ACQUAVIVA DELLE FONTI Bari, Puglia Ita 3
❒ ACQUI (Ovada, Alessandria, Piemonte) Ita 3
❒ ADAMOS (Adamov) Siebenbuergen Hun 1
❒ ADAMUZ Cordoba Spa 1 2
❒ ADELNAU (Odolanow) Posen Ger 1
❒ ADELSHEIM Baden Ger 1 6
❒ ADENAU Rheinland Ger 1
❒ ADERNO (Catania) Ita 3
❒ ADERNO Sicilia Ita 3
❒ ADLER Ger 3 4
❒ ADLWANG OO Aus 1
❒ ADMONT Steiermark Aus 1
❒ ADOLFSHUETTE Hessen-Nassau Ger 1 7
❒ ADORF/ VOGTLAND Sachsen Ger 1 2 14
❒ ADRA Almeria Spa 1
❒ ADZANETA Castellon Spa 1
❒ AELBEKE West Flanders Bel 1
❒ AELST Limbourg Bel 1
❒ AELTRE East Flanders Bel 1
❒ AERTRYCKE West Flanders Bel 10
❒ AFFREVILLE (Khemis Miliana) Alg 1
❒ AFJORD Nor 14
❒ AFLENZ Steiermark Aus 1
❒ AGATHARIED Bayern Ger 6
❒ AGEN Lot et Garonne Fan 1 2 3
❒ AGEN-ALLIANCE Lot-et-Garonne Fan 1
❒ AGEN-RUCHE Lot-et-Garonne Fan 1
❒ AGEN-STE L'AGENOISE Lot-et-Garonne Fan 1
❒ AGER Lerida Spa 1
❒ AGGSBACH NO Aus 1
❒ AGNANO-TERME Napoli Ita 3
❒ AGNETENDORF/ RIESENGEBIRGE (Jagniatkow) Schiesien Ger 1
❒ AGRAMON Albacete Spa 2
❒ AGRAMUNT Lerida Spa 1
❒ AGRES Alicante Spa 1
❒ AGUAVIVA Teruel Spa 2
❒ AGUDO Ciudad Real Spa 1
❒ AGUIAR DA BEIRA Guarda Por 1 2
❒ AGUILAR DE SEGARRA Barcelona Spa 1
❒ AGUILAR DEL ALFAMBRA Teruel Spa 1
❒ AGUILAS Murcia Spa 1 2
❒ AGUILLANA Gerona Spa 1
❒ AGULLENTE Valencia Spa 1
❒ AHLBECK Pommern Ger 1 8
❒ AHLEN/ WERSE Westfalen Ger 1 2 5 6
❒ AHMEDNAGAR Maharashtra Ind 15
❒ AHRENSBOEK Oldenburg-Eutin Ger 1
❒ AHRWEILER & ADENAU Rheinland Ger 1
❒ AHRWEILER/ AHR Rheinland Ger 1 6 7
❒ AIBLING/ BAD Bayern Ger 1 6
❒ AICH Kaernten Aus 1
❒ AICH OO Aus 1
❒ AICHACH/ PAAR Bayern Ger 2
❒ AICHKIRCHEN OO Aus 1
❒ AIDENBACH Bayern Ger 1 7
❒ AIGEN OO Aus 1
❒ AIGEN Salzburg Aus 1
❒ AIGEN Steiermark Aus 1
❒ AIGES-VIVES Gard Fan 6
❒ AIGNES Haute Garonne Fan 1
❒ AIGREFEUILLE D'AUNIS Charente Inf Fan 2
❒ AIGUAMURCIA Tarragona Spa 1
❒ AIGUES TOSSES DEL LLOBREGAT (Sant Andreu de la Barca) Barcelona Spa 1
❒ AIGUESBONES (Sant Quinten de Mediona) Barcelona Spa 1
❒ AIGUESBONES DE MONTBUI (Santa Margarida de Montbui) Barcelona Spa 1
❒ AIGUFREDA Barcelona Spa 1
❒ AIGUILLON Lot-et-Garonne Fan 2
❒ AIGUMURCIA Tarragona Spa 1
❒ AINSA Huesca Spa 2
❒ AISEAU Hainaut Bel 1
❒ AISNE-ARDENNES-MARNE Fan 1 2
❒ AISNE-ET-ARDENNES Fan 1
❒ AISONVILLE ET BERNOVILLE Fan 1
❒ AISTAIG/ OBERNDORF Wuerttemberg Ger 7
❒ AISTERSHEIM OO Aus 1
❒ AISTHOFEN OO Aus 1
❒ AITONA Lerida Spa 1
❒ AIX Nord Fan 1 7
❒ AIX LA PROVENCE Ita 14
❒ AIX-EN-PROVENCE Bouches du Rhone Fan 2 6 7
❒ AIX-LES-BAINS Savoie Fan 1
❒ AJACCIO Corse Fan 7
❒ AJACCIO ET BASTIA Corse Fan 1
❒ AJOFRIN Toledo Spa 1
❒ AKEN/ ELBE (Acken) Provinz Sachsen Ger 1
❒ AKMOLINSK Rus 1
❒ AKUTIKHA Rus 1
❒ ALACON Teruel Spa 1
❒ ALAINCOURT Aisne Fan 1
❒ ALAINCOURT-BERTHENICOURT Aisne Fan 1
❒ ALAIS (Ales) Gard Fan 1 2 7
❒ ALAMILLO Ciudad Real Spa 1
❒ ALANDROAL Evora Por 1 2
❒ ALARCON Cuenca Spa 1
❒ ALBA DEL VALLES (Sant Fost de Campsentelles) Barcelona Spa 1
❒ ALBACETE Albacete Spa 1 2 12
❒ ALBADALEJO Ciudad Real Spa 1
❒ ALBAGES Lerida Spa 1
❒ ALBAIDA Valencia Spa 1
❒ ALBALAT DE LA RIBERA Valencia Spa 1
❒ ALBALAT DE TARONCHERS Valencia Spa 1
❒ ALBALATE DE CINCA Huesca Spa 1
❒ ALBALATE LUCHADOR Teruel Spa 1
❒ ALBALATILLO Huesca Spa 2
❒ ALBANCHEZ Almeria Spa 1

❒ ALBATARRECH Lerida Spa 1
❒ ALBATERA Alicante Spa 1
❒ ALBELDA Huesca Spa 1
❒ ALBENTOSA Teruel Spa 1
❒ ALBERGARIA Por 2
❒ ALBERIQUE Valencia Spa 2
❒ ALBERNDORF OO Aus 1
❒ ALBERSDORF, BAD Schleswig-Holstein Ger 1
❒ ALBERSWEILER Pfalz Ger 7
❒ ALBERT Somme Fan 2 3 7
❒ ALBESA Lerida Spa 1
❒ ALBEVILLE Somme Fan 1
❒ ALBI Tarn Fan 1 2 6 7
❒ ALBI-FARENC Tarn Fan 1
❒ ALBI-FERRET Tarn Fan 1
❒ ALBI-FOURNIALES Tarn Fan 1
❒ ALBI-ROBERT Tarn Fan 1
❒ ALBI, L'Lerida Spa 1
❒ ALBIOL, L'Tarragona Spa 1
❒ ALBLASSERDAM South Holland Net 14
❒ ALBOCACER Castellon Spa 1
❒ ALBOLODUY Almeria Spa 1
❒ ALBONDON Granada Spa 1
❒ ALBONS Gerona Spa 1
❒ ALBOX Almeria Spa 1
❒ ALBUDEITE Murcia Spa 1
❒ ALBUFEIRA Faro Por 1 2
❒ ALBUNOL Granada Spa 1
❒ ALCACER DO SAL Setubal Por 1 2
❒ ALCALA DE CHIVERT Castellon Spa 1
❒ ALCALA DE LA SELVA Teruel Spa 2
❒ ALCALA DEL JUCAR Albacete Spa 1
❒ ALCALHALI Alicante Spa 1
❒ ALCAMPEL Huesca Spa 1 2
❒ ALCANAR Tarragona Spa 1
❒ ALCANENA Santarem Por 2
❒ ALCANIZ Teruel Spa 1
❒ ALCANO Lerida Spa 1
❒ ALCANTARA DEL JUCAR Valencia Spa 1
❒ ALCARACEJOS Cordoba Spa 1
❒ ALCARRAS Lerida Spa 1
❒ ALCAUDETE Jaen Spa 1
❒ ALCAZARES, LOS Murcia Spa 1
❒ ALCHEL Fan 2
❒ ALCIRA Valencia Spa 1
❒ ALCOBA Ciudad Real Spa 1
❒ ALCOBACA Leiria Por 1 2
❒ ALCOCHETE Setubal Por 1
❒ ALCOLEA Almeria Spa 1
❒ ALCOLEA DE CINCA Huesca Spa 1 2
❒ ALCOLECHA Alicante Spa 1
❒ ALCOLETGE Lerida Spa 1
❒ ALCONTAR Almeria Spa 1
❒ ALCORIZA Teruel Spa 2
❒ ALCOUTIM Faro Por 2
❒ ALCOVER Tarragona Spa 1
❒ ALCOY Alicante Spa 1
❒ ALCUBIERE Huesca Spa 2
❒ ALCUBLAS Valencia Spa 1
❒ ALCUDIA DE CARLET Valencia Spa 1
❒ ALCUDIA DE CRESPINS Valencia Spa 1
❒ ALDAYA Valencia Spa 1
❒ ALDEA DE SAN BENITO Cuidad Real Spa 1
❒ ALDEA DEL REY (Cuidad Real) Spa 1
❒ ALDEANUEVA DE BARRARROYA Toledo Spa 1
❒ ALDEGALEGA Setubal Por 1
❒ ALDEIRE Granada Spa 1
❒ ALDEKERK Rheinland Ger 1
❒ ALDI FREDDO Ita 3
❒ ALDOVER Tarragona Spa 1
❒ ALELLA Barcelona Spa 1
❒ ALENCON Orne Fan 1 7
❒ ALENCON ET FLEURS Orne Fan 1
❒ ALENQUER Lisboa Por 2
❒ ALENYA Pyrenees-Orientales Fan 1 2
❒ ALESSANDRIA Piemonte Ita 3
❒ ALESUND Nor 14
❒ ALET LES BAINES Aude Fan 1 2
❒ ALEXANDRIA (Alexandrija) Rus 1 14
❒ ALEXANDROPOL (Leninaken) Rus 1
❒ ALEXANDROV-KUJAWSKI Rus 1
❒ ALEXANDROVSK (Central Russia) Rus 1
❒ ALEXANDROVSK (Olexandrivsk) Rus 1
❒ ALEXANDROVSK (Ukraine) Rus 1
❒ ALEXANDROVSK-GRUSHEVSKI (Shachty, Shakhty) Rus 1
❒ ALEXANDROVSK-SAKHALINSKI Rus 1
❒ ALEXANDROVSKOI Rus 1
❒ ALEXEJEWSKOJE (Alexeevsk) Rus 1
❒ ALFAFARA Alicante Spa 1
❒ ALFAMBRA Teruel Spa 2
❒ ALFANDEGA DA FE Braganca Por 1
❒ ALFARA Tarragona Spa 1
❒ ALFARRAS Lerida Spa 1
❒ ALFAZ DEL PI Alicante Spa 1
❒ ALFELD/ LEINE Hannover Ger 1 2 6 7 11
❒ ALFES Lerida Spa 1
❒ ALFONDEGUILLA Castellon Spa 1
❒ ALFORJA Tarragona Spa 1
❒ ALGAR DE PALANCIA Valencia Spa 1
❒ ALGARD Nor 14
❒ ALGEMESI Valencia Spa 1
❒ ALGER Alg 1 2 6 7 11 12
❒ ALGINET Valencia Spa 2
❒ ALGRINGEN (Algrange) Lothringen Ger 6
❒ ALGUAIRE Lerida Spa 1
❒ ALGUENA Alicante Spa 1
❒ ALHABIA Almeria Spa 1
❒ ALHAMA DE MURCIA Murcia Spa 1
❒ ALHAMA DE SALMERON Almeria Spa 1
❒ ALHAMBRA Ciudad Real Spa 1
❒ ALIAGA Teruel Spa 1
❒ ALICANTE Alicante Spa 1
❒ ALIJO Vila Real Por 2
❒ ALIO Tarragona Spa 1
❒ ALJEZUR Faro Por 1
❒ ALJUSTREL Beja Por 1 2
❒ ALKMAAR North Holland Net 8
❒ ALKOVEN OO Aus 1
❒ ALLAND NO Aus 1
❒ ALLARMONT Vosges Fan 1
❒ ALLEMAND Aisne Fan 1
❒ ALLENDORF-SOODEN/ WERRA Hessen Nassau Ger 2
❒ ALLENDORF/ WERRA Hessen-Nassau Ger 1
❒ ALLENSTEIN/ ALLE (Olsztyn) Ostpreussen Ger 1 2 12
❒ ALLENTSTEIG NO Aus 1
❒ ALLEPUZ Teruel Spa 1
❒ ALLERHEILIGEN OO Aus 1
❒ ALLERSBERG Bayern Ger 7
❒ ALLEVARD-FORGES-ULTENBACH Isere Fan 1
❒ ALLOZA Teruel Spa 1 2
❒ ALLSTEDT (Allstaedt) Sachsen-Wei-Eisen Ger 1 2 6
❒ ALM-ATA (Vyerny) Rus 1
❒ ALMACELLES Lerida Spa 1
❒ ALMADA Setubal Por 1 2
❒ ALMADEN Ciudad Real Spa 1 2
❒ ALMADENEJOS Ciudad Real Spa 1
❒ ALMAGRO Ciudad Real Spa 1
❒ ALMANSA Albacete Spa 1
❒ ALMASFUEZITOE Hun 2
❒ ALMATRET Lerida Spa 1
❒ ALMEDINA Ciudad Real Spa 1
❒ ALMEIDA Guarda Por 1
❒ ALMEIRIM Santarem Por 1
❒ ALMENAR Lerida Spa 1
❒ ALMERIA Almeria Spa 1 2
❒ ALMKERK North Brabant Net 14
❒ ALMODOVAR Beia Por 1
❒ ALMODOVER DEL CAMPO Ciudad Real Spa 2
❒ ALMOLDA, LA Zaragoza Spa 1
❒ ALMONACID Toledo Spa 1
❒ ALMONACID DE LA CUBA Zaragoza Spa 2
❒ ALMORADI Alicante Spa 1
❒ ALMOSTER Tarragona Spa 1
❒ ALMSICK Westfalen Ger 1 3 4 5
❒ ALMUNIA DE CINCA Zaragoza Spa 2
❒ ALMURADIEL Ciudad Real Spa 1
❒ ALMUSAFES Valencia Spa 1
❒ ALORA Malaga Spa 2
❒ ALP Gerona Spa 1
❒ ALPAIRCA Santarem Por 1
❒ ALPERA Albacete Spa 1
❒ ALPHEN/ RIJN South Holland Net 8
❒ ALPIRSBACH/ KINZIG Wuerttemberg Ger 1 2
❒ ALSDORF Rheinland Ger 1 2 3 5 7
❒ ALSENBORN Pfalz Ger 1
❒ ALSFELD/ SCHWALM Hessen Ger 1 6
❒ ALSODUX Almeria Spa 1
❒ ALT ROHLAU (Stara Role) Cze 2
❒ ALT-GAARZ (Alt-Garz) Mecklenburg-Schwerin Ger 2
❒ ALT-NEISSBACH/ GLATZ Schiesien Ger 2
❒ ALT-PFIRT Elsass Ger 1
❒ ALT-RAHLSTEDT Schleswig-Holstein Ger 1 2
❒ ALT-STRELITZ Mecklenburg-Strelitz Ger 2

❒ ALTA OO Aus 1
❒ ALTAFULLA Tarragona Spa 1
❒ ALTAIST OO Aus 1
❒ ALTAS Rus 1
❒ ALTDAMM/ PLOENE (Szczecin Dabie) Pommern Ger 1 4
❒ ALTDORF/ SCHWARZACH Bayern Ger 6 7
❒ ALTEN Sachsen Ger 7
❒ ALTEN-GRABOW Provinz Sachsen Ger 3
❒ ALTEN-UND FRAUEN-BREITUNGEN Sachsen-Meiningen Ger 1
❒ ALTENAU/ HARZ Hannover Ger 1 3
❒ ALTENBACH Elsass Ger 1
❒ ALTENBERG Bel 14
❒ ALTENBERG NO Aus 2
❒ ALTENBERG OO Aus 1
❒ ALTENBERG/ ERZGEBIRGE Sachsen Ger 1 5
❒ ALTENBURG Sachsen-Altenburg Ger 1 2 6 8 12 13
❒ ALTENBURG-KOTTERITZ Thueringen Ger 2
❒ ALTENDERNE Westfalen Ger 3 4
❒ ALTENDORF/ RUHR Westfalen Ger 3
❒ ALTENESSEN Rheinland Ger 1 3
❒ ALTENFELD Thueringia Ger 2 9
❒ ALTENFELDEN OO Aus 1
❒ ALTENGLAN Pfalz Ger 1
❒ ALTENKIRCHEN & WALDBROEL Rheinland Ger 1
❒ ALTENKIRCHEN/ WIED Rheinland Ger 1
❒ ALTENKUNDSTADT Bayern Ger 1
❒ ALTENMARKT Steiermark Aus 1
❒ ALTENMARKT IM PONGAU Salzburg Aus 1
❒ ALTENMARKT/ TRIESTING NO Aus 1
❒ ALTENMARKT/ YSPER NO Aus 1
❒ ALTENSTEIG/ NAGOLD (Alltenstaig) Wuerttemberg Ger 1 2
❒ ALTENVOERDE (Ennepetal) Westfalen Ger 2
❒ ALTENWERDER U. FINKENWAERDER Hamburg Ger 1
❒ ALTENWIED Rheinland Ger 2
❒ ALTER DO CHAO Portalegre Por 1
❒ ALTFELDE (Stare Pole) Westpreussen Ger 2
❒ ALTHAIN/ DITTERSBACH Schlesien Ger 1 2
❒ ALTHANN-DUMENIL Haut-Rhin Fan 1
❒ ALTHANN-PIENOZ Haut-Rhin Fan 1
❒ ALTHEIDE, BAD (Polanica-Zdroj) Schlesien Ger 1 2
❒ ALTHEIM OO Aus 1
❒ ALTKIRCH Elsass Ger 2
❒ ALTKLOSTER/ ESTE (Buxtehude) Hannover Ger 1 2
❒ ALTLENGBACH NO Aus 1
❒ ALTMITTWEIDA Sachsen Ger 1
❒ ALTMORSCHEN Hesse-Nassau Ger 1
❒ ALTMUENSTER OO Aus 1
❒ ALTOETTING Bayern Ger 1
❒ ALTONA/ ELBE Schleswig-Holstein Ger 1 2 3 7 8 9 14
❒ ALTORRICON Huesca Spa 1 2
❒ ALTPORT Haut-Rhin Fan 1
❒ ALTSCHWENDT OO Aus 1
❒ ALTTHANN Elsass Ger 1
❒ ALTTHANN Haut Rhin Fan 1
❒ ALTUSRIED Bayern Ger 1 2 14
❒ ALTWASSER (Szczawnica Zdroj) Schlesien Ger 1 2 3 5
❒ ALUPKA (Aloupka) Rus 1
❒ ALUSIAK Ger 3
❒ ALVAIAZERE Leiria Por 1
❒ ALVITO Beja Por 1 2
❒ ALYATY Rus 1
❒ ALZENAU/ UNTERFRANKEN Bayern Ger 1
❒ ALZEY/ SELZ Hessen Ger 1 6 8 11
❒ ALZONNE Aude Fan 1
❒ AMARANTE Porto Por 2
❒ AMAY Liege Bel 1
❒ AMBERG/ VILS Bayern Ger 1 2 4 5 6 7 8 9 10 13 12
❒ AMBERIEU Ain Fan 10
❒ AMBOISE Indre et Loir Fan 7
❒ AMEL (Ambleve) Liege Bel 14
❒ AMELIA Ita 3
❒ AMELIE-LES-BAINS Pyrenees Orientales Fan 2
❒ AMELINGHAUSEN Niedersachsen Ger 1 14
❒ AMER Gerona Spa 1
❒ AMERIKA/ MULDE Sachsen Ger 2
❒ AMERSFOORT Utrecht Net 15
❒ AMETLLA DE MAR Tarragona Spa 1
❒ AMETLLA DE MEROLA Barcelona Spa 1
❒ AMETLLA DEL VALLES Barcelona Spa 6
❒ AMIENS Somme Fan 1 2 3 6 7 12
❒ AMMENDORF Provinz Sachsen Ger 2
❒ AMMERSCHWEIGER Elsass Ger 1
❒ AMMERSCHWIR Haut-Rhin Fan 1 2
❒ AMOENEBURG Hessen-Nassau Ger 1
❒ AMORBACH/ MUDAU Bayern Ger 1 2
❒ AMOUGIES East Flanders Bel 1
❒ AMPFLWANG OO Aus 1
❒ AMPLEPIUS Rhone Fan 7
❒ AMPOLLA Tarragona Spa 1
❒ AMPOSTA Tarragona Spa 1
❒ AMPSIN Liege Bel 1 14
❒ AMSTENRADE Limburg Net 14
❒ AMSTERDAM North Holland Net 1 2 8
❒ AMSTETTEN NO Aus 1 2
❒ ANADIA Aveiro Por 1
❒ ANANIEV (Ananyev, Ananiev, Ananjew) Rus 1
❒ ANAPA Rus 1
❒ ANDENNE Namur Bel 1 2
❒ ANDERBECK Provinz Sachsen Ger 2
❒ ANDERLUES Hainaut Bel 2
❒ ANDERNACH Rheinland Ger 1 2
❒ ANDERNACH & MAYEN Rheinland Ger 1
❒ ANDERSDORF (Przysieczna) Schlesien Ger 7
❒ ANDIJAN Rus 1
❒ ANDISHAN (Andizhan) Rus 1
❒ ANDORF OO Aus 1
❒ ANDORRA Teruel Spa 2
❒ ANDREASBERG Westfalen Ger 2
❒ ANDREYEV (Jedrzejow) Rus 1
❒ ANDRICHSFURT OO Aus 1
❒ ANDRIMONT Liege Bel 1
❒ ANDRYCHOW Galicia Rpl 2
❒ ANDUJAR Jaen Spa 2
❒ ANGARA Rus 1
❒ ANGELRODA Sachsen-Weimar Ger 9
❒ ANGERBURG/ ANGERAP (Wegorzewo) Ostpreussen Ger 1
❒ ANGERE Rus 1
❒ ANGERMUENDE Brandenburg Ger 1 2
❒ ANGERMUND Rheinland Ger 1
❒ ANGERS Maine et Loire Fan 1 11 14
❒ ANGERSBERG OO Aus 1
❒ ANGLES Gerona Spa 1
❒ ANGLEUR Liege Bel 1 2
❒ ANGOULEME Charente Fan 1 2 7 10 11
❒ ANGUILCOURT-LE-PORT Aisne Fan 1
❒ ANHALT Anhalt Ger 1 6
❒ ANHIERS Nord Fan 1
❒ ANIANE-BOULANGE Herault Fan 1
❒ ANICHE Nord Fan 1 2
❒ ANIF Salzburg Aus 1
❒ ANIZY-LE-CHATEAU Aisne Fan 1
❒ ANKLAM/ PEENE (Anclam) Pommern Ger 1 2 7
❒ ANNA Valencia Spa 1
❒ ANNA PAULOWNA North Holland Net 14
❒ ANNABERG NO Aus 1
❒ ANNABERG & MARIENBERG Sachsen Ger 1
❒ ANNABERG/ ERZGEBIRGE Sachsen Ger 1 7 8
❒ ANNABURG Provinz Sachsen Ger 1 7 8
❒ ANNAHUETTE Brandenburg Ger 2 5 7
❒ ANNECY Haute Savoie Fan 1 7 10
❒ ANNEMASSE Haute Savoie Fan 2 7
❒ ANNEMASSE-BAUD-CHAR Haute-Savoie Fan 1
❒ ANNEN Westfalen Ger 1 2 7
❒ ANNEUX Nord Fan 1
❒ ANNOIS Aisne Fan 1
❒ ANNONAY Ardeche Fan 1 7
❒ ANNWEILER/ QUEICH Pfalz Ger 1 6 7
❒ ANOR Nord Fan 1 7
❒ ANRATH Rheinland Ger 1 2

❒ ANSBACH/ REZAT (Anspach) Bayern Ger 1 2 7 8 9
❒ ANSEGHEM West Flanders Bel 1
❒ ANSEREMME Namur Bel 1
❒ ANSEROEUL Hainaut Bel 1
❒ ANSFELDEN OO Aus 1
❒ ANSPRUNG Sachsen Ger 1
❒ ANTALDES Hun 1
❒ ANTALOCZ (Antalovci) Cze 2
❒ ANTALOCZ Hun 3
❒ ANTAS Almeria Spa 1
❒ ANTFELD Westfalen Ger 2
❒ ANTHEIT Liege Bel 1
❒ ANTHERING Salzburg Aus 1
❒ ANTHIERS Nord Fan 1
❒ ANTIESENHOFEN OO Aus 1
❒ ANTOING Hainaut Bel 1
❒ ANTONIENHUETTE (Huta Antonia; Wirek) Schlesien Ger 1 2
❒ ANTONINI Rus 1
❒ ANTONIOW Poland Ger 1
❒ ANTONY Seine Fan 1
❒ ANTWERP (Antwerpen, Anvers) Antwerp Bel 1 2 11
❒ ANUCHINO (Anoutchino, Anutchino) Rus 1
❒ ANVAING Hainaut Bel 2
❒ ANZBACH NO Aus 1
❒ ANZHERO-SUDZHENSK (Anzhersky, Anscher Grube) Rus 1
❒ ANZIN Nord Fan 1
❒ APELDOORN Gelderland Net 14 1
❒ APENRADE (Abenraa, Denmark) Schleswig-Holstein Ger 1 2 7
❒ APLERBECK/ DORTMUND Westfalen Ge 2 3
❒ APOLDA Sachsen-Weimar-Eisenach Ger 1 2 6 8
❒ APPELN Hannover Ger 1
❒ APPEN Schleswig-Holstein Ger 1
❒ APPENWEIER Baden Ger 2
❒ APPILLY Fan 1
❒ AQUILA Abruzzo Ita 3
❒ ARAD Hun 1
❒ ARAD Rom 1 2
❒ ARAHAL Sevilla Spa 6
❒ ARBE Ita 3 14
❒ ARBECA Lerida Spa 1
❒ ARBING OO Aus 1
❒ ARBOC Tarragona Spa 1
❒ ARBRE (Aubres) Hainaut Bel 1
❒ ARBUCIES Gerona Spa 1
❒ ARC-AINIERES Hainaut Bel 1
❒ ARC-LES-GRAY Fan 11
❒ ARCHANGEL (Arckangel) Rus 1 2
❒ ARCHENA Murcia Spa 1
❒ ARCHES Vosges Fan 1 2
❒ ARCHON Ardennes Fan 1
❒ ARCHS Lerida Spa 1
❒ ARCHSUM/ SYLT Schleswig-Holstein Ge 1
❒ ARCOS DE VALDEVEZ Viana do Castelo Por 1 2
❒ ARCUEIL Val de Marne Fan 7 11
❒ ARCUEIL-CACHAN Seine Fan 7 9
❒ ARDAGGER NO Aus 1
❒ ARDOYE West Flanders Bel 1
❒ AREN Huesca Spa 1
❒ ARENAS DE SAN JUAN Ciudad Real Spa 1
❒ ARENDSEE Mecklenburg-Schwerin Ger 2
❒ ARENS DE LLEDO Teruel Spa 1
❒ ARENYS DE MAR Barcelona Spa 1 6
❒ ARENYS DE MUNT Barcelona Spa 1
❒ AREZZO Ita 3 14
❒ ARGAMASILLA DE ALBA Ciudad Real Spa 1
❒ ARGELAGUER Gerona Spa 1
❒ ARGENSOLA Barcelona Spa 1
❒ ARGENTAN Orne Fan 11
❒ ARGENTERA Tarragona Spa 1
❒ ARGENTIERE-LA-BASSEE Hautes Alps Fan 7
❒ ARGENTONA Barcelona Spa 1
❒ ARIEGE Ariege Fan 1
❒ ARJONA Jaen Spa 2
❒ ARJONILLA Jaen Spa 1
❒ ARLEN Baden Ger 2 9
❒ ARLES (Arelate) Bouches du Rhone Fan 2 7
❒ ARLES-S/ TECH Pyrennees Orientales Fan 2
❒ ARLEUX Nord Fan 1
❒ ARMAMAR Viseu Por 2
❒ ARMAVIR Rus 1 2
❒ ARMEE AMERICAINE EN Fan 10
❒ ARMEE-LES-FOYERS du Soldat Fan 10
❒ ARNES Tarragona Spa 1
❒ ARNEY Liege Bel 1
❒ ARNHEIM Gelderland Net 8
❒ ARNSBERG (Podgorze) Schlesien Ger 2
❒ ARNSBERG (Arensberg) Westfalen Ger 1 2 6
❒ ARNSTADT/ GERA Thueringen Ger 1 2 6 8 11
❒ ARNSTORF Bayern Ger 2
❒ ARNSWALDE Brandenburg Ger 12
❒ AROLSEN Waldeck Ger 1
❒ AROUCA Aveiro Por 1 2
❒ ARQUATA SCRIVIA Alessandria Genova Ita 3 14
❒ ARRAIOLOS Evora Por 1 2
❒ ARRAS Pas de Calais Fan 1 3 11
❒ ARRONCHES Portalegre Por 1 2
❒ ARRUDA DOS VINHOS Lisboa Por 2
❒ ARSEGUEL Lerida Spa 1
❒ ARSIMONT Namur Bel 1
❒ ARTEMOVSK Rus 1
❒ ARTEMOVSK-RUDNIK (Bachmut Artemovsk, Bakhmout) Rus 1
❒ ARTEMPS Aisne Fan 1
❒ ARTERN Provinz Sachsen Ger 1 2 6
❒ ARTES Barcelona Spa 1
❒ ARTESA DE LLEIDA Lerida Spa 1
❒ ARTESA DE SERGE Lerida Spa 1
❒ ARTSTETTEN NO Aus 1
❒ ARVANT Haute Loire Fan 7
❒ ARVILLE Luxembourg Bel 1
❒ ARVOINGT Nord Fan 1
❒ ARYES (Orzysz) Ostpreussen Ger 1 3 8
❒ ARZAMAS Rus 1
❒ ARZBERG Bayern Ger 1 2 6 7 9
❒ ASCH (As) Boehmen Cze 1 2 9
❒ ASCHACH OO Aus 1
❒ ASCHACH Steyr Aus 1
❒ ASCHACH/ DONAU OO Aus 1 3
❒ ASCHAFFENBURG/ MAIN Bayern Ger 1 2 6 7 8
❒ ASCHBACH NO Aus 1
❒ ASCHBACH OO Aus 1
❒ ASCHERSLEBEN/ EINE Provinz Sachsen Ger 1 2 7 8 9 11
❒ ASCO Tarragona Spa 1
❒ ASCOLI PICENO Ita 14
❒ ASHKHABAD (Askhabad, Aschabad, Poltoratsk) Rus 1
❒ ASINARA Sardinia Ita 3
❒ ASKIM Nor 14
❒ ASNIERES Seine Fan 2 3
❒ ASPA Lerida Spa 1
❒ ASPACH OO Aus 1
❒ ASPE Alicante Spa 1
❒ ASPERG (Asberg) Wuerttenberg Ger 15
❒ ASPERHOFEN NO Aus 1
❒ ASPRES Hautes Alpes Fan 1
❒ ASSCHE Brabant Bel 1
❒ ASSEBROUCK (Assebroek) West Flanders Bel 1 14
❒ ASSELN (Dortmund) Westfalen Ger 2 4
❒ ASSELN UND BRAKEL (Dortmund) Westfalen Ger 2
❒ ASSEN Drenthe Net 1
❒ ASSENS Den 11
❒ ASSINGHAUSEN Westfalen Ger 2
❒ ASSISI Ita 3
❒ ASTEN OO Aus 1
❒ ASTI Piemonte ita 3
❒ ASTRAKHAN Rus 1
❒ ASTURIAS Y LEON Spa 1 6
❒ ATH Hainaut Bel 1
❒ ATHIES S/ LAON Aisne Fan 1
❒ ATTAFS Les Alger Alg 2
❒ ATTENDORN Westfalen Ger 1 2 6
❒ ATTERSEE OO Aus 1
❒ ATTNANG-PUCHHEIM OO Aus 1
❒ ATZBACH OO Aus 1
❒ ATZENBRUGG NO Aus 1
❒ AU BEIM HOHEN STEG OO Aus 1
❒ AU/ DONAU OO Aus 1
❒ AUBEL Liege Bel 1
❒ AUBENAS Ardeche Fan 1 7
❒ AUBENAS-VAL Ardeche Fan 12
❒ AUBENCHEUL AU BAC Nord Fan 1
❒ AUBENCHEUL AU BOIS Aisne Fan 1
❒ AUBERCHICOURT Nord Fan 1
❒ AUBERG OO Aus 1
❒ AUBERVILLIERS (Notre Dame des Vertus) Seine Fan 1 2
❒ AUBIGNY AUX KAISNES Aisne Fan 1
❒ AUBIGNY-AU-BAC Nord Fan 1

❒ AUBING Bayern Ger 1
❒ AUBONE Meurthe et Moselle Fan 1 2
❒ AUBY Nord Fan 1
❒ AUCH Gers Fan 2 3 6
❒ AUCHEL Pas de Calais Fan 1 2
❒ AUCHY-LES-ORCHIES Nord Fan 1
❒ AUDEGEM East Flanders Bel 1
❒ AUDEMETZ Bel 1
❒ AUDENARDE (Audenaerde) East Flanders Bel 1
❒ AUDENARDEE-ST. GEORGES Seine Bel 7
❒ AUDERGHEM Brabant Bel 1
❒ AUDEWARDE Bel 1
❒ AUDIGNY Aisne Fan 1
❒ AUDINCOURT Doubs Fan 1 7
❒ AUE/ ERZEBIRGE Sachsen Ger 1 2 9
❒ AUEN Kaernten Aus 1
❒ AUENBUELL (Aunboel) Den 1
❒ AUERBACH Bayern Ger 7
❒ AUERBACH/ VOGTLAND Sachsen Ger 1 2 8
❒ AUERSWALDE Sachsen Ger 1
❒ AUGSBURG Bayern Ger 1 2 7 8 9 12 14
❒ AUGUSTENBURG Den 1
❒ AUGUSTENBURG (Augustenborg, Denmark) Schleswig-Holstein Ger 2
❒ AUGUSTFEHN Oldenburg Ger 7
❒ AUGUSTUSBURG/ ERZGEBIRGE Sachsen Ger 1
❒ AULNOY S/ LAON Aisne Fan 1
❒ AULT Pas de Calais Fan 1
❒ AUMA/ ORLA Sachsen-Weimar-Eisenach Ger 1 2
❒ AUMALE (Sour al-Ghozlane) Medea Alg 1
❒ AU MUEHL Steiermark Aus 9
❒ AUMUND-VEGESACK Hannover Ger 7
❒ AURA/ SAALE Bayern Ger 14
❒ AU RACH OO Aus 1
❒ AU RAS/ ODER (Uraz) Schlesien Ger 1
❒ AURICH/ OSTFRIESLAND Hannover Ger 1 2
❒ AURIGNAC Haute Garonne Fan 1
❒ AURILLAC Cantal Fan 1 3
❒ AURILLAC AND CANTAL Cantal Fan 1 2 3
❒ AUROLZMUENSTER OO Aus 1
❒ AURORA DE LLUCANES (Sant Boi de Llucanes) Barcelona Spa 1
❒ AUSSEE, BAD Steiermark Aus 1
❒ AUSSERFELDEN Salzburg Aus 5
❒ AUSSERNZELL Baden Ger 2
❒ AUSSIG (Ustinad Labem) Boehmen Cze 1 9 12
❒ AUTEUIL Hauts-de-Seine Fan 2 7
❒ AUTEUIL-LONGCHAMP Hauts-de-Seine Fan 7
❒ AUTREMENCOU RT Aisne Fan 1
❒ AUTREVILLE Fan 1
❒ AUTRYVE West Flanders Bel 1
❒ AUVELAIN East Flanders Bel 1
❒ AUVELAIS Namur Bel 1
❒ AUVILLAR Tarn-et-Garonne Fan 1 2
❒ AUXERRE Yonne Fan 1 3
❒ AUZAT-SUR-ALLIER Puy-de-Dome Fan 7
❒ AVDOTINO Rus 1
❒ AVEIRO Aveiro Por 1
❒ AVELGEM (Avelghem) West Flanders Bel 1 2
❒ AVENBUELL (Avnboel, Denmark)
❒ Schleswig-Holstein Ger 1
❒ AVENTOFT Schleswig-Holstein Ger 2
❒ AVERSA Ita 14
❒ AVESNES Nord Fan 1 2
❒ AVESNES ET SOLESMES Nord Fan 1 2
❒ AVESNES-LE-SEC Nord Fan 1
❒ AVESNES-LES-AUBERT Nord Fan 1 2
❒ AVESNES-SUR-HELPE Nord Fan 1 2
❒ AVEYRON Fan 1
❒ AVEZZANO Abruzzo Ita 3
❒ AVEZZANO Aquila Ita 3
❒ AVIA Barcelona Spa 1
❒ AVIETO Ita 3
❒ AVIGNON Vaucluse Fan 1 3 6 7 12
❒ AVIGNONNET Haute-Garonne Fan 2
❒ AVILES Asturias Spa 2 12
❒ AVINYO Barcelona Spa 1
❒ AVION Pas-de-Calais Fan 1
❒ AVIRONS Eure Fan 2
❒ AVIZ Portalegre Por 2
❒ AVORD Cher Fan 10
❒ AWANS Liege Bel 2
❒ AWIRES, LES Liege Bel 2
❒ AWOINGT Bel 1
❒ AWOINGT Nord Fan 1
❒ AX-LES THERMES Ariege Fan 1 2
❒ AY Marne Fan 1 7
❒ AYELO Valencia Spa 2
❒ AYODAR Castellon Spa 1
❒ AYWAILLE Liege Bel 2
❒ AZAMBUJA Lisboa Por 1
❒ AZANUY Huesca Spa 1 2
❒ AZAY RIDEAU Indre-et-Loire Fan 2
❒ AZILLE Aisne Fan 1
❒ AZILLE Aude Fan 2
❒ AZILLE Nord Fan 2
❒ AZINCOURT (Agincourt) Nord Fan 1
❒ AZINO Ita 3
❒ AZUARA Zaragoza Spa 1

B

❒ BAARN Utrecht Net 8
❒ BABENHAUSEN Bayern Ger 1
❒ BABOEUF Oise Fan 1
❒ BAC SAINT-MAUR Pas de Calais Fan 2
❒ BACARES Almeria Spa 1
❒ BACCARAT Meurthe-et-Moselle Fan 2
❒ BACELLA Lerida Spa 1
❒ BACH Steiermark Aus 1
❒ BACHANT Nord Fan 1
❒ BACHEM Rheinland Ger 2 7
❒ BACHMANNING OO Aus 1
❒ BACHY Nord Fan 1 2
❒ BACKNANG Wuerttemberg Ger 1 2 6
❒ BADALONA Barcelona Spa 2
❒ BADBERGEN Hannover Ger 1 2
❒ BADEN Baden Ger 1
❒ BADEN NO Aus 1
❒ BADEN-BADEN Baden Ger 1 2 6 7 8 9
❒ BADENWEILER Baden Ger 11
❒ BADERSLEBEN Provinz Sachsen Ger 1
❒ BADETZ Anhalt Ger 1
❒ BADONVILLER Meurthe-et-Moselle Fan 7
❒ BAELEN SUR VESDRE (Baelgen) West Flanders Bel 14
❒ BAELLS Huesca Spa 1
❒ BAERENSTEIN Sachsen-Meiningen Ger 1 9
❒ BAERENWALDE (Barwice; Blincze) Westpreussen Ger 7
❒ BAERNAU Bayern Ger 1
❒ BAERWALDE (Mieszkowice; Barwice) Pommern Ger 1 9
❒ BAERWALDE Sachsen Ger 2
❒ BAEUMENTHEIM Bayern Ger 7 9
❒ BAEZA Jaen Spa 1
❒ BAGA Barcelona Spa 1
❒ BAGES Pyrennes Orientales Fan 2 7
❒ BAGES D'EN SELVES (Sant Mateu de Bages) Barcelona Spa 1
❒ BAGNARIA D'ARSA Ita 3
❒ BAGNERS-DE-BIGORRE Haute Pyrennees Fan 2 11
❒ BAIA Ita 14
❒ BAIA MARE Rom 1 2
❒ BAIENFURT Wuerttember Ger 2
❒ BAIERSBRONN Wuerttemberg Ger 1
❒ BAILEN Jaen Spa 1 2
❒ BAILLEUL (Bailloeul) Hainaut Bel 1
❒ BAILLEUL Nord Fan 1 2
❒ BAISIEUX Hainaut Bel 1
❒ BAISIEUX Nord Fan 1
❒ BAIVES Nord Fan 1
❒ BAIX MONTSENY (Sant Celoni) Barcelona Spa 1
❒ BAJENOVO Rus 1
❒ BAKU (Bakou) Rus 1
❒ BALACLAVA (Balaklava) Rus 1
❒ BALAGUER Lerida Spa 1
❒ BALAKLEYA (Balakleia) Rus 1
❒ BALAN Ardennes Fan 1 2
❒ BALBIGNY Loire Fan 7
❒ BALDENBURG (Bialy Dwor) Westpreussen Ger 1
❒ BALENYA Barcelona Spa 1
❒ BALESTRATE Ita 3
❒ BALF (Wolfs) Hun 1
❒ BALINGEN Wuerttemberg Ger 1 2 6

❒ BALLENSTEDT/ HARZ Anhalt Ger 1 2 11
❒ BALLESTAR Castellon Spa 1
❒ BALLESTEROS DE CALATRAVA Ciudad Real Spa 1
❒ BALLYKINDAR Ire 15
❒ BALONES Alicante Spa 1
❒ BALSARENY Barcelona Spa 1
❒ BALTA Rus 1
❒ BALTALPASHINSK (Batalpachinsk) Rus 1
❒ BALVE Westfalen Ger 1
❒ BAMAKO Sud 1
❒ BAMBERG Bayern Ger 1 2 6 7 9 10 12
❒ BAMBERG-GAUSTADT Bayern Ger 2
❒ BANERES Alicante Spa 2
❒ BANGALORE Ind 3
❒ BANGSUND Nor 14
❒ BANOS Jaen Spa 1
❒ BANSIN, SEEBAD Pommern Ger 2
❒ BANTEUX Nord Fan 1
❒ BANTOUZELLES Nord Fan 1
❒ BANYERES Tarragona Spa 1
❒ BANYOLES Gerona Spa 1
❒ BAPAUME Pas de Calais Fan 1
❒ BAR Rus 1
❒ BAR-LE-DUC Meuse Fan 1
❒ BARALLE Pas-de-Calais Fan 1
❒ BARBAIRA Aude Fan 1 7
❒ BARBASTE Lot-et-Garonne Fan 1
❒ BARBASTRO Huesca Spa 1
❒ BARBAZAN Haute-Garonne Fan 2
❒ BARBENS Lerida Spa 1
❒ BARBERA DE LA CONCA Barcelona Spa 1
❒ BARBERA DEL VALLES Barcelona Spa 1
❒ BARBY/ ELBE Provinz Sachsen Ger 1 2
❒ BARCELLOS (Barcelos) Braga Por 1 2
❒ BARCELONA Barcelona Spa 1 2 8 9 11 12
❒ BARCHETA Valencia Spa 1
❒ BARCHFELD/ WERRA Hessen-Nassau Ger 1
❒ BARCS Hun 1
❒ BARDI Ita 14
❒ BARENTON-BEL Ain Fan 1
❒ BARENTON-BUGNY Aisne Fan 1
❒ BARENTON-CEL Aisne Fan 1
❒ BARGTEHEIDE Schleswig-Holstein Ger 2
❒ BARGUZIN (Bargousin) Rus 1
❒ BARIG Valencia Spa 1
❒ BARILE Ita 3
❒ BARISIS Ain Fan 1
❒ BARMEN-LANGERFELD Rheinland Ger 7
❒ BARMEN-RITTERSHAUSEN Rheinland Ger 2
❒ BARMEN-UNTER ESCHBACH Rheinland Ger 2
❒ BARMEN-WICHLINGHAUSEN Rheinland Ger 2
❒ BARMEN/ WIPPER Rheinland Ger 1 2 3 4 5 6 7 8 9 11
❒ BARMSTEDT Schleswig-Holstein Ger 2
❒ BARNAUL (Barnaoul) Rus 1 3
❒ BARNOVKA Rus 1
❒ BARNTRUP Lippe Ger 2
❒ BARONIA DE RIALB Lerida Spa 1
❒ BARONISSI Campania Ita 3
❒ BARONISSI Salerno Ita 3
❒ BARRANCOS Beja Por 1
❒ BARRAX Albacete Spa 1
❒ BARREIRO Setubal Por 1 2
❒ BARRIO DE ABAJO Ciudad Real Spa 2
❒ BARRY Hainaut Bel 1
❒ BARSINGHAUSEN Hannover Ger 1
❒ BARTENSTEIN/ ALLE (Bartoszyce O.L.) Ostpreussen Ger 1
❒ BARTH (Bardt) Pommern Ger 1 2
❒ BARUTH Brandenburg Ger 1 2
❒ BARWALDE N.M. Brandenburg Ger 1 6
❒ BARZDORF (Bozanov) Cze 2
❒ BARZY Aisne Fan 1
❒ BAS-OHA Liege Be] 1
❒ BAS-WARNETON West Flanders Bel 1
❒ BASCHENOVO (Bazhenovo) Rus 1
❒ BASECLES Hainaut Bel 1
❒ BASEL East Flanders Bel 1
❒ BASKO Yug 1
❒ BASSE-BODEUX Liege Bel 1
❒ BASSE-INDRE, LA Loire Inferieure Fan 7 9
❒ BASSES Fan
❒ BASSES Alpes Fan 1
❒ BASSONES Fan 1
❒ BASSOUES Gers Fan 1
❒ BASSUM Hannover Ger 2
❒ BASTIA Corse Fan 3 4
❒ BASTIDE-DE-BESPLAS Ariege Fan 2
❒ BASTOGNE Luxembourg Bel 1 2
❒ BASUEL Nord Fan 1
❒ BATAREINAIA (Batarejnaja) Rus 1 3
❒ BATEA Tarragona Spa 1
❒ BATERE Mines Fan 7
❒ BATUM (Batoum) Rus 1
❒ BAU (Bov, Denmark) Schleswig-Holstein Ger 2
❒ BAUDRE-MOUCHARD Jura Fan 7
❒ BAUERWITZ/ ZINNA (Baborow) Schlesien Ger 1
❒ BAUGNIES Hainaut Bel 1
❒ BAULE, LA Loire Inferieure Fan 6
❒ BAUMGARTEN 00 Aus 1
❒ BAUMGARTENBERG 00 Aus 1
❒ BAUMHOLDER Rheinland Ger 2
❒ BAUSTETTEN Wuerttemberg Ger 1
❒ BAUTZEN/ SPREE (Budissin) Sachsen Ger 1 2 4 7 8 9
❒ BAUWIN Nord Fan 1
❒ BAVICHOVE (Bavikhove) West Flanders Bel 1
❒ BAYARQUE Almeria Spa 1
❒ BAYERHOF Bayern Ger 7
❒ BAYEUX Calvados Fan 7
❒ BAYONNE Basses-Pyrenees Fan 1 2 6 7 14
❒ BAYREUTH/ RED MAIN (Bai Reuth) Bayern Ger 1 2 3 4 7 8 9 11
❒ BAZA Granada Spa 1
❒ BAZANCOURT Marne Fan 1
❒ BAZAS Gironde Fan 2
❒ BAZEILLES Ardennes Fan 1 2
❒ BAZHENOVO Rus 1
❒ BAZIEGES Haute Garonne Fan 1 2
❒ BEAS DE SEGURA Jaen Spa 1
❒ BEAUCOURT Doubs Fan 7 9
❒ BEAUCOURT Territoire de Belfort Fan 2 9 14
❒ BEAUDIGNIER Nord Fan 1
❒ BEAULIEU Ardennes Fan 1 6
❒ BEAULIEU Herault Fan 1 7
❒ BEAULIEU Nord Fan 1
❒ BEAUMONT Haute Savoie Fan 2
❒ BEAUMONT Nord Fan 1
❒ BEAUMONT DE LOMAGNE Tarn et Garonne Fan 1 2
❒ BEAUMONT EN BEIVE Aisne Fan 1
❒ BEAUMONT ET PERSAN Val d'Oise Fan 1
❒ BEAUNE Cote d'Or Fan 2 7
❒ BEAUNETZ LES CAMBRAC Pas de Calais Fan 1
❒ BEAUREVOIR Aisne Fan 1 2
❒ BEAUTOR Aisne Fan 7
❒ BEAUVAIS Oise Fan 1
❒ BEAUVAIS Somme Fan 6 7
❒ BEAUVOIS Aisne Fan 1
❒ BEAUVOIS-EN-CAMBRESIS Nord Fan 1
❒ BECEITE Teruel Spa 1
❒ BECHI Castellon Spa 1
❒ BECHYNE Cze 1
❒ BECHYNE Bohemia Aus 1
❒ BECKUM/ BALVE Westfalen Ger 1 2 6
❒ BECLERS Hainaut Bel 1
❒ BECQUIGNY Aisne Fan 1 2
❒ BEDAR Almeria Spa 1
❒ BEDARIEUX Herault Fan 2 7
❒ BEDERUNGEN Ger 1
❒ BEDESBACH Pfalz Ger 1
❒ BEDMAR Jaen Spa 1
❒ BEDNO-DEMYANSK (Spask) Rus 1
❒ BEDZIN Rus 1
❒ BEEK Limburg Net 14
❒ BEELITZ Brandenburg Ger 1
❒ BEENDORF Provinz Sachsen Ger 2
❒ BEENDORF/ HALDENSLEBEN Braunschweig Ger 2
❒ BEERNEM West Flanders Bel 1
❒ BEESKOW/ SPREE Brandenburg Ger 1 3
❒ BEETZENDORF Provinz Sachsen Ger 1
❒ BEGET Gerona Spa 1
❒ BEGIJAR Jaen Spa 1
❒ BEGUDA Gerona Spa 1
❒ BEGUDA ALTA Barcelona Spa 1
❒ BEGUES Barcelona Spa 1

❒ BEGUR Gerona Spa 1
❒ BEHAMBERG NO Aus 2
❒ BEHO Luxembourg Bel 14
❒ BEHRING ISLAND Rus 1
❒ BEIERFELD Sachsen Ger 1 2 9
❒ BEIERSDORF Sachsen Ger 1
❒ BEILNGRIES/ ALTMUEHL Bayern Ger 1 2 6
❒ BEIRA Moz 1
❒ BEJA Beja Por 1 2
❒ BEKESCSABA Hun 1
❒ BELALCAZAR Cordoba Spa 1
❒ BELAYA GLINA Rus 1
❒ BELCELE East Flanders Bel 1
❒ BELCHATOW (Piotrkow Trybunalski) Rpi 2
❒ BELCHATOW (Belkhatov) Rus 1
❒ BELFORT (Territoire de Belfort) Haute-Rhin Fan 1 2 6
❒ BELGARD/ PERSANTE (Bialogard) Pommern Ger 1 2
❒ BELGERN/ ELBE Provinz Sachsen Ger 1 6
❒ BELIANES Lerida Spa 1
❒ BELILLA DE CINCA Huesca Spa 2
❒ BELL-LLOC D'URGELL Lerida Spa 1
❒ BELLAGUARDA (La Pobleta de la Granadella) Lerida Spa 1
❒ BELLCAIRE D'URGELL Lerida Spa 1
❒ BELLEBEN Provinz Sachsen Ger 2
❒ BELLEGARDE Ain Fan 7
❒ BELLEM East Flanders Bel 1
❒ BELLEME Orne Fan 2
❒ BELLENBERG Bayern Ger 1 14
❒ BELLENGLISE Aisne Fan 1
❒ BELLERNAUX Bel 14
❒ BELLEVAUX Luxembourg Bel 14
❒ BELLEVAUX-LIGNEUVILLE Bel 14
❒ BELLEY Ain Fan 2 10
❒ BELLHEIM/ SPIEGELBACH Pfalz Ger 1
❒ BELLICAIRE D'EMPORDA Gerona Spa 1
❒ BELLICOU RT Aisne Fan 1
❒ BELLMUNT D'URGELL Lerida Spa 1
❒ BELLONE Fan 1
❒ BELLPUIG D'URGELL Lerida Spa 1
❒ BELLREGUART Valencia Spa 1
❒ BELLSERRAT (Sant Pere de Torello) Barcelona Spa 1
❒ BELLTALL Tarragona Spa 1
❒ BELLUNO Ita 14
❒ BELLVEI Tarragona Spa 1
❒ BELLVERDECERDANYA Lerida Spa 1
❒ BELLVIS Lerida Spa 1
❒ BELMEZ Cordoba Spa 2
❒ BELMONT-CHAVANOZ Isere Fan 2
❒ BELMONTE Cuenca Spa 1
❒ BELORETZ (Beloretsk) Rus 1
❒ BELPECH Aude Fan 2
❒ BELVAL Vosges Fan 1
❒ BELVES Dordogne Fan 1 2
❒ BELVIS DE LA JARA Toledo Spa 1
❒ BELZIG Brandenburg Ger 2
❒ BEN-AHIN Liege Bel 1
❒ BENABARRE Huesca Spa 2
❒ BENAHADUX Almeria Spa 1
❒ BENAJAMA Alicante Spa 1
❒ BENALUA DE GUADIX Granada Spa 1 2
❒ BENALUA DE LAS VILLAS Granada Spa 1
❒ BENAMAUREL Granada Spa 2
❒ BENASAL Castellon Spa 1
❒ BENASQUE Huesca Spa 1
❒ BENATAE Jaen Spa 2
❒ BENAVENT DE SEGRIA Lerida Spa 1
❒ BENAVENTE Santarem Por 1 2
❒ BENAVITES Valencia Spa 1
❒ BENAY Aisne Fan 1
❒ BENDLEWO Posen Ger 9
❒ BENDSIN (Bedzina; Bendzin) Schlesien Ger 1 2 14
❒ BENEDIKTBEUREN (Benedictbeuren) Bayern Ger 3
❒ BENEJUZAR Alicante Spa 1
❒ BENETUSER Valencia Spa 1
❒ BENEVENTO Campania Ita 3
❒ BENFELD Fan 2
❒ BENFELD Elsass Ger 2
❒ BENGUELA Ang 1 2
❒ BENI-SAF Tlemcen Alg 2
❒ BENIAMINOW Rpl 2 3
❒ BENIARBEIG Alicante Spa 1
❒ BENIARDA Alicante Spa 1
❒ BENIARJO Valencia Spa 1
❒ BENIARRES Alicante Spa 1
❒ BENIATJAR Valencia Spa 1
❒ BENICARLO Castellon Spa 1
❒ BENICASIM Castellon Spa 1
❒ BENIDORM Alicante Spa 1
❒ BENIEL Murcia Spa 1
❒ BENIFAIRO DE VALLDIGNA Valencia Spa 2
❒ BENIFALLET Tarragona Spa 1
❒ BENIFALLIM Alicante Spa 1
❒ BENIFATO Alicante Spa 1
❒ BENIFAYO Valencia Spa 1
❒ BENIGANIM Valencia Spa 1
❒ BENILLOBA Alicante Spa 1
❒ BENIMANTELL Alicante Spa 1
❒ BENIMASOT Alicante Spa 1
❒ BENINAR Almeria Spa 1
❒ BENIPEIXCAR Valencia Spa 2
❒ BENISA Alicante Spa 2
❒ BENISSANET Tarragona Spa 1
❒ BENLLOCH Castellon Spa 1
❒ BENNECKENSTEIN/ HARZ Provinz Sachsen Ger 1
❒ BENNUNGEN/ SANGERHAUSEN Provinz Sachsen Ger 1
❒ BENQUERENCIA Caceres Spa 1
❒ BENRATH Rheinland Ger 1 2 3 7 9
❒ BENSBERG Rheinland Ger 1 2
❒ BENSEN (Benesov nad Ploucnic) Boehmen Cze 1 2
❒ BENSHEIM Hessen Ger 1 4 6
❒ BENTARIQUE Almeria Spa 2
❒ BENTHEIM Westfalen Ger 1
❒ BENTSCHEN (Zbaszyn) Posen Ger 1
❒ BEOGRAD (Belgrad) Yug 1
❒ BERCHEM East Flanders Bel 1
❒ BERCHIDDA Sardegna Ita 3
❒ BERCHIDDA Sassari Ita 3
❒ BERCHING/ OBERPFALZ Bayern Ger 6
❒ BERCHTESGADEN Bayern Ger 1
❒ BERDICHEZ (Berditchev) Rus 1
❒ BERDYANSK Rus 1
❒ BEREGSRASZ Hun 1
❒ BEREHOVO (Beregszasz) Cze 1
❒ BERENT/ FERSE (Behrend, Koscierzyna) Westpreussen Ger 1
❒ BEREZNIK Rus 1
❒ BEREZOVKA Rus 1
❒ BERG OO Aus 1
❒ BERGA Barcelona Spa 1
❒ BERGA/ ELSTER Thueringia Ger 1 2
❒ BERGEDORF Hamburg Ger 1 2 6 9
❒ BERGEN Nor 14
❒ BERGEN OP ZOOM North Brabant Net 1 14
❒ BERGEN/ DUMME Hannover Ger 1 8
❒ BERGEN/ RUEGEN Pommern Ger 1
❒ BERGERAC Dordogne Fan 1 2 7
❒ BERGERDAMM/ NAUEN Brandenburg Ger 3
❒ BERGERHOF Rheinland Ger 2
❒ BERGHAREN Gelderland Net 14
❒ BERGHEIM Salzburg Aus 1
❒ BERGHEIM/ ERFT Rheinland Ger 2 4 5
❒ BERGHEM North Brabant Net 14
❒ BERGISCH-GLADBACH Rheinland Ger 1 2
❒ BERGNEUSTADT Rheinland Ger 1 2
❒ BERGNEUSTADT & VOLLMERSHAUSEN Rheinland Ger 2
❒ BERGUES-SU R-SAMBRE Aisne Fan 1
❒ BERGUSIN (Barguzin) Rus 1
❒ BERGZABERN BAD/ ERLBACH Pfalz Ger 1 6
❒ BERIKAI Rus 1
❒ BERIKUL (Berikulski) Rus 1
❒ BERJA Almeria Spa 1 2
❒ BERKA, BAD/ WERRE Sachsen-Weimar-Eisenach Ger 1 9
❒ BERLAER Brabant Bel 1
❒ BERLAIMONT Nord Fan 1 2
❒ BERLEBURG, BAD Westfalen Ger 1 2 6
❒ BERLIN UND NOWAWES (Babelsberg) Ger 2
❒ BERLIN-BRITZ Brandenburg Ger 2 7
❒ BERLIN-CHARLOTTENBURG Brandenburg Ger 1 2 3 7 9 11 13
❒ BERLIN-COEPENICK Ger 1
❒ BERLIN-DESSAU Brandenburg Ger 2
❒ BERLIN-FRIEDRICHSHAGEN Brandenburg Ger 2
❒ BERLIN-HASENHEIDE Brandenburg Ger 7

❒ BERLIN-JOHANNISTHAL Brandenburg Ger 1
❒ BERLIN-KOEPENICK (Berlin-Coepenick) Brandenburg Ger 1 9
❒ BERLIN-LICHTENBERG Brandenburg Ger 2 7
❒ BERLIN-LUDWIGSHAVEN (See Wuerttemberg) Ger 2
❒ BERLIN-NEUKOELLN Brandenburg Ger 2 8
❒ BERLIN-NIEDERSCHOENEWEIDE Brandenburg Ger 1 2
❒ BERLIN-OBERSCHOENEWEIDE Brandenburg Ger 2
❒ BERLIN-PANKOW Brandenburg Ger 7
❒ BERLIN-RAUXEL Westfalen Ger 2
❒ BERLIN-SCHOENEBERG Brandenburg Ger 2 7
❒ BERLIN-SIEMENSSTADT Brandenburg Ger 2
❒ BERLIN-SPANDAU Brandenburg Ger 1 2 7 8 12
❒ BERLIN-TEGEL Brandenburg Ger 3 7
❒ BERLIN-TEMPELHOF Brandenburg Ger 7
❒ BERLIN-TREPTOW Brandenburg Ger 1 7
❒ BERLIN-WEDDING Brandenburg Ger 7
❒ BERLIN-WILMERSDORF Brandenburg Ger 7
❒ BERLIN-WITTENAU Brandenburg Ger 8
❒ BERLIN-ZEHLENDORF Brandenburg Ger 7
❒ BERLIN/ SPREE Brandenburg Ger 1 2 3 7 8 9 11 12 13
❒ BERLINCHEN (Barlinek) Brandenburg Ger 1
❒ BERN (Berne) Swi 2
❒ BERNAU Brandenburg Ger 1
❒ BERNAY Eure Fan 7 11
❒ BERNBURG/ SAALE Anhalt Ger 1 2 7 12
❒ BERNCASTEL-CUES/ MOSELLE (Bernkastel) Rheinland Ger 1 2 11
❒ BERNDORF NO Aus 1 3 4 7 9
❒ BERNE Oldenburg Ger 2
❒ BERNECK/ FICHTELGEBIRGE AM WHITE MAIN Bayern Ger 1 14
❒ BERNHARDSLEITEN OO Aus 1
❒ BERNISSART Hainaut Bel 1
❒ BERNDT Aisne Fan 1
❒ BERNSBACH Sachsen Ger 1
❒ BERNSTADT Sachsen Ger 1 2
❒ BERNSTADT (Bierutow) Schlesien Ger 1 2
❒ BEROLZHEIM Bayern Ger 7
❒ BERROUAGHIA Alg 1
❒ BERSENBRUECK Hannover Ger 1
❒ BERSILLIES L'ABBAYE Hainaut Bel 1
❒ BERTAUCOURT-EPOURDON Aisne Fan 1 2
❒ BERTHENICOURT Nord Fan 1
❒ BERTREE Liege Bel 1
❒ BERTRICH Rheinland Ger 6 7
❒ BERUY Nord Fan 1
❒ BERXEN Hannover Ger 3 4
❒ BERZDORF/ EIGEN Schlesien Ger 2
❒ BESALU Gerona Spa 1
❒ BESANCON Doubs Fan 1 2 6 7
❒ BESCANO Gerona Spa 1
❒ BESIGHEIM/ NECKAR-ENZ Wuerttemberg Ger 2 9 1 1
❒ BESORA Gerona Spa 1
❒ BESSIERES Haute Garonne Fan 1 6
❒ BESTWIG Westfalen Ger 1
❒ BETECOM (Betekom, Beauvechain) Brabant Bel 1
❒ BETERA Valencia Spa 1
❒ BETHEL/ BIELEFELD Westfalen Ger 1 7
❒ BETHENCOURT Somme Fan 1
❒ BETHENY Marne Fan 1
❒ BETHUNE Pas de Calais Fan 1 2 6
❒ BETTEMBOURG Lux 1
❒ BEUCHEN Bayern Ger 1
❒ BEUEL Rheinland Ger 1 2
❒ BEUGNIES Nord Fan 1
❒ BEULAY Vosges Fan 1
❒ BEUTHEN-CARLSHOF Schlesien Ger 2 8
❒ BEUTHEN-FREUDENSHUETTE Schlesien Ger 2
❒ BEUTHEN-HINDENBURG (Bytom) Schlesien Ger 2 8
❒ BEUTHEN/ ODER (Bytom Odrzanski) Schlesien Ger 1 2 3 5 8 9 14
❒ BEUTSCHEN (Zbaszyn) Posen Ger 1
❒ BEUVRY Pas de Calais Fan 1
❒ BEUVY-LEZ-ORCHIES Nord Fan 1
❒ BEVENSEN Hannover Ger 2
❒ BEVERCE Liege Bel 14
❒ BEVERE-BIJ-AUDENAERDE East Flander Bel 1
❒ BEVEREN-LEZ-COURTRAI (Beveren-Leie) West Flanders Bel 1
❒ BEVEREN-WAAS (Beveren-Waes) East Flanders Bel 1
❒ BEVERLOO Limbourg Bel 3
❒ BEVERN Schleswig-Holstein Ger 1
❒ BEVERN-BIJ-ROUSELARE West Flanders Bel 1
❒ BEVERSTEDT Hannover Ger 1
❒ BEVERUNGEN/ WESER Westfalen Ger 1
❒ BEVERWIJK North Holland Net 8 14
❒ BEXBACH Pfalz Ger 7
❒ BEYENBURG Rheinland Ger 2
❒ BEYERNAUMBURG Provinz Sachsen Ger 2
❒ BEZHETSK Rus 1
❒ BEZIERS Herault Fan 1 2 3 6 7
❒ BHOPAL Ind 3
❒ BIACHE SAINT VAAST Pas de Calais Fan 1
❒ BIALLA (Biala Piska) Ostpreussen Ger 1 2
❒ BIALYSTOK (Belostok) Rpl 1
❒ BIAR Alicante Spa 1
❒ BIARRITZ Pyrenees Atlantiques Fan 1 1
❒ BIBBIANO Arezzo. Ita 3
❒ BIBBIANO Toscana Ita 3
❒ BIBERACH/ RISS Wuerttemberg Ger 1 2
❒ BIBERBACH NO Aus 1
❒ BIBRA, BAD Provinz Sachsen Ger 1 2
❒ BICHANCOURT Aisne Fan 1
❒ BIEBRICH/ RHEIN (Bieberich; Biberich) Hessen-Nassau Ger 1 7 8
❒ BIECHLACH OO Aus 1
❒ BIEDENKOPF/ LAHN Hessen-Nassau Ger 1 2 14
❒ BIEDERMANNSDORF NO Aus 1
❒ BIELEFELD Westfalen Ger 1 6 7 11
❒ BIELITZ (Bilsko, Bielsko) Cze 1
❒ BIELITZ/ BIALA RIVER (Bielsk Podlaski; Bielsko; Sielice) Schlesien Ger 1 2 7 14
❒ BIELSCHOWITZ (Bielszowice) Schlesien Ger 1 5 7
❒ BIELSK Rus 15
❒ BIELSTEIN Rheinland Ger 1 2 14
❒ BIENSERVIDA Albacete Spa 1
❒ BIERBEEK (Sint Camillus) Brabant Bel 14
❒ BIERE Provinz Sachsen Ger 7 9
❒ BIERSTADT Hessen-Nassau Ger 1
❒ BIESME (Biesmes) Namur Bel 1
❒ BIETIGHEIM Wuerttemberg Ger 1 2
❒ BIGGE Westfalen Ger 1
❒ BIGUES Barcelona Spa 1
❒ BIISK (Bijsk, Bisk, Biysk) Rus 1 3
❒ BIKANER Ind 3
❒ BILLANCOURT Seine Fan 2 7
❒ BILLY-MONTIGNY Pas-de-Calais Fan 1
❒ BILSEN Schleswig-Holstein Ger 1
❒ BILSTAIN Liege Bel 1
❒ BINACED Huesca Spa 1
❒ BINCHE Hainaut Bel 1 2
❒ BINEFAR Huesca Spa 1 2
❒ BINGEN/ RHEIN Hessen Ger 1 6
❒ BINGERBRUECK Rheinland Ger 1 2
❒ BIOSCA Lerida Spa 1
❒ BIRKENFELD Rheinland Ger 1 2
❒ BIRKENHAIN (Brzezina) Schlesien Ger 1 5
❒ BIRKENWERDER Brandenburg Ger 2
❒ BIRKEROED Den 11
❒ BIRNBACH Bayern Ger 2
❒ BIRNBAUM/ WARTA (Miedzychod) Posen Ger 1
❒ BIRSTEIN Hessen-Nassau Ger 1
❒ BISAURA DE TER (Sant Quirze de Besora) Spa 1
❒ BISBAL DE FALSET Tarragona Spa 1
❒ BISBAL DEL PENEDES, LA Tarragona Spa 1
❒ BISBAL, LA Gerona Spa 1
❒ BISCHOFFERODE Provinz Sachsen Ger 2

❐ BISCHOFSBURG/ DIMMER (Biskupiec) Ostpreussen Ger 1
❐ BISCHOFSGRUEN Bayern Ger 1 2
❐ BISCHOFSHEIM/ RHOEN Bayern Ger 1
❐ BISCHOFSHOFEN Salzburg Aus 1 2
❐ BISCHOFSTEIN (Bisztynek, Poland) Ostpreussen Ger 1
❐ BISCHOFSTETTEN NO Aus 1
❐ BISCHOFSWERDA Sachsen Ger 1 2
❐ BISCHWALDE/ LOEBAU Westpreussen Ger 2
❐ BISMARCK Provinz Sachsen Ger 1
❐ BISMARCKHUETTE (Hajduki Wielkie; Hajducka) Schlesien Ger 1 5
❐ BISPINGEN Hannover Ger 1
❐ BISSEGEM (Bisseghem) West Flanders Bel 1
❐ BISSINGEN/ ENZ Wuerttenberg Ger 1 7
❐ BISTRITZ Aus 3
❐ BITBURG/ EIFEL Rheinland Ger 1 6
❐ BITCHE Moselle Fan 7
❐ BITCHWEILER Ober Alsace Fan 1 2
❐ BITETTO Bari Ita 3
❐ BITETTO Puglia Ita 3
❐ BITSCH (Bitche) Lothringen Ger 5 10
❐ BITSCHWEILER (Bitschwiller) Elsass Ger 1 2
❐ BITTERFELD/ MULDE Provinz Sachsen Ger 1 2 6 7 8 13
❐ BJELORETZKIJE ZAVOD (Beloretz) Rus 1
❐ BJOLDERUP Den 1 2
❐ BJOLDERUP SOGNERAD (Bjolderup) Den 1 2
❐ BLACHE-ST. VAAST Pas del Calais Fan 1
❐ BLAESVELT (Blaasveld) Antwerp Bel 1
❐ BLAGODARNOYE Rus 1
❐ BLAGOVESCHENSK Rus 1
❐ BLAICHACH Bayern Ger 2 7
❐ BLANC-MISSERON-CRESPIN Nord Fan 1
❐ BLANCA Murcia Spa 2
❐ BLANCAFORT Tarragona Spa 1
❐ BLANDAIN Hainaut Bel 1
❐ BLANES Gerona Spa 1
❐ BLANKENBERGE (Blankenberghe) West Flanders Bel 1
❐ BLANKENBURG/ HARZ (Bad Blankenburg) Provinz Sachsen Ger 2 3
❐ BLANKENBURG, Bad/ THUR Provinz Sachsen Ger 1 6
❐ BLANKENESE/ ELBE Schleswig-Holstein Ger 1 2
❐ BLANKENHAIN (Blankenhayn) Thueringen Ger 1 2
❐ BLANKENSTEIN/ RUHR Westfalen Ger 7
❐ BLANKENSTEIN/ SAALE Thueringen Ger 1 6
❐ BLANQUEFORT Lot-et-Garonne Fan 2
❐ BLANZY-LES-MINES Saone et Loire Fan 7
❐ BLASHKI (Blaszki) Rus 1
❐ BLATON Hainaut Bel 1
❐ BLAUBEUREN/ BLAU Wuerttemberg Ger 1
❐ BLAYE Gironde Fan 3
❐ BLECKEDE/ ELBE Hannover Ger 1
❐ BLEHARIES Hainaut Bel 1
❐ BLEHARIES, ERE, ETC. Hainaut Bel 1
❐ BLEICHERODE/ BUDE-HARZ Provinz Sachsen Ger 1 2
❐ BLENDECQUES Fan 11
❐ BLENHORST, BAD Hannover Ger 3 5 9
❐ BLERANCOURT Aisne Fan 1
❐ BLESA Teruel Spa 1
❐ BLEXEN Oldenburg Ger 1 2 6
❐ BLICQUY Hainaut Bel 1
❐ BLIDA Alger Alg 1
❐ BLINDENMARKT NO Aus 1 2
❐ BLITZEN ROD Hessen Ger 1
❐ BLOIS Loire et Cher Fan 1 6
❐ BLOMBERG/ DISTEL Lippe Ger 1 2
❐ BLOTTENDORF (Polevski) Cze 1
❐ BLUMAU Steiermark Aus 1
❐ BLUMBERG/ DOEBLITZ Pommern Ger 1
❐ BLUMENTHAL Hannover Ger 1 2
❐ BLUMENTHAL-ROENNEBECK Hannover Ger 2
❐ BNIN (Bninska) Posen Ger 6
❐ BOBERA Lerida Spa 1
❐ BOBINGEN Bayern Ger 2
❐ BOBISCHAU/ MITTELWALDE Schlesien Ger 2
❐ BOBREK Schlesien Ger 1 2 3 5 7
❐ BOBRUISK (Bobrouisk) Rus 1
❐ BOCAIRENTE Valencia Spa 1
❐ BOCHNIA Galicia Rpl 1 2
❐ BOCHOLT/ AA (Bochold) Westfalen Ger 1 2 7 14
❐ BOCHUM Westfalen Ger 1 3 5 6 7 9 11 12 14
❐ BOCHUM-HARPEN Westfalen Ger 2
❐ BOCHUM, ESSEN Westfalen Ger 1
❐ BOCHUM, GELSENKIRCHEN, HATTINGEN Westfalen Ger 6
❐ BOCKENEM Hannover Ger 2
❐ BOCKSWIESE-HAHNENKLEE Hannover Ger 1
❐ BOCKWITZ N.L. Brandenberg Ger 2
❐ BODEGRAAF Net 8
❐ BODENBACH-TETSCHEN (Podmokly-Decin) Boehmen Cze 1 2
❐ BODENBURG Niedersachsen Ger 14
❐ BODENDORF OO Aus 1
❐ BODENFELDE Hannover Ger 2
❐ BODENMAIS Bayern Ger 7
❐ BODENWERDER/ WESER Hannover Ger 1 2
❐ BOEBLINGEN Wuerttemberg Ger 1
❐ BOEBLINGEN UND SINDELFINGEN Wuerttemberg Ger 1 6
❐ BOECKINGEN Wuerttemberg Ger 1
❐ BOEDEFELD Westfalen Ger 2
❐ BOEEL Schleswig-Holstein Ger 1
❐ BOEHEIMKIRCHEN NO Aus 1
❐ BOEHL Pfalz Ger 1
❐ BOEHLEN Sachsen Ger 2 9 15
❐ BOEHLITZ-EHRENBERG Sachsen Ger 1 2
❐ BOEHMERWALD UlrichsbergAus 1
❐ BOEHMISCHKRUT NO Aus 2
❐ BOEHRINGEN/ RUDOLFZELL Baden Ger 1
❐ BOELE Westfalen Ger 1
❐ BOENNINGHEIM Wuerttemberg Ger 2
❐ BOENNINGSTEDT Schleswig-Holstein Ger 1
❐ BOESDORF/ ELSTER Sachsen Ger 1
❐ BOGEN/ STRAUBING Bayern Ger 2 6
❐ BOGENSE Den 11
❐ BOGENTREICH Westfalen Ger 2
❐ BOG HARI (Ksar el Boukhari) Alg 1
❐ BOGLIACCO Ita 14
❐ BOGOSLOVSK (Bogoslov) Rus 1
❐ BOGTRYK Den 11
❐ BOGUTCHAR Rus 1
❐ BOHAIN Aisne Fan 1 2 7
❐ BOHAIN Nord Fan 1 2
❐ BOI RY-NOTRE DAME Pas de Calais Fan 1
❐ BOIS BERNARD Pas de Calais Fan 1
❐ BOIS COLOMBES Hauts de Seine Fan 2 7
❐ BOIS LES PARGNY Aisne Fan 1
❐ BOISSET Herault Fan 7
❐ BOIX DE NOGUERA (Trago de Noguera) Lerida Spa 1
❐ BOIZENBURG/ ELBE (Boitzenburg) Mecklenburg-Schwerin Ger 1 2
❐ BOKEL Schleswig-Holstein Ger 1
❐ BOKELSESS Schleswig-Holstein Ger 1
❐ BOLAMO Portuguese Guinea Prg 1
❐ BOLANOS Ciudad Real Spa 1
❐ BOLBAITE Valencia Spa 1
❐ BOLBEC Seine Inferieure Fan 1 2
❐ BOLBEC-LILLEBONNE Seine Inferieure Fan 1 2
❐ BOLDIXUM Schleswig-Holstein Ger 13
❐ BOLDOGASSZONY Hun 3
❐ BOLDOGESSZONY (Boldogaszony) Frauenkirchen Aus 3
❐ BOLECHOW (Stanislawow Ukraine, Bolekhov, USSR, Ivano Frankovsk) Galicia Rpl 2
❐ BOLKENHAIN/ NEISSE (Bolkow) Ger 1 2
❐ BOLLWEILER (Bollwiller) Elsass Ger 1
❐ BOLLWEILER Haut-Rhin Fan 1

❒ BOLOGNA Mantova Lombardia Ita 3 14
❒ BOLSHOI TOKMAK (Bol Choi) Rus 1
❒ BOLSWARD Friesdland Net 2
❒ BOLTANA Huesca Spa 1
❒ BOLTENHAGEN (Ostseebad) Mecklenburg-Schwerin Ger 2
❒ BOLZANO Ita 14
❒ BOMBARRAL Leiria Por 1 2
❒ BOMMERN Westfalen Ger 1 9
❒ BOMMERSHOVEN Limbourg Bel 1
❒ BOMPAS Pyrenees Orientales Fan 1 2 7
❒ BOMST (Babimost) Posen Ger 1
❒ BON-SECOURS Hainaut Bel 1
❒ BONASTRE Tarragona Spa 1
❒ BONAVENTO SIENA Ita 3
❒ BONCELLES Liege Bel 1
❒ BONDIOUJSK (Bondyuzhski, Bondjuschskij) Rus 1
❒ BONDUES Nord Fan 1
❒ BONE (Annaba) Bone Alg 6 7
❒ BONETE Albacete Spa 1
❒ BONIKOW Posen Ger 7 9
❒ BONN Rheinland Ger 1 2 6 7 8 9 11 13
❒ BONNEVILLE Haute Savoie Fan 1 2
❒ BONORVA Sardegna Ita 3
❒ BONY Aisne Fan 1
❒ BOOM Antwerp Bel 1
❒ BOPFINGEN/ EGER Baden-Wuerttemberg Ger 1 7
❒ BOPPARD (Boppart) Rheinland Ger 1 6
❒ BORBA Evora Por 1
❒ BORBECK Rheinland Ger 8 9
❒ BORCULO Gelderland Net 14
❒ BORDEAUX Gironde Fan 1 3 7 10 11 12
❒ BORDELUM Schleswig-Holstein Ger 1
❒ BORDES-SUR-AZIZE Ariege Fan 2
❒ BORDES, LES Lerida Spa 1
❒ BORDESHOLM Schleswig-Holstein Ger 1
❒ BORDIGHERE English Ita 3
❒ BORDILS Gerona Spa 1
❒ BORDJ-BOU-ARRERIDJ Setif Alg 1 6
❒ BORDJ-MENAIEL Tizi-Ouzou Alg 1
❒ BORDONECCHIA English Ita 3
❒ BOREK (Borken) Posen Ger 1
❒ BORGER Drenthe Net 1 14
❒ BORGES BLANQUES, LES Lerida Spa 1
❒ BORGES DEL CAMP Tarragona Spa 1
❒ BORGHORST Westfalen Ger 1 2
❒ BORGLOON Limbourg Bel 1
❒ BORGO D'ALE Novara Ita 3
❒ BORGO D'ALE Piemonte Ita 3
❒ BORGO DI S. DONNINO Emilia Ita 3
❒ BORGO DI S. DONNINO Parma Ita 3
❒ BORGO FORTE Lombardia Ita 3
❒ BORGO FORTE Mantova Ita 3
❒ BORISOGLEBSK Rus 1
❒ BORK Westfalen Ger 1 2 7
❒ BORKEN Westfalen Ger 1 14
❒ BORKUM Hannover Ger 1
❒ BORLOO (Borlo) Limbourg Bel 1
❒ BORNA Sachsen Ger 1 2 9 10
❒ BORNE Net 8
❒ BORNHEIM Hessen-Nassau Ger 7 9
❒ BORNSTEDT Provinz Sachsen Ger 2
❒ BOROVITCHY (Borovitchi) Rus 1
❒ BORRASSA Gerona Spa 1
❒ BORREDA Barcelona Spa 1
❒ BORSIGWERK (Zaklady Borsiga) Schlesien Ger 1 5 9
❒ BORSTEL Schleswig-Holstein Ger 1
❒ BORSTENDORF/ ERZGEBIRGE Sachsen Ger 1
❒ BORY (Borysa) Ger 2
❒ BORYSLAW (Borisov, Borislav, Galicia) Rus 2
❒ BOSAU Schleswig-Holstein Ger 1 9
❒ BOSMONT Aisne Fan 1
❒ BOSOST Lerida Spa 1
❒ BOSSUYT (Bossuit) West Flanders Bel 1
❒ BOT Tarragona Spa 1
❒ BOTARELL Tarragona Spa 1
❒ BOTTROP Westfalen Ger 1 2 6 7
❒ BOTTROP, GLADBECK UND OSTERFELD Westfalen Ger 1
❒ BOU-THALES (Bou-Thale) Alg 7
❒ BOUCHAIN Nord Fan 1
❒ BOUCLE-SAINT BLAISE East Flanders Bel 1
❒ BOUE Aisne Fan 1
❒ BOUFARIK (Bufarik) Alger Alg 1
❒ BOUFFIOULX Hainaut Bel 1 2
❒ BOUGIE (Bejaia) Alg 1 6
❒ BOUGIE-SETIF Constantine Alg 1
❒ BOUGLAI Rus 1
❒ BOUILLON Luxembourg Bel 1
❒ BOULE LA Loire-Atlantique Fan 7
❒ BOULOC Haute Garonne Fan 2
❒ BOULOGNE Seine Fan 7 12
❒ BOULOGNE SUR GESSE Haute Garonne Fan 2
❒ BOULOGNE SUR HELPE Nord Fan 1
❒ BOULOGNE-BILLANCOURT Hauts de Seine Fan 7 12
❒ BOULOGNE-SUR-MER Pas de Calais Fan 1 7 9 12
❒ BOULOU, LE Pyrenees Orientales Fan 2
❒ BOULT-S/ SUIPPE Marne Fan 1
❒ BOULZICOU RT Ardennes Fan 1
❒ BOURBON Pas de Calais Fan 1
❒ BOURBOULE, LA Puy-de-Dome Fan 7
❒ BOURG Aix Fan 2 10
❒ BOURG DE SOMMEVOIRE Haute Marne Fan 14
❒ BOURG EN BRESSE Ain Fan 1 7 10
❒ BOURG-ARGENTAL Loire Fan 7
❒ BOURG-DE-PEAGE Drome Fan 7
❒ BOURG-LEOPOLD Limbourg Bel 1
❒ BOURGANEUF Creuse Fan 2
❒ BOURGES Cher Fan 1 2 7 9
❒ BOURGET, LE Seine Fan 1 7 10
❒ BOURGOIN Isaere Fan 6 7
❒ BOURLON Pas de Calais Fan 1
❒ BOURRET Tarn et Garonne Fan 1
❒ BOUSBECQUE Nord Fan 1
❒ BOUSIES Nord Fan 2
❒ BOUVIGNIES Nord Fan 1
❒ BOV (Bau) Den 2
❒ BOZEN Ita 1 14
❒ BOZKOV Cze 3
❒ BRA-SUR-LIENNE Liege Bel 1
❒ BRACHT Rheinland Ger 1
❒ BRACKEL/ DORTMUND Westfalen Ger 5
❒ BRACKENHEIM/ LABER Wuerttemberg Ger 1
❒ BRAENDSTRUP Den 2
❒ BRAENDSTRUP Schleswig-Holstein Ger 2
❒ BRAEUNLINGEN Baden Ger 1
❒ BRAFIM Tarragona Spa 1
❒ BRAGA Braga Por 1 2
❒ BRAGANCA Braganca Por 1 2
❒ BRAINE-LE-COMTE Hainaut Bel 1
❒ BRAKE (Braake) Oldenburg Ger 1 2
❒ BRAKEL Gelderland Net 14
❒ BRAKEL/ HOEXTER Westfalen Ger 1
❒ BRAMBACH, BAD Vogtland Sachsen Ger 1
❒ BRAMBAUER/ DORTMUND Westfalen Ger 3 5
❒ BRAMFELD Schleswig-Holstein Ger 1
❒ BRAMSTEDT, BAD/ BRAMAUE Schleswig-Holstein Ger 1
❒ 8 RANCOU RT Aisne Fan 1
❒ BRANCOURT LE GRAND Aisne Fan 1
❒ BRAND-ERBISDORF Sachsen Ger 1 2
❒ BRAND/ AACHEN Rheinland Ger 7
❒ BRANDE-HOERNERKIRCHEN Schleswig-Holstein Ger 1
❒ BRANDENBERG Tirol Aus 1
❒ BRANDENBURG Ger 1 2 3
❒ BRANDENBURG/ HAVEL Brandenburg Ger 1 2 3 7 8 9 10 12
❒ BRANDIS Sachsen Ger 1 2
❒ BRANDSTATT OO Aus 1

❒ BRANICE Rpl 1
❒ BRANNENBURG/ INN Bayern Ger 2
❒ BRASMENIL Hainaut Bel 1
❒ BRASSCHAAT (Brasschaet) Antwerp Bel 1
❒ BRATISLAVA (Pressburg) Cze 1 2
❒ BRAUBACH/ RHEIN Hessen-Nassau Ger 1 6 7
❒ BRAUNAU (Broumov) Boehmen Cze 2
❒ BRAUNAU/ INN OO Aus 1 2 3 4
❒ BRAUNLAGE/ HARZ Braunschweig Ger 1 7
❒ BRAUNSBERG/ PASSARGE (Braniewo) Ostpreussen Ger 1
❒ BRAUNSCHWEIG Braunschweig Ger 1 2 6 7 8 9 11 12
❒ BRAUX-NOUZON Ardennes Fan 1
❒ BRAY ST. CHRISTOPHE Fan 1
❒ BRAYE EN THIERACHE Aisne Fan 1 2
❒ BRAZATORTAS Ciudad Real Spa 1
❒ BRAZLAV (Bratslav) Rus 1
❒ BREBACH Pfalz Ger 9
❒ BREBIERES Pas de Calais Fan 1 2
❒ BRECHT Antwerp Bel 1
❒ BRECKERFELD Westfalen Ger 1 3
❒ BREDA Gerona Spa 1
❒ BREDE North Brabant Net 8
❒ BREDENSCHEID Westfalen Ger 3
❒ BREDSTEDT Scheswig-Holstein Ger 1
❒ BREE Limbourg Bel 1
❒ BREGENZ Vorarlberg Aus 1 9
❒ BREHNA Provinz Sachsen Ger 1
❒ BREISACH/ RHEIN Baden Ger 1 6
❒ BREITENBACH/ HERZBERG Hessen-Nassau Ger 2
❒ BREITENBERG OO Aus 1
❒ BREKKVASSEL Nor 14
❒ BREMEN/ WESER Ger 1 2 3 6 7 8 9 10 11 12
❒ BREMERHAVEN/ WESER Bremen Ger 1 2 5 7 8 9 11 12
❒ BREMERHAVEN, GEESTEMUENDE, LEHE Bremen Ger 1 2
❒ BREMERVOERDE/ OSTE Hannover Ger 1
❒ BRESCIA Castello/ Lombardia Ita 3 14
❒ BRESLAU/ ODER (Wroclaw) Schlesien Ger 1 2 3 5 6 7 8 11 12 13
❒ BRESSOUX Liege Bel 2
❒ BRESSUIRE Deux-Sevres Fan 3
❒ BREST Finistere Fan 3 7 12
❒ BRETIGNY Oise Fan 1
❒ BRETLEBEN/ ARTERN Provinz Sachsen Ger 2
❒ BRETNIG Sachsen Ger 1 2
❒ BREUIL Fan 6
❒ BREVIK Nor 14
❒ BREYELL Rheinland Ger 1
❒ BREZNICE (Breznicka) Cze 1
❒ BRIANCON Hautes Alpes Fan 7
❒ BRIATEXTE Tarn Fan 1 2
❒ BRIEG/ ODER (Brzeg) Schlesien Ger 1 2 7
❒ BRIESEN/ GRAN (Bries; Wabrzezno) Westpreussen Ger 1 6
❒ BRIEULLES Ardennes Fan 1
❒ BRIFFOEIL Bel 1
❒ BRILLON Meuse Fan 1
❒ BRILON Westfalen Ger 1 2
❒ BRIN-SUR-SEILLE Meurthe & Moselle Fan 7
❒ BRISSY Aisne Fan 1
❒ BRITZ Brandenburg Ger 5 7
❒ BRIVE Correze Fan 1 2 6
❒ BRIXLEGG Tirol Aus 1
❒ BROA Yug 1
❒ BROACKER (Broager, Denmark) Schleswig Holstein Ger 1
❒ BROAGER (Broacker) Den 2
❒ BROCKAU (Brochow; Brockow) Schlesien Ger 1 2 7
❒ BROCKESWALDE/ CUXHAVEN Hamburg Ger 2
❒ BROCKHAGEN Westfalen Ger 5
❒ BROCKWITZ Sachsen Ger 2 7
❒ BRODE Hun 1
❒ BRODY Rus 1
❒ BRODY Ukraine Rpl 1
❒ BROECHEM Antwerp Bel 1
❒ BROERUP Den 11
❒ BROERUP-OMEGN Den I 1
❒ BROMBACH Baden Ger 1
❒ BROMBERG NO Aus 1
❒ BROMBERG/ BRAHE (Bydgoszcz) Posen Ger 1 6 7 10 12
❒ BRONAU (Bronow) Schlesien Ger 7
❒ BRONCHALES Teruel Spa 1
❒ BRONS (Broons) Cotes du Nord Fan 7
❒ BROTO Huesca Spa 1
❒ BROTTERODE Thueringia Ger 1
❒ BROUCHY Somme Fan 1
❒ BRUAY EN ARTOIS Pas de Calais Fan 1 2 3
❒ BRUCH (Lom u Mostu) Boehmen Cze 1
❒ BRUCH, EL Barcelona Spa 1
❒ BRUCHHAUSEN/ HUESTEN Westfalen Ger 2
❒ BRUCHSAL/ SALZBACH Baden Ger 1 8
❒ BRUCK OO Aus 1 9
❒ BRUCK IM PINZGAU Salzburg Aus 1
❒ BRUCK-WAASEN OO Aus 1
❒ BRUCK/ MUR Steiermark Aus 9
❒ BRUDERSDORF/ NABBURG Bayern Ger 2
❒ BRUDERZECHE Ger 5
❒ BRUDZEW (Broudzew) Rpl 1 2
❒ BRUECKEN/ BIRKENFELD Rheinland Ger 2
❒ BRUECKENAU Bayern Ger 1 2
❒ BRUEEL Mecklenburg-Schwerin Ger 1
❒ BRUEGGEN Rheinland Ger 1 2 6 7
❒ BRUEHL/ KOELN Rheinland Ger 1 2
❒ BRUENN (Brno) Maehren Cze 1 2
❒ BRUESAU (Brezova nad Svitavou) Maehren Cze 1
❒ BRUEX (Most) Boehmen Cze 1 3
❒ BRUEX Most, Czechoslovakia Aus 3
❒ BRUGES (Brugge) West Flanders Bel 1 10
❒ BRUILLE ST, AMAND Nord Fan 1
❒ BRUILLE-LES-MARCHIENNES Nord Fan 1
❒ BRULL Barcelona Spa 1
❒ BRUNDE ROTHENKRUG Den 1
❒ BRUNDE-ROTHENKRUG Schleswig-Holstein Ger 1
❒ BRUNDOEBRA Sachsen Ger 1
❒ BRUNEMONT Nord Fan 1 2
❒ BRUNN AM GEBIRGE NO Aus 1 3 9
❒ BRUNNENTHAL OO Aus 1
❒ BRUNOY (Boulangerie) Bouryaillat Fan 14
❒ BRUNSBUETTELKOOG Schleswig-Holstein Ger 1 2
❒ BRUNSHAUPTEN Mecklenburg-Schwerin Ger 1
❒ BRUNSSUM Limburg Net 14
❒ BRUSAND Nor 14
❒ BRUSSELS (Bruxelles) Brabant Bel 1
❒ BRUYELLE (Bruyelles) Hainaut Bel 1
❒ BRUYERES ET MONTBERAULT Aisne Fan 1
❒ BRZESKO Galicia Rpl 2
❒ BRZESZCZE Rpl 2
❒ BRZEZANY (Berezhany, Ukraine) Galicia Rpl 2
❒ BRZEZOWITZ (Brzozowice) Schlesien Ger 1 3
❒ BUBENDORF, MEILERSDORF, WOLFSBACH NO Aus 1
❒ BUBLITZ (Bobolice) Pommern Ger 1 6
❒ BUCH NO Aus 1
❒ BUCH OO Aus 1
❒ BUCHA/ KOENITZ Sachsen-Weimar-Eisenach Ger 2
❒ BUCHAU-FEDERSEE Wuerttemberg Ger 2
❒ BUCHBRUNN Bayern Ger 1 14
❒ BUCHENAU Hessen-Nassau Ger 1
❒ BUCHENWALD/ WEIMAR Sachsen Ger 15
❒ BUCHHOLZ Sachsen Ger 1 2 9
❒ BUCHKIRCHEN OO Aus 1
❒ BUCHSWEILER (Bouxwiller; Bouxviller; Buchswiller) Elsass Ger 1 6
❒ BUCOVICE Cze 1 2 3
❒ BUCURESTI (Bucharest) Rom 1 2 12
❒ BUDAPEST Hun 1 2 14
❒ BUDAPEST-KOEBANYA Hun 2
❒ BUDELIERE-CHAMBUR Creuse Fan 14
❒ BUDENNOVSK (Svyatoi Krest) Rus 1

❒ BUDOS Gironde Fan 2
❒ BUDZIN (Budsin) Posen Ger 1
❒ BUECHEN Schleswig-Holstein Ger 1
❒ BUECHEN-BAHNHOF Hannover Ger 1
❒ BUECKEBURG Schaumburg-Lippe Ger 1 2 8
❒ BUEDELSDORF Schleswig-Holstein Ger 1 2 9
❒ BUEDERICH Nordrhein-Westfalen Ger 14
❒ BUEDERICH-MEERBUSCH Westfalen Ger 2
❒ BUEDINGEN Hessen Ger 1 6 8
❒ BUEHL Baden Ger 1 2
❒ BUELLINGEN (Bullange) Liege Bel 14
❒ BUENDE Westfalen Ger 1
❒ BUENOS AI RES Arg 11
❒ BUER (now Gelsenkirchen) Westfalen Ger 1 5 6
❒ SUEREN Westfalen Ger 1 5
❒ BUEREN BEI COESFELD Westfalen Ger 5 7
❒ BUERGEL Sachsen-Weimar-Eisenach Ger 1 2 9
❒ BUERGSTEIN (Sloup) Cze 1
❒ BUESUM Schleswig-Holstein Ger 1 2
❒ BUETGENBACH Bel 14
❒ BUETOW (Bytow) Pommern Ger 1 3 4
❒ BUETTGEN Rheinland Ger 1
❒ BUETZOW Mecklenburg-Schwerin Ger 1 6
❒ BUGGENHOUT East Flanders Bel 1
❒ BUGNICOURT Nord Fan 1
❒ BUGURUSLAN Rus 1
❒ BUIA Ita 1
❒ BUIRONFOSSE Aisne Fan 1
❒ BUISSENAL Hainaut Bel 1
❒ BUISSIERE, LA Hainaut Bel 1
❒ BUJALANCE Cordoba Spa 2
❒ BUKHARA Rus 1
❒ BUKOWSKO Galicia Rpi 2
❒ BULLAS Murcia Spa 1
❒ BULLENKUHLEN Schleswig-Holstein Ger 1
❒ BUNDE Limburg Net 14
❒ BUNOL Valencia Spa 1
❒ BUNZLAU (Boleslawiec) Schlesien Ger 1 2 6 7 9 11 13
❒ BUONO CONVENTO (Toscana) Ita 3
❒ BURDINNE Liege Bel 1
❒ BURG Provinz Sachsen Ger 1 2 3
❒ BURG Schleswig-Holstein Ger 1
❒ BURG-MAGDEBURG/ IHLE Provinz Sachsen Ger 1 4 9
❒ BURG/ FEHMARN Schleswig-Holstein Ger 1 6
❒ BURG/ WUPPER (Wipper) Rheinland Ger 1
❒ BURGAU Bayern Ger 1 6
❒ BURGBROHL Rheinland Ger 7
❒ BURGDORF/ AA Hannover Ger 1 2
❒ BURGHASLACH Bayern Get- 6 7
❒ BURGHAUSEN/ SALZACH Bayern Ger 1 2 6 7
❒ BURGHT Bel 1
❒ BURGHT East Flanders Bel 1
❒ BURGKIRCHEN OO Aus 1
❒ BURGKUNDSTADT/ MAIN Bayern Ger 2
❒ BURGLENGENFELD/ NAAB Bayern Ger 1 2 6
❒ BURGOS Burgos Spa 1 6
❒ BURGRIEDEN/ LAUPHEIM Wuerttemberg Ger 2 7
❒ BURGSCHLEINITZ NO Aus 1
❒ BURGSTAEDT Sachsen Ger 1 2
❒ BURGSTEINFURT Westfalen Ger 1 2 4 6
❒ BU RHAVE Oldenburg Ger 1
❒ BURJASOT Valencia Spa 1
❒ BURKERSDORF/ ERZGEBIRGE Sachsen Ger 1 2
❒ BURKHARDTSDORF Sachsen Ger 1
❒ BURKHARDTSDORF & TALHEIM Sachsen Ger 1
❒ BURRIANA Castellon Spa 1
❒ BURSCHEID (Borcette; Burtscheid) Rheinland Ger 1
❒ BURY Hainaut Bel 1
❒ BUSAURA DE TER (Sant Quirze de Besora) Spa 1
❒ BUSCHWEILLER (Bishchwiller) Haut Rhin Fan 1
❒ BUSENDORF (Bouzonville) Lothringen Ger 7
❒ BUSQUISTAR Granada Spa 1
❒ BUSSEY Fan 1
❒ BUSSOM North Holland Net 8
❒ BUTGENBACH Liege Bel 14
❒ BUTOW Pommern Ger 4
❒ BUTTENHEIM Bayern Ger 7
❒ BUTTENWIESEN Bayern Ger 14
❒ BUTTLAR Hessen Ger 1
❒ BUTTSTAEDT (Buttstadt) Thueringen Ger 1 2
❒ BUTURLINOVKA Rus 1
❒ BUTZBACH (Boutschbach) Hessen Ger 1
❒ BUVIK Nor 14
❒ BUXTEHUDE/ ESTE Hannover Ger 1 2 7 9
❒ BUZET Hainaut Bel 1
❒ BUZET-S/ TARN Haute Garonne Fan 1
❒ BUZULUK (Busuluk) Rus 1
❒ BYSTRICE nad Pernstejnem Cze 1
❒ BYVAABEN Den 11

C

❒ CABANABONA Lerida Spa 1
❒ CABANES Castellon Spa 1
❒ CABASSERS Tarragona Spa 1
❒ CABEZA DE BUEY Badajoz Spa 2
❒ CABEZARADOS Cuidad Real Spa 1
❒ CABEZARRUBIAS DEL PUERTO Cuidad Real Spa 1
❒ CABRA (Cabra del Santo Cristo) Jaen Spa 2
❒ CABRA D'ANOIA Barcelona Spa 1
❒ CABRA DEL CAMP Tarragona Spa 1 2
❒ CABRERA DE MATARO Barcelona Spa 1
❒ CABRILS Barcelona Spa 1
❒ CACAK Ser 1
❒ CACHTEM West Flanders Bel 1
❒ CADAQUES Gerona Spa 1
❒ CADAVAL Lisboa Por 1
❒ CADIAR Granada Spa 1
❒ CADILLAC Gironde Fan 1 2 6 7
❒ CADOURS Haute-Garonne Fan 1 2
❒ CAEMMERSWALDE Sachsen Ger 1
❒ CAEN Calvados Fan 3 6 7 14
❒ CAEN ET HONFLEUR Calvados Fan 1 3 6 14
❒ CAENEGHEM West Flanders Bel 1
❒ CAGLIARI Sardegna Ita 3
❒ CAGNAC Tarn Fan 1
❒ CAGNICOURT Pas de Calais Fan 1
❒ CAGNONCLES Nord Fan 1
❒ CAGNY Fan 14
❒ CAHORS Lot Fan 1 3 6 7
❒ CALACEITE Teruel Spa 1 2
❒ CALAF Barcelona Spa 1
❒ CALAFELL Tarragona Spa 1
❒ CALAIS Pas de Calais Fan 1 2 3 6 7 12
❒ CALAIS LA CAPELLE Pas de Calais Fan 6
❒ CALAMATA Gre 14
❒ CALANDA Teruel Spa 2
❒ CALANDA DE DIA Teruel Spa 1
❒ CALASPARRA Murcia Spa 1
❒ CALAU N.L. Brandenburg Ger 1 2
❒ CALBE/ MILDE (Kalbe) Provinz Sachsen Ger 2
❒ CALBE/ SAALE Provinz Sachsen Ger 1 9
❒ CALCAR/ RHINE (Kalkar) Rheinland Ger 1
❒ CALCE Bari Ita 3
❒ CALCE Puglia Ita 3
❒ CALCE Sicilia Ita 3
❒ CALCI Pisa Ita 3
❒ CALCI Toscana Ita 3
❒ CALDAS DA RAINHA Leiria Por 1 2
❒ CALDERS Barcelona Spa 1
❒ CALDES D'ESTRAC Barcelona Spa 1
❒ CALDES DE MALAVELLA Gerona Spa 1
❒ CALDES DE MONTBUI Barcelona Spa 1
❒ CALELLA Barcelona Spa 1
❒ CALH ETA Angra do Heroismo Azs 1 2
❒ CALIG Castellon Spa 1
❒ CALL/ EIFEL (Kall) Rheinlkand Ger 2
❒ CALLDETENES Barcelona Spa 1
❒ CALLENELLE Hainaut Bel 1
❒ CALLOO East Flanders Bel 1
❒ CALLOSA DE ENSARRIA Alicante Spa 1
❒ CALLOSA DE SEGURA Alicante Spa 2
❒ CALLUS Barcelona Spa 1
❒ CALMBACH Wuerttemberg Ger 1
❒ CALONGE DE LA COSTA BRAVA Gerona Spa 1

❒ CALONGE DE SEGARRA Barcelona Spa 1
❒ CALONNE Hainaut Bel 1
❒ CALPE Alicante Spa 1
❒ CALVOERDE Braunschweig Ger 2
❒ CALW Wuerttemberg Ger 1 2 6
❒ CALZADA DE CALATRAVA Cuidad Real Spa 1
❒ CAMAIORE Lucca Toscana Ita 3
❒ CAMALDOLI Genova Ita 3
❒ CAMARASA Lerida Spa 1
❒ CAMARENA Teruel Spa 1
❒ CAMARILLAS Teruel Spa 1
❒ CAMARLES Tarragona Spa 1
❒ CAMBERG Hessen-Nassau Ger 1 6
❒ CAMBIL Jaen Spa 1
❒ CAMBRAI Nord Fan 1 2
❒ CAMBRILS DE MAR Tarragona Spa 1
❒ CAMBURG/ SAALE Sachsen-Meiningen Ger 1 2 6 7
❒ CAMEROUNS (Kamerun) Cam 1
❒ CAMINHA Viana do Castelo Por 1 2
❒ CAMMIN/ KAMIONKA (Kamien Pomorski) Pommern Ger 1 6 9
❒ CAMP AVIGNON Fan 3
❒ CAMP BARNES Fij 14
❒ CAMP BORNHOFEN Hessen-Nassau Ger 1
❒ CAMP KNOX Ice 14
❒ CAMP SEVEN INT.CAMP (Camp Hay) Aul 14
❒ CAMP TRICHINOPOLY Cey 3
❒ CAM PAG NA Compania Ita 3
❒ CAMPAGNA Salerno Ita 3
❒ CAMPAGNE Ariege Fan 2
❒ CAMPANARIO Badajoz Spa 1
❒ CAMPANETA, LA Alicante Spa 2
❒ CAMPDEVANOI Gerona Spa 1
❒ CAMPELLO Alicante Spa 1
❒ CAMPILLO Cuenca Spa 1
❒ CAMPILLO DE ALTOBUEY Cuenca Spa 1
❒ CAMPILLO DE ARENAS Jaen Spa 1 2
❒ CAMPILLO DE LA JARA, EL Toledo Spa 1
❒ CAMPINA Rom 1
❒ CAMPLI Abruzzi Ita 3
❒ CAMPLI Terrano Ita 3
❒ CAMPO Huesca Spa 2
❒ CAMPO BASSO Ita 3
❒ CAMPO FELICE Ita 3
❒ CAMPO MAIOR Portalegre Por 1
❒ CAMPO RUS Cuenca Spa 1
❒ CAMPORROBLES Valencia Spa 1
❒ CAMPOS DEL RIO Murcia Spa 1
❒ CAMPOTEJAR Granada Spa 1
❒ CAMPREDO Tarragona Spa 1
❒ CAMPRODON Gerona Spa 1
❒ CAMUNAS Toledo Spa 1
❒ CANADA Alicante Spa 1
❒ CANALS Valencia Spa 1 2
❒ CANCON Lot-et-Garonne Fan 2
❒ CANDASNOS Huesca Spa 1 2
❒ CANENA Jaen Spa 1
❒ CANET DE MAR Barcelona Spa 1
❒ CANET LO ROIG Castellon Spa 1
❒ CANETE DE LAS TORRES Cordoba Spa 2
❒ CANILES Granada Spa 2
❒ CANJAYAR Almeria Spa 1 2
❒ CANNES Alpes Maritimes Fan 2 7
❒ CANNSTADT/ NECKAR (Bad Cannstadt) Wuerttemberg Ger 1 2 6 7 9
❒ CANONJA, LA Tarragona Spa 1
❒ CANORS Ita 14
❒ CANTAING Nord Fan 1
❒ CANTAL Fan 1
❒ CANTALLOPS Gerona Spa 1
❒ CANTANHEDE Coimbra Por 2
❒ CANTAVIEJA Teruel Spa 2
❒ CANTH (Katy Wroclawskie) Schlesien Ger 1 7
❒ CANYA, LA Gerona Spa 1
❒ CAPAFONTS Tarragona Spa 1
❒ CAPCANES Tarragona Spa 1
❒ CAPELLADES Barcelona Spa 1
❒ CAPELLE A/ D IJSSEL South Holland Net 14
❒ CAPELLE, LA Aisne Fan 1 6 7
❒ CAPELLE, LA Nord Fan 1 7
❒ CAPILLA Badajoz Spa 2
❒ CAPRAIAL Genova Ita 3
❒ CAPRAIAL Isola Ita 3
❒ CAPRAIAL Liguria Ita 3
❒ CAPSECH Gerona Spa 2
❒ CAPUA-CASERTA Ita 14
❒ CARAMAN Haute Garonne Fan 1 2
❒ CARAVACA Murcia Spa 1
❒ CARBONERAS Almeria Spa 1
❒ CARBONNE Haute-Garonne Fan 1 2
❒ CARCAGENTE Valencia Spa 1
❒ CARCASSONE Aude Fan 1 2 3 6 7
❒ CARCER Valencia Spa 1
❒ CARCHELEJO Jaen Spa 2
❒ CARDEDEU Barcelona Spa 1
❒ CARDENA Cordoba Spa 2
❒ CARDONA Barcelona Spa 1
❒ CARINI Palermo Ita 3
❒ CARINI Sicilia Ita 3
❒ CARLET Valencia Spa 1
❒ CARLOW Mecklenburg-Strelitz Ger 1
❒ CARLSFUND Provinz Sachsen Ger 2
❒ CARLSHAFEN (Karlshafen) Hessen-Nassau Ger 1 8
❒ CARLSHOF (Karluszowiec/ Tarnowitz) Schlesien Ger 2
❒ CARMAUX Tarn Fan 2 7
❒ CARME Barcelona Spa 1
❒ CARNALLS FREUDE GRUBE (Beuthen) Schlesien Ger 5
❒ CARNIERES Hainaut Bel 2
❒ CARNOT Alger Alg 2
❒ CAROLINA, LA Jaen Spa 1 2
❒ CARPENTRAS Vaucluse Fan 3 7
❒ CARPI (Modena) Ita 14
❒ CARPIAGNE Marseilles Fan 3
❒ CARRION DE CALATRAVA Ciudad Real Spa 1
❒ CARRIZOSA Ciudad Real Spa 1
❒ CARTEGENA Murcia Spa 1 2
❒ CARTIGNIES Somme Fan 1
❒ CARTIGNY Fan 1 2
❒ CARVIN Pas de Calais Fan 1 2
❒ CASABIANDA Aleria Corse Fan 3 4 10
❒ CASABLANCA (Dar el Beida) Mor 7
❒ CASAGIOVE Napoli Ita 3
❒ CASAL Cremona Ita 3
❒ CASAL Lombardia Ita,3
❒ CASAL Maggiore Ita 3
❒ CASAL D'ALTAMURA Ita 3
❒ CASALE Alessandria Ita 3
❒ CASALE Monferrato Ita 3
❒ CASALE Piemonte Ita 3
❒ CASAS BAJAS Valencia Spa 1
❒ CASAS DE HARO Cuenca Spa 1
❒ CASAS DE JUAN NUNEZ Albacete Spa 1
❒ CASAS IBANEZ Albacete Spa 1 2
❒ CASCAIS Lisboa Por 2
❒ CASERES Tarragona Spa 1
❒ CASERTA Aldifreddo Ita 3
❒ CASERTA Campania Ita 3
❒ CASERTA Caserma Ita 3
❒ CASERTA CASERMA Padiglione Ita 3
❒ CASINO Colli d'Asti Ita 3
❒ CASLAV Cze 1
❒ CASPE Zaragoza Spa 1
❒ CASSA DE LA SELVA Gerona Spa 1
❒ CASSANO Avellino Ita 3
❒ CASSEL-IHRINGHAUSEN Hessen-Nassau Ger 7
❒ CASSEL/ FULDA (Kassel) Hessen-Nassau Ger 1 2 3 4 6 7 9 11 14
❒ CASSENUIL Lot-et-Garrone Fan 2
❒ CASSINO Campania Ita 3
❒ CASSINO Caserta Ita 3
❒ CASSINO Molini Milla Ita 3
❒ CASTALLA Alicante Spa 1
❒ CASTANESA Huesca Spa 1
❒ CASTEJON DE SOS Huesca Spa 1 2
❒ CASTEL Franco Ita 3
❒ CASTEL DE CABRA Teruel Spa 1
❒ CASTEL ROCCHERE Alessandria Ita 3
❒ CASTEL ROCCHERE Piemonte Ita 3
❒ CASTEL URSINO Catania Ita 3
❒ CASTEL URSINO Sicilia Ita 3
❒ CASTELJALOUX Lot-et-Garonne Fan 1 2
❒ CASTELL DE FERRO Granada Spa 1
❒ CASTELLANA Bari Ita 3

❒ CASTELLANA Puglia Ita 3
❒ CASTELLAR Jaen Spa 1
❒ CASTELLAR DE N'HUG Barcelona Spa 1
❒ CASTELLAR DE SANTIAGO Ciudad Real Spa 1
❒ CASTELLAR DEL VALLES Barcelona Spa 1
❒ CASTELLBELL I EL VILAR Barcelona Spa 1
❒ CASTELLBO, VALL DE Lerida Spa 1
❒ CASTELLCIUTAT Lerida Spa 1
❒ CASTELLDANS Lerida Spa 1
❒ CASTELLDEFELS Barcelona Spa 1
❒ CASTELLET DE LLOBREGAT (Sant Vicent de Castellet) Barcelona Spa 1
❒ CASTELLFOLLIT DE LA ROCA Gerona Spa 1
❒ CASTELLFULLIT DE RIUBREGOS Barcelona Spa 1
❒ CASTELLFULLIT DEL BOIX Barcelona Spa 1
❒ CASTELLIGALI Barcelona Spa 1
❒ CASTELLNOU DE BAGES Barcelona Spa 1
❒ CASTELLNOU DE SEANA Lerida Spa 1
❒ CASTELLO Allessandria Piemonte Ita 3
❒ CASTELLO D'EMPURIES Gerona Spa 1
❒ CASTELLO DE FARFANYA Lerida Spa 1
❒ CASTELLO DEL TREBBIO Firenza Toscana Ita 3
❒ CASTELLOLI Barcelona Spa 1
❒ CASTELLON DE LA PLANA Spa 1
❒ CASTELLOTE Teruel Spa 1
❒ CASTELLSARROCA (Sant Marti Sarroca) Barcelona Spa 1
❒ CASTELLSERA Lerida Spa 1
❒ CASTELLTERSOL Barcelona Spa 1
❒ CASTELLVELL Tarragona Spa 1
❒ CASTELLVI DE LA MARCA Barcelona Spa 1
❒ CASTELMORON Lot et Garonne Fan 1 2
❒ CASTELNAU-D'AUZAN Gers Fan 1
❒ CASTELNAU-MONTRATIER Lot Fan 1
❒ CASTELNAUDARY Aude Fan 7 6 2
❒ CASTELNOU Teruel Spa 1
❒ CASTELO BRANCO Castelo Branco Por 1 2
❒ CASTELO DE PAIVA Aveiro Por 1 2
❒ CASTELO DE VIDE Portalegre Por 1
❒ CASTELSARRASIN Tarn et Garonne Fan 2 6 7 14
❒ CASTELSERAS Teruel Spa 1
❒ CASTERA-VERDUZAN Gers Fan 1 2
❒ CASTIGALEU Huesca Spa 1
❒ CASTILLO DE LOCUBIN Jaen Spa 1
❒ CASTILLON (Castillon la Bataille) Gironde Fan 1 2 7
❒ CASTRES Tarn Fan 2 3 6 7 10
❒ CASTRIL Granada Spa 1
❒ CASTRO DAIRE Viseu Por 1
❒ CASTRO MARIM Faro Por 1
❒ CASTRO VERDE Beja Por 1
❒ CASTRO-URDIALES Santander Spa 1
❒ CASTROP (Castrop-Rauxel) Westfalen Ger 1 2 3 5 7 12
❒ CASTUERA Badajoz Spa 1
❒ CATANIA Sicilia Ita 3
❒ CATEAU, LE Nord Fan 1 2
❒ CATELET, LE Aisne Fan 1
❒ CATILLON Nord Fan 2
❒ CATLLAR EL Tarragona Spa 1
❒ CATRAL Alicante Spa 1
❒ CATTENIERES Nord Fan 1
❒ CAUB/ RHEIN (Kaub) Hessen-Nassau Ger 1 7
❒ CAUDEBEC-LES-ELBEUF Seine Inferieur Fan 1
❒ CAUDELBEC-LES-ELBEUF Seine Inferieur Fan 2
❒ CAUDETE Albacete Spa 1
❒ CAUDETE DE LAS FUENTES Valencia Spa 1
❒ CAUDIES Pyrenees Orientales Fan 2
❒ CAUDRY Nord Fan 1 2
❒ CAULAINCOURT Aisne Fan 1
❒ CAULERY Nord Fan 1
❒ CAUNES-MINERVOIS Aude Fan 1
❒ CAUROIR Nord Fan 1
❒ CAUSSADE Tarn et Garonne Fan 1 2
❒ CAUTERETS Hautes Pyrenees Fan 2
❒ CAUZE, LE Tarn et Garonne Fan 1
❒ CAVA Hospital Ita 3
❒ CAVA, LA (Tarragona) Spa 1
❒ CAVI Alessandria Piemonte Ita 3
❒ CAVI Castello Ita 3
❒ CAYLUS Tarn et Garonne Fan 1 2
❒ CAZALLA DE LA SIERRA Sevilla Spa 6
❒ CAZIERES Haute-Garonne Fan 1 7
❒ CAZORLA Jaen Spa 2
❒ CECHTICE Cze 1
❒ CECILIA DE VOLTREGA Barcelona Spa 1
❒ CEFALONIA Gre 14
❒ CEFALU Palermo Ita 3
❒ CEFALU Sicilia Ita 3
❒ CEHEGIN Murcia Spa 1
❒ CELAKOVICE Cze 1
❒ CELLE SCHLOSS Hannover Ger 4
❒ CELLE/ ALLER Hannover Ger 1 2 4 8 9 12
❒ CELLELAGER Hannover Ger 3
❒ CELLERA DE TER, LA Gerona Spa 1
❒ CELLIEU Loire Fan 7
❒ CELLULE Puy-de-Dome Fan 1 3
❒ CELORICO DA BEIRA Guarda Por 1
❒ CELORICO DE BASTO Braga Por 2
❒ CELRA Gerona Spa 1
❒ CENTELLES Barcelona Spa 1
❒ CENTO Emilia Ita 3
❒ CENTO Ferrara Ita 3
❒ CERIGNOLA Abruzzo Ita 3
❒ CERIGNOLA Foggia Ita 3
❒ CERISY Fan 1
❒ CERIZY Aisne Fan 1
❒ CERNY LES BUSSY Aisne Fan 1
❒ CERTA (Serta) Castelo Branco Por 1 2
❒ CERTOSA Ita 3
❒ CERTOSA Di PADULA Ita 3
❒ CERVELLO Barcelona Spa 1
❒ CERVERA Lerida Spa 1 2
❒ CERVERA DE LLANO Cuenca Spa 1
❒ CERVERA DEL MAESTRO Castellon Spa 1
❒ CERVIA Lerida Spa 1
❒ CERVIA DE TER Gerona Spa 1
❒ CERVIONE Corse Fan 1 3
❒ CESENA Forli Ita 3
❒ CESENA Marche Ita 3
❒ CESKA TREBOVA Boehmen Cze 1
❒ CESSIERES Aisne Fan 1
❒ CETINJE (Cettinje) Mon 2
❒ CETTE (Sete) Herault Fan 1 3 6 7
❒ CEUTI Murcia Spa 1
❒ CEZIMBRA (Sesimbra) Setubal Por 1 2
❒ CHABIELICE Rpl 2
❒ CHAGNAT EN LIMAGNE Fan 3
❒ CHAGNY Saone et Loire Fan 7
❒ CHALANDRY Aisne Fan 1 7
❒ CHALEASSIERE St. Etienne Fan 2 7
❒ CHALINDREY Haute Marne Fan 7
❒ CHALON SUR SAONE Saone et Loire Fan 7
❒ CHALON-SUR-SAONE Autin & Louhans Fan 1
❒ CHALON-TOURNUS-CHAGNY Saone et Loire Fan 7
❒ CHALONS SUR MARNE Marne Fan 3 6 7
❒ CHAM/ CHAM Bayern Ger 1 2 6
❒ CHAMBERY Savoie Fan 1 3 7 14
❒ CHAMBON LE Haute Loire Fan 7
❒ CHAMBRY S/ LAON Aisne Fan 1
❒ CHAMBUSCA (Santarem) For 2
❒ CHAMONIX Haute Savoie Fan 1 2 7
❒ CHAMOUX Haute-Savoie Fan 2
❒ CHAMPAGNOLE Jura Fan 7
❒ CHAMPIGNEULES Yonne Fan 7
❒ CHANXHE-POULSEUR Liege Bel 2
❒ CHAPELLE-A-WATTINES Hainaut Bel 1

❐ CHAPON-SERAING
Liege Bel 1
❐ CHARDZHUI Rus 1
❐ CHARENTONNEAU Fan 14
❐ CHARLEROI Hainaut Bel 2
❐ CHARLEVILLE
Ardennes Fan 7 10 12
❐ CHARLEVILLE & SEDAN
Ardennes Fan 6
❐ CHARLEVILLE-MEZIERES
Ardennes Fan 1 2
❐ CHARLEVILLE-MEZIERES-
MOHON Ardennes Fan 3
❐ CHARLIEU Loire Fan 3 6 7
❐ CHARLOTTEGRUBE (Czernica;
Czernice) Schiesien Ger 2
❐ CHARLOTTENBRUNN (Jedlina-
Zdroj) Schlesien Ger 2 7 9
❐ CHARLOTTENBURG/ BERLIN-
SPREE Brandenburg Ger 13
❐ CHARMES Aisne Fan 1
❐ CHARTRES
Eure et Loire Fan 3 6 10 11
❐ CHARVIEN Isere Fan 2
❐ CHASSE Isere Fan 3 14
❐ CHATEAU D'ESTOUILLY-
HAM Somme Fan 1
❐ CHATEAU SALINS
Moselle Fan 1
❐ CHATEAU-REGNAULT-
BOGNY Ardennes Fan 1
❐ CHATEAU-SALINS
Elsass Ger 2
❐ CHATEAUNEUF
Ille et Vilaine Fan 4
❐ CHATEAURENARD
Bouches-du-Rhone Fan 2
❐ CHATEAUROUX
Indre Fan 1 2 3 4 7 10
❐ CHATELET Hainaut Bel 1 2 14
❐ CHATELINEAU
Hainaut Bel 1 2
❐ CHATELLERAULT
Vienne Fan 6 7 11
❐ CHATENOIS
Territoire de Belfort Fan 7
❐ CHATILLON S/ OISE
Aisne Fan 1
❐ CHATILLON-LE-DUC Fan 3
❐ CHATOU Yvelines Fan 1 6
❐ CHAUMONT Haute-
Marne Fan 7 10
❐ CHAU NY Aisne Fan 1 2 3
❐ CHAUNY & PONT-
L'EVEQ Oise Fan 1
❐ CHAVES (Vila Real) Por 1 2
❐ CHAVILLE
Hautes de Seine Fan 1
❐ CHAZELLES
Saone et Loire Fan 7
❐ CHECY-CHATEAUNEUF-SULLY-VIRTY
(Sully-Vitry) Loire Fan 6
❐ CHEDDE Haute Savoie Fan 7
❐ CHELIABNISK (Chelyabinsk,
Tscheljabinsk) Rus 1
❐ CHEMNITZ-FURTH
Sachsen Ger 2
❐ CHEMNITZ-GABLENZ
Sachsen Ger 2
❐ CHEMNITZ-HILBERSDORF
Sachsen Ger 2
❐ CHEMNITZ-KAPPEL
Sachsen Ger 2
❐ CHEMNITZ-SCHOENAU
Sachsen Ger 2
❐ CHEMNITZ/ CHEMNITZ (Karl
Marx Stadt) Sachsen Ger 1 2 3 5 7
8 11 12 14

❐ CHENEE Liege Bel 1
❐ CHERATTE Liege Bel 1
❐ CHERBOURG
Loire-Atlantique Fan 1 6 7
❐ CHERCHELL (Shershell
Caesarea) Al-Asnam Alg 1
❐ CHERCQ Hainaut Bel 1
❐ CHERDYN (Tscherdyn) Rus 1
❐ CHEREMKHOVO
(Tcheremkhovo) Rus 1
❐ CHEREPOVETZ
(Tscernevitz) Rus 1
❐ CHERKASSKOE
(Tchersasskoe) Rus 1
❐ CHERKASSY Rus 1
❐ CHERNIS ANOUI S
(Tchernij Anou) Rus 1
❐ CHERNOISTOCHINSK
Rus 1
❐ CHERNOVETZ
(Tchernevetz) Rus 1
❐ CHEROEY Charente Fan 7
❐ CHERT Castellon Spa 2
❐ CHERY LES POUILLY
Fan 1
❐ CHESTE Valencia Spa 1
❐ CHEVRESIS-MONCEAU
Aisne Fan 1 2
❐ CHEZLADZ (Czeladz) Rus 1
❐ CHIAVARI Ita 14
❐ CHIEVRES Hainaut Bel 1
❐ CHIGNY Aisne Fan 1
❐ CHILLON Ciudad Real Spa 1
❐ CHINCHILLA Albacete Spa 1
❐ CHI RIVEL Almeria Spa 1
❐ CHISTOPOL
Tchistopol Rus 1
❐ CHITA Tchita Rus 1 3
❐ CHIVA Valencia Spa 1
❐ CHIVA DE MORELLA
Castellon Spa 1
❐ CHLUDOWO Posen Ger 2
❐ CHODECZ (Khodetch,
Kodetch) Rpl 2
❐ CHODOROW (Chodorov
USSR) Galicia Rpl 1
❐ CHODZIEZ Posen Ger 2
❐ CHOLET
Maine et Loire Fan 1 2 3 4 7 10
❐ CHOMUTOV (Komatau,
Komotau) Boehmen Cze 1 2
❐ CHORZOW (Chorzowska)
Schlesien Ger 1 5
❐ CHOTEBOR
(Obcanska Zalozna) Cze 1
❐ CHRISTBURG/ SORGE (Dziezgan)
Westpreussen Ger 1 2
❐ CHRISTIANSFELD Den 1
❐ CHRISTIANSFELD
(Kristiansfelt, Denmark)
Schleswig-Holstein Ger 1
❐ CHRISTIANSTADT/ BOBER
(Krzystkowice)
Brandenburg Ger 2
❐ CHRISTOFEN NO Aus 1 2
❐ CHRIZANOW Galicie Aus 1
❐ CHROSCZUETZ
(Chroscice) Schlesien Ger 1 2
❐ CH RZANOW
(Krenau) Galicia Rpl 2
❐ CHUDIWA
(Chudenin) Boehmen Cze 2
❐ CHU LI LLA Valencia Spa 1 2
❐ CHURSDORF Sachsen Ger 2
❐ CHWALLOWITZ (Chwalowice; Chwalkowska)
Schlesien Ger 2
❐ CHYSKY Cze 1

❐ CICAGNA Ita 3
❐ CIECHOCINEK
(Tcheckhotsinek, Hermannsbad,
Wloclawek) Rpl 2
❐ CIECHOCINEK Rus 1
❐ CIELCE Rpl 2
❐ CIELCE (Kielce) Rus 1
❐ CIEZA Murcia Spa 1 2
❐ CIEZKOWICE
(Cieskowice) Galicia Rpl 2
❐ CINCO OLIVAS
Zaragoza Spa 2
❐ CINCTORRES
Castellon Spa 2
❐ CINQ-CANTONS-ANGLET
Basses-Pyrenees Fan 2
❐ CINTE-GABELLE Fan 2
❐ CIRERER DE LLOBREGAT, EL
(Sant Climent de Llobregat)
Barcelona Spa 1
❐ CIREY
Meurthe-et-Moselle Fan 1 6
❐ CIREY-BLAMONT-XURES
Fan 1
❐ CITE Fan 7
❐ CITTA'DUCALE
Abruzzo Ita 3
❐ CITTA'DUCALE
Aquila Ita 3
❐ CIUDAD REAL
Ciudad Real Spa 1 2
❐ CIUTADILLA
Lerida Spa 1
❐ CIVIDALE Ita 3
❐ CIVITA CASTELLANA
Lazio Ita 3
❐ CIVITA CASTELLANA
Roma Ita 3
❐ CLAIRAC
Lot-et-Garonne Fan 1 2
❐ CLARVALLS Lerida Spa 1
❐ CLASTRES Aisne Fan 1
❐ CLAUSSNITZ Sachsen Ger 1
❐ CLAUSTHAL/ HARZ
Hannover Ger 1 3 5 14
❐ CLAYETTE, LA
(Saone et Loire) Fan 7
❐ CLEMENT TOWN Ind 3
❐ CLERCQ Hainaut Bel 1
❐ CLERMONT L'HERAULT
Herault Fan 1
❐ CLERMONT-AULNAT
Fan 3
❐ CLERMONT-FERRAND
Puy-de-Dome Fan 2 6 7 10 12
❐ CLERMONT-SOUS-HUY
Liege Bel 1
❐ CLERMONT-SUR-BERWINNE
Liege Bel 1
❐ CLETTENBERG
Provinz Sachsen Ger 2
❐ CLEVE Rheinland Ger 1 2 8
❐ CLICHY LA GARENNE
Hautes de Seine Fan 1
❐ CLOETZE (Kloetze)
Provinz Sachsen Ger 9
❐ CLOPPENBU RG
Oldenburg Ger 1
❐ CLOS MORTIER
Haute-Marne Fan 2
❐ CLUJ
(Klausenburg) Rom 2
❐ CLUSES
Haute-Savoie Fan 2
❐ COBDAR
Almeria Spa 1
❐ COBLENZ
(Koblenz) Rheinland Ger 1 2 6 7 11

❒ COBLENZ-LUETZEL Rheinland Ger 2 7 11
❒ COBLENZ-NEUENDORF Rheinland Ger 2
❒ COBURG/ ITZ (Sachsen-Coburg) Bayern Ger 1 2 6 7 8 9
❒ COCCONATE D'ASTI Alessandia Piemonte Ita 3
❒ COCENTAI NA Alicante Spa 1
❒ COCHEM-SIMMERN-ZELL Rheinland Ger 1
❒ COCHEM/ MOSEL (Kochem) Rheinland Ger 1
❒ CODINES DE VALLES Barcelona Spa 1
❒ COEETQUIDAN Fan 3
❒ COENNERN (Koennern) Provinz Sachsen Ger 9
❒ COESFELD Westfalen Ger 1 2 5
❒ COETHEN (Koethen) Anhalt Ger 1 2 9
❒ COEVRDEN Drenthe Net 1 14
❒ COFRENTES Valencia Spa 1
❒ COGNAC Charente Fan 1 2 7 11
❒ COGUL Lerida Spa 1
❒ COIMBRA Coimbra Por 1 2
❒ COLBERG, BAD (Sachsen-Meiningen) Ger 1 4 14
❒ COLDITZ/ MULDE (Kolditz) Sachsen Ger 1 2
❒ COLL DE NARGO Lerida Spa 1
❒ COLLBATO Barcelona Spa 1
❒ COLLDEJOU Tarragona Spa 1
❒ COLLE DI TENDA Cunei Ita 3
❒ COLLE DI TENDA Liguria Ita 3
❒ COLLIO Ita 14
❒ COLLSESPINA (Collsuspina) Barcelona Spa 1
❒ COLMAR Haut Rhin Fan 1 2 6 14
❒ COLMAR/ LAUCH Elsass Ger 1 7 9
❒ COLOGNE Gers Fan 2
❒ COLOMBIES Aveyron Fan 2
❒ COLOMERA Granada Spa 1
❒ COLONFAY Aisne Fan 1
❒ COLONNOWSKA Schlesien Ger 2
❒ COMBLAIN-AU-PONT Liege Bel 1
❒ COMINES Nord Fan 1
❒ COMINES West Flanders Bel 1
❒ COMO Ita 3
❒ COMPIEGNE Oise Fan 1 3
❒ CONCA D'ORO Sicilia Ita 3
❒ CONDEIXA A NOVA Coimbra Por 1
❒ CONDOM Gers Fan 1 2
❒ CONFRIDES Alicante Spa 1 2
❒ CONQUES Aude Fan 2
❒ CONQUISTA Cordoba Spa 1
❒ CONSTANCIA Santarem Por 1 2
❒ CONSTANTI Tarragona Spa 1 2
❒ CONSTANTIN Westfalen Ger 4
❒ CONSTANTINE (Cirta) Constantine Alg 1 6 7
❒ CONSTMETTINGEN Wuerttemberg Ger 1
❒ CONSUEGRA Toledo Spa 1
❒ CONTES-LES-PINS Alpes Maritimes Fan 7
❒ CONTESCOURT Aisne Fan 1
❒ CONTICH Antwerp Bel 1
❒ CONTRES Loir et Cher Fan 7
❒ CONVERSANO Bari Puglia Ita 3
❒ COPITZ/ ELBE Sachsen Ger 2
❒ COPONS Barcelona Spa 1
❒ COPUA-CASERTA Ita 14
❒ CORBACH/ ITTER (Korbach) Waldeck Ger 1
❒ CORBEEK-LOO Brabant Bel 1
❒ CORBEHEM Pas de Calais Fan 1
❒ CORBEIL ET ETAMPES Seine-et-Oise Fan 1
❒ CORBERA DE LLOBREGAT Barcelona Spa 1
❒ CORBERA DE TERRA ALTA Tarragona Spa 1 2
❒ CORBIE Somme Fan 1
❒ CORBINS Lerida Spa 1
❒ CORDES Tarn Fan 1
❒ CORDINGEN Hannover Ger 2
❒ CORMONS Ita 3
❒ CORNELLA DE LLOBREGAT Barcelona Spa 1
❒ CORNESSE Liege Bel 1
❒ CORNIMONT Vosges Fan 1 2
❒ CORNUDELLA Tarragona Spa 1
❒ CORNUDELLA DE MONTSANT Tarragona Spa 1
❒ CORONADA, LA Badajoz Spa 1
❒ CORONATO Genova Ita 3
❒ CORONATO Hospital Ita 3
❒ CORPHALIE-LEZ-HUY Liege Bel 1
❒ CORRAL DE ALMAGUER Toledo Spa 1
❒ CORRAL DEL CALATRAVA Ciudad Real Spa 1
❒ CORRAL-RUBIO Albacete Spa 1
❒ CORRE Haute Saone Fan 1
❒ CORREZE Fan 1
❒ CORSE Fan 14
❒ CORTE Corse Fan 3 4 7
❒ CORTE Maggiore Ita 3
❒ CORTE Piacenza Ita 3
❒ CORTES DA PALLAS Valencia Spa 1
❒ CORTIJO ALTO Ciudad Real Spa 1
❒ CORUCHE Santarem Por 1 2
❒ COSEL (Kozle) Schlesien Ger 1 2 7
❒ COSNE Allier Fan 7 14
❒ COSNE-SUR-LOIRE Nievre Fan 14
❒ COSSMANNSDORF Sachsen Ger 2
❒ COSWIG/ ELBE (Koswigk) Provinz Sachsen Ger 1 2 7
❒ COTE-CHAUDE Fan 7
❒ COTEAU, LE Loire Fan 2
❒ COTES-DU-NORD Nord Fan 14
❒ COTTBUS/ SPRED (Kottbus) Brandenburg Ger 1 2 3 6 12 14
❒ COUCKELAERE West Flanders Bel 1
❒ COUCY LE CHATEAU Aisne Fan 1
❒ COUEERON Loire Atlantique Fan 7
❒ COUILLET Hainaut Bel 1
❒ COULOMMIERS Seine et Marne Fan 11
❒ COUR-SUR-HEURE Hainaut Bel 1
❒ COURCELLES Hainaut Bel 1
❒ COURCELLES-LES-LENS Pas de Calais Fan 1
❒ COURCHETTES Nord Fan 1
❒ COURNEUVE, LA Seine-Saint Denis Fan 1 2 7 11
❒ COURRIERES Namur Bel 1
❒ COURRIERES Pas de Calais Fan 1 2
❒ COURSAN Aude Fan 2
❒ COURSEL Limbourg Bel 1
❒ COUTANCES Manche Fan 11
❒ COUTHUIN Liege Bel 1
❒ COUTICHES Nord Fan 1 2
❒ COVILHA Castelo Branco Por 1
❒ COX Alicante Spa 1
❒ CRAILSHEIM/ JAXT (Krailsheim) Wuerttemberg Ger 1 6 7 9
❒ CRANENBURG (Kranenburg) Rheinland Ger 1
❒ CRANSAC Aveyron Fan 1
❒ CRANZAHL Sachsen Ger 1
❒ CRATO Portalegre For 1 2
❒ CRAUX Ardennes Fan 7
❒ CRECY-EN-BRIE Seine-et-Marne Fan 6
❒ CRECY-SUR SERRE Aisne Fan 1 6 7
❒ CREFELD Rheinland Ger 1 2 3 4 5 6 7 8 9 11 12
❒ CREFELD-GLADBACH-GREVENBROICHKEMPEN-NEUSS Rheinland Ger 1 2
❒ CREFELD-UARDINGEN Rheinland Ger
❒ CREFELD/ DUISBURG Rheinland Ger 2
❒ CREIXELL DE MAR Tarragona Spa 1
❒ CREMONA Ita 14
❒ CRENGELDANZ Westfalen Ger 5 7
❒ CREPY-EN-LAONNOIS Aisne Fan 1
❒ CRESPIN Nord Fan 1
❒ CRESSY-OMENCOURT Somme Fan 1
❒ CRETAS Teruel Spa 2
❒ CREULLY Calvados Fan 7
❒ CREUSE (Gueret et Aubusson) Creuse Fan 1
❒ CREUSOT, LE (Le Creuzot) Saone et Loire Fan 2 3 7
❒ CREUSSEN/ OBERFRANKEN Bayern Ger 1
❒ CREVECOEUR S/ ESCAUT Nord Fan 1

❒ CREVILLENTE
Alicante Spa 2
❒ CREZY-SUR-SERRE
Aisne Fan 6
❒ CRIGNY Aisne Fan 1
❒ CRIMMITSCHAU/ PLEISSE
(Crimmitzschau)
Sachsen Ger 1 2 8 11
❒ CRINCY Nord Fan 1
❒ CRIPTANA
Ciudad Real Spa 1
❒ CRIVITZ (Krivitz)
Mecklenburg-Schwerin Ger 1
❒ CROEBA Sachsen Ger 1
❒ CROEBERN/ LEIPZIG
Sachsen Ger 1
❒ CROISIC, LE (Loire Inferieure)
Loire Atlantique Fan 7
❒ CROIX Haute-Marne Fan 1 2
❒ CROIX ET WASQUEHAL
Nord Fan 1
❒ CROIX-FONSOMME Fan 1
❒ CROIX-MOLIGNEAUX
Somme Fan 1
❒ CROMBACH Liege Bel 14
❒ CRONE/ BRAHE
(Koronowo) Posen Ger 1
❒ CRONENBERG
Rheinland Ger 1 2 8
❒ CROSNES
Seine et Oise Fan 7
❒ CROSSEN/ ODER & BOBER
(Krosno; Krossen)
Brandenburg Ger 1 3 6 7 9
❒ CROSTA-ADOLFSHUETTE
Sachsen Ger 2
❒ CROTTENDORF/ ERZGEBIRGE
(Krottendorf) Sachsen Ger 1
❒ CRUPILLY Aisne Fan 1
❒ CRUYSHAUTEM
East Flanders Bel 1
❒ CSOT Hun 3
❒ CUATRETONDETA
Alicante Spa 1
❒ CUBA Beja Por 1 2
❒ CUBELLS Lerida Spa 1
❒ CUERNE West Flanders Bel 1
❒ CUESTRIN (Kostrzyn;
Kostrzynska)
Brandenburg Ger 1 2 3 6
8 12 13
❒ CUEVAS DE ALMONZORA
Almeria Spa 1
❒ CUEVAS DE CANART
Teruel Spa 1
❒ CUEVAS DE VINROMA
Castellon Spa 1 2
❒ CUINCY Nord Fan 1
❒ CUISEAUX
Saone-et-Loire Fan 2
❒ CUKMANTL
(Zuckmantel) Cze 1
❒ CUKROWNIA/
ZNIN Posen Ger 2
❒ CULEMBORG
Gelderland Net 1
❒ CULLAR-BAZA Granada Spa 1 2
❒ CULLERA Valencia Spa 1 2
❒ CULM (Kulm; Chelmno,
Chelmska) Westpreussen
Ger 1
❒ CULMSEE (Kulmsee; Chelmza;
Chelmska) Wespreussen
Ger 1
❒ CUNEO Piemonte Ita 3
❒ CUNEWALDE Sachsen Ger 1 2
❒ CURRAGH Ire 15
❒ CU RSDORF
Thueringen Ger 1
❒ CURVILLE
Haute-Marne Fan 7
❒ CUTS Oise Fan 1
❒ CUXAC D'AUDE
Aude Fan 7
❒ CUXHAVEN Hamburg Ger 1 2 9
❒ CYPRUS Cyr 14
❒ CYSOING Nord Fan 1 2
❒ CZARNKOW (Czarnikau)
Posen Ger 1
❒ CZEGLED (Cegled) Hun 1
❒ CZELADZ (Tcheliadz,
Tscheliads) Silesia Ger 2
❒ CZEMPIN Posen Ger 1 2
❒ CZERNITZ (Czernica)
Schlesien Ger 1 2 3
❒ CZERNOWITZ (Chernovtsy,
Chernovitsy, Cernauti, Romania,
Cernovoy, USSR) Hun 1 3
❒ CZERSK (Marienwalde)
Westpreussen Ger 1 2
❒ CZERWIONKA
Schlesien Ger 2
❒ CZESTOCHOWA (Chenstokhov,
Tchenstovok) Rus 1
❒ CZESTOCHOWA (Tchenstokov;
Chenstokhov; Czenstochau)
Schlesien Ger 1 2
❒ CZYZYNY
(Czyzynska) Rpl 2

D

❒ D'URVILLE,
Bateau Dumont Fan 1
❒ DABER (Dobra)
Pommern Ger 1
❒ DABIE (Dombe) Rus 1
❒ DABIE (Dombe, Altdamm)
Galicia Ger 1
❒ DABIE (Dombe, Altdamm)
Galicia Rpl 1
❒ DABROWA GORNICZA
Rus 1
❒ DABROWA GORNICZA (Dombrau;
Dombrova) Schlesien Ger 1 2 6
❒ DABROWSKIE ZAGLEBIE
Rus 1
❒ DACHAU/ AMMER
Bayern Ger 7 9 14
❒ DACKNAM
East Flanders Bel 1
❒ DADIZEELE
West Flanders Bel 1
❒ DAENISCHBURG
Luebeck Ger 1
❒ DAGANZO Madrid Spa 2
❒ DAHLEN Sachsen Ger 1 2
❒ DAHLENBURG
Hannover Ger 1 14
❒ DAHLERAU
Rheinland Ger 7
❒ DAHLERBRUECK
Westfalen Ger 14
❒ DAHLHAUSEN/ WUPPER
Rheinland Ger 1 2 7
❒ DAHME/ DAHME
Brandenburg Ger 1
❒ DAHOMEN
(Dahomey, Benin) Fwa 1
❒ DAIGNY Aisne Fan 1
❒ DAIMIEL Ciudad Real Spa 2
❒ DAKAR Sen 6 7
❒ DALANE Nor 14
❒ DALER (Dabler) Den 1
❒ DALER
Schleswig-Holstein Ger 1
❒ DALHAUSEN/ HOEXTER
Westfalen Ger 1 2 7
❒ DALHEM Liege Bel 1
❒ DALIAS Almeria Spa 1 2
❒ DALLON Aisne Fan 1
❒ DALSHEIM Hessen Ger 7
❒ DAMAZAN
Lot-et-Garonne Fan 2
❒ DAMIATTE Tarn Fan 7
❒ DAMME Oldenburg Ger 2
❒ DAMPREMY Hainaut Bel 1
❒ DAMRE Liege Bel 2
❒ DAN DOWKA Rpl 2
❒ DANDOWKA Rus 1
❒ DANIZY Aisne Fan 1 2
❒ DANNEFELD
Provinz Sachsen Ger 2
❒ DANNENBERG/
JEETZE Hannover Ger 1
❒ DANTON Ita 14
❒ DANTUMADEEL Net 1
❒ DANZIG-LANGFUHR
(Gdansk-Wrzeszcz)
Westpreussen Ger 2
❒ DANZIG-TROYL (Gdansk Przerobka)
Westpreussen Ger 4 5
❒ DANZIG/ VISTULA (Gdansk)
Westpreussen Ger 1 2 6 7 9 12
❒ DAR-ES-SALAAM
(Mzizima) Gea 7
❒ DARFELD
Westfalen Ger 3 14
❒ DARGUN/ KLOSTERSEE
Mecklenburg-Schwerin Ger 1 2
❒ DARKEHMEN/ ANGERAPP
(Oziersk) Ostpreussen Ger 1
❒ DARLINGERODE
Provinz Sachsen Ger 1
❒ DARMOS Tarragona Spa 1
❒ DARMSTADT/ DARM
Hessen Ger 1 2 6 7 8 9
❒ DARRO
Granada Spa 1
❒ DASSEL Hannover Ger 2
❒ DASSOW
Mecklenburg-Schwerin Ger 1
❒ DATTELN
Westfalen Ger 1 2 3
❒ DAUN Rheinland Ger 1 6 7
❒ DAURIA Rus 1
❒ DAX Landes Fan 6 7
❒ DE CLINGE (Deklinge)
East Flanders Bel 1
❒ DEAUVILLE Calvados Fan 3 7
❒ DEBRA Rus 1
❒ DECAZEVILLE
Aveyron Fan 2
❒ DECHY Nord Fan 1
❒ DECK (Swierklaniec)
Schlesien Neu 1
❒ DEERLYCK (Deerlijk)
West Flanders Bel 1
❒ DEERSHEIM Sachsen Ger 7
❒ DEESBACH U. LICHTENHAIN
Thueringen Ger 1
❒ DEGGENDORF/ DANUBE
(Deckendorf) Bayern Ger 1 2 6 7 15
❒ DEHESA DE GUADIX
Granada Spa 1
❒ DELBRUECK
Westfalen Ger 1 2 9
❒ DELDEN Overijssel Net 2
❒ DELFELD Westfalen Ger 2
❒ DELFT South Holland Net 8
❒ DELITZSCH/ LOBER
Provinz Sachsen Ger 1 2

❒ DELMENHORST/ DELME Oldenburg Ger 1 2
❒ DEMITZ-THUMITZ Sachsen Ger 1
❒ DEMMIN/ TOLLENSE & TREBEL Pommern Ger 1 2
❒ DENAIN Nord Fan 1 2
❒ DENDERBELLE East Flanders Bel 1
❒ DENDERMONDE East Flanders Bel 1
❒ DENEKAMP Overijssel Net 14
❒ DENIA Alicante Spa 1 2
❒ DENKLINGEN Rheinland Ger 1
❒ DEOLI Ind 3
❒ DERBENT Rus 1
❒ DERCY Aisne Fan 1
❒ DERENBURG/ HARZ Provinz Sachsen Ger 1
❒ DEREY Aisne Fan 1
❒ DERFELD Westfalen Ger 1
❒ DERGNEAU Hainaut Bel 1
❒ DERMBACH/ RHOEM Sachsen-Wei-Eisen Ger 1 2 7
❒ DERNE Westfalen Ger 5 7
❒ DERSCHLAG Rheinland Ger 1
❒ DESCHENITZ (Desenice) Boehmen Cze 2
❒ DESSAU/ MULDE (Dessaw) Anhalt Ger 1 2 7 12
❒ DESSELBRUNN OO Aus 1
❒ DESSELGHEM (Desselgem) West Flanders Bel 1
❒ DESTNA Cze 1
❒ DETMOLD/ WERRA Lippe Ger 1 9
❒ DETTINGEN/ ERMS Wuerttemberg Ger 7
❒ DETTINGEN/ MAIN Bayern Ger 2 7 9
❒ DEURNE North Brabant Net 14
❒ DEUTSCH GABEL (Nemecke Jablonne) Cze 3
❒ DEUTSCH PIEKAR (Piekary Wielkie) Schlesien Ger 1
❒ DEUTSCH WERNERSDORF (Vernerovice) Cze 2
❒ DEUTSCH-ALTENBURG NO Aus 2
❒ DEUTSCH-EYLAU (Elk Ilawa) Westpreussen Ger 1 6
❒ DEUTSCH-GABEL Boehemen Aus 3 4
❒ DEUTSCH-KRONE (Walcz) Westpreussen Ger 1 7
❒ DEUTSCH-RUMBACH Elsass Ger 2
❒ DEUTSCH-WAGRAM NO Aus 1
❒ DEUTSCHENBORA Sachsen Ger 1
❒ DEUTSCHLANDSBERG Steiermark Aus 9
❒ DEUTSCHRUMBACH Haut-Rhin Fan 2
❒ DEUX SEVRES Fan 1 6
❒ DEUX-ACREN Hainaut Bel 1
❒ DEVENTER Overijssel Net 8 14
❒ DEYNZE (Deinze) East Flanders Bel 1
❒ DEZMA Granada Spa 2
❒ DIEBAN (Dziewin) Schlesien Ger 7
❒ DIEBURG/ GERSPRENZ Hessen Ger 6
❒ DIEDENHOFEN Lothringen Ger 1 2 3 6 7 9 10 12
❒ DIEDENHOFEN-NIEDERJEUTZ Lothringen Ger 3 7
❒ DIEPENBEEK Limbourg Bel 1
❒ DIEPHOLZ/ HUNTE Hannover Ger 1
❒ DIEPPE Seine Maritime Fan 1 3
❒ DIERINGHAUSEN Rheinland Ger 1 2 7
❒ DIERSBACH OO Aus 1
❒ DIESSEN-ST. GEORGEN Bayern Ger 2
❒ DIESSEN/ AMMERSEE Bayern Ger 1 2
❒ DIEST Brabant Bel 1 3
❒ DIETERSDORF OO Aus 1
❒ DIETESHEIM Hessen Ger 7 9
❒ DIETFURT Bayern Ger 7
❒ DIETFURT/ ALTMUEHL Bayern Ger 1 2
❒ DIETRICHSCHLAG BEI AIGEN OO Aus 1
❒ DIETRICHSCHLAIG BEI LEONFELDEN OO Aus 1
❒ DIETZ/ LAHN Hessen-Nassau Ger 1
❒ DIEUPENTALE Tarn-et-Garonne Fan 1 2
❒ DIFFERDINGEN (Differdange) Lux 7
❒ DIGOIN Saone-et-Loire Fan 7
❒ DIGOIN-EST- Saone-et-Loire Fan 7
❒ DIJON Cote-d'Or Fan 1 6 7 11
❒ DILLENBURG/ DILLE Hessen-Nassau Ger 1
❒ DILLINGEN/ DONAU Bayern Ger 1 2 4 5 6
❒ DILLINGEN/ SAAR Rheinland Ger 4 5
❒ DILLKREIS Hessen-Nassau Ger 1 6
❒ DIMBACH OO Aus 1
❒ DINAN Cotes du Nord Fan 3
❒ DINANT Namur Bel 1
❒ DINARD Ille et Vilaine Fan 2 7
❒ DINGELSTAEDT/ UNSTRUT Provinz Sachsen Ger 1 2 6
❒ DINGOLFING/ ISAR Bayern Ger 1 2 6
❒ DINKELSBUEHL/ WERNITZ Bayern Ger 6
❒ DINSLAKEN Rheinland Ger 1 3 6 7
❒ DINTERLOORD North Brabant Net 1
❒ DINXPERLO Gelderland Net 14
❒ DIOSGYOER Hun 1
❒ DIPPOLDISWALDE/ WEISSERITZ Sachsen Ger 1 2
❒ DIRE DAOUA (Dire Dawa) Eth 2
❒ DIRLEWANG Bayern Ger 1
❒ DIRNWAGRAM OO Aus 1
❒ DI RSCHAU/ VISTULA (Tczew) Westpreussen Ger 1 2 7
❒ DISCARD Fan 7
❒ DISON Liege Bel 1
❒ DITFURT Provinz Sachsen Ger 1
❒ DITTERSBACH (Jetrichov) Cze 2
❒ DITTERSBACH (Walbrzych; Starsow) Schlesien Ger 1
❒ DITTERSDORF/ ERZGEBIRGE Sachsen Ger 1 2
❒ DITTMANNSDORF Sachsen Ger 2
❒ DIVES Calvados Fan 1 7
❒ DIZY LE GROS Aisne Fan 1
❒ DJALMAN-KIL-BOUROUN Rus 1
❒ DJANKOI Rus 1
❒ DJIBOUTI (Afars, Issas) Fsl 1 6
❒ DJIDJELLI Constantine Alg 7
❒ DMITRIEV-CONSTANTINOFF (Dmitriev-Poselok) Rus 1
❒ DMITRIEVSK (Dmitriyevsk) Rus 1
❒ DNEPROPETROVSK (Ekaterinoslav) Rus 1
❒ DOBERAN (Bad Doberan) Mecklenburg-Schwerin Ger 1
❒ DOBRA (Poland) Rus 1
❒ DOBRA/ LIMANOWA Galicia Rpl 2
❒ DOBRIS Cze 1
❒ DOBRZELIN/ PLOCK Rpl 2
❒ DOEBELN Sachsen Ger 1 2 3 4 8 12
❒ DOEBERITZ Brandenburg Ger 2 3 10
❒ DOEBERN N.L. Brandenburg Ger 2 6
❒ DOEL East Flanders Bel 1
❒ DOEMITZ Mecklinburg-Schwerin Ger 1 2 7
❒ DOERFL Steiermark Aus 1
❒ DOETINCHEM Gelderland Net 14
❒ DOKKUM Friesland Net 8
❒ DOLAR Granada Spa 1
❒ DOLCEDO Liguria Ita 3
❒ DOLCEDO Porto Maurizio Ita 3
❒ DOLE Jura Fan 7
❒ DOLLBERGEN Hannover Ger 2
❒ DOLORES Alicante Spa 1
❒ DOLSTHAIDA Provinz Sachsen Ger 1
❒ DOMB (Dab) Schlesien Ger 1 5
❒ DOMBROVA (Dabrowa Gornicza) Rus 1
❒ DOMBROVSKIE KOPI (Dabrowskie Zaglebie) Rus 1
❒ DOMBROWO (Dabrowo; Dabrowki) Posen Ger 2
❒ DOME, PUY DE Puy de Domb Fan 1
❒ DOMENYS DEL PENEDES Tarragona Spa 1
❒ DOMMELSTADL/ PASSAU Bayern Ger 2
❒ DOMMITSCH/ ELBE (Dommitsh) Provinz Sachsen Ger 1
❒ DOMNAU (Domnowo) Ostpreussen Ger 1
❒ DOMPIERRE Nord Fan 1
❒ DON BENITO Badajoz Spa 1 2
❒ DONA MARIA OCANA Almeria Spa 1

❒ DONAUESCHINGEN/ BRIGACH & BREGE Baden Ger 1 2 6 7 9
❒ DONAUTALNOTGELD OO Aus 1
❒ DONAUWOERTH/ WERNITZ & DANUBE Bayern Ger 1 2
❒ DONAWITZ Steiermark Aus 9
❒ DONCHERY Ardennes Fan 1
❒ DONGE North Brabant Net 1
❒ DONNDORF Provinz Sachsen Ger 2
❒ DONSTIENNES Hainaut Bel 1
❒ DONZELL D'URGELL Lerida Spa 1
❒ DONZERE Drome Fan 7
❒ DOPIEWO (Wanenfeld) Posen Ger 2
❒ DOPPL OO Aus 1
❒ DORDORF/ DORNBURG Thueringen Ger 14
❒ DORDRECHT South Holland Net 8
❒ DORENPT Aisne Fan 1
❒ DORF AN DER PRAM OO Aus 1
❒ DORFBACH Bayern Ger 1
❒ DORFCHEMNITZ Sachsen Ger 1
❒ DORFGASTEIN Salzburg Aus 1
❒ DORMAGEN Rheinland Ger 2
❒ DORNAP Rheinland Ger 1 2 3 5 7
❒ DORNBACH NO Aus 1
❒ DORNBURG/ SAALE Sachsen-Weimar-Eisenach Ger 1
❒ DORNDORF/ RHOEN Thueringen Ger 2
❒ DORNSTETTEN Wuerttemberg Ger 1
❒ DORSTEN/ LIPPE Westfalen Ger 1
❒ DORSTFELD Westfalen Ger 5
❒ DORTAN Ain Fan 1 2 9
❒ DORTMUND Westfalen Ger 2 5 6 7 9 11 14
❒ DORTMUND UND HOERDE Westfalen Ger 1
❒ DORUM Hannover Ger 2
❒ DOS TORRES Cordoba Spa 1 2
❒ DOSRIUS Barcelona Spa 1
❒ DOTTERNHAUSEN Baden-Wuerttemberg Ger 14
❒ DOTTIGNIES West Flanders Bel 1
❒ DOUAI Nord Fan 1 2 3 14
❒ DOUAI-CARVIN Nord Fan 1
❒ DOUCHY Aisne Fan 1
❒ DOUDLEBY U KOSTELCE Cze 2
❒ DOUERA Alg 1
❒ DOUGLAS (CAMP) Ism 15
❒ DOUILLY Somme Fan 1
❒ DOUR Hainaut Bel 2
❒ DOURGES Pas de Calais Fan 1
❒ DRA-EL-MIZAN Alg 1
❒ DRABENDERHOEHE Nord Rhein-Westfalen Ger 14
❒ DRACHSELSRIED Bayern Ger 2
❒ DRAGUIGNAN Tarn et Garonne Fan 2 3 7

❒ DRAMBURG/ DRAGE (Drawsko Pomorskie) Pommern Ger 1
❒ DRAMMEN Nor 14
❒ DRANGEDAL Nor 14
❒ DRASCHWITZ Sachsen Ger 7 9
❒ DRASENDORF Kaernten Aus 1
❒ DREBACH Sachsen Ger 1 2
❒ DREISCHOR Zeeland Net 1
❒ DREIWERDEN Sachsen Ger 2
❒ DRENKE/ HOEXTER Westfalen Ger 1
❒ DRENTE Net 14
❒ DRESDEN & RADEBERG Sachsen Ger 2
❒ DRESDEN-ALTSTADT Sachsen Ger 1 7 12
❒ DRESDEN-HEIDENAU Sachsen Ger 2
❒ DRESDEN-LAUBEGAST Sachsen Ger
❒ DRESDEN-LEUBEN Sachsen Ger 2
❒ DRESDEN-LOCKWITZGRUND Sachsen Ger 2
❒ DRESDEN-NEUSTADT Sachsen Ger 1 9
❒ DRESDEN-NEUSTADT-ALTSTADT Sachsen Ger 1
❒ DRESDEN-RADEBEUL Sachsen Ger 7
❒ DRESDEN-STETZSCH Ger
❒ DRESDEN-TRACHAU Sachsen Ger 2
❒ DRESDEN-ZITTAU Sachsen Ger 11
❒ DRESDEN/ ELBE Sachsen Ger 1 2 7 9 11 12 13
❒ DRESOW Pommern Ger 7
❒ DREWER Brandenburg Ger 2
❒ DRIBURG, BAD Westfalen Ger 1 7
❒ DRIEL Gelderland Net 14
❒ DRIENCOURT Fan 1
❒ DRIESEN/ NETZE (Drezdenko) Brandenburg Ger 1 6
❒ DROCOURT Pas de Calais Fan 1 2
❒ DROHOBYCZ (Drogobyc, USSR) Galicia Rpl 1 2
❒ DROLSHAGEN Westfalen Ger 1
❒ DRONGEN (Tronchiennes) East Flanders Bel 1
❒ DROSENDORF NO Aus 1
❒ DROSS NO Aus 1
❒ DROSSEN (Osno Lubuskie) Brandenburg Ger 1
❒ DROYSSIG Provinz Sachsen Ger 2
❒ DRUTEN Gelderland Net 14
❒ DRUZHKOVKA (Droujkovka) Rus 1
❒ DUALA Cam 1
❒ DUBENSKOGRUBE Schlesien Ger 1
❒ DUBNO (Doubno, Ukraine) Galicia Rpl 1 2
❒ DUDERSTADT/ HAHLE Provinz Sachsen Ger 1
❒ DUEBEN Provinz Sachsen Ger 1
❒ DUELKEN Rheinland Ger 1 2
❒ DUELMEN Westfalen Ger 1 2 4

❒ DUEMMLINGHAUSEN Rheinland Ger 2
❒ DUENEBERG Hamburg Ger 7
❒ DUENTH (Dynt, Denmark) Schleswig-Holstein Ger 1
❒ DUEPPEL (Dybboel, Denmark) Schleswig-Holstein Ger 1
❒ DUEREN Rheinland Ger 1 2 6 7 9
❒ DUERKHEIM, BAD Pfalz Ger 1
❒ DUERNAU OO Aus 1
❒ DUERNSTEIN NO Aus 1
❒ DUERREN Wuerttemberg Ger 2
❒ DUERRKUNZENDORF Rheinland Ger 7
❒ DUESAIGUES Tarragona Spa 1
❒ DUESSELDORF Rheinland Ger 1 2 3 5 7 9 11 14
❒ DUESSELDORF-DERENDORF Rheinprovinz Ger 2 7
❒ DUESSELDORF-GERRESHEIM Rheinprovinz Ger 2 7
❒ DUESSELDORF-GRAFENBERG Rheinland Ger 2
❒ DUESSELDORF-HEERDT Rheinland Ger 2
❒ DUESSELDORF-OBERKASSEL Rheinland Ger 2
❒ DUESSELDORF-RATH Rheinland Ger 2
❒ DUESSELDORF-RATINGEN Rheinland Ger 2
❒ DUFFEL Antwerp Bel 1
❒ DUISBURG Rheinland Ger 1 2 4 5 7 11 14
❒ DUISBURG-BEEK Rheinland Ger 11
❒ DUISBURG-HOCHFELD Rheinland Ger 2
❒ DUISBURG-MEIDERICH Rheinland Ger 2 5
❒ DUISBURG-MUELHEIM Rheinland Ger 2
❒ DUISBURG-RUHRORT Rheinland Ger 2 3
❒ DUISBURG-WANHEIM Rheinland Ger 2
❒ DUISDORF Rheinland Ger 7
❒ DUNA-SZERDAHLEY (Dunajska Streda, Dunaszerdahely) Cze 3
❒ DUNAJEVZY (Dunayevtzi, Dunayeuzy) Rus 1
❒ DUNASZERDAHELY Hun 3
❒ DUNIERES Haute Loire Fan 7
❒ DUNKELSTEIN NO Aus 1
❒ DUNKERQUE Nord Fan 1 2 6 7 11
❒ DU RAS Lot et Garonne Fan 1 2
❒ DURBAN Aude Fan 2
❒ DURLACH/ PFINZ Baden Ger 1 7
❒ DURRACH OO Aus 1
❒ DU RY Aisne Fan 1
❒ DURY Nord Fan 1
❒ DUSSEN North Brabant Net 14
❒ DUX (Duchov, Duchcov) Boehmen Cze 1
❒ DYBBOEL (Dueppel, Schleswig-Holstein, Germany) Den 1
❒ DYNT (Duenth) Den 1
❒ DYON Cote d'Or Fan 1

❐ DYROTZ Brandenburg Ger 3
❐ DZIALOSZYCE (Dzialochitzi) Rpl 2
❐ DZIALOSZYCE (Dzialochitzi, Dzyaloshitse) Rus 1
❐ DZIEDZICE (Dziedzicka) Rpl 2
❐ DZIKOW (Dzikownowy, Tarnobrzeg) Galicia Rpl 2

E

❐ EAUZE Gers Fan 1 2
❐ EBBERUP Den 11
❐ EBELSBERG OO Aus 1
❐ EBEN OO Aus 1
❐ EBEN/ ACHENSEE Tirol Aus 1
❐ EBENHAUSEN Bayern Ger 7
❐ EBENSEE OO Aus 1 9
❐ EBENTHAL Kaernten Aus 1
❐ EBERBACH/ NECKAR Baden Ger 1 6 7 8
❐ EBERGASSING NO Aus 9
❐ EBERNBURG Rheinland Ger 2
❐ EBERSBACH Sachsen Ger 1 2 8
❐ EBERSBERG Bayern Ger 1 2
❐ EBERSCHWANG OO Aus 1
❐ EBERSDORF Thueringen Ger 1
❐ EBERSDORF/ HABELSCHWERDT (Bystrzyca Klodzka) Glatz Ger 2
❐ EBERSTALLZELL OO Aus 1
❐ EBERSWALDE Brandenburg Ger 1 2 7 12 14
❐ EBINGEN/ SCHMIECHA Wuerttemberg Ger 1 2 6 9
❐ EBREICHSDORF NO Aus 1
❐ EBSTORF Hannover Ger 2
❐ ECAUSSINES-D'ENGHIEN Hainaut Bel 1 2
❐ ECAUSSINES-LALAING Hainaut Bel 1 2
❐ ECHTSBERG OO Aus 1
❐ ECKARTSAU NO Aus 1
❐ ECKARTSBERGA Provinz Sachsen Ger 1 6 7 9
❐ ECKENHAGEN Rheinland Ger 1
❐ ECKERNFOERDE Schleswig-Holstein Ger 1 2 8
❐ ECKKAMP Rheinland Ger 1
❐ ECOURT ST. QUENTIN Nord Fan 1 2
❐ EDE Gelderland Net 8
❐ EDELAERE East Flanders Bel 1
❐ EDENKOBEN Pfalz Ger 1
❐ EDLBACH OO Aus 1
❐ EDLING Bayern Ger 1
❐ EDOLO Brescia Ita 3
❐ EDOLO Lombardia Ita 3
❐ EDT BEI LAMBACH OO Aus 1
❐ EENAME East Flanders Bel 1
❐ EERBEEK N.V. Gelderland Net 14
❐ EERNEGHEM West Flanders Bel 1
❐ EFERDING OO Aus 1 2
❐ EGEDESMINDE Grn 14
❐ EGELN/ BODE Provinz Sachsen Ger 14
❐ EGELSEE NO Aus 1
❐ EGENBUETTEL Schleswig-Holstein Ger 1
❐ EGER (Cheb) Boehman Cze 2
❐ EGERSUND Nor 14
❐ EGG Kaernten Aus 1
❐ EGGE/ VOLMARSTEIN Westfalen Ger 2
❐ EGGELSBERG OO Aus 1
❐ EGGENBERG OO Aus 1
❐ EGGENBURG NO Aus 1 2
❐ EGGENDORF OO Aus 1
❐ EGGENFELDEN/ ROTT Bayern Ger 1 2 6
❐ EGGERDING OO Aus 1
❐ EGGOLSHEIM Bayern Ger 7
❐ EGHEM (Eeghem) West Flanders Bel 1
❐ EGING/ VILSHOFEN Bayern Ger 2
❐ EGLOSHEIM Wuerttemberg Ger 3
❐ EHEIN Liege Bel 1
❐ EHINGEN/ DONAU Wuerttemberg Ger 1 2 6
❐ EHMEN/ FALLERSLEBEN (Wolfsberg, Niedersachsen) Hannover Ger 2
❐ EHRANG/ KYLL & MOSEL Rheinland Ger 2
❐ EHRENBREITSTEIN/ RHINE Rheinland Ger 1 8
❐ EHRENFRIEDERSDORF Sachsen Ger 1 2
❐ EIBAU/ RUMBURGE (Eybau) Sachsen Ger 1 2 11
❐ EIBENBERG Sachsen Ger 1
❐ EIBENSTOCK Sachsen Ger 1 2 9
❐ EIBISWALD Steiermark Aus 9
❐ EICH Lux 1 2
❐ EICHBERG Steiermark Aus 1
❐ EICHENDORF Bayern Ger 2
❐ EICHRODT-WUTHA Sachsen-Weimar-Eisenach Ger 1
❐ EICHSTAETT/ ALTMUEHL (Aichstadt) Bayern Ger 1 4 10 14
❐ EICKEL (Wanne-Eickel) Westfalen Ger 1 2 9
❐ EICKELBORN Westfalen Ger 9
❐ EIDELSTADT Hamburg Ger 1 2
❐ EIDELSTEDT Schleswig-Holstein Ger 1 2
❐ EIDENBERG OO Aus 1
❐ EIDSHAUG Nor 14
❐ EILENBURG/ MULDE Provinz Sachsen Ger 1 2 6 7 8 9
❐ EILSEN, BAD/ AU Schaumburg-Lippe Ger 7 8 9 12 13
❐ EILSLEBEN Provinz Sachsen Ger 1
❐ EINBECK Hannover Ger 1
❐ EINBRUCH/ RUHR Westfalen Ger 1
❐ EINDHOVEN North Brabant Net 8
❐ EINOELLEN Pfalz Ger 1
❐ EINSIEDEL/ GOLNITZ Sachsen Ger 1 2
❐ EINSWARDEN Oldenburg Ger 2
❐ EISBERGEN Westfalen Ger 1
❐ EISDEN Limbourg Bel 1 14
❐ EISDORF/ HARZ Provinz Sachsen Ger 2.
❐ EISENACH Sachsen-Weimar-Eisenach Ger 1 2 6 7 9 11 12 13
❐ EISENBACH/ HOERSEL Baden Ger 2
❐ EISENBERG Sachsen-Altenburg Ger 1 2 9
❐ EISENERZ Steiermark Aus 1 9
❐ EISENSTEIN Bayern Ger 7
❐ EISFELD Sachsen-Meiningen Ger 1 2 6
❐ EISK Rus 1
❐ EISLEBEN Provinz Sachsen Ger 1 2 7 12 13
❐ EITORF Rheinland Ger 1 2 7 14
❐ EITRHEIM Nor 14
❐ EIZENDORF OO Aus 1
❐ EKATERINBURG Rus 1
❐ ELABUGA (Elabouga, Yelabuga) Rus 1
❐ ELBAU Ger 11
❐ ELBERFELD-BARMEN Rheinland Ger 11
❐ ELBERFELD/ WIPPER Rheinland Ger 1 2 3 4 6 7 8 9 11 12
❐ ELBEUF Seine-Inferieure Fan 1 2 6
❐ ELBING/ ELBING (Elblag) Westpreussen Ger 1 6 8
❐ ELBINGERODE (Provinz Sachsen) Hannover Ger 2 7
❐ ELCHE Alicante Spa 2
❐ ELCHE DE LA SIERRA Albacete Spa 1
❐ ELDA Alicante Spa 1
❐ ELDAGSEN Hannover Ger 1 6
❐ ELETS (Eletz, Yelets) Rus 1
❐ ELGERSBURG Sachsen-Coburg-Gotha Ger 1 7 9
❐ ELINIKI (Elninsk) Rus 1
❐ ELISABETHSTADT (Ibasfalau, Dumbraveni) Rom 1
❐ ELISAVETGRAD (Elizabethgrad, Lisavethrad, Jelisavetgrad) Rus 1
❐ ELISENFELD/ ARZBERT Bayern Ger 2
❐ ELIZABETHPOL Rus 1
❐ ELLAR Jaen Spa 2
❐ ELLEFELD/ VOGTLAND Sachsen Ger 1
❐ ELLERBEK Schleswig-Holstein Ger 1
❐ ELLERHOOP Als Fan 1
❐ ELLEZELLES East Flanders Bel 1
❐ ELLGUTH-STEINAU (Ligota-Scienawska) Schlesien Ger 2
❐ ELLINGEN Bayern Ger 2
❐ ELLRICH/ HARZ Provinz Sachsen Ger 1 2
❐ ELLWANGEN/ JAGST Wuerttemberg Ger 1 2 3 6
❐ ELMSCHENHAGEN Schleswig-Holstein Ger 1 13
❐ ELMSHORN/ ELBE Schleswig-Holstein Ger 1 2 6 7
❐ ELNE Pyrenees-Orientales Fan 2
❐ ELPE Westfalen Ger 2
❐ ELSASS/ LOTHRINGEN Ger 1
❐ ELSEN Rheinland Ger 2
❐ ELSENAU (Domaslawek) Posen Ger 1 2
❐ ELSENBORN Liege Bel 14

❒ ELSENBORN/ MALMEDY Rheinland Ger 10
❒ ELSENTHAL Bayern Ger 7
❒ ELSLOO Limburg Net 14
❒ ELSNIGK Sachsen Ger 7
❒ ELST Gelderland Net 14
❒ ELSTER, BAD/ LITTLE ELSTER Sachsen Ger 1 2 9
❒ ELSTERBERG/ WHITE ELSTER Sachsen Ger 1 2
❒ ELTERLEIN Sachsen Ger 1
❒ ELTMAN N/ MAI N Bayern Ger 1 6 7
❒ ELTVILLE/ RHEIN (Elfeld) Rheinland Ger 1 7
❒ ELVAS Portalegre Por 2
❒ ELVERDISSEN Westfalen Ger 2
❒ ELVERLINGSEN/ ALTENA Westfalen Ger 1 5
❒ ELVERSELE (Elverseele) East Flanders Bel 1
❒ ELZACH Baden Ger 1
❒ ELZE Hannover Ger 1
❒ EMANUELSSEGEN Schlesien Ger 5 9
❒ EMBOURG Liege Bel 1
❒ EMDEN (Embden) Hannover Ger 1 2 8 14
❒ EMELGHEM (Emelgem) West Flanders Bel 1 14
❒ EMILIA Ita 14
❒ EMMAGRUBE (Kopalina Emma) Schlesien Ger 2 5
❒ EMMEN Drenthe Net 14
❒ EMMENDINGEN/ ELTZ Baden Ger 1 6 8 9
❒ EMMERICH/ RHEIN (Emrich) Rheinland Ger 1 6 8
❒ EMMERSDORF NO Aus 1
❒ EMMERTHAL Hannover Ger 2
❒ EMPORI, LA VILA D' (Sant Pere Pescador) Gerona Spa 1
❒ EMS, BAD/ LAHN Hessen-Nassau Ger 1 8 9 11
❒ EMSDETTEN Westfalen Ger 1 2 11 14
❒ ENAKIYEVO (Yenakyevo, Enakievo, Yevo, Yenaki) Rus 1
❒ ENDORF/ SAUERLAND Westfalen Ger 7
❒ ENGELHARTSZELL OO Aus 1
❒ ENGELSDORF Sachsen Ger 1 2
❒ ENGELSKIRCHEN Rheinland Ger 1
❒ ENGEN Baden Ger 1
❒ ENGERWITZDORF OO Aus 1
❒ ENGHIEN-LES-BAINS Val d'Oise Fan 7
❒ ENGLANCOURT Aisne Fan 1
❒ ENGLEFONTAINE Nord Fan 2
❒ ENGUERA Valencia Spa 1
❒ ENIX Almeria Spa 2
❒ ENKENBACH Pfalz Ger 1
❒ ENKHUIZEN North Holland Net 8
❒ ENNEPE Westfalen Ger 1
❒ ENNEVELIN Nord Fan 1
❒ ENNIGERLOH Westfalen Ger 1 7

❒ ENNS OO Aus 1 2
❒ ENNSDORF NO Aus 1
❒ ENSCHEDE Overijssel Net 1 14
❒ ENSEN/ KOELN Rheinland Ger 2
❒ ENSIVAL Liege Bel 1
❒ ENYING Hun 3
❒ ENZESFELD NO Aus 1
❒ EPE (Eep) Westfalen Ger 7
❒ EPEHY Somme Fan 1
❒ EPERNAY Marne Fan 1 2 7
❒ EPINAL Vosges Fan 1 7 10
❒ EPINOY Pas de Calais Fan 1
❒ EPPE-SAUVAGE Nord Fan 1
❒ EPPEGHEM (Eppegem) Brabant Bel 1
❒ EPPELBORN Rheinland Ger 1
❒ EPPELBORN-DIRMINGEN Rheinland Ger 1
❒ EPPENDORF (Eppindorf) Sachsen Ger 1 2
❒ EPPEVILLE Somme Fan 1 2
❒ ERBACH-REISKI RCHEN Pfalz Ger 1
❒ ERBACH/ DONAU Wuerttemberg Ger 1
❒ ERBACH/ ODENWALD Hessen Ger 1
❒ ERBENDORF/ WAALDNAAB Bayern Ger 1 2 6
❒ ERBLAND Nordhein-Westfalen Ger 14
❒ ERCHEU Somme Fan 1
❒ ERDING Bayern Ger 2
❒ ERDMANNSDORF OO Aus 1
❒ ERE (Erre) Hainaut Bel 1
❒ ERFDE Schleswig-Holstein Ger 1
❒ ERFENSCHLAG Sachsen Ger 1 2
❒ ERFURT Provinz Sachsen Ger 1 2 7 9 10 11 13 12
❒ ERGOLDSBACH Bayern Ger 1
❒ ERING Bayern Ger 1
❒ ERIVAN Rus 1
❒ ERKELENZ Rheinland Ger 1 2
❒ ERKRATH Rheinland Ger 1
❒ ERLA NO Aus 1
❒ ERLA Sachsen Ger 2
❒ ERLACH OO Aus 1
❒ ERLANGEN Bayern Ger 1 2 8 9 10 11
❒ ERLAU/ EGER Sachsen Ger 2 7 9
❒ ERLAUF IM NIBELUNGENGAU NO Aus 1 2
❒ ERLBACH/ VOGTLAND Sachsen Ger 1
❒ ERLENBACH/ MAIN Bayern Ger 1
❒ ERLON Aisne Fan 1
❒ ERLOY Aisne Fan 1
❒ ERMANNSDORF Sachsen Ger 1 2 9
❒ ERMELO Gelderland Net 14
❒ ERMETON-SUR-BIERT Namur Bel 1
❒ ERMSLEBEN/ HARZ Provinz Sachsen Ger 1
❒ ERNSTBRUNN NO Aus 1
❒ ERNSTHOFEN NO Aus 1
❒ ERQUELINNES Hainaut Bel 1
❒ ERRE Nord Fan 1
❒ ERSTEIN Elsass Ger 6 7

❒ ERTL NO Aus 2
❒ ERWITTE-ANROECHTE Westfalen Ger 1
❒ ERZSBETFALA (Pestszenterzsebet, Erzsebetfalva, Leninvaros, Pesterzsebet Hun 2
❒ ESBJERG Den 11 12
❒ ESCALE, L'Gerona Spa 1
❒ ESCANUELA Jaen Spa 1
❒ ESCARMAIN Nord Fan 1
❒ ESCATALENS Tarn-et-Garonne Fan 2
❒ ESCATRON Zaragoza Spa 1
❒ ESCAUDAIN Nord Fan 1 7
❒ ESCAUDOEUVRES Nord Fan 1
❒ ESCAUFORT Aisne Fan 1 2
❒ ESCH-SUR-ALZETTE Lux 1 2
❒ ESCHENAU OO Aus 1
❒ ESCHENAU IM PINZGAU Salzburg Aus 1
❒ ESCHERFELD/ BORNA Sachsen Ger 2
❒ ESCHERSHAUSEN/ LENNE Braunschweig Ger 1 2
❒ ESCHWEGE/ WERRA Hessen-Nassau Ger 13 4 6 14
❒ ESCHWEILER Rheinland Ger 1 3 6 7 9
❒ ESCHWEILER & STOLBERG Rheinland Ger 1 2
❒ ESCORIAL DE LA SIERRA (San Lorenzo del Escorial) Madrid Spa 1
❒ ESCUCHA Teruel Spa 1
❒ ESENS Hannover Ger 1
❒ ESINGEN Schleswig-Holstein Ger 1
❒ ESLARN Bayern Ger 7
❒ ESLOHE Westfalen Ger 1
❒ ESMERY-HALLON Somme Fan 1 2
❒ ESNEUX Liege Bel 1
❒ ESPALOIS Tarn-et-Garonne Fan 2
❒ ESPARRAGOSA DE LARES Badajoz Spa 2
❒ ESPARREGUERA (Esparraguera) Barcelona Spa 1 2
❒ ESPELUY Jaen Spa 1
❒ ESPERGAERDE Den 11
❒ ESPIERRES West Flanders Bel 1
❒ ESPINELVES Gerona Spa 1
❒ ESPINHO Aveiro For 2
❒ ESPLECHIN Hainaut Bel 1
❒ ESPLUGA CALVI Lerida Spa 1
❒ ESPLUGA DE FRANCOLI Tarragona Spa 1
❒ ESPLUGUES Barcelona Spa 1
❒ ESPLUS Huesca Spa 1
❒ ESPOLLA Gerona Spa 1
❒ ESPOZENDE (Esposende) Braga Por 2
❒ ESQUELMES Hainaut Bel 1
❒ ESQUERCHIN Nord Fan 1
❒ ESQUERIES Aisne Fan 1
❒ ESRUM Den 11
❒ ESSEN Rheinland Ger 1 2 3 4 5 6 7 8 11 12 14
❒ ESSEN-ALTENESSEN Rheinland Ger 2
❒ ESSEN-BORBECK Rheinland Ger 2 3
❒ ESSEN-FRILLENDORF Rheinland Ger 2

❒ ESSEN-KARNAP Rheinland Ger
❒ ESSEN-RUETTENSCHEID Rheinland Ger 2
❒ ESSIGNY-LE-GRAND Aisne Fan 1
❒ ESSIGNY-LE-PETIT Aisne Fan 1
❒ ESSINGEN Pfalz Ger 7
❒ ESSLINGEN Wuerttemberg Ger 1 2 7 8 9
❒ ESSWEILER Pfalz Ger 1 6
❒ EST Banlieue Fan 7
❒ EST-TAGLIAMENTO Ita 14
❒ ESTADA Huesca Spa 1
❒ ESTADILLA Huesca Spa 1 2
❒ ESTAIMBOURG Hainaut Bel 1
❒ ESTAMPES Seine et Oise Fan 4
❒ ESTANY L'Barcelona Spa 1
❒ ESTARREJA Aveiro Por 2
❒ ESTERCUEL Teruel Spa 1 2
❒ ESTERN Westfalen Ger 2
❒ ESTERNBERG OO Aus 1
❒ ESTERRI D'ANEU Lerida Spa 1
❒ ESTICHE DE CINCA Huesca Spa 2
❒ ESTIVELLA Valencia Spa 1
❒ ESTOPINAN Huesca Spa 1
❒ ESTOUILLY Somme Fan 1
❒ ESTREES Aisne Fan 1
❒ ESTREES Nord Fan 1
❒ ESTREMOZ Evora Por 1 2
❒ ESZTERGOM Hun 1
❒ ETAING Pas-de-Calais Fan 1
❒ ETAMPES Seine et Oise Fan 3 4
❒ ETAVES-ET-BOCQUIAUX Aisne Fan 1
❒ ETCHEBERRYGAAY Fan 6
❒ ETERPIGNY Pas-de-Calais Fan 1
❒ ETHE Luxembourg Bel 1
❒ ETRAT Loire Fan 7
❒ ETREAUPONT Aisne Fan 1
❒ ETREILLES Aisne Fan 1
❒ ETREUX Aisne Fan 1
❒ ETSDORF NO Aus 1
❒ ETTAL Bayern Ger 1 2
❒ ETTEN EN LEUR North Brabant Net 14
❒ ETTENHEIM Baden Ger 1 6
❒ ETTLINGEN/ ALB Baden Ger 1 6 7 8 9 10
❒ ETZDORF Sachsen-Altenburg Ger 7
❒ ETZERSTETTEN NO Aus 2
❒ EULAU-WILHELMSHUETTE Schlesien Ger 2
❒ EUPEN Liege Bel 14
❒ EUPEN/ VESDRE Rheinland Ger 1 6 9
❒ EURATSFELD NO Aus 1
❒ EURE ET LOIRE Fan 1 6
❒ EURVILLE Haute Marne Fan 7
❒ EUSKIRCHEN Rheinland Ger 1 7
❒ EUTIN Schleswig-Holstein Ger 1 2 3
❒ EUZKADI Vizcaya Spa 6
❒ EVENKAMP Westfalen Ger 7 9
❒ EVERSBERG Westfalen Ger 1
❒ EVIAN-LES-BAINS Haute Savoie Fan 2
❒ EVIN-MALMAISON Pas de Calais Fan 1
❒ EVINGSEN Westfalen Ger 2
❒ EVORA Evora Por 2
❒ EVREGNIES Hainaut Bel 1
❒ EVREUX Eure Fan 1 3 6 7 11 14
❒ EXIN (Kcynia) Posen Ger 1
❒ EYDTKUHNEN (Kybartai, Lithuanian USSR) Ostpreussen Ger 7
❒ EYMET Dordogne Fan 1
❒ EYNATTEN East Flanders Bel 14
❒ EYNE East Flanders Bel 1
❒ EYSSET Dordogne Fan 1
❒ EYZIN-PINET Isere Fan 1 2

F

❒ FABARA Zaragoza Spa 1 2
❒ FABREZAN Aude Fan 1
❒ FACHECA Alicante Spa 1
❒ FACHES-THUMESNIL Nord Fan 1
❒ FAHR Rheinland Ger 2
❒ FAHRAFELD NO Aus 2
❒ FALAISE Calvados Fan 7
❒ FALKEN Sachsen Ger 1
❒ FALKENAU-KITTLITZ (Falknov-Kytlice, Falkenou-Kittlitz, Eger, Sokolov) Boehmen Cze 2
❒ FALKENAU/ HOHENSTEIN-ERNSTTHAL Sachsen Ger 1 2
❒ FALKENAU/ OHRI (Falknov/ Eger) Boehmen Cze 1
❒ FALKENBERG Provinz Sachsen Ger 2
❒ FALKENBERG (Niemodlin) Schlesien Ger 1 2
❒ FALKENBURG (Zlocieniec) Pommern Ger 1 2
❒ FALKENSTEIN/ VOGTLAND Sachsen Ger 1 2 7 8
❒ FALLAIS Liege Bel 1
❒ FALLERSLEBEN Hannover Ger 1
❒ FALLINGBOSTEL Hannover Ger 1 6
❒ FALLINGBOSTEL & WALSRODE Hannover Ger 1
❒ FALSET Tarragona Spa 1
❒ FAMORCA Alicante Spa 1
❒ FAMPOUX Pas de Calais Fan 1
❒ FANNA Ita 14
❒ FANNREM Nor 14
❒ FARCIENNES Hainaut Bel 1
❒ FARGNIERS Aisne Fan 1
❒ FARNERS DE LA SELVA (Santa Coloma de Farners) Gerona Spa 1
❒ FARNRODA Sachsen-Gotha Ger 2
❒ FARO Faro Por 1 2
❒ FARSUND Nor 14
❒ FATARELLA, LA Tarragona Spa 1
❒ FAUCOUCOURT Aisne Fan 1
❒ FAULQUEMONT Lorraine Fan 3 14
❒ FAUMONT Nord Fan 1
❒ FAURA Valencia Spa 1
❒ FAVRIL Nord Fan 1
❒ FAYET Aisne Fan 1
❒ FAYMONVILLE Liege Bel 14
❒ FAYON Zaragoza Spa 1
❒ FEBRO, LA Tarragona Spa 1
❒ FECAMP Seine Inferieure Fan 1 9 11
❒ FECAMP-FOURNEAUX Seine Inferieure Fan 7 9
❒ FECHAIN Nord Fan 1 2
❒ FEDA Nor 14
❒ FEDOSIA (Foudziadian, Fudziadian) Rus 1
❒ FEHRENBACH Thueringia Ger 2
❒ FEIGNIES Nord Fan 1
❒ FEIRA Aveiro Por 1 2
❒ FELDBACH Kaernten Aus 3
❒ FELDBERG Mecklenburg-Strelitz Ger 1
❒ FELDBERGER HOF/ SCHWARZWALD Baden Ger 1
❒ FELDEGG OO Aus 1
❒ FELDKI RCH Voralberg Aus 2 9
❒ FELDKIRCHEN/ DONAU OO Aus 1
❒ FELDKIRCHEN/ INN 0O Aus 1
❒ FELDMUEHL OO Aus 1
❒ FELED Hun 1
❒ FELGUEIRAS Porto Por 1
❒ FELGUERA, LA Asturias Spa 2
❒ FELIX Almeria Spa 1
❒ FELLBACH Wuerttemberg Ger 1
❒ FELLERINGEN Elsass Ger 1
❒ FELLERINGEN Haut-Rhin Fan 1
❒ FELLHAMMER (Boguszow) Schlesien Ger 1
❒ FELSOSAG Hun 3
❒ FENAIN Nord Fan 1
❒ FENESTRELE Piemonte Ita 3
❒ FERDINANDSGRUBE (Kopalnia Ferdynand) Schlesien Ger 5
❒ FERE, LA Aisne Fan 1 2
❒ FERIER Nord Fan 1
❒ FERIN Nord Fan 1
❒ FERNANCABALLERO Ciudad Real Spa 1
❒ FERREIRA Granada Spa 1
❒ FERREIRA DO ALENTEJO Beja Por 2
❒ FERREIRA DO ZEZERE Santarem Por 1 2
❒ FERSCHNITZ NO Aus 1 2
❒ FERTE-ALAIS, LA Seine et Oise Fan 7
❒ FERTE-CHEVRESIS, LA Aisne Fan 1
❒ FERTE-MACE, LA Orne Fan 2 3
❒ FERTOEBOZ (Holing) Hun
❒ FERTOERAKOS (Kroisbach) Hun
❒ FESNY Aisne Fan 1
❒ FESTENBERG (Twardagora) Schlesien Ger 2
❒ FEUCHT Bayern Ger 6
❒ FEUCHTWANGEN/ SULZ (Feuchtwang) Bayern Ger 6
❒ FEUCHY Pas-de-Calais Fan 1
❒ FEUDINGEN Westfalen Ger 2
❒ FEUERBACH Wuerttemberg Ger 1 6 9
❒ FEUERSBRUNN NO'Aus 1
❒ FEUQUIERES Somme Fan 4 7
❒ FEURS Fan 7

❒ FIEBERBRUNN Tirol Aus 1
❒ FIESOLE Hospital Ita 3
❒ FIEULAINE Aisne Fan 1
❒ FIGOLS DE SEGRE Lerida Spa 1
❒ FIGUEIRA DA FOZ Coimbra Por 1 2
❒ FIGUEIRA DE CASTELO RODRIGO Guarda Por 1
❒ FIGUEIRO DOS VINHOS Leiria Por 1 2
❒ FIGUERES Gerona Spa 1 2
❒ FIGUEROLA D'ORCAU Lerida Spa 1
❒ FILEHNE/ NETZE (Wielen, Wulen) Posen Ger 1
❒ FILLINGES Haute Savoie Fan 1 2
❒ FINALMARINA Castelfranco Ita 3
❒ FINALMARINA Forte Ita 3
❒ FINALMARINA Genova Ita 3
❒ FINALMARINA Liguria Ita 3
❒ FINANA Almeria Spa 1
❒ FINESTRAT Alicante Spa 1
❒ FINESTRES Gerona Spa 1
❒ FINHAN Tarn-et-Garonne Fan 2
❒ FINISTERE Fan 3 12
❒ FINKENWALDE/ SZCZECIN Pommern Ger 2
❒ FINNENTROP Westfalen Ger 2
❒ FINS Tarn Fan 1
❒ FINSTERBERGEN Thueringen Ger 7 9
❒ FINSTERWALDE N L Brandenburg Ger 1 2 6 8
❒ FIREJOW (Ferlejuv USSR) Rpl 1 2
❒ FIRENZE Ita 3
❒ FIRMINY Loire Fan 2 3 7
❒ FIRSCHING OO Aus 1
❒ FISCHAMEND NO Aus 1
❒ FISCHELN/ KREFELD Rheinland Ger 1
❒ FISCHLHAM OO Aus 1
❒ FISLIS Elsass Ger 1
❒ FISLIS Haut-Rhin Fan 1
❒ FIUME (Rieka, Rijeka, Yugoslavia) Ita 1 14
❒ FIUME (Rijeka) Yug 1
❒ FLA Nor 14
❒ FLACA Gerona Spa 1
❒ FLADUNGEN Bayern Ger 2
❒ FLAMENGRIE, LA Aisne Fan 1
❒ FLATOW (Zlotow, Zlotowo, Czlotowo) Westpreussen Ger 1
❒ FLATVALSUNDET Nor 14
❒ FLAVIGNY-LE-GRAND-BEURAIN Fan 1
❒ FLAVIGNY-LE-PETIT Aisne Fan 1 2
❒ FLAVY LE MELDEUX Somme Fan 1
❒ FLAVY-LE-MARTEL Aisne Fan 1 2
❒ FLAYOSC Var Fan 7
❒ FLAYOX Var Fan 7
❒ FLEKKEFJORD Nor 14
❒ FLEMALLE-GRANDE Liege Bel 1 6
❒ FLEMALLE-HAUTE Liege Bel 1
❒ FLENSBURG (Flensborg) Schleswig-Holstein Ger 1 2 6 7 8 9 10 14
❒ FLERS-EN-ESCREBIEUX Nord Fan 1
❒ FLEURANCE Fan 1 2
❒ FLINES-LEZ-RACHES Nord Fan 1
❒ FLISA Nor 14
❒ FLIX Tarragona Spa 1
❒ FLOBECQ Hainaut Bel 1
❒ FLOEHA Sachsen Ger 1 11
❒ FLOERSHEIM/ MAIN Hessen-Nassau Ger 1
❒ FLOING Ardennes Fan 1
❒ FLOREAL DEL RASPEIG Alicante Spa 1
❒ FLOREFFE Namur Bel 1
❒ FLORENSAC Herault Fan 7
❒ FLORESTA, LA Lerida Spa 1
❒ FLORY LE MELDEUX Oise Fan 1
❒ FLOSS Bayern Ger 1
❒ FLOSSENBURG Bayern Ger 15
❒ FLOSSMUEHLE/ BORSTENDORF Sachsen Ger 2
❒ FLOYOX Var Fan 7
❒ FLUQUIERES Aisne Fan 1
❒ FOCKBEK (Fokbek) Schleswig-Holstein Ger 2
❒ FOCKENDORF Thueringen Ger 2 7
❒ FOHNSDORF Steiermark Aus 9
❒ FOIX Arriege Fan 1 2
❒ FOIXA Gerona Spa 1
❒ FOLEMBRAY Aisne Fan 1 2
❒ FOLGUEROLES Barcelona Spa 1
❒ FOLLAFOSS Nor 14
❒ FOLSCHVILLER Lorraine Fan 3 14
❒ FONDON Almeria Spa 1
❒ FONELAS Granada Spa 1
❒ FONOLLOSA Barcelona Spa 2
❒ FONSOMME Aisne Fan 1
❒ FONTAINE AU PIRE Nord Fan 1
❒ FONTAINE NOTRE DAME Nord Fan 1
❒ FONTAINE-L'EVEQUE Hainaut Bel 1 2
❒ FONTAINE-LES-CLERCS Aisne Fan 1
❒ FONTAINE-UTERTE Aisne Fan 1
❒ FONTAINE-VALMONT Hainaut Bel 1
❒ FONTANARES Valencia Spa 1
❒ FONTE D'AMORE DI SYLMONA Ita 3 14
❒ FONTENAY LE COMTE Vendee Fan 7
❒ FONTENAY-AUX-ROSES Hautes de Seine Fan 1
❒ FONTENELLE Aisne Fan 1
❒ FONTENOY-BOURGEON Hainaut Bel 1
❒ FONTS DE SACALM (Sant Hilari Sacalm) Gerona Spa 1
❒ FONZ Huesca Spa 1
❒ FORBACH Lothringen Ger 1 2 6 14
❒ FORBACH Moselle Fan 1 2 3 14
❒ FORBACH/ MURG Baden Ger 1 6
❒ FORCA, LA Barcelona Spa 1
❒ FORCALL Castellon Spa 2
❒ FORCHHEIM Sachsen Ger 1 2
❒ FORCHHEIM/ REGNITZ Bayern Ger 1 7 9
❒ FORCHIES-LA-MARCHE Hainaut Bel 1
❒ FORDON Posen Ger 1
❒ FORENVILLE Nord Fan 1
❒ FORES Tarragona Spa 1
❒ FOREST Nord Fan 1
❒ FOREST-LEZ-BRUXELLES Brabant Bel 1
❒ FOREST-LEZ-FRASNES Hainaut Bel 1
❒ FORESTE Aisne Fan 1 2
❒ FORGES DE GUEUGNON Fan 1
❒ FORLI Marche Ita 3
❒ FORMENTERA DEL SEGURA Alicante Spa 1
❒ FORNELLES DE LA SELVA Gerona Spa 1
❒ FORNELLI Sardegna Ita 3
❒ FORNOS DE ALGODRES Guarda Por 2
❒ FORST Pfalz Ger 1
❒ FORST/ LAUSITZ Brandenburg Ger 1 2 6 11 12
❒ FO RSTH U B OO Aus 1
❒ FORT DE SENNECEY Fan 3
❒ FORT DE VAROIS Fan 3
❒ FORT DU MURIER Isere Fan 3
❒ FORTANETE Teruel Spa 1
❒ FORTUNA Murcia Spa 1
❒ FOS Haute-Garonne Fan 2
❒ FOSSANO Cueno Ita 3
❒ FOSSANO Piemonte Ita 3
❒ FOSSE Namur Bel 1
❒ FOSSLANDSOSEN Nor 14
❒ FOSSOMBRONE Ita 3
❒ FOUGERES Ille et Vilaine Fan 3 7
❒ FOUILLOUSE Loire Fan 7
❒ FOURCHAMBAULT Fan 14
❒ FOURCHAMBAULT Nievre Fan 14
❒ FOURMIES Nord Fan 1 2
❒ FOURMIES ET TRELON Nord Fan 7
❒ FOURQUEVAUX Haute Garonne Fan 1
❒ FOUSSERET Haute Garonne Fan 1
❒ FOYOS Valencia Spa 1
❒ FOZ-CALANDA Teruel Spa 1
❒ FRAENKISCH-CRUMBACH Hessen Ger 1
❒ FRAGA Huesca Spa 1 2
❒ FRAHAM OO Aus 1
❒ FRAILES Jaen Spa 1
❒ FRAISANS Jura Fan 7
❒ FRAISSE Loire Fan 7
❒ FRAITURE-EN-CONDROZ Liege Bel 1
❒ FRANCILLY-SELENCY Aisne Fan 1
❒ FRANKENBERG/ EDER Hessen-Nassau Ger 1
❒ FRANKENBERG/ ZSCHOPAU Sachsen Ger 1 2 8
❒ FRANKENBURG OO Aus 1 2
❒ FRANKENFELS NO Aus 1
❒ FRANKENHAUSEN/ KYFFHAUSEN (Bad Frankenhausen) Thueringen Ger 1 2 6

❐ FRANKENMARKT OO Aus 1
❐ FRANKENSTEIN (Zabkowice) Schlesien Ger 1 2 5 6 7 9
❐ FRANKENTHAL Pfalz Ger 1 6 7 8 9
❐ FRANKENTHAL/ GERA Thueringen Ger 2
❐ FRANKFURT-HEDDERNHEIM Hessen-Nassau Ger 7 8
❐ FRANKFURT/ MAIN Hessen-Nassau Ger 1 2 3 4 6 7 8 9 10 11 12
❐ FRANKFURT/ MAIN-GRIESHEIM Hessen-Nassau Ger 8
❐ FRANKFURT/ MAIN-ROEDELHEIM Hessen-Nassau Ger 7
❐ FRANKFURT/ MAIN-WEST Hessen-Nassau Ger 7
❐ FRANKFURT/ ODER (Sublice) Brandenburg Ger 1 2 3
❐ FRANQUESES, LES Barcelona Spa 1
❐ FRANZBERG OO Aus 1
❐ FRANZBURG Pommern Ger 1 2
❐ FRASNES-LEZ-BUISSENAL Hainaut Bel 1
❐ FRATTAMAGGIORE Ita 11
❐ FRAUENAU Bayern Ger 1 6 7
❐ FRAUENDORF (Wroblin) Schlesien Ger 7
❐ FRAUENKOPF Rus 1
❐ FRAUENSTEIN/ ERZGEBIRGE Sachsen Ger 1 2
❐ FRAUENWALDAU/ TREBNITZ Schlesien Ger 2
❐ FRAUENZELL Bayern Ger 14
❐ FRAUREUTH Thueringen Ger 2
❐ FRAUSTADT (Wschowa) Schlesien Ger 1 2
❐ FRAUWALDAU/ TREBNITZ Schlesien Ger 2
❐ FRECHEN Rheinland Ger 1 3 7 9
❐ FREDBURG Westfalen Ger 1
❐ FREDEN/ LEINE Hannover Ger 2 7
❐ FREDERICIA Den 11
❐ FREDERIKSBJERG-TROJBORG Den 12
❐ FREDERIKSBORG Den 11
❐ FREDERIKSHAVN Den 11
❐ FREDERIKSSUND Den 11
❐ FREGINALS Tarragona Spa 1
❐ FREIBERG Sachsen Ger 1 2 7 8 10 11 13
❐ FREIBURG (Swiebodzice) Schlesien Ger 1 2
❐ FREIBURG/ Breisgau, KONSTANZ SCHOPFHEIM und VILLIGEN Baden Ge 1 2
❐ FREIBURG/ ELBE Hannover Ger 2
❐ FREIBURG/ TREISAM-BREISGAU Baden Ger 1 2 7 8 9 11 13
❐ FREIENOHL (Freiheit) Westfalen Ger 1
❐ FREIENWALDE/ ODER (Oberbarnim, Moorbad; Bad Freienwalde) Brandenburg Ger 1 2
❐ FREIENWALDE/ ODER (Chociwel) Pommern Ger 1

❐ FREILASSING Bayern Ger 1 2
❐ FREINBERG OO Aus 1
❐ FREISING/ ISAR Bayern Ger 1 2 7
❐ FREISTADT (Frystat, Frystak) Cze 2
❐ FREISTADT OO Aus 1 2 3 4
❐ FREITAL Sachsen Ger 1 2
❐ FREIXANET (Sant Guim Estacio) Lerida Spa 1
❐ FREIXO DE ESPADA A CINTA Braganca Por 2 1
❐ FREMDISWALDE Sachsen Ger 2
❐ FRENCH OCEANIA Foa 1
❐ FRENDA Alg 1
❐ FREREN Hannover Ger 1
❐ FRERENT Nord Fan 7
❐ FRESNE S/ ESCAUT Nord Fan 2
❐ FRESNEDA, LA Teruel Spa 1
❐ FRESNES Nord Fan 2
❐ FRESNES LES MANTAUBAN Fan 1
❐ FRESNOY-LE-GRAND Aisne Fan 1
❐ FRESSAIN Nord Fan 1
❐ FRESSIES Nord Fan 1
❐ FRESVIK Nor 14
❐ FRETOY Somme Fan 1
❐ FREUDENSTADT UND BAIERSBRONN Wuerttemberg Ger 1 2
❐ FREUDENSTADT/ MURG Wuerttemberg Ger 1 6 7
❐ FREUDENTHAL/ WANDERSLEBEN Provinz Sachsen Ger 1
❐ FREVENT Pas-de-Calais Fan 7
❐ FREVENT & ENVIRONS Pas de Calais Fan 7
❐ FREYBURG/ UNSTRUT Provinz Sachsen Ger 1
❐ FREYENSTEIN/ OSTPRIGNITZ Brandenburg Ger 1
❐ FREYSTADT (Kozuchow) Schlesien Ger 1 2 6
❐ FREYSTADT (Freistadt) Westpreussen Ger 1
❐ FREYUNG/ WALD Bayern Ger 1 2 6 7
❐ FRIAUL (Friuli) Venice Ita 14
❐ FRICKENHAUSEN/ MAIN Wuerttemberg Ger 2
❐ FRIEDBERG Bayern Ger 1 2
❐ FRIEDBERG Hessen Ger 1 2 3 4 5
❐ FRIEDEBERG Bayern Ger 1
❐ FRIEDEBERG/ PEZA-NEUMARK (Strzelce Krajenskie, Poland) Brandenburg Ger 1
❐ FRIEDEBERG/ QUEIS (Mirsk) Schlesien Ger 1
❐ FRIEDENFELS Bayern Ger 6
❐ FRIEDENSAU Provinz Sachsen Ger 7
❐ FRIEDENSGRUBE (Kopalnia Pokoj) Schlesien Ger 4 5
❐ FRIEDENSHUETTE (Huta Pokoj) Schlesien Ger 1 2 3 4 5 7
❐ FRIEDLAND Mecklenburg-Strelitz Ger 1 2
❐ FRIEDLAND MAERKISCH (Prawdinsk; Pravdinsk) Ostpreussen Ger 1 8

❐ FRIEDLAND/ STEINAU Schlesien Ger 1 2 7
❐ FRIEDRICH-AUGUSTHUETTE Oldenburg Ger 2
❐ FRIEDRICHRODA Sachsen-Gotha Ger 1
❐ FRIEDRICHSBRUNN/ HARZ Provinz Sachsen Ger 1
❐ FRIEDRICHSDORF (Bykowina) Schlesien Ger 1 4
❐ FRIEDRICHSDORF/ TAUNUS Hessen-Nassau Ger 1 7
❐ FRIEDRICHSFELD/ WESEL Rheinland Ger 1 3
❐ FRIEDRICHSHAFEN/ BUCHHORN Wuerttemberg Ger 1 2 6 8
❐ FRIEDRICHSHAIDE Ruess j. Linie Ger 7
❐ FRIEDRICHSHAIN Brandenburg Ger 7 9
❐ FRIEDRICHSRODA Thueringen Ger 1 2
❐ FRIEDRICHSTADT Schleswig-Holstein Ger 1 2 8
❐ FRIEDRICHSTHAL-SAAR Rheinland Ger 1
❐ FRIEDRICHSUETTE-LAASPHE Westfalen Ger 2
❐ FRIEDRICHSWERTH Sachsen-Gotha Ger 2 7
❐ FRIELENDORF Hessen Ger 5
❐ FRIERES-FAILLOUEL Aisne Fan 1
❐ FRIESACH Brandenburg Ger 1 8
❐ FRIESLAND Net 14
❐ FRIESOYTHE/ SOESTE Oldenburg Ger 1
❐ FRIGOLET Bouches du Rhone Fan 3 4 10 15
❐ FRITZLAR Hessen Ger 1 14
❐ FROENDENBERG/ RUHR Westfalen Ger 1 2
❐ FROHBURG Sachsen Ger 1 2
❐ FROHNAU/ ERZGEBIRGE Sachsen Ger1
❐ FROHSE/ ELBE Provinz Sachsen Ger 1
❐ FROIDMONT Hainaut Bel 1
❐ FRONCLES Haute-Marne Fan 2
❐ FRONTEIRA Portalegre Por 1 2
❐ FRONTENHAUSEN/ VILS Bayern Ger 2
❐ FRONTON Haut Garonne Fan 2
❐ FROSE Anhalt Ger 1
❐ FROSINONE Ita 14
❐ FROSTA Nor 14
❐ FROYENNES Hainaut Bel 1
❐ FRUECHT/ EMS Hessen-Nassau Ger 1
❐ FRUITERS (Castellbisbal) Barcelona Spa 1
❐ FUCHSBERG Hannover Ger 3
❐ FUENFKIRCHEN (Pecs) Hun 2
❐ FUENLABRADA DE LOS MONTES Badajoz Spa 1
❐ FUENTE Cuenca Spa 2
❐ FUENTE DEL FRESNO Ciudad Real Spa 2
❐ FUENTE LA HUGUERA Valencia Spa 1
❐ FUENTE LA LANCHA Cordoba Spa 1

❒ FUENTE-ENCARROZ Valencia Spa 1
❒ FUENTEALAMO Albacete Spa 1
❒ FUENTEALBILLA Albacete Spa 1
❒ FUENTESPALDA Teruel Spa 1
❒ FUERSTENAU Hannover Ger 1
❒ FUERSTENBERG Mecklenburg-Strelitz Ger 1
❒ FUERSTENBERG/ ODER (Stalinstadt, Eisenhuettenstadt) Brandenburg Ger 3
❒ FUERSTENBERG/ WESER Westphalia Ger 1
❒ FUERSTENFELDBRUCK Bayern Ger 2
❒ FUERSTENFELDE N M (Boleszkowice) Brandenburg Ger 6
❒ FUERSTENGRUBE Ger 5
❒ FUERSTENHAUSEN/ SAAR Rheinland Ger 3 7
❒ FUERSTENWALDE/ SPREE Brandenburg Ger 1 2 6 9
❒ FUERSTENZELL Bayern Ger 2 14
❒ FUERTH Bayern Ger 1 2 6 7 8 9 10 11 13
❒ FUESSEN Bayern Ger 1 2 4 5 7 9
❒ FULDA Hessen-Nassau Ger 1 2 6 8 9
❒ FULIOLA, LA Lerida Spa 1
❒ FULLEDA Lerida Spa 1
❒ FUMAL Liege Bel 1
❒ FUMAY Ardennes Fan 1 2
❒ FUMEL Lot et Garonne Fan 2 7
❒ FUNCHAL Madeira Mai 2
❒ FUNDAO Castelo Branco For1 2
❒ FURNEAUX (Furnaux) Namur Bel 1
❒ FURTH NO Aus 1
❒ FURTH/ WALDE Bayern Ger 1 2 6
❒ FURTWANGEN Baden Ger 1 6 9
❒ FUSCHL/ SEE Salzburg Aus 1

G

❒ GAANSAGER Den 2
❒ GAANSAGER (Gaansager, Denmark) Schleswig-Holstein Ger 1 2
❒ GABIN (Gombin) Rus 1
❒ GABLONZ/ NEISSE (Jablonec nad Nisou) Boehmen Cze 1 2
❒ GABON Fwa 6
❒ GACY-SUR-EURE Eure Fan 7
❒ GADEBUSCH Mecklenburg-Schwerin Ger 1
❒ GADOR Almeria Spa 1
❒ GAFLENZ OO Aus 1
❒ GAFSA Tun 2
❒ GAGGENAU/ MURG Baden Ger 1 2 9
❒ GAGNY Seine et Oise Fan 14
❒ GAGRI (Gagry) Rus 1
❒ GAHLEN Westfalen Ger 5
❒ GAIA Por 6 13
❒ GAILDORF/ KOCHER Wuerttemberg Ger 2 6 13
❒ GAILLAC Tarn Fan 1 2
❒ GAILLAC-TOULZA Haute-Garonne Fan 1 2
❒ GAIMERSHEIM Bavaria Ger 10
❒ GAINFARN NO Aus 1
❒ GAISIN Rus 1
❒ GALAGUER Lerida Spa 1
❒ GALATI Rom 12
❒ GALERA Granada Spa 1
❒ GALERA DEL PLA, LA Tarragona Spa 1
❒ GALLAIX Hainaut Bel 1
❒ GALLARDOS, LOS Almeria Spa 1
❒ GALLICIAN Gard Fan 7
❒ GALLNEUKIRCHEN OO Aus 1
❒ GALLSPACH OO Aus 1
❒ GALVEZ Toledo Spa 1
❒ GALZOV Rus 1
❒ GAMING NO Aus 1
❒ GAMPERN OO Aus 1
❒ GAND (Guisland) East Flanders Bel 14
❒ GANDDAL Nor 14
❒ GANDERKESEE Oldenburg Ger 2
❒ GANDERSHEIM/ GANDE Braunschweig Ger 2 14
❒ GANDESA Tarragona Spa 1
❒ GANDIA Valencia Spa 1
❒ GANGELT Rheinland Ger 1
❒ GANGES Herault Fan 7
❒ GARBAYUELA Badajoz Spa 1
❒ GARBUS Thueringia Ger 2
❒ GARCIA Tarragona Spa 1 2
❒ GARD Fan 6 7
❒ GARD-HERAULT-AUDE Fan 14
❒ GARDELEGEN Provinz Sachsen Ger 1 2 3 6 7 9
❒ GARENNE, LA Seine Fan 7
❒ GARGALLO Teruel Spa 1
❒ GARGANTA, LA Ciudad Real Spa 2
❒ GARIBALDI Genova Ita 3
❒ GARIBALDI Hospital Ita 3
❒ GARMISCH/ LOISACH Bayern Ger 1 2 6 7
❒ GARRIGA, LA Barcelona Spa 1 2
❒ GARRIGUELLA Gerona Spa 1
❒ GARRUCHA Almeria Spa 1
❒ GARS/ KAMP NO Aus 1 2
❒ GARSTEDT Schleswig-Holstein Ger 1
❒ GARSTEN OO Aus 1
❒ GASPOLTSHOFEN OO Aus 1
❒ GASTEIN, BAD Salzburg Aus 1
❒ GATA DE GORGOS Alicante Spa 1
❒ GATCHINA (Trotzk) Rus 1
❒ GATERSLEBEN Provinz Sachsen Ger 1
❒ GAUCHY Aisne Fan 1
❒ GAUDRAIN-RAMECROIX Hainaut Bel 1
❒ GAUTSCH/ LEIPZIG Sachsen Ger 1 2 9
❒ GAVA Barcelona Spa 1 2
❒ GAVI Ligure Ita 3
❒ GAVI CASTELLO Alessandria Piemonte Ita 3
❒ GAVIAO Portalegre Por 1 2
❒ GAVRELLE Pas-de-Calais Fan 1
❒ GAYANES Alicante Spa 2
❒ GDYNIA/ DANZIG (Gdingen) Westpreussen Ger 2
❒ GEBESEE/ GERA Provinz Sachsen Ger 1
❒ GEBOLTSKIRCHEN OO Aus 1
❒ GEBWEILER Elsass Ger 1
❒ GEERAARDSBERGEN East Flanders Bel 1
❒ GEESTEMUENDE (Bremerhaven) Hannover Ger 1 2
❒ GEFREES Rheinland Ger 9
❒ GEHOFEN Provinz Sachsen Ger 1
❒ GEHREN Schwarzburg-Sonderhausen Ger 2 9
❒ GEIERSBERG OO Aus 1
❒ GEILENKIRCHEN & HEINSBERG Rheinland Ger 1
❒ GEILENKIRCHEN/ WURM Rheinland Ger 1
❒ GEINBERG OO Aus 1
❒ GEISA/ ULSTER Thueringen Ger 1 2
❒ GEISELHOERING/ KLEIN LABER Bayern Ger 6
❒ GEISENHEIM/ RHEIN Hessen-Nassau Ger 7 8 9
❒ GEISHAUSEN Elsass Ger 1
❒ GEISHAUSEN Haut-Rhin Fan 1
❒ GEISING Sachsen Ger 1
❒ GEISLINGEN/ STEIG Wuerttemberg Ger 1 2 9
❒ GEISSFOERTH Hessen-Nassau Ger 1
❒ GEISWEID Westfalen Ger 2 9
❒ GEITHAIN (Geiten) Sachsen Ger 2
❒ GELDERN Rheinland Ger 1 2
❒ GELEEN Limberg Net 14
❒ GELENAU Sachsen Ger 1 2
❒ GELIDA Barcelona Spa 1
❒ GELNHAUSEN/ KINZIG Hessen-Nassau Ger 1 8
❒ GELSA Zaragoza Spa 1
❒ GELSENKIRCHEN Westfalen Ger 1 3 5 6 8 9 11
❒ GELSENKIRCHEN-BISMARCK Westfalen Ger 2
❒ GELSENKIRCHEN-ROTTHAUSEN Westfalen Ger 1 6
❒ GELTING Schleswig-Holstein Ger 2
❒ GEMBITZ (Gebice) Posen Ger 1
❒ GEMMENICH Liege Bel 1 14
❒ GEMUENDEN/ MAIN Bayern Ger 1 6
❒ GENERAC Gard Fan 2
❒ GENERARGUES Gard Fan 7
❒ GENEVILLIERS Hauts-de-Seine Fan 7
❒ GENGENBACH/ KINZIG Baden Ger 1 2 6
❒ GENK (Genck) Limbourg Bel 1 14
❒ GENOA Ita 3
❒ GENSUNGEN Hessen-Nassau Ger 1
❒ GENT (Ghent, Gant, Gand) East Flanders Bel 1 6
❒ GENTHIN Provinz Sachsen Ger 1
❒ GENTILLY Seine Fan 7

❒ GEOPPERSDORF Sachsen Ger 1 2
❒ GEORGENDORF Kaernten Aus 1
❒ GEORGENSGMUEND Bayern Ger 7
❒ GEORGESHUETTE Silesia Ger 1
❒ GEORGESWALDE Sachsen Ger 2
❒ GEORGIYEVSK Rus 1
❒ GEORGSMARIENHUETTE Hannover Ger 9
❒ GEORGSWALDE Cze 1
❒ GERA Reuss j.L Ger 1 2 7 8 9 11 12 14
❒ GERA-DEBSCHWITZ Thueringen Ger 2
❒ GERA-ZWOETZEN Thueringen Ger 2
❒ GERA/ ELGERSBURG Sachsen-Gotha Ger 2 6 7 8 9 11
❒ GERABRONN Wuerttemberg Ger 1 2
❒ GERBSTEDT Provinz Sachsen Ger 2
❒ GERCY Saone et Loire Fan 7
❒ GERDAISES Tarn-et-Garonne Fan 2
❒ GERERSDORF NO Aus 1
❒ GERETSBERG OO Aus 1
❒ GERGAL Almeria Spa 1
❒ GERGNY Aisne Fan 1
❒ GERHARDSBRUNN OO Aus 1
❒ GERINGSWALDE Sachsen Ger 1
❒ GERLEVE Westfalen Ger 3
❒ GERMAINE Aisne Fan 1 2
❒ GERMERSHEIM/ RHEIN Pfalz Ger 1 6 7
❒ GERNRODE/ HARZ Anhalt Ger 1
❒ GERNSBACH/ MURG Baden Ger 1 2
❒ GEROLDSGRUEN Bayern Ger 1
❒ GEROLSTEIN Rheinland Ger 2 9
❒ GEROLZHOFEN Bayern Ger 6
❒ GEROTTEN UN POETZLES NO Aus 1
❒ GERRESHEIM/ DUESSELDORF Rheinland Ger 7
❒ GERRI DE LA SAL Lerida Spa 1
❒ GERS Fan 1
❒ GERSDORF/ ROSSWEIN Sachsen Ger 1 2
❒ GERSFELD Hessen Ger 1 14
❒ GERSTETTEN Wuerttemberg Ger 1
❒ GERTHE (Bochum) Westfalen Ger 1 2 3 5 7
❒ GERWERMINGHOFF Grube Schlesien Ger 3
❒ GESCHER Westfalen Ger 1 2
❒ GESCHWENDA Thueringen Ger 2
❒ GESEKE Westfalen Ger 2
❒ GEULLE Limburg Net 14
❒ GEVELSBERG Westfalen Ger 1 2 8 11
❒ GEVELSBERG-NORD Westfalen Ger 2
❒ GEX Ain Fan 6 7
❒ GEXONNE Meurthe-et-Moselle Fan 7
❒ GEYER Sachsen Ger 1
❒ GEYERSDORF Sachsen Ger 1
❒ GEYRIAC MINERVOIS Aude Fan 7
❒ GFOEHL NO Aus 1
❒ GHEEL Antwerp Bel 1
❒ GHELUWE West Flanders Bel 1
❒ GHILARZA Sardegna Ita 3
❒ GHINAGLIA Ita 14
❒ GIBEON Ged 1
❒ GIBERCOU RT Aisne Fan 1
❒ GIBRALTAR Gib 14
❒ GIENGEN/ BRENZ Wuerttemberg Ger 1 2
❒ GIERSDORF (Grottkau; Galaszczyce) Schlesien Ger 2
❒ GIESENKIRCHEN/ RHEYDT Rheinland Ger 1
❒ GIESSEN North Brabant Net 14
❒ GIESSEN/ LAHN Hessen-Nassau Ger 1 2 6 7 8 12
❒ GIESSHUEBL NO Aus 1
❒ GIESSUEBEL Thueringen Ger 2
❒ GIFHORN/ ALLER Hannover Ger 1 2
❒ GIHEL Fan 2
❒ GIJON Asturias Spa 2
❒ GILDENHALL/ FREILAND SIEDLUNG Brandenburg Ger 1
❒ GILENKIRCHEN & HEINSBERG Rheinland Ger 1
❒ GILGENBERG OO Aus 1
❒ GILGENBURG (Dabrowno) Ostpreussen Ger 1 6
❒ GILLY Hainaut Bel 1
❒ GIMINAGNO Siena Ita 3
❒ GIMONT Gers Fan 1 2
❒ GIN-NICE Alpes Maritimes Fan 7
❒ GINESTAR D'ERBE Tarragona Spa 1
❒ GINGEN/ FILS Wuerttemberg Ger 2
❒ GINGHELOM (Gingelom) Limbourg Bel 1
❒ GINOUSE Pyrenees Orientales Fan 7
❒ GIONIURAGGIO Sardegna Ita 3
❒ GIRAUD Fan 7
❒ GIRONA Gerona Spa 1
❒ GIRONELLA Barcelona Spa 1
❒ GISCLARENY Barcelona Spa 1
❒ GISLEY Den 11
❒ GISPERSLEBEN Sachsen Ger 7
❒ GITS West Flanders Bel 1
❒ GITTELDE Braunschweig Ger 7
❒ GIVET Ardennes Fan 2
❒ GIVORS Rhone Fan 1 2 7
❒ GJEMLESTAD Nor 14
❒ GJERPEN Nor 14
❒ GLADBACH (Bergisch Gladbach) Rheinland Ger 1 2 4 14
❒ GLADBECK Westfalen Ger 1 3 5
❒ GLADENBACH Hessen-Nassau Ger 1
❒ GLAESENDORF/ FRANKENSTEIN (Szklary) Schlesien Ger 5 7
❒ GLAGEON Nord Fan 1 2
❒ GLASHUETTE Sachsen Ger 1 2
❒ GLASOV (Glazov) Rus 1
❒ GLATZ/ NEISSE (Kladsko; Klodzko) Schlesien Ger 1 2 6 11
❒ GLAUCHAU/ MULDE Sachsen Ger 1 2 8 11
❒ GLEHN Rheinland Ger 1
❒ GLEIDINGEN/ INNERSTE Hannover Ger 2
❒ GLEINACH Kaernten Aus 1
❒ GLEINK OO Aus 1
❒ GLEIWITZ/ KLODNITZ (Gilwice;Gliwicka) Schlesien Ger 1 2 3 5 7 11
❒ GLEIZE, LA Liege Bel 1
❒ GLEVINYOL DE TER (Les Masies de Sant Hipolit) Barcelona Spa 1
❒ GLINDE Schleswig-Holstein Ger 2
❒ GLINK MARIAMPOLSKI Rpl 2
❒ GLOESA Sachsen Ger 1
❒ GLOETHE/ FOERDERSTEDT Provinz Sachsen Ger 2 7
❒ GLOGAU/ HOTZENPLOTZ (Glogow; Zielona Gora) Schlesien Ger 1 2 7 9 10
❒ GLOGGNITZ NO Aus 9
❒ GLOMFJORD Nor 14
❒ GLUCHOV (Glukhov, Gloukov) Rus 1
❒ GLUECKFRIED Ger 5
❒ GLUECKSBURG Schleswig-Holstein Ger 1 7
❒ GLUECKSTADT/ ELBE Schleswig-Holstein Ger 1 2 7
❒ GLUTVIN (Goloutvin) Rus 1
❒ GMUEND NO Aus 1 3 9
❒ GMUEND SCHWAEBISCH Wuerttemberg Ger 1 7
❒ GMUNDEN OO Aus 1
❒ GNADENFREI (Pilawa Gorna) Schlesien Ger 1 2 3 4 7
❒ GNARRENBURG Hannover Ger 1
❒ GNEISENAU Ger 4
❒ GNEIXENDORF NO Aus 1
❒ GNESEN (Gniezno) Posen Ger 1 2 6 10 14
❒ GNESEN UND WITKOWO (Gniezno) Posen Ger 1
❒ GNOIEN Mecklenburg-Schwerin Ger 1
❒ GOCH/ NIERS Rheinland Ger 1 7 8
❒ GODALL Tarragona Spa 1
❒ GODELHEIM/ HOEXTER Westfalen Ger 1
❒ GODESBERG/ BAD/ RHEIN Rheinland Ger 1 8 11
❒ GODULLASCHACHT Schlesien Ger 5
❒ GOEDOELLOE Hun 14
❒ GOEGGINGEN Bayern Ger 2 8 11
❒ GOELLERSDORF Aus 2
❒ GOELTZSCH Thueringen Ger 2
❒ GOEPPERSDORF Sachsen Ger 1 2
❒ GOEPPINGEN/ FILS Wuerttemberg Ger 1 2 6 7 8 14
❒ GOERCHEN Posen Ger 1 7
❒ GOERGENSGMUEND Bayern Ger 7
❒ GOERKAU (Jirkov) Cze 1

❒ GOERLITZ/ NEISSE (Zgorzelec) Schlesien Ger 1 2 3 4 7 8 9 12 14
❒ GOERNE Brandenburg Ger 7
❒ GOERSDORF Sachsen Ger 2
❒ GOERZKE Ger 13
❒ GOES Zeeland Net 1 8
❒ GOESING AM WAGRAM NO Aus 2
❒ GOESSNITZ/ PLEISSE Thueringen Ger 1 2 6 11
❒ GOESTLING NO Aus 1 2
❒ GOETTINGEN/ LEINE Hannover Ger 1 2 3 8
❒ GOETTWEIG NO Aus 2
❒ GOETZENDORF NO Aus 1
❒ GOEULZIN Nord Fan 1
❒ GOHFELD Westfalen Ger 1
❒ GOISE LA Nord Fan 1
❒ GOISERN OO Aus 1
❒ GOIX-TERRON Ardennes Fan 6
❒ GOLANCOURT Oise Fan 1
❒ GOLDAP/ GOLDAPP Ostpreussen Ger 1
❒ GOLDBACH Elsass Ger 1
❒ GOLDBACH Haut-Rhin Fan 1
❒ GOLDBACH Sachsen Ger 2
❒ GOLDBERG Mecklenburg-Schwerin Ger 1
❒ GOLDBERG/ KATZBACH (Zlotoryja) Schlesien Ger 1
❒ GOLDLAUTER Provinz Sachsen Ger 7
❒ GOLDSCHMIEDEN (Wroclaw Zlotniki) Schlesien Ger 3
❒ GOLDWOERTH OO Aus 1
❒ GOLEGA Santarem Por 2
❒ GOLENCIN Posen Ger 2
❒ GOLINA Rpl 2
❒ GOLINA Rus 1
❒ GOLLANTSCH (Golancz) Posen Ger 1 2
❒ GOLLING Salzburg Aus 1
❒ GOLLNOW (Goleniow) Pommern Ger 1 13
❒ GOLMES Lerida Spa 1 2
❒ GOLPA Provinz Sachsen Ger 2 7
❒ GOLZERN/ MULDE Sachsen Ger 3
❒ GOLZWARDEN Oldenburg Ger 2
❒ GOMEL Rus 1
❒ GOMPERSDORF Schlesien Ger 7
❒ GONARS Ita 14
❒ GONDOMAR Porto Por 1
❒ GONDRIN Gers Fan 6 7
❒ GONESSE Seine-Maritime Fan 1
❒ GONSAWA (Gasawa) Posen Ger 1
❒ GONSENHEIM Hessen Ger 1
❒ GONT-SUR-SEINE Aube Fan 7
❒ GONTAUD Lot et Garonne Fan 1 2
❒ GONTENBACH Aus 1
❒ GONY Aisne Fan 1
❒ GONY/ BELLONE Pas-de-Calais Fan 1
❒ GOR Granada Spa 1
❒ GORA Posen Ger 1 2
❒ GORAFE Granada Spa 1
❒ GORASDZE (Gorazdze) Schlesien Ger 2
❒ GORGA Alicante Spa 1
❒ GORGAST Brandenburg Ger 10
❒ GORINCHEM South Holland Net 8
❒ GORIZIA Yug 14
❒ GORKI (Nizhne Novgorod) Rus 1
❒ GORLICE (Reszow, Reichshof) Ger 1 2
❒ GORLUVKA Rus 1
❒ GORNOSLASKI OKREG PRZEMYSLOWY Schlesien Ger 1
❒ GORNSDORF/ ERZGEBIRGE Sachsen Ger 1 2
❒ GORODOK Rus 1
❒ GORZEWO/ GROSS GOLLE Posen Ger 2
❒ GORZKOWICE Rpl 2
❒ GORZKOWICE Rus 1
❒ GORZNO (Gohren) Westpreussen Ger 1
❒ GOSAU OO Aus 1
❒ GOSLAR-LANGELSHEIM Hannover Ger 1
❒ GOSLAR/ OCKER Hannover Ger 1 2 9 14
❒ GOSOL Lerida Spa 1
❒ GOSSAM NO Aus 1
❒ GOSSELIES Hainaut Bel 1 2
❒ GOSSLERSHAUSEN (Sadlinek) Westpreussen Ger 1 7
❒ GOSSWITZ Sachsen-Altenburg Ger 7
❒ GOSTYN (Gostingen) Posen Ger 1 2 6
❒ GOTEBORG Swe 2
❒ GOTHA Sachsen-Gotha Ger 1 2 6 7 8 9 12 13 14
❒ GOTHMUND-LUEBECK Schleswig-Holstein Ger 1
❒ GOTSCHDORF (Hostalkovy) Maehren Cze 1
❒ GOTT MIT UNS GRUBE (Lazisk) Schlesien Ger 5
❒ GOTTESBERG (Boguszow; Boguslawskiego) Schlesien Ger 1 2 5 7
❒ GOTTESZELL Bayern Ger 1
❒ GOTTLEUBA Sachsen Ger 1
❒ GOTTMADINGEN Baden Ger 2
❒ GOTTSCHALP/ PLESSEN Westpreussen Ger 2
❒ GOTTSDORF NO Aus 2
❒ GOUGNIES Hainaut Bel 2
❒ GOURNAY-EN-BRAY Seine Inferieure Fan 7
❒ GOU RZOUF (Gurzuf) Rus 1
❒ GOUVEIA Guarda Por 2
❒ GOUY Aisne Fan 1
❒ GOUY-SOUS-BELLONE Pas de Calais Fan 1
❒ GOUZEAUCOURT Nord Fan 1
❒ GOVORRANO Piemonte Ita 3
❒ GOZEE Hainaut Bel 1
❒ GRAACH/ MOSEL Rheinland Ger 2
❒ GRAAL (Graal-Mueritz) Mecklenburg-Schwerin Ger 2
❒ GRABOW Mecklenburg-Schwerin Ger 1 2 7
❒ GRACE-BERLEUR Liege Bel 1
❒ GRADIGNAN Gironde Fan 7 11
❒ GRAEFENHAIN Sachsen-Coburg-Gotha Ger 1 7
❒ GRAEFENHAINICHEN Provinz Sachsen Ger 1
❒ GRAEFENRODA Sachsen-Weimar Ger 1 2 7
❒ GRAEFENTHAL Sachsen-Meiningen Ger 1 7
❒ GRAEFRATH (Solingen) Rheinland Ger 1 6
❒ GRAESTED Den 11
❒ GRAETZ (Grodzisk) Posen Ger 1
❒ GRAF ELSENTHALENAU Bayern Ger 7
❒ GRAF VON BALLESTRANISCHE Werke Schlesien Ger 5
❒ GRAFELFING Bayern Ger 7
❒ GRAFEN STADEN Haut-Rhin Fan 1 2
❒ GRAFENAU Bayern Ger 1 7
❒ GRAFENSCHLAG NO Aus 1
❒ GRAFENSTADEN Elsass Ger 1 2
❒ GRAFENWOEHR Bayern Ger 3 5 7 10
❒ GRAFING Bayern Ger 6
❒ GRAINET Bayern Ger 1 2
❒ GRAISSESSAC Herault Fan 2 3
❒ GRAMASTETTEN OO Aus 2
❒ GRAMAT Lot Fan 2
❒ GRAMBY Den 1
❒ GRAMBY (Denmark) Schleswig-Holstein Ger 1
❒ GRAMENET DEL BESOS Barcelona Spa 1
❒ GRANADA DEL PENEDES Barcelona Spa 1
❒ GRANADA, LA Barcelona Spa 1
❒ GRANADELLA, LA Lerida Spa 1
❒ GRANATULA Ciudad Real Spa 1
❒ GRAND BOMAND Haute-Saone Fan 2
❒ GRAND DU ROI Gard Fan 7
❒ GRAND HORNU Hainaut Bel 2
❒ GRAND RENG Hainaut Bel 1
❒ GRAND VERLY Aisne Fan 1
❒ GRAND-BORNAND Haute Savoie Fan 2
❒ GRAND-METZ Hainaut Bel 1
❒ GRANDE COMBE, LA Gard Fan 3 6 7 14
❒ GRANDE COMORE Gra 7
❒ GRANDE-SUR-ADOUR Landes Fan 2
❒ GRANDGLISE (Grandglisse) Hainaut Bel 1
❒ GRANDOLA Setubal Por 1
❒ GRANEN Huesca Spa 1
❒ GRANER DE BAGES (Santpedor) Barcelona Spa 2
❒ GRANJA DE ESCARPE (Granja D'ESCARP) Lerida Spa 1 2
❒ GRANJUELA, LA Cordoba Spa 1
❒ GRANOLLERS Barcelona Spa 1
❒ GRANSEE Brandenburg Ger 1
❒ GRANVILLE (Douglas) Ism 15
❒ GRANVILLE Mance Fan 1 6

❒ GRANVILLE-CHERBOURG Marne Fan 1
❒ GRANVILLIERS Oise Fan 7
❒ GRANYENA DE LES GARRIGUES Lerida Spa 1
❒ GRANYENA DE SEGARRA Lerida Spa 1
❒ GRASLITZ (Kraslice) Boehmen Cze 1
❒ GRASSAU Bayern Ger 1
❒ GRATALLOPS Barcelona Spa 6
❒ GRATKORN Steiermark Aus 2
❒ GRAU-DU-ROI Gard Fan 1 7
❒ GRAUDENZ/ VISTUAL (Grudziadz) Westpreussen Ger 1 3 7 8 9 10 12
❒ GRAULHET Tarn Fan 1 2 7
❒ GRAUS Huesca Spa 1 2
❒ GRAVE North Brabant Net 14
❒ GRAVENHAGE South Holland Net 1 8
❒ GRAVENSTEIN (Graesten) Den 1
❒ GRAVENSTEIN (Graasten, Denmark) Schlesqig-Holstein Ger 1
❒ GRAY Haute-Saone Fan 14
❒ GRAY ET VESOUL Haute-Saone Fan 1
❒ GRAY-VESOUL-LURE Haute Saone Fan 14
❒ GRAZ Steiermark Aus 1 2 3 9 11
❒ GREECE Gre 11
❒ GREFRATH/ CREFELD Rheinland Ger 1 2
❒ GREIFENBERG/ REGA (Gryfice; Gryfow) Pommern Ger 1 2 4 9
❒ GREIFENHAGEN (Gryfino) Pommern Ger 1 2 6
❒ GREIFENSTEIN NO Aus 1
❒ GREIFENSTEIN/ BLANKENBURG Thueringer Ger 2
❒ GREIFFENBERG (Gryfow Slask) Schlesien Ger 1 2 6 7
❒ GREIFSWALD/ RYCK (Gripeswold) Pommern Ger 1 6 9 12
❒ GREIN OO Aus 1 2
❒ GREIZ UND ZEULENRODA Thueringen Ger 2
❒ GREIZ-DOELAU Thueringen Ger 2
❒ GREIZ/ WHITE ELSTER Thueringen Ger 1 2 8 11
❒ GREMBERGEN East Flanders Bel 1
❒ GRENAA Den 12
❒ GRENADE-SUR-GESSE Gard Fan 1
❒ GRENADE, HAUTE Garonne Fan 1 2
❒ GRENOBLE Isere Fan 1 2 7 9 11
❒ GRENZENDORF (Graniczna, Glatz) Schlesien Ger 2
❒ GREPPIN Sachsen Ger 7
❒ GRESSVIK Nor 14
❒ GRESTEN NO Aus 1 2
❒ GREUSSEN Schwarzburg-Sondershausen Ger 1
❒ GREVEN/ EMS Westfalen Ger 9
❒ GREVENBROICH Rheinland Ger 1 2 7
❒ GREVENBROICH-JUECHEN NORD. Westfalen Ger 14
❒ GREVESMUEHLEN Mechlenburg-Schwerin Ger 1
❒ GRICOURT Aisne Fan 1
❒ GRICOURT-NIAY-RENANSART Aisne Fan 1
❒ GRIENDTSVEEN Limburg Net 2
❒ GRIES OO Aus 1
❒ GRIES AM BRENNER Tirol Aus 1
❒ GRIESBACH/ ROTTAL Bayern Ger 2
❒ GRIESHEIM/ MAIN Hessan-Nassau Ger 2 5 7 8
❒ GRIESKIRCHEN OO Aus 1 2
❒ GRIESSBACH/ ZSCHOPAUTAL Sachsen Ger 1
❒ GREITHAUSEN/ KLEVE Rheinland Ger 2 5 7
❒ GRIGNASCO Ita 3
❒ GRIGNOLS Dordogne Fan 1 2
❒ GRIMMA/ MULDE Sachsen Ger 1 2 7 9
❒ GRIMMEN/ TREBEL (Grimme) Pommern Ger 1 2
❒ GRIMSTAD Nor 14
❒ GRISOLLES Tarn-et-Garonne Fan 2
❒ GRIVENGNEE Liege Bel 1
❒ GROBBENDONCK (Brobbondonk) Antwerp Bel 1
❒ GRODEK JAGIELLONSKI (Gorodok, Lvov Oblast, W Ukrainia) Galicia Rpl 2
❒ GRODNO (Gardinas, Belorussiya USSR) Rpl 2
❒ GRONDO (Gardinas) Rus 1
❒ GRODZISK: (Grodzisk Mazowiecki) Posen Ger 2
❒ GRODZTEZ (Grodziec, Grodzetz) Rus 1
❒ GROEBA/ ELBE Sachsen Ger 1 2
❒ GROEMBMING Steiermark Aus 1
❒ GROEDEN Provinz Sachsen Ger 1
❒ GROEDIG Salzburg Aus 1 2 3 4
❒ GROEDITZ/ RIESA Sachsen Ger 2
❒ GROEMITZ Schleswig-Holstein Ger 1
❒ GROENINGEN Wuerttemberg Ger 2
❒ GROSSGSTOETTEN OO Aus 1
❒ GROHN-VEGESACK Hannover Ger 2
❒ GROHN/ BREMEN Hannover Ger 2
❒ GROISE, LA Nord Fan 1
❒ GROITZSCH Sachsen Ger 1 2
❒ GRONAU/ LEINE Westfalen Ger 1 2 6
❒ GRONINGEN Net 14
❒ GROOTFONTEIN Ged 2
❒ GROSAGE Hainaut Bel 1
❒ GROSCHOWITZ (Groszowice) Schlesien Ger 1 2 3 5
❒ GROSLAY Val-d' Oise Fan 1
❒ GROSNYJ (Grozny) Rus 1
❒ GROSS DOMBROWKA (Dabrowo) Schlesien Ger 1
❒ GROSS HAMMER (Velke Hamry) Boehmen Cze 1
❒ GROSS OTTERSLEBEN Sachsen Ger 8
❒ GROSS PORITSCH Sachsen Ger 3 10
❒ GROSS SOLSCHEN (Gross Solchen) Hannover Ger 9
❒ GROSS STREHLITZ (Strzelce) Schlesien Ger 1 2 5 7
❒ GROSS ZIEGENORT (Trzebiez) Pommern Ger 2
❒ GROSS-APENBURG Provinz Sachsen Ger 2
❒ GROSS-AUHEIM Hessen-Nassau Ger 2 7 9
❒ GROSS-BORN (Borne; Gross-Boernecke) Ger 3
❒ GROSS-BREESEN Brandenburg Ger 2
❒ GROSS-DUENGEN Hannover Ger 2
❒ GROSS-EULAU/ SPROTTAU (Ilawa) Schlesien Ger 1
❒ GROSS-FLOTTBEK Schleswig-Holstein Ger 1 2
❒ GROSS-GERAU Hessen Ger 1
❒ GROSS-GRABEN (Grabowno Wielkie) Schlesien Ger 2
❒ GROSS-ILSEDE Hannover Ger 2
❒ GROSS-KALDENBERG Rheinland Ger 11
❒ GROSS-KAYNA Sachsen Ger 2
❒ GROSS-KOSCHEN Brandenburg Ger 7
❒ GROSS-LUCKOW/ BLUMENHAGEN Brandenburg Ger 2
❒ GROSS-NENNDORF Hannover Ger 2
❒ GROSS-NORDENDE Schleswig-Holstein Ger 1
❒ GROSS-OSTHEIM Bayern Ger 2
❒ GROSS-PANIOW Schlesien Ger 2
❒ GROSS-PERTHOLZ NO Aus 1
❒ GROSS-RAUDEN (Rudy) Schlesien Ger 1
❒ GROSS-REKEN Westfalen Ger 1
❒ GROSS-ROSEN (Rogozinski; Strzelce) Schlesien Ger 15
❒ GROSS-ROSENBURG Provinz Sachsen Ger 2 7
❒ GROSS-SALZA (Bad Salzelmen) Provinz Sachsen Ger 1 6
❒ GROSS-SCHLIEWITZ (Sliwice) Westpreussen Ger 2
❒ GROSS-SCHWEIDNITZ Sachsen Ger 1 2
❒ GROSS-SIEGHARTS NO Aus 1
❒ GROSS-UMSTADT Hessen Ger 1
❒ GROSS-WARTENBERG (Sycow) Schlesien Ger 1 6 13
❒ GROSS-WIRSCHLEBEN Provinz Sachsen Ger 1
❒ GROSS-ZIMMERN Hessen Ger 1
❒ GROSSALMERODE Hessen-Nassau Ger 1 7 9
❒ GROSSARL Salzburg Aus 1
❒ GROSSBOTHEN Sachsen Ger 2
❒ GROSSBREITENBACH Thueringen Ger 1 2 9

❒ GROSSDEUBEN Sachsen Ger 1
❒ GROSSENBAUM/ DUISBURG Rheinland Ger 2 11
❒ GROSSENHAIN/ ROEDER (Groszenhain) Sachsen Ger 1 2 8
❒ GROSSHARTMANNSDORF Sachsen Ger 1 2
❒ GROSSHOFEN NO Aus 1
❒ GROSSKAMSDORF Provinz Sachsen Ger 1
❒ GROSSKOENIGSDORF Rheinland Ger 1
❒ GROSSLUGA Sachsen Ger 7
❒ GROSSPRIESEN (Velke Brezno) Cze 2
❒ GROSSRAMING OO Aus 1
❒ GROSSROEHRSDAORF/ ROEDER Sachsen Ger 1 2 9
❒ GROSSRUDESTEDT Sachsen-Weimar-Eisenach Ger 1
❒ GROSSRUECKERSWALDE/ ERZGEBIRGE Sachsen Ger 1
❒ GROSSSCHOENAU (Velky Senov) Dze 1
❒ GROSSSCHOENAU Sachsen Ger 2 8
❒ GROSSWEIL/ KOCHEL Bayern Ger 2
❒ GROSSZOESSEN Sachsen Ger 1
❒ GROSSZSCHOCHER Sachsen Ger 2
❒ GROSZ-SCHOENAU Hun 1
❒ GROTTKAU (Grodkow) Schlesien Ger 1
❒ GROUGIS Aisne Fan 1
❒ GROUPES COMMERCEAUX du Gard Fan 7
❒ GRUBE ILSE N.L. Brandenburg Ger 2
❒ GRUBEN Steiermark Aus 1
❒ GRUCHET LE VALASSE Seine Inferieur Fan 1 2
❒ GRUENA Sachsen Ger 1 2 9
❒ GRUENAU NO Aus 1
❒ GRUENAU OO Aus 1
❒ GRUENBACH AM SCHNEEBERG NO Aus 1
❒ GRUENBACH BEI FREISTADT OO Aus 1
❒ GRUENBACH/ VOGTLAND Sachsen Ger 1
❒ GRUENBERG Hessen Ger 1
❒ GRUENBERG (Zielona Gora) Schlesien Ger 1 2 6 9 13
❒ GRUENBURG OO Aus 1
❒ GRUENHAIN Sachsen Ger 1 2 6
❒ GRUENHAINICHEN/ FLOEHA Sachsen Ger 1
❒ GRUENSTADT Pfalz Ger 1 8
❒ GRUENTHAL Bayern Ger 7 9
❒ GRUENZENHAUSEN/ ALTMUEHL Bayern Ger 1 2 6
❒ GRUESSOW Pommern Ger 9
❒ GRUGIES Aisne Fan 1 2
❒ GRUMBACH Sachsen Ger 1
❒ GRUMELLO Ita 14
❒ GRUND, BAD Hannover Ger 1 2
❒ GRUNDHOF/ ANGELN Schleswig-Holstein Ger 1
❒ GRUPPIGNANO Ita 3
❒ GRUSHEVSKI (Alexandrovsk-Grushevski) Rus 1
❒ GRYBOW Galicia Rpl 2
❒ GSCHWANDT OO Aus 1
❒ GSTOETTENAU OO Aus 1
❒ GUADAHORTUNA Granada Spa 1
❒ GUADALAJARA Guadalajara Spa 1
❒ GUADAMUR Toledo Spa 1
❒ GUADASUAR Valencia Spa 1
❒ GUADIX Granada Spa 1 2
❒ GUALBA Barcelona Spa 1
❒ GUALCHOS Granada Spa 2
❒ GUARDA Guarda Por 1 2
❒ GUARDAMAR DEL SEGURA Alicante Spa 1
❒ GUARDIA DE NOGUERA Lerida Spa 1
❒ GUARDIA, LA Jaen Spa 1
❒ GUARDIOLA DE GARGES (Sant Salvador de Guardiola) Barcelona Spa 1
❒ GUARDIOLA DE BERGA Barcelona Spa 1
❒ GUARDIOLA DEL PENEDES (Font-Rubi) Barcelona Spa 2
❒ GUARROMAN Jaen Spa 1
❒ GUEN (Gubin, Zielonogorskie) Brandenburg Ger 1 3 6 8 10
❒ GUDAUTI (Goudaouty) Rus 1
❒ GUEBWILLER (Gebweiler) Haute-Rhin Fan 1
❒ GUECKELSBERG-FLOEHA Sachsen Ger 2
❒ GUEMAPPE Pas-de-Calais Fan 1
❒ GUENTHERSFELD Sachsen-Meiningen Ger 2
❒ GUENZBURG/ DONAU Bayern Ger 1 2 6
❒ GUERGOUR Alg 7
❒ GUERIGNY Vievre Fan 7
❒ GUESNAIN Nord Fan 1 2
❒ GUENSTEN Anhalt Ger 1
❒ GUESTROW/ NEBEL Mecklenburg-Schwerin Ger 1 2 4 9
❒ GUETERSLOH Westfalen Ger 1 3 4 9
❒ GUETZKOW Pommern Ger 1
❒ GUETZOW Mecklenburg-Schwerin Ger 1 6
❒ GUEUGNON Saone-et-Loire Fan 7
❒ GUGU OO Aus 1
❒ GUHRAU (Gora Slask) Schlesien Ger 1 2
❒ GUIAMETS, LES Tarragona Spa 1
❒ GUIDOTT Huette Schlesien Ger 5
❒ GUIGNIES Hainaut Bel 1
❒ GUIJO, EL Cordoba Spa 1
❒ GUILLS DEL CANTO Lerida Spa 1
❒ GUIMARAES Braga Por 1 2
❒ GUIMERA Lerida Spa 1
❒ GUISCARD Oise Fan 1 2
❒ GUISE Aisne Fan 1 7
❒ GUISSONA Lerida Spa 1
❒ GUIXOLS Gerona Spa 1 2
❒ GULLEGHEM (Gullegem) West Flanders Bel 1
❒ GULSKOGEN Nor 14
❒ GUMBINNEN (Gusiew USSR) Ostpreussen Ger 1 8
❒ GUMMERSBACH Rheinland Ger 1 2 6 14
❒ GUMPOLDSKIRCHEN NO Aus 1
❒ GUNSKIRCHEN OO Aus 1
❒ GUNTRAMSDORF NO Aus 1
❒ GUNY Oise Fan 2
❒ GURAHUMORA (Provinz Bukowinia, Gura Humorului, Rumania) Hun 3
❒ GURGL Tirol Aus 1
❒ GURIEV (Gurjev) Rus 1
❒ GURTEN OO Aus 1
❒ GUSSWERK Steiermark Aus 1
❒ GUSTAVSBURG Hessen-Nassau Ger 1 7 9 14
❒ GUTACH Baden Ger 2 7
❒ GUTAU OO Aus 1
❒ GUTTENBRUN-HEILIGENKREUZ NO Aus 1
❒ GUTTENBRUNN NO Aus 1
❒ GUTOW/ PLESCHEN (Pleszew) Posen Ger 1 2
❒ GUTTENTAG (Dobrodzien) Schlesien Ger 1 2
❒ GUTTSTADT (Dobre Miasto) Ostpreussen Ger 1
❒ GUYENNE & GASCOGNE Aude Fan 6
❒ GYLAND Nor 14
❒ GYOER (Raab) Hun 1 2
❒ GYSEGEM East Flanders Bel 1

H

❒ HAAG Bayern Ger 1 2
❒ HAAG AM HAUSBRUCK OO Aus 1
❒ HAAG DORF NO Aus 1 2
❒ HAAN Rheinland Ger 1 2 3 6
❒ HAAR/ MUENCHEN Bayern Ger 2 10
❒ HAARBRUECK Westfalen Ger 1
❒ HAARBY Den II
❒ HAARLEM North Holland Net 14
❒ HAARLEMMERMEER North Holland Net 14
❒ HABELSCHWERDT (Bystrzyca Klodzka) Schlesien Ger 1 2 6 7
❒ HABINGHORST Westfalen Ger 2
❒ HACHENBURG Hessen-Nassau Ger 1 7
❒ HACKLBRUNN OO Aus 1
❒ HADAMAR Hessen Ger 14
❒ HADELN/ OTTENDORF Hannover Ger 1
❒ HADEMARSCHEN Schleswig-Holstein Ger 2
❒ HADERSDORF AM KAMP NO Aus 1 2
❒ HADERSDORF-WIEDLINGAU NO Aus 1
❒ HADERSFELD NO (Wood) Aus 1
❒ HADERSLEBEN (Haderslev) Den 2 11 14
❒ HADERSLEBEN (Haderslev, Denmark) Schleswig-Holstein Ger 1 2 9
❒ HADRES NO Aus 1 2
❒ HAELTERT East Flanders Bal 1
❒ HAEMMERN Rheinland Ger 7
❒ HAENIGSEN Hannover Ger 2
❒ HAESDONCK East Flanders Bel 1
❒ HAGEN Westfalen Ger 1 2 3 5 6 7 9 11 12 14

❒ HAGEN & BERLIN Brandenburg Ger 11
❒ HAGEN-ECKESEY Westfalen Ger 2
❒ HAGEN-GRUENTHALER Westfalen Ger 1
❒ HAGEN/ BREMEN Bremen Ger 1
❒ HAGENAU Elsass Ger 6 7 9 10
❒ HAGENBERG OO Aus 1
❒ HAGENDINGEN Lorthringen Ger 1 3
❒ HAGENDINGEN Moselle Fan 1 2
❒ HAGENOW Mecklenburg-Schwerin Ger 1
❒ HAGFELD OO Aus 1
❒ HAHNEMUEHLE Hannover Ger 2
❒ HANKENKLEE Hannover Ger 2
❒ HAI-SHEN-WEI (Vladivostok) Rus 1
❒ HAIBACH OO Aus 1
❒ BAIBACH BEI ASCHACH Salzburg Aus 1
❒ HAID Hun 14
❒ HAID BEI MATUHAUSEN OO Aus 1 15
❒ HAIDA (Hajda, Novy Bor) Cze 2
❒ HAIDEMUEHLE Provinz Sachsen Ger 2
❒ HAIDENAU Ger 7
❒ HAIDERSHOFFEN NO Aus 1
❒ HAIDHOF Bayern Ger 7
❒ HAIGER Hessen-Nassau Ger 1 5 7
❒ HAIGERMOOS OO Aus 1
❒ HAINBURG NO Aus 1 2 9
❒ HAINDORF NO Aus 1
❒ HAINEWALDE Sachsen Ger 1
❒ HAINFELD NO Aus 2
❒ HAINHOLZ Schleswig-Holstein Ger 1
❒ HAINICHEN Sachsen Ger 1 2 8
❒ HAINITZ Sachsen Ger 7
❒ HAINSBERG Sachsen Ger 2
❒ HAINSPACH (Hanspach, Lipova) Boehmen Cze 1
❒ HAINSTADT Baden Ger 7
❒ HAINSTADT Hessen Ger 7
❒ HAIPHONG Fic 7
❒ HAIZENDORF NO Aus 1
❒ HAJMASKER Hun 1 3
❒ HALBAU Schlesien Ger 2
❒ HALBERG GRUBE (Lohmar) Rheinland Ger 7
❒ HALBERSTADT Provinz Sachsen Ger 1 2 6 7 8 10 11 12
❒ HALBSTADT (Mezimesti) Boehmen Cze 2
❒ HALDEN Westfalen Ger 2
❒ HALDERN Rheinland Ger 1
❒ HALEBUELL Schleswig-Holstein Ger 1
❒ HALEN East Flanders Bel 1
❒ HALL IN TIROL Tirol Aus 1 2
❒ HALL, BAD OO Aus 1
❒ HALL, SCHWAEBISCH Wuerttemberg Ger 6 7 8 9 10
❒ HALLBACH Sachsen Ger 1
❒ HALLE Westfalen Ger 1 7
❒ HALLE-CROELLWITZ Provinz Sachsen Ger 2
❒ HALLE-TROTHA Provinz Sachsen Ger 12
❒ HALLE/ SAALE Provinz Sachsen Ger 1 2 3 4 5 6 7 9 12
❒ HALLEIN Salzburg Aus 1 2
❒ HALLENBERG Westfalen Ger 1
❒ HALLIGEN Schleswig-Holstein Ger 1
❒ HALLMONSOEDT OO Aus 1
❒ HALLSTATT OO Aus 1
❒ HALLUIN Nord Fan 1 2
❒ HALLWANG Salzburg Aus 1
❒ HALSTENBEK Schleswig-Holstein Ger 1
❒ HALTERN Westfalen Ger 1 6
❒ HALVER Westfalen Ger 1
❒ HAM Somme Fan 1 6 7
❒ HAM-NOYON-ST.SIMON Haute Saone Fan 1
❒ HAM-SUR-HEURE Hainaut Bel 1
❒ HAM-SUR-SAMBRE Namur Bel 1
❒ HAMBLAIN-LES-PRES Pas-de-Calais Fan 1
❒ HAMBORN Rheinland Ger 1 2 3 5 6 7 11
❒ HAMBRUNN Bayern Ger 1
❒ HAMBURG Hamburg Ger 1 2 3 5 6 7 8 11 12 13 14
❒ HAMBURG-HARBURG Hamburg Ger 2
❒ HAMBURG-HARVESTEHUDE Hamburg Ger 2
❒ HAMBURGER HALLIG Schleswig-Holstein Ger 2
❒ HAMEGIGOURT Aisne Fan 1 3
❒ HAMEL Nord Fan 1
❒ HAMELN Hannover Ger 1 2 3 12 14
❒ HAMFELDE Schleswig-Holstein Ger 2
❒ HAMM Westfalen Ger 1 2 5 6 7 9 11 12 14
❒ HAMME East Flanders Bel 1
❒ HAMMELBURG Bayern Ger 1 3 4 6 7 10
❒ HAMMERSTEIN Rheinland Ger 3 6 14
❒ HAMMERSTEIN (Czarne) Westpreussen Ger 3 6
❒ HAMMERTHAL Westfalen Ger 3
❒ HAMOIS-EN-CONDROZ Namur Bel 2
❒ HANAU/ MAIN Hessen-Nassau Ger 1 7 8 9
❒ HANCOURT Somme Fan 1
❒ HANDENBERG OO Aus 1
❒ HANGDAO-KHETSZY Rus 1
❒ HANKENSBUETTEL Hannover Ger 1
❒ HANNAPES Aisne Fan 1
❒ HANNOGNE Ariege Fan 1
❒ HANNOVER Hannover Ger 1 2 5 7 8 9 10 11 12 13 14
❒ HANNOVER & HELDESHEIM Hannover Ger 1
❒ HANNOVER-BRINK Hannover Ger 2
❒ HANNOVER-DOEHREN Hannover Ger 1 3
❒ HANNOVER-HAINHOLZ Hannover Ger 2
❒ HANNOVER-HERRENHAUSEN Hannover Ger 2 3
❒ HANNOVER-LAATZEN Hannover Ger 2 3
❒ HANNOVER-LANGENHAGEN Hannover Ger 2 3
❒ HANNOVER-LIMMER Hannover Ger 2 3
❒ HANNOVER-LINDEN Hannover Ger 2 3 7
❒ HANNOVER-WALDHAUSEN Hannover Ger 2 3
❒ HANNOVER-WUELFEL Hannover Ger 2 3
❒ HANNOVERISCHE-MUENDEN Hannover Ger 1 2 3 11 14
❒ HANOI Fic 7
❒ HANSBEKE East Flanders Bel 1
❒ HANSDORF/ PAKOSCH (Piechocin) Posen Ger 2
❒ HANSINELLE (Hanzinelle) Namur Bel 1
❒ HANTES-WIHERIES Hainaut Bel 1
❒ HANZINNE Namur Bel 1
❒ HAPPENCOURT Aisne Fan 1
❒ HARBACH Kaernten Aus 1
❒ HARBIN (Charbin, Kharbin) Rus 1 2
❒ HARBKE Provinz Sachsen Ger 5 7
❒ HARBURG/ ELBE Schleswig-Holstein Ger 1 2 7 9 13
❒ HARBY Somme Fan 6
❒ HARCHIES Hainaut Bel 1
❒ HARDENBERG-NEVIGES Rheinland Ger 1
❒ HARDEWIJK Gelderland Net 14
❒ HARELBEKE West Blanders Bel 1
❒ HARESKOV Den 11
❒ HARGELSBERG OO Aus 1
❒ HARGICOURT Aisne Fan 1
❒ HARKA (Harkau) Hun 1
❒ HARKORTEN (Haspe) Westfalen Ger 2
❒ HARLY Aisne Fan 1
❒ HARLY PRES ST. QUENTIN Somme Fan 7
❒ HARNES Pas de Calais Fan 1
❒ HARPEN Westfalen Ger 2
❒ HARRAN Nor 14
❒ HART OO Aus 1
❒ HART BEI AMSTETTEN Aus 3
❒ HARTENSTEIN Sachsen Ger 1
❒ HARTHA/ CHEMNITZ Sachsen Ger 1 2 8
❒ HARTHAU Sachsen Ger 1 2
❒ HARTHEIM OO Aus 2
❒ HARTKIRCHEN (Pocking) Bayern Ger 6 7
❒ HARTKIRCHEN OO Aus 1
❒ HARTMANNSDORF Sachsen Ger 1 2 9
❒ HARZBURG BAD Braunschweig Ger 1 9
❒ HARZGERODE Anhalt Ger 1
❒ HASELBACH Steiermark Aus 1
❒ HASELDORF Schleswig-Holstein Ger 2
❒ HASELUENNE Hannover Ger 1
❒ HASLACH OO Aus 1
❒ HASLCAH/ KINZIGTAL Baden Ger 1
❒ HASLACH, HAUSACH, SCHILTACH U. WOLFACH Baden Ger 1

❒ HASLACH, HAUSACH, SCHILTACH, WOLFACH U. Baden Ger 1
❒ HASLOH Schleswig-Holstein Ger 1
❒ HASNON Nord Fan 1 2
❒ HASPE (Hagen) Westfalen Ger 1 2 5 7 8 9
❒ HASPRES Nord Fan 1 2
❒ HASSELT Limbourg Bel 1
❒ HASSENBERG Sachsen-Coburg Ger 4
❒ HASSFURT Bayern Ger 1 6
❒ HASSLINGHAUSEN (Sprockhoevel) Westfalen Ger 1 2 9
❒ HASSLOCH Pfalz Ger 2
❒ HATTEM Gelderland Net 14
❒ HATTINGEN/ RUHR Westfalen Ger 1 2 3 6 11
❒ HATTORF/ OSTERODE Hannover Ger 2
❒ HAUBOURDIN Nord Fan 11
❒ HAUCOURT Pas-de-Calais Fan 1
❒ HAUGE Nor 14
❒ HAUNERSDORF Bayern Ger 1
❒ HAUNOLDSTEIN NO Aus 1
❒ HAUPTMANNSDORF (Hejtmankovice) Boehmen Cze 2
❒ HAUS/ GRAFENAU Bayern Ger 1
❒ HAUSACH Baden Ger 1
❒ HAUSBERGE/ WESER Westfalen Ger 1
❒ HAUSEN-REITBACH Baden Ger 2
❒ HAUSET Liege Bel 14
❒ HAUSHAM Lothringen Ger 7
❒ HAUSHAM/ AGATHARIED Bayern Ger 7
❒ HAUSHAM/ OBERBAYERN Bayern Ger 2 7
❒ HAUSMANING OO Aus 1
❒ HAUSMENING NO Aus 1
❒ HAUT-CONGO Fea 7
❒ HAUTE LOIRE Fan 3
❒ HAUTERIVE (Hautes-Rives) Aisne Fan 7
❒ HAUTEVILLE Aisne Fan 1
❒ HAUTMONT Manche Fan 1
❒ HAUTMONT (Hautmond) Nord Fan 7
❒ HAUZENBERG Bayern Ger 2 6 7
❒ HAVELBERG Brandenburg Ger 2 3 6
❒ HAVELTE Drenthe Net 14
❒ HAVELUY Nord Fan 1
❒ HAVINNES Hainaut Bel 1
❒ HAVRE West Flanders Bel 1 14
❒ HAVRE, LE Seine Inferieure Fan 1 2 3 7 10 11 12
❒ HAYENCOURT Nord Fan 1
❒ HAYINGEN (Hayange) Lothringen Ger 6 7
❒ HAYNAU (Chojnow) Schlesien Ger 1 2 6 7
❒ HAZTARTAS Hun 2
❒ HEBERTSFELDEN Bayern Ger 7
❒ HEBETSBERG OO Aus 1
❒ HECHINGEN Hohenzollern Ger 1 6
❒ HECHINGEN U. HAIGERLOCH Hohenzollern Wuerttemberg Ger 1
❒ HECHTEL Limbourg Bel 1
❒ HECKLINGEN Anhalt Ger 1
❒ HEDDERNHEIM/ FRANKFURT/ M Hessen-Nassau Ger 7
❒ HEDEL Gelderland Net 14
❒ HEDIMONT Bel 1
❒ HEEDE Schleswig-Holstein Ger 1
❒ HEEMSTEDT North Holland Net 1 8 14
❒ HEER Limburg Net 14
❒ HEEREN (Kamen-heeren-Werve) Westfalen Ger 5 7
❒ HEERENVEEN Friesland Net 14
❒ HEERLEN Limburg Net 1 14
❒ HESSEN, BAD/ Eilsen Lippe Ger 1
❒ HEESTERT West Flanders Bel 2
❒ HEIDE Schleswig-Holstein Ger 1 8 9
❒ HEIDELBERG Baden Ger 1 6 8 9 13
❒ HEIDENAU Sachsen Ger 2 7 8 9
❒ HEIDENAU-NORD Sachsen Ger 1
❒ HEIDENHEIM/ BRENZ Wuerttemberg Ger 1 2 7 9 14
❒ HEIDENREICHSTEIN NO Aus 1
❒ HEIDERSDORF (Gosciejowice) Schlesien Ger 2
❒ HEIDGRABEN Schleswig-Holstein Ger 1
❒ HEIDHAUSEN/ RUHR Rheinland Ger 2
❒ HEIDINGSFELD Bayern Ger1
❒ HEIERSDORF/ ERZGEBIRGE Sachsen Ger 2
❒ HEILBROWN Wuerttemberg Ger 1 2 6 7 12
❒ HEILIGENBERG OO Aus 1
❒ HEILGENDAMM (Bad Doberan) Mecklenburg-Schwerin Ger 2
❒ HEILIGENFELDE Hannover Ger 2
❒ HEILIGENHAFEN Schleswig-Holstein Ger 1 2 6
❒ HEILGENHAUS Rheinland Ger 1 8
❒ HEILGENKRUEZ Steiermark Aus1
❒ HEILIGENSTADT (Heilbad Heiligenstadt) Provinz Sachsen Ger 1 6 9
❒ HEILIGENSTADT U. WORBIS Provinz Sachsen Ger 1 6
❒ HEILSBERG (Lidzbark Warminski) Ostpreussen Ger1
❒ HEIMDAL Nor 14
❒ HEINRICHAU/ MUENSTERBERG (Glinno) Schlesien Ger 2
❒ HEINRICHSDORF/ RAMSBEC Westfalen Ger 2
❒ HEINRICHSGRUEN Aus 3
❒ HEINRICHSHALL (Koestritz) Thueringen Ger 2
❒ HEINSBERG Rheinland Ger 1
❒ HEINUM Hannover Ger 2
❒ HEINZENDORF (Hyncice) Cze 2
❒ HEISTERBACH Rheinland Ger 1
❒ HEKELGEM Brabant Bel 1
❒ HELCHEREN-ZOLDER East Flanders Bel 1 14
❒ HELCHIN West Flanders Bel1
❒ HELDBURG Bayern Ger 2
❒ HELDBURG Sachsen-Miningen Ger 1
❒ HELDER, DEN North Holland Net 14
❒ HELDRITT Sachsen-Coburg Ger 7
❒ HELDRUNGEN Provinz Sachsen Ger 1 2 6 7
❒ HELECHAL Badajoz Spa 2
❒ HELENE & AMALIA (Essen) Rheinland Ger 5
❒ HELESMES (Mellemes) Nord Fan 1 7
❒ HELFENBERG OO Aus 1
❒ HELGOLAND Schleswig-Holstein Ger 1 2 8
❒ HELLELAND Nor 14
❒ HELLIN Albacete Spa 11
❒ HELMARSHAUSEN Hessen-Nassau Ger 1
❒ HELMBRECHTS Bayern Ger 1 2
❒ HELMOND North Brabant Net 8 14
❒ HELMSDORF Baden Ger 7
❒ HELMSDORF Provinz Sachsen Ger 1 2 7
❒ HELMSTEDT, BAD Brauschweig Ger 2 3 9 11
❒ HELPFAU-UTTENDORF OO Aus 1
❒ HELSINGE Den 11
❒ HELSINGOER Den 11
❒ HELSINKI (Helsingfors) Uusimaa Fin 1
❒ HEM Nord Fan 1
❒ HEM-LENGLET Nord Fan 1
❒ HEMAU Bayern Ger 2
❒ HEMDINGEN Schleswig-Holstein Ger 1
❒ HEMELINGEN (Bremen) Hannover Ger 2 7
❒ HEMER Westfalen Ger 2
❒ HEMIXEM Antwerp Bel 1
❒ HENDRIK-IDO-AMBRACHT South Holland Net 14
❒ HENGELO Overijssel Net 14
❒ HENGERSBERG Bayern Ger 7
❒ HENHART OO Aus 1
❒ HENIN-LIETARD Pas de Calais Fan 1 7
❒ HENINEL Pas-de-Calais Fan 1
❒ HENNEF/ SIEG Rheinland Ger 1 8
❒ HENRI-CHAPELLE Liege Bel 14
❒ HENRIETTENHEUTTE (Opalanki; Przemkow) Schlesien Ger 2 7
❒ HEPPENBACH Liege Ger 14
❒ HEPPENHEIM/ BERGSTEIN Hessen Ger 1 6
❒ HEPPENSEN (Wilhelmshaven) Hannover Ger 2
❒ HEPPIGNIES Hainaut Bel 1
❒ HERAULT Fan 1 6 7
❒ HERBILLON Alg 10
❒ HERBOLZHEIM/ BREISGAU Baden Ger 2 7
❒ HERBRECHTINGEN Wuerttemberg Ger 1
❒ HERCK-ST. LAMBERT Lombourg Bel 1
❒ HERDECKE Westfalen Ger 1 2
❒ HERENCIA Ciudad Real Spa 1

❒ HERENT Brabant Bel 1
❒ HERENTHALS (Herentals) Antwerp Bel 1
❒ HERENTHOUT Antwerp Bel 1
❒ HEREFORD Westfalen Ger 1 2 9 11
❒ HERGENRATH Liege Bel 14
❒ HERGNIES Nord Fan 1 2
❒ HERIE LA VIEVILLE LA Aisne Fan 1
❒ HERINNES-LEZ-PECQ Hainaut Bel 1
❒ HERMALLE-SOUS-HUY Liege Bel 1
❒ HERMANNSTADT/ ZIBIN (Nagy Szeben, Sibiu) Rom 2 12
❒ HERMEE Liege Bel 1
❒ HERMSDORF (Hermankovice) Boehmen Cze 2
❒ HERMSDORF Sachsen Ger 1 2
❒ HERMSDORF-KLOSTERLAUSNITZ Thueringen Ger 1 2
❒ HERMSDORF/ KYNAST (Sobieszow) Schlesien Ger 1
❒ HERMUELHEIM Rheinland Ger 5
❒ HERNE Westfalen Ger 1 3 5 9 11
❒ HERNING Den 11
❒ HEROLD Sachsen Ger 1
❒ HEROLDSBERG Bayern Ger 2
❒ HERON Liege Bel 1
❒ HERPEN North Brabant Net 14
❒ HERRENBERG Wuerttemberg Ger 1 6
❒ HERRENWYK Luebeck Ger 1
❒ HERRERA DE LOS NAVARROS Zaragoza Spa 1 2
❒ HERRNHUT Sachsen Ger 1
❒ HERRNSTADT (Wasosz) Schlesien Ger 1
❒ HERSBRUCK Bayern Ger 1 2 6
❒ HERSCHBACH/ UNTERWESTER-WALDKREIS Hessen-Nassau Ger 1
❒ HERSEAUX West Flanders Bel 1 14
❒ HERSFELD (Bad Hersfeld) Hessen-Nassau Ger 1 6 9
❒ HERSTAL Liege Bel 2
❒ HERSTELLE/ HOEXTER Westfalen Ger 1
❒ HERTEN Westfalen Ger 1 2 3
❒ HERTOGENBOSCH South Holland Net 8 14
❒ HERTWIGSWALDAU (Snowizda/ Jawor, Chotkow/ Zagan, Doboszowice/ Zabkowice) Schlesien Ger 2
❒ HERVE Liege Bel 1
❒ HERVEST-DORSTEN (Dorsten) Westfalen Ger 3 5
❒ HERVILLY Aisne Fan 1 2
❒ HERWIGSDORF Sanchsen Ger 1
❒ HERZBERG/ ELSTER Provinz Sachsen Ger 1
❒ HERZBERG/ HARZ Hannover Ger 2
❒ HERZHORN Schleswig-Holstein Ger 1
❒ HERZLAKE Hannover Ger 2
❒ HERZOG-JULIUSHUETTE Braunschweig Ger 1
❒ HERZOGENAURACH Bayern Ger 1
❒ HERZOGENBURG NO Aus 1 2
❒ HERZOGENRATH Rheinland Ger 2 9
❒ HERZOGDORF OO Aus 1
❒ HERZOGSWALDE/ GLATZ (Nagodzice) Schlesien Ger 2
❒ HESEPE Hannover Ger 3
❒ HESKESTAD Nor 14
❒ HESSISCH-OLDENBURG Hessen-Nassau Ger 1
❒ HESTRE, LA Hainaut Bel 1
❒ HETEREN Gelderland Net 14
❒ HETTENLEIDELHEIM Pfalz Ger 1
❒ HETTSTEDT Provinz Sachsen Ger 1
❒ HEUBACH (Gross-Umstadt) Hessen-Nassau Ger 7
❒ HEUBERG Baden Ger 7 10
❒ HEUDICOURT Somme Fan 1 2
❒ HEULE West Flanders Bel 1
❒ HEUSDEN Brabant Net 8
❒ HEUSY Liege Bel 1
❒ HEVERLE (Heverlee) Barbant Bel 1
❒ HEX Limbourg Bel 1
❒ HEYDEKRUG/ MEMELGEBIET (Silute, Luthuanian SSR) Ostpreussen Ger 1
❒ HEYST-AAN-ZEE West Flanders Bel 1
❒ HIDRASUNDET Nor 14
❒ HIESFELD Rheinland Ger 1
❒ HIGUERUELA Albacete Spa 1
❒ HIJAR Teruel Spa 2
❒ HILDBURGHAUSEN Sachsen-Meiningen Ger 1 2
❒ HILDBURGHAUSEN, EISFELD, THEMAR, ETC Ger 1
❒ HILDEN Rheinland Ger 1 2 8
❒ HILDESHEIM Hannover Ger 1 2 6 7 8 9 12 14
❒ HILDESHEIM Sachsen-Meiningen Ger 1
❒ HILLEGOM South Holland Net 14
❒ HILLEROD Den 12
❒ HILPOLTSTEIN/ MITTELFRANKEN Bayern Ger 7
❒ HILVERSUM North Holland Net 8
❒ HIMBERG NO Aus 1
❒ HINAJOSA DEL DUQUE Cordoba Spa 1
❒ HINDENBURG (Zabrze) Schlesien Ger 1 3 6 7 8
❒ HINTENBERG OO Aus 1
❒ HINTENBERG 00 Aus 1
❒ HINTERBRUEHL NOT Aus 1
❒ HINTERNAH Sachsen-Coburg Ger 7 9
❒ HINTERSTODER OO Aus 1
❒ HINZENBACH OO Aus 1
❒ HIRACOURT Aisne Fan 1
❒ HIRSCHBACH OO Aus 1
❒ HIRSCHBERG (Eberfing) Bayern Ger 4
❒ HIRSCHBERG (Herborn) Hessen-Nassau Ger 7
❒ HIRSCHBERG (Jelenia) Schlesien Ger 1 2 4 7 9
❒ HIRSCHBERG JELENIA GORA LUDEWENBERG U. S Schlesien Ger 1 7 9
❒ HIRSCHBERG/ SAALE Thueringen Ger 1 2 7 9
❒ HIRSCHBERG, SCHLOSS Bayern Ger 3 4 7
❒ HIRSCHENWIES Kaernten Aus 1
❒ HIRSCHFELD Sachsen Ger 2 7 9
❒ HIRSCHFELDE Sachsen Ger 1 2 7
❒ HIRSIGEN Ober Elsass Ger 1
❒ HIRON Aisne Fan 1 6 7
❒ HIRSTINGEN Oberelsass Fan 1
❒ HITDORF Rheinland Ger 1
❒ HJERMITSLEV Den 11
❒ HJOERRING Den 11
❒ HNATNICE Cze 2
❒ HOBOKEN Antwerp Bel 1
❒ HOBRO Den 11
❒ HOCHBURG-ACH OO Aus 1
❒ HOCHEMMERICH (Diergardt) Ger 4
❒ HOCHEMMERICH (Duisburg) Ger 3 5 11
❒ HOCHFILZEN Tirol Aus 1
❒ HOCHHEIM/ MAIN Hessen-Nassau Ger 1
❒ HOCHHUB OO Aus 1
❒ HOCHNEUKIRCH Rheinland Ger 1 2
❒ HOCHSTEIN Pfalz Ger 1
❒ HOCKENSBUELL Schleswig-Holstein Ger 1
❒ HODIMONT Liege Bel 1
❒ HOECHST/ MAIN Hessen-Nassau Ger 1 7 9
❒ HOECHSTAEDT/ AIRSCH Bayern Ger 1 6 7
❒ HOEHN Hessen-Nassau Ger 5 7
❒ HOEHR Rheinland Ger 13
❒ HOEHSCHEID/ SOLINGEN Rheinland Ger 1 6
❒ HOEJER (Hoyer) Den 1 2
❒ HOELLRIEGELSKREUTH Bayern Ger 7
❒ HOELONDA Nor 14
❒ HOENNETHAL Westfalen Ger 2 3
❒ HOENSBROCK Limburg Net 14
❒ HOENTROP/ BOCHUM Westfalen Ger 6
❒ HOERDE (Dortmund) Westfalen Ger 1 3 5 6 7 8 12
❒ HOERDT Pfalz Ger 1
❒ HOERNERKIRCHEN Schleswig-Holstein Ger 1
❒ HOERSCHING OO Aus 1 2
❒ HOERSTE Westfalen Ger 3
❒ HOEVENEN Antwerp Bel 1
❒ HOEXTER Westfalen Ger 1
❒ HOEYANGER Nor 14
❒ HOEYHEIMSVIK Nor 14
❒ HOEYLAND Nor 14
❒ HOF Bayern Ger 1 2 6 7 12
❒ HOFFNUNGSTHAL Rheinland Ger 1 2
❒ HOFGASTEIN Salzburg Aus 1
❒ HOFGEISMAR/ WESER (Horengeismar) Hessen-Nassau Ger 1
❒ HOFHEIM/ TAUNUS Hessen Ger 1
❒ HOFHEIM/ UNTERFRANKEN Bayern Ger 1 2
❒ HOFKIRCHEN AN DER TRATTNACH OO Aus 1

❒ HOFKIRCHEN IM MUEHLKREIS OO Aus 1
❒ HOFKIRCHEN IM TRAUNKREIS OO Aus 1
❒ HOFSTETTEN B BRIENZ Swi 1
❒ HOHEN-NEUENDORF Brandenburg Ger 1 2
❒ HOHENASPERG Wuerttemberg Ger 3
❒ HOHENBERG NO Aus 1
❒ HOHENBUDBERG Rheinland Ger 3
❒ HOHENERXLEBEN Anhalt Ger 2
❒ HOHENERXLEBEN Provinz Sachsen Ger 2
❒ HOHENFELS/ STOCKACH Baden Ger 14
❒ HOHENFELS Sachsen Ger 1
❒ HOHENFRIEDEBERG (Dobromierz) Schlesien Ger 1
❒ HOHENLEIPISCH Provinz Sachsen Ger 1
❒ HOHENZOLLERISCH-SIGMARINGEN Hohenzollern Ger 1
❒ HOHENZOLLERN Hohenzollern Ger 1
❒ HOHENZOLLERNBRUECKE Hohenzollern Ger 1
❒ HOHNDORF/ CHEMNITZ Sachsen Ger 1
❒ HOHNSTEIN Sachsen Ger 1
❒ HOLBAEK Den 11
❒ HOLENBRUNN/ WUNSIEDEL Bayern Ger 7
❒ HOLICE Cze 2
❒ HOLLAIN (Hainaut) Bel 1
❒ HOLLENBURG A.D. DONAU NO Aus 2
❒ HOLLENSTEIN NO Aus 1
❒ HOLNIS Schleswig-Holstein Ger 1
❒ HOLNON Aisne Fan 1
❒ HOLSTEBRO Den 11
❒ HOLTE Westfalen Ger 3
❒ HOLTENAU (Kiel-Holtenau) Schleswig-Holstein Ger 1
❒ HOLTHAUSEN/ PLETTENBERG Westfalen Ger 2 9
❒ HOLTWICK Westfalen Ger 2
❒ HOLZHAUSEN Nordhein-Westfalen Ger 6 14
❒ HOLZHAUSEN OO Aus 1
❒ HOLHAUSEN/ LEIPZIG Sachsen Ger 2
❒ HOLZHEIM Rheinland Ger 1
❒ HOLZKIRCHEN Bayern Ger 6
❒ HOLZMINDEN Braunschweig Ger 1 2 3
❒ HOLWICKEDE Westfalen Ger 2 5
❒ HOMBERG/ DUISBURG Rheinland Ger 1 3 5
❒ HOMBERG/ KASSEL Hessen-Nassau Ger 1
❒ HOMBLEUX Somme Fan 1
❒ HOMBLEY Somme Fan 1
❒ HOMBLIERES Aisne Fan 1
❒ HOMBOURG (Homburg) Liege Bel 1 14
❒ HOMBURG/ SAAR Pfalz Ger 1
❒ HOMBURG, BAD V.D. HOEHE Hessen-Nassau Ger 1 6 8 9 11 14
❒ HOMECOURT Lothringen Ger 1 3
❒ HOMECOURT Meurthe-et-Moselle Fan 1 2
❒ HOMMELVIK Nor 14
❒ HOMOKSZIL Hun 2 3
❒ HOMOLJSKOG Yug 1
❒ HONFLEUR Calvados Fan 11
❒ HONG KONG Hkg 14
❒ HONNECOURT Nord Fan 1
❒ HONNEF/ RHEIN (Bad Honnef) Rheinland Ger 1 2 9
❒ HOORN North Holland Net 14
❒ HORASITZ Aus 3
❒ HORB/ NECKAR Wuerttemberg Ger 1 2 6
❒ HORCAJO Cuenca Spa 1
❒ HORDAIN Nord Fan 1
❒ HORDEL Westfalen Ger 1 5
❒ HOREPNIK Cze 1
❒ HOREPNIKU Hun 3
❒ HORGEN/ ROTTWEIL Wuerttemberg Ger 1
❒ HORMAING Nord Fan 1
❒ HORME Loire Fan 3 7
❒ HORMERSDORF/ ERZGEBRIRGE Sachsen Ger 1 2
❒ HORN NO Aus 1 2
❒ HORN/ WESTFALEN Lippe Ger 1 4
❒ HORNAING Nord Fan 1
❒ HORNBERG Baden Ger 1
❒ HORNBOSTEL Hannover Ger 2
❒ HORNEBURG/ UNTER ELBE Hannover Ger 2
❒ HORNOS DE SEGURA Jaen Spa 1
❒ HORREM/ BOCHUM Rheinland Ger 1 5
❒ HORSENS Den 12
❒ HORST Limburg Net 1
❒ HORST-EMSCHER (Gelsenkirchen) Westfalen Ger 1 2 6
❒ HORST/ LEGDEN Westfalen Ger 3 11
❒ HORSTMAR Westfalen Ger 1
❒ HORTA Horta Azs 1 2
❒ HORTA DE TERRA ALTA (Horta de Sant Joan) Tarragona Spa 1
❒ HORTS DEL LLOBREGAT (Sant Vincenc dels Horts) Barcelona Spa 1
❒ HOSTALETS DE PIEROLA Barcelona Spa 1
❒ HOSTALRIC Gerona Spa 1
❒ HOSTOLES (Sant Feliu de Pallarols Gerona Spa 1
❒ HOSZCA (Hoszcza, Goskcha) Rus 1
❒ HOSZCZA (Hoszca) Rpl 2
❒ HOUDAN Yvelines Fan 1
❒ HOUDENG West Flanders Bel 1
❒ HOUILLES Yvellines Fan 1
❒ HOUSSET Aisne Fan 1
❒ HOUTAING Hainaut Bel 1
❒ HOUTHEM West Flanders Bel 1
❒ HOVIN Nor 14
❒ HOWARDRIES Hainaut Bel 1
❒ HOYANGER Nor 14
❒ HOYER (Hoejer, Denmark) Schleswig-Holstein Ger 1 2
❒ HOYERSWERDA Schlesien Ger 1
❒ HOYM Anhalt Ger 1
❒ HOYMGRUBE Schlesien Ger 1
❒ HRONOVE (Hronow, Hronov) Cze 1 3
❒ HUCCORGNE Liege Bel 1
❒ HUCKINGEN/ DUISBURG Rheinland Ger 2 5
❒ HUDE Niedersachsen Ger 14
❒ HUECKELHOVEN Rheinland Ger 2
❒ HUECKESWAGEN Rheinland Ger 1 2 5 9
❒ HUEFINGEN Baden Ger 1 2
❒ HUELS Rheinland Ger 1 2 8
❒ HUELSENBUSCH Rheinland Ger 1
❒ HUELZWEILER Rheinland Ger 1
❒ HUENFELD Hessen-Nassau Ger 1 6
❒ HUEPSTEDT Provinz Sachsen Ger 7
❒ HUERCAL-OVERA Almeria Spa 1
❒ HUERM NO Aus 2
❒ HUERTEZUELAS Ciudad Real Spa 1
❒ HUERTH/ KOELN Rheinland Ger 11
❒ HUESA Jaen Spa 1
❒ HUESCAR Granada Spa 1
❒ HUESSEREN-GROS ROMAN Haut-Rhin Fan 1
❒ HUESSEREN-PETIT Haut-Rhin Fan 1
❒ HUESSEREN-WESSERLING Elsass Ger 1
❒ HUESSERN-WESSERLING Ober Elsass Fan 1
❒ HUESTEN (Neheim-Huesten) Westfalen Ger 1 2 11
❒ HUETE Cuenca Spa 1 2
❒ HUETTAU Salzburg Aus 1
❒ HUETTE OO Aus 1
❒ HUETTENHAUSEN Rheinland Ger 2
❒ HUFEN Ostpreussen Ger 1 2
❒ HUGH ZWANG GRUBE Schlesien Ger 5
❒ HUISSEN Gelderland Net 14
❒ HUIZEN North Holland Net 14
❒ HULSTE West Flanders Bel 1
❒ HUMPOLEC Cze 1 2
❒ HUNDESTED Den 11
❒ HUNDSBERG OO Aus 1
❒ HUNDSBERG OO Aus 1
❒ HOHENLIMBURG Westfalen Ger 1 2
❒ HOHENLINDE (Lagiewniki) Schlesien Ger 1 2
❒ HOHENLOHEHUETTE (Katowice) Schlesien Ger 5
❒ HOHENMOELSEN Provinz Sachsen Ger 1 7 9
❒ HOHENOELLEN Pfalz Ger 1
❒ HOHENSALZA (Inowroclaw) Posen Ger 1 6 11
❒ HOHENSCHAMBACH (Hemau) Bayern Ger 2 7
❒ HOHENSTEIN Provinz Sachsen Ger 1 3
❒ HOHENSTEIN-ERNSTTHAL Sachsen Ger 1 2 7 8
❒ HOHENWESTEDT Schleswig-Holstein Ger 1 7

❒ HOHENZELL OO Aus 1
❒ HUNDSHUEBEL/ ERZGEBIRGE Sachsen Ger 1
❒ HURTH Aus 3
❒ HURUP Den 11
❒ HURWENEN Gelderland Net 14
❒ HUSBY Schleswig-Holstein Ger 1
❒ HUSBYHOLZ Schleswig-Holstein Ger 1
❒ HUSUM Schleswig-Holstein Ger 1 9 14
❒ HUSZT (Chust) Cze 2
❒ HUTCHISON CAMP (Douglas) Ism 15
❒ HUY Liege Bel 1

I

❒ IAKAVLEVSKAIA Rus 1
❒ IBARS DE NOGUERA Lerida Spa 1
❒ IBBENBUEREN Westfalen Ger 1 2 9
❒ IBI Alicante Spa 6
❒ IBIECA Huesca Spa 2
❒ IBORRA (Misspelling of Ivorra) Lerida Spa 1
❒ IBROS Jaen Spa 1
❒ ICHENHAUSEN Bayern Ger 6
❒ ICHSTEDT Schwarzburg-Rudolstadt Ger 7
❒ ICHTEGEM West Flanders Bel 1
❒ ICHTERSHAUSEN Thueringen Ger 2 9
❒ IDANHA A NOVA Castelo Branco Por 2
❒ IDAR Oldenburg-Birkenfeld Ger 1 2
❒ IDAR-MUENSTER Rheinland Ger 2
❒ IDAR-OBERSTEIN Rheinland Ger 2
❒ IDRIA (Idrija) Yug 1
❒ IDSTEIN Hessen-Nassau Ger 1 6
❒ IDUNA Hamburg Ger 2
❒ IDUNY Ger 1
❒ IGELSHIEB Sachsen-Meiningen Ger 1
❒ IGLESUELA DEL CID Teruel Spa 2
❒ IGLS Tirol Aus 1
❒ IGUALDA Barcelona Spa 1 2
❒ IGUMEN (Igoumen, Cherven) Rus 1
❒ IJSSELMONDE South Holland Net 14
❒ IJSSELSTEIN South Holland Net 2
❒ ILFELD Hannover Ger 1
❒ ILHAVO Aveiro Por 1 2
❒ ILLE Pyrenees Orientales Fan 2
❒ ILLE-ET-VILAINE Fan 14
❒ ILLERTISSEN Bayern Ger 2
❒ ILLKIRCH Elsass Ger 2
❒ ILLSCHWANG Bayern Ger 1
❒ ILMENAU Sachsen-Weimar-Eisenach Ger 1 2 6 7 9
❒ ILSE, GRUBE Brandenburg Ger 2
❒ ILSENBURG Provinz Sachsen Ger 1 2 9
❒ ILSENHAGEN Hannover Ger 1
❒ ILSHOFEN Wuerttemberg Ger 2
❒ IMAN Rus 1
❒ IMBACH NO Aus 1
❒ IMMENSTADT/ ALLGAEU Bayern Ger 1 2 6 9
❒ IMMIGRATH Rheinland Ger2
❒ IMOLA Ita 3
❒ IMST Tirol Aus 1
❒ INCHY-EN-ARTOIS Pas-de-Calais Fan 1
❒ INDRE Fan 4
❒ INDRET Loire Inferieure Fan 7
❒ INFANTES Ciudad Real Spa 1
❒ INGELMUNSTER West Flanders Bel 1
❒ INGOLSTADT Bayern Ger 1 4 7 9
❒ INGOYGHEM West Flanders Bel 1
❒ INGUTOSU Bau Ita 3
❒ INGUTOSU Sandegna Ita 3
❒ INHAMBANE Moz 2
❒ INNERNSTEIN OO Aus 2
❒ INNERSCHWANDT OO Aus 1
❒ INNSBRUCK Tirol Aus 1 2 9
❒ INSTERBURG (Czerniachowsk) Ostpreussen Ger 1 2 8
❒ INSTINCION Almeria Spa 1
❒ INZERSDORF OO Aus 1
❒ IPEK (Pec) Mon 1
❒ IRDNING Steiermark Aus 2
❒ IRGERSDORF Sachsen Ger 2
❒ IRKUTSK (Irkoutsk) Rus 1 2
❒ IRMAPIGEN Den 11
❒ IRMSTOETTEN OO Aus 1
❒ IRON Aisne Fan 1
❒ IRRINGSTORF OO Aus 1
❒ IRYTSH Rus 1
❒ ISBERGUES Pas-de-Calais Fan 1
❒ ISCHL, BAD OO Aus 1
❒ ISEGHEIM (Iseghem) West Flanders Bel 1 14
❒ ISENHAGEN/ WITTINGEN Hannover Ger 2
❒ ISEO Brescia Ita 3
❒ ISEO Lombardia Ita 3
❒ ISERLOHN Westfalen Ger 1 2 6 8 11
❒ ISERNIA Campo Basso Ita 3
❒ ISHIM (Ichim) Rus 1
❒ ISJUM (Izium, Isyoum) Rus 1
❒ ISLE-ADAIN Fan 1
❒ ISLE-EN-JOURDAIN Gers Fan 1 2
❒ ISLE-ET-DODON Haute Garonne Fan 1 2
❒ ISNY/ ALLGAEU Wuerttemberg Ger 1 6
❒ ISOLA di Ponsa Ita 3
❒ ISONA Lerida Spa 1
❒ ISSELBURG Rheinland Ger 2
❒ ISSERVILLE Alg 1
❒ ISSIGEAC Dordogne Fan 1
❒ ISSOIRE Puy de Dome Fan 7
❒ ISSOUDUN Indre Fan 3
❒ ISTRES Bouches du Rhone Fan 7 10
❒ ISTRIA (Pola) Yug 1
❒ ITANCOURT Aisne Fan 1
❒ ITHAK Gre 14
❒ ITS SULMONA AQUILA AGREZZO Ita 3
❒ ITTENBACH Rheinland Ger 1
❒ ITTENBEUREN-RAVENSBURG Wuerttemberg Ger 2
❒ ITZEHOE Schleswig-Holstein Ger 1 2 6 8 9 14
❒ IUNCEWO (Iwonicka) Posen Ger 1
❒ IVANOVO-VEZNESSENSK Rus 1
❒ IVANOVSKOE Rus 1
❒ IVARS D'URGELL Lerida Spa 1
❒ IVORRA Lerida Spa 1
❒ IWUY Nord Fan 1 2
❒ IXELLES Brabant Bel 1
❒ IZEL Luxembourg Bel 1
❒ IZEL-LES-EQUERCHIN Pas-de-Calais Fan 1
❒ IZIEUZ Loire Fan 7
❒ IZNALLOZ Granada Spa 2

J

❒ JABLONNE/ ORLICI Cze 1
❒ JABLONOW/ LUCZKA (Gesslershausen) Rpl 1
❒ JACOBSHAGEN (Dobrzany) Pommern Ger 1
❒ JAEGERNDORF (Krnov) Maehren Cze 1 2
❒ JAEGERSPRIS Den 11
❒ JAEN Jaen Spa 2
❒ JAHNSBACH Sachsen Ger 1
❒ JAKOBSBERG Westfalen Ger 1
❒ JAKOBSDORF Brandenburg Ger 2
❒ JAKOBSHAGEN (Dobrzany) Ostpreussen Ger 1
❒ JALANCE Valencia Spa 1
❒ JALON Alicante Spa 1
❒ JAMNITZ (Jemnice) Maehren Cze 2
❒ JANOW Schlesien Ger 1
❒ JANOWITZ (Janowiec) Posen Ger 1 2
❒ JARATSCHEWO (Jaraczewo) Posen Ger 1
❒ JARMEN Pommern Ger 1
❒ JARNAC Charente Fan 2 7
❒ JAROMER Cze 2
❒ JAROTSCHIN (Jarocin) Posen Ger 1
❒ JASCHINE (Jasienie) Schlesien Ger 2
❒ JASENICKOG Yug 1
❒ JASLO (Jessel) Galicia Rpl 1 2
❒ JASTROW (Jastrowie) Westpreussen Ger 1
❒ JATIEL Teruel Spa 1
❒ JATIVA Valencia Spa 1
❒ JAUER (Jawor) Schlesien Ger 1 2
❒ JAUERNIG (Javornik) Cze 1 2
❒ JAVEA Alicante Spa 1 2
❒ JAWORZNIE (Javorzno, Jaworzno) Rpl 2
❒ JEANCOURT Aisne Fan 1
❒ JEDLICZE (Jedlice) Rpl 2
❒ JEDRZEJOW Rpl 1 2
❒ JEGUN Gers Fan 1 2
❒ JEMEPPE-SUR-MEUSE Liege Bel 1
❒ JEMPPE-SUR-SAMBRE Namur Bel 1
❒ JENA Sachsen-Weimar-Eisenach Ger 1 2 7 9 11 12

❒ JERESA Valencia Spa 1
❒ JEREZ DEL MARQUESADO Granada Spa 1
❒ JERICA Castellon Spa 1
❒ JERICHOW (Jericho) Provinz Sachsen Ger 1 7
❒ JESCHUETZ (Jezyce) Schlesien Ger 7
❒ JESSEN Provinz Sachsen Ger 1
❒ JESSENITZ Mecklenburg-Schwerin Ger 1 7
❒ JESSNITZ Anhalt Ger 1 7
❒ JESTETTEN Baden Ger 1 2
❒ JEUCK (Goyer) Limbourg Bel 1
❒ JEUTENDORF NO Aus 1
❒ JEVER Oldenburg Ger 1 2
❒ JEZIORKI (Seeheim) Posen Ger 2
❒ JIHLAVA Iglau Cze 1
❒ JIJONA Alicante Spa 2
❒ JIMENA Jaen Spa 1
❒ JINDRICHUV HRADEC Cze 1 2
❒ JOCHBERG Tirol Aus 1
❒ JOCKGRIM Pfalz Ger 1
❒ JODAR Jaen Spa 2
❒ JOEHSTADT Sachsen Ger 1
❒ JOEUF Meurthe-et-Moselle Fan 1
❒ JOHANNESBERG (Honsberk) Cze 1
❒ JOHANNESBERG (Janovice, Janovicky) Cze 2
❒ JOHANNGEORGENSTADT Sachsen Ger 1 2
❒ JOHANNISBURG (Jansborg; Pisz) Ostpreussen Ger 1
❒ JOINVILLE-LE-PONT Seine Fan 7 10
❒ JOLLAIN-MERLIN Hainaut Bel 1
❒ JONCOURT Aisne Fan 1 2
❒ JONQUERA, LA Gerona Spa 1
❒ JONZAC Charente Inferieure Fan 7
❒ JORBA Barcelona Spa 1
❒ JORK Hannover Ger 1
❒ JORQUERA Albacete Spa 1
❒ JOSEFSTADT Aus 3
❒ JOUGUET Cotes-du-Nord Fan 2 3
❒ JOUZIEUX Loire Fan 7
❒ JUDENAU NO Aus 1
❒ JUDENBACH Sachsen-Meiningen Ger 7 9
❒ JUDENBURG Steiermark Aus 9
❒ JUDENDORF OO Aus 1
❒ JUDENDORF-LEOBEN Steiermark Aus 9
❒ JUECHEN Rheinland Ger 1 9
❒ JUELICH Rheinland Ger 1
❒ JUETERBOG Brandenburg Ger 1 10 12
❒ JUIA Gerona Spa 1
❒ JUIST Hannover Ger 1
❒ JULIUSBURG (Radzijow) Schlesien Ger 2
❒ JUMET Hainaut Bel 1
❒ JUMILLA Murcia Spa 1
❒ JUNCEWO (Junkers) Posen Ger 2
❒ JUNCOSA DE LES GARRIGUES (Juncosa) Lerida Spa 2
❒ JUNEDA Lerida Spa 1
❒ JUNGBUNZLAU Aus 3
❒ JUNGENTHAL Rheinland Ger 2
❒ JUNKERSDORF Bayern Ger 14
❒ JUST DESVERN Barcelona Spa 1
❒ JUTROSCHIN (Jutrosin) Posen Ger 1
❒ JUVISY-SUR-ORGE Seine et Oise Fan 7 10

K

❒ KABEL (Hagen-Kabel) Westfalen Ger 2
❒ KADOM Rus 1
❒ KAENDLER Sachsen Ger 1
❒ KAERNTNER (Landes Kasse) Kaernten Aus 1
❒ KAESMARK (Kezmarok) Cze 2
❒ KAHLA Sachsen-Altenburg Ger 1 2
❒ KAHLA-LEUCHTENBURG Thueringen Ger 2
❒ KAIN Hainaut Bel 1
❒ KAISERODA Sachsen-Weimar-Eisenach Ger 7
❒ KAISERSLAUTERN Pfalz Ger 1 2 6 8 11 12
❒ KAISERSTEINBRUCH NO Aus 14
❒ KAISERSWERTH (Duesseldorf-Kaiserswerth) Rheinland Ger 1
❒ KALBSREITH/ GOLDENEN AUE Provinz Sachsen Ger 1
❒ KALDENKIRCHEN Rheinland Ger 1 2
❒ KALICH (Kalisz) Rus 1
❒ KALISZ (Kalich, Kalisz Pomorski, Kallies) Rpl 1 2
❒ KALLHAM OO Aus 1
❒ KALLIES (Kalisz/ Pomorski) Pommern Ger 1
❒ KALLMUENZ Bayern Ger 1
❒ KALMIERSCHUETZ Posen Ger 3
❒ KALOCSA Hun 14
❒ KALTENLEUTGEBEN NO Aus 9
❒ KALTENNORDHEIM Thueringen Ger 1 2
❒ KALVARIENBERG Steiermark Aus 1
❒ KAMCHATKA Rus 1
❒ KAMEN Westfalen Ger 1
❒ KAMENETZ-PODILSK (Kamenetz-Podolsk) Rus 1
❒ KAMENZ Sachsen Ger 1 2 10
❒ KAMIN (Kamien; Kamienna) Schlesien Ger 1
❒ KAMIN (Kamien) Westpreussen Ger 1
❒ KAMINSK Rus 1
❒ KAMMENZ Sachsen Ger 1
❒ KAMMERN AM KAMP NO Aus 1
❒ KAMNITZ (Ceska Kamenice) Boehmen Cze 1
❒ KAMPEN Overijssel Net 14
❒ KAMPEN/ SYLT Schleswig-Holstein Ger 2
❒ KAMSTIGALL/ PILLAU (Kaukehmen) Ostpreussen Ger 1 3
❒ KANAL Yug ..1
❒ KANDEL Pfalz Ger 1
❒ KANDERN Baden Ger 1 6
❒ KANDRZIN-POGORZELLETZ (Kedzierzyn-Pogorzelee) Schlesien Ger 2
❒ KANSK Rus 1 3
❒ KAPELLEN NO Aus 2
❒ KAPELLEN Rheinland Ger 1
❒ KAPFENBERG Steiermark Aus 9
❒ KAPOSVAR Hun 1 14
❒ KAPPELN Schleswig-Holstein Ger 1 2
❒ KAPUSTJANY (Kapustin) Rus 1
❒ KARA-KILIS Rus 1
❒ KARAKUS Rus 1
❒ KARANSEBES Hun 1
❒ KARBY Schleswig-Holstein Ger 2
❒ KARF (Karb) Schlesien Ger 1
❒ KARGOPOL Rus 1
❒ KARIBIB Ged 2
❒ KARIBIB AND OMARURU Ged 2
❒ KARKEN Rheinland Ger 2 14
❒ KARLINGBERG OO Aus 1
❒ KARLINGEN Lothringen Ger 1
❒ KARLINGEN Marne Fan 1
❒ KARLOVAC (Karlstadt) Rom 1
❒ KARLOVAC (Karlstadt) Yug 1
❒ KARLSBAD (Karlovy Vary) Boehmen Cze 1 2
❒ KARLSMARKT (Karlowice) Schlesien Ger 1 7
❒ KARLSRUHE Baden Ger 1 2 3 7 9 11 12
❒ KARLSTADT/ MAIN Bayern Ger 1 2 6 7
❒ KARNAP (Essen) Rheinland Ger 2 5
❒ KARNTNER LANDESKASSE Karnten Aus 1
❒ KARPINSKI (Bogoslovsk, Bogoslov) Rus 1
❒ KARS Rus 1
❒ KARSUN Rus 1
❒ KARTHAUS (Kartuzy) Westpreussen Ger 1
❒ KARTUZY Rpl 1
❒ KASAN (Kazan) Rus 1 2
❒ KASIMOV Rus 1
❒ KASTEN NO Aus 1
❒ KATARSKI ZAVOD Rus 1
❒ KATERINOSLAV (Ekaterinoslav, Yekaterinoslav) Rus 1
❒ KATERNBERG Rheinland Ger 2 3
❒ KATSCHER (Kietrz) Schlesien Ger 1
❒ KATTOWITZ (Katowice) Schlesien Ger 1 2 5 7 9
❒ KATY Hun 2
❒ KATZENAU BEI LINZ OO Aus 3 4
❒ KATZENSTEIN Provinz Sachsen Ger 1
❒ KATZENSTEIN/ OSTERODE Hannover Ger 2
❒ KATZHUETTE Schwarzburg-Rudolstadt Ger1 2 7 9
❒ KAUFBEUREN Bayern Ger 1 2 6 7
❒ KAUFFUNG/ KATZBACK (Wojcieszow) Schlesien Ger1 7

❒ KAUKAZKAYA (Kavkazskaya) Rus 1
❒ KAUKEHMEN Ostpreussen Ger 1 12
❒ KAWALLEN (Kowale) Schlesien Ger 7
❒ KAYES Sen 6
❒ KAYNA Provinz Sachsen Ger 9
❒ KAYSERBERG Haut Rhin Fan 1
❒ KAYSERBERG-WEIBEL Haut-Rhin Fan 1
❒ KAYSERSBERG Elsass Ger 1 2
❒ KAZALINSK (Kasalinsk, Kasli) Rus 1
❒ KAZAMERZH (Kazimierz, Kasimerj) Rus 1
❒ KAZIMIERZ (Kazimerj) Rpl 1 2
❒ KCHBANSKI SOYUZ Rus 1
❒ KDYNE Cze 2
❒ KECSKEMET Hun 1
❒ KEDABEK Rus 1
❒ KEFERNMARKT OO Aus 1
❒ KEHL/ RHEIN Baden Ger 1 2 6 7
❒ KEILHAU Schwarzburg-Rudolstadt Ger 1
❒ KEITUM/ SYLT Schleswig-Holstein Ger 1 2
❒ KELABERDA Rus 1
❒ KELBRA/ KYFFHAEUSER Provinz Sachsen Ger 1 6
❒ KELHEIM/ DONAU Bayern Ger 1 6 7
❒ KELLINGHUSEN, BAD Schlesig-Holstein Ger 1 6 8
❒ KELTSY (Kielce) Rus 1
❒ KEMATEN NO Aus 1
❒ KEMATEN AN DER KREMS OO Aus 1
❒ KEMATEN BEI WELS OO Aus 1
❒ KEMBERG Provinz Sachsen Ger 1
❒ KEMMELBACH NO Aus 1 2
❒ KEMNATH Bayern Ger 1 2 6
❒ KEMPEN (Kepno) Posen Ger 1 6
❒ KEMPEN/ RHEIN Rheinland Ger 1 2 6 8
❒ KEMPTEN/ ALLGAEU Bayern Ger 1 2 6 79
❒ KEMSEKE East Flanders Bel 1
❒ KENADSA Alg 1 7
❒ KENYERMEZOE Hun 3 4
❒ KENZINGEN Baden Ger 1
❒ KERB Rus 1
❒ KERTCH-YENIKALE (Kerch) Rus 1
❒ KESSEL-LOO (Kessel-Lo) Brabant Bel 1
❒ KESZTHELY Hun 14
❒ KET-TENIS Liege Bel 14
❒ KETTENREITH NO Aus 1
❒ KETTWIG Rheinland Ger 1 2 7
❒ KETY Rpl 2
❒ KEVELAER Rheinland Ger 1
❒ KHAILAR Rus 1
❒ KHARKIV (Kharkov, Charkov) Rus 1
❒ KHERSON Rus 1
❒ KHODECH (Khodetch, Chodecz) Rus 1
❒ KHOJENT (Khodzhent) Rus 1
❒ KIAKHTA (Kjachta) Rus 1
❒ KICHTIM Rus 1
❒ KIEL Schleswig-Holstein Ger 1 2 7 9 10 11 12 14
❒ KIEL-EIGENTHEIM-PRITS-FRIEDRICHSORT Schleswig-Holstein Ger 1
❒ KIEL-ELMSHENHAGEN Schleswig-Holstein Ger 1
❒ KIEL-GAARDEN Schleswig-Holstein Ger 2
❒ KIEL-HOLTENAU Schleswig-Holstein Ger 2
❒ KIEL-NEUMUEHLEN-DIETRICHSDORF Schleswig-Holstein Ger 1
❒ KIEL-WELLINGDORF Schleswig-Holstein Ger 2
❒ KIELCZYGLOW Rus 1
❒ KIELCZYGLOW Posen Ger 2
❒ KIELDRECHT West Flanders Bel 1
❒ KIERSPE Westfalen Ger 1
❒ KIEV (Kiiv, Kiyev) Rus 1
❒ KILB NO Aus 1 2
❒ KIM (Santo) Rus 1
❒ KIMRATHSHOFEN Bayern Ger 14
❒ KINDELBRUECK Provinz Sachsen Ger 1 2
❒ KIPFENBERG Bayern Ger 2
❒ KIRCHBERG Sachsen Ger 1
❒ KIRCHBERG AM WAGRAM NO Aus 1
❒ KIRCHBERG AM WALDE NO Aus 1
❒ KIRCHBERG AN DER DONAU OO Aus 1
❒ KIRCHBERG AN DER PIELACH NO Aus 1
❒ KIRCHBERG BEI LINZ OO Aus 1
❒ KIRCHDORF AM INN OO Aus 1
❒ KIRCHDORF AN DER KREMS OO Aus 1
❒ KIRCHENDEMENREUTH Bayern Ger 7
❒ KIRCHENLAMITZ Bayern Ger 6
❒ KIRCHENPOPOWO (Popowo Koscielne) Posen Ger 1
❒ KIRCHHAIN Bayern Ger 1
❒ KIRCHHAIN Brandenburg Ger 1
❒ KIRCHHAIN Hessen-Nassau Ger 1
❒ KIRCHHAM OO Aus 1
❒ KIRCHHEIM Bayern Ger 2 7
❒ KIRCHHEIM OO Aus 1
❒ KIRCHHEIM/ TECK Wuerttemberg Ger 1 2 6
❒ KIRCHHEIMBOLANDEN Pfalz Ger 1 7
❒ KIRCHHELLEN Westfalen Ger 1
❒ KIRCHSCHLAG NO Aus 1
❒ KIRCHZARTEN Baden Ger 1
❒ KIRCHZELL Bayern Ger 1
❒ KIRKEHAVN Nor 14
❒ KIRKNESVA Nor 14
❒ KIRN/ NAHE Rheinland Ger 1 6
❒ KIRSCHAU Sachsen Ger 2 7
❒ KISEL (Kizel) Rus 1
❒ KISKUNHALAS Hun 14
❒ KISLAR (Kizlyar) Rus 1
❒ KISLOVODSK Rus 1
❒ KISSINGEN (Bad Kissingen) Bayern Ger 1 2 6
❒ KISSINGEN-MUENNERSTADT Bayern Ger 1
❒ KISSLEGG/ ALLGAEU Wuerttemberg Ger 2 6
❒ KITZBUEHEL Tirol Aus 1
❒ KITZINGEN Bayern Ger 1 2 6 13
❒ KIZYL-KIIA Rus 1
❒ KLAEDEN Provinz Sachsen Ger 2
❒ KLAFFENBACH/ CHEMNITZ Sachsen Ger 1
❒ KLAFFER OO Aus 1
❒ KLAGENFURT Kaernten Aus 1 2 9
❒ KLAMM OO Aus 1
❒ KLANXBUELL Schleswig-Holstein Ger 1
❒ KLATTAU (Klatovy) Boehmen Cze 2
❒ KLAUS OO Aus 1
❒ KLAUSDORF Schleswig-Holstein Ger 1
❒ KLAUSEN-LEOPOLDSDORF NO Aus 1
❒ KLECHEV (Kleczew, Kletchev) Rus 1
❒ KLECZEW (Kletchev) Rpl 1
❒ KLEIN WANZLEBEN Provinz Sachsen Ger 2 7
❒ KLEIN-AUHEIM Hessen-Nassau Ger 7
❒ KLEIN-NORDENDE-LIETH Schleswig-Holstein Ger 1
❒ KLEIN-PODLESS/ GROSS-KLINSCH Westpreussen Ger 2
❒ KLEIN-WINDHUK Ged 2
❒ KLEINEN BAD Mecklenburg-Schwerin Ger 1
❒ KLEINHEUBACH/ MAIN Bayern Ger 1 2
❒ KLEINLAUFENBURG Baden Ger 1
❒ KLEINMUENCHEN OO Aus 1 3 4 5 9
❒ KLEINNEUSCHOENBERG Sachsen Ger 2
❒ KLEINPOECHLARN NO Aus 1
❒ KLEINSAUBERNITZ Sachsen Ger 2 7
❒ KLEINSCHMALKALDEN Thueringen Ger 1
❒ KLEINSORGE Ostpreussen Ger 7
❒ KLEINSTEINBERG Sachsen Ger 2
❒ KLEINZELL IM MUEHLKREIS OO Aus 1
❒ KLEMENSOW (Szczebrzeszyn) Rpl 2
❒ KLEMENSOW Rus 1
❒ KLENKA (Kleka) Posen Ger 1 2
❒ KLEPZIG Anhalt Ger 7
❒ KLESCHKAU (Kleszczewo) Westpreussen Ger 2
❒ KLETTENDORF (Klecina) Schlesien Ger 1 2 3
❒ KLETZKO (Kloetzen; Klecko) Posen Ger 1
❒ KLEVE (Cleve) Rheinland Ger 4 5 7
❒ KLEY/ DORTMUND Westfalen Ger 5 14
❒ KLIMINTOW Rpl 2
❒ KLIMONTOW Rus 1

❒ KLINGENBERG/ MAIN Bayern Ger 1
❒ KLINGENTHAL Sachsen Ger 1 2 11
❒ KLINGET OO Aus 1
❒ KLINTSKY (Klintzy) Rus 1
❒ KLODNITZ-ODERHAFEN (Klodnica) Schlesien Ger 1
❒ KLOSTER ZINNA Brandenburg Ger 1
❒ KLOSTERMANSFELD Provinz Sachsen Ger 2
❒ KLOSTERNEUBURG NO Aus 2
❒ KLOTZSCHE Sachsen Ger 9
❒ KLUETZ Mecklenburg-Schwerin Ger 1
❒ KLUNDERT North Brabant Net 1
❒ KNABEN Nor 14
❒ KNAPPSACK Rheinland Ger 2
❒ KNEITLINGEN Braunschweig Ger 1
❒ KNIVSBERG (Knivsbjerg) Den 2
❒ KNIVSBERG (Knivsbjerg, Denmark) Schleswig-Holstein Ger 1
❒ KNIZHKA Rus 1
❒ KNOKE (Knokke) West Flanders Bel 1
❒ KNUROW Schlesien Ger 1 2 3 7
❒ KOBENHAVN (Copenhagen) Den 11 12
❒ KOBERG Schleswig-Holstein Ger 1
❒ KOCHEL Bayern Ger 2
❒ KOCHLOWITZ (Kochlowice) Schlesien Ger 1 2
❒ KODETCH (Chodecz) Rus 1
❒ KOEBEN/ ODER (Chobienia) Schlesien Ger 1
❒ KOEBLITZ Sachsen Ger 2
❒ KOED-FLAESK Den 11
❒ KOEGE Den 11
❒ KOELLN-REISIEK Schleswig-Holstein Ger 1
❒ KOELN Rheinland Ger 1 2 5 7 8 9 11 12 13
❒ KOELN-BAYENTHAL Rheinland Ger 2 7
❒ KOELN-BRAUNSFELD Rheinland Ger 11
❒ KOELN-BRUEHL Rheinland Ger 1
❒ KOELN-DELLBRUECK Rheinland Ger 2 11
❒ KOELN-DUETZ Rheinland Ger 2
❒ KOELN-EHRENFELD Rheinland Ger 2
❒ KOELN-GRUBE FORTUNA Rheinland Ger 5
❒ KOELN-GRUHLWERK Rheinland Ger 5
❒ KOELN-HOLWEIDE Rheinland Ger 2
❒ KOELN-KALK Rheinland Ger 2 11
❒ KOELN-KLETTENBERG Rheinland Ger 1 7
❒ KOELN-LENDENTHAL Rheinland Ger 2
❒ KOELN-MUELHEIM Rheinland Ger 7
❒ KOELN-MUELHEIM, WIPPERFUERTH Rheinland Ger 2 7
❒ KOELN-NIPPES Rheinland Ger 2 7
❒ KOELN-PAFFRATH Rheinland Ger 2
❒ KOELN-POLL Rheinland Ger 2
❒ KOELN-RIEHL Rheinland Ger 2
❒ KOELN-ROTTWEIL Rheinland Ger 5
❒ KOELN-SUELZ Rheinland Ger 2
❒ KOELN-TROISDORF Rheinland Ger 7
❒ KOELN-ZOLLSTOCK Rheinland Ger 2
❒ KOELTSCHEN Brandenburg Ger 2
❒ KOENIGLICH NEUDORF Schlesien Ger 1 2
❒ KOENIGSAU OO Aus 1
❒ KOENIGSAUE Provinz Sachsen Ger 1
❒ KOENIGSBERG (Kaliningrad; Krolowiec) Ostpreussen Ger 1 2 7 12
❒ KOENIGSBERG/ FRANKEN Bayern Ger 1 2 6
❒ KOENIGSBERG/ NEUMARKT (Krzywka) Brandenburg Ger 1
❒ KOENIGSBRUECK Sachsen Ger 1 3
❒ KOENIGSEE Thueringen Ger 1 6 9
❒ KOENIGSHOF Aus 3
❒ KOENIGSHOF (Kraluv Dvur) Cze 2
❒ KOENIGSHOFEN/ GRABFELD Bayern Ger 1
❒ KOENIGSHUETTE (Krolewska Huta) Schlesien Ger 1 2 3 5 8
❒ KOENIGSSEE Bayern Ger 1
❒ KOENIGSSTEELE-HORST Westfalen Ger 2
❒ KOENIGSSTEELE/ ESSEN Westfalen Ger 1 2 7 8
❒ KOENIGSTEIN/ ELBE Sachsen Ger 1 2 3 6
❒ KOENIGSTEIN/ TAUNUS Hesse-Nassau Ger 1
❒ KOENIGSTHOR (Neuruppin) Brandenburg Ger 7
❒ KOENIGSWALDE Schlesien Ger 1 3
❒ KOENIGSWARTHA Sachsen Ger 2
❒ KOENIGSWIESEN OO Aus 1
❒ KOENIGSWINTER & HONNEF Rheinland Ger 2
❒ KOENIGSWINTER/ RHEIN Rheinland Ger 1
❒ KOENIGSWUSTERHAUSEN Brandenburg Ger 1
❒ KOENNERN Provinz Sachsen Ger 1
❒ KOEPPELSDORF Sachsen-Meiningen Ger 7
❒ KOERLIN/ PERSANTE (Karlino) Pommern Ger 1
❒ KOERNER Sachsen-Gotha Ger 1 7
❒ KOESCHING Bayern Ger 6
❒ KOESEN, BAD Provinz Sachsen Ger 1 2
❒ KOESLIN (Koszalin) Pommern Ger 1 6 12
❒ KOESSEN Tirol Aus 1
❒ KOESTENDORF Salzburg Aus 1
❒ KOESTRITZ (Bad Koestritz) Reuss j. l Ger 1 7
❒ KOETHENSDORF-REITZENHAIN Sachsen Ger 1
❒ KOETITZ/ COSWIG Sachsen Ger 2 7
❒ KOETSCHENBRODA (Radebeul) Sachsen Ger 1 2 8
❒ KOETTWITZ Sachsen Ger 2
❒ KOETZTING/ WALD Bayern Ger 1 2 6
❒ KOEYLIOE Fin 3
❒ KOG EL Steiermark Aus 1
❒ KOHLSCHEID Rheinland Ger 2
❒ KOHREN Sachsen Ger 1
❒ KOKAND Rus 1
❒ KOKCHANSK (Kokshaisk Zavod, Kokschajski Zavod) Rus 1
❒ KOLASIN Mon 1
❒ KOLBERG (Colberg; Kolobrzeg) Pommern Ger 1 2 4 6 7 11
❒ KOLBERMOOR Bayern Ger 2
❒ KOLCHUGINO (Leninsk-Kuznetski) Rus 1
❒ KOLDING Den 11 12
❒ KOLLMITZBERG NO Aus 1
❒ KOLLNAU/ BREISGAU Baden Ger 2
❒ KOLLUMERLAND Friesland Net 14
❒ KOLMAR (Chodziez) Posen Ger 1 2 6
❒ KOLO Rus 1
❒ KOLO Posen Ger 1
❒ KOLOZSVAR Hun 1
❒ KOLUSZKI (Kolyschki, Kolyushki) Rus 1
❒ KOMAROM (Komorn, Komaromujvaros) Hun 3
❒ KOMEN West Flanders Bel 6
❒ KOMOTAU, SEBASTIANSBERG, GOERKAU (Chomutov, Jirkov, Hora) Cze 1 2
❒ KONARZEWO Posen Ger 6
❒ KONETSPOL (Koniecpol) Rus 1
❒ KONGSBERG Nor 14
❒ KONIECPOL Rpl 2
❒ KONIN Rpl 1 2
❒ KONIN (Konsk, Konskie) Rus 1
❒ KONITZ (Chojnice) Westpreussen Ger 1 6 9 14
❒ KONSKIE (Konsk, Konski) Rpl 2
❒ KONSTADT (Wolczyn) Schlesien Ger 1 7
❒ KONSTANZ Baden Ger 1 2 6 7 8
❒ KOPERVIK Nor 14
❒ KOPFING OO Aus 1
❒ KOPHAZA (Kohlnhof) Hun
❒ KOPPELSDORF Sachsen-Meiningen Ger 7
❒ KOPPERA Nor 14
❒ KOPPITZ Schlesien Ger 1 2
❒ KOPRIVNICA (Koprzywnica, Koprivnice) Rus 1
❒ KOPRIVNICE Cze 2
❒ KOPRZYWNICA Rpl 2
❒ KORBECK Rus 1
❒ KORNER Sachsen-Gotha Ger 7

❒ KORNEUBURG NO Aus 1 9
❒ KORNTAL Wuerttemberg Ger 1
❒ KORNWESTHEIM/ STUTTGART Wuerttemberg Ger 1 2
❒ KORSCHENBROICH Rheinland Ger 1
❒ KORSOER Den 11
❒ KORTENBERG Sint Jozef Bel 14
❒ KORTEZ (Korzec, Korets) Rus 1
❒ KORTRIJK (Courtrai) West Flanders Bel 1
❒ KORTRIJK-DUTZEL (Cortryck-Dutzel) Brabant Bel 1
❒ KORZEC (Korec, Koretz) Rpl 1
❒ KOSCHMIN (Kozmin) Posen Ger 1 6
❒ KOSLIN (Koszalin) Pommern Ger 1 6 12
❒ KOSLOWAGORA (Kozlowagora) Schlesien Ger 1
❒ KOSTEN (Koscian) Posen Ger 1
❒ KOSTSCHIN (Kostrzyn) Posen Ger 1
❒ KOTELNICH (Kotelnitsch) Rus 1
❒ KOTTERN (Kempten) Bayern Ger 2 7
❒ KOTTHAUSEN Rheinland Ger 1
❒ KOUIF Mor 7
❒ KOURGAN (Kurgan) Rus 1
❒ KOUTAIS (Kutais) Rus 1
❒ KOUTNO (Kutno) Rus 1
❒ KOUZMINSK ROUNDNIK (Kuzminsk Rudnik) Rus 1
❒ KOVAL (Kowal) Rus 1
❒ KOVNO (Kaunas) Rus 1
❒ KOVROV Rus 1
❒ KOWAL Rpl 2
❒ KOWNO (Kaunas) Lit 1
❒ KOWNO (Kaunas) Posen Ger 1
❒ KOZICHOVICE Cze 2
❒ KOZICHOVICE Hun 1
❒ KOZLOV (Michurinsk, Eupatoria, Evaptoriya) Rus 1
❒ KRAGEROE Nor 14
❒ KRAGUJEVAC Ser 1
❒ KRAIBURG/ INN Bayern Ger 1
❒ KRAKEROEY Nor 14
❒ KRAKOW (Krakau, Crakow) Galicia Rpl 2
❒ KRAKOW Mecklenburg-Schwerin Ger 1
❒ KRAMATORSKAJA (Kramatovskaya, Kramatorskaia) Rus 1
❒ KRANICHFELD Sachsen-Meiningen Ger 1
❒ KRAPPAMUEHLE (Krupskimlyn) Schlesien Ger 7
❒ KRAPPITZ (Krapkowice) Schlesien Ger 1 2 7
❒ KRAS Ita 14
❒ KRAS Yug 1
❒ KRASINIEC Rus 1
❒ KRASNAIA RETSKA (Krasnaya Rechka,Krasnaja Rjetschka) Rus 1 3
❒ KRASNODAR (Ekaterinodar, Ekaterinburg, Jekaterinodar, Kouban) Rus 1
❒ KRASNOE SELO Rus 1
❒ KRASNOUFIMSK Rus 1
❒ KRASNOYARSK (Krasnoiarsk) Rus 1
❒ KRAUSCHWITZ Schlesien Ger 7
❒ KREISBACH NO Aus 1
❒ KREISCHA Sachsen Ger 1
❒ KREITH Tirol Aus 1
❒ KREMENCHUG (Kreminchuk, Krementchoug) Rus 1
❒ KREMENETZ (Kremenez, Krzemieniec) Rus 1
❒ KREMLIN BICETRE Val de Marne Fan 11
❒ KREMPE Schleswig-Holstein Ger 1
❒ KREMS NO Aus 1 2 9 14
❒ KREMSMUENSTER OO Aus 1 2
❒ KREUZBERG Steiermark Aus 1
❒ KREUZBERG/ WALD Bayern Ger 7
❒ KREUZBURG (Kluczbork) Schlesien Ger 1 2 7
❒ KREUZEN OO Aus 1
❒ KREUZNACH (Bad Kreuznach) Rheinland Ger 1 2 6 8
❒ KREUZTAL Westfalen Ger 1
❒ KREUZWALD (Creutzwald) Lothringen Ger 7
❒ KRIEBENAU (Kriebethal) Sachsen Ger 9
❒ KRIEBITSCH Sachsen Ger 2
❒ KRIEBSTEIN/ WALDWHEIM Sachsen Ger 2 9
❒ KRIEGLACH Steiermark Aus 1 2
❒ KRIEWALD Schlesien Ger 6
❒ KRIEWEN (Krzywin) Posen Ger 1
❒ KRIFT OO Aus 1
❒ KRIM Rus 1
❒ KRIMML Salzburg Aus 1
❒ KRIMPEN/ IJSSEL South Holland Net 1 2 14
❒ KRIMPEN/ LEK South Holland Net 1 14
❒ KRIPP/ RHEIN (Remagan) Rheinland Ger 7
❒ KRIPPEN Sachsen Ger 6
❒ KRISTIANIA Nor 11
❒ KRISTIANSFELT (Christiansfeld) Den 1
❒ KRISTIANSUND Nor 14
❒ KRITZENDORF NO Aus 1
❒ KRIVI RIH (Krivoy Rog) Rus 1
❒ KROEBEN (Krobia) Posen Ger 1
❒ KROELPA Provinz Sachsen Ger 1
❒ KROEPELIN Mecklinburg-Schwerin Ger 1
❒ KROISBACH OO Aus 1
❒ KRONACH Baden Ger 1 6
❒ KRONACH Bayern Ger 1 2 6
❒ KRONSTADT (Cronstadt) Rus 1
❒ KRONSTORF OO Aus 1
❒ KROPP Schleswig-Holstein Ger 10
❒ KROSCIENKO (Dunajcem/ Chyrov) Galicia Rpl 2
❒ KROSNEVETSK (Krosniewice, Krosnevitsi, Xenievka) Rus 1
❒ KROSNIEWICE (Krosnevitsi) Rpl 2
❒ KROSNO Galicia Rpl 2
❒ KROTOSCHIN (Krotoszyn) Posen Ger 1 6
❒ KRUEMMEL (Geesthacht) Schleswig-Holstein Ger 2 3 7
❒ KRUET Alsace Fan 1
❒ KRUET Elsass Ger 1
❒ KRUIBEKE (Cruybeke) East Flanders Bel 1
❒ KRUMAU AM KAMP NO Aus 1
❒ KRUMBACH Bayern Ger 1 6
❒ KRUMHERMERSDORF/ ERZGEBIRGE Sachsen Ger 1 2
❒ KRUMMNUSSBAUM NO Aus 1
❒ KRUPPAMUEHLE Schlesien Ger 7
❒ KRUSCHIN/ NAYMOWO (Kruszyna) Westpreussen Ger 2 6
❒ KRUSCHWITZ (Kruszwica) Posen Ger 1
❒ KRUSEVAC Ser 1
❒ KRYNICA-ZDROJ Galicia Rpl 1
❒ KRYUKOV (Krioukovo) Rus 1
❒ KRZEMIENIEC (Kremenetz, Kremenets) Rpl 1 2
❒ KRZEMIENIEC Rus 1
❒ KRZESZOWICE (Kressendorf) Galicia Rpl 1
❒ KSENYEVKA (Ksenievskaya) Rus 1
❒ KUCHEN Wuerttemberg Ger 2
❒ KUDOWA, BAD (Kudowa-Zdroj) Schlesien Ger 1
❒ KUEHNHAIDE/ ZWOENITZ Sachsen Ger 1 2
❒ KUEHNRING NO Aus 1
❒ KUEKOELLODOMBO Hun 1
❒ KUELLENHAIN/ ELBERFELD Rheinland Ger 2
❒ KUENZELSAU Wuerttemberg Ger 1 2 6
❒ KUEPPERSTEG Rheinland Ger 2
❒ KUEPPSTEG Rheinland Ger 2
❒ KUEPS Bayern Ger 7 9
❒ KUERNBERG NO Aus 1
❒ KUFSTEIN Tirol Aus 1 2
❒ KULIBAK (Koulebaki) Rus 1
❒ KULKWITZ Rheinland Ger 2
❒ KULMBACH Bayern Ger 1 2 6 7 11
❒ KUMMERFELD Schleswig-Holstein Ger 1
❒ KUNZENDORF (Konczyce) Schlesien Ger 1 3
❒ KUPFERDREH (Essen) Rheinland Ger 1 2 3 57
❒ KUPFERHAMMER-GRUENTHAL Sachsen Ger 2
❒ KUPFERMUEHLE Schleswig-Holstein Ger 2
❒ KUPIANSK (Koupiansk) Rus 1
❒ KURMISH (Kurmysh) Rus 1
❒ KURNIK (Kornik) Posen Ger 1
❒ KURZENMOOR Schleswig-Holstein Ger 1
❒ KUSCHVA (Kushva, Kursk) Rus 1
❒ KUSEL Pfalz Ger 1 14

❒ KUSEY/ ALT MARK Provinz Sachsen Ger 2 7
❒ KUSMINSKOJE (Kuzminskoye) Rus 1
❒ KUSNETZK (Kuznetsk) Rus 1
❒ KUTNO (Koutno) Rpl 2
❒ KUTTLAU (Kotla) Schlesien Ger 2 7
❒ KUZLE/ LUBESIN Posen Ger 2
❒ KVAL Nor 14
❒ KVINESDAL Nor 14
❒ KYAKHTA (Troitskosavsk) Rus 1
❒ KYLLBURG/ EIFEL Rheinland Ger 2
❒ KYRITZ Brandenburg Ger 1 2
❒ KYRKJEBOE Nor 14
❒ KYRKSAETEROERA Nor 14
❒ KYSCHTYMSKIJ (Kyshtym) Rus 1
❒ KYSPERK (Supi Hora) Cze 2

L

❒ L'GOV Rus 1
❒ L'UBICE (Leibicz) Cze 3
❒ LAA A. D. THAYA NO Aus 1
❒ LAAGE Mecklenburg-Schwerin Ger 1
❒ LAAKIRCHEN OO Aus 1
❒ LAASPHE Westfalen Ger 2
❒ LABAND (Labady) Schlesien Ger 5
❒ LABATLAN Hun 1
❒ LABES (Lobez) Pommern Ger 1 2 6
❒ LABIAU (Polessk) Ostpreussen Ger 1
❒ LABINSK (Labinskaya) Rus 1
❒ LABISCHIN (Labiszyn) Posen Ger 1
❒ LABOE Schleswig-Holstein Ger 1 7
❒ LABUERDA Huesca Spa 1
❒ LACCONI Cagliari Ita 3
❒ LACCONI Sardegna Ita 3
❒ LACEPEDE Lot-et-Garonne Fan 2
❒ LADENBURG Baden Ger 1 2
❒ LADEUZE Hainaut Bel 1
❒ LADIJIN (Ladyschin) Rus 1
❒ LAEGERDORF Schleswig-Holstein Ger 1 2
❒ LAEHN (Wlen) Schlesien Ger 1 2
❒ LAEKEN Brabant Bel 1
❒ LAENESTROL Den 11
❒ LAERDAL Nor 14
❒ LAFAYETTE (Bougaa) Alg 7
❒ LAFITTE Lot et Garonne Fan 1
❒ LAFRANCAISE Tarn et Garonne Fan 2
❒ LAGATA Zaragoza Spa 2
❒ LAGE Lippe Ger 1
❒ LAGISZA Rpl 2
❒ LAGISZA Rus 1
❒ LAGOS Faro For 1 2
❒ LAGRASSE Aude Fan 2
❒ LAGUARRES Huesca Spa 1
❒ LAGUEPIE Tarn et Garonne Fan 2
❒ LAHR Baden Ger 1 2 7 8
❒ LAIBACH (Ljubljana) Yug 1
❒ LAIGNEVILLE Oise Fan 7
❒ LAIMBACH OO Aus 2
❒ LAINECK/ BAYREUTH Bayern Ger 2
❒ LAKESVAG Nor 14
❒ LALANDE Dordogne Fan 3
❒ LALLAING Nord Fan 1
❒ LALUEZA Huesca Spa 1
❒ LAMBACH OO Aus 1
❒ LAMBERMONT Liege Bel 1
❒ LAMBERSART Hainaut Bel 1
❒ LAMBRECHT Pfalz Ger 1 6 8
❒ LAMBRECHTEN OO Aus 1
❒ LAMBRES Nord Fan 1
❒ LAMEGO Viseu Por 1
❒ LAMONTZEE Liege Bel 1
❒ LAMOTTE-BEUVRON Loir et Cher Fan 7
❒ LAMOURA Jura Fan 7
❒ LAMPERTHEIM Hessen Ger 1
❒ LAMPERTSMUEHLE Pfalz Ger 1 7
❒ LAMPRECHTSHAUSEN Salzburg Aus 1
❒ LAMSPRINGE Hannover Ger 1
❒ LANAYE Limbourg Bel 1
❒ LANDAS Nord Fan 1 6 7
❒ LANDAU Pfalz Ger 1 6 8
❒ LANDAU/ ISAR Bayern Ger 1 2
❒ LANDE, LA Dordogne Fan 3
❒ LANDECK, BAD (Ladek-Zdroj) Schlesien Ger 1 2 6 8
❒ LANDEGG NO Aus 3
❒ LANDELIES Hainaut Bel 1
❒ LANDENNE-SUR-MEUSE Liege Bel 1
❒ LANDERDING OO Aus 1
❒ LANDES Nord Fan 6 7
❒ LANDESHUT (Kamienna Gora) Schlesien Ger 1 2 6 7
❒ LANDFRIEDSTETTEN NO Aus 1
❒ LANDIFAY Fan 1
❒ LANDKIRCHEN/ FEHMARN Schleswig-Holstein Ger 1
❒ LANDRECIES Nord Fan 1
❒ LANDSBERG (Koszalin; Ledyczek; Gorzow Slask) Schlesien Ger 1 2 6 8
❒ LANDSBERG/ LECH Bayern Ger 1 2 3 6 7 9
❒ LANDSBERG/ WARTHE (Gorzow) Brandenburg Ger 1 2 6 7 8
❒ LANDSHUT Bayern Ger 1 2 3 4 7 11
❒ LANDSKRON (Lanskroun) Maehren Cze 2 9
❒ LANDSTUHL Pfalz Ger 2
❒ LANGACKER OO Aus 1
❒ LANGANGEN Nor 14
❒ LANGAU (Oberviechtach) Bayern Ger 7
❒ LANGBURKERSDORF Sachsen Ger 1
❒ LANGELN Schleswig-Holstein Ger 1
❒ LANGELOHE Schleswig-Holstein Ger 1
❒ LANGELSHEIM Braunschweig Ger 2
❒ LANGENALTHEIM Bayern Ger 1
❒ LANGENAU Sachsen Ger 1
❒ LANGENBERG Rheinland Ger 1 2 7
❒ LANGENBERG-REUSS (Gera) Thueringen Ger 2 8
❒ LANGENBIELAU Schlesien Ger 2
❒ LANGENBRUCK Bayern Ger 7 8
❒ LANGENBURG Wuerttemberg Ger 7
❒ LANGENDREER (Bochum) Westfalen Ger 1 2 3 5 9 11
❒ LANGENESS-NORDMARSCH Schleswig-Holstein Ger 1
❒ LANGENHORN/ HUSUM Schleswig-Holstein Ger 1
❒ LANGENLEUBA Sachsen Ger 2
❒ LANGENLOIS NO Aus 1
❒ LANGENOELS (Olszyna) Schlesien Ger 1 2 7
❒ LANGENSALZA Provinz Sachsen Ger 1 2 3
❒ LANGENSCHWALBACH Hessen-Nassau Ger 1 6
❒ LANGENSTEIN OO Aus 1
❒ LANGENZENN Bayern Ger 14
❒ LANGERFELD/ BARMEN (Wuppertal) Westfalen Ger 7
❒ LANGESUND Nor 14
❒ LANGEWIESEN Schwarzburg-Sondershausen Ger 1
❒ LANGGUHLE (Golina Wielka) Posen Ger 2
❒ LANGON Gironde Fan 2
❒ LANGQUAID Bayern Ger 1
❒ LANK (Meerbusch) Rheinland Ger 1 6
❒ LANNACH Steiermark Aus 2
❒ LANNEPAX Ger Fan 1
❒ LANNOY Nord Fan 1
❒ LANTREMANCE (Lantremange) Liege Bel 1
❒ LANZENBERG OO Aus 1
❒ LAON Aisne Fan 1 3 7 14
❒ LAPLAIGNE (Bleharies, Ere, etc.) Hainaut Bel 1
❒ LAPYSCHTA Rus 1
❒ LAREN North Holland Net 14
❒ LAROCHE Fan 3
❒ LAROCHETTE/ FELS Lux 1
❒ LAROQUE D'OLMES (Laroques) Ariege Fan 1 6 7
❒ LARRAZET Tarn et Garonne Fan 1
❒ LARZAC Dordogne Fan 3 14
❒ LASBERG OO Aus 1
❒ LASBORDES Aude Fan 1
❒ LASCUARRE Huesca Spa 1
❒ LASPAULES Huesca Spa 1
❒ LASPUNA Huesca Spa 1
❒ LASSAN Pommern Ger 1 2 7
❒ LATERNIA Ita 14
❒ LATINNE Liege Bel 1
❒ LATISANA Ita 3
❒ LAUBAN (Luban) Schlesien Ger 1 2 4 6 7 8
❒ LAUBAU Schlesien Ger 6
❒ LAUCHA Provinz Sachsen Ger 1
❒ LAUCHERTHAL Hohenzollern Ger 1
❒ LAUCHHAMMER Provinz Sachsen Ger 2
❒ LAUCHSTEDT BAD Provinz Sachsen Ger 1 13
❒ LAUENBURG (Lebork) Pommern Ger 1 2 4 6
❒ LAUENBURG/ ELBE Schleswig-Holstein Ger 1 2 6

❒ LAUENSTEIN Bayern Ger 1
❒ LAUF/ PEGNITZ Bayern Ger 1 2 6
❒ LAUFEN Bayern Ger 1 6
❒ LAUFEN-TITTMONING Bayern Ger 1
❒ LAUFFEN/ NECKAR Wuerttemberg Ger 1
❒ LAUINGEN/ DONAU Bayern Ger 1 2 6
❒ LAUJAR Almeria Spa 2
❒ LAUN (Louny) Boehmen Cze 1 2
❒ LAUPHEIM Wuerttemberg Ger 1 2
❒ LAURAHUETTE (Huta Laura) Schlesien Ger 1 2 3 6 7
❒ LAUSA BEI LOSENSTEIN OO Aus 1
❒ LAUSCHA Sachsen-Meiningen Ger 1 7
❒ LAUSICK, BAD Sachsen Ger 1
❒ LAUTA Brandenburg Ger 1 7
❒ LAUTAWERK Brandenburg Ger 2
❒ LAUTENBACH Elsass Ger 2
❒ LAUTENBURG (Lidzbark) Westpreussen Ger 1
❒ LAUTENTHAL/ HARZ Hannover Ger 1
❒ LAUTER Sachsen Ger 2 6
❒ LAUTERBACH Hessen Ger 1 6
❒ LAUTERBACH Wuerttemberg Ger 2
❒ LAUTERBACH/ GLATZ Schlesien Ger 2
❒ LAUTERBERG/ HARZ (Bad Lauterberg/ Harz) Hannover Ger 1 2
❒ LAUTERECKEN Pfalz Ger 1
❒ LAUTERN Ostpreussen Ger 2
❒ LAUW (Lowaige) Limbourg Bel 1
❒ LAUWE West Flanders Bel 1
❒ LAUWIN-PLANQUE Nord Fan 1
❒ LAUZERTE Tarn et Garonne Fan 2
❒ LAUZIERE, LA charente Inferieure Fan 7
❒ LAUZUN Lot et Garonne Fan 2
❒ LAVAL Mayenne Fan 14
❒ LAVAQUERESSE Aisne Fan 1
❒ LAVARDEUS Gers Fan 2
❒ LAVAUR Tarn Fan 1
❒ LAVELANET Ariege Fan 2
❒ LAVERGIES Aisne Fan 1
❒ LAVIT DE LOMAGNE Tarn et Garonne Fan 1
❒ LAVOIR Liege Bel 1
❒ LAVORO Ita 14
❒ LAXENBURG NO Aus 1
❒ LAYOS Toledo Spa 1
❒ LAZISK Schlesien Ger 5 7
❒ LE MANS Sarthe Fan 14
❒ LEBA Pommern Ger 4
❒ LEBBEKE East Flanders Bel 1
❒ LEBING OO Aus 1
❒ LEBUS Brandenburg Ger 1
❒ LECCE Ita 3
❒ LECERA Zaragoza Spa 2
❒ LECHENICH Nordrhein-Westfalen Ger 14
❒ LECHERIE-VIEVILLE Fan 1
❒ LECHFELD Bayern Ger 3 9 10
❒ LECINA DE CINCA Huesca Spa 1
❒ LECK Schleswig-Holstein Ger 1
❒ LECTOU RE Gers Fan 1
❒ LECZYCA (Lenchitsa, Lentchitsa) Rus 1
❒ LECZYCA (Lentichitsa, Lentschuetz) Galicia Rpl 2
❒ LEDEBERG East Flanders Bel 1
❒ LEDEC Cze 1
❒ LEDEGHEM (Ledegem) West Flanders Bel 1
❒ LEER Hannover Ger 2 6 8
❒ LEERNES Hainaut Bel 1
❒ LEERS Nord Fan 1
❒ LEERS-NORD Hainaut Bel 1
❒ LEEUWARDEN Friesland Net 8
❒ LEFOREST Pas de Calais Fan 1
❒ LEHAUCOURT Aisne Fan 3
❒ LEHE Hannover Ger 1 8
❒ LEHESTEN Sachsen-Meiningen Ger 1 2 6 7 9
❒ LEHRTE Hannover Ger 1 9
❒ LEIBEN OO Aus 1
❒ LEIBICZ Hun 3
❒ LEICHLINGEN Rheinland Ger 1 6
❒ LEIDSCHENDAM South Holland Net 14
❒ LEIPHEIM Bayern Ger 6
❒ LEIPZIG Sachsen Ger 1 2 7 8 9 11 12 13 14
❒ LEIPZIG-BOEHLITZ-EHRENBERG Sachsen Ger 2
❒ LEIPZIG-CONNEWITZ Sachsen Ger 2
❒ LEIPZIG-DOELITZ Sachsen Ger 2
❒ LEIPZIG-EUTRITZSCH Sachsen Ger 2
❒ LEIPZIG-GAUTZSCH Sachsen Ger 2
❒ LEIPZIG-GOHLIS Sachsen Ger 2 7
❒ LEIPZIG-GROSSZSCHOCHER Sachsen Ger 2
❒ LEIPZIG-HEITERBLICK Sachsen Ger 7
❒ LEIPZIG-LEUTZSCH Sachsen Ger 2
❒ LEIPZIG-LIEBERTWOLKWITZ Sachsen Ger 2
❒ LEIPZIG-LINDENAU Sachsen Ger 2
❒ LEIPZIG-MOELKAU Sachsen Ger 2 7
❒ LEIPZIG-OETZSCH-MARKKLEEBERG Sachsen Ger 2
❒ LEIPZIG-PAUNSDORF Sachsen Ger 2
❒ LEIPZIG-PLAGWITZ Sachsen Ger 2 7
❒ LEIPZIG-REUDNITZ Sachsen Ger 2
❒ LEIPZIG-SCHOENAU Sachsen Ger 2
❒ LEIPZIG-SELLERHAUSEN Sachsen Ger 2
❒ LEIPZIG-STOETTERITZ Sachsen Ger 2
❒ LEIPZIG-THONBERG Sachsen Ger 2
❒ LEIPZIG-VO Sachsen Ger 2
❒ LEIPZIG-WAHREN Sachsen Ger 2
❒ LEIRIA Leiria Por 1 2
❒ LEITMERITZ (Litomerice) Boehmen Cze 2
❒ LEKKERKERK South Holland Net 1
❒ LEKNO Posen Ger 1
❒ LEMBACH OO Aus 1
❒ LEMBECK (Dorsten) Westfalen Ger 6
❒ LEMBECQ-LEZ-HAL Barbant Bel 1
❒ LEMBEK-ALTSCHERMBECK Westfalen Ger 1
❒ LEMBERG (Lvov, Lviv, Lwow) Rus 1
❒ LEMBERG (Lwow, L'vov, Ukraine) Galicia Rpl 1 23
❒ LEME Aisne Fan 1
❒ LEMGO Westfalen Ger 1
❒ LEMVIG Den 11
❒ LEND Salzburg Aus 1
❒ LENDELEDE West Flanders Bel 1
❒ LENDRINGSEN (Soest) Westfalen Ger 5
❒ LENGAU OO Aus 1
❒ LENGEFELD/ ERZGEBIRGE-VOGTLAND Sachsen Ger 1 2 8 13
❒ LENGERICH Westfalen Ger 1 2 7
❒ LENGFURT/ MAIN (Triefenstein) Bayern Ger 7
❒ LENGGRIES Bayern Ger 1 6
❒ LENNEP (Remscheid) Rheinland Ger 1 2 6 7 8
❒ LENS Pas de Calais Fan 1 2 3 6 12 14
❒ LENS Somme Fan 7 9 1 2
❒ LENZEN/ ELBE Brandenburg Ger 1
❒ LEOBERSDORF NO Aus 9
❒ LEOBSCHUETZ (Glubczyce) Schlesien Ger 1 2 6 8
❒ LEONBERG Wuerttemberg Ger 1 7
❒ LEONDING OO Aus 1
❒ LEONFELDEN OO Aus 1 2
❒ LEOPOLDSBURG Limbourg Bel 1
❒ LEOPOLDSCHLAG OO Aus 1
❒ LEOPOLDSHALL Anhalt Ger 1
❒ LEPSINSK Rus 1
❒ LERBACH Hannover Ger 1
❒ LERIGNEAUX Fan 7
❒ LES Lerida Spa 1
❒ LESCHELLE Fan 1
❒ LESDAIN Hainaut Bel 1
❒ LESDINS Aisne Fan 1
❒ LESPIGNAN Herault Fan 7
❒ LESQUIELLE-ST. GERMAIN Aisne Fan 1
❒ LESQUIELLES Fan 1
❒ LESSEN Westpreussen Ger 6
❒ LESSINES Hainaut Bel 1
❒ LESTELLE Basses Pyrenees Fan 2
❒ LESUM Hannover Ger 2
❒ LETICHEV (Letitchev) Rus 1
❒ LETMATHE Westfalen Ger 1 2 5 67
❒ LETTE/ MUENSTER (Oelde) Westfalen Ger 3 7
❒ LETTENREUTH (Michelau) Bayern Ger 7
❒ LETUR Albacete Spa 1

❒ LEUBNITZ Sachsen Ger 1
❒ LEUBSDORF Sachsen Ger 1
❒ LEUKERSDORF Erzgebeit Sachsen Ger 1
❒ LEUNA WERKE (Leuna Werke "Walter Ulbricht") Provinz Sachsen Ger 2
❒ LEUPEGEM East Flanders Bel 1
❒ LEUTENBERG Schwarzburg-Rudolstadt Ger 1 6 7
❒ LEUTERSDORF O.L. Sachsen Ger 1 9
❒ LEUTKIRCH/ ALLGAEU Wuerttemberg Ger 1 6 7
❒ LEUTZSCH/ LEIPZIG Sachsen Ger 2 7
❒ LEUVEN (Louvain) Brabant Bel 1
❒ LEUZE Hainaut Bel 1
❒ LEVAL Nord Fan 1
❒ LEVAL-TRAHEGNIES Hainaut Bel 1
❒ LEVANGER Nor 14
❒ LEVASHOVO Rus 1
❒ LEVERGIES Aisne Fan 1
❒ LEVERKUSEN Rheinland Ger 2 3 4 5 8 14
❒ LEVERKUSEN-WIESDORF Rheinland Ger 2
❒ LEWARDE Nord Fan 1
❒ LEWIN (Lewin Klodzki) Schlesien Ger 1
❒ LEZAT Ariege Fan 2
❒ LEZIGNAN Aude Fan 1
❒ LIAISON DES VOSGES Fan 2
❒ LIANCOURT Oise Fan 7
❒ LIBAU (Libava, Liepaja) Rus 1
❒ LIBLAR (Erftstadt) Rheinland Ger 5
❒ LIBOURNE Gironde Fan 1
❒ LIBRILLA Murcia Spa 1
❒ LICH Hessen Ger 1
❒ LICHTENAU OO Aus 1
❒ LICHTENAU (Loreba) Schlesien Ger 2 7
❒ LICHTENBERG OO Aus 1
❒ LICHTENBERG/ ERZGEBIRGE Sachsen Ger 7
❒ LICHTENBUCH OO Aus 1
❒ LICHTENBURG/ TORGAU Sachsen Ger 15
❒ LICHTENEGG OO Aus 1
❒ LICHTENFELS/ MAIN Bayern Ger 1 2 6 8 14
❒ LICHTENHAIN (Schwarzburg-Rudolstadt) Ger 7
❒ LICHTENHORST Hannover Ger 2 3
❒ LICHTENSEE Sachsen Ger 2
❒ LICHTENSTEIN-CALLNBERG Sachsen Ger 1 2
❒ LICHTENTAL Baden Ger 7
❒ LICHTENTANNE Sachsen Ger 1
❒ LICHTENWALDE/ GLATZ Schlesien Ger 2
❒ LICHTERVELDE (Litchtervelda) West Flanders Bel 1 14
❒ LIDA Rus 1
❒ LIDA Beloussiya Rpl 2
❒ LIDMAN Cze 1
❒ LIEBAU (Lubawka) Schlesien Ger 1 2 6 7
❒ LIEBENAU OO Aus 1
❒ LIEBENSTEIN BAD Sachsen-Meiningen Ger 1
❒ LIEBENWERDA (Bad Liebenwerda) Provinz Sachsen Ger 1 7
❒ LIEBEROSE Brandenburg Ger 1
❒ LIEBERTWOLKWITZ Sachsen Ger 1 14
❒ LIEBSTADT (Milakowo, Poland) Ostpreussen Ger 1 2
❒ LIECHTENSTEIN Lie 1
❒ LIEGE Liege Bel 1
❒ LIEGNITZ (Legnica) Schlesien Ger 1 2 8 11 12
❒ LIEPGARTEN Pommern Ger 1
❒ LIER Antwerp Bel 1
❒ LIERNEAUX Liege Bel 1
❒ LIESEN Westfalen Ger 2
❒ LIESSIES Nord Fan 1
❒ LIETOR Albacete Spa 1
❒ LIEVIN Pas de Calais Fan 1 2 7
❒ LIEZ Aisne Fan 1
❒ LIGNE Hainaut Bel 1
❒ LIGURIA Ita 14
❒ LIJAR Almeria Spa 1
❒ LIKNES Nor 14
❒ LILIENFELD NO Aus 1 2 9
❒ LILIENTHAL Hannover Ger 1
❒ LILLA Tarragona Spa 1
❒ LILLE Nord Fan 1 2 3 7 11
❒ LILLEBONNE Seine-Inferieure Fan 1 2
❒ LILLO Toledo Spa 1
❒ LIMANOWA (Ilmenau) Galicia Rpl 1 2
❒ LIMBACH (Limbach-Oberfrohna) Sachsen Ger 1 2 7
❒ LIMBOURG Limbourg Bel 1
❒ LIMBURG/ LAHN Hessen-Nassau Ger 1 7 11
❒ LIMOGES Haute Vienne Fan 1 6 7 10 12
❒ LIMOGES-PONT DE CHERUY Isere Fan 7 2
❒ LIMOUX Aude Fan 1
❒ LINARES Jaen Spa 1
❒ LINDABRUNN NO Aus 1
❒ LINDAS Nor 14
❒ LINDAU UND WEILER Bayern Ger 1
❒ LINDAU/ BODENSEE Bayern Ger 1 2 7 14
❒ LINDAU/ HARZ Hannover Ger 1 7
❒ LINDBERG Kaernten Aus 1
❒ LINDEN Brabant Bel 1
❒ LINDEN-DAHLHAUSEN (Bochum) Westfalen Ger 6
❒ LINDEN/ HANNOVER Hannover Ger 2 7
❒ LINDENAU (Leipzig) Sachsen Ger 7
❒ LINDENBERG/ ALLGAEU Bayern Ger 1 2 14
❒ LINDENTHAL/ LEIPZIG Sachsen Ger 1
❒ LINDERODE N-L (Lipinki; Luzyskie) Brandenburg Ger 2
❒ LINGEN Hannover Ger 1
❒ LINNICH Rheinland Ger 1
❒ LINSOUX Aude Fan 1 2
❒ LINTFORT (Kamp-Lintfort) Rheinland Ger 2 4
❒ LINTORF Rheinland Ger 2
❒ LINYOLA Lerida Spa 1
❒ LINZ OO Aus 1 2 3 9
❒ LINZ/ RHEIN Rheinland Ger 1 2 6
❒ L.IOUSTDORF Rus 1
❒ LIPECK (Lipetsk, Lipetzk) Rus 1
❒ LIPINE (Lipiny) Schlesien Ger 1 2 3
❒ LIPNO (Leipe) Rpl 1
❒ LIPNO Rus 1
❒ LIPPE Lippe Ger 1 6
❒ LIPPEHNE (Lipiany) Brandenburg Ger 1 6
❒ LIPPSPRINGE BAD Westfalen Ger 1
❒ LIPPSTADT Westfalen Ger 1 6 11 13
❒ LISBOA (Lisbon) Lisboa Por 1 2
❒ LISDORF (Saarlouis) Rheinland Ger 7
❒ LISIEUX Calvados Fan 2
❒ LISLE SUR TARN Tarn Fan 1
❒ LISSA (Leszno) Posen Ger 1 6
❒ LISSE South Holland Net 14
❒ LIST/ SYLT Schleswig-Holstein Ger 1
❒ LISVA (Lysva, Lysvensk) Rus 1
❒ LITSCHAU NO Aus 1
❒ LITZMANNSTADT (Lodz) Rpl 1 2 9 15
❒ LIVADIA Rus 1
❒ LIVAROT ET ST. PIERRE-SUR-DIVES Calvados Fan 7
❒ LIVORNO CASERMA Cavalleria Toscana Ita 3
❒ LIZEAC Tarn et Garonne Fan 2
❒ LLACUNA Barcelona Spa 1 2
❒ LLADO Gerona Spa 1
❒ LLAGOSTA, LA Barcelona Spa 1
❒ LLAGOSTERA, Gerona Spa 1
❒ LLANES Asturias Spa 1
❒ LLARDECANS Lerida Spa 1
❒ LLAVANERES Barcelona Spa 1
❒ LLAVANERES DE MONTAL (Sant Vicent de Montal) Barcelona Spa 1
❒ LLAVORSI Lerida Spa 1
❒ LLEIDA Lerida Spa 1 2
❒ LLEVANTI DE MAR (Sant Antoni de Mar) Gerona Spa 1
❒ LLIBER Alicante Spa 2
❒ LLICA DE MUNT Barcelona Spa 1
❒ LLINARS Barcelona Spa 1
❒ LLIVIA Gerona Spa 1
❒ LLOA Tarragona Spa 1
❒ LLOMBAY Valencia Spa 1 2
❒ LLORENC DE MORUNYS Lerida Spa 1
❒ LLORENS D'HORTONS Barcelona Spa 1
❒ LLORENS DEL PANADES Tarragona Spa 1
❒ LLORET DE MAR Gerona Spa 1
❒ LLORIANA DE TER (Sant Vicenc de Torello) Barcelona Spa 1
❒ LLUCA Barcelona Spa 1
❒ LOANDA Ang 1
❒ LOBBERICH Rheinland Ger 1 2
❒ LOBEDA Sachsen-Weimar-Eisenach Ger 1
❒ LOBENSTEIN Thueringen Ger 1 2

❒ LOBSDORF Sachsen Ger 2
❒ LOBSENS (Lobzenica) Posen Ger 1
❒ LOBSTAEDT Sachsen Ger 1
❒ LOCHEN OO Aus 1
❒ LOCKSTEDT Schleswig-Holstein Ger 1 2 10
❒ LODELINSART Hainaut Bel 1
❒ LODZ Rus 1
❒ LOEBAU Sachsen Ger 1 2
❒ LOEBAU (Lubawa) Westpreussen Ger 1
❒ LOEBEJUEN Provinz Sachsen Ger 1
❒ LOEBERITZ/ BITTERFELD Provinz Sachsen Ger 2
❒ LOEBERSDORF Aus 9
❒ LOECKNITZ Pommern Ger 2
❒ LOEFFINGEN Baden Ger 1
❒ LOEGUMKLOSTER (Luegumkloster) Den 1
❒ LOERRACH Baden Ger 1 2 6 8 9
❒ LOESSNITZ/ ERZGEBIRGE Sachsen Ger 1 2
❒ LOETZEN (Lec; Gizycko) Ostpreussen Ger 1
❒ LOEWEN (Lewin Brzeski) Schlesien Ger 1
❒ LOEWENBERG (Lwowek Slask) Schlesien Ger 1 2 6 7
❒ LOFER Salzburg Aus 1
❒ LOFFRE Nord Fan 1
❒ LOGOISK (Logoysk, Lohojsk) Rus 1
❒ LOHMEN Sachsen Ger 1
❒ LOHNSBU RG OO Aus 1
❒ LOHR/ MAIN Bayern Ger 1 2 6 7
❒ LOICH NO Aus 1
❒ LOIRET (Comtes de Checy-Chateauneuf-Sully-Vitry) Fan 6
❒ LOITZ Pommern Ger 1 8
❒ LOKEREN East Flanders Bel 1
❒ LOLLAR Hessen Ger 7
❒ LOMBARDA Ita 14
❒ LOMMATZSCH Sachsen Ger 1 7
❒ LOMMERSWEILER Liege Bel 14
❒ LONGAGES Haute Garonne Fan 1
❒ LONGAVESNES Somme Fan 1
❒ LONGUYON Est Fan 2
❒ LONGWY Lorraine Fan 2
❒ LONS-LE-SAUNIER Jura Fan 1 7 14
❒ LONTZEN Liege Bel 14
❒ LOON OP ZAND North Brabant Net 14
❒ LOOSDORF NO Aus 1
❒ LOPERA Jaen Spa 2
❒ LOPISCHEWO (Lopiszewo/ Ritschenwalde) Posen Ger 1 2
❒ LORA DEL RIO Sevilla Spa 6
❒ LORCA Murcia Spa 1
❒ LORCH Hessen-Nassau Ger 1
❒ LORCH OO Aus 1
❒ LORCH Wuerttemberg Ger 2 7
❒ LORENZDORF (Lawszowa) Schlesien Ger 7
❒ LORENZENBERG Kaernten Aus 1
❒ LORIENT Morbihan Fan 1 7 10 11
❒ LOSA DEL OBISPO Valencia Spa 1
❒ LOSCHWITZ (Dresden) Sachsen Ger 7
❒ LOSENSTEIN OO Aus 1
❒ LOSENSTEINLEITHEN OO Aus 1
❒ LOSLAU (Wodzislawska) Schlesien Ger 1 6
❒ LOSONCZ (Lucenec) Cze 2
❒ LOSSEN (Losina; Losiow) Schlesien Ger 7
❒ LOT Fan 6
❒ LOTHRINGEN Lothringen Ger 1
❒ LOULE Faro Por 1 2
❒ LOURCHES Nord Fan 1
❒ LOURENCO MARQUES Moz 1 12
❒ LOURES Lisboa Por 1
❒ LOURINHA Lisboa Por 1 2
❒ LOUVIERE, LA Hainaut Bel 1
❒ LOUVIERS Eure Fan 1
❒ LOUZA Coimbra Por 1
❒ LOUZADA Porto Por 1 2
❒ LOVEDAY (South Australia) Aul 14
❒ LOVERVAL Hainaut Bel 1
❒ LOVERVALEFanl
❒ LOVITCH (Lowicz) Rus 1
❒ LOWAIGE (Lauw) Liege Bel 1
❒ LOWICZ (Lovitch) Rpl 1 2
❒ LUBAN (Lubau) Posen Ger 1 2 3
❒ LUBANGO Ang 1
❒ LUBICHOW (Lubiechowo) Westpreussen Ger 1
❒ LUBLIN (Lioublin, Lyublin) Rus 1
❒ LUBLIN (Lueben; Lioublin) Schlesien Ger 1 2
❒ LUBLINITZ (Lubliniec) Schlesien Ger 1
❒ LUBRANIEC Rpl 2
❒ LUBRIN Almeria Spa 2
❒ LUCAINENA DE LAS TORRES Almeria Spa 1
❒ LUCCA Ita 14
❒ LUCENA DEL CID Castellon Spa 1
❒ LUCHON Huate-Garonne Fan 1 2
❒ LUCHON ET CANTON Haute Garonne Fan 1
❒ LUCK (Loutsk) Rpl 1
❒ LUCK (Loutsk, Lutsk) Rus 1
❒ LUCKA OO Aus 1
❒ LUCKA Sachsen-Altenburg Ger 1
❒ LUCKAU Brandenburg Ger 1 13
❒ LUCKENWALDE Brandenburg Ger 1 2 7
❒ LUDENDORF Rheinland Ger 1
❒ LUDWIGSBURG Wuerttemberg Ger 1 3 6 7 8
❒ LUDWIGSDORF Schlesien Ger 3
❒ LUDWIGSHAFEN/ RHEIN Pfalz Ger 1 2 3 6 7 8
❒ LUDWIGSHUETTE/ BIEDENKOPF Hessen-Nassau Ger 2
❒ LUDWIGSLUST Mecklenburg-Schwerin Ger 1
❒ LUDWIGSSTADT Bayern Ger 1
❒ LUDWIGSTEIN Hessen-Nassau Ger 1
❒ LUEBBECKE Westfalen Ger 1
❒ LUEBBEN/ SPREE Brandenburg Ger 1 14
❒ LUEBCHEN (Lubow; Lubin) Schiesien Ger 7 10
❒ LUEBECK Schleswig-Holstein Ger 1 2 3 7 10 14
❒ LUEBEN (Lubin) Schlesien Ger 1 2 7
❒ LUEBTHEEN Mecklenburg-Schwerin Ger 1
❒ LUEBZ Mecklenburg-Schwerin Ger 1
❒ LUECHOW Hannover Ger 1
❒ LUECHTRINGEN Westfalen Ger 1
❒ LUEDENSCHEID Westfalen Ger 1 2 6 8
❒ LUEDERITZBUCH Ged 2
❒ LUEDERSDORF Brandenburg Ger 2
❒ LUEDINGHAUSEN Westfalen Ger 1 5 7
❒ LUEGDE Westfalen Ger 1 3 7
❒ LUEGUMKLOSTER (Loegumkloster, Denmark) Schleswig-Holstein Ger 1
❒ LUENEBURG Hannover Ger 1 2 6 7 14
❒ LUENEN Westfalen Ger 1 5 7
❒ LUENOW/ ANGERMUENDE Brandenburg Ger 2
❒ LUETGENDORTMUND (Dortmund) Westfalen Ger 1 5 11
❒ LUETJENBURG Schleswig-Holstein Ger 1 2
❒ LUETTRINGHAUSEN Rheinland Ger 1 2
❒ LUETZELHAUSEN Elsass Ger 1
❒ LUETZEN Sachsen Ger 6 13
❒ LUETZSCHENA Sachsen Ger 7
❒ LUFTENBERG OO Aus 1
❒ LUGA Sachsen Ger 7
❒ LUGAU Sachsen Ger 1 7
❒ LUGAU Schlesien Ger 5
❒ LUGHOF OO Aus 1
❒ LUGOS (Stava Lubovna) Slovakia Cze 1
❒ LUGROS Granada Spa 1
❒ LUINGNE West Flanders Bel 1
❒ LUJAR Granada Spa 1
❒ LUKAVEC Cze 1
❒ LUNDAMO Nor 14
❒ LUNDE Nor 14
❒ LUNDEN Schleswig-Holstein Ger 1
❒ LUNDERSKOV Den 11
❒ LUNDERUP (Roeten Krug, Roede kro) Den 1
❒ LUNDERUP (Roten Krug; Roede Kro, Denmark) Schleswig-Holstein Ger 1
❒ LUNEL Herault Fan 2 7
❒ LUNEVILLE Meurthe et Moselle Fan 1
❒ LUNOW/ ANGERMUENDE Brandenburg Ger 2
❒ LUNZ AM SEE NO Aus 1
❒ LUNZENAU/ MULDE Sachsen Ger 1
❒ LUPION Jaen Spa 1
❒ LURE Haute-Saone Fan 1 14
❒ LUSERNA S. Giovanni Ita 3
❒ LUSERNA Torino Piemonte Ita 3

❒ LUSSAT Fan 1
❒ LUTTER/ BARENBERGE Braunschweig Ger 1 2
❒ LUTTERBACH Elsass Ger 1
❒ LUTZHOEFT Schleswig-Holstein Ger 1
❒ LUXEMBURG Lux 1 11
❒ LUXEMBURG-HOLLERICH Ruhr Ger 7
❒ LUZENAC Ariege Fan 2
❒ LUZNICKOG Yug 1
❒ LUZOIR Aisne Fan 3
❒ LYCHEN Brandenburg Ger 2 7
❒ LYCK Ostpreussen Ger 1
❒ LYON Rhone Fan 1 2 3 7 10 11 12
❒ LYON-GRANCHE-BLANCHE Fan 3
❒ LYS-LEZ-LANNOY Nord Fan 1 2
❒ LYUBERTZY (Lioubertz) Rus 1

M

❒ MAADI Zemplin Hun 14
❒ MAADID Alg 2
❒ MAAZIZ Algerie Alg 2
❒ MACAEL Almeria Spa 2
❒ MACANET DE LA SELVA Gerona Spa 1
❒ MACAO Mac 1 2
❒ MACERADA Ita 14
❒ MACON Saon et Loire Fan 1
❒ MACON-BOURG Saone et Loire Fan 1
❒ MACOT Savoy Fan 14
❒ MACZEIKOWITZ (Maciejkowice) Schlesien Ger 1
❒ MADAGASCAR Mad 2 7 11
❒ MADDALON Campania Ita 3
❒ MADDALON Caserta Ita 3
❒ MADE North Brabant Net 14
❒ MADEBACH Sachsen-Gotha Ger 1
❒ MADJANY Rus 1
❒ MADRID Madrid Spa 1 2 6
❒ MADRIDEJOS Toledo Spa 1
❒ MADRIGUERAS Albacete Spa 1
❒ MADUESEE (Miedwie) Pommern Ger 2
❒ MAEHRISCH NEUSTADT (Unicov) Cze 1
❒ MAEHRISCH TRUEBAU (Moravska Trebova) Cze 2
❒ MAELLA Zaragoza Spa 1
❒ MAELOEY Nor 14
❒ MAERE Nor 14
❒ MAERKE-KERKHEM (Maarke-Kerkem) West Flanders Bel 1
❒ MAERZDORF (Martinkovice) Cze 2
❒ MAFFERSDORF (Vratislavice nad Nis) Boehmen Cze 1 2 6 7
❒ MAFFLE (Maffles) Hainaut Bel 1
❒ MAFRA Lisboa Por 1 2
❒ MAGDEBURG Provinz Sachsen Ger 1 2 3 4 6 7 9 11
❒ MAGDEBURG UND HALBERSTADT Provinz Sachsen Ger 1 2
❒ MAGDEBURG-BUCKAU Provinz Sachsen Ger 2 7
❒ MAGDEBURG-SUEDOST Provinz Sachsen Ger 7
❒ MAGDEBURG/ NEUSTADT Provinz Sachsen Ger 2 3
❒ MAGNY-LA-FOSSE Aisne Fan 1
❒ MAHORA Albacete Spa 1
❒ MAIA DE MONTCAL Gerona Spa 1
❒ MAIALS Lerida Spa 1
❒ MAIKAMMER Pfalz Ger 1
❒ MAILLERAYE, LA Seine Inferieure Fan 3 14
❒ MAILLY Aube Fan 7 10
❒ MAINBERNHEIM Bayern Ger 1
❒ MAINBURG Bayern Ger 2 6
❒ MAINVAULT Hainaut Bel 1
❒ MAINZ Hessen Ger 1 2 3 4 5 6 7 8 9 10 11
❒ MAINZ-WIESBADEN Hessen Ger 11
❒ MAISACH Bayern Ger 4
❒ MAISHOFEN Salzburg Aus 1
❒ MAISONS-LAFITTE Seine et Oise Fan 7
❒ MAISSAU NO Aus 1
❒ MAISSENY Aisne Fan 1
❒ MAKEYEVKA (Dmitrievsk) Rus 1
❒ MAKINSK KHUTORA (Makinskie Khoutora) Rus 1
❒ MALAGON Ciudad Real Spa 1
❒ MALAKOFF Hauts-de-Seine Fan 6
❒ MALAPANE (Ozimek) Schlesien Ger 3 7
❒ MALCHIN Mecklenburg-Schwerin Ger 1
❒ MALCHOW Mecklenburg-Schwerin Ger 1
❒ MALDA Lerida Spa 1
❒ MALDEGEM East Flanders Bel 1
❒ MALE CHYSCE Hun 2
❒ MALENTE-GREMSMUEHLEN Schleswig-Holstein Ger 1
❒ MALGRAT Barcelona Spa 1
❒ MALIN Rus 1
❒ MALLA I MIRAMBERC Barcelona Spa 1
❒ MALLMITZ (Malomice) Schlesien Ger 1 2
❒ MALM Nor 14
❒ MALMEDY Liege Bel 14
❒ MALMERSBACH Alsace Fan 1
❒ MALMERSPACH Elsass Ger 1
❒ MALO-LES-BAINS Nord Fan 7
❒ MALPARTIDA DE LA SERENA Badajoz Spa 1
❒ MALPICA DE TAJO Toledo Spa 1
❒ MALTSCHAWE (Malazow) Schlesien Ger 1 7
❒ MALZY Aisne Fan 1
❒ MAMMING Bayern Ger 1
❒ MAMOLA, LA Granada Spa 2
❒ MANCHA REAL Jaen Spa 1
❒ MANCHURCIA STATION (Mantchjouria) Rus 1
❒ MANDAS Sicilia Ita 3
❒ MANDE Fan 6
❒ MANDERFELD Liege Bel 14
❒ MANEBACH Sachsen-Gotha Ger 1 7
❒ MANGLBURG OO Aus 1
❒ MANGUALDE Viseu Por 1
❒ MANHARTSBERG NO Aus 1
❒ MANIOWY Germany Rpl 2
❒ MANISES Valencia Spa 1
❒ MANJIBAR Jaen Spa 1
❒ MANK NO Aus 1
❒ MANLLEU Barcelona Spa 1
❒ MANNERSDORF NO Aus 1
❒ MANNHEIM Baden Ger 1 2 6 7 11 12 14
❒ MANNHEIM-WALDHOF Baden Ger 2
❒ MANNING OO Aus 1
❒ MANRESA Barcelona Spa 1 2
❒ MANRESANA LA Barcelona Spa 1
❒ MANS, LE Sarthe Fan 1 3 11 14
❒ MANSFELD-LANGENDREER Zeche Westfalen Ger 5
❒ MANSFELD/ SEEKREIS Sachsen Ger 1
❒ MANTEIGAS Guarda Por 1
❒ MANTOVA Lombardia Ita 3 14
❒ MANTUA Ita 14
❒ MANUEL Valencia Spa 1
❒ MANZANARES Ciudad Real Spa 1
❒ MARAMURES Rom 2
❒ MARAUSSAN Herault Fan 7
❒ MARBACH NO Aus 1
❒ MARBACH/ FLOEHATAL Sachsen Ger 1
❒ MARBACH/ NECKAR Wuerttemberg Ger 1 2 6 13
❒ MARBAIX-LA-TOUR Hainaut Bel 1
❒ MARBURG/ LAHN Hessen-Nassau Ger 1 6 10 11 12
❒ MARC-EN-OSTREVENT Alg 1
❒ MARCA Tarragona Spa 1 2
❒ MARCHE Luxembourg Bel 1
❒ MARCHE-LEZ-ECAUSSINES Hainaut Bel 1
❒ MARCHEGG NO Aus 1
❒ MARCHENA Sevilla Spa 6
❒ MARCHIENNE-AU-PONT Hainaut Bel 1
❒ MARCHIENNES Nord Fan 1
❒ MARCHIENNES-CAMPAGNE Nord Fan 1
❒ MARCHIN Liege Bel 1
❒ MARCHTRENK OO Aus 1 3 4
❒ MARCIAC Gers Fan 2
❒ MARCILLY-LE-PAVE Loire Fan 3 7
❒ MARCINELLE Hainaut Bel 1
❒ MARCKE West Flanders Bel 1
❒ MARCO DE CANAVEZES Porto Por 2
❒ MARCOING Fan 2
❒ MARCQ EN OSTREVENT Nord Fan 1
❒ MARE LE Isere Fan 3
❒ MAREMMA Sardegna Ita 3
❒ MARENGO (Hadjout) Alg 1
❒ MARENNES Fan 11
❒ MAREST Oise Fan 1
❒ MAREST-DAMPCOURT Oise Fan 1
❒ MARGALEF DE MONTSANT Tarragona Spa 1
❒ MARGANELL Barcelona Spa 2

❒ MARGGRABOWA (Marggrabowo, Treuburg, Olecko, Oletzko)Ostpreusse Ger 1
❒ MARIA Almeria Spa 1
❒ MARIA LAAB Aus 1
❒ MARIA LAACH NO Aus 1
❒ MARIA LAAH OO Aus 1
❒ MARIA LANZENDORF NO Aus 1
❒ MARIA SCHMOLLN OO Aus 1
❒ MARIA TAFERL NO Aus 1 2
❒ MARIA-ENZERSDORF NO Aus 1
❒ MARIAZELL Steiermark Aus 1 2
❒ MARIBOR (Marburg/ Drau) Yug 1 3
❒ MARIEMONT Hainaut Bel 2
❒ MARIENBAD (Marianske Lazne) Cze 1
❒ MARIENBERG Hessen-Nassau Ger 1 7
❒ MARIENBERG Sachsen Ger 1
❒ MARIENBERG/ WUERZBURG Bayern Ger 3
❒ MARIENBERGHAUSEN Rheinland Ger 1
❒ MARIENBURG (Maiborg) Westpreussen Ger 1 2
❒ MARIENHAGEN Hannover Ger 2 7
❒ MARIENHEIDE Rheinland Ger 1
❒ MARIENHOEHE/ SCHWETZ Posen Ger 2
❒ MARIENHUETTE Schlesien Ger 1
❒ MARIENSTEIN Bayern Ger 1 3 7
❒ MARIENTHAL Bayern Ger 2
❒ MARIENTHAL Schlesien Ger 2
❒ MARIENWERDER/ LITTLE NOGAT (Kwidzyn) Westpreussen Ger 1 2 6
❒ MARIGNANE Bouches du Rhone Fan 7
❒ MARINHA GRANDE Leiria Por 1
❒ MARIUPOL (Marioupol, Mariiupil) Rus 1
❒ MARJALIZA Toledo Spa 1
❒ MARKDORF Baden Ger 1
❒ MARKERSDORF/ LEIPZIG Sachsen Ger 1 2 7
❒ MARKIRCH (Sainte-Marie-aux-Mines) Elsass Ger 1 2
❒ MARKIRCH (Sainte-Marie-aux-Mines) Haut Rhin Fan 1
❒ MARKLISSA/ QUEISS (Lesna, Nowe Hajduki) Schlesien Ger 2 7
❒ MARKNEUKIRCHEN Sachsen Ger 1
❒ MARKRANSTAEDT Sachsen Ger 1 2
❒ MARKSTAEDT (Miescisko) Posen Ger 1 6
❒ MARKTBIBART/ EHE Bayern Ger 6
❒ MARKTHEIDENFELD Bayern Ger 1 6
❒ MARKTLEUTHEN Bayern Ger 2 6
❒ MARKTREDWITZ Bayern Ger 1 2 6
❒ MARKTSCHORGAST Bayern Ger 1 6
❒ MARL Westfalen Ger 1 2 3
❒ MARLE Aisne Fan 1
❒ MARLES Pas de Calais Fan 1
❒ MARLINNE Limbourg Bel 1
❒ MARLOW (Mecklenburg-Schwerin) Ger 1
❒ MARMANDE Lot et Garonne Fan 2
❒ MARMOLEJO Jaen Spa 1
❒ MARNE Fan 1
❒ MARNE Schleswig-Holstein Ger 1 2
❒ MARNEFFE Liege Bel 1
❒ MAROC Mor 7
❒ MAROILLES Nord Fan 1
❒ MARQUIN Hainaut Bel 1
❒ MARRAKESCH Mor 9
❒ MARSALA Sicilia Ita 3
❒ MARSALA Trapani Ita 3
❒ MARSBACH OO Aus 1
❒ MARSEILLAN Herault Fan 7
❒ MARSEILLE Bouches de Rhone Fan 1 2 3 6 7 10
❒ MARSILLARGUES Herault Fan 2
❒ MARTEL Lot Fan 2
❒ MARTEN Westfalen Ger 1
❒ MARTENVILLE-ATTILLY Aisne Fan 1
❒ MARTERBUESCHEL Sachsen Ger 2
❒ MARTINIQUE Mar 1
❒ MARTINRODA Sachsen-Gotha Ger 7
❒ MARTINS Liege Bel 1
❒ MARTINSBERG NO Aus 1
❒ MARTORELL Barcelona Spa 1
❒ MARTORELLES DE BAIX Barcelona Spa 1
❒ MARTOS Jaen Spa 1
❒ MARTRES D'ARTIERES Puy-de-Dome Fan 2
❒ MARTRES-TOLOSANE Haute Garonne Fan 1
❒ MARVAO Portalegre Por 1
❒ MAS D'AGENAIS Lot et Garonne Fan 2
❒ MAS DE BARBERANS Tarragona Spa 1
❒ MAS DE LAS MATAS Teruel Spa 2
❒ MAS-ELOI, LE Fan 3
❒ MASCARA Mostaganem Alg 1
❒ MASDENVERGE Tarragona Spa 1
❒ MASMUENSTER Elsass Ger 1 2
❒ MASNIERES Nord Fan 7
❒ MASNOU, EL Barcelona Spa 1
❒ MASO Tarragona Spa 2
❒ MASPUJOLS Tarragona Spa 1
❒ MASQUEFA Barcelona Spa 1
❒ MASROIG Tarragona Spa 1
❒ MASSALCOREIG Lerida Spa 1
❒ MASSANES Gerona Spa 1
❒ MASSEN/ UNNA Westfalen Ger 2 3 5 7
❒ MASSING/ ROTT Bayern Ger 1
❒ MASSOW (Maszewo, Mascewo) Pommern Ger 1
❒ MATARO Barcelona Spa 1 2
❒ MATEO DE LAS FUENTES (San Mateo) Castellon Spa 1
❒ MATERA Bari Ita 3
❒ MATERA Puglia Ita 3
❒ MATOSINHOS Porto Por 1
❒ MATTEOTTI (Rino de Mono) Ita 14
❒ MATTIGHOFEN OO Aus 1 2
❒ MATTSEE Salzburg Aus 1
❒ MATZLEINSDORF NO Aus 1
❒ MAUBEUGE Nord Fan 1 2 3 7
❒ MAUBEUGE & SOIRE Le Chateau Nord Fan 1 2
❒ MAUBRAY Hainaut Bel 1
❒ MAUDACH Pfalz Ger 7
❒ MAUER-OEHLING NO Aus 1
❒ MAUERKIRCHEN OO Aus 1
❒ MAUGUIO Herault Fan 7 10
❒ MAULBRONN Wuerttemberg Ger 1 6
❒ MAULBURG Baden Ger 1
❒ MAULDE Hainaut Bel 1
❒ MAULEON Basses Pyrennees Fan 7
❒ MAURAGE Hainaut Bel 1
❒ MAUROIS Nord Fan 1
❒ MAUROY Aisne Fan 1
❒ MAUTERN NO Aus 1
❒ MAUTH Niederbayern Ger 1
❒ MAUTHAUSEN OO Aus 1 3 14
❒ MAUVEZIN Gers Fan 1
❒ MAXGLAN Salzburg Aus 1
❒ MAXIMILIANSAU Pfalz Ger 1
❒ MAYEN Rheinland Ger 1 2 6 7 8 11
❒ MAYEN UND ANDERNACH Rheinland Ger 1
❒ MAYENNE Mayenne Fan 1 6 14
❒ MAZAMET Tarn Fan 2 6 7
❒ MAZARRON Murcia Spa 1 2
❒ MAZERES Ariege Fan 2
❒ MAZET, LA-ST. VOY Haute Loire Fan 7
❒ MEALHADA Aveiro Por 1
❒ MECHELEN (Malines) Antwerp Bel 1
❒ MECHERNICH Rheinland Ger 1 2
❒ MECINA BOMBARON Granada Spa 1 2
❒ MECKENHEIM Rheinland Ger 1
❒ MECKLENBURG-SCHWERIN Ger 1
❒ MECKLENBURG-STRELITZ (Neustrelitz) Ger 1
❒ MEDA Guarda Por 1 2
❒ MEDEA Medea Alg 1
❒ MEDEBACH (Medebeke) Westfalen Ger 1 2 7
❒ MEDEROESTERREICH Land Aus 1
❒ MEDIONA Barcelona Spa 1
❒ MEDJIBOJ Rus 1
❒ MEDVEZHYE (Molotovskoye, Yevdokimovskoye) Rus 1
❒ MEERANE Sachsen Ger 1 7 8
❒ MEERANE & MUELSEN-ST. JAKOB Sachsen Ger 2
❒ MEERDONCK East Flanders Bel 1

❒ MEERLO Limburg Net 14
❒ MEERSSEN Limburg Net 14
❒ MEGGENHOFEN OO Aus 1
❒ MEHLEM/ RHEIN Rheinland Ger 2
❒ MEHLIS (Zella-Mehlis, Melis) Sachsen-Gotha Ger 1 7
❒ MEHLSACH (Olsztyn, Pienieznc) Ostpreussen Ger 2 7
❒ MEHRNBACH OO Aus 1
❒ MEIDERICH (Duisburg) Rheinland Ger 7
❒ MEILERSDORF NO Aus 1
❒ MEILLERAIE, LA Fan 3
❒ MEINERSDORF/ ERZGEBIRGE Sachsen Ger 1 2
❒ MEINERSEN Hannover Ger 2
❒ MEINERZHAGEN Westfalen Ger 1
❒ MEININGEN Sachsen-Meiningen Ger 1 2 7
❒ MEISENHEIM/ GLAN Rheinland Ger 1
❒ MEISSEN/ ELBE Sachsen Ger 1 2 7 8 12 13
❒ MEISSEN/ MINDEN Westfalen Ger 2
❒ MEKTA-EL-HADID Alg 1
❒ MELDORF Schleswig-Holstein Ger 2
❒ MELEDA Ita 14
❒ MELEKESS Rus 1
❒ MELFI FOTENZA Balilicata Ita 3
❒ MELGACO Viana do Castelo For 2
❒ MELHUS Nor 14
❒ MELIANA Valencia Spa 1
❒ MELILLA (Riff) Spanish Morocco Spa 1
❒ MELK NO Aus 1 2
❒ MELLE East Flanders Bel 1
❒ MELLE/ ELSE Hannover Ger 1
❒ MELLENBACH Schwarzburg-Rudolstadt Ger 1 2
❒ MELLET Hainaut Bel 1
❒ MELLRICHSTADT/ SAALE Bayern Ger 1
❒ MELSELE East Flanders Bel 1 14
❒ MELSUNGEN/ FULDA Hessen-Nassau Ger 1 6
❒ MELUN Seine-et-Marne Fan 1 7
❒ MEMBACH Liege Bel 1 14
❒ MEMEL/ DAMGE NEMAN, NEMUNAS NIEMAN (Klaipeda) Ostpreussen Ger 1
❒ MEMEL/ DAMGE NEMAN, NEUMUNAS NIEMEN (Memelburg) Ostpreussen Ger 1
❒ MEMMINGEN Bayern Ger 1 14
❒ MENAGUENS Lerida Spa 1
❒ MENASALBAS Toledo Spa 1
❒ MENDE Lozere Fan 1
❒ MENDEN Westfalen Ger 1 6 7
❒ MENDRISIO Sicilia Ita 3
❒ MENEN (Meenen, Menin) West Flanders Bel 1
❒ MENGEDE Westfalen Ger 1
❒ MENGEN/ DANUBE Wuerttemberg Ger 1 2 6
❒ MENJIBAK Jaen Spa 1
❒ MENNESSIS Aisne Fan 1
❒ MENNEVRET Aisne Fan 1
❒ MENORCA Spa 6
❒ MENQUINENZA Zaragoza Spa 1
❒ MENTERODA Provinz Sachsen Ger 1 2 7
❒ MENTON Alpes Maritimes Fan 7
❒ MEPPEN/ EMS Hannover Ger 1 2 7 14
❒ MERAKER Nor 14
❒ MERBES-LE-CHATEAU Hainaut Bel 2
❒ MERGELSTETTEN Wuerttemberg Ger 2
❒ MERGENTHEIM, BAD/ TAUBER (Marienthal) Wuerttemberg Ger 1 6
❒ MERGO Ita 3
❒ MERICOURT Pas de Calais Fan 1
❒ MERKEBEKK Nor 14
❒ MERLEBACH Fan 3 14
❒ MERLEBACH Lothringen Fan 14
❒ MERLENBACH Lothringen Ger 6
❒ MERN Den 11
❒ MERSEBURG/ SAALE Sachsen Ger 1 2 3 6 9 13
❒ MERTOLA Beja Por 1 2
❒ MERV Rus 1
❒ MERXPLAS Antwerp Bel 1
❒ MERY SUR SEINE Aube Fan 2
❒ MERY-TILEF (Mery-Tilff) Liege Bel 2
❒ MERZDORF (Marcinkowice, Zagan) Schlesien Ger 5 7
❒ MERZIG-WADERN/ SAAR Rheinland Ger 2
❒ MERZIG/ SAAR Rheinland Ger 1
❒ MESCHEDE/ RUHR Westfalen Ger 1 2 9
❒ MESERITZ/ OBRA (Miedzyrzecs) Posen Ger 1 6
❒ MESNAY Jura Fan 6 7
❒ MESNIL ST. NICAISE Fan 1
❒ MESNIL-L'ESTRE Fan 1
❒ MESNIL-SAINT-LAURENT Fan 1
❒ MESSEL Hessen Ger 7
❒ MESSINGHAUSEN BEI BRILON Westfalen Ger 2
❒ MESTRE Ita 14
❒ METTENDORF Rheinland Ger 2
❒ METTERSDORF Kaernten Aus 1
❒ METTLACH Rheinland Ger 1 2
❒ METTMACH OO Aus 1
❒ METTMANN/ DUESSEL Rheinland Ger 1 2 6 7
❒ METZ Moselle Fan 1
❒ METZ/ MOSELLE-SEILLE Lothringen Ger 1
❒ METZERAL Elsass Ger 2
❒ METZINGEN Wuerttemberg Ger 1
❒ MEUKERKEN-WAAS (Nieukerken) East Flanders Bel 14
❒ MEULEBEKE West Flanders Bel 1 14
❒ MEU RA Thueringen Ger 1
❒ MEURCHIN Pas de Calais Fan 2
❒ MEUSELBACH Thueringen Ger 1 6
❒ MEUSELWITZ Thueringen Ger 1 2 6 7 11
❒ MEWE/ VISTULA (Gniew nad Wisla) Westpreussen Ger 1 3 4
❒ MEYENBURG/ PRIGNITZ Brandenburg Ger 1
❒ MEYERODE Liege Bel 14
❒ MEZIERES Ardennes Fan 1
❒ MEZIERES-SUR-OISE Aisne Fan 1
❒ MEZIN Lot et Garonne Fan 1
❒ MEZOETUR Hun 14
❒ MEZQUITA DE JARQUE Teruel Spa 1
❒ MGHLIN (Mglin) Rus 1
❒ MIATCHEV ET MICHKOW (Mijaczow et Myazkow) Rus 1
❒ MICHAELNBACH OO Aus 1
❒ MICHAELSTHAL/ GLATZ Schlesien Ger 1 2
❒ MICHALKOWITZ (Michalkowice, Michalowskiego Piotra) Schlesien Ger
❒ MICHELAU Bayern Ger 1
❒ MICHELBACH/ ODENWALD Hessen Ger 1
❒ MICHELDORF OO Aus 1
❒ MICHELSTADT Hessen-Nassau Ger 4 7
❒ MICHENDORF Brandenburg Ger 2
❒ MICHEVILLE Meurthe et Moselle Fan 2
❒ MIDDELBURG Zeeland Net 2
❒ MIDDELFART Den 11
❒ MIDWOUD North Holland Net 14
❒ MIECHOWITZ (Miechowice, Miechowska) Schlessien Ger 1 5
❒ MIELEC Galicia Rpl 2
❒ MIELEN-BOVEN-AELST Limbourg Bel 1
❒ MIERZYN Rpl 2
❒ MIERZYN Rus 1
❒ MIESBACH Bayern Ger 1 2 6 7 9
❒ MIETINGEN Wuerttemberg Ger 1
❒ MIGUEL ESTEBAN Toledo Spa 1
❒ MIGUELTURRA Ciudad Real Spa 1
❒ MIJACZOW (Mijaczow et Myszkow, Miatchev et Michkov) Rpl 2
❒ MIKOLAJOW/ BRODY (Mikhaylouka USSR, Mikhaylovka, Mikhalpol) Galicia Rpl 2
❒ MIKOLOW Schlesien Ger 1
❒ MIKULTSCHUETZ (Mikulskiego) Schlesien Ger 1 5
❒ MILA, EL Tarragona Spa 1
❒ MILANO Ita 11 14
❒ MILAZZO Ita 3 14
❒ MILBERTSHOFEN Bayern Ger 2
❒ MILDENAU/ ERZGEBIRGE Sachsen Ger I
❒ MILERES Asturias Spa 2
❒ MILETTO Catania Ita 3
❒ MILETTO Sicilia Ita 3
❒ MILEVSKA Aus 1
❒ MILEVSKO Cze 1
❒ MILHAU (Millau) Aveyron Fan 11
❒ MI LIANA Alg 1

❐ MILITSCH (Milicz, Milicka) Schlesien Ger 1
❐ MILLINGEN Rheinland Ger 1
❐ MILOSLAW (Miloslau) Posen Ger 1
❐ MILOVICE Cze 2
❐ MILOWITZ Aus 3
❐ MILOWITZ Ita 3
❐ MILSPE Westfalen Ger 1 2
❐ MILTENBERG/ MAIN Bayern Ger 1 2 14
❐ MILTITZ Sachsen Ger 2
❐ MINAS DEL HORCAJO Ciudad Real Spa 1
❐ MINDELHEIM/ MINDE Bayern Ger 1 4 7 8
❐ MINDEN Westfalen Ger 1 2 3 4 7 8
❐ MINERALNIYE VODI (Mineralni Vodi) Rus 1
❐ MINES DE BLANZY Saone et Loire Fan 3
❐ MINES DE LA LOIRE Fan 3
❐ MINGLANILLA Cuenca Spa 1
❐ MINING OO Aus 1
❐ MINISTER ACHENBACH Ger 5
❐ MINKOVCY (Minkovtsy) Rus 1
❐ MINSK Rus 1
❐ MI RAFLOR Alicante Spa 1
❐ MIRAMAR Valencia Spa 1
❐ MIRAMAS Bouches du Rhone Fan 3
❐ MIRAMONT Courcelettes Bel 1
❐ MIRAMONT Haute Garonne Fan 2
❐ MIRAMONT Iries Bel 1
❐ MIRANDA DO CORVO Cormbra Por 1
❐ MIRANDE Gers Fan 2
❐ MIRANDELA Braganca Por 1
❐ MIRAUMONT Communes Fan 1
❐ MIRAVET Tarragona Spa 1
❐ MIROW Mecklenburg-Strelitz Ger 1 2
❐ MISBURG Hannover Ger 2
❐ MISDROY (Miedzyzdroje) Pommern Ger
❐ MISKOLCZ (Miskolc, Borsod-Abauj-Zemplen) Hun 1
❐ MISLATA Valencia Spa 1
❐ MISTELBACH NO Aus 1 9
❐ MISTELBACH/ LAYA Bayern Ger 1
❐ MISTLBERG OO Aus 1
❐ MITAU (Yelgava, Jelgava) Lat 1 11
❐ MITAU (Mitava, Jelgava, Yelgava) Rus 1
❐ MITICHTCHI (Mytischi) Rus 1
❐ MITTEL-LAZISK Schlesien Ger 1
❐ MITTELBACH/ CHEMNITZ Sachsen Ger 2
❐ MITTELBERG NO Aus 1
❐ MITTELFROHNA Sachsen Ger 1
❐ MITTELSTEINE Schlesien Ger 2
❐ MITTELWALDE (Miedzylesie) Schlesien Ger 1 2 7
❐ MITTENDORF Aus 3
❐ MITTENWALD/ ISAR Bayern Ger 1
❐ MITTER-ARNSDORF NO Aus 1
❐ MITTERBACH NO Aus 1 2
❐ MITTERHAUSLEITEN NO Aus 1
❐ MITTERNDORF Steiermark Aus 1 3
❐ MITTERSILL Salzburg Aus 1
❐ MITTERTEICH Bayern Ger 1 2 7 9
❐ MITTWEIDA/ ZSCHOPPAU Sachsen Ger 1 2 7 8
❐ MITZACH Fan 1
❐ MITZACH Elsass Ger 1 7 8
❐ MLADA BOLESLAV Cze 2
❐ MLAVA (Mlawa) Rus 1
❐ MLAWA (Mielau) Rpl 2
❐ MOCAMEDES Ang 1
❐ MOCHENWANGEN Wuerttemberg Ger 2
❐ MODENA Ita 3 14
❐ MOEDLING NO Aus 1 2 9
❐ MOEGELTOENDER (Moegeltondern) Den 1
❐ MOEGELTONDERN (Moegeltoender, Denmark) Schleswig-Holstein Ger 1
❐ MOELKAU-LEIPZIG Sachsen Ger 1
❐ MOELKE (Milko, Silkowska) Schlesien Ger 2 4 5 7
❐ MOELKE-LUDWIGSDORF Schlesien Ger 5
❐ MOELLENBECK Hessen-Nassau Ger 1
❐ MOELLENBECK Schaumburg Ger 1
❐ MOELLN Schleswig-Holstein Ger 1 2
❐ MOEN West Flanders Bel 1
❐ MOERBEKE East Flanders Bel 1
❐ MOERKERKE West Flanders Bel 1
❐ MOERS Rheinland Ger 1 2
❐ MOERSCHWANG OO Aus 1
❐ MOERZEKE East Flanders Bel 1
❐ MOGADOURO Breganca Por 1
❐ MOGENTE Valencia Spa 1
❐ MOGILEV (Moghilev) Rus 1
❐ MOGILEV-PODOLSK (Moghilev-Podolsk) Rus 1
❐ MOGILNO (Gembitz, Gebice) Posen Ger 1 6 14
❐ MOHACS Hun 14
❐ MOHLSDORF/ GREIZ Reuss j.L. Ger 2 7
❐ MOHON Ardennes Fan 7
❐ MOHRKIRCH Schleswig-Holstein Ger 14
❐ MOHRUNGEN (Morag) Ostpreussen Ger 1
❐ MOI Nor 14
❐ MOIA Barcelona Spa 1
❐ MOIGNELEE Namur Bel 1
❐ MOIMENTA DA BEIRA Viseu Por 1
❐ MOISSAC Tarn et Garonne Fan 2
❐ MOITA Setubal Por 1
❐ MOJACAR Almeria Spa 1
❐ MOLAIN Aisne Fan 1
❐ MOLDE Nor 14
❐ MOLENBEEK-ST. JEAN Brabant Bel 1
❐ MOLIERES Tarn et Garonne Fan 2
❐ MOLINO Ita 3
❐ MOLINS DE LLORBREGAT (Molins de Rei) Barcelona Spa 1
❐ MOLL Antwerp Bel 1
❐ MOLLAU Elsass Ger 1
❐ MOLLAU Upper Elsass Fan 1
❐ MOLLERUSSA Lerida Spa 1
❐ MOLLN OO Aus 1
❐ MOLOCHANSK (Molotchansk) Rus 1
❐ MOMBACH Hessen Ger 7
❐ MOMBRACELLI D'ASTI Piemonte Ita 3
❐ MONACO Mco 1 11
❐ MONASTIR Cagliari Ita 3
❐ MONASTIR Sardegna Ita 3
❐ MONASTYREK Rus 1
❐ MONBRUN Aude Fan 2
❐ MONCAO Viana do Castelo Por 1 2
❐ MONCEAU-SUR-SAMBRE Hainaut Bel 1
❐ MONCENISIO Piemonte Ita 3
❐ MONCENISIO Torino Ita 3
❐ MONCHECOURT Nord Fan 1
❐ MONCHIQUE Faro Por 1
❐ MONCLAR Tarn et Garonne Fan 1 2
❐ MONDESCOURT Oise Fan 1
❐ MONDREPUIS Aisne Fan 1
❐ MONDSEE OO Aus 1
❐ MONFALCONE Yug 14
❐ MONFORT Gers Fan 1
❐ MONFORTE Alicante Spa 1
❐ MONFORTE Portalegre Por 1 2
❐ MONHEIM Rheinland Ger 2
❐ MONIGO (Treviso) Ita 14
❐ MONISTROL (Monistrol de Calders) Barcelona Spa 1
❐ MONISTROL DE BAGES Barcelona Spa 1
❐ MONJOS DEL PENEDES (Santa Margariday Els Monjos) Barcelona Spa 1
❐ MONOPOLI Ita 3
❐ MONOVAR Alicante Spa 1
❐ MONPAZIER Dordogne Fan 2
❐ MONREALE Palermo Ita 3
❐ MON REALE Sicilia Ita 3
❐ MONS Hainaut Bel 1
❐ MONS Haute-Loire Fan 3 4
❐ MONSCHAU Rheinland Ger 1
❐ MONSEGUR Gironde Fan 2
❐ MONT D'ORIGNY Aisne Fan 1
❐ MONT-DE-MARSAN Landes Fan 1 2
❐ MONT-DORE LE Puy-de-Dome Fan 7
❐ MONT-RAL Tarragona Spa 1
❐ MONT-ROIG Tarragona Spa 1
❐ MONT-SAINTE-ALDEGONDE Hainaut Bel 1
❐ MONT-SUR-MARCHIENNE Hainaut Bel 1
❐ MONTABAUR Hessen-Nassau Ger 1 3 4 5 6 7
❐ MONTAGNAC Herault Fan 7 12
❐ MONTAGUT DE FLUVIA Gerona Spa 1
❐ MONTAIGU Vendee Fan 1
❐ MONTALBAN Teruel Spa 1

❐ MONTANANA Huesca Spa 1
❐ MONTARGIS Loiret Fan 1
❐ MONTAUBAN Tarn et Garonne Fan 1 2 3 7
❐ MONTAY Nord Fan 9
❐ MONTBELLIARD Doubs Fan 2
❐ MONTBLANC Tarragona Spa 1
❐ MONTBREHAIN Aisne Fan 1
❐ MONTBRIO DEL CAMP Tarragona Spa 1
❐ MONTBRISON Loire Fan 3 7
❐ MONTBRUN Aude Fan 2
❐ MONTCADA I REIXAC Barcelona Spa 1
❐ MONTCEAU-LES-MINES Saone Fan 3 7 14
❐ MONTCLAR Barcelona Spa 1
❐ MONTCORTES Lerida Spa 1
❐ MONTCUQ Lot Fan 2
❐ MONTE NARBA Sardegna Ita 3
❐ MONTEALEGRE DEL CASTILLO Albacete Spa 1
❐ MONTECH Tarn-et-Garonne Fan 2
❐ MONTEGNEE Liege Bel 1 7
❐ MONTELIMAR Drome Fan 1 1
❐ MONTELLA I MARTINET Lerida Spa 1
❐ MONTEMALE Genua Ita 14
❐ MONTEMOR 0 VELHO Coimbra Por 1 2
❐ MONTEMOR-0-NOVA Evora Por 2
❐ MONTENEGRO Mon 1
❐ MONTERRUBIO DE LA SERENA Badajoz Spa 1
❐ MONTESA Valencia Spa 1
❐ MONTESCOURT-LIZEROLLES Aisne Fan 1
❐ MONTESQUIEU-VOLVESTRE Haute Garonne Fan 2
❐ MONTESQUIOU Gers Fan 2
❐ MONTFERRI Tarragona Spa 1
❐ MONTGAT Barcelona Spa 1
❐ MONTI Sardegna Ita 3
❐ MONTIEL Ciudad Real Spa 1
❐ MONTIGNIES-SAINT-CHRISTOPHE Hainaut Bel 1
❐ MONTIGNY-EN-ARROUAISE Aisne Fan 1
❐ MONTIGNY-EN-GOHELLE Pas de Calais Fan 1
❐ MONTIGNY-LE-TILLEUL (Montignies-le-Tilleul) Hainaut Bel 1
❐ MONTIGNY-SUR-SAMBRE (Montignies-sur-Sambre) Bel 1
❐ MONTILLANA Granada Spa 1
❐ MONTLUCON Allier Fan 3 7
❐ MONTLUCON-GANNAT Allier Fan 1 2 3 7
❐ MONTMAGNY Seine et Oise Fan 7
❐ MONTMANEU Barcelona Spa 1
❐ MONTMANY FIGARO Barcelona Spa 1
❐ MONTMEDY Meuse Fan 1
❐ MONTMELO Barcelona Spa 1
❐ MONTMORENCE Seine et Oise Fan 7
❐ MONTOIRE Loire et Cher Fan 3
❐ MONTOLIEU Aude Fan 1 7
❐ MONTOLIEU Rhone Fan 7
❐ MONTORNES Lerida Spa 1
❐ MONTORO Cordoba Spa 2
❐ MONTPELLIER Herault Fan 1 7
❐ MONTPEZAT Tarn et Garonne Fan 1
❐ MONTREAL Aude Fan 1 2 6
❐ MONTREUIL-SUR-MER Pas de Calais Fan 1
❐ MONTRICOUX Tarn et Garonne Fan 1
❐ MONTROS Lerida Spa 1
❐ MONTSENY Barcelona Spa 1
❐ MONTZEN Liege Bel 1 14
❐ MONZA Lombardia Ita 3
❐ MONZA Milano Ita 3
❐ MONZON Huesca Spa I
❐ MOORSELEN (Moorsele) West Flanders Bel 1
❐ MOOS Bayern Ger 1
❐ MOOS Kaernten Aus 1
❐ MOOSBACH OO Aus 1
❐ MOOSBURG/ ISAR Bayern Ger 1 3 7
❐ MOOSCH Elsass Ger 1 7
❐ MOOSDORF OO Aus 1
❐ MOOSH Alsace Fan 1
❐ MORA Evora Por 2
❐ MORA D'EBRE (Mora de Ebro) Tarragona Spa 1
❐ MORA DE RUBIELOS Teruel Spa 1
❐ MORA LA NOVA Tarragona Spa 1
❐ MORAL DE CALATRAVA Ciudad Real Spa 1
❐ MORATALLA Murcia Spa 1
❐ MORAVSKE BUDEJOVICE Maehren Cze 1
❐ MORAVSKOG (Moravskog-Nis, Morava) Yug 1
❐ MORCOURT Aisne Fan 1
❐ MOREDA Granada Spa 1
❐ MORELL, EL Tarragona Spa 1
❐ MORELLA Castellon Spa 1 2
❐ MORESNET Liege Bel 1 14
❐ MORGENROTH Kreis Beuthen Schlesien Ger 5
❐ MORINGEN Hannover Ger 2
❐ MORLAIX Finistere Fan 1 1
❐ MORSBACH Rheinland Ger 1
❐ MORSHANSK Rus 1
❐ MORSUM/ SYLT Schleswig-Holstein Ger 1
❐ MORTIERS Aisne Fan 1
❐ MORTSEL (Sint-Amedus) Liege Bel 14
❐ MORUNYS Lerida Spa 1
❐ MORZG Salzburg Aus 1
❐ MOSBACH Baden Ger 1 2 6
❐ MOSCOW (Moskova) Rus 1
❐ MOSDOK (Mozdok) Rus 1
❐ MOSINA Rpl 2
❐ MOSON (Mosony, Wieselburg) Hun 1
❐ MOSQUERUELA Teruel Spa 1
❐ MOSS Nor 14
❐ MOSTAGANEM Alg 1 2 7
❐ MOSTER Nor 14
❐ MOSVIK Nor 14
❐ MOSYR (Mozyr) Rus 1
❐ MOTILLEJA Spa 1
❐ MOTRIL Granada Spa 2
❐ MOTTE-D'AVEILLANS Isere Fan 3 14
❐ MOUCHAN Gers Fan 1
❐ MOUGERES Herault Fan 3
❐ MOULBAIX Hainaut Bel 1
❐ MOULINS Allier Fan 1 3
❐ MOULINS Nievre Fan 7
❐ MOULINS ET LAPALISSE Allier Fan 1 3
❐ MOULLEAU, LE Gironde Fan 6 7
❐ MOURA Beja Por 1 2
❐ MOURAO Evora Por 1 2
❐ MOUSCRON West Flanders Bel 1 14
❐ MOUSSOULENS Aude Fan 2
❐ MOUSTIER Hainaut Bel 1
❐ MOUVAUX Bel 1
❐ MOUVY Oise Fan 1
❐ MOUY Oise Fan 1 7
❐ MOY Aisne Fan 1
❐ MOYS Schlesien Ger 1 2
❐ MOYUELA Zaragoza Spa 2
❐ MROTSCHEN (Mrocza) Posen Ger 1
❐ MUCH Rheinland Ger 1
❐ MUCHENITZ (Mechnice) Schlesien Ger 1
❐ MUECHELN/ GEISSELBACH Provinz Sachsen Ger 1 2 7
❐ MUECKENBERG Provinz Sachsen Ger 1
❐ MUEGELN Sachsen Ger 1
❐ MUEGLITZ (Mohelnice) Maehren Cze I
❐ MUEHLACKER Wuerttemberg Ger 7
❐ MUEHLAU/ CHEMNITZ Sachsen Ger 1 2
❐ MUEHLBERG/ ELBE Provinz Sachsen Ger 1 6 14
❐ MUEHLDORF-NEUMARKT/ ROTT Bayern Ger 6
❐ MUEHLDORF/ INN Bayern Ger 1 2
❐ MUEHLEN Rheinland Ger 2
❐ MUEHLHAUSEN (Thomas Muentzer-StadtMuehlhausen) Provinz Sachsen Ger 1 2 6 7 8 12
❐ MUEHLHAUSEN. WORBIS & HEILIGENSTADT Provinz Sachsen Ger 2
❐ MUEHLHEIM OO Aus 1
❐ MUEHLHEIM/ MAIN Hessen-Nassau Ger 1 6 7
❐ MUEHLING OO Aus 3 4 5
❐ MUEHLWAND/ VOGTLAND Sachsen Ger 2
❐ MUELHAUSEN/ ILL (Mulhouse) Elsass Ger 1 7 10 14
❐ MUELHEIM Elsass Ger 7
❐ MUELHEIM/ RUHR Rheinland Ger 1 2 3 5 6 7 10 11 12
❐ MUELLHEIM Baden Ger 1 6
❐ MUELSEN-ST. JAKOB Sachsen Ger 1
❐ MUELSEN-ST. MICHELN Sachsen Ger 1
❐ MUENCHBERG/ PULSNITZ Bayern Ger 1 2 6
❐ MUENCHEBERG Brandenberg Ger 3 6
❐ MUENCHEHAGEN Hannover Ger 2

❒ MUENCHEN-FREISING Bayern Ger 7
❒ MUENCHEN-GIESING Bayern Ger 7
❒ MUENCHEN-GLADBACH (Moenchen Gladbach) Rheinland Ger 1 2 7 8
❒ MUENCHEN-GLADBACH & RHEYDT Rheinland Ger 1 2 8
❒ MUENCHEN-MOOSACH Bayern Ger 7
❒ MUENCHEN-NEUAUBING Bayern Ger 2
❒ MUENCHEN-NYMPHENBURG Bayern Ger 2
❒ MUENCHEN-PASING Bayern Ger 1
❒ MUENCHEN-PERLACH Bayern Ger 2
❒ MUENCHEN-SOLLN Bayern Ger 2
❒ MUENCHEN-SUED Bayern Ger 7
❒ MUENCHEN/ ISAR Bayern Ger 1 2 3 6 7 8 9 10 11 12 14
❒ MUENCHENBERNSDORF Thueringen Ger 1 2
❒ MUENCHHAUSEN Aus 2
❒ MUENDEN (Hannoverisch-Muenden) Hannover Ger 4 6 11
❒ MUENDER/ DEISTER (Bad Muender) Hannover Ger 2
❒ MUENNERSTADT Bayern Ger 1
❒ MUENSINGEN Wuerttemberg Ger 3 4 6
❒ MUENSTER Elsass Ger 1
❒ MUENSTER Tirol Aus 1
❒ MUENSTER Westfalen Ger 1 2 3 4 6 7 11 14
❒ MUENSTER/ NECKAR Wuerttemberg Ger 4 6 7
❒ MUENSTERBERG/ OHLAU (Ziebice) Schlesien Ger 1 6 7 13
❒ MUENSTEREIFEL/ ERFT Rheinland Ger 1
❒ MUENSTERMAIFELD (Muenster-Mayfeld) Rheinland Ger 1
❒ MUENZBACH OO Aus 1
❒ MUENZKI RCHEN OO Aus 1
❒ MUERITZ/ OSTSEEBAD (Graal-Mueritz) Mecklenburg-Schwerin Ger 2
❒ MUERWIK Schleswig-Holstein Ger 2 10
❒ MUERZZUSCHLAG Steiermark Aus 1 2 9
❒ MUESCHEDE (Arnsberg) Westfalen Ger 7
❒ MUILLE-VILLETTE Somme Fan 1
❒ MUKACEVO (Munkacs) Cze 1 2
❒ MULA Murcia Spa 1
❒ MU LDA Sachsen Ger 1
❒ MULDENSTEIN Provinz Sachsen Ger 7
❒ MULHOUSE (Muelhausen) Alsace Fan 1 7 10 14
❒ MULHOUSE (Muelhausen) Haute Rhin Fan 1 7 10 14
❒ MUMSDORF Provinz Sachsen Ger 2 7
❒ MUNDERFING OO Aus 1 2
❒ MUNDERKINGEN/ DANUBE Wuerttemberg Ger 1 6
❒ MUNIESA Teruel Spa 2
❒ MUNKACS (Mukachevo USSR) Hun 1
❒ MUNSTERLAGER Hannover Ger 2 3 10
❒ MURA Barcelona Spa 1
❒ MURAU Steiermark Aus 1
❒ MURCA Vila Real For 1
❒ MURCIA Murcia Spa 1 2
❒ MURE, LA Fan 3 14
❒ MURES-ALCALA LA REAL Jaen Spa 2
❒ MURET Haute Garonne Fan 1 2
❒ MURG Baden Ger 1 2
❒ MURLA Alicante Spa 1
❒ MURMANSK (Mourmansk) Rus 1
❒ MURNAU Bayern Ger 1 2 14
❒ MURO DEL ALCOY Alicante Spa 2
❒ MURO LUCANO Basilicata Ita 3
❒ MURO LUCANO Potenza Ita 3
❒ MUROM (Mourom) Rus 1
❒ MURRHARDT/ MURR Wuerttemberg Ger 1 2 6
❒ MURTAS, COJAYAR Y MECINA TEDEL Granada Spa 1
❒ MUSKAU/ NEISSE (Bad Muskau) Schlesien Ger 1 2
❒ MUTTERS Tirol Aus 1
❒ MUTZSCHEN (Mutzchen) Sachsen Ger 1
❒ MUY, LE Fan 7
❒ MYLAU/ Vogtland Sachsen Ger 1 2 7
❒ MYRA Nor 14
❒ MYSLENICE Galicia Rpl 1
❒ MYSLOWITZ (Myslowice) Schlesien Ger 1

N

❒ NAARN OO Aus 1
❒ NABBURG/ NAAB Bayern Ger 1 2
❒ NACERADEC Cze 1
❒ NACHA Huesca Spa 1
❒ NACHOD/ METTAU Westfalen Ger 7
❒ NACHRODT Westfalen Ger 2 5 7
❒ NACHTERSTADT Provinz Sachsen Ger 1
❒ NACIMIENTO Almeria Spa 1
❒ NADEJKOV Cze 1
❒ NADESCHDINSKY (Nadezhdinsky, Nadejdinsk) Rus 1
❒ NAERBOE Nor 14
❒ NAESTVED Den 11
❒ NAGOLD-ALTENSTEIG Wuerttemberg Ger 2
❒ NAGOLD/ NAGOLD Wuerttemberg Ger 1 2 6
❒ NAGYBANYA (Baia Mare, Rumania) Hun 1
❒ NAGYCZENK (Grosszinkendorf) Hun 1
❒ NAGYKAROLYFALVA (Velke Karlovice) Hun 1
❒ NAGYMEGYER Hun 3
❒ NAGYMEGYER (Nagy-megyer, Velky Meder) Slovakia Cze 3
❒ NAGYSZALONTA (Nagy-Szalatna, Salonta, Rumania) Hun 1
❒ NAGYSZOELLOES (Nagy-Szollos, Vinogradov, USSR) Hun 1
❒ NAILA Bayern Ger 1 2 6
❒ NAIVASKA Ken 14
❒ NAKEL/ NETZKE (Naklo, Nackel) Posen Ger 1
❒ NAKSKOV Den 11
❒ NALCHIK (Naltchik) Rus 1
❒ NALEC Lerida Spa 1
❒ NALINNES Hainaut Bel 1
❒ NAMSLAU/ WEIDA (Namyslow) Schlesien Ger 1 2
❒ NAMUR Namur Bel 1
❒ NANCY Meurthe et Moselle Fan 1 2 3 7 11 14
❒ NANDLSTADT Bayern Ger 2
❒ NANDRIN Liege Bel 1
❒ NANTERRE Hauts de Seine Fan 3
❒ NANTES Loire Inferieure Fan 1 3 12 14 7
❒ NANUROY Aisne Fan 1
❒ NAPOLI Castel Ita 3
❒ NAPOLI S. Elmo Ita 3
❒ NAQUERA Valencia Spa 1
❒ NARBONNE Aude Fan 1 2 6 7 12
❒ NARNI Perugia Ita 3
❒ NARNI Umbria Ita 3
❒ NARVA Est 2
❒ NARVIK Nor 14
❒ NASSAU/ LAH N Hessen-Nassau Ger 1
❒ NASTAETTEN/ MUEHLBACK Hessen-Nassau Ger 1 8
❒ NATTERNBACH OO Aus 1
❒ NATTHEIM Wuerttemberg Ger 1
❒ NAUEN/ OSTHAVELLAND Brandenburg Ger 1 7
❒ NAUGARD (Nowogard) Pommern Ger 1
❒ NAUHEIM BAD Hessen Ger 1 8
❒ NAUMBURG/ QUEISS Schlesien Ger 2
❒ NAUMBURG/ SAALE Provinz Sachsen Ger 1 2 6 8 9 10
❒ NAUNDORF/ KOETZSCHENBRODA Sachsen Ger 1 2
❒ NAUNHOF/ PAARDE Sachsen Ger 1 2 7 13
❒ NAUPLIA Gre 14
❒ NAU ROY Aisne Fan 1
❒ NAVAHERMOSA Toledo Spa 1
❒ NAVAL Huesca Spa 2
❒ NAVALMORALES Toledo Spa 1
❒ NAVALUCILLOS Toledo Spa 1
❒ NAVARCLES Barcelona Spa 1
❒ NAVAS (Castelladral) Barcelona Spa 1
❒ NAVAS DE SAN JUAN Jaen Spa 1
❒ NAVATA Gerona Spa 1
❒ NAZARE Leiria Por 1 2
❒ NEBRA/ UNSTRUT Provinz Sachsen Ger 1
❒ NECKARGEMUEND/ ELSENZ & NECKAR Baden Ger 1
❒ NECKARSULM/ SULM & NECKAR Wuerttemberg Ger 1 2 6
❒ NECKENDORF (Lutherstadt Eisleben) Provinz Sachsen Ger 7
❒ NEDER-EENAME East Flanders Bel 1
❒ NEDERBRAKEL East Flanders Bel 1

❒ NEEROETEREN Limbourg Bel 1
❒ NEERPELT Limbourg Bel 1
❒ NEG REPELISSE Tarn et Garonne Fan 1
❒ NEHEIM/ RUHR & WOEHNE Westfalen Ger 1 2 6
❒ NEIDENBURG (Nidzica, Nidborg) Ostpreussen Ger 1 6
❒ NEIDENFELS Pfalz Ger 1
❒ NEINBERG Bremen Ger 14
❒ NEINDORF/ HEDWIGSBURG Braunschweig Ger 2
❒ NEINSTEDT/ HARZ Provinz Sachsen Ger 1 7
❒ NEISSE-NEULAND Schlesien Ger 1
❒ NEISSE/ NEISSE NYSA, NYSKA Schlesien Ger 1 2 3 4 6 8 9
❒ NEKOR Cze 2
❒ NELAS Viseu Por 1 2
❒ NEMECKY BROD Cze 1
❒ NEMOURS Seine et Marne Fan 11
❒ NEPSZAVA UTALVANY Hun 1
❒ NERAC Lot et Garonne Fan 1 2
❒ NERCHAU/ MULDE Sachsen Ger 1 2
❒ NERCHINSK (Nertchinsk) Rus 1
❒ NERESHEIM Wuerttemberg Ger 1 2
❒ NERKEWITZ/ JENA Thueringen Ger 14
❒ NERPIO Albacete Spa 1
❒ NERVIEUX Loire Fan 7
❒ NESLANDSVATN Nor 14
❒ NESLE Somme Fan 1
❒ NESSELWANG Bayern Ger 1 8
❒ NESVETEVKHEVO (Nesvetevitchi) Rus 1
❒ NETZEKREIS (Schoenlanke, Trzcianka) Pommern Ger 1
❒ NETZSCHKAU/ VOGTLAND Sachsen Ger 1 2 9
❒ NEU ASTENBERG Westfalen Ger 1
❒ NEU EIBENBERG Sachsen Ger 2
❒ NEU ROETHENBACH Bayern Ger 7
❒ NEU ULM Bayern Ger 1 6
❒ NEU WEISSTEIN (Kamionek) Schlesien Ger 2
❒ NEU-MORESNET Bel 14
❒ NEU-MORESNET Liege Bel 14
❒ NEUBAMBERG Hessen Ger 1
❒ NEUBECKUM Westfalen Ger 1 2
❒ NEUBERG (Podhradi) Cze 9
❒ NEUBERUN (Nowy Bierun) Schlesien Ger 7
❒ NEUBRANDENBURG Mecklenburg-Strelitz Ger 1 2 14
❒ NEUBUKOW Mecklenburg-Schwerin Ger 12
❒ NEUBURG/ DONAU Bayern Ger 1 2 6
❒ NEUBURG/ INN Bayern Ger 1
❒ NEUBURG/ KAMMEL Bayern Ger 3
❒ NEUDAMM (Debno) Brandenburg Ger 1 6
❒ NEUDAMM/ FRANKFURT/ MAIN Hessen-Nassau Ger 6
❒ NEUDECK (Swierklaniec) Schlesien Ger 2
❒ NEUDORF (Nowa Wies) Schlesien Ger 1 2
❒ NEUDORF/ ERZGEBIRGE Sachsen Ger 1
❒ NEUEIBAU Sachsen Ger 2
❒ NEUENAHR, BAD Rheinland Ger 1 2 7
❒ NEUENBUERG/ ERZ Wuerttemberg Ger 2 6
❒ NEUENGAMME/ HAMBURG Hamburg Ger 15
❒ NEUENHAUS/ HILGEN Rheinland Ger 2
❒ NEUENKIRCHEN Westfalen Ger 3 4
❒ NEUENMARKT Bayern Ger 14
❒ NEUENRADE Westfalen Ger 1 2 3
❒ NEUENSCHWAND (Bodenwoehr) Ger 9
❒ NEUENSTADT/ KOCHER Wuerttemberg Ger 2
❒ NEUERBURG Rheinland Ger 2
❒ NEUERN (Nyrsko) Boehmen Cze 2 9
❒ NEUFCHATEAU Vosges Fan 7
❒ NEUFELDEN OO Aus 1 2
❒ NEUFFEN Wuerttemberg Ger 1
❒ NEUGERSDORF Sachsen Ger 1 2
❒ NEUGRABEN-HAUSBRUCH (Hamburg) Schleswig-Holstein Ger 1
❒ NEUHALDENSLEBEN Sachsen Ger 1 2
❒ NEUHAMMER Schlesien Ger 3
❒ NEUHAUS NO Aus 1
❒ NEUHAUS Sachsen-Meiningen Ger 2 6
❒ NEUHAUS Thueringen Ger 2 6
❒ NEUHAUS/ ELBE Hannover Ger 1 2 3
❒ NEUHAUS/ INN Bayern Ger 2
❒ NEUHAUS/ OSTE Hannover Ger 1
❒ NEUHAUS/ OSTSEE Mecklenburg-Schwerin Ger 2
❒ NEUHAUS/ RENNWEG Schwarzburg-Rudolstadt Ger 1 6
❒ NEUHAUS/ Solling Westfalen Ger 1
❒ NEUHAUSEN/ ERZGEBIRGE Sachsen Ger 1 2
❒ NEUHEIDUK (Nowe Hajduki, Hajducka) Schlesien Ger 1
❒ NEUHEUSIS Ged 2
❒ NEUHOF Hessen-Nassau Ger 1
❒ NEUHOF OO Aus 1
❒ NEUHOFEN AN DER KREMS OO Aus 2
❒ NEUHOFEN AN DER YBBS NO Aus 1
❒ NEUHOFEN IM INNKREIS OO Aus 1
❒ NEUILLY-SUR-SEINE Hautes de Seine Fan 7
❒ NEUKALEN Mecklenburg-Schwerin Ger 1
❒ NEUKEMATEN OO Aus 1
❒ NEUKIRCH (Nowa Cerkwia, Kerekwie) Schlesien Ger 2 7
❒ NEUKIRCHEN AM OSTRONG NO Aus 2
❒ NEUKIRCHEN AM WALDE OO Aus 1
❒ NEUKIRCHEN AN DER ENKNACH OO Aus 1
❒ NEUKIRCHEN BEI LAMBACH OO Aus 1
❒ NEUKIRCHEN/ HEIL BLUT Bayern Ger 1 6
❒ NEUKIRCHEN/ PLEISSE Sachsen Ger 2
❒ NEUKIRCHEN/ VOECKLA OO Aus 1
❒ NEUKIRCHEN/ VOGTLAND Sachsen Ger 1
❒ NEUKIRCHEN/ WYHRA Sachsen Ger 2
❒ NEUKIRCHHOF Fantasy City Ger 1
❒ NEUKLOSTER Mecklenburg-Schwerin Ger 1
❒ NEULENGBACH NO Aus 1
❒ NEUMARK Sachsen Ger 2
❒ NEUMARK-BEDRA Provinz Sachsen Ger ·
❒ NEUMARK/ DREWENZ (Nowe Miasto, Lubawskie) Westpreussen Ger 2 6
❒ NEUMARKT Salzburg Aus 1
❒ NEUMARKT (Sroda Slask) Schlesien Ger 1 2 6 7
❒ NEUMARKT Steiermark Aus 1
❒ NEUMARKT AN DER YBBS NO Aus 1
❒ NEUMARKT IM HAUSRUCKKREIS OO Aus 1
❒ NEUMARKT IM MUEHLKREIS OO Aus 1
❒ NEUMARKT/ ROTT (Neumarkt-St. Veit, Neumarkt-St. Veit) Bayern Ger 2 6 7
❒ NEUMARKT/ SULZ Bayern Ger 1 6 7
❒ NEUMARKT/ WALD (Nowry Targ) Galicia Rpl 1
Bayern Ger 2
❒ NEUMUEHLEN-DIETRICHSDORF Schleswig-Holstein Ger 2
❒ NEUMUENSTER Schleswig-Holstein Ger 1 2 7 14
❒ NEUNBURG/ WALD Bayern Ger 1
❒ NEUNDORF Anhalt Ger 1
❒ NEUNDORF/ GLATZ Schlesien Ger 1 2
❒ NEUNHOFEN Sachsen-Weimar-Eisenach Ger 1
❒ NEUNKIRCHEN NO Aus 9
❒ NEUNKIRCHEN Rheinland Ger 1 3 9
❒ NEUOETTING Bayern Ger 1 2
❒ NEUOETTING/ ALTOETTING Bayern Ger 2
❒ NEUOFFSTEIN Pfalz Ger 7
❒ NEUPETERSHAIN N. L. Brandenburg Ger 2
❒ NEURATH Rheinland Ger 7
❒ NEURODE/ EULENGEBIRGE (Nowa Ruda) Schlesien Ger 1 2 4 5 6

❒ NEURUPPIN Brandenburg Ger 2 6 8
❒ NEUSALZ/ ODER (Nowa Sol) Schlesien Ger 1 2 6 7 11
❒ NEUSALZA-SPREMBERG Sachsen Ger 1 2
❒ NEUSS/ ERFT Rheinland Ger 1 2 3 7 8 14
❒ NEUSSAU/ BUCHEN Schleswig-Holstein Ger 7
❒ NEUSTADT Baden Ger 1 2 6 7
❒ NEUSTADT (Unicov) Maehren Cze 1
❒ NEUSTADT Sachsen Ger 1 2 8
❒ NEUSTADT (Prudnik) Schlesien Ger 1 2 6 7
❒ NEUSTADT Schleswig-Holstein Ger 1 8 14
❒ NEUSTADT/ AISCH Bayern Ger 1 6
❒ NEUSTADT/ DONAU Bayern Ger 1 6
❒ NEUSTADT/ ELDE Mecklenburg-Schwerin Ger 1
❒ NEUSTADT/ HAARDT Pfalz Ger 1 6 8
❒ NEUSTADT/ KULM Bayern Ger 1
❒ NEUSTADT/ METTAU Bohemia Cze 1
❒ NEUSTADT/ ORLA Thueringen Ger 1 7
❒ NEUSTADT/ PINNE (Lwowek) Posen Ger 1
❒ NEUSTADT/ REHDE (Weihersfrei, Wejherowo) Westpreussen Ger 1
❒ NEUSTADT/ RUEBENBERG Hannover Ger 1
❒ NEUSTADT/ SAALE Bayern Ger 1 2 6
❒ NEUSTADT/ WALDNABB Bayern Ger 1
❒ NEUSTADT/ WARTHE (Nowe Miasto, Pomorze) Posen Ger 1
❒ NEUSTADTL A.D. DONAU NO Aus 1
❒ NEUSTAEDTEL (Nowe Miasteczke) Schlesien Ger 1
❒ NEUSTETTIN (Szczecinek) Pommern Ger 1 2 6 7
❒ NEUSTIFT OO Aus 1
❒ NEUSTIFT IM STUBAL Tirol Aus 1
❒ NEUSTIFT-INNERMANZING NO Aus 1
❒ NEUSTRELITZ Mecklenburg-Strelitz Ger 1
❒ NEUTEICH (Nytych, Nowy Staw) Danzig Westpreussen Ger 1 2
❒ NEUTOMISCHEL (Nowy Tomsyl) Posen Ger 1 2
❒ NEUVILETTE Somme Fan 1
❒ NEUVILLE-LES-RAON, LA Vosges Fan 1 2
❒ NEUVILLY Nord Fan 2
❒ NEUWEDEL (Drawno) Brandenburg Ger 1 7
❒ NEUWERK/ OELZE Thueringen Ger 2
❒ NEUWIED-RASSELSTEIN Rheinland Ger 12
❒ NEUWIED/ RHEIN Rheinland Ger 1 2 6 8 11 12
❒ NEUWIESE Sachsen Ger 1
❒ NEUX-LES-MINES Pas de Calais Fan 1
❒ NEVEKLOV Boehmen Cze 2
❒ NEVERS Nievre Fan 1 3 7 14
❒ NEVIGES Rheinland Ger 2 8
❒ NEZSIDER Hun 3
❒ NICE Alpes Maritimes Fan 1 2 6 7 10 11
❒ NICKLASDORF NO Aus 1
❒ NIEBUELL Schleswig-Holstein Ger 1
❒ NIECHCICE Rpl 2
❒ NIECHCICE Rus 1
❒ NIED/ MAIN Hessen-Nassau Ger 1 2 9
❒ NIEDER HERMSDORF/ WALDENBURG Schlesien Ger 1
❒ NIEDER INGELHEIM/ RHEIN (Ingelheim) Hessen Ger 1
❒ NIEDER MARSBERG Sachsen Ger 1
❒ NIEDER MARSBERG Westfalen Ger 1 2
❒ NIEDER RYDULTAU (Rydultowy Dolne) Schlesien Ger 1
❒ NIEDER ULLERSDORF (Mirostowice) Brandenburg Ger 2
❒ NIEDER ZWOENITZ Sachsen Ger 1
❒ NIEDERCUNNERSDORF Sachsen Ger 1
❒ NIEDERDORF/ ERZGEBIRGE Sachsen Ger 2
❒ NIEDEREINSIEDEL (Dolni Poustevna) Cze 1
❒ NIEDERFRIEDERSDORF Sachsen Ger 2
❒ NIEDERHADAMAR Hessen Ger 14
❒ NIEDERHARTMANNSDORF/ SAGAN Schlesien Ger 1
❒ NIEDERKAUFUNGEN Hessen-Nassau Ger 1
❒ NIEDERKRUECHTEN Rheinland Ger 2
❒ NIEDERLAHNSTEIN Hessen-Nassau Ger 1
❒ NIEDERLAHNSTEIN-OBERLAHNSTEIN Rheinland Ger 2
❒ NIEDERLAUSITZ Sachsen Ger 7
❒ NIEDERLEIS NO Aus 1
❒ NIEDERLUNGWITZ Sachsen Ger 1
❒ NIEDERMENDIG Rheinland Ger 1
❒ NIEDERNEUKIRCHEN OO Aus 1
❒ NIEDERODERWITZ Sachsen Ger 1 2 7
❒ NIEDEROESTERREICH Land Aus 1
❒ NIEDERRAMSTADT Hessen Ger 7
❒ NIEDERSACHSWERFEN Sachsen Ger 2
❒ NIEDERSALZBRUNN Schlesien Ger 1 2
❒ NIEDERSCHELD (Dillenburg) Hessen-Nassau Ger 1 7
❒ NIEDERSCHELDEN Westfalen Ger 2 5
❒ NIEDERSCHLEMA Sachsen Ger 2 7
❒ NIEDERSEDLITZ Sachsen Ger 2
❒ NIEDERSEIFFENBACH Sachsen Ger 1 2
❒ NIEDERSFELD Westfalen Ger 2
❒ NIEDERTHALHEIM OO Aus 1
❒ NIEDERULLERSDORF (Morostowice-DLN) Cze 2
❒ NIEDERWALDKIRCHEN OO Aus 1
❒ NIEDERWIESA Sachsen Ger 1
❒ NIEDERWUERSCHNITZ Sachsen Ger 1
❒ NIEDOBSCHUETZ Schlesien Ger 5
❒ NIEHEIM Westfalen Ger 2
❒ NIEL Antwerp Bel 1
❒ NIENBURG/ SAALE Sachsen Ger 2 9
❒ NIENBURG/ WESER Hannover Ger 1 2
❒ NIENDORF (Hamburg) Hamburg Ger 2
❒ NIENDORF/ OSTSEEBAD Schleswig-Holstein Ger 1
❒ NIENHAGEN Mecklenburg-Schwerin Ger 2
❒ NIENSTEDTEN Schleswig-Holstein Ger 2 9
❒ NIEPOLOMICE Galicia Ger 2
❒ NIESKY O.L. Schlesien Ger 2
❒ NIEUKERKEN-WAAS (Nieukerken) East Flanders Bel 1
❒ NIEUPORT BAINS Calvados Fan 7
❒ NIEUWERKERK/ IJSSEL South Holland Net 14
❒ NIEVERN Hessen-Nassau Ger 1
❒ NIEZYCHOWO/ SEEHEIM Posen Ger 2
❒ NIJAR Almeria Spa 1
❒ NIJMEGEN Gelderland Net 14
❒ NIKITOVKA Rus 1
❒ NIKOLAEV (Mikolaiv) Rus 1
❒ NIKOLAI (Mikolow) Schlesien Ger 1 2
❒ NIKOLSK-USSURIISKY (Nicolsk-Oussourisky) Rus 1 3
❒ NIKOPIL (Nikopol) Rus 1
❒ NIKSIC Mon 1
❒ NIMES Gard Fan 1 3 7 11
❒ NIMPTSCH (Niemcza) Schlesien Ger 1 2
❒ NINGPO (Lotu) Chi 11
❒ NININO/ RITSCHENWALDE Posen Ger 2
❒ NIS (Nish) Serbia Yug 1
❒ NISA (Niza) Portalegre Por 1 2
❒ NISIDA Isole Ita 3
❒ NITTENAU/ REGEN Bayern Ger 6
❒ NIVELLES Brabant Bel 1 2
❒ NIXDORF (Mikulasovice) Cze 1
❒ NIZHNE NOVGOROD Rus 1
❒ NIZZA Fan 6
❒ NOALEJO Jaen Spa 1 2
❒ NOBLEJAS Toledo Spa 1
❒ NOCERA Ita 3
❒ NOCERA UMBRA BAGNI Sardegna Ita 3
❒ NOEBISFELDE-KALTENDORF Provinz Sachsen Ger 1

❒ NOECHLING NO Aus 1 2
❒ NOERDLINGEN/ GOLDBACH Bayern Ger 1 6
❒ NOERENBERG (Insko) Pommern Ger 1
❒ NOERRE LOEGUM Den 1
❒ NOESCHENRODE Provinz Sachsen Ger 1
❒ NOESTVED Den 12
❒ NOEUX-LES-MINES Pas de Calais Fan 1 2
❒ NOGENT LE ROTROU Eure Fan 11
❒ NOGENT SUR MARNE Val de Marne Fan 7
❒ NOGENT-EN-BASSIGNY Haute Marne Fan 7
❒ NOGUERONES DE ALCAUDETE Jaen Spa 1
❒ NOIRETABLE Loire Fan 7
❒ NOLA CASERTA Campania Ita 3
❒ NOMAIN Nord Fan 1
❒ NONASPE Zaragoza Spa 1
❒ NOORDGOUWE Zeeland Net 1
❒ NORD Fan 1
❒ NORD-AISNE-OISE Fan 1
❒ NORD-PAS-DE-CALAIS Fan 1
❒ NORDDORF/ AMRUM Schleswig-Holstein Ger 2
❒ NORDEN Hannover Ger 1 11 14
❒ NORDENHAM Hannover Ger 1 2 6
❒ NORDENHAM-EINSWARDEN Hannover Ger 2
❒ NORDER-UND SUEDERDITHMARSCHEN Schleswig-Holstein Ger 1
❒ NORDERNEY Hannover Ger 1 7
❒ NORDERWIJCK (Noorderwijk, Norderwyck) Antwerp Bel 1
❒ NORDHALBEN-RODACH Bayern Ger 2 6
❒ NORDHAUSEN/ ZORGE Provinz Sachsen Ger 1 2 6
❒ NORDHORN/ VECHTE Hannover Ger 1 2 8 14
❒ NORTE PEQUENO Azs 2
❒ NORTHEIM Hannover Ger 1 2 6
❒ NORTORF Schleswig-Holstein Ger 1
❒ NOSSEN/ MULDE Sachsen Ger 1 2
❒ NOTO PALAZZOLO Syrakus Sicilia Ita 3 14
❒ NOTODDEN Nor 14
❒ NOUVELLE-CALEDONIE New 1 11
❒ NOUVION EN THIERACHE Aisne Fan 1 6 7
❒ NOUVO SARDEGNA Sardegna Ita 3
❒ NOUZON Ardennes Fan 7
❒ NOVA GOA Goa Ind 1
❒ NOVAYA USHITSA (Novo-Utchitsa, Nowa Uszyca, Nowes Uszyey, Novo-Ouchitsa Rus 1
❒ NOVE BENATKY nad Boleslav Cze 1
❒ NOVE MESTO nad Metuji Cze 2
❒ NOVELDA Alicante Spa 1
❒ NOVES DE SEGRE Lerida Spa 1
❒ NOVGOROD Rus 1
❒ NOVI Ligure Ita 3
❒ NOVO-VORONIKOVSK Rus 1
❒ NOVOCHERKASSK (Novotcherkassk) Rus 1
❒ NOVOGRAD VOLYINSK (Novograd Volynsi, Volinsk) Rus 1
❒ NOVOGROD VELIKI Rus 1
❒ NOVOROSSISK (Novorossijsk) Rus 1
❒ NOVOSYBKOV Novozybkov) Rus 1
❒ NOVOZYBKOV Rus 1
❒ NOVY MARGELAN (Fergana) Rus 1
❒ NOWA SACZ (Neu-Sandec, Neu-Sandez) Rpl 2
❒ NOWAWES (Babelsberg) Brandenburg Ger 2 7 9
❒ NOWOGRODEK (Novogrovkok) Rpl 1
❒ NOWORADOMSK (Radomsko) Rpl 2
❒ NOYELLES-GODAULT Pas de Calais Fan 1 3 14
❒ NOYON Oise Fan 1 3
❒ NOYON-CHAUNY-LA-FERE Oise Fan 1
❒ NUCIA Alicante Spa 2
❒ NUEMBRECHT Rheinland Ger 1
❒ NUENCHWITZ Sachsen Ger 1
❒ NUERNBERG REICHELSDORF Bayern Ger 1
❒ NUERNBERG UND FUERTH Bayern Ger 1
❒ NUERNBERG-FUERTH Bayern Ger 2 12
❒ NUERNBERG-REICHELSDORF U. SCHWABACH Bayern Ger 2
❒ NUERNBERG/ PEGNITZ Bayern Ger 1 2 3 4 6 7 8 9 10 11
❒ NUERTINGEN/ NECKAR Wuerttemberg Ger 1 2 6 9 14
❒ NUGHEDU, SAN NICOLO Sardegna Ita 3
❒ NUGHEDU, SAN NICOLO Sasari Ita 3
❒ NUKERKE East Flanders Bel 1
❒ NULES Castellon Spa 1
❒ NULLES Tarragona Spa 1 2 6
❒ NUSSBACH IM KREMSTAL OO Aus 1
❒ NUSSDORF AM ATTERSEE OO Aus 1
❒ NUSSDORF AN DER TRAISEN NO Aus 1
❒ NUSSENDORF-ARTSTETTEN NO Aus 1
❒ NUTH Net 14
❒ NUTTELN Oldenburg Ger 6 7
❒ NYIREGYHAZA Hun 1
❒ NYKOEBING Den 11

O

❒ OBER DITTMANNSDORF Sachsen Ger 2
❒ OBER ELSASS Elsass Ger 1
❒ OBER EULA Sachsen Ger 2
❒ OBER LESCHEN (Lezno Gorne) Schlesien Ger 2
❒ OBER NIEWIADOM (Niewiadom) Schlesien Ger 4 5 7
❒ OBER SALZBRUNN (Szczawno -zdrot) Schlesien Ger 1
❒ OBER UND UNTER-GRAINAU (Grainau) Bayern Ger 6
❒ OBER-SALZBRUNN (Szczawno -zdrot) Schlesien Ger 2
❒ OBERACHMANN OO Aus 1
❒ OBERALM Steiermark Aus 1
❒ OBERAMMERGAU/ AMMER Bayern Ger 1 6
❒ OBERBACH-RHOEN Bayern Ger 1 2
❒ OBERBARNIM Brandenburg Ger 1
❒ OBERBERGISCHER Nordrhein-Westfalen Ger 14
❒ OBERBRUCH/ HEINSBERG Rheinland Ger 2
❒ OBERCASSEL Rheinland Ger 1
❒ OBERCUNNERSDORF Sachsen Ger 1
❒ OBERDORF (Horni Ves) Cze 2
❒ OBERDORF, MARKT Bayern Ger 1 2
❒ OBERDORLA Provinz Sachsen Ger 1
❒ OBERELSBACH Bayern Ger 7
❒ OBERESSLINGEN Wuerttemberg Ger 2
❒ OBERESTERREICH Land Aus 1
❒ OBERFRIEDERSDORF Sachsen Ger 1
❒ OBERFROHNA Sachsen Ger 1 2
❒ OBERGEBRA Provinz Sachsen Ger 2
❒ OBERGELERA Sachsen Ger 1
❒ OBERGEORGENTHAL (Bruex) Boehmen Cze 1
❒ OBERGLOGAU (Glogowek, Glozowek) Schlesien Ger 1 6 8
❒ OBERGRAFENDORF NO Aus 1 2
❒ OBERGUENZBURG Bayern Ger 2
❒ OBERHAGEN Westfalen Ger 3 7
❒ OBERHAUSEN Rheinland Ger 1 2 3 4 5 6 7 8 9
❒ OBERHEIM Wuerttemberg Ger 1
❒ OBERHELDRUNGEN Sachsen Ger 1
❒ OBERHESSEN Hessen Ger 1
❒ OBERHOF Sachsen-Gotha Ger 1
❒ OBERHOFEN Elsass Ger 1 3 7 10
❒ OBERHOHNDORF Sachsen Ger 1
❒ OBERHOLLABRUNN NO Aus 1 3
❒ OBERKAPPEL OO Aus 1
❒ OBERKIRCH Baden Ger 1
❒ OBERKIRCH, OPPENAU U. BAD PETERSTAL Baden Ger 1
❒ OBERKIRCHEN Westfalen Ger 2 4 5
❒ OBERLAHNKREIS (Weilburg) Hessen-Nassau Ger 1

❒ OBERLAHNSTEIN Hessen-Nassau Ger 1 2 7
❒ OBERLANGENBIELAU (Bielawa) Schlesien Ger 1 2
❒ OBERLENNINGEN Wuerttemberg Ger 2
❒ OBERLICHTENAU Sachsen Ger 1
❒ OBERLIND (Sonneberg) Sachsen-Meiningen Ger 1 7
❒ OBERLOEDLA-LOSSEN Thueringen Ger 10
❒ OBERLUNGWITZ Sachsen Ger 1 2
❒ OBERLUSTADT Pfalz Ger 1
❒ OBERNBERG AM BRENNER Tirol Aus 1
❒ OBERNBERG AM INN OO Aus 1 2
❒ OBERNBURG/ MAIN Bayern Ger 1 2
❒ OBERNDORF (St. Johann) Tirol Aus 1
❒ OBERNDORF A.D. EBENE NO Aus 2
❒ OBERNDORF AN DER SALZACH Salzburg Aus 1
❒ OBERNDORF/ NECKAR Wuerttemberg Ger 1 2 6 7
❒ OBERNDORF, REDLHAM (& SCHLATT) OO Aus 1
❒ OBERNEUHUETTENDORF Ger 7
❒ OBERNEUKIRCH Sachsen Ger 1 2
❒ OBERNEUKIRCHEN OO Aus 1
❒ OBERNEUSCHOENEBERG/ ERZGEBIRGE Sachsen Ger1
❒ OBERNHEIM Wuerttemberg Ger 2
❒ OBERNIEWIADOM (Niewiadom) Schlesien Ger 2
❒ OBERNKIRCHEN Hessen-Nassau Ger 1
❒ OBERNZELL/ DONAU Bayern Ger 6
❒ OBERODERWITZ Sachsen Ger 1 2
❒ OBERRAD/ MAIN Hessen-Nassau Ger 7
❒ OBERRARBACH Westfalen Ger 7
❒ OBERRENGERSDORF O.L. Schlesien Ger 2
❒ OBERROEBLINGEN/ SEE Provinz Sachsen Ger 2
❒ OBERROEDINGHAUSEN Westfalen Ger 2
❒ OBERROTTENDORF Sachsen Ger 2
❒ OBERSACHSENBERG/ VOGTLANDSachsen Ger 1
❒ OBERSCHADEN OO Aus 1
❒ OBERSCHLESIEN (Gorny Slask) Schlesien Ger 1 6 12 13
❒ OBERSCHLIERBACH OO Aus 1
❒ OBERSITZKO (Obrzycko, Obesrsitsko, Obersycko, Oberzyko) Schlesien Ger 1
❒ OBERSTDORF Bayern Ger 2
❒ OBERSTEIN Rheinland Ger 1 2 6
❒ OBERSTEIN UND IDAR Rheinland Ger 1
❒ OBERSTUETZENGRUEN Sachsen Ger 1
❒ OBERTRUM Salzburg Aus 1
❒ OBERURSEL/ TAUNUS Hessen-Nassau Gerl
❒ OBERVIECHTACH Bayern Ger 7
❒ OBERVORMARKT OO Aus 1
❒ OBERWEILER-TIEFENBACH Pfalz Ger 1
❒ OBERWEISSBACH Thueringen Ger 1
❒ OBERWEISSBACH, CURSDORF DEESBACH Thueringen Ger 1
❒ OBERWEISSENBACH (und Bernhardschlag) OO Aus 1
❒ OBERWESEL Rheinland Ger 1 2 6
❒ OBERWESTERWALDKREIS Hessen-Nassau Ger 1
❒ OBERWIESENTHAL Sachsen Ger 1
❒ OBERWOELBLING NO Aus 1
❒ OBERWOLFACH Baden Ger 2
❒ OBERWOLFERN OO Aus 1
❒ OBERWUERSCHNITZ Sachsen Ger 1
❒ OBERZWIESELAU (Lindberg) Bayern Ger 7
❒ OBIDOS (Leiria) Por 1
❒ OBLADIS Tirol Aus 2
❒ OBORNIK/ WARTA (Oborniki) Posen Ger 16
❒ OBRIGHOVEN-LACKHAUSEN Rheinland Gerl
❒ OBRITZBERG NO Aus 1
❒ OCANA Toledo Spa 1
❒ OCHEMCHIRI (Otchemtchiri) Rus 1
❒ OCHSENFURT/ MAIN Bayern Ger 1 2 6
❒ OCHSENHAUSEN Wuerttemberg Ger 1
❒ OCHTRUP/ VECHTE Westfalen Ger 1 2 7
❒ OCKERT NO Aus 1
❒ ODDA Nor 14
❒ ODDENSE Den 11
❒ ODEMIRA Beja Por 1
❒ ODENA Barcelona Spa 1
❒ ODENKIRCHEN/ NIERS Rheinland Ger 1
❒ ODENSE Den 12
❒ ODERBERG/ ODER Brandenburg Ger 1
❒ ODERN Elsass Ger 1
❒ ODESSA (Jelisawetgrad) Rus 1 2 14
❒ ODONOV Rus 1
❒ OEBLARN IM ENNSTALE Steiermark Aus 1
❒ OED NO Aus 1
❒ OEDENBURG (Sopron) Hun 1
❒ OEDERAN Sachsen Ger 1 2 8 9
❒ OEDESSE Hannover Ger 2
❒ OEDT-ST. HUBERT Rheinland Ger 2 7
❒ OEDT/ NIERS (Grafrath) Rheinland Ger 7
❒ OEHLING NO Aus 1
❒ OEHRINGEN/ OHR Wuerttemberg Ger 1 2 6
❒ OEIE Nor 14
❒ OELBERG (Olivetin) Cze 9
❒ OELDE Westfalen Ger 1 2 6
❒ OELKINGHAUSEN (Schwelm) Ger 5 7
❒ OELS/ OELS (Olesnica, Olesnicka) Schlesien Ger 1 2 6 7 8
❒ OELSNITZ/ ELSTER Sachsen Ger 1 2 8
❒ OELZE Thueringen Ger 2
❒ OEPPING OO Aus 1
❒ OERLINGHAUSEN Lippe Ger 1 7
❒ OERNHOEJ Den ll
❒ OESTFOLD Nor 14
❒ OETTINGEN/ WERNITZ Bayern Ger 6
❒ OETZSACH-MARKKLEEBERG Sachsen Ger 1
❒ OEVENTROP Westfalen Ger 2
❒ OEYNHAUSEN, BAD Westfalen Ger 1 2 7
❒ OFFENBACH/ MAIN Hessen-Nassau Ger 1 6 7 8 9 11 12
❒ OFFENBURG/ KINZIG Baden Ger 1 2 6 7
❒ OFFENHAUSEN OO Aus 1 2
❒ OFFLEBEN Provinz Sachsen Ger 1
❒ OFTERING OO Aus 1
❒ OGASSA Gerona Spa 1
❒ OGGERSHEIM Pfalz Ger 1
❒ OGRODZIENIEC Rpl 2
❒ OGRODZIENIEC Rus 1
❒ OHAIN Nord Fan 1
❒ OHANES Almeria Spa 2
❒ OHEIMGRUBE/ KATTOWITZ (Kopalnia Wujek) Schlesien Ger 5
❒ OHLAU/ ODER (Olawa) Schlesien Ger 1 2 7 8
❒ OHLE (Altena) Misspelling Westfalen Ger 2
❒ OHLEN/ ALTENA (Ahlen) Westfalen Ger 5
❒ OHLIGS Rheinland Ger 1 2 3 4 6 11
❒ OHLSTORF OO Aus 1
❒ OHRA Hun 9
❒ OHRDRUF Sachsen-Coburg-Gotha Ger 1 2 4 6
❒ OIGNIES Nord Fan 1
❒ OIGNIES Pas de Calais Fan 1
❒ OIGNIES-AISEAU Hainaut Bel 2
❒ OISSEL Seine Inf. Fan 3
❒ OISTERWIJK Brabant Net 8
❒ OISY Aisne Fan 1
❒ OIX Gerona Spa 1
❒ OJOS Murcia Spa 1 2
❒ OKAHAN DA Ged 2
❒ OKER/ OKER (Ocker) Braunschweig Ger 2
❒ OKHAO Faro Por 1 2
❒ OKOCIM Rpl 2
❒ OKULOVKA (Okoulovka) Rus 1
❒ OLAND (Hallig) Schleswig-Holstein Ger 13 1
❒ OLBA Spa 1
❒ OLBERNHAU Sachsen Ger 1
❒ OLBERSDORF Sachsen Ger 2
❒ OLDAU Hannover Ger 2
❒ OLDENBURG Oldenburg Ger 1 2 6 7 10
❒ OLDENBURG/ HUNTE Oldenburg Ger 1 2
❒ OLDENBURG/ LITTLE BROEKAUE Schleswig-Holstein Ger 1 2

❒ OTTERNDORF/ ELBE Hannover Ger 1 8
❒ OTTMACHAU/ NEISSE (Otmuchow) Schlesien Ger 1 2 6
❒ OTTNANG OO Aus 1
❒ OTTOBEUREN Bayern Ger 7
❒ OTTWEILER Rheinland Ger 1
❒ OUCKENE West Flanders Bel 1
❒ OUDERKERK/ IJSSEL South Holland Net 14
❒ OUED-EL-ALLEUG Alg 1
❒ OUENZA Alg 7
❒ OUGREE Liege Bel 2
❒ OULLINS Loiret Fan 7
❒ OULU (Uleaborg) Oulu Prov. Fin 2
❒ OUM-THEBOUL Alg 1
❒ OUPEYE Liege Bel 1
❒ OUTSCHEID/ EIFEL Rheinland Ger 2
❒ OUVEILLAN Aude Fan 7
❒ OVADA Ita 3
❒ OVAR Aveiro Por 1
❒ OVERHALLA Nor 14
❒ OVERIJSSEL Net 14
❒ OVERMEIRE East Flanders Bel 1
❒ OVERRATH Rheinland Ger 1
❒ OVERSCHIE South Holland Net 14
❒ OYBIN Sachsen Ger 2
❒ OYONNAX Ain Fan 7
❒ OYONNAX-BELLEGARDE Ain Fan 6 7
❒ OZORKOW Rpl 2
❒ OZORKOW (Ozyurkov) Rus 1

P

❒ P CAMP Ism 15
❒ PAAL Limbourg Bel 14
❒ PABNEUKIRCHEN OO Aus 1
❒ PACHECO Murcia Spa 1
❒ PACHIA (Pashiya) Rus 1
❒ PACOS DE FERREIRA Porto Por 2
❒ PACOV Cze 1 2
❒ PACOVE Hun 1
❒ PACY-SUR-EURE Eure Fan 6 7
❒ PADERBORN/ PADER Westfalen Ger 1 2 4 7
❒ PADOVA Ita 3 14
❒ PADUELES Almeria Spa 1
❒ PADULA Campania Ita 3
❒ PADULA Salerno Ita 3
❒ PAENTCHNO (Pajeczno) Rus 1
❒ PAIMBOEUF Loire Inferieure Fan 1 7
❒ PAIPORTA Valencia Spa 2
❒ PAJECZNO Rpl 2
❒ PAKOSCH (Pakosc) Posen Ger 1
❒ PALAFOLLS Barcelona Spa 1
❒ PALAFRUGELL Gerona Spa 1
❒ PALAMOS Gerona Spa 1
❒ PALAU D'ANGLESOLA Lerida Spa 1
❒ PALAU SACOSTA Gerona Spa 1
❒ PALAU-SABARDERA Gerona Spa 1 2
❒ PALAU-SOLITA Barcelona Spa 1
❒ PALAUTORDERA Barcelona Spa 1
❒ PALAVAS Herault Fan 7
❒ PALAVAS LES FLOTS Fan 7
❒ PALENBERG Rheinland Ger2
❒ PALISSE, LA Ardeche Fan 7
❒ PALLARUELO DE MONEGROS Huesca Spa 1
❒ PALLEJA Barcelona Spa 1
❒ PALLUEL Pas de Calais Fan 1
❒ PALMA Nova Ita 3
❒ PALMA D'EBRE Tarragona Spa 1
❒ PALMA DE CERVELLO, LA Barcelona Spa 1
❒ PALMERA Valencia Spa 1
❒ PALS Gerona Spa 1
❒ PALS Pommern Ger 1
❒ PALSCHAU (Palczewo) Westpreussen Ger 1
❒ PALTING-PERWANG OO Aus 1
❒ PAMIERS Ariege Fan 3 7
❒ PANEVEZHIS (Panevezys) Rus 1
❒ PANTANO DEL CIJARES Caceres Spa 1
❒ PAPA Hun 1
❒ PAPENBURG Hannover Ger 1 2
❒ PAPIGNIES Hainaut Bel 1
❒ PAPIOL Barcelona Spa 1
❒ PAPPENHEIM/ ALTMUEHL Bayern Ger 6
❒ PARCHIM/ ELBE (Parchen) Mecklenburg-Schwerin Ger 1 7 11
❒ PARDINES Gerona Spa 1
❒ PARDO, EL Madrid Spa 1
❒ PAREDES Porto Por 1 2
❒ PAREDES DE COU RA Viana do Castelo Por 2
❒ PARETS DEL VALLES Barcelona Spa 2
❒ PAREY/ ELBE Provinz Sachsen Ger 1 2
❒ PARIS Fan 1 2 4 6 7 10 11 12 3
❒ PARIS-BOULOGNE-BILLANCOURT Fan 14
❒ PARMA Ita 14
❒ PARNIK Cze 2
❒ PARRAS DE CASTELLOTE Teruel Spa 1
❒ PARTALOA Almeria Spa 1
❒ PARTENKIRCHEN (Garmisch-Partenkirchen) Bayern Ger 6
❒ PARUSCHOWITZ (Paruszowiec) Schlesien Ger2 3
❒ PARZ OO Aus 1
❒ PASCHING OO Aus 1
❒ PASEWALK/ UCKER (Passewalk) Pommern Ger 1 2
❒ PASING Bayern Ger 1 2
❒ PASSANANT Tarragona Spa 1
❒ PASSAU/ INN, DANUBE Bayern Ger 1 2 7
❒ PATRAS Gre 14
❒ PATSCHKAU/ NEISSE (Paczkow) Schlesien Ger 1
❒ PATTIGHAM OO Aus 1
❒ PATURAGES Hainaut Be[2
❒ PAU Basses Pyrenees Fan 3 6 7 10
❒ PAU Gerona Spa 1
❒ PAU DE SERT (Santa Pau) Gerona Spa 1
❒ PAUDORF NO Aus 1
❒ PAUILLAC Gironde Fan 7
❒ PAULINZELLA Schwarzburg-Rudoistadt Ger 1
❒ PAULS Tarragona Spa 1
❒ PAULSBORN Bayern Ger 7
❒ PAULSDORF (Pawlow) Schlesien Ger 1
❒ PAUNSDORF Sachsen Ger 1
❒ PAVIA Ita 3 14
❒ PAVLOHRAD (Pavlograd) Rus 1
❒ PAVLOVO Rus 1
❒ PAVLOVSK Rus 1
❒ PAYERBACH NO Aus 1
❒ PEAL DE BECERRO Jaen Spa 2
❒ PECHBRUNN Bayern Ger 7
❒ PECHINA Almeria Spa 1
❒ PECHLUNA Aude Fan 2
❒ PECKING OO Aus 1
❒ PECQ Hainaut Bel 1
❒ PECQUENCOURT Nord Fan1
❒ PECS Hun 1 14
❒ PEDERNOSO, EL Cuenca Spa 1
❒ PEDREGUER Alicante Spa 2
❒ PEDRO MARTINEZ Granada Spa 1
❒ PEDRO MUNOZ Ciudad Real Spa 1
❒ PEDROCHE Cordoba Spa 1
❒ PEDRONERAS Cuenca Spa 1
❒ PEGAU/ WHITE ELSTER Sachsen Ger 1 2
❒ PEGNITZ/ PEGNITZ Bayern Ger 6
❒ PEGO Alicante Spa 1
❒ PEINE Hannover Ger 1 2 6 7 13
❒ PEISERN/ WARTA (Pyzdry) Schlesien Ger 1
❒ PEISSENBERG Bayern Ger 1 6
❒ PEIZE Drenthe Net 14
❒ PELAGO Toscana Ita 3
❒ PELAGO Villa Paterno Ita 3
❒ PELHRIMOV Cze 1
❒ PENAFIEL Porto Por 1 2
❒ PENAGUILLA Alicante Spa 1
❒ PENALBA Huesca Spa 1
❒ PENALSORDO Badajoz Spa 1
❒ PENALVA DO CASTELO Viseu Por 1 2
❒ PENARROYA DE TASTAVINS Teruel Spa 1
❒ PENELA Coimbra Por 1
❒ PENELLES Lerida Spa 1
❒ PENHOET Morbihan Fan 7
❒ PENICHE Leiria Por 1 2
❒ PENIG/ MULDE Sachsen Ger 1 2 7
❒ PENKING OO Aus 1
❒ PENKUN Pommern Ger 1
❒ PENNE Let et Garonne Fan 6
❒ PENNEWANG OO Aus 1
❒ PENSA (Penza) Rus 1
❒ PENSICOLA Castellon Spa 1
❒ PENZBERG Bayern Ger 1 2 7
❒ PENZIG O.L. (Piensk) Schlesien Ger 1 2 7
❒ PENZLIN Mecklenburg-Schwerin Ger 1
❒ PEPINSTER Liege Bel 1
❒ PERA, LA Gerona Spa 1

❒ PERAFITA Barcelona Spa 1
❒ PERAFORT Tarragona Spa 1
❒ PERAMOLA Lerida Spa 1
❒ PERCHTOLDSDORF NO Aus 1 2
❒ PERELLO Tarragona Spa 1
❒ PERESLAV (Pereslavl-Zalesski) Rus 1
❒ PERG OO Aus 1 2
❒ PERGKIRCHEN OO Aus 1
❒ PERIGUEUX Dordogne Fan 1 6 7
❒ PERK OO Aus 2
❒ PERLEBERG/ STEPNITZ Brandenburg Ger 1 8
❒ PERM (Motovilika) Rus 1
❒ PERNAU OO Aus 1
❒ PERNERSDORF NO Aus 2
❒ PERONNE Somme Fan 1 6 7
❒ PERONNE-LEZ-ANTOING (Peronnes lez-Antoing) Hainaut Bel 1
❒ PERPETUA DE MOGUDA Spa 1
❒ PERPIGNAN Pyrenees Orientales Fan 1 2 6 7 10
❒ PERREUX, LA Seine Fan 3 7
❒ PERSENBEUG NO Aus 1
❒ PERUGIA Ita 14
❒ PESCANTINA Veneto Ita 3
❒ PESCANTINA Verona Ita 3
❒ PESO DA REGUA Vila Real Por 1 2
❒ PESSAC Gironde Fan 7
❒ PESTCHANKA Rus 3
❒ PESTI HIRLAP Hun 2
❒ PETEGHEM East Flanders Bel 1
❒ PETERGHEM-AUDENAERDE East Flanders Bel 1
❒ PETERSDORF Schleswig-Holstein Ger 14
❒ PETERSDORF/ ZACKEN (Piechowice) Schlesien Ger 1 2
❒ PETERSHAGEN/ WESER Brandenburg Ger 2
❒ PETERSKIRCHEN OO Aus 1
❒ PETERSTAL Baden Ger 1
❒ PETIT-BOURG Seine et Oise Fan 7
❒ PETIT-RECHAIN Liege Bel 1
❒ PETITE-ROSELLE Kleinrosseln Moselle Fan 3 14
❒ PETR-ALEXANDROVSK (Turtkul) Rus 1
❒ PETREL Alicante Spa 1
❒ PETRIKAU (Piotrkow) Rus 1
❒ PETROGRAD (Leningrad) Rus 1 2
❒ PETROIO Ita 3
❒ PETROKOV (Piotrkow) Rus 1
❒ PETROKOV-KOUJAVSKI (Piotrkow Kujawski) Rus 1
❒ PETROLA Albacete Spa 1
❒ PETRONELL NO Aus 1
❒ PETROPAVLOSK (Petropavlosk-S. Kamtchatke) Rus 1
❒ PETROVSK (Petrovskoye, Petroskaya) Rus 1
❒ PETROWITZ (Piotrowice, Piotrkowska) Schlesien Ger 1
❒ PETROZAVODSK Rus 1
❒ PETTENBACH OO Aus 1 2
❒ PETZENKIRCHEN NO Aus 1
❒ PEUERBACH OO Aus 1 2
❒ PEVERIL (Peel) Ism 15
❒ PEXONNE Meurthe et Moselle Fan 7
❒ PEYRIAC-MINERVOIS Aude Fan 7
❒ PFAFFENDORF Rheinland Ger 1
❒ PFAFFENHAUSEN Bayern Ger 2
❒ PFARRKIRCHEN BEI BAD HALL OO Aus 1
❒ PFARRKIRCHEN IM MUEHLKREIS OO Aus 1
❒ PFARRWERFEN Salzburg Aus 1
❒ PFEDDERSHEIM Hessen Ger 1
❒ PFOERRING/ DONAU Bayern Ger 1 2 6
❒ PFOERTEN N.L. Brandenburg Ger 1
❒ PFORZHEIM/ ENZ, NAGOLD Baden Ger 1 2 6 7 8 11
❒ PFULLENDORF Baden Ger 1
❒ PFULLINGEN Wuerttemberg Ger 1 2
❒ PHILIPPEVILLE (Skikda, Constantine) Alg 1
❒ PHILIPPEVILLE Namur Bel 2
❒ PHILIPPSTHAL Hessen-Nassau Ger 1
❒ PHILLIPPSBURG Baden Ger 1
❒ PI DE LLOBREGAT Barcelona Spa 1
❒ PIACENZA Ita 3 14
❒ PIANOSA Isole Ita 3
❒ PIAVE Ita 14
❒ PIAZZA ARMERINA Caltanisetta Ita 3
❒ PIAZZA ARMERINA Sicilia Ita 3
❒ PIBERBACH OO Aus 1
❒ PICANA Valencia Spa 1
❒ PICCHETTA Ita 3
❒ PICHL BEI WELS OO Aus 1
❒ PICHL BEI WINDISCHGARSTEN OO Aus 1
❒ PIECHCIN Rpl 2
❒ PIEDRABUENA Ciudad Real Spa 1
❒ PIEGUT Dordogne Fan 2 6 7
❒ PIERA Barcelona Spa 1
❒ PIERBACH OO Aus 1
❒ PIERREFITTE Hautes-Pyrenees Fan 3 14
❒ PIERRELATTE Drome Fan 7
❒ PIESTANY Cze 2
❒ PIESTERITZ/ HALLE Provinz Sachsen Ger 2
❒ PIETON Hainaut Bel 1
❒ PIETRA Ligure Ita 3
❒ PIGNAN Herault Fan 7
❒ PILAR DE LA HONRADADA Alicante Spa 2
❒ PILENKOVA (Pilenkovo) Rus 1
❒ PILES Valencia Spa 1
❒ PILIAV (Pilawa) Rpl 2
❒ PILIAV Rus 1
❒ PILICA (Pilitsa) Rpl 2
❒ PILLAU (Baltijsk, USSR) Ostpreussen Ger 1 6
❒ PILLKALLEN (Dobrowolsk, USSR) Ostpreussen Ger 1 2
❒ PILSEN (Plzen) Boehmen Cze 2
❒ PINAR Granada Spa 1
❒ PINATAR Murcia Spa 1 2
❒ PINCHOV (Pinczow) Rus 1
❒ PINCZOW Rpl 1
❒ PINEDA Barcelona Spa 1 2
❒ PINEDA DE SEGARRA (Freixenet de Segarra) Lerida Spa 1
❒ PINEDES DE LLOBREGAT (Santa Coloma de Cervello) Barcelona Spa 1
❒ PINELL Lerida Spa 1
❒ PINELL DE BRAI Tarragona Spa 1
❒ PINEROLO Ita 3 14
❒ PINHEL Guarda Por 1
❒ PINNE (Pniewy) Posen Ger 1
❒ PINNEBERG Schleswig-Holstein Ger 1 2 6 8
❒ PINOSO Alicante Spa 1
❒ PINOUSE, MINES DE LA Pyrennes Orientales Fan 7
❒ PINS DEL VALLES Barcelona Spa 1
❒ PINSDORF OO Aus 1
❒ PINTE, DE East Flanders Bel 1
❒ PIOTRKOW (Pitrokov, Belorussiya, USSR) Rpl 2
❒ PIOTRKOW TRYBUNALSKI (Piotrkow) Rus 1
❒ PIPAIX Hainaut Bel 1 14
❒ Pi RA Tarragona Spa 1
❒ PIRCHHORN OO Aus 1
❒ PIRMASENS Pfalz Ger 1 2 6 7
❒ PIRNA/ ELBE Sachsen Ger 1 2 5 7 8
❒ PIROGOVSK (Pirogovskoe) Rus 1
❒ PIRONCHAMPS Hainaut Bel 1
❒ PISA Toscana Ita 3
❒ PISCHELSDORF OO Aus 1
❒ PITSCHEN (Byczyna) Schlesien Ger 1 2
❒ PITZENBERG OO Aus 1
❒ PIZZIGHETTONE Cremona Ita 3
❒ PIZZIGHETTONE Lombardia Ita 3
❒ PJATIGORSK (Pyatigorsk, Piatigorsk) Rus 1
❒ PJESTSCHANKA (Pestchanka) Rus 1
❒ PLA DE CABRA, EL Tarragona Spa 1 2
❒ PLA DE CADI Lerida Spa 1
❒ PLA DE TER (Santa Eugenia de Ter) Gerona Spa 1
❒ PLA DEL PENEDES, EL Barcelona Spa 1
❒ PLAN Aus 3
❒ PLANA DE RIUCORP (Sant Martide Malda) Lerida Spa 1
❒ PLANEGG/ MUENCHEN Bayern Ger 2
❒ PLANES D'HOSTOLES, LES Gerona Spa 1
❒ PLANES DE MONTSIA (Santa Barbera) Tarragona Spa 1
❒ PLANOLES Gerona Spa 1
❒ PLASSENBURG (Kulmbach) Bayern Ger 3 4
❒ PLASSENBURG-KULMBACH Bayern Ger 4
❒ PLATHE (Ploty) Pommern Ger 1
❒ PLATTING/ ISAR Bayern Ger 1 2

❒ PLAU Mecklenburg-Schwerin Ger 1
❒ PLAUE-BERNSDORF Sachsen Ger 1
❒ PLAUE/ HAVEL Sachsen Ger 1 2 7
❒ PLAUEN/ WHITE ELSTER Sachsen Ger 1 2 7 8 12
❒ PLEINE-SELVE Aisne Fan 1
❒ PLEISSA Sachsen Ger 1 2
❒ PLESCHEN (Pleszew) Posen Ger 1 2
❒ PLESS (Pszczyna) Schlesien Ger 1 5
❒ PLESSA Provinz Sachsen Ger 1
❒ PLESSER GRUBE Schlesien Ger 4
❒ PLESZEW (Pleschen) Rpl 1 2
❒ PLETTENBERG/ ELSE Westfalen Ger 1 2
❒ PLIEGO Murcia Spa 1
❒ PLJEVLJA Mon 1
❒ PLOCHINGEN/ NECKAR Wuerttemberg Ger 2
❒ PLOCHWALD OO Aus 1
❒ PLOCK (Plozk, Plotsk, Schroettersburg) Rpl 1 2
❒ PLOEN Schleswig-Holstein Ger 1 2
❒ PLOETZ Provinz Sachsen Ger 2
❒ PLONSK (Ploehnen) Rpl 2
❒ PLOU Teruel Spa 2
❒ PLOUVAIN Fan 1
❒ PNIOWITZ (Pniowiec) Schlesien Ger 2 3
❒ POAL Lerida Spa 1
❒ POBERSHAU Sachsen Ger 1
❒ POBLA DE CIERVOLES Lerida Spa 1
❒ POBLA DE CLARAMUNT Barcelona Spa 1
❒ POBLA DE LILLET, LA Barcelona Spa 1
❒ POBLA DE MASSALUCA Tarragona Spa 1
❒ POBLA DE MONTORNES Tarragona Spa 1 2
❒ POBLA DE MUFAMET Tarragona Spa 1
❒ POBLA DE SEGUR Lerida Spa 1
❒ POBLE DE CEDO Lerida Spa 1
❒ POBLE DEL LLIERCA (Sant Jaume de Llierca) Gerona Spa 1
❒ POBOLEDA Tarragona Spa 2
❒ POCKAU/ FLOEHATAL Sachsen Ger 1
❒ POCKING Bayern Ger 2
❒ PODEBRADY (Podiebrad) Boehmen Cze 1
❒ PODEJUCH (Podjuchy) Pommern Ger 2
❒ PODGORICA (Titograd) Mon 1
❒ PODGORZE Galicia Rpl 2
❒ PODOLIN/ WAPNO Posen Ger 2
❒ POECHLARN NO Aus 1
❒ POEDEROIJN Gelderland Net 14
❒ POEGGSTALL NO Aus 2
❒ POELFING-BRUNN Steiermark Aus 9
❒ POELITZ (Police) Pommern Ger 1
❒ POELZIG Sachsen-Altenburg Ger 1
❒ POENDORF OO Aus 1
❒ POESSNECK Sachsen-Meiningen Ger 1 2 6 7
❒ POETTING OO Aus 1
❒ POETTMES Bayern Ger 1 6
❒ POGORZELA (Pogoschella, Pogorzela) Posen Ger 1
❒ POHLSDORF (Pazdziorno) Schlesien Ger 7
❒ POISSY Seine et Oise Fan 7
❒ POITIERS Vienne Fan 1 3 4 6 10 11
❒ POITIERS & LA VIENNE Vienne Fan 1
❒ POIX-TERRON Ardennes Fan 1 6
❒ POLA Ita 3 14
❒ POLAN Toledo Spa 1
❒ POLAUN (Polubny) Cze 2
❒ POLENINO Huesca Spa 1
❒ POLENZ Sachsen Ger 2
❒ POLESIE/ KRAKOW Rpl 1
❒ POLEY Brandenburg Ger 5
❒ POLICAR Granada Spa 1
❒ POLINYA Barcelona Spa 1
❒ POLLEUR Liege Bel 1
❒ POLLNOW (Polanow) Pommern Ger 1
❒ POLOPOS Granada Spa 2
❒ POLTAVA Rus 1
❒ POLTORADSK (Poltoratsk, Askhabad) Rus 1
❒ POLZIN, BAD (Polczyn Zdroj) Pommern Ger 1 6
❒ POMAROLO Torino Piemonte Ita 3
❒ POMBAL Leiria Por 2
❒ POMEROLS Herault Fan 7
❒ POMMEREUIL Nord Fan 1
❒ POMONAHUEGEL Ged 2
❒ POMORZE (Pomorska) Pommern Ger 3
❒ POMPIGNAN Tarn-et-Garonne Fan 2
❒ PONEVEJ (Panevezys, Ponevezh) Rus 1
❒ PONHOLZ (Oberpfalz) Bayern Ger 2
❒ PONT AUDEMER Eure Fan 7
❒ PONT D'ARMENTERA Tarragona Spa 1
❒ PONT DE CHERUY Isere Fan 7
❒ PONT DE CHERUY-TIGNEU Isere Fan 2
❒ PONT DE SUERT Lerida Spa 1
❒ PONT DE VILOMARA, EL Barcelona Spa 1
❒ PONT-A-MOUSSON Meurthe et Moselle Fan 3 7
❒ PONT-SUR-SAMBRE Nord Fan 1
❒ PONT-SUR-SEINE Aube Fan 7
❒ PONTE DA BARCA Viana do Castelo Por 2
❒ PONTE DE LIMA Viana do Castelo Por 2
❒ PONTE DE LOUP Hainaut Bel 1
❒ PONTE DO SOR Portalegre Por 2
❒ PONTOISON Manche Fan 7
❒ PONTONS Barcelona Spa 1
❒ PONTRUET Fan 1
❒ PONTS Lerida Spa 1
❒ POORTUGAAL South Holland Net 14
❒ POPPENBUET-TEL Schleswig-Holstein Ger 1
❒ PORCUNA Jaen Spa 2
❒ POREBA (Poremba) Rus 1
❒ POREBA Posen Ger 2 3
❒ PORRERA Tarragona Spa 1
❒ PORSGRUNN Nor 14
❒ PORT BOU Gerona Spa 1
❒ PORT DE LA SELVA Gerona Spa 1
❒ PORT KUNDA Est 2
❒ PORT KUNDA Rus 14
❒ PORT MIOU Bouches du Rhone Fan 1 6
❒ PORTA WESTPHALICA Westfalen Ger 1
❒ PORTALEGRE Portalegre Por 1 2
❒ PORTEL Evora Por 1 2
❒ PORTELL DE MORELLA Castellon Spa I
❒ PORTELLA, LA Lerida Spa 1
❒ PORTELLADA, LA Teruel Spa 1 2
❒ PORTIMAO Faro Por 1 2
❒ PORTO Porto Por 2
❒ PORTO DE MOZ Leiria Por 2
❒ PORTO ERCOLE Grosseto Liguria Ita 3
❒ PORTO FERRAIO isola d'Elba Ita 3
❒ PORTO TORRES Sardegna Ita 3
❒ PORTO TORRES Sassari Ita 3
❒ PORVOO (Borga) Uusimaa Fin 2
❒ PORZ-URBACH Rheinland Ger 2
❒ PORZ/ RHEIN Rheinland Ger 2 7
❒ PORZUNA Ciudad Real Spa 1 2
❒ POSADOWO Posen Ger 1 2
❒ POSEN-OST (Poznan) Posen Ger 1
❒ POSEN-WEST(Poznan, Zachod) Posen Ger 1 2
❒ POSEN/ WARTA (Poznan) Posen Ger 1 2 6 7 8 10
❒ POSSENDORF Sachsen Ger 2
❒ POSTERHOLT Net 1
❒ POTARZYCE Posen Ger 1
❒ POTENZA Basilicata Ita 3
❒ POTRIES Valencia Spa 1
❒ POTSDAM/ RUTHE & HAVEL Brandenburg Ger 1 2 7
❒ POTTENBRUNN NO Aus 1 2
❒ POTTENDORF NO Aus 1 9
❒ POTTENSTEIN NO Aus 1 2 9
❒ POTULICE/ NAKEN (Potulitz) Posen Ger 1
❒ POUCH Provinz Sachsen Ger 1 9
❒ POUILLY Loire Fan 7
❒ POUILLY ET CHARLIEU Loire Fan 7
❒ POULIGUEN, LE Loire-Inferieure Fan 2

❑ POULSEUR Liege Bel 1 2
❑ POUSSET Liege Bel 1
❑ POUZAUGES Vendee Fan 11
❑ POVOA DE LANHOSO Braga Por 2
❑ POVOA DE VARZIM Porto Por 1 2
❑ POXRUCK OO Aus 1
❑ POYSDORF NO Aus 1
❑ POZAREVACKOG (Pozarevac) Yug 1
❑ POZO RUBIO DE SANTIAGO Cuenca Spa 1
❑ POZO-ALCON Jaen Spa 2
❑ POZO-ESTRECHO Murcia Spa 2
❑ POZOBLANCO Cordoba Spa 1 2
❑ POZUELO DE CALATRAVA Ciudad Real Spa 1
❑ POZZOLO Ita 3
❑ PRACHATITZ (Prachatice) Cze 2
❑ PRADELL Tarragona Spa 1
❑ PRADES Tarragona Spa 1
❑ PRAEGARTEN OO Aus 1
❑ PRAHA (Prague) Boehmen Cze 8 1 12
❑ PRAIA DA GRACIOSA Azs 2
❑ PRAM OO Aus 1
❑ PRAMBACHKIRCHEN OO Aus 1
❑ PRAMBERG OO Aus 1
❑ PRAMET OO Aus 1
❑ PRAT DE COMPTE Tarragona Spa 1
❑ PRAT DE LLOBREGAT Barcelona Spa 1
❑ PRATDIP Tarragona Spa 1
❑ PRATS D'ANOIA (Els Prats de Rei)Barcelona Spa 1
❑ PRATS DE LLUCANES Barcelona Spa 1
❑ PRAUST/ DANZIG (Prause, Pruszcz Gdanski) Westpreussen Ger 2
❑ PREETZ/ PORETZ Schleswig-Holstein Ger 1 2 6
❑ PREHAC Landes Fan 1
❑ PREINSBACH NO Aus 1
❑ PREIXANA Lerida Spa 1
❑ PREIXENTS (A Freixens) Lerida Spa 1
❑ PREMIA Barcelona Spa 1
❑ PREMIA DE MAR Barcelona Spa 1
❑ PREMING OO Aus 1
❑ PREMNAGAR AT DEHRA DUN Ind 15
❑ PREMNITZ Brandenburg Ger 2
❑ PREMONT Aisne Fan 1
❑ PRENZLAU/ UCKER (Prenzlow) Brandenburg Ger 1 2 3 6 13
❑ PRERAU (Prerov) Cze 2
❑ PRERAU-WIEN NO Aus 2
❑ PRESES, LES Gerona Spa 1
❑ PRESIDIO Di TRAPANI Sicilia Ita 3
❑ PRESSATH Bayern Ger 6 7
❑ PRESSBAUM NO Aus 1
❑ PRESSECK Bayern Ger 7
❑ PRESSIG Bayern Ger 7
❑ PRESTE, LA Bazes Pyrennees Fan 7
❑ PRETZSCH Provinz Sachsen Ger 1
❑ PREUSSISCH HOLLAND (Paslek) Ostpreussen Ger 1 3
❑ PREUSSISCH-EYLAU (Bagrationowsk) Ostpreussen Ger 1
❑ PREUSSISCH-STARGARD (Stargard Gdanski, Starogard) Westpreussen Ger 1
❑ PREUX-AU-BOIS Nord Fan 1
❑ PRICHSENSTADT Bayern Ger 7
❑ PRIEBUS/ NEISSE (Prezewoz) Schlesien Ger 1 2
❑ PRIEGO Cuenca Spa 1
❑ PRIEN Bayern Ger 1
❑ PRIES-FRIEDRICHSORT Schleswig-Holstein Ger 2
❑ PRIESTERATH Nordrhein-Westfalen Ger 14
❑ PRIESTERITZ-HALLE/ SAALE Sachsen Ger 2
❑ PRIKUMSK (Svyatoi Krest) Rus 1
❑ PRILUKI Rus 1
❑ PRIN-DEYRANCON Deux-Sevres Fan 3 14
❑ PRISCHES Nord Fan 1
❑ PRISDORF Schleswig-Holstein Ger 1
❑ PRITZWALK/ DOMNITZ Brandenburg Ger 1 7
❑ PROBSTZELLA Sachsen-Meiningen Ger 1
❑ PROENCA A NOVA Castelo Branco Por 2
❑ PROESSDORF Sachsen-Altenburg Ger 1 2
❑ PROFEN Provinz Sachsen Ger 2
❑ PROISY Aisne Fan 1
❑ PROIVILLE Nord Fan 1
❑ PRORA-Pommern Ger 7
❑ PROSCHWITZ/ NEISSE (Prosec nad Nisou) Boehmen Cze 2
❑ PROSKURIV (Proskurov, Proskottrov) Rus 1
❑ PROTZTRUM OO Aus 1
❑ PROVENCE Alais Fan 1 6
❑ PROVENCE Arles Gap et Toulon Fan 1 6
❑ PROVENCE Avignan Fan 1 6
❑ PROVENCE Marseille Fan 1 6
❑ PROVENCE Nimes Fan 1 6
❑ PROVENCIO, EL Cuenca Spa 1
❑ PROVIEND Net 1
❑ PRUEM Rheinland Ger 1 2 6
❑ PRY Namur Bel 1
❑ PRZEDBORZ (Przedborska) Rpl 2
❑ PRZEMYSL (Peremyshl, Deutsch Przemysl) Galicia Rpl 2
❑ PRZYROW Rpl 2
❑ PRZYROW Rus 1
❑ PRZYSCHETZ (Przyrzecz) Schlesien Ger 1
❑ PSCHOW/ RYBNIK Schlesien Ger 5
❑ PSKOV (Pskow, Pieskau) Rus 1
❑ PUCHBERG AM SCHNEEBERG N0 Aus 1
❑ PUCHBERG BEI WELS OO Aus 1
❑ PUCHBERG IM MACHLAND OO Aus 1
❑ PUCHENAU OO Aus 1
❑ PUCHHEIM Bayern Ger 4 7
❑ PUCHKIRCHEN AM TRATTEBERG OO Aus 1
❑ PUCKING OO Aus 1
❑ PUEBLA DE ALMORADIEL Toledo Spa 1
❑ PUEBLA DE CASTRO Huesca Spa 2
❑ PUEBLA DE CAZALLA Sevilla Spa 6
❑ PUEBLA DE D. FADRIQUE Granada Spa 1
❑ PUEBLA DE RODA, LA Huesca Spa 1
❑ PUEBLA DEL DU, C Valencia Spa 1
❑ PUEBLA LARGA Valencia Spa 1
❑ PUEBLA NUEVA Toledo Spa 1
❑ PIEBLA TORNESA Castellon Spa 1
❑ PUECHERSREUTH Bayern Ger 2
❑ PUEHRET OO Aus 1
❑ PUELZHEIM Pfalz Ger 1
❑ PUENTE DE GENAVE Jaen 'Spa 1
❑ PUERBACH -NO Aus 1
❑ PUERNSTEIN OO Aus 1
❑ PUERSTLING OO Aus 1
❑ PUERTA DE SEGURA, LA Jaen Spa 1
❑ PUERTO HURRACO Badajoz Spa 1
❑ PUERTO LAPICE Ciudad Real Spa 1
❑ PUERTOLAS Huesca Spa 1
❑ PUERTOLLANO Ciudad Real Spa 1
❑ PUETTLINGEN Rheinland Ger 8
❑ PUIG (Sant Mori) Gerona Spa 1
❑ PUIG Valencia Spa 1
❑ PUIG-ALT DE TER Gerona Spa 1 2
❑ PUIGCERDA Gerona Spa 1
❑ PUIGPELAT Tarragona Spa 1
❑ PUIGREIG Barcelona Spa 1
❑ PUIGVERD D'AGRAMUNT Lerida Spa 1
❑ PUISIEUX ET CLANLIEU Aisne Fan 1
❑ PULPI Almeria Spa 1 2
❑ PULSNITZ (Pulssnitz) Sachsen Ger 1 2 10
❑ PUNITZ (Poniec) Posen Ger 1
❑ PUPPING OO Aus 1 14
❑ PURCHENA Almeria Spa 1 2
❑ PURGSTALL NO Aus 1 2
❑ PURKERSDORF NO Aus 1
❑ PURMEREND North Holland Net 14
❑ PUSSAY Seine et Oise Fan 7
❑ PUSSEMANGE Luxembourg Bel 1
❑ PUT-BUS (Ruegen) Pommern Ger 1
❑ PUTLITZ Brandenburg Ger 2 7
❑ PUTNOK Hun 1 2
❑ PUTZIG (Puck) Westpreussen Ger 1 7
❑ PUTZLEINSDORF OO Aus 1

❒ PUY DE DOME
Puy de,Dome Fan 1
❒ PUY L'EVEQUE Lot Fan 2
❒ PUY, LE (Le'Puy en Velay)
Haute Loire Fan 1 4 7
❒ PUYLAROQUE
Tarn et Garonne Fan 2
❒ PUYLAURENS Tarn Fan 1
❒ PUZOL Valencia Spa 1
❒ PYATIGORSK Rus 1
❒ PYRENEES
ORIENTALES Fan 1
❒ PYRITZ
(Pyrzyce) Pommern Ger 1
❒ PYRMONT, BAD
Waldeck Ger 1 7 14
❒ PYZDRY Rus 1
❒ PYZDRY Posen Ger 1

Q

❒ QUADRATH Rheinland Ger 2
❒ QUAKENBRUECK
Hannover Ger 1 6
❒ QUAREMONT.
East Flanders Bel 1
❒ QUARMBY Ism 14
❒ QUAROULLE Nord Fan 7
❒ QUASN ITZ Sachsen Ger 1
❒ QUEDLINBURG/ BODE
Provinz Sachsen Ger 1 2 3 7
8 9 13
❒ QUELIMANE Moz 1 2
❒ QUERALBS Gerona Spa 1
❒ QUERCIA Rome Latina Ita 3
❒ QUERCY Fan 6
❒ QUERFURT/ QUERN (Quernfurt)
Provinz Sachsen Ger 1 2 6
❒ QUERN
Schleswig-Holstein Ger 1
❒ QUEROL Tarragona Spa 2
❒ QUESN.OY LE Nord Fan 1
❒ QUIBERON Morbihan Fan 3
❒ QUICKBORN
Schleswig-Holstein Ger 7
❒ QUIERSCHIED
Rheinland Ger 1 2
❒ QUIEVRAIN Hainaut Bel 1
❒ QUILLAN Aude Fan 1
❒ QUIMPER Finistere Fan 1
❒ QUIMPER-BREST
Finistere Fan 1
❒ QUINCY Aisne Fan 1
❒ QUINTANA DE LA SERENA
BadaJoz Spa 1
❒ QUINTANAR Cuenca Spa 1
❒ QUINTANAR DE: LA ORDEN
Toledo Spa 2

R

❒ RAA-BESENBECK
Schleswig-Holstein Ger 1
❒ RAAB OO Aus 1
❒ RAABS NO Aus 1
❒ RAAMSDONK
North Brabant Net 14
❒ RABASTENS Tarn Fan 1
❒ RABAUL Gng 1
❒ RABENSBURG NO Aus 1
❒ RABENSTEIN NO Aus 1 2
❒ RABENSTEIN (Karl-Marx-
Stactt) Sachsen Ger 2 8
❒ RABENTAL OO Aus 1
❒ RABKA Rpl 2
❒ RACHES Nord Fart 1 2
❒ RACHTIG/ MOSEL
Rheinland Ger 2
❒ RACOT, (Rakoly, Rakoty)
Posen Ger 1
❒ RADAUTZ (Radauit) Rom 2
❒ RADEBERG Sachsen Ger 1 2 7
❒ RADEBEUL Sachsen Ger 2 7 9
❒ RADEVORMWALD
Rheinland Ger 1 2
❒ RADLBERG NO Aus 1
❒ RADLIN Schlesien Ger 7
❒ RADOLFSZELL
Baden Ger 1 2 6
❒ RADOM Rpl 2
❒ RADSTADT Salzburg Aus 1
❒ RADZIEJOW
(Radzeieov) Rpl 1
❒ RADZIONKAU (Radzionkow)
Schlesien Ger 1 2 3 5 7 9
❒ RAEREN Liege Bel 14
❒ RAFAL Alicante Spa 1
❒ RAFELBUNOL
Valencia Spa 1
❒ RAFELCOFER
Valencia Spa I
❒ RAFELGUARAF
Valencia Spa 1
❒ RAFFINGS NO Aus 1
❒ RAFOL DE SALEM
Valencia Spa 1
❒ RAGNIT/ NIEMAN
Ostpreussen Ger 1
❒ RAGOL Almeria Spa 1
❒ RAGUHN/ MULDE
Anhalt Ger l 2
❒ RAIMBEAUCOURT
Nord Fan 1
❒ RAIN Kaernten Aus 1
❒ RAINBACH OO Aus 1
❒ RAINBERG OO Aus 1
❒ RAINCY,
LE Seine et Oise Fan 1
❒ RAIPOLTENBACH
NO Aus 1
❒ RAISTI NG
Bayern Ger 2
❒ RAJADELL
Barcelona Spa 1
❒ RAKKESTAD Nor 14
❒ RAKOSFALVA Hun 1
❒ RAKOW (Rakowska) Rpl 2
❒ RAKWITZ
(Rakoniewice) Rosen Ger 1
❒ RAMBOUILLET
Seine-et-Oise Fan 10
❒ RAMEGRIES-CHIN
Hainaut Bel 1
❒ RAMGARH Ind 15
❒ RAMMELSBACH Pfalz Ger 1
❒ RAMSBECK Westfalen Ger 2
❒ RAMSDORF/ AS
(Velen) Westfalen Ger 7
❒ RAMSEL Barbant Bel 1
❒ RANCE Hainaut Bel 1
❒ RANDEGG NO Aus 1
❒ RANDERS Den 12
❒ RANDOW Pommern Ger 1
❒ RANHEIM Nor 14
❒ RANIS Provinz Sachsen Ger 1
❒ RANNARI EDL A.D.
DONAU OO Aus 1
❒ RANSART Hairnaut Bel 1
❒ RANSHOFEN OO Aus 1
❒ RANSPACH Elsass Gerl
❒ RANSPACH
Ober Elsass Fan 1
❒ RANST Antwerp Bel 1
❒ RAPITADELS ALFACS, LA (Sant Caries de
La Rapita) Tarragona Spa 1
❒ RAPPOLTSWEILER
Elsass Ger 1
❒ RAS-EL-MA
(Bedeau) Alg 1 7
❒ RASCHAU/ ERZGEBIRGE
Sachsen Ger 1
❒ RASCHEWITZ (Raszowice, Zmigrod)
Schlesien Ger 7
❒ RASCHKOW (Raschkau,
Raszkow) Posen Ger 1
❒ RASPAY Murcia -Spa 2
❒ RASQUERA Tarragona Spa 1
❒ RASTATT Baden Ger 1 2 6 8
❒ RASTENBERG,BAD Sachsen-
Weimar-Eisenach Ger 1 2
❒ RASTENBURG (Ketrzyn)
Ostpreussen Ger 1
❒ RASTENFELD NO Aus 1
❒ RASZKOW Rpl 1
❒ RATHEIM Rheinland Ger 2
❒ RATHENOW/ HARD (Rathenau)
Brandenburg Ger 1 2 7 11
❒ RATIBOR/ ODER
(Raciborz) Schlesien Ger 1 2 3 4
5 6 7
❒ RATINGEN Rheinland Ger 1 2
❒ RATINGEN-DUESSELDORF
Rheinland Ger 2
❒ RATTENBERG Tirol Aus 1
❒ RATZEBUHR
(Okonek) Pommern Ger 1
❒ RATZEBURG (Racisburg)
Schleswig-Holstein Ger 1 2
❒ RATZERSDORF NO Aus 1
❒ RAUCOU RT Ardennes Fan 7
❒ RAUENSTEIN
Sachsen-Meiningen Ger 1 2 7
❒ RAUNHEIM Hessen Ger 1
❒ RAURIS Salzburg Aus 1
❒ RAUSCHA O.L.
(Ruszuw) Schlesien Ger 12
❒ RAUSCHEN (Ryn, Svetlogorsk,
USSR) Ostpreussen Ger 1
❒ RAUXEL Westfalen Ger 1 2 3 5 6 7
❒ RAVEL Puy de Dome Fan 7
❒ RAVENSBRUECK
Brandenburg Ger 15
❒ RAVENSBURG
Wuerttemberg Ger 1 6 7 13
❒ RAVENSTEIN
North Brabant Net 14
❒ RAVIERES Yonne Fan 7
❒ RAWITSCH
(Rawicz) Posen Ger 1 2 7
❒ RAXENDORF NO Aus 2
❒ RAYMOT Lerida Spa 2
❒ REAL DE GANDIA
Valencia Spa 1
❒ REAL DE MONTROY
Valencia Spa 1
❒ REALMONT Tarn Fan 2 7
❒ REBBELROTH
Rheinland Ger 2
❒ RECHENBERG
Sachsen Ger 1
❒ RECHT Liege Bel 14
❒ RECKEM
West Flanders Bel 1
❒ RECKHEIM Fan 6
❒ RECKLINGHAUSEN
Westfalen Ger 1 2 3 5 7 8
❒ RECKLINGHAUSEN-'SUED
Westfalen Ger 23
❒ REDONDO Evora Por 1 2
❒ REERSLEV Den 1 1
❒ REES Rheinland Ger 1 2 3
❒ REES-ESS-ERDEN
Rheinland Ger 2

❒ REETZ/ IHNA (Recz, Poland) Brandenburg Ger 1
❒ REGAU OO Aus 1
❒ REGEN ZWIESEL, OSTERHOFEN Bayern Ger7
❒ REGEN/ REGEN Bayern Ger2 7
❒ REGENHUETTE Bayern Ger2
❒ REGENSBURG/ DANUBE (Ratisbon) Bayern Ger 1 2 4
❒ REGENSTAUF Bayern Ger 1
❒ REGENWALDE/ REGA (Resko) Pommern Ger 1 6
❒ REGGIA Ita 14
❒ REGGIO EMILIA Ita 3 14
❒ REGIS/ PLEISSE (Regis-Breitingen) Sachsen Ger 1
❒ REGNYAsine Fan 1
❒ REGUENGOS DE MONSARAZ Evora Por 1
❒ REHAU/ GRUENEBACH (Rechau) Bayern Ger 1 26
❒ REHBERG NO Aus 1
❒ REHBURG Hannover Ger 1
❒ REHMEN Sachsen-Meiningen Ger 1
❒ REHNA Mecklenburg-Schwerin Ger 1
❒ REICHENAU Sachsen Ger 1 2 11
❒ REICHENBACH (Dzierzoninow) Ostpreussen Ger 1
❒ REICHENBACH Sachsen Ger 1 2 7 89
❒ REICHENBACH (Dzierzoniow) Schlesien Ger 1 2 7 8
❒ REICHENBACH/ REGEN Bayern Ger 1 7
❒ REICHENBERG Aus 3
❒ REICHENBERG (Liberec) Boehmen Cze 1 2 4 12
❒ REICHENBRAND Sachsen Ger 2
❒ REICHENFELS Reuss juengere Linie Ger 2
❒ REICHENHAIN Sachsen Ger 2 7
❒ REICHENHALL Bad/ Saal Ger 1 2 6 8
❒ REICHENHALL Bayern Ger 1 2 6 8
❒ REICHENHALL/ FILS Wuerttemberg Ger 2
❒ REICHENSTEIN (Zlotystok) Schlesien Ger 7
❒ REICHENTAL IM MUEHLKREIS OO Aus 1
❒ REICHENWEIER (Riquewihr) Elsass Ger 1 2
❒ REICHERSBERG AM INN OO Aus 1
❒ REICHERSDORF NO Aus 2
❒ REICHMANNSDORF/ WITTENBERG Sachsen-Meiningen Ger 7
❒ REICHRAMING OO Aus 1
❒ REID BEI MAUTHAUSEN OO Aus 1
❒ REID BEI TRAUNKREIS OO Aus 1
❒ REID, LA Liege Bel 1
❒ REIFENSTEIN Aus 3
❒ REIFENSTEIN Hun 1
❒ REIMS Marne Fan 1 2 3 7
❒ REINERZ, BAD/ WEISTRITZ (Duszniki-Zdroj) Schlesien Ger 1 2
❒ REINFELD Schlesien Ger 1
❒ REINFELD Schleswig-Holstein Ger 2
❒ REINOSA Santander Spa 1
❒ REINSDORF Provinz Sachsen Ger 2 7
❒ REIPOLTSKIRCHEN Pfalz Ger 1
❒ REISEN (Rydzyna, Leszno) Posen Ger 4
❒ REISGARN NO Aus 2
❒ REISHOLZ/ DUESSELDORF Rheinland Ger 2 5 7
❒ REITERSCHLAG Kaernten Aus 1
❒ REITH Tirol Aus 1
❒ REITZENHAIN Sachsen Ger1
❒ REJET DE BEAULIEU Nord Fan 1
❒ REKUM Hannover Ger 7
❒ RELIZANE (Ighil, Izane) Alg 1
❒ RELLINARS Barcelona Spa 1
❒ RELLINGEN Schleswig-Holstein Ger 1
❒ REMAGEN/ RHEIN (Rheinmagen)
❒ Rheinland Ger 1 2 7 9 11 14
❒ REMAUCOU RT Aisne Fan 1
❒ REMDA/ RINNE Thueringen Ger 1 2
❒ REMIGNY Aisne Fan 1
❒ REMIREMONT Calvados Fan 2
❒ REMIREMONT Vosges Fan 1 7
❒ REMOUCHAMPS Liege Bel1
❒ REMPTENDORF Reuss Altere Linie Ger 7.
❒ REMSCHEID Rheinland Ger 1 2 3 5 11 14
❒ REMSCHEID-BLOMBACHT Rheinland, Ger 2
❒ REMSCHEID-HASTEN Rheinland Ger 2
❒ REMSCHEID-VIERINGHAUSEN Rheinland Ger 2
❒ RENAIX (Rosne) East Flanders Bel 1 14
❒ RENANSART (Renausart) Aisne Fan 1
❒ RENCHEN/ RENCH Baden Ger 1
❒ RENDSBURG/ EYDER Schleswig-Holstein Ger 1 2 8
❒ RENGERSDORF (Krosnowice) Schlesien Ger2
❒ RENICCI Arezzo Ita 14
❒ RENLIES Hainaut Bel 1
❒ RENNES (Roazon, Breton) Ille et Vilaine Fan 1 4 7 10 14
❒ RENNES-ST. MALO Ille et Vilaine Fan 1 7
❒ REOLE, LA Gironde Fan 2 6 7
❒ REPPEN Brandenburg Ger 1 2
❒ REQUEJO Santander Spa 2
❒ 0EQUENA Valencia Spa 2
❒ RETHEL Ardennes Fan 1
❒ RETHY Antwerp Bel 1
❒ RETTGENSTEDT/ COELLEDA Provinz Sachsen Ger 2
❒ RETZ NO Aus 1
❒ REULAND Liege Bel 14
❒ REULBACH/ RHOEN Hessen-Nassau Ger 2
❒ REUMONT Nord Fan 1
❒ REUNION Reu 1 2 6
❒ REUS Tarragona Spa 1 2
❒ REUTH Sachsen Ger 2
❒ REUTLINGEN/ ESCHATZ Wuerttemberg Ger 1 2 6 7 8
❒ REVAL (Tallin, Revel) Est 1
❒ REVDA Rus 1
❒ REVEL Haute Garonne Fan 1
❒ REVES Hainaut Bel 1
❒ REVIGNY Meuse Fan 4 7 10
❒ REYERSHAUSEN Hannover Ger 2
❒ REZEKNE (Rositten, Rezhitsa) Rus 1
❒ REZENDE Viseu Por 1
❒ RHEDA/ EMS Westfalen Ger1
❒ RHEDEN Gelderland Net 8
❒ RHEIN Ostpreussen Ger 1
❒ RHEINBACH Rheinland Ger1
❒ RHEINE Westfalen Ger 1 6 11 14
❒ RHEINFELDEN Baden Ger 1 2
❒ RHEINGAUKREIS (Ruedesheim) Hessen-Nassau Ger 1
❒ RHEINHAUSEN Rheinland Ger 1 2
❒ RHEINISCH Westfalen Ger 5
❒ RHEINPROVINZ Rheinland Ger 1
❒ RHEINSBERG Brandenburg Ger 1
❒ RHEINZABERN/ ERLBACH Pfalz Ger 1
❒ RHENEN Gelderland Net 1
❒ RHEURDT-SCHAEPHUYSEN Rheinland Ger 1
❒ RHEYDT/ NIERS (Rheidt, Rheid, Rheyd)
❒ Rheinland Ger 1 2 7 14
❒ RHINOW (Rhin) Brandenburg Ger 2
❒ RHODT Pfalz Ger 1
❒ RIALP Lerida Spa 1
❒ RIBA, LA Tarragona Spa 1
❒ RIBADESELLA Asturias Spa 1
❒ RIBARROJA Valencia Spa 1
❒ RIBARROJA D'EBRE Tarragona Spa 1 2
❒ RIBBERTWERKE/ HERMUELHEIM Rheinland Ger 5
❒ RIBE Den 1 1
❒ RIBEMONT Aisne Fan 1
❒ RIBERA DE CARDOS Lerida Spa 1
❒ RIBES DE FRESER Gerona Spa 1
❒ RIBES DEL PENEDES (Sant pere de Ribes) Barcelona Spa 1
❒ RIBINSK Rus 1
❒ RIBNITZ/ RECKNITZ Mecklenburg-Schwerin Ger 1
❒ RIBOLLA Grosseto Toscana Ita 3
❒ RICKELSHAUSEN Baden Ger 2
❒ RICOTE Murcia Spa 1
❒ RICTORIA Ita 3
❒ RIDAURA Gerona Spa 1
❒ RIDDER (Leninogorsk) Rus 1
❒ RIED bei Mauthausen OO Aus 1
❒ RIED bei Traunkreis OO Aus 1
❒ RIED IM INNKREIS OO Aus 1
❒ RIEDAU OO Aus 1
❒ RIEDENBURG Bayern Ger 1 2 3
❒ RIEDENBURG Salzburg Aus 1
❒ RIEDER/ OSTHARZ Anhalt Ger 1

❒ RIEDLINGEN/ DANUBE Wuerttemberg Ger 1 2
❒ RIELLS DE MONTSENY Gerona Spa 1
❒ RIELLS DEL FAI Barcelona Spa 1
❒ RIERA DE GAIA, LA Barcelona Spa 1
❒ RIESE/ ELBE (Riesa) Sachsen Ger 1 2 12
❒ RIESENBURG (Prabuty, Poland) Westpreussen Ger 1 6
❒ RIETBERG/ EMS Westfalen Ger 1
❒ RIETI Ita 14
❒ RIETSCHEN Schlesien Ger 1 2
❒ RIEULAY Fan 1
❒ RIEUMES Haute Garonne Fan 2
❒ RIGA Rus 1
❒ RIGOROSO Sciura Ita 3
❒ RIJSWIJK South Holland Net 1 8 14
❒ RIMBERG Westfalen Ger 2
❒ RIMOGNE Ardennes Fan 1
❒ RINDLBERG OO Aus 1
❒ RINGENBERG Rheinland Ger 2
❒ RINGKOEBING Den 11
❒ RINGSTED Den 1 1
❒ RINKENAES (Rinkenis) Den 1
❒ RINKENIS (Rinkenaes, Denmark) Schleswig-Holstein Ger 1
❒ RINTELN/ WESER Hessen-Nassau Ger 1 7
❒ RIO MAIOR Santarem Por 1
❒ RIODEVA Teruel Spa 1
❒ RIOJA Almeria Spa 2
❒ RIOM Puy de Dome Fan 2 3
❒ RIONANSA Santander Spa 1
❒ RIPOLL Gerona Spa 1
❒ RIPOLL DEL VALLES (Sant Lorenc Savall) Barcelona Spa 1
❒ RIPOLLET Barcelona Spa 1
❒ RITSCHENWALDE (Ryczlow) Posen Ger 2
❒ RITTERHUDE Hannover Ger 1
❒ RIUDARENES Gerona Spa 1
❒ RIUDECANYES Tarragona Spa 1
❒ RIUDECOLS Tarragona Spa 1
❒ RIUDIBITLLES Barcelona Spa 1
❒ RIUDOMS Tarragona Spa 1
❒ RIUDOR DE BAGES (Sant Fruitos de Bages) Barcelona Spa 1
❒ RIVNE (Rowne) Rus 1
❒ RIXHEIM (Rexen) Elsass Ger 1
❒ ROANNE Loire Fan 1 2 3 6 7 10
❒ ROBERTVILLE Liege Bel 14
❒ ROBRES Huesca Spa 1
❒ ROCA DEL VALLES Barcelona Spa 1
❒ ROCAFORT DE BAGES Barcelona Spa 2
❒ ROCAFORT DE QUERALT Tarragona Spa 1
❒ ROCAFORT DE VALLBONA Lerida Spa 1
❒ ROCALLAURA Lerida Spa 1
❒ ROCHE-ARNAUD Le Puy de Dome Fan 7
❒ ROCHE-BIESSARD Fan 3
❒ ROCHE-CHALAIS, LA Dordogne Fan 2
❒ ROCHE-LA-MOLIERE Loire Fan 1 2
❒ ROCHE-MAURICE Fan 3
❒ ROCHE, LA Sur-Yon Fan 7
❒ ROCHE, LA Sur-Yon Vendee Fan 1
❒ ROCHEFORT-SUR-MER Charente Inferieure Fan 1 2 4 6 7
❒ ROCHELLE, LA Charente Inferieure Fan 1 3 6 7 10 12
❒ ROCHERATH Liege Bel 1 14
❒ ROCHLITZ/ MULDE Sachsen Ger 1 2 7
❒ ROCHSBURG Sachsen Ger 2
❒ RODA Sachsen-Altenburg Ger 1 2 7
❒ RODA DE BARA Tarragona Spa 1
❒ RODA DE TER Barcelona Spa 1
❒ RODA, LA Albacete Spa 1
❒ RODACH/ RODACH Coburg-Bayern Ger 1 2 6 7
❒ RODAUN NO Aus 1
❒ RODEWISCH Sachsen Ger 1 2 7 8
❒ RODEZ ET MILLAU (Milhau) Aveyron Fan 1
❒ RODI Sicilia Ita 3
❒ RODIGKAU Provinz Sachsen Ger 2
❒ RODING/ REGEN Bayern Ger 1
❒ RODLEBEN Anhalt Ger 2
❒ RODONYA Tarragona Spa 1
❒ ROEBEL Mecklenburg-Schwerin Ger 1
❒ ROEBELN Mecklenburg-Schwerin Ger 1
❒ ROEDBY Den 2
❒ ROEDDING Den 1 2
❒ ROEDDING (Roedding, Denmark) Schleswig-Holstein Ger 1 2
❒ ROEDELNSTEIN Westfalen Ger 2
❒ ROEDVIG Den 11
❒ ROEHLINGSHAUSEN Westfalen Ger 2
❒ ROEHRIGSHOF/ WERRA Hessen-Nassau Ger 1
❒ ROEHRSDORF Sachsen Ger 1
❒ ROELLFELD Bayern Ger 1
❒ ROEMERSTADT (Rymarov) Cze 1
❒ ROEMHILD Sachsen-Meiningen Ger 1 2
❒ ROENNEBECK Hannover Ger 2
❒ ROERA Nor 14
❒ ROERMOND Limburg Net 8
❒ ROEROS Nor 14
❒ ROESA Provinz Sachsen Ger 9
❒ ROESCHITZ NO Aus 1
❒ ROESKILDE Den 11
❒ ROESRATH Rheinland Ger 2
❒ ROESSEL (Reszel) Ostpreussen Ger 1 2
❒ ROETHA/ PLEISSE Sachsen Ger 1 2
❒ ROETHENBACH/ PEGNITZ Bayern Ger 2 7 13
❒ ROGACHEV (Rogatchev, Rogarschev) Rus 1
❒ ROGASEN/ WETNA (Rogozno, Rogozinska) Posen Ger 1
❒ ROGOWO Posen Ger 1
❒ ROHR Bayern Ger 1 2
❒ ROHRBACH OO Aus 1 2
❒ ROHRBACH/ HEIDELBERG Baden Ger 1 27
❒ ROISDORF Rheinland Ger 2
❒ ROISEL Somme Fan 1
❒ ROITHAM OO Aus 1
❒ ROITZSCH/ BITTERFELD Provinz Sachsen Ger 1 2 7 9
❒ ROJALES Alicante Spa 1
❒ ROKIETNICE (Rokietnicka) Posen Ger 2
❒ ROKITTNITZ (Rokitnica) Silesien Ger 1
❒ ROLLEGHEMCAPELLE (Rollegem-Kapelle) West Flanders Bel
❒ ROLLSHAUSEN Hannover Ger 1 2
❒ ROMANA, LA Alicante Spa 1
❒ ROMANS Fan 3
❒ ROMBACH Lothringen Ger 2 3
❒ ROMBURG/ HOHENSALZA Posen Ger 2
❒ ROME Ita 11 14
❒ ROMILLY-SUR-SEINE Aube Fan 14
❒ ROMMETVEIT Nor 14
❒ ROMORANTIN Loire et Cher Fan 3
❒ RONCHAMP Haute-Saone Fan 4
❒ RONCQ Nord Fan 1
❒ RONDA Malaga Spa 2
❒ RONDORF/ RODENKIRCHEN Rheinland Ger 1
❒ RONGY Hainaut Bel 1
❒ RONNEBURG Sachsen-Altenburg Ger 1 2 7
❒ RONSDORF Rheinland Ger 1 2 11
❒ RONSSOY Somme Fan 1
❒ ROOBORST East Flanders Bel 1
❒ ROOST-WARENDIN Nord Fan 1
❒ ROPPENZWEILER Elsass Ger 1
❒ ROQUES D'OSONA (Sant Marti de Sobremunt) Barcelona Spa 1
❒ ROQUETAS DE MAR Almeria Spa 1
❒ ROQUETES (Roquetas) Tarragona Spa 1
❒ ROSBACH/ SIEG Rheinland Ger 1
❒ ROSCHKOW (Roszkow) Posen Ger 1
❒ ROSDZIN (Rozdzien) Schlesien Ger 1
❒ ROSEGG Steiermark Aus 1
❒ ROSELL Castellon Spa 1
❒ ROSENAU-ISARMOOS Bayern Ger 1
❒ ROSENBERG-KRONACH Bayern Ger 4
❒ ROSENBERG/ OBERPFALZ Bayern Ger 2 4 7 9
❒ ROSENBERG/ STOBER (Olesno, Olesnicka) Schlesien Ger 1

❒ ROSENBURG NO Aus 1 2
❒ ROSENBURG (Susz) Westpreussen Ger 1
❒ ROSENHEIM Westpreussen Ger 1
❒ ROSENHEIM/ INN Bayern Ger 1 2 6 7
❒ ROSENTHAL (Rozmital) Cze 2
❒ ROSENTHAL-REUSS Thueringen Ger 2
❒ ROSENTHAL/ GLATZ Schlesien Ger 2
❒ ROSES Gerona Spa 1
❒ ROSES DE LLOBREGAT (Sant Feliu de Llobregat) Barcelona Spa 1
❒ ROSITZ Sachsen-Altenburg Ger 2 7
❒ ROSMALEN North Brabant Net 14
❒ ROSSATZ IN DER WACHAU NO Aus 1
❒ ROSSBACH Pfalz Ger 1 7
❒ ROSSBACH Provinz Sachsen Ger 1 7
❒ ROSSBACH/ ROSSBACH Hessen-Nassau Ger 7
❒ ROSSBERG Wuerttemberg Ger 5
❒ ROSSELLO Lerida Spa 1
❒ ROSSLA Provinz Sachsen Ger1 7
❒ ROSSLAU/ ELBE Anhalt Ger1 2
❒ ROSSLEBEN/ UNSTRUT Provinz Sachsen Ger 2
❒ ROSSUM Gelderland Net 14
❒ ROSSWEIN/ MULDE Sachsen Ger 1 2
❒ ROSTOCK/ WARNOW Mecklenburg-Schwerin Ger 1 2 7 12
❒ ROSTOKINO Rus 1
❒ ROSTOV/ DON (Rostow) Rus 1
❒ ROSWADZE (Rozwada) Schlesien Ger 2 3
❒ ROTENBURG Hannover Ger 1 2 3 6
❒ ROTENBURG/ FULDA Hessen-Nassau Ger 1
❒ ROTH/ REDNITZ Bayern Ger 2 6 7
❒ ROTHAUS Baden Ger 4
❒ ROTHEN OO Aus 1
❒ ROTHENBACH/ LANDESHUT Schlesien Ger 1 2 7
❒ ROTHENBACHL OO Aus 1
❒ ROTHENBURG/ NEISSE Schlesien Ger 2 7
❒ ROTHENBURG/ TAUBER Bayern Ger 1 2 6
❒ ROTHENKIRCHEN/ VOGTLAND Sachsen Ger 1 7
❒ ROTHENKRUG Den 1
❒ ROTHSELBERG Pfalz Ger 1
❒ ROTHWASSER O.L. Schlesien Ger 1 6
❒ ROTTENBACH OO Aus 1
❒ ROTTENBACH/ THUERINGEN Saxe-Coburg Ger 7
❒ ROTTENBURG/ LAABER Bayern Ger 1 6
❒ ROT-TENBURG/ NECKAR Wuerttemberg Ger 1 2 6
❒ ROTTENMANN Steiermark Aus 1
❒ ROTTERDAM South Holland Net 1 8 14
❒ ROTTHALMUENSTER Bayern Ger 1 2
❒ ROTTHAUSEN Rheinland Ger 1 7 8
❒ ROTTHAUSEN Westfalen Ger 1 2
❒ ROTTLUFF Sachsen Ger 1
❒ ROTTWEIL/ NECKAR Wuerttemberg Ger 1 5 6 7
❒ ROUBAIX Nord Fan 1 7
❒ ROUBOIX-TOURCOING Nord Fan 1
❒ ROUCOURT Hainaut Bel 1
❒ ROUEN Seine Inferieur Fan 1 3 6 7 11 14
❒ ROUEN-LEVASSEUR Seine Inferieure Fan 3
❒ ROUEN-QUAI DE FRANCE Seine Inferieure Fan 3
❒ ROUGIERS Var Fan 7
❒ ROUPY Aisne Fan 1
❒ ROU RELL, EL Tarragona Spa 1
❒ ROUSSELARE (Roulers) West Flanders Bet 2
❒ ROUV-LE-GRAND Somme Fan 1
❒ ROUVEROY Hainaut Bel 1
❒ ROUVROY Pas de Calais Fan 1
❒ ROUX Hainaut Bel 1 2
❒ ROVNO (Rowne, Rovnoye) Rus 1
❒ ROWNE/ DUKLA (Wolyn, Rovno, Ukraine, Reichenstein, Zloty Stok) Rpl 2 14
❒ ROYAN Charente Maritime Fan 6 7
❒ ROYAT LES BAI NS Puy de Dome Fan 2 7
❒ ROZIERES Haute Marne Fan 2
❒ ROZPRZA Rpl 2
❒ ROZSNTO (Roznava) Cze 1
❒ ROZSNYO (Rosenau, Roznava, Czechoslovakia) Hun 1
❒ RUBI Barcelona Spa 1 2
❒ RUBIELOS DE MORA Teruel Spa 1
❒ RUBITE Granada Spa 1
❒ RUDA Schlesien Ger 1 5 7
❒ RUDELSBURG/ BAD KOESEN Provinz Sachsen Ger 2 7
❒ RUDOLSTADT/ SAALE Thueringen Ger 1 2 6 7 8
❒ RUEBELAND/ BODE Braunschweig Ger 2
❒ RUEDESHEIM/ RHEIN Rheinland Ger 1 8
❒ RUEGEN Pommern Ger 2
❒ RUEGENWALDE (Darlowo) Pommern Ger 1 2 6
❒ RUEGENWALDERMUEND (Darlowko, Ruegenwalde) Pommern Ger 1
❒ RUEHRING OO Aus 1
❒ RUEIL Seine et Oise Fan 2
❒ RUELZHEIM Pfalz Ger 1
❒ RUENDEROTH Rheinland Ger 1 2 14
❒ RUESSELSHEIM/ MAIN Hessen-Nassau Ger 1 7 8 11
❒ RUESTORF OO Aus 1
❒ RUESTRINGEN (Wilhelmshaven) Oldenburg Ger 1 2
❒ RUETHEN/ MOEHNE Westfalen Ger 1
❒ RUFACH Elsass Ger 1
❒ RUFFEC Charente Fan 7
❒ RUFISQUE Sen 6
❒ RUHLA/ RUHE Sachsen-Gotha Ger 1 7
❒ RUHLAND/ ELSTER Schlesien Ger 7
❒ RUHLSDORF Brandenburg Ger 7
❒ RUHMANNSFELDEN Bayern Ger 2
❒ RUHNOW Pommern Ger 2
❒ RUHPOLDING Bayern Ger 1
❒ RUHR & RHEINE Westfalen Ger 7
❒ RUISBROEK Brabant Bel 1
❒ RUMBEKE West Flanders Bel 1 14
❒ RUMBURG (Rumburk) Boehmen Cze 1
❒ RUMELINGEN Lux 7
❒ RUMILLIES Hainaut Bel 1
❒ RUMILLY Fan 1
❒ RUMMELSBURG (Miastko) Pommern Ger 1 7
❒ RUMPST Antwerp Bel 1
❒ RUPELMONDE East Flanders Bet 1
❒ RUPIA Gerona Spa 1
❒ RUPIT Barcelona Spa 1
❒ RUPPERSDORF (Ruprechtice) Boehmen Cze2
❒ RUPPERSDORF (Wyszonowice) Schlesien Ger 1 7
❒ RUPPERSTHAL NO Aus 1
❒ RUPRECHTSHOFEN OO Aus 1
❒ RUS Jaen Spa 1
❒ RUSS/ NIEMEN Ostpreussen Ger 1
❒ RUSSDORF Sachsen Ger 1
❒ RUSSDORF/ ROTTAL Bayern Ger 1 2
❒ RUSSEIGNIES East Flanders Bel 1
❒ RUTE Kaernten Aus 1
❒ RUTSWEILER/ LAUTER Pfalz Ger 1
❒ RUTTEN Limbourg Bel 1
❒ RUTZENHAM OO Aus 1
❒ RUYEN East Flanders Bel 1
❒ RUYSSELEDE West Flanders Bel 1
❒ RUZOMBEROK Cze 2
❒ RYATIGORSK Rus 1
❒ RYAZAN (Rjazan) Rus 1
❒ RYBNIK/ RUDKA (Rynsk) Schlesien Ger 1 2 7
❒ RYCKEVORSEL Antwerp Bel 1
❒ RYGGE Nor 14
❒ RYKOVO (Yenakyevo) Rus 1
❒ RYMANOW (Rzeszow) Galicia Ger 2
❒ RYPIN (Rippin) Rpl 2

S

❒ SAALBACH Salzburg Aus 2
❒ SAALBURG Reuss juengere Linie Ger 1
❒ SAALFELD (Zalewo) Ostpreussen Ger 1 6
❒ SAALFELD UND RODOLSTADT Thueringen Ger 1
❒ SAALFELD/ SAALE Thueringen Ger 1 2 6 7
❒ SAALFELDEN Salzburg Aus 1

❒ SAAR-BUCKENHEIM Lothringen Ger 6
❒ SAARALBEN Lothringen Ger 7
❒ SAARALEBEN Lorraine Fan 7
❒ SAARAU (Zarow) Schlesien Ger 1 9
❒ SAARBRUCKEN HEIM Lothringen Fan 6
❒ SAARBRUECKEN Rheinland Ger 1 2 3 7 8 12
❒ SAARBRUECKEN-BURBACH Rheinland Ger 2
❒ SAARBURG/ LOTHRINGEN Ger 6
❒ SAARBURG/ TRIER Rheinland Ger 1 2 6
❒ SAARGEMUEND Lothringen Ger 1 2 6
❒ SAARLAUTERN (Saarlouis) Rheinland Ger 1 3
❒ SAATZIG (Szadko) Pommern Ger 1
❒ SAAZ (Zatec) Boehmen Cze 1
❒ SABAC Ser 1
❒ SABADELL Barcelona Spa 1 2
❒ SABLES D'OLONNE, LES Vendee Fan 7
❒ SABLETTES-LES-BAINS Var Fan 7
❒ SABORWITZ (Zaborowice) Schlesien Ger 6 7
❒ SABROSA Vila Real Por 1
❒ SABUGAL Guarda For 1
❒ SACHSA, BAD Hannover Ger 1
❒ SACHSEN Ger 1 4
❒ SACHSENBURG Sachsen Ger 1 2
❒ SACHSENHAUSEN Hessen-Nassau Ger 7 15
❒ SAD Rus 1
❒ SADURNI D'ANOIA Barcelona Spa 1
❒ SAECKINGEN Baden Ger 1
❒ SAERCHEN N. L. (Annahuette) Brandenburg Ger 7
❒ SAEUSENSTEIN NO Aus 1
❒ SAGAN (Zagan) Schlesien Ger 1 3 4 6 7 8 14
❒ SAGRA Alicante Spa 1
❒ SAGUNTO Valencia Spa 1 2
❒ SAIL-SUR-COUZAN Loire Fan 7
❒ SAILLY LEZ LANNOY Nord Fan 1
❒ SAILLY-EN-OSTREVENT Pas de Calais Fan 1
❒ SAINS-RICHAUMONT Aisne Fan 1
❒ SAINT AGENAU Fan 3
❒ SAINT ANDRE DE L'EURE Eure Fan 7
❒ SAINT ANTOINE Fan 2
❒ SAINT ANTONIN Tarn et Garonne Fan 1
❒ SAINT AUGUSTIN Seine-et-Marne Fan 7
❒ SAINT BARTHELEMY Dordogne Fan 1
❒ SAINT BRIEUC Cotes du Nord Fan 1 2 14
❒ SAINT CERE Lot Fan 2
❒ SAINT CHAMOND Loire Fan 7
❒ SAINT CLAR Gers Fan 1
❒ SAINT CLAUDE Jura Fan 7
❒ SAINT CLOUD Hauts de Seine Fan 11
❒ SAINT DENIS Seine Fan 7
❒ SAINT DIDIER LA STAUVE Loire Fan 7
❒ SAINT DIE Vosges Fan 1
❒ SAINT DIZIER Haute-Marne Fan 1 7
❒ SAINT EFIENNE du Rouvray Fan 3
❒ SAINT ETIENNE Loire Fan 1 2 3 7 11 12 14
❒ SAINT ETIENNE-FIRMINY Loire Fan 7
❒ SAINT ETILENNE DU ROUVRAY Fan 3
❒ SAINT FELIX Haute Garonne Fan 2
❒ SAINT FONS Rhone Fan 7
❒ SAINT GAUDENS Haute Garonne Fan 1 7
❒ SAINT GENEST LERPT Loire Fan 2
❒ SAINT GERMAIN en Laye Yvelines Fan 6 7 11
❒ SAINT GOBAIN Aisne Fan 1 7
❒ SAINT HIPOLITE Fan 1
❒ SAINT HIPPOLYTE DU FORT Gard Fan 7 10
❒ SAINT JEAN DE LUZ Basses Pyrenees Fan 7
❒ SAINT JEAN DU GARD Gard Fan 6
❒ SAINT JEAN LE COMTAL Gers Fan 1
❒ SAINT JUERY Tarn Fan 7
❒ SAINT JUST EN CHEVALET Loire Fan 7
❒ SAINT LAURENT DE CERDANS Pyrenees Orientales Fan 2
❒ SAINT LAURENT DE LA L'Aude Fan 1
❒ SAINT LAU RENT DE LA CABRERISSE L'Aude Fan 1 2
❒ SAINT LAURENT-LE-MINIER Gard Fan 3 14
❒ SAINT LIZAIGNE Indre Fan 7
❒ SAINT LO Manche Fan 14
❒ SAINT LOUIS DU RHONE Bouches-du-Rhone Fan 9
❒ SAINT MACAARE Gironde Fan 1
❒ SAINT MALO Cotes du Nord Fan 7 12
❒ SAINT MALO Ille-et-Vitaine Fan 7 12
❒ SAINT MANDE Seine Fan 7
❒ SAINT MARIE AUX MINES Haut Rhin Fan 7
❒ SAINT MARTIN DE CRAU Bouches du Rhone Fan 2
❒ SAINT MARTIN DE RE Fan3
❒ SAINT MARTIN LA LANDE Aude Fan 1
❒ SAINT MARTIN-VALMEROUX Aisne Fan 2
❒ SAINT MARTORY Haute Garonne Fan 2
❒ SAINT MATHIEUDE-TREVIERS Herault Fan 7
❒ SAINT MAURICE Fan 14
❒ SAINT MAXIENT L'ECOLE Deux Sevres Fan 10 7
❒ SAINT MAXIMIN Var Fan 6
❒ SAINT MEDARD EN JALLES Gironde Fan 3 7 14
❒ SAINT MONTANT Gard Fan 6
❒ SAINT NAZAIRE Haute-Loire Fan 4 7
❒ SAINT NICOLAS DE LA GRAVE Tarn-et-Garonne Fan 2
❒ SAINT OMER Pas de Calais Fan 1 7
❒ SAINT PAUL-EN-JAREZ Loire Fan 7
❒ SAINT PIERRE SUR/ DIVES Calvados Fan 7
❒ SAINT PORQUIER Tarn et Garonne Fan 2
❒ SAINT PUY Gers Fan 1
❒ SAINT QUEN Seine-St. Denis Fan 7
❒ SAINT QUENTIN Aisne Fan 1 2 3 7 14
❒ SAINT QUENTIN AND Guise Aisne Fan 1
❒ SAINT QUENTIN-LE-PETIT Ardennes Fan 1
❒ SAINT QUIRC Ariege Fan 2
❒ SAINT RAMBERT Loire Fan 7
❒ SAINT RAMBERT EN BUGEY Ain Fan 2 3 7
❒ SAINT REMY DE PROVENCE Bouches du Rhone Fan 4 7
❒ SAINT SERNIN DE DURAS Gironde Fan 2
❒ SAINT SU LPICE Tarn Fan 1 7
❒ SAINT SULPICE SUR LEZE Haute Garonne Fan 1
❒ SAINT SYMPHORIEN Indre-et-Loire Fan 7
❒ SAINT TROPEZ Var Fan 3 4 7
❒ SAINT VITH Liege Bel 14
❒ SAINT-GENOIS West Flanders Bel 1
❒ SAINT-GEORGES-SUR-MEUESE Liege Bel 1
❒ SAINT-GILLES-BRUXELLES Brabant Bel 1
❒ SAINT-HUBERT Luxembourg Bel 1
❒ SAINT-LEGER Hainaut Bel 1
❒ SAINT-MAUR Hainaut Bel 1
❒ SAINT-REMY-GEEST Brabant Bel 1
❒ SAINT-SEVERIN Liege Bel 1
❒ SAINTE CROIX Ariege Fan 1
❒ SAINTE DE SAINT VINCENTE DE PAUL Herault Fan 7
❒ SAINTE MENEHOULD Marne Fan 7
❒ SAINTE SIGOLENE Haute-Loire Fan 7
❒ SAINTES Charente Inferieure Fan 7
❒ SAKI Rus 1
❒ SAKSHAUG Nor 14
❒ SALA Consirliana Ita 3
❒ SALARDU Lerida Spa 1
❒ SALAS ALTAS Huesca Spa 2
❒ SALAS DE PALLARS Lerida Spa 1

❒ SALDINSKY (Nizhne Saldinsky) Rus 1
❒ SALEM Baden Ger 7
❒ SALEM Valencia Spa 1
❒ SALERNE Var Fan 7
❒ SALIES-DU-SALAT Haute Garonne Fan 2
❒ SALINAS Alicante Spa 2
❒ SALINDRES Gard Fan 2
❒ SALINES DU CAP-VERT Cav 6
❒ SALINS DE GIRAUD Bouches du Rhone Fan 7
❒ SALINS LES BAINS Jura Fan 7 10 14
❒ SALISBURY Rhd 14
❒ SALLANCHES Haute Savoie Fan 1 2
❒ SALLANCHES-MONT BLANC Haute Savoie Fan 1
❒ SALLENT Barcelona Spa 1
❒ SALLES-SUR-L'HERS Aude Fan 2
❒ SALLY-LEZ-LANNOY Nord Fan 1
❒ SALO Turku Ja Pori Fin 1
❒ SALOMO Tarragana Spa 1
❒ SALON Bouches-du-Rhone Fan 6
❒ SALSADELLA Castellon Spa 1
❒ SALTOS DE FLIX Tarragona Spa 1
❒ SALUSSOLE Piemonte Ita a
❒ SALVAGNAC Tarn Fan 1
❒ SALVATERRA DE MAGOS Santarem Por 1
❒ SALZBRUNN, BAD (Szczawno-Zdroj) Schlesien Ger12
❒ SALZBURG (Salzbwrg) Land and Stadt Aus 1 2 9
❒ SALZBURGHOEN Bayern Ger 1
❒ SALZDETFURTH, BAD Hannover Ger 2 14
❒ SALZGITTER Hannover Ger 2 9
❒ SALZIG BAD Rheinland Ger 1
❒ SALZUFLEN, BAD Lippe-Detmold Ger 1 10
❒ SALZUNGEN (Bad Salzungen) Thueringen Ger 16
❒ SALZWEDEL Provinz Sachsen Ger 1 2 3
❒ SAMARA Rus 1
❒ SAMARKAND Rus 1
❒ SAMATAN & LOMBEZ Fan 2
❒ SAMBOR/ DNIESTER (Sambora) Galicia Rpl 2
❒ SAMBUCA Zabut Ita 3
❒ SAMEON Nord Fan 1
❒ SAM0A Gec 2
❒ SAMOEENS Haute Savoie Fan 2
❒ SAMOSTRZEL Posen Ger 1 2
❒ SAMOTSCHIN (Szamocin) Posen Ger 1 2
❒ SAMPER DE CALANDA Teruel Spa 1
❒ SAMTER (Szamotulska, Szamotuly) Posen Ger 1
❒ SAN CARLOS DEL VALLE Ciudad Real Spa 1
❒ SAN CLEMENTE Cuenca Spa 1
❒ SAN FELICE (Verona) Ita3 14
❒ SAN FELICE Caserma Ita 3 14
❒ SAN FELICE Veneta Ita 3 14
❒ SAN GIMIGNANO Siena Ita 3
❒ SAN GIMIGNANO Toscana Ita 3
❒ SAN GIOVANNI LA PUNTA Sicilia Ita 3
❒ SAN GIOVANNI VALDARNO Avezzano Piemonte Ita. 3
❒ SAN JAVIER Murcia Spa 1 2
❒ SAN LAZARO Parmense Ita 3
❒ SAN LORENZO DE CALATRAVA Ciudad Real Spa 1
❒ SAN MIGUEL DEL SALINAS Alicante Spa 1
❒ SAN PIETRO Ita 3
❒ SAN RAFAEL DEL RIO Castellon Spa 1
❒ SAN REMO Hospital Ita 3
❒ SAN REMO Liguria Ita 3
❒ SAN SEVERINO Macerata Marche Ita 3
❒ SAN TIAGO Cav 1
❒ SAN VITO Cagliari Sardegna Ita 3
❒ SAN LAVINERA D'ANOIA (Sant Pere Sallavinera) Barcelona Spa 1
❒ SANAHUJA Lerida Spa 1
❒ SANCOURT Fan 1
❒ SANDAU/ ELBE Sachsen Ger SANDBERG (Piaski) Posen Ger 1
❒ SANDBOSTEL Bremen Ger 14
❒ SANDE Schleswig-Holstein Ger 1 2
❒ SANDEFJORD Nor 14
❒ SANDHILL PARK Grb 3
❒ SANDL OO Aus 1
❒ SANDNES Nor 14
❒ SANDOMIERZ/ SAN AND VISTULA (Sandomier, Sandomir) Rpl 1 2
❒ SANDOW (Cottbus) Pommern Ger 7
❒ SANET Y NEGRALS Alicante Spa
❒ SANGEHAUSEN Provinz Sachsen Ger 1 2 6
❒ SANIS DU NORD Nord Fan 1 2
❒ SANKT AEGIDI OO Aus 1
❒ SANKT AEGYD/ NEUWALD NO Aus 1
❒ SANKT AGATHA OO Aus 1
❒ SANKT AMARIN Elsass-Ger 1 2
❒ SANKT ANDREASBERG. Hannover Ger 1 2
❒ SANKT ANDREASBERG-SILBERHUETTE Hannover Ger. 2
❒ SANKT ANDREASBERG-WALDHAUS Hannover Ger 2
❒ SANKT AVOLD Lothringen Ger 6
❒ SANKT BLASIEN Baden Ger 1 2
❒ SANKT EGIDIEN Sachsen Ger 1 7
❒ SANKT FLORIAN GO Aus 1 2
❒ SANKT FLORIAN Steiermark Aus 1
❒ SANKT FLORIAN/ INN OO Aus 1
❒ SANKT GALLEN Steiermark Aus 1 2
❒ SANKT GEORGEN UND TOLLETT 00 Aus 1
❒ SANKT GEORGEN/ ATTERGAU OO Aus 1 2
❒ SANKT GEORGEN/ GUSEN OO Aus 1
❒ SANKT GEORGEN/ LEYS NO Aus 1
❒ SANKT GEORGEN/ REITH NO Aus 1
❒ SANKT CEORGEN/ SCHWARZWALD Baden Ger 1 6 7
❒ SANKT GEORGEN/ WALD OO Aus 1
❒ SANKT GEORGEN/ YBBSPELDE NO A 11
❒ SANKT GILGEN Salzburg Aus 1
❒ SANKT GOAR Rheinland Ger 1
❒ SANKT GOARSHAUSEN Hessen Ger 1
❒ SANKT GOARSHEIM Hessen Ger 1
❒ SANKT GOTTHARD OO Aus 1
❒ SANKT HUBERT Rheinland Ger 1
❒ SANKT INGBERT Pfalz Ger 1 9
❒ SANKT JOACHIMSTAL (Jachymov) Boehmen Cze 1
❒ SANKT J0HANN Tirol Aus 1
❒ SANKT JOHANN/ ENGSTETTEN NO Aus
❒ 'SANKT JOHANN/ PONGAU Salzburg Aus 1 2
❒ SANKT JOHANN/ WALDE OO Aus 1
❒ SANKT JOHANN/ WIMBERG OO Aus
❒ SANKT KONRAD OO Aus 1
❒ SANKT LAU RENZ OO Aus 1
❒ SANKT MAGNUS/ BREMEN Hannover Ger 1
❒ SANKT MARIEN OO Aus 1
❒ SANKT MARIENKIRCHEN AM HAUSRUCK OO Aus 1
❒ SANKT MARIENKIRCHEN BEI SCHAERDING OO Aus 1
❒ SANKT LEONHARD BEI FREISTADT 00 Aus 1
❒ SANKT LEONHARD/ FORST UND REPRECHTSHOFEN NO Aus 1
❒ SANKT LEONHARD/ WALDE NO Aus I
❒ SANKT LORENZE/ MONDSEE OO Aus 1
❒ SANKT LORENZEN Kaernten Aus 1
❒ SANKT MAGDALENA BEI LINZ OO Aus 1
❒ SANKT MARIENKIRCHEN/ POLSENZ OO Aus 1
❒ SANKT MARTIN BEI LINZ OO Aus 1
❒ SANKT MARTIN BEI TRAUN OO Aus 9
❒ SANKT MARTIN IM INNKREIS OO Aus 1
❒ SANKT MARTIN IM MUEHLKREIS OO Aus 1

❒ SANKT MARTIN UND KARLSBACH NO Aus 1
❒ SANKT NIKOLA/ DONAU OO Aus 1
❒ SANKT OSWALD NO Aus 1 2
❒ SANKT OSWALD BEI FREISTADT OO Aus 1
❒ SANKT OSWALDE BEI HASLACH OO Aus 1
❒ SANKT PANKRAZ OO Aus 1
❒ SANKT PANTALEON NO Aus 1
❒ SANKT PANTALEON OO Aus 1
❒ SANKT PETER Kaernten Aus 1
❒ SANKT PETER IN DER AU NO Aus 1
❒ SANKT PETER/ HART OO Aus 1
❒ SANKT PETER/ WIMBERG OO Aus 1
❒ SANKT POELTEN NO Aus 1 2 14
❒ SANKT ROMAN OO Aus 1
❒ SANKT SEBASTIAN BEI MARIAZELL Steiermark Aus 1
❒ SANKT STEFAN AM WALD OO Aus 1
❒ SANKT THOMAS AM BLASENSTEI N 00 Aus 1
❒ SANKT THOMAS BEI WAIZENKIRCHEN 00 Aus 1
❒ SANKT TOENIS Rheinland Ger 1
❒ SANKT ULRICH OO Aus 1
❒ SANKT VALENTIN NO Aus 1
❒ SANKT VEIT AN DER GOELSEN NO Aus 1
❒ SANKT VEIT/ MUEHLKREIS OO Aus 1
❒ SANKT VEIT/ PONGAU Salzburg Aus 1
❒ SANKT VEIT/ TRIESTING NO Aus 1
❒ SANKT WENDEL Rheinland Ger 1
❒ SANKT WI LLI BALD OO Aus 1
❒ SANKT WOLFGANG OO Aus 1
❒ SANNIKI Rpl 2
❒ SANNOIS Seine-et-Oise Fan 7
❒ SANOK Galicia Rpl 2
❒ SANT CRUZ Almeria Spa 1
❒ SANT GUIM ESTACIO (Freixanet) Lerida Spa 1
❒ SANT MARTI DEL BAS Barcelona Spa 1
❒ SANT POL DE MAR Barcelona Spa 1
❒ SANTA COMBA DAO Viseu Por 1
❒ SANTA CREU DE XUTGLAR Barcelona Spa 1
❒ SANTA CRUZ DE GRACIOSA Azs 2
❒ SANTA CRUZ DE LA ZARZA Toledo Spa 1
❒ SANTA CRUZ DE LOS CANAMOS Ciudad Libre Spa 1
❒ SANTA CRUZ DE MUDELA Ciudad Real Spa 1
❒ SANTA ELENA Jaen Spa 1
❒ SANTA EU FEM IA Cordoba Spa 1
❒ SANTA FE Almeria Spa 1
❒ SANTA LECINA Huesca Spa 1
❒ SANTA MARIA Capua Ita 3
❒ SANTA MARIA Caserta Ita 3
❒ SANTA MARIA Compania Ita 3
❒ SANTA MARIA Vetere Ita 3
❒ SANTA POLA Alicante Spa 1
❒ SANTANDER, PALENCIA Y BURGOS Santander Spa 6
❒ SANTAREM Santarem Por 1 2
❒ SANTES CREUS Tarragona Spa 2
❒ SANTIAGO DE CACEM Setubal Por 1
❒ SANTIAGO DE LA ESPADA Jaen Spa 1
❒ SANTISTEBAN DEL PUERTO Jaen Spa 2
❒ SANTO TIRSO Porto Por 1 2
❒ SANTOMISCHEL (Zaniemysl) Posen Ger 1 2
❒ SANTORENS Huesca Spa 1
❒ SANTULUSORGIO Cagliari Ita 3
❒ SANTULUSORGIO Sardegna Ita 3
❒ SAO BRAS DE ALPORTEL Faro Por 1 2
❒ SAO PEDRO DO SUL Viseu Por 2
❒ SAO ROQUE DO PICO Horta Azs 2
❒ SAO TOME Sao Tome e Principe Sap 1
❒ SAPRAIA Isola Ita 3
❒ SARAMON Gers Fan 1
❒ SARCELLES Val d'Oise Fan 1
❒ SARDANOLA-RIPOLLET Barcelona Spa 2
❒ SARDAR ABAD Rus 1
❒ SARDARA Cagliari Ita 3
❒ SARDARA Sardegna Ita 3
❒ SARDARABAD (Oktemberyan) Yerevan prov. Arm 1
❒ SARDOAL Santarem Por 1 2
❒ SAREJEVO (Serajevo) Yug 1 2
❒ SARIENA Huesca Spa 1
❒ SARLEINSBACH OO Aus 1
❒ SARMINGSTEIN IM STRUDENGAU OO Aus 2
❒ SAROSPATAK Hun 1
❒ SARPSBORG Nor 14
❒ SARRAL Tarragona Spa 1
❒ SARRE-MINES DE LA Fan 1
❒ SARRIA DE TER Gerona Spa 1
❒ SARRION Teruel Spa 1 2
❒ SARROCA DE SEGRE Lerida Spa 2 6
❒ SARS-LA-BUISSIERE Hainaut Bel 1
❒ SARS-POTERIES Nord Fan 1
❒ SARSTEDT Hannover Ger 2 7
❒ SART Liege Bel 1
❒ SASSARI Sardegna Ita 3
❒ SASSEGNIES Nord Fan 1
❒ SASSENHEIM South Holland Net 14
❒ SASSERRA Barcelona Spa 1
❒ SASTIGO Zaragoza Spa 1
❒ SATORALJAUJIHELY (Gruenhut) Hun 1
❒ SATRUP (Sottrup, Denmark) Schleswig-Holstein Ger 1
❒ SATTLERN OO Aus 1
❒ SATZUNG Sachsen Ger 1
❒ SAUDA Nor 14
❒ SAULGAU Wuerttemberg Ger 1 2 6
❒ SAULTAIN Fan 11
❒ SAULZOIR Nord Fan 7
❒ SAUPERSDORF Sachsen Ger 1 2
❒ SAVERDUN Ariege Fan 2
❒ SAVIGLIANO Hospital Ita 3
❒ SAVONA Genova Ita 3
❒ SAVONA Liguria Ita 3
❒ SAVY Fan 1
❒ SAX Alicante Spa 1
❒ SAYDA Sachsen Ger 1
❒ SCANDIANO Emilia Ita 3
❒ SCANDIANO Reggio Emilia Ita 3
❒ SCARPANTO Isola Ita 3
❒ SCHAALA Schwarzburg-Rudolstadt Ger 1
❒ SCHAEDLITZ/ PLESS Schlesien Ger 2
❒ SCHAERDING/ INN OO Aus 1
❒ SCHAESBERG Limburg Net 1
❒ SCHAESSBURG (Sighisoara) Rom 2
❒ SCHAFSTAEDT Provinz Sachsen Ger 1 2
❒ SCHALCHEN OO Aus 1
❒ SCHALKAU Sachsen-Meiningen Ger 1
❒ SCHALKSMUEHLE Westfalen Ger 7
❒ SCHANDAU BAD Sachsen Ger 1
❒ SCHANZ OO Aus 1
❒ SCHARDENBERG OO Aus 1
❒ SCHARFENORT (Ostrorog) Posen Ger 1
❒ SCHARLEY (Szarlej) Schlesien Ger 1 2 7 9
❒ SCHARMBECK (Osterholz-Scharmbeck) Hannover Ger 1 7
❒ SCHARNHORST/ DORTMAND Westfalen Ger 4
❒ SCHARTEN OO Aus 1
❒ SCHATTLEITEN UND SCHWEINSEGG OO Aus 1
❒ SCHAUBERG Bayern Ger 2
❒ SCHAUENSTEIN/ OBERNKIRCHEN Hessen-Nassau Ger 1 2 7
❒ SCHAUMBURG Hessen-Nassau Ger 1
❒ SCHAUMBURG Lippe Ger 1
❒ SCHAUMBURG-LIPPE Ger 1
❒ SCHEESSEL Hannover Ger 1
❒ SCHEIBBS NO Aus 1
❒ SCHEIBENBERG Sachsen Ger 1
❒ SCHEIDEGG/ ALLGAUE Bayern Ger 14
❒ SCHELEJEWO (Szelejewo) Posen Ger 1

❒ SCHELLENBERG Sachsen Ger 1
❒ SCHELSEN Rheinland Ger 1
❒ SCHENKENFELDEN OO Aus 1
❒ SCHERMBECK Rheinland Ger 1
❒ SCHERPENHEUVEL (Schaarbeek, Montaigu) Brabant Bel 1
❒ SCHERREBECK (Skaerbaek, Denmark) Scheswig-Holstein Ger 1
❒ SCHIEDAM South Holland Net 8 14
❒ SCHIEFBAHN Rheinland Ger 1
❒ SCHIERAU/ DOMBROWKA Posen Ger 2
❒ SCHIERKE Provinz Sachsen Ger 2
❒ SCHIFFBEK (Hamburg) Scheswig-Holstein Ger 2 7 13
❒ SCHIFFERSTADT Pfalz Ger 1
❒ SCHIFFWEILER/ SAAR Rheinland Ger 1
❒ SCHILDBERG Nor 14
❒ SCHILDBERG (Ostrzeszow) Posen Ger 1
❒ SCHILDHORST/ FREDEN Hannover Ger 1 2
❒ SCHILDORN OO Aus 1
❒ SCHILTACH Baden Ger 1 2
❒ SCHIRGISWALDA Sachsen Ger 1 2
❒ SCHIRMECK/ MOLSHEIM Elsass Ger 1
❒ SCHIRNDING Bayern Ger 2
❒ SCHIRRHEIN BEI HAGENAU Elsass Ger 1
❒ SCHIVELBEIN (Slawno, Swidwin) Pommern Ger 1
❒ SCHKEUDITZ Provinz Sachsen Ger 1
❒ SCHLAEGL OO Aus 1
❒ SCHLAG/ GABLONZ (Gablonz-Jablonec nad Nisou, Czechoslovakia) Hun 9
❒ SCHLAG/ NISOU (Jablonekce Paseky) Boehmen Cze 2
❒ SCHLAWE (Slawno) Pommern Ger 1 6
❒ SCHLEBUSCH Rheinland Ger 1 2
❒ SCHLEBUSCH-MONTFORT (Schlebusch-Manfort) Rheinland Ger 2
❒ SCHLEID Rheinland Ger 2
❒ SCHLEIDEN Rheinland Ger 1
❒ SCHLEISSHEIM OO Aus 1
❒ SCHLEIZ Reuss J.L. Ger 1 2 7 13
❒ SCHLESIENGRUBE (Chropaczow) Ger 1 2 3 5
❒ SCHLESIENGRUBE (Kopalnia Slask) Schlesien Ger 1 2 3 5
❒ SCHLESWIG Schleswig-Holstein Ger 1 2 3 10
❒ SCHLESWIG-HOLSTEIN Ger 1 7
❒ SCHLETTAU Sachsen Ger 1
❒ SCHLETTSTADT (Selestat) Elsass Ger 1 6
❒ SCHLEUSINGEN Thueringen Ger 1 2 7
❒ SCHLICHT Bayern Ger 2
❒ SCHLICHT Oberpfalz Ger 2
❒ SCHLIERBACH (Brachttal) Hessen-Nassau Ger 1 7 13
❒ SCHLIERBACH OO Aus 1
❒ SCHLIERSEE Bayern Ger 1
❒ SCHLITZ Hessen-Nassau Ger 7
❒ SCHLOCHAU (Schochau, Czluchow) Westpreussen Ger 1
❒ SCHLOSSVIPPACH Sachsen-Weimar-Eisenach Ger 1
❒ SCHLOTHEIM Thueringen Ger 1 2
❒ SCHLUCKENAU (Sluknov) Boehmen Cze 1
❒ SCHLUECHTERN Hessen-Nassau Ger 1
❒ SCHMALKALDEN Hessen-Nassau Ger 1 2 6 7
❒ SCHMALLENBERG Wastfalen Ger 1
❒ SCHMIEDEBERG/ RIESENGBIRGE (Bad Schmiedeberg, Kowary) Schlesien Ger 1 2
❒ SCHMIEDEBERG, BAD (Eisenmoorbad) Provinz Sachsen Ger 1 2 6 7
❒ SCHMIEDEFELD Provinz Sachsen Ger 1 2 6 7 9
❒ SCHMIEGEL (Szmigiel, Smigiel) Posen Ger 1 2 6
❒ SCHMOELLN Sachsen Altenburg Ger 1 2 6
❒ SCHMOELZ (Kueps) Bayern Ger 6 7
❒ SCHNEEBERG Bayern Ger 1
❒ SCHNEEBERG-NEUSTAEDTEL Sachsen Ger 1 2
❒ SCHNEEBERG/ ERZGEBIRGE Sachsen Ger 1 8
❒ SCHNEIDEMUEHL (Pila) Posen Ger 1 3 4 6
❒ SCHNELSEN Schleswig-Holstein Ger 1
❒ SCHNEUZLREIT Aus 2
❒ SCHNEVERDINGEN Hannover Ger 1
❒ SCHNUFENHOFEN Bayern Ger 6
❒ SCHOBUELL Schleswig-Holstein Ger 1
❒ SCHOEMBERG (Szombierki, Szymrych) Schlesien Ger 1 2 5
❒ SCHOENAICH/ STUTTGART Wuerttemberg Ger 7
❒ SCHOENAU NO Aus 1
❒ SCHOENAU IM MUEHLKREIS OO Aus 1
❒ SCHOENAU-SCHALLERBACH OO Aus 1
❒ SCHOENAU/ CHEMNITZ Sachsen Ger 2
❒ SCHOENAU/ KATZBACH (Swierzawa, Glatz) Schlesien Ger 1 2
❒ SCHOENAU/ TRIESTING NO Aus 1
❒ SCHOENAU/ WIESEN Baden Ger 1 2
❒ SCHOENBACH (Krasna) Cze 2
❒ SCHOENBACH Sachsen Ger 1 2
❒ SCHOENBERG (Sumperk/ Desse, Sumburk Maehrisch) Cze 1 2
❒ SCHOENBERG Liege Bel 14
❒ SCHOENBERG Mecklinburg-Strelitz Ger 1 7
❒ SCHOENBERG OO Aus 1
❒ SCHOENBERG O.L. (Sulikow) Schlesien Ger 1 2
❒ SCHOENBERG/ GRAFENAU Bayern Ger 6 7
❒ SCHOENBERG/ LANDSHUT (Schoemberg, Szombierki, Szymbork, Szymrych, Sulikow) Schlesien Ger 1 2 5
❒ SCHOENBICHL NO Aus 1
❒ SCHOENBUEHEL/ DONAU NO Aus 1
❒ SCHOENEBECK & GROSS-SALZA Provinz Sachsen Ger 1
❒ SCHOENEBECK/ ELBE Provinz Sachsen Ger 1 2
❒ SCHOENECK (Skarzcewy, Skarszewy) Westpreussen Ger 1 7
❒ SCHOENECK/ VOGTLAND Sachsen Ger 1 6 7
❒ SCHOENECKEN-WETTELDORF Rheinland Ger 1
❒ SCHOENENBERG Nordhein-Westfalen Ger 14
❒ SCHOENENBUCHEN Baden Ger 1
❒ SCHOENENTHAL Rheinland Ger 2
❒ SCHOENFELD/ GLATZ (Klodzka) Schlesien Ger 1 2 7
❒ SCHOENFELD/ ZSCHOPAUTAL Sachsen Ger 1 2 7
❒ SCHOENFLIESS (Trzeinsko-Zdroj) Brandenburg Ger 6
❒ SCHOENHAGEN Hannover Ger 2 7
❒ SCHOENHEIDE Sachsen Ger 1 2
❒ SCHOENINGEN Braunschweig Ger 7
❒ SCHOENINGSDORF Hannover Ger 2
❒ SCHOENLANKE (Trzcianka) Posen Ger 1 6 7
❒ SCHOENTHAL Schlesien Ger 2
❒ SCHOENWALD Bayern Ger 1 2 6
❒ SCHOEPPENSTAEDT Braunschweig Ger 1
❒ SCHOERFLING AM ATTERSEEOO Aus 1
❒ SCHOETMAR Lippe Ger 1
❒ SCHOKKEN (Skoki) Posen Ger 1
❒ SCHOLVEN Westfalen Ger 3
❒ SCHONAICH/ STUTTGART Baden Ger 7
❒ SCHONDORF Ammersee Ger 14
❒ SCHONDORF Bayern Ger 14
❒ SCHONFLIESS/ ODER Brandenburg Ger 6
❒ SCHONGAU Bayern Ger 1 7
❒ SCHONINGEN Braunschweig Ger 7
❒ SCHOORISSE East Flanders Bel 1
❒ SCHOOTEN Antwerp Bel 1
❒ SCHOPFHEIM Baden Ger 1 2 7
❒ SCHOPPNITZ (Szopienice) Schlesien Ger 2
❒ SCHORNDORF Wuerttemberg Ger 1 2 7
❒ SCHOTTEN Hessen Ger 1
❒ SCHRAM BERG Wuerttemberg Ger 1 2 6 7 8 9 13

- ❒ SCHREIBERHAU (Szklarska Poreba) Schlesien Ger 1 7
- ❒ SCHREMS NO Aus 1
- ❒ SCHRETZHEIM Bayern Ger 7
- ❒ SCHRIESHEIM Baden Ger 1
- ❒ SCHRIMM (Srem) Posen Ger 1
- ❒ SCHROBENHAUSEN Bayern Ger 1 2 6
- ❒ SCHRODA (Sroda) Posen Ger 1 2 6
- ❒ SCHUBIN (Szubin) Posen Ger 1
- ❒ SCHUEREN/ HOERDE Westfalen Ger 3 5
- ❒ SCHUETTORF Hannover Ger 1
- ❒ SCHUETZENDORF (Wilemowice, Strzawa) Schlesien Ger 7
- ❒ SCHULITZ (Solec) Posen Ger 1
- ❒ SCHULTERZUCKER OO Aus 1
- ❒ SCH USSEN RI ED Wuerttemberg Ger 2
- ❒ SCHWAAN Mecklenburg-Schwerin Ger 1
- ❒ SCHWABACH Bayern Ger 1 2 7
- ❒ SCHWABEN UND NEUBURG Bayern Ger 1
- ❒ SCHWABEN/ ERDING Bayern Ger 2
- ❒ SCHWABMUENCHEN Bayern Ger 1
- ❒ SCHWABSTEDT Schleswig-Holstein Ger 2
- ❒ SCHWADORF NO Aus 2
- ❒ SCHWAEBISCH GMUEND Wuerttemberg Ger 1 2 7
- ❒ SCHWAEBISCH HALL Wuerttemberg Ger 1 2 6
- ❒ SCHWALLENBACH/ DONAU NO Aus 1
- ❒ SCHWAND IM INNKREIS OO Aus 2
- ❒ SCHWANDORF-WACKERSDORF Bayern Ger 2
- ❒ SCHWANDORF/ OBERPFALZ Bayern Ger 1 2 7 9
- ❒ SCHWANEBECK Provinz Sachsen Ger 1 2
- ❒ SCHWANENSTADT OO Aus. 1
- ❒ SCHWARMSTEDT Hannover Ger 4
- ❒ SCHWARZA/ SAALE Schwarzburg-Rudolstadt Ger 1
- ❒ SCHWARZACH IM PONGAU Salzburg Aus 1
- ❒ SCHWARZBURG Schwarzburg-Rudolstadt Ger 1 7
- ❒ SCHWARZBURG Schwarzburg-Sonderhausen Ger 6
- ❒ SCHWARZBURG-SONDERHAUSEN Ger 6
- ❒ SCHWARZENAU NO Aus 1
- ❒ SCHWARZENBACH/ SAALE Bayern Ger 1 2 6
- ❒ SCHWARZENBECK Schleswig-Holstein Ger 2
- ❒ SCHWARZENBERG OO Aus 1
- ❒ SCHWARZENBERG Sachsen Ger 1 2 7 14
- ❒ SCHWARZENFELD Bayem Ger 2
- ❒ SCHWARZENHAMMER Bayern Ger 2
- ❒ SCHWARZENTHAL OO Aus 1
- ❒ SCHWARZFELD Niedersachsen Ger 14
- ❒ SCHWARZGRAEBEN OO Aus 1
- ❒ SCHWARZHOFEN, Bayern Ger 1
- ❒ SCHWARZWALDAU Schlesien Ger 2
- ❒ SCHWAZ Tirol Aus 1
- ❒ SCHWECHAT NO Aus 9
- ❒ SCHWEDT/ ODER Brandenburg Ger 1 2
- ❒ SCHWEGENHEIM Pfalz Ger 1
- ❒ SCHWEICH/ MOSEL Rheinland Ger 2
- ❒ SCHWEIDNITZ (Swidnica) Schlesien Ger 1 2 3 4
- ❒ SCHWEINA Thueringen Ger 1
- ❒ SCHWEINFURT Bayern Ger 1 2 6 7 11 12
- ❒ SCHWEINITZ Provinz-Sachsen Ger 1
- ❒ SCHWEIZERTAL Sachsen Ger 2
- ❒ SCHWENNINGEN/ NECKAR Wuerttemberg Ger 1 2 7
- ❒ SC14WEPNITZ Sachsen Ger 1
- ❒ SCHWERIN Mecklinburg-Schwerin Ger 1 2 6 12
- ❒ SCHWERIN/ WARTHE (Kierszkowo, Skwierzyna) Posen Ger 1 2 6 7
- ❒ SCHWERSENZ (Swarzedz) Posen Ger 1
- ❒ SCHWERTBERG OO Aus 1
- ❒ SCHWERTE Westfalen Ger 2 3 7 15
- ❒ SCHWETZ (Swiecie) Westpreussen Ger 1
- ❒ SCHWETZINGEN Baden Ger 1 8
- ❒ SCHWIEBUS (Swiebodzin, Poland) Brandenburg Ger 1 2
- ❒ SCHWIECHELDT/ PEINE Hannover Ger 2
- ❒ SCHWIENTOCHLOWITZ (Swietochlowice) Schlesien Ger 1 2 3 5
- ❒ SCHWOEDIAU OO Aus 1
- ❒ SCIACCA Ita 3
- ❒ SCORDEVOLE Novara Ita 3
- ❒ SCORDEVOLE Piamonte Ita 3
- ❒ SCORZE Carelle Ita 3
- ❒ SEAUVE, LA Haute Loire Fan 7
- ❒ SEBAS,TIANSBERG (Hora Sv Sebestiana) Cze 1
- ❒ SEBNITZ Sachsen Ger 1 2 8 13
- ❒ SEBONCOURT Aisne Fan 1
- ❒ SECLIN Nord Fan 1
- ❒ SEDAN Ardermes Fan 1
- ❒ SEDAVI Valencia Spa 1
- ❒ SEDIERES Correze Fan 4
- ❒ SEDLCANY Cze 1
- ❒ SEDLEC Cze 1
- ❒ SEEBACH Sachsen-Weimar-Eisenach Ger 7
- ❒ SEEBERGEN Sachsen, -Coburg-Gotha Ger 7
- ❒ SEEBURG (Jeziorany) Ostpreussen Ger 1
- ❒ SEEGEFELD (Falkensee) Brandenburg Ger 7
- ❒ SEEHAUSEN/ ALTMARK Provinz Sachsen Ger 1
- ❒ SEEHEIM (Jeziorki) Posen Ger 2
- ❒ SEEKIRCHEN Salzburg Aus 1
- ❒ SEELINGSTAEDT/ GRIMMA Sachsen Ger 2
- ❒ SEELZE Hannover Ger 7
- ❒ SEESEN Braunschweig Ger 2 8
- ❒ SEETH Schleswig-Holstein Ger 1
- ❒ SEETH-ECKHOLT Schleswig-Holstein Ger 1
- ❒ SEEWALCHEN AM ATTERSEE OO Aus 1
- ❒ SEFFERN/ EIFEL Rheinland Ger 2
- ❒ SEGARRA DE GAIA (Santa Coloma de Queralt) Tarragona Spa. 1 6
- ❒ SEGEBERG BAD Schleswig-Holstein Ger 12 6 8
- ❒ SEGURIES DE TER Gerona Spa 1
- ❒ SEHMA Sachsen Ger 1 7
- ❒ SEHNDE Hannover Ger 2
- ❒ SEIDENBERG O.L. (Zawidow) Schlesien Ger 1 2
- ❒ SEIFERSDORF/ RADEBERG Sachsen Ger 2
- ❒ SEIFFEN Sachsen Ger 1
- ❒ SEIFHENNERSDORF Sachsen Ger 1 2
- ❒ SEILLES Liege Bel 1
- ❒ SEIRA Huesca Spa 1
- ❒ SEITENBERG/ GLATZ (Stronie Slaskie) Schlesien Ger 1 6 14
- ❒ SEITENDORF/ DRESDEN Sachsen Ger 2
- ❒ SEITENDORF/ GLATZ Schlesien Ger 2
- ❒ SEITENSTETTEN NO Aus 1
- ❒ SEIXAL Setubal Por 1
- ❒ SELB Bayern Ger 1 2 6 13
- ❒ SELBITZ Bayern Ger 2
- ❒ SELBU Nbr 14
- ❒ SELESNEVKA Rus 1
- ❒ SELGUA Huesca Spa 1
- ❒ SELIGENSTADT Hessen Ger 1 7
- ❒ SELLIN/ RUEGEN Pommern Ger 1
- ❒ SELM Westfalen Ger 5 7
- ❒ SELSBAK Nor 14
- ❒ SELSINGEN Hannover Ger 1
- ❒ SELTERS Rheinland Ger 14
- ❒ SELVA DE MAR Gerona Spa 1
- ❒ SELVA DEL CAMP, LA Tarragona Spa 1
- ❒ SELZTAL Steiermark Aus 1 9
- ❒ SEMINARIO SAN GIOVANNI Ita 3
- ❒ SEMIPALATINSK Rus 1
- ❒ SEMPIGNY Oisne Fan 1
- ❒ SENA Huesca Spa 1
- ❒ SENDALAMULA-CARACOLLERA Ciudad Real Spa 2
- ❒ SENDEN Bayern Ger 2
- ❒ SENEGAL Sen 1 6
- ❒ SENFTENBACH OO Aus 1
- ❒ SENFTENBERG Brandenburg Ger 1 2
- ❒ SENFTENBERG NO Aus 1
- ❒ SENGHILEI (Sengilei) Rus 1
- ❒ SENIA, LA Tarragona Spa 1

❒ SIENLIS Oise Fan 11
❒ SENNE Westfalen Ger 3 4 7
❒ SENNHEIM Elsass Ger 1 2
❒ SENONES Vosges Fan 6
❒ SENS Yonne Fan 1
❒ SENSBURG (Mragowo O.L.) Ostpreussen Ger 1 6
❒ SENTEIN Ariege Fan 3 14
❒ SENTERADA Lerida Spa 1
❒ SENTIU, LA Lerida Spa 1
❒ SENTMENAT Barcelona Spa 1
❒ SEPOLNO (Krainski, Zempelburg) Rpl 1
❒ SEPPENRADE Westfalen Ger 3
❒ SEPSISZENTGYOERGYOEN (Sfintu Gheorghe) Transylvania Rom 1
❒ SEPTFONDS Tarn-et-Garonne Fan 7
❒ SERAIN Aisne Fan 1
❒ SERAING-SUR-MEUSE Liege Bel 1 2
❒ SERGINSKIZAVOD Rus 1
❒ SERGLUINSK-GUFALEISK Rus 1
❒ SERMANCELHE Viseu Por 1
❒ SERON Almeria Spa 1
❒ SEROS Lerida 1 2
❒ SERPA BeJa For 1 2
❒ SERRA D'ALMOS Tarragona Spa 1
❒ SERVIAN Herault Fan 7
❒ SERVIEReS Correze Fan 3 4
❒ SERVIGLIANO Ascoli Ita 3
❒ SERY-LES-MEZIERES Aisne Fan 1
❒ SESGARRIGUES DEL IPENFDES (Sant Cugat Sesgarrigues) Barcelona Spa 2
❒ SESROVIRES Barcelona Spa 1
❒ SESUEIOLES Barcelona Spa 1
❒ SETIF Setif Alg 7
❒ SETLA Y MIRARROSA Alicante Spa 1
❒ SETTE Fan 1
❒ SETTRUP (Hoexter) Westfalen Ger 11
❒ SETUBAL Setubal Por 1 2
❒ SEU D'URGELLLA (Seo de Urge) Lerida Spa 1 2
❒ SEVA Barcelona Spa 1
❒ SFVASTOPIL (Sevastopol, Sebastorpol) Rus 1
❒ SEVENEEKEN East Flanders Bel 1
❒ SEVER DO VOUGA Aveiro Por 2
❒ SEVERINSBERG Rhein provinz Ger 11
❒ SEVILLEJA DE LA JARA Toledo Spa 1
❒ SEVLUS VELKY (Szoelloes Nagyszoelloes) Cze 2
❒ SEVRES Seine-et-Oise Fan 6
❒ SEYCHES Lot et Garonne Fan 2
❒ SEZAN NE Marne Fan 7
❒ SHALYGINO (Schalygina) Rus 1
❒ SHANGHAI Chi 11
❒ SHCHERBI.NOVKA (Dzerzhinsk, Chtcherbinovka) Rus 1
❒ SHCHERKOV (Shchertovsov, Szczercow, Chtchertsov) Rus 1
❒ SHENKURSK (Chenkoursk, Chenkursk) Rus 1
❒ SHEPETOVKA (Schepetovka, Chepetovka) Rus 1
❒ SHUYA (Schuja) Rus 1
❒ SIADI (Siady) Rus 1
❒ SIDI-BEL-ABBES Oran Alg 1 2 7
❒ SIEBENLEHN Sachsen Ger 2
❒ SIEBIGERODE Provinz Sachsen Ger 2
❒ SIEBLEBEN Sachsen-Gotha Ger 1
❒ SIEDENBURG Hannover Ger 2
❒ SIEDING OO Aus 1
❒ SIEDLCE (Sedletz) Rpl 1
❒ SIEDLINGHAUSEN Westfalen Ger 2
❒ SIEGBURG Rheinland Ger 1 8 14
❒ SIEGEN Westfalen Ger 1 2 6 8
❒ SIEGERSLEBEN Provinz Sachsen Ger 2
❒ SIEGKREIS Rheinland Ger 1 2
❒ SIEGMAR Sachsen Ger 1 2 8
❒ SIEMIANOWITZ (Siemianowice) Schlesien Ger 1 2 3
❒ SIEMIANOWITZ-GEORGSHUETTE (Siemianowice-Huta Jerzy) Schlesien Ger 2
❒ SIEMIANOWITZ-LAURAHUETTA (Siemianowice-Huta Laura) Schlesien Ger 2
❒ SIERADZ (Seradz) Rus 1
❒ SIERADZ/ WARTA (Sieraje, Seradz, Schieratz) Rpl 1 2
❒ SIERNING OO Aus 1
❒ SIERPC (Sichelberg) Rpl 2
❒ SIERPC (Sierpec, Serpets) Rus 1
❒ SIERRO Almeria Spa 2
❒ SIERSLESEN Provinz SachsenGer 2 6 11
❒ SIERSZA (Sierszy) Schlesien Ger 2
❒ SIEZENHEIM Salzburg Aus 1
❒ SIGEAN Aude Fan 6
❒ SIGHARTING OO Aus 1
❒ SIGHETUL MARMATIEI Rom 2
❒ SIGMARINGEN Hohenzollern Ger 1 6 7
❒ SIGMUNDSHERBERG NO Aus 1 3
❒ SIGOLSHEIM Elsass Ger 1
❒ SILACH Westfalen Ger 1
❒ SILBERBERG (Srebrna) Schlesien Ger 1
❒ SILBERHUTTE Anhalt Ger 2 7
❒ SILENRIEUX Namur Bel 2
❒ SILES Jaen Spa 2
❒ SILJAN Nor 14
❒ SILS Gerona Spa 1
❒ SILSCHEDE Westfalen Ger 2
❒ SILVES Faro Por 1 2
❒ SIMAT DE VALLDIGNA Valencia Spa 1
❒ SIM BACH/ INN Bayern Ger 1 2 6
❒ SIMEBURSK (Simbirsk) Rus 1
❒ SIMFEROPOL Rus 1 2
❒ SIMMERN Rheinland Ger 1 3
❒ SIMORRE-ET-VILLEFRANCHE Gers Fan 2
❒ SIMPELVELD Limburg Net 14
❒ SIMSK (Sim, Simski Zavod) Rus 1
❒ SIN-LE-NOBLE Nord Fan 1
❒ SINAAI-WAAS East Flanders Bel 1 14
❒ SINCENY Fan 1
❒ SINDELBURG NO Aus 1
❒ SIN Di Est 2
❒ SINES Setubal For 1
❒ SINGEN Baden Ger 1 7
❒ SINGEN-HOHENTWIEL Baden Ger 1 2
❒ SINGHOFEN Hessen-Nassau Ger 7
❒ SINNAI Sardegna Ila 3
❒ SINSHEIM/ ELSENZ Baden Ger 2 6
❒ SINT-AMANDS Antwerp Bel 1
❒ SINT-ANDRIES West Flanders Bel 1
❒ SINT-BLASIUS-BOUCLE East Flanders Bel 1
❒ SINT-CORNELIS-HOOREBEKE East Flanders Bel 1
❒ SINT-GILLIS-BIJ-DENDERMONDE East Flanders Bel 1
❒ SINT-GILLIS-WAAS East Flanders Bel 1
❒ SINT-HUIBRECHTS-ILILLE Limbourg Bel 1
❒ SINT-LENAARTS Antwerp Bel 1
❒ SINT-LIEVENS-HOUTEM East Flanders Bel 1
❒ SINT-MICHIELS West Flanders Bel 2
❒ SINT-NIKOLAAS-WAAS East fLanders Bel 1 14
❒ SINT-PAUWELS-WAAS East Flanders Bel 1
❒ SINT-PIETERS-LEEUW Brabant Bel 1
❒ SINT-TRUIDEN Limbourg Bel 1 14
❒ SINTE-KATHELIJNE-WAVER Antwerp Bel 11
❒ SINTE-KRUIS West Flanders Bel 1
❒ SINTRA Lisboa Por 1
❒ SINZIG Rheinland Ger 1 2 6
❒ SIPBACHZELL OO Aus 1
❒ SIPPENAEKEN Liege-Bel 14
❒ SIRADAN Hautes Pyrenees 'Fan 2
❒ SIRAN Herault Fan 7
❒ SIRDALSVATNET Nor 14
❒ SIREVAG Nor 14
❒ SIRNES Nor 14
❒ SISANTE Cuenca Spa 1 2
❒ SITGES Barcelona Spa 1 2
❒ SITTENDORF NO Aus 1
❒ SITZENBERG NO Aus 1
❒ SITZENDORF Thueringen Ger 2
❒ SIVRY Hainaut Bel 1
❒ SKAERBAEK (Scherrebeck) Den 1
❒ SKAEVINGE Den 11
❒ SKALA PODALS-KAYA (Skala nad, Zbruczem) Rus 1
❒ SKALICA Cze 2

❒ SKALMIERSCHUETZ (Skalmierzyce) Posen Ger 1 3 4
❒ SKALOLCZA (Slowakel, Skalicz, Hungary, Skalica, Czechoslovakia)Hungary Hun 2
❒ SKANDERBORG Den 11
❒ SKATVAL Nor 14
❒ SKELUND Den 11
❒ SKERKSENY Hun 1
❒ SKIEN Nor 14
❒ SKIVE Den 11
❒ SKJEBERG Nor 14
❒ SKJERN Den 11
❒ SKOBELEV (Fergana, Skobelef) Rus 1 3
❒ SKOGN Nor 14
❒ SKUDENESHAMN Nor 14
❒ SKURZ (Skorcz, Skurcz) Westpreussen Ger 1 2
❒ SLAVUSCHA Rus 1
❒ SLAVYANSK (Slaviansk) Rus 1
❒ SLAWKOW Rpl 2
❒ SLAWSK Rpl 2
❒ SLIDEDRECHT South Holland Net 14
❒ SLIKKERVEER Net 14
❒ SLOMOWO Posen Ger 7
❒ SLUPCA (Slouptsy, Sloutsk) Rus 1
❒ SLUPCA (Slouptsy) Posen Ger 2
❒ SMEDEREVO Ser 1
❒ SMELA Rus 1
❒ SMIGIEL Rpl 1
❒ SMOLENSK Rus 1
❒ SNEJNY Rus 1
❒ SOBERNHEIM Rheinland Ger 1
❒ SOBESLAV Cze 1
❒ SOCHI (Stochi) Rus 1
❒ SOCIETE NORMANDE de Meltallurgie Fan 3
❒ SOCOVOS Albacete Spa 1
❒ SOCUELLAMOS Ciudad Libre Spa 1
❒ SODENTORF (Bad Soden) Hessen-Nassau Ger 7
❒ SODINGEN (Herne) Westfalen Ger 1 2 3 5
❒ SOELDE (Dortmund) Westfalen Ger 2 5
❒ SOEMMERDA Provinz Sachsen Ger 1 6 7
❒ SOENDER SEJERSLEV (Seierslev) Den 2
❒ SOENDERBORG Den 1 12
❒ SOEN DERBORG-AABEN RAA Den 11
❒ SOENDERBY Den 11
❒ SOENDERHO Den 11
❒ SOENDERSKOV (Suederholz) Den 1
❒ SOERGJAESLINGAN Nor 14
❒ SOERNEWITZ/ MEISSEN (Coswig) Sachsen Ger 7
❒ SOERUP Schleswig-Holstein Ger 1 14
❒ SOEST Utrecht Net 14
❒ SOEST Westfalen Ger 1 2 3 6 7
❒ SOHEIT-TINLOT (Soheit-Tinlet) Liege Bel 1
❒ SOHLAND/ SPREE Sachsen Ger 1 2 7
❒ SOHRAU (Zory) Schlesien Ger 1
❒ SOHREN Rheinland Ger 7 14
❒ SOIGNIES Hainaut Bel 1 2
❒ SOKAL/ BUG Galicia Rpl 1
❒ SOLANA, LA Ciudad Real Spa 1
❒ SOLDAU (Dzialdowo) Ostpreussen Ger 6 10
❒ SOLDEN (Mysliborz, Poland) Brandenburg Ger 1
❒ SOLDIN N.M. (Mysliborz) Brandenburg Ger 1 6
❒ SOLEC (Schulitz, Solecka) Posen Ger 1
❒ SOLERA Jaen Spa 1
❒ SOLERAS, EL Lerida Spa 1
❒ SOLESMES Nord Fan 1 7
❒ SOLI VELLA Tarragona Spa 2
❒ SOLIKAMSK Rus 1
❒ SOLINGEN Rheinland Ger 1 2 6 7 11 12 14
❒ SOLINGEN-WEYER Rheinland Ger 2
❒ SOLLANA Valencia Spa 1
❒ SOLNHOFEN Bayern Ger 1
❒ SOLRE-LE-CHATEAU Nord Fan 6
❒ SOLRE-SUR-SAMBRE Hainaut Bel 1
❒ SOLSONA Lerida Spa 1
❒ SOLTAU Hannover Ger 1 2 7
❒ SOMAIN EN OSTREVENT Nord Fan 1
❒ SOMMEREIN (Samorin, Somorja) Cze 3
❒ SOMMERFELD (Lubsko, Poland) Brandenburg Ger 1
❒ SOMMERHAUSEN Bayern Ger 6
❒ SOMMEVOIRE Haute Marne Fan 1 2 14
❒ SOMMIERES Gard Fan 7
❒ SOMONTIN Almeria Spa 1 2
❒ SOMORJA Hun 3
❒ SOMPOLNO Rus 1
❒ SONDERBURG (Soenderborg, Denmark) Schleswig-Holstein Ger 1 2 7
❒ SONDERNACH Elsass Ger 1
❒ SONDERNHEIM Pfalz Ger 1
❒ SONDERSHAUSEN Schwarzburg-Sondershausen Ger 1 2 7
❒ SONNBERG OO Aus 1
❒ SONNBERG Salzburg Aus 1
❒ SONNEBERG Thueringen Ger 1 2 6 7
❒ SONNENBURG/ NEUMARK Sachsen Ger 2
❒ SONNTAGSBERG NO Aus 1
❒ SONSBECK Rheinland Ger 2
❒ SONSECA CON CASALGORDO Toledo Spa 1
❒ SONTHEIN/ N Wuerttemberg Ger 1 2
❒ SONTHOFEN Bayern Ger 6
❒ SONTHOFEN-IMMENSTADT Bayern Ger 1
❒ SONTRA Hessen Ger 1
❒ SOOCHOW (Wuhsien, Wu-shi) Chi 11
❒ SOODEN/ WERRA (Bad) Hessen-Nassau Ger 1
❒ SOPRONNYEK (Sopron, Oldenburg, Germany) Hun 3
❒ SORAU N.L. (Zary, Poland) Brandenburg Ger 1 11
❒ SORBAS Almeria Spa 1
❒ SORGUES Vaucluse Fan 7
❒ SORT Lerida Spa 1
❒ SOS Lot et Garonne Fan 1
❒ SOSES Lerida Spa 1
❒ SOSNOWIEC (Sosnowice, Sosnovitsy) Schlesien Ger 2
❒ SOSOYE Namur Bel 1
❒ SOTTEVILLE-LES-ROUEN Fan 3
❒ SOTTORF Niedersachsen Ger 14
❒ SOTTRUP Den 1
❒ SOUDJENKA (Sudzhenka) Rus 1
❒ SOUILLAC Lot Fan 2
❒ SOULAC-SUR-MER Gironde Fan 7
❒ SOURE Coimbra Por 1 2
❒ SOUS REGION Economique d'Orleans Fan 1
❒ SOUTCHAN (Sutchan) Rus 1
❒ SOUVRET Hainaut Bel 1
❒ SOUZEL Portalegre Por 1
❒ SPA Liege Bel 1 14
❒ SPAICHINGEN Wuerttemberg Ger 1 8
❒ SPANDAU Brandenburg Ger 1 7 8 12 14
❒ SPANGDAHLEM Rheinland Ger 10
❒ SPANGENBERG Hessen-Nassau Ger 14
❒ SPARBACH NO Aus 1
❒ SPARBU Nor 14
❒ SPARNECK Bayern Ger 1
❒ SPEICHER/ EIFEL Rheinland Ger 1 2
❒ SPETZERFEHN/ OSTFR. Hannover Ger 2
❒ SPEYER/ RHEIN Pfalz Ger 1 6 7 8 14
❒ SPIEGELAU Bayern Ger 7
❒ SPILLUM/ NAMDALEN Nor 14
❒ SPINETO DI CASTELLAMIENTE Ita 14
❒ SPINNMUEHLE-REICHENBACH/ Vogtland Sachsen Ger 2
❒ SPITAL/ PHYRN OO Aus 1
❒ SPITTAL/ DRAU Carinthia Aus 14
❒ SPITZ/ DONAU NO Aus 1
❒ SPITZKUNNERSDORF Sachsen Ger 2
❒ SPLIT (Spalto, Spljet) Yug 1
❒ SPLITTER (Tilsit-Splitter) Ostpreussen Ger 1
❒ SPOLETA Ita 3
❒ SPORYSZ/ ZYWCA Rpl 2
❒ SPRATZERN Aus 3
❒ SPREMBERG/ LAUSITZ Brandenburg Ger 1 2 6 7
❒ SPRENDLINGEN (Dreieich) Hessen-Nassau Ger 7 9
❒ SPRIMONT Liege Bel 1 2
❒ SPRINGE Hannover Ger 1 2
❒ SPROCKHOEVEL Westfalen Ger 5
❒ SPROTTAU (Szprotawa) Schlesien Ger 1 2 3 4 5 6 7
❒ SPY Namur Bel 1
❒ SREM Rpl 1
❒ SRETENSK Rus 3
❒ ST DENIS Reu 1
❒ STAAKEN Brandenburg Ger 7
❒ STADE Hannover Ger 1 8 14

❒ STADL-PAURA OO Aus 1
❒ STADTAMHOF Bayern Ger 2 7
❒ STADTHAGEN Lippe Ger 2 9
❒ STADTILM Schwarzburg-Rudolstadt Ger 1 7
❒ STADTKYLL Rheinland Ger2
❒ STADTLENGSFELD Sachsen-Weimar-Eisenach Ger 1 2 13
❒ STADTLOHN Westfalen Ger 2 7
❒ STADTOLDENDORF Braunschweig Ger 1 2 7
❒ STAFFELSTEIN Bayern Ger 1
❒ STAHLHEIM (Amneville) Lothringen Ger 7
❒ STAHLMARK (Wengern) Rheinland Ger 2
❒ STAINBRUGES (Stambruges) Hainaut Bel1
❒ STAINS Seine Fan 7
❒ STAINZ Steiermark Aus 9
❒ STAJERSKA Yug 14
❒ STALLUPOENEN (Niesterow) Ostpreussen Ger 1
❒ STAMMBACH Bayern Ger 1
❒ STAMNAN Nor 14
❒ STANDHARDT OO Aus 1
❒ STANISLAWOW (Stanislav, Stanislau, Ivano-Frankovsk) Galicia Rpl 2
❒ STANZTHAL Kaernten Aus 1
❒ STARACHOWICE Rpl 2
❒ STARBACH Sachsen Ger 2
❒ STARGARD Mecklenburg-Strelitz Ger 1
❒ STARGARD (Starogard, Starndworska, Stargard Szezecinski) Westpreussen Ger 1 2 3 4 14
❒ STARI BAR Mon 1
❒ STARI OSKOL (Stary Oskol) Rus 1
❒ STARKSTADT (Starkov) Boehmen Cze 2
❒ STARO-KONSTANTINOV (Volhynie) Rus 1
❒ STASSFURT Provinz Sachsen Ger 1 2
❒ STATHELLE Nor 14
❒ STATTERSDORF NO Aus 1
❒ STAUCHITZ Sachsen Ger 2
❒ STAUFEN/ BREISGAU Baden Ger 1
❒ STAVANGER Nor 14
❒ STAVELOT Liege Bel 1
❒ STAVENHAGEN Mecklenburg-Schwerin Ger 1 6
❒ STAVNITSA Rus 1
❒ STAVROPOL Rus 1
❒ STAWISZYN Rpl 2
❒ STAZZANO Alessandria Ita 3
❒ STAZZANO Piemonte Ita 3
❒ STECHAU/ HERZBERG AM ELSTER Provinz Sachsen Ger 2
❒ STECKLENBERG/ HARZ Provinz Sachsen Ger 1
❒ STEDESAND Schleswig-Holstein Ger 1
❒ STEEGEN OO Aus 1
❒ STEELE Rheinland Ger 3 5 8
❒ STEENBERGEN North Brabant Net 1
❒ STEENDORP East Flanders Bel 1
❒ STEENWIJK Overijssel Net 1
❒ STEFANSHART NO Aus 1
❒ STEIN Bayern Ger 2 6 7
❒ STEIN Kaernten Aus 1
❒ STEIN Limburg Net 14
❒ STEIN AN DER DONAU NO Aus 1
❒ STEINACH Sachsen-Meiningen Ger 1 6
❒ STEINAKIRCHEN AM FORST NO Aus 1 2
❒ STEINAU/ ODER (Scinawa) Schlesien Ger 1
❒ STEINAWEG NO Aus 1
❒ STEINBACH Sachsen-Meiningen Ger 1
❒ STEINBACH AM ZIEHBERG OO Aus 1
❒ STEINBACH-HALLENBERG Hessen-Nassau Ger 1 2
❒ STEINBACH/ GLATZ Schlesien Ger 1 2
❒ STEINBACH/ STEYR OO Aus 1
❒ STEINBACH/ WALD Bayern Ger 2
❒ STEINBRUCK OO Aus 1
❒ STEINBRUECKEN Hessen-Nassau Ger 7
❒ STEINBURG Schleswig-Holstein Ger 1
❒ STEINEN Baden Ger 1 2
❒ STEINERKIRCHEN AN DER TRAUN 00 Aus 1
❒ STEINERKIRCHEN/ INNBACH OO Aus 1
❒ STEINFELD Schleswig-Holstein Ger 1
❒ STEINFELS (Parkstein) Bayern Ger 7
❒ STEINFOERDE Hannover Ger 2
❒ STEINFOERDE-WIETZ Hannover Ger 1
❒ STEINFURT Westfalen Ger 1
❒ STEINHAUS BEI WELS OO Aus 1
❒ STEINHEID Sachsen-Meiningen Ger 1
❒ STEINHEIM Westfalen Ger 1
❒ STEINIGTWOHNSDORF O.L. Sachsen Ger 1
❒ STEINKJER Nor 14
❒ STEINKLAMM NO Aus 2 3
❒ STEINKREUZ OO Aus 1
❒ STEINWALD OO Aus 1
❒ STEINWIESEN Bayern Ger 6 7
❒ STEKENE East Flanders Bel 1
❒ STELLAU Schleswig-Holstein Ger 2
❒ STELLINGEN (Hamburg) Schleswig-Holstein Ger 1 7 8
❒ STELLINGEN-LANGENFELDE Schleswig-Holstein Ger 1
❒ STEMBERT Liege Bel 1
❒ STENDAL Provinz Sachsen Ger 1 2 3 7 8 12
❒ STENDSITZ Westpreussen Ger 2
❒ STENSCHEWO (Steszew) Posen Ger 1
❒ STEPENITZ/ CAMMIN (Stepnica) Pommern Ger 2
❒ STERKRADE Rheinland Ger 1 3 6
❒ STERLITAMAK Rus 1
❒ STERNBERG Mecklenburg-Schwerin Ger 1
❒ STESZEWO (Steszewska) Posen Ger 1
❒ STETTIN (Szececin) Pommern Ger 1 2 5 6 7 11 12
❒ STEUDNITZ/ DORNBURG Thueringen Ger 2 7
❒ STEYR OO Aus 1 2 9
❒ STEYR-SELZTHAL ST. MICHAEL OO Aus 9
❒ STEYREGG OO Aus 1
❒ STEYREMUEHL OO Aus 9
❒ STIFTUNG BEI LEONFELDEN OO Aus 1
❒ STINNES ZECHE (Essen-Karnap) Rheinland Ger 3 4
❒ STJOERDAL Nor 14
❒ STOCKACH Baden Ger 1
❒ STOCKELSDORF Schleswig-Holstein Ger 1
❒ STOCKERAU NO Aus 1 9
❒ STOCKHAUSEN/ LAHN Hessen-Nassau Ger 11
❒ STOCKHEIM Bayern Ger 7
❒ STOCKHEIM Limbourg Bel 1
❒ STOECKHEIM Hannover Ger 1 7
❒ STOEREN Nor 14
❒ STOERMEDE (Geseke) Westfalen Ger 3
❒ STOESSEN Provinz Sachsen Ger 1
❒ STOESSING NO Aus 1 2
❒ STOKKOEY Nor 14
❒ STOKSUND Nor 14
❒ STOLBERG Rheinland Ger 1
❒ STOLBERG/ HARZ Provinz Sachsen Ger 1
❒ STOLLBERG/ ERZGEBIRGE Sachsen Ger 1 2 14
❒ STOLNBERG OO Aus 1
❒ STOLP (Slupsk) Pommern Ger 1 2
❒ STOLPEN Sachsen Ger 1 2
❒ STOLZENAU/ WESER Hannover Ger 1 2
❒ STOLZENBURG Pommern Ger 7
❒ STOLZENHAGEN Brandenburg Ger 7
❒ STOPNICA Rpl 2
❒ STOPNICA Rus 1
❒ STORAS Nor 14
❒ STORCHNEST (Osieczna) Posen Ger 1 2
❒ STORD Nor 14
❒ STORKENSAUSEN/ OBERELSASS Elsass Ger 1
❒ STORKOW Brandenburg Ger1
❒ STORMARN Schleswig-Holstein Ger 1
❒ STORMEDE Westfalen Ger 3
❒ STOSSBERG Cze 1
❒ STOSSWEIER Elsass Ger 1
❒ STOTEL Hannover Ger 1
❒ STRAELEN Rheinland Ger 1 2
❒ STRAHWALDE-HERRNHUT Sachsen Ger 2 11
❒ STRALKOWO (Strahlau, Strzalkowo) Posen Ger 3 10
❒ STRALSUND Pommern Ger 1 2 3 4 6 7 8 10 12
❒ STRALSUND-DAENHOLM Pommern Ger 3 4

❒ STRASBOURG Bas-Rhin Fan 1
❒ STRASBURG (Brodnice, Brodnica) Westpreussen Ger 1 2 3 6 7
❒ STRASBURG/ UCKERMARK Brandenburg Ger 1 2 6
❒ STRASS Kaernten Aus 1
❒ STRASS NO Aus 1
❒ STRASS OO Aus 1
❒ STRASSBURG (Strasbourg) Elsass Ger 1 3 6 7 10
❒ STRASSEBERSBACH (Dietzhoelztal) Hessen-Nassau Ger 6
❒ STRASSEN Steiermark Aus 1
❒ STRASSWALCHEN Salzburg Aus 1
❒ STRAUNBING Bayern Ger 1 2 7 10
❒ STRAUSBERG Brandenburg Ger 1 2 7
❒ STREHLEN (Strzelin) Schlesien Ger 1 2 6 7
❒ STREHLITZ (Strzelce) Schlesien Ger 7
❒ STRELA/ ELBE Sachsen Ger 1 2
❒ STRELITZ (Altstrelitz) Mecklenburg-Strelitz Ger 1 2 3 7
❒ STRELNO (Strzelno) Posen Ger 1
❒ STRENGBERG NO Aus 1
❒ STRETTI Sardegna Ita 3
❒ STRETWIESEN NO Aus 2
❒ STRICHE (Stryschek, Stryszek) Posen Ger 1
❒ STRIEGAU (Strzegom) Schleslen Ger 1 2 4 5 7
❒ STROEBECK Provinz Sachsen Ger 1
❒ STROEHEN Hannover Ger 3
❒ STROHEIM OO Aus 1
❒ STRONSDORF NO Aus 2
❒ STRUER Den 11
❒ STUEHLINGEN Baden Ger 1
❒ STUER BAD IX Armeekorps Ger 3 10
❒ STUETZERBACH Provinz Sachsen Ger 1 2 7 9
❒ STUHM (Sztum) Westpreussen Ger 1
❒ STUTTGART Wuerttemberg Ger 1 2 3 6 7 8 9 10 11 13 14
❒ STUTTGART-0BERTUERKHEIM Wuerttemberg Ger 2
❒ STUTTHOF (Sztutowo, Koebyly) Westpreussen Ger 15
❒ SUBEN OO Aus 1
❒ SUBIACO Ita 3
❒ SUBIRATS Barcelona Spa 1
❒ SUCHSDORF Schleswig-Holstein Ger 1
❒ SUCHUM (Sukhum) Rus 1
❒ SUCZAWA (Suceava) Rom 1
❒ SUD-EST Fan 7
❒ SUDANELL Lerida Spa 1
❒ SUDER-DITHIMARSCHEN Schleswig-Holstein Ger 1
❒ SUDERODE, BAD Provinz Sachsen Ger 1 SUECA Valencia Spa 1
❒ SUECHTELN Rheinland Ger 1 8
❒ SUEDERBRARUP Schleswig-Holstein Ger 1 2
❒ SUEDERHOLZ (Soenderskov, Denmark) Schleswig-Holstein Ger 1
❒ SUELZE Mecklenburg-Schwerin Ger 1
❒ SUEPPLINGENBURG Braunschweig Ger 2
❒ SUERTH/ KOELN Rheinland Ger 2
❒ SUESEL Schleswig-Holstein Ger 2
❒ SUESSENBACH NO Aus 2
❒ SUHL Provinz Sachsen Ger 1 2 6 7 8
❒ SUKHONA (Soukhona) Rus 1
❒ SULIN (Sulinovskoye, Krasny Sulin) Rus 1
❒ SULITJELMA Nor 14
❒ SULMIRSCHUETZ (Sulmierzyce) Posen Ger 1
❒ SULMONE Aquila Abruzzo Ita 3
❒ SULSIQUE East Flanders Bel 1
❒ SULZ Elsass Ger 1
❒ SULZA, BAD Sachsen-Weimar-Eisenach Ger 1 3
❒ SULZBACH-SAAR Rheinland Ger 1
❒ SULZBACH/ OBERPFALZ Bayern Ger 1
❒ SULZERN Elsass Ger 1
❒ SULZMATT Elsass Ger 1
❒ SUMY Rus 1
❒ SUNDERN Westfalen Ger 2
❒ SUNDREMDA Thueringen Ger 2
❒ SUNDS Den 11
❒ SUNDWIG Westfalen Ger 2
❒ SUNYER Lerida Spa 1
❒ SURIA Barcelona Spa 1
❒ SURIGEDHO Asinara Ita 3
❒ SUSQUEDA Gerona Spa 1
❒ SUTTHOF (Elbing) Westpreussen Ger 15
❒ SUTTROP Nordhein-Westfalen Ger 14
❒ SVELGEN Nor 14
❒ SVENDBORG Den 11 14
❒ SVERDLOVSK (Ekaterinburg) Rus 1
❒ SVORKMO Nor 14
❒ SWAKOPMUND Ged 2
❒ SWARZEDZ Schlesien Ger 1
❒ SWEREZEELE Bel 14
❒ SWEVEGHEM West Flanders Bel 1
❒ SWIERKLANIEC (Neudeck) Schlesien Ger 2
❒ SWIETOCHLOWICE (Schwientochlowitz) Schlesien Ger 1
❒ SWINEMUENDE (Swinoujscie) Pommern Ger l 6 8
❒ SWINESNUTEN Scherzscheine Ger 2
❒ SYLT Schleswig-Holstein Ger 10
❒ SYRIA Syr 7
❒ SYSERT (Sysertski Zavod) Rus 1
❒ SYSSEELE West Flanders Bel 1
❒ SZABAD NEP UTALVANY Hun 1
❒ SZAKOLCA (Szakolcza, Skalicz, Skalica) Cze 1 2
❒ SZAKOLCZA (Slowakei) Hun 1
❒ SZAKOLCZA Rpl 2
❒ SZCERCU (Szcerecz) Hun 1
❒ SZCERCU/ LEMBERG Galicia Rpl 3
❒ SZCZAKOWA Rpl 2
❒ SZCZERCOW (Chtchertsov) Rpl 1 2
❒ SZCZERZEC (Shchirets, Scirec USSR) Galicia Rpl 2
❒ SZECZENY Hun 1
❒ SZEFESHERVAR Hun 1
❒ SZEGED Hun 1
❒ SZELEJEWO Rpl 1
❒ SZENT MARGITSZIGET Hun 1
❒ SZENTGOTTHARD Hun 1
❒ SZERENCS Hun 1
❒ SZERSZARD Hun 14
❒ SZIGETVAR Hun 14
❒ SZOMBATHELY (Steinamanger) Hun 1
❒ SZYMANOWICE (Chimanowitsy) Rpl 1 2

T

❒ TABAL Almeria Spa 2
❒ TABANELLO English Ita 3
❒ TABERNAS Almeria Spa 1
❒ TABERNES DE VALLDIGNA Valencia Spa 1
❒ TABOR (Tabora) Boehmen Cze 1 2
❒ TABOR Pont Hun 14
❒ TABORA Gea 1 14
❒ TAFELBERG OO Aus 1
❒ TAGAMANENT Barcelona Spa 1
❒ TAGANROG Rus 1
❒ TAGGIA Liguria Ita 3
❒ TAGGIA San Remo Ita 3
❒ TAGUIL (Nizhne Taguil) Rus 1
❒ TAHANRIH (Taganrog) Rus 1
❒ TAILFINGEN (Albstadt) Wuerttemberg Ger 1 2 6 9
❒ TAISKIRCHEN OO Aus 1
❒ TAISNIERES Nord Fan 1
❒ TALAMANCA Barcelona Spa 2
❒ TALARRUBIAS Badajoz Spa 1
❒ TALAUDIERE, LA Loire Fan 7
❒ TAMAN Rus 1
❒ TAMARIS Fan 11
❒ TAMARITE Huesca Spa 1 2
❒ TAMBACH-DIETHARZ Sachsen-Gotha Ger 1
❒ TAMBOV Rus 1
❒ TAMINES Namur Bel 1
❒ TANGERHUETTE Provinz Sachsen Ger 2 6
❒ TANGERMUENDE Provinz Sachsen Ger 1 2 6
❒ TANGSTEDT Schleswig-Holstein Ger 1
❒ TANINGES Haute Savoie Fan 2
❒ TANNA Reuss j. L. Ger 1
❒ TANNENBERG/ ERZGEBIRGE achsen Ger 1
❒ TANNENBERGSTHAL/ VOGTLAND Sachsen Ger 1
❒ TANNHAUSEN Schlesien Ger 1 2 7 13
❒ TANNHAUSEN-WUESTEIGEFZSDORF Schlesien Ger 2
❒ TANNRODA Sachsen-Weimar-Eisenach Ger 1

❒ TANNUTUVA Rus 1
❒ TARADELL Barcelona Spa 1
❒ TARANCON Cuenca Spa 1
❒ TARARE Rhone Fan 1
❒ TARARE, AMPLEPUIS, (Thizy, Lamure) Rhone Fan 1
❒ TARASCON Bouches-du-Rhone Fan 7
❒ TARASOVKA Rus 1
❒ TARAZONA Albacete Spa 2
❒ TARBES Hautes Pyrenees Fan 1 6 7
❒ TARN Fan 1
❒ TARNOBRZEG Galicia RPL 1
❒ TARNOPOL/ SERED (Ternopol USSR) Galicia Rpl 1
❒ TARNOW/ BIALA Galacia Rpl 2
❒ TARNOWITZ (Tarnowskie Gory) Schlesien Ger 1 2 7 9 11
❒ TAROUCA Viseu Por 1
❒ TARRAGONA Tarragona Spa 1
❒ TARRANA SARENA Ita 14
❒ TARREGA Lerida Spa l 2
❒ TARROS Lerida Spa 1
❒ TARSDORF OO Aus 1
❒ TASHKENT (Taschkent, Tachkent) Rus 1
❒ TATARSKAYA Rus 1
❒ TAUBENBRUNN OO Aus 1
❒ TAUBENHEIM/ SPREE Sachsen Ger 1
❒ TAUBERBISCHOFSHEIM Baden Ger 1 6
❒ TAUFKIRCHEN/ PRAM OO Aus 1
❒ TAUFKIRCHEN/ TRATTNACH OO Aus 1
❒ TAURA Sachsen Ger 1 2
❒ TAUSENBLUM NO Aus 1
❒ TAVAUX Jura Fan 1
❒ TAVAUX ET PONTSERICOURT Aisne Fan 1
❒ TAVERNELLO Ita 14
❒ TAVIRA Faro Por 2
❒ TCHARDJOUI Rus 1
❒ TCHERDYN (Tcherdin) Rus 1
❒ TEBESSA Annaba Alg 7
❒ TECKLENBURG Westfalen Ger 1
❒ TEGERNSEE Bayern Ger 1
❒ TEIA Barcelona Spa 1
❒ TEICHHUETTE/ HARZ (Gittelde) Braunschweig Ger 2
❒ TEICHWALD OO Aus 1
❒ TEISENDORF Bayern Ger 1 2
❒ TEISNACH Bayern Ger 1 2 7
❒ TELC Cze 1
❒ TELFS Tirol Aus 1
❒ TEMESVAR (Timisoara) Rom 1 2
❒ TEMESVAR/ ALT-BEGA (Timisoara) Galacia Rpl 2
❒ TEMESVAR/ ALT-BEGA (Temeswar, Temeschwar, Temesar Banat) Galicia Rpl 2
❒ TEMPELBURG (Dzarlinek, Czaplinek) Pommern Ger 1 2 6
❒ TEMPLEUVE Hainaut Bel 1
❒ TEMPLIN Brandenburg Ger 1 2
❒ TEMSCHE (Tamise) East Flanders Bel 1
❒ TENES (El Bayadh) Alg 2
❒ TENINGEN Baden Ger 1 2
❒ TENNSTEDT Provinz Sachsen Ger 1
❒ TEPLITZ (Teplice) Cze 14
❒ TEPLITZ-SCHOENAU (Teplice-Sanov) Boehmen Cze 1
❒ TEREK Rus 1
❒ TERESA DE COFRENTES Valencia Spa 1
❒ TERGERNSEE-ROTTACH (Tegernsee) Bayern Ger 6
❒ TERGNIER Aisne Fan 1 7
❒ TERGNIER-FARGNIERS Quessy-et-Voueel Fan 1
❒ TERHAGEN Antwerp Be] 1
❒ TERMENS Lerida Spa 1
❒ TERNBERG OO Aus 1
❒ TERNEUZEN Net 14
❒ TERNI Ita 14
❒ TERNITZ NO Aus 9
❒ TERRASOLA I LAVIT Barcelona Spa 1
❒ TERRASSA Barcelona Spa 1
❒ TERRASSINI Palermo Ita 3
❒ TERRASSINI Sicilia Ita 3
❒ TERRENOIRE Loire Fan 3 7
❒ TERRINCHES Ciudad Real Spa 1
❒ TERSCHELLING Net 14
❒ TERTRE Hainaut Bel 2
❒ TESCHEN (Tesin, Cieszyn, Decin) Cze 1
❒ TESCHEN/ OLSA (Cieszyn, Cesky Tesin) Galicia Rpl 1
❒ TESSENDERLOO Limbourg Bel 1
❒ TESSIN Mecklenburg-Schwerin Ger 1
❒ TETE Moz 1
❒ TETEROW Mecklenburg-Schwerin Ger 1 6 7
❒ TETTAU (Mainleus) Bayern Ger 2 1 3
❒ TETTENBORN Provinz Sachsen Ger 2
❒ TETTNANG Wuerttemberg Ger 1 2 6
❒ TEUCHERN Provinz Sachsen Ger 1 2 7
❒ TEUDITZ (Grosskorbetha) Provinz Sachsen Ger 7
❒ TEUQUIERES Somme Fan 7
❒ TEUSCHNITZ Bayern Ger 1 7
❒ TEUTSCHENTHAL Sachsen Ger 7
❒ TEVAR Cuenca Spa 1
❒ TEVEREN Nordrhein-Westfalen Ger 14
❒ TEXING NO Aus 1
❒ THALE/ HARZ Provinz Sachsen Ger 1 2 6 7
❒ THALGAU Salzburg Aus 1
❒ THALHEIM Provinz Sachsen Ger 2
❒ THALHEIM Sachsen Ger 2 1
❒ THALHEIM BEI WELS OO Aus 1
❒ THANN Elsass Ger 1 2 6
❒ THANN Haut Rhin Fan 1 6
❒ THANN OO Aus 1
❒ THANNDORF/ GLATZ Schlesien Ger 1 2
❒ THANNHAUSEN Bayern Ger 1
❒ THANSTETTEN OO Aus 1
❒ THAON-LES-VOSGFS Vosges Fan 7
❒ THEISBERGSTEGEN Pfalz Ger 1
❒ THEISSEN Provinz Sachsen Ger 7
❒ THEMAR Thueringen Ger 2 7
❒ THENELLES Aisne Fan 1
❒ THEODOSIE Rus 1
❒ THERESIENFELD NO Aus 1
❒ THERESIENSTADT Aus 3
❒ THERESIENSTADT (Terezin) Boehmen Cze 3 5
❒ THESDORF Schelswig-Holstein Ger 1
❒ THEUX Liege Bel 1
❒ THEZAN Aude Fan 1
❒ THIAUCOURT ET St. Mihiel Fan 1
❒ THIELRODE-WAAS East Flanders Bel 1
❒ THIELT West Flanders Bel 1
❒ THIERACHE Aisne Fan 7
❒ THIERSHEIM/ OBERFRANKEN Bayern Ger 2
❒ THIESI Ita 3
❒ THIEULAIN Hainaut Bel 1
❒ THILLOT LE Vosges Fan 2
❒ THIMISTER Liege Bel 1
❒ THISTED Den 11
❒ THIVENCELLES-FRESNES sur Escaut Fan 1
❒ THIVIERS Dordogne Fan 7
❒ THOMASROITH OO Aus 2 9
❒ THOMMEN Liege Bel 14
❒ THONBERG Sachsen Ger 2
❒ THONON LES BAINS Haute Savoie Fan 11
❒ THOREBY Den 11
❒ THORN (Torun) Westpreussen Ger 1 6 12 14
❒ THORSHAVN Faeroeer Islands Den 14
❒ THOUROUT West Flanders Bel 1
❒ THRAEHNA S.A. Thueringen Ger 2
❒ THUIN Hainaut Bel 1
❒ THULIN Hainaut Bel 1
❒ THUM/ ERZGEBIRGE Sachsen Ger 1 2
❒ THY-LE-BAUDHUIN-(Thy-le-Baudin) Namur Bel 1
❒ THY-LE-CHATEAU Namur Bel 1
❒ TIANA Barcelona Spa 1
❒ TICHAU (Tichy) Schlesien Ger 2
❒ TIEFENFURT (Parowa) Schlesien Ger 2 7
❒ TIEFGRABEN OO Aus 1
❒ TIEFURT/ WEIMAR Sachsen Ger 1
❒ TIEGENDORF/ DANZIG WestpTeussen Ger 1
❒ TIEGENHOF/ DANZIG (Nowy Dwor Dworska) Westpreussen Ger 1
❒ TIENEN (Thienen) Barbant Bel 1
❒ TIENEN-TIENSE Brabant Bel 14
❒ TIENGEN Baden Ger 1 2
❒ TIFLIS Rus 1 2
❒ TIHANGE Liege Bel 1
❒ TIJOLA Almeria Spa 1 2
❒ TILBURG North Brabant Net 8
❒ TILLEUL, LE Seine-Inferieure Fan 7

❒ TILLEUR Liege Bel 2
❒ TILLOY Nord Fan 1
❒ TILSIT (Sovetsk, Sowietsk, Sowjetsk, USSR) Ostpreussen Ger 1 6 7 8 12
❒ TIMELKAM OO Aus 1
❒ TINGLEFF (Tinglev, Denmark) Schleswig-Holstein Ger 1 2
❒ TINGIEV (Tingleff) Den 1 2
❒ TINNUM/ SYLT Schleswig-Holstein Ger 1
❒ TIRIG Castellon Spa 2
❒ TIROLER Landkasse Aus 1
❒ TIRSCHENREUTH Bayern Ger 1 2 7
❒ TIRSCHTIEGEL (Trziel) Posen Ger 1
❒ TIRVIA Lerida Spa 1
❒ TITTMONING Bayern Ger 1 2
❒ TIUMEN (Tioumen) Rus 1
❒ TIURANA Lerida Spa 1
❒ TIVENYS Tarragona Spa 1
❒ TIVISSA Tarragona Spa 1
❒ TKIBULI (Tkvibuli, Tkvibouli) Rus 1
❒ TOBARRA Albacete Spa 1
❒ TOBOLSK Rus 1
❒ TOBOSO, EL Toledo Spa 1
❒ TOCKENDORF Sachsen-Altenburg Ger 7
❒ TODTNAU Baden Ger 1 2
❒ TOELZ BAD Bayern Ger 1 6 8
❒ TOENNING Schleswig-Holstein Ger 2 6
❒ TOENSBERG Nor 14
❒ TOKMAK (Bolshoi Tokmak) Rus 1
❒ TOMACHPOL Rus 1
❒ TOMAR (Thomar) Santarem Por 1 2
❒ TOMASZOW RAWSKI/ PILICA (Tomachov-Ravsky) Rpl 2
❒ TOMBARINI Sardegna Ita 3
❒ TOMELLOSO Ciudad Real Spa 1
❒ TOMSK Rus 1
❒ TONA Barcelona Spa 1
❒ TONADELA Viseu Por 1 2
❒ TONDERN (Toender) Den 1 11
❒ TONDERN (Toender, Denmark) Schleswig-Holstein Ger 1 7
❒ TONGEREN Limbourg Bel 1
❒ TONNDORF-LOHE Scheswig-Holstein Ger 1
❒ TONNEINS Lot et Garonne Fan 1 11
❒ TONNING Schleswig-Holstein Ger 6
❒ TORA Lerida Spa 1
❒ TORA DE RIUBREGOS Lerida Spa 1
❒ TORDA (Turda, Rumania) Hun 1
❒ TORDERA Barcelona Spa 1
❒ TORELLO Barcelona Spa 1 2
❒ TORGAU Provinz Sachsen Ger 1 2 3 6 8 10 13
❒ TORGELOW Pommern Ger 1 6
❒ TORINI Ita 3 11
❒ TORLA Huesca Spa 1
❒ TORMS, ELS Lerida Spa 1
❒ TORNABOUS Lerida Spa 1
❒ TORRALBA DE ARAGON Huesca Spa 1
❒ TORRALBA DE CALATRAVA Ciudad Real Spa 1
❒ TORRE CARDELA Granada Spa 1
❒ TORRE DE CABDELLA Lerida Spa 1
❒ TORRE DE CLARAMUNT Barcelona Spa 2
❒ TORRE DE L'ESPANYOL Tarragona Spa 1 2
❒ TORRE DE MONCORVO Braganca Por 1
❒ TORREBESSES Lerida Spa 1
❒ TORREBLANCA Castellon Spa 1
❒ TORREBLASCOPEDRO Jaen Spa 1
❒ TORRECAMPO Cordoba Spa 1
❒ TORRECILLA DE ALCANIZ Spa 2
❒ TORREDELCAMPO Jaen Spa 2
❒ TORREDEMBARA Tarragona! Spa 1
❒ TORREDONJIMENO Jaen Spa 1
❒ TORREFARRERA Lerida Spa 2
❒ TORREG ROSSA Lerida Spa 1
❒ TORRELAMEU Lerida Spa 1
❒ TORRELLES'DE FOIX Barcelona Spa 1
❒ TORRELLES DE LLOBREGAT Barcelona Spa 1
❒ TORREMANZANAS Alicante Spa 1
❒ TORRENTE DE CINCA Huesca Spa 2
❒ TORRENUEVA Ciudad Real Spa 1
❒ TORREPERROGIL Jaen Spa 1
❒ TORRES DE ALBANCHEZ Jaen Spa 1
❒ TORRES DE SEGRE Lerida Spa 1
❒ TORRES DEL OBISPO Huesca Spa, 1
❒ TORRES NOVAS Santarem Por 2
❒ TORRES VEDRAS Lisboa Por 1 2
❒ TORREVELILLA Teruel Spa 2
❒ TORREVIEJA Alicante Spa 2
❒ TORROELLA DE FLUVIA Gerona Spa 1
❒ TORROELLA DE MONTGRI Gerona Spa 1
❒ TORROJA Tarragona Spa 1
❒ TORTELLA Gerona Spa 1
❒ TORTONA Alessandria Piemonte Ita 3
❒ TORTOSA Tarragona Spa 1 2
❒ TORVIZCON Granada Spa 1
❒ TOSCANO Ita 14
❒ TOSES DE LA MONTANYA Gerona Spa 1
❒ TOSSA Gerona Spa 1
❒ TOST (Toszek) Schlesien Ger 1 2
❒ TOSTEDT Hannover Ger 1
❒ TOTANA Murcia Spa 1
❒ TOUFFLERS Nord Fan 1
❒ TOUL Meurthe-et-Moselie Fan 2
❒ TOULIS Fan 1
❒ TOULON AND VAR Fan 3 7 11 12
❒ TOULOUSE Haute Garonne Fan 1 2 3 7 11 14
❒ TOURCOING Nord Fan 1
❒ TOURNAI Hainaut Bel 1
❒ TOURNAI, ANTOING, CALONNE, ETC. Hainaut Bel 1
❒ TOURNEVILLE Eure Fan 10
❒ TOURNHOUT (Turnhout) Antwerp Bel 1
❒ TOURNON-D'AGENAIS Lot-et-Garonne Fan 2
❒ TOURS Indre-et-Loire Fan 1 3 7
❒ TOUS D'ANOIA Barcelona Spa 1
❒ TRAAR Rheinland Ger 1
❒ TRABEN-TRARBACH Rheinland Ger 2
❒ TRACHENBERG (Zmigrod) Schlesien Ger 1 2
❒ TRADIGIST NO Aus 2
❒ TRAGO DE NOGUERA Lerida Spa 1
❒ TRAGWEIN OO Aus 1
❒ TRAISEN NO Aus 1 3
❒ TRAISKIRCHEN NO Aus 1
❒ TRAISMAUER NO Aus 1
❒ TRAIT, LE Seine Inferieure Fan 3 14
❒ TRANCOSO (Trancozo) Guarda Por 1 2
❒ TRANG-DA Fic 7
❒ TRAPPSTADT Bayern Ger 1
❒ TRATTEN Kaernten Aus 1
❒ TRAUN OO Aus 1
❒ TRAUNKIRCHEN OO Aus 1
❒ TRAUNSTEIN Bayern Ger 1 2 3 4 6
❒ TRAUTZSCHE Sachsen Ger 2
❒ TRAVECY Aisne Fan 1 10
❒ TRAVEMUENDE Schleswig-Holstein Ger 2
❒ TREBITSCH (Trebic) Hun 1
❒ TREBITSCH (Trebic) Maehren Cze 2
❒ TREBITSCH (Trebic) Moravia Aus 2
❒ TREBNITZ (Trzebinia) Schlesien Ger 1 2 8 11
❒ TREBOUKHOVETZ Rus 1
❒ TREBSEN/ MULDE Sachsen Ger 1 2
❒ TREFFURT Provinz Sachsen Ger 1
❒ TRELON Nord Fan 1
❒ TREMESSEN (Trzemeszno, Trzemeszenska) Posen Ger 1 6
❒ TRENNFURT/ MAIN Bayern Ger 1 2
❒ TRENTINO Ita 14
❒ TREPORT, LE Seine-Inferieure Fan 1
❒ TREPTOW/ REGA (Trzebiatow) Pommern Ger 1 2
❒ TREPTOW/ TOLLENSEE (Altentreptow) Pommern Ger 1 2
❒ TREST Cze 2
❒ TREUBACH OO Aus 1
❒ TREUCHTLINGEN Bayern Ger 1 2 6
❒ TREUCHTLINGEN-WEISSENBURG Bayern Ger 1 2
❒ TREUEN Sachsen Ger 1 2
❒ TREUENBRIETZEN Brandenburg Ger 1
❒ TREVISO Ita 3 14
❒ TREVISO English Ita 3 14

❒ TREYSA Hessen-Nassau Ger 1
❒ TREZELLES Allier Fan 7
❒ TRIBERG Baden Ger 1 6 14
❒ TRIBSEES Pommern Ger 1 2
❒ TRIEBEL N.L. Brandenburg Ger 2
❒ TRIEBES Thueringen Ger 1 2
❒ TRIER Rheinland Ger 1 2 3 6 7 11
❒ TRIESTE Ita 14
❒ TRIFTERN Bayern Ger 1
❒ TRIGNAC Loire-Atlantique Fan 7
❒ TRIGOLET Bouches-du-Rhone Fan 7
❒ TRINEC (Trzyniec) Cze 2
❒ TRINO NOVARA Piemonte Ita 3
❒ TRIPTIS Thueringen Ger 1 2
❒ TRITTAU Schleswig-Holstein Ger 1
❒ TROIS VIERGES Lux 7
❒ TROISCHEN/ ROSSWEIN Sachsen Ger 2
❒ TROISDORF Rheinland Ger 1 2 7
❒ TROISV!LLES Nord Fan 1
❒ TROITSK (Troizk) Rus 1
❒ TROIZKOSSAWSK (Troitskosavsk) Rus 1
❒ TROLDHEDE Den 2
❒ TROMPELOUP Fan 3
❒ TRONDHEIM Nor 14
❒ TROPPAU (Opava) Maehren Cze 2 11
❒ TROSSINGEN Wuerttemberg Ger 1 2 6 7
❒ TROSTBERG Bayern Ger 1 2 7
❒ TROUVILLE-SUR-MER Salvados Fan 7 11 14
❒ TROYES Aube Fan 1 7
❒ TRUEBAU (Moravska Trebova) Maehren Cze 1 2
❒ TSARITSIN (Tsaritsyn) Rus 1
❒ TSCHERBENEY/ GLATZ Schlesien Ger 2
❒ TSCHEREMCHOVO (Cheremkhovo) Rus 1
❒ TSCHEREPOVEZ (Cherepovetz) Rus 1
❒ TSCHERNO-ISTOTSCHINSKIJ (Chernoistochinsk) Rus 1
❒ TSEKHOTSINEK (Ciechocinek) Rus 1
❒ TSINANFU Shantung Chi 7
❒ TSUMEB Ged 2
❒ TUAPSE (Touapse) Rus 1
❒ TUCHEL (Tuchola) Westpreussen Ger 1 4
❒ TUEBINGEN Wuerttemberg Ger 1 2 6 14
❒ TUERKHEIM Bayern Ger 1 2
❒ TUERNITZ NO Aus 1
❒ TUGNY LE PONT Fan 1
❒ TULA (Toula) Rus 1
❒ TULA Sardegna Ita 3
❒ TULCHIN (Toultchin) Rus 1
❒ TULISHKOV (Tuliszkow, Toulichkov) Rus 1
❒ TULISZKOW (Toulichkov) Rpl 1
❒ TULLE Correze Fan 1 3 14
❒ TULLE ET USSEL Correze Fan 1
❒ TULLN NO Aus 1
❒ TULLNERBACH NO Aus 1
❒ TUMELTSHAM OO Aus 1
❒ TUNE Nor 14
❒ TUNGENDORF Schleswig-Holstein Ger 1
❒ TUNIS Tun 1 2 7
❒ TUNTSCHENDORF (Tlumaczow) Schlesien Ger 4
❒ TUPIGNY Fan 1
❒ TURA Ita 14
❒ TUREK (Tourek) Rpl 1 2
❒ TUREW (Turwia) Posen Ger 1 2
❒ TURIN (Turino) Ita 14
❒ TURINSKI RUDNIK (Turjinskie) Rus 1
❒ TURON Guadalajara Spa 1
❒ TU RRE Almeria Spa 1
❒ TUSTANOWICE Rpl 1
❒ TUTTLINGEN Wuerttemberg Ger 1 6 7
❒ TVER Rus 1
❒ TWISTRINGEN Hannover Ger 1
❒ TYN NAD VLTAVOU Cze 1
❒ TYNSET Nor 14
❒ TYSSA (Tisa) Cze 2
❒ TYSSEDAL Nor 14

U

❒ UALAND Nor 14
❒ UBACH/ WORMS Limburg Net 14
❒ UBEDA Jaen Spa 1
❒ UCCLE Brabant Bel 1
❒ UDEN North Brabant Net 1
❒ UDINE Ita 3 14
❒ UEBERLINGEN Baden Ger 1 2 6 7
❒ UEBERRUHR Rheinland Ger 2
❒ UEBIGAU Provinz Sachsen Ger 1
❒ UECKERMUENDE Pommern Ger 1 7
❒ UEDEM-KEPPELN Rheinland Ger 1
❒ UELZEN Hannover Ger 1 2 7
❒ UERDINGEN Rheinland Ger 1 2 3 4 5 6 8
❒ UETERSEN Schleswig-Holstein Ger 1 2
❒ UETNKE-CETINJE Montenegro Yug 14
❒ UFA (Oufa) Rus 1
❒ UFER OO Aus 2
❒ UFFENHEIM Bayern Ger 1 2 6
❒ UFFHOLZ Elsass Ger 1
❒ UGIJAR Granada Spa 1
❒ UGINE Savoie Fan 7
❒ UGNY-L'EQUIPEE Somme Fan 1
❒ UGOLNY (Bogoslovsk) Rus 1
❒ UHLI RSKE JANOVICE Cze 1
❒ UHYST/ TAUCHER Sachsen Ger 2
❒ UJEST (Ujazd) Schlesien Ger 1
❒ UK (Uge) Den 1
❒ UK (Uge, Denmark) Schleswig-Holstein Ger 1
❒ ULAN-UDE (Verkhneudinsk) Rus 1
❒ ULEA Murcia Spa 1
❒ ULEFOSS Nor 14
❒ ULEILA DEL CAMPO Almeria Spa 1
❒ ULFLINGEN Lux 7
❒ ULLASTRELL Barcelona Spa 1
❒ ULLDECONA Tarragona Spa 1 2
❒ ULLDEMOLINS Tarragona Spa 1
❒ ULLERSRICHT Bayern Ger 2
❒ ULM-EINSINGEN Wuerttemberg Ger 2
❒ ULM/ DONAU Wuerttemberg Ger 1 2 4 7 8 12 13
❒ ULMERFELD NO Aus 1 2
❒ ULRICHSBERG OO Aus 1
❒ ULTRAMORT Gerona Spa 1
❒ ULYANOVSK (Ulyanovka, Sablino, Simbursk) Rus 1
❒ UMAN (Ouman) Rus 1
❒ UMANSKAYA (Leningradskaya) Rus 1
❒ UNGENACH OO Aus 1
❒ UNGVAR (Uzhorod) Cze 1
❒ UNIEJOW/ WARTA Rpl 10
❒ UNIEUX Loire Fan 7
❒ UNION, LA Murcia Spa 1
❒ UNKEL Pfalz Ger 14
❒ UNKEL-SCHEUREN Rheinland Ger 2
❒ UNNA Westfalen Ger 1 2 5 6 11
❒ UNNA-KOENIGSBORN Westfalen Ger 5
❒ UNRUHSTADT (Kargowa) Posen Ger 1
❒ UNTER ELSASS Elsass Ger 1
❒ UNTER PEISSENBERG Bayern Ger 6
❒ UNTER-LOIBEN NO Aus 1
❒ UNTER-RATZERSDORF NO Aus 2
❒ UNTER-SCHADEN OO Aus 1
❒ UNTER-THUMRITZ NO Aus 2
❒ UNTER-VORMARKT OO Aus 1
❒ UNTER-WEISSENBACH OO Aus 1
❒ UNTER-WEITERSDORF OO Aus 1
❒ UNTER-WOLFERN OO Aus 1
❒ UNTERACH OO Aus 1
❒ UNTERBARMEN Rheinland Ger 2
❒ UNTERBREIZBACH/ RHOEN Sachsen-Meiningen Ger 2
❒ UNTERESCHBACH Rheinland Ger 2
❒ UNTERGAISBACH OO Aus 1
❒ UNTERGRIESBACH Bayern Ger 2
❒ UNTERHACHING/ MUENCHEN Bayern Ger 2
❒ UNTERHART OO Aus 1
❒ UNTERHAUSEN Wuerttemberg Ger 1
❒ UNTERKOCHEN Wuerttemberg Ger 2 7
❒ UNTERKREUZBERG VOR WALD Bayern Ger 7
❒ UNTERNEUBRUNN Thueringen Ger 2
❒ UNTERPOERLITZ Sachsen-Meiningen Ger 2 9
❒ UNTERSACHSENBERG Sachsen Ger 1
❒ UNTERTAUNUSKREIS Hessen-Nassau Ger 1

❒ UNTERTEUTSCHENTHAL Provinz Sachsen Ger 1
❒ UNTERTUERKHEIM Bayern Ger 7 14
❒ UNTERWALD OO Aus 1
❒ UNTERWEISSBACH Schwarzburg-Rudolstadt Ger 1
❒ UNTERWELLENBORN Thueringen Ger 2
❒ UNTERWESERSTAEDTE (Bremerhaven) Bremen Ger 2 6
❒ UNTERWESTERWALDKREIS Hessen-Nassau Ger 1
❒ UNZMARKT Aus 9
❒ UPICE Cze 9
❒ URACH Wuerttemberg Ger 1
❒ URALSK (Ouralsk) Rus 1
❒ URBANIA Pesaro Ita 3
❒ URBIS Elsass Ger 1
❒ URDA Toledo Spa 1
❒ URFAHR OO Aus 1 2
❒ URK North Holland Net 14
❒ URMATT Elsass Ger 1 2
❒ URRACEL Almeria Spa 1
❒ URREA DE GAEN Teruel Spa 1
❒ URTG Gerona Spa 1
❒ URUGUAY Uru 11
❒ URUILLERS Fan
❒ URVILLE Bateau Dumont Fan 1
❒ USCH (Ujscie) Posen Ger 1 6
❒ USCILUG Rpl 2
❒ USEDOM Pommern Ger 1 7
❒ USEDOM-WOLLIN Pommern Ger 1
❒ USHITSA (Uszycy, Novo-Utichitsa) Rus 1
❒ USINGEN Hessen-Nassau Ger 1 6
❒ USLAR Hannover Ger 1 2
❒ USOLYE (Ousole, Bereznik) Rus 1
❒ UST-KATAVSKI ZAVOD (Ust-Katay) Rus 1
❒ USTILUG (Uscilug) Rus 1
❒ USTRON Cze 2
❒ USTRON Schlesien Ger 2
❒ UTIEL Valencia Spa 1
❒ UTRECHT Utrecht Net 8 14
❒ UTRILLAS Teruel Spa 1
❒ UTZENAICH OO Aus 1
❒ UTZENFELD Baden Ger 1
❒ UZICE (Titovo Uzice) Ser 1

V

❒ VAALS Limburg Net 1 14
❒ VACARISSES (Vaquerisses) Barcelona Spa 1
❒ VACHA Thueringen Ger 1 2
❒ VACQUI RES Haute Garonne Fan 1
❒ VADHEIM Nor 14
❒ VAETHEN-TANGERHUETTE Provinz Sachsen Ger 2 7
❒ VAFOSS Nor 14
❒ VAGARSHAPAD Rus 1
❒ VAGOS Aveiro Por 1
❒ VAIHINGEN/ ENZ Wuerttemberg Ger 1 3 14
❒ VAL CHIAMPO Ita 14
❒ VALBERT Westfalen Ger 1
❒ VALDEALGORFA Teruel Spa 1
❒ VALDELTORMO Teruel Spa 1
❒ VALDEPENAS Ciudad Real Spa 1 2
❒ VALDEPENAS DE JAEN Jaen Spa 1
❒ VALDERROBLES Teruel Spa 1 2
❒ VALDOIE Territoire de Belfort Fan 7
❒ VALENCA Viana do Castelo Por 1 2
❒ VALENCE AND DROME Fan 1 3 7 14
❒ VALENCE-D'AGEN Tarn-et-Garonne Fan 2
❒ VALENCIA Valencia Spa 2
❒ VALENCIENNES Nord Fan 1 2 3 11 14
❒ VALENTIGNEY Doubs Fan 2 7
❒ VALENZUELA Cordoba Spa 2
❒ VALENZUELA DE CALATRAVA Ciudad Real Spa 1
❒ VALJEVO Ser 1
❒ VALJUNQUERA Teruel Spa 1
❒ VALKENSWAARD North Brabant Net 8 14
❒ VALL DE GALLINERA Alicante Spa 1
❒ VALL DE UXO Castellon Spa 1
❒ VALLALTA DEL MARESME Barcelona Spa 1
❒ VALLBONA D'ANOIA Barcelona Spa 1
❒ VALLBONA DE LOS MONGES Lerida Spa 1
❒ VALLCEBRE Barcelona Spa 1
❒ VALLCLARA Tarragona Spa 1
❒ VALLE DE LA SERENA Badajoz Spa 1
❒ VALLEE-MULATRE LA Aisne Fan 1
❒ VALLENDAR Rheinland Ger 1
❒ VALLFLORIDA (Sant Esteve de Palautordera) Barcelona Spa 1
❒ VALLFOGONA DE BALAGUER Lerida Spa 1
❒ VALLFOGONA DE RIUCORP Tarragona Spa 1 2
❒ VALLGORGUINA Barcelona Spa 1
❒ VALLIBONA Castellon Spa 1
❒ VALLMOLL Tarragona Spa 1
❒ VALLS Tarragona Spa 1
❒ VALLVERT D'URGELL (Vallvert) Lerida Spa 1
❒ VALONGO Porto Por 2
❒ VALOR Granada Spa 1
❒ VALPACOS Vila Real Por 1
❒ VALSEQUILLO Cordoba Spa 1
❒ VALVERDE DEL JUCAR Cuenca Spa 1
❒ VAMBERK Cze 2
❒ VANDELLOS Tarragona Spa 1
❒ VANDSBURG (Wiecbork) Westpreussen Ger 1
❒ VANNES Morbihan Fan 6
❒ VANVES Hautes de Seine Fan 1 6
❒ VARA DE REY Cuenca Spa 1
❒ VARCHAVA Rus 1
❒ VARDE Den 11
❒ VAREL Oldenburg Ger 2 7
❒ VARENNE, LA Seine Fan 7
❒ VARHAUG Nor 14
❒ VARNAES (Warnitz) Den 2
❒ VAROSKI-BEOGRAD (Varoski-Belgrade) Yug 1
❒ VAROSSZALONAK Hun 3
❒ VARZI Ita 14
❒ VAS (Eisenburg) Hun 1
❒ VASILKOV Rus 1
❒ VASMEGYE Hun 1
❒ VAUCIENNES Oise Fan 7
❒ VAULX Hainaut Bel 1
❒ VAULX-LEZ-TOURNAI Hainaut Bel 1
❒ VAUX-AUDIGNY Aisne Fan 1
❒ VAYRAC Lot Fan 2
❒ VECHTA Oldenburg Ger 1 2
❒ VEEN North Brabant Net 14
❒ VEENDAM Groningen Net 1
❒ VEGESACK Bremen Ger 1 2 3 5 8
❒ VEILSDORF Sachsen-Meiningen Ger 7
❒ VEJBAEK (Veibaek, Weibaek) Den 1 2
❒ VEJLBY Den 12
❒ VEJLE Den 11 12 14
❒ VELAINES-LEZ-TOURNAI Hainaut Bel 1
❒ VELAS Angra do Heroismo Azs 1
❒ VELBERT Rheinland Ger 1 2 6
❒ VELEFIQUE Almeria Spa 1
❒ VELEN-RAMSDORF Westfalen Ger 3
❒ VELEZ-BLANCO Almeria Spa 1
❒ VELEZ-RUBIO Almeria Spa 1
❒ VELIKI (Novgorod Veliki) Rus 1
❒ VELILLA DE EBRO Zaragoza Spa 1
❒ VELKE MEZIRICI Cze 1
❒ VELP North Brabant Net 14
❒ VELSEN North Holland Net 8
❒ VELSEN Rheinland Ger 5
❒ VELTEN Brandenburg Ger 1 2 7
❒ VELVARY Cze 1
❒ VENDELLES Aisne Fan 1
❒ VENDEUIL Aisne Fan 1
❒ VENDHUILE Aisne Fan 1
❒ VENDRAY (Venray) Limburg Net 14
❒ VENDRELL, EL Tarragona Spa 1
❒ VENETO Ita 14
❒ VENICE Ita 14
❒ VENLO Limburg Net 1 8
❒ VENNESHAMN Nor 14
❒ VENNISSIEUX Rhone Fan 3 14
❒ VENOSA Basilicata Ita 3
❒ VENOSA Potenza Ita 3
❒ VENTSPILS (Vindava, Windau, Vindau) Rus 1
❒ VENUSBERG Sachsen Ger 2
❒ VERA Almeria Spa 1
❒ VERCHNYATSK (Verchnjatschka) Rus 1
❒ VERDAL Nor 14
❒ VERDEN/ ALLER Hannover Ger 1
❒ VERDUN Meuse Fan 3 14

❒ VERFEIL Haute-Garonne Fan 2
❒ VERGEL Alicante Spa 1
❒ VERGES Gerona Spa 1
❒ VERGUIER, LE Aisne Fan 1
❒ VERKHNE SALDINSKI ZAVOD (Verkhne-Saldin, Verkhnyaya Salda) Ru 1
❒ VERKHNE-ISSETSK Rus 1
❒ VERKHNEDNIEPROVSK (Verchnednjeprovsk, Verhne-Dnyeprovsk) Rus 1
❒ VERMAND Aisne Fan 1
❒ VERNER-D'ARIEGE Ariege Fan 3 14
❒ VERNEUIL-SUR-SERRE Fan 1
❒ VERONA Ita 14
❒ VERRASTRANDA Nor 14
❒ VERREBROECK East Flanders Bel 1
❒ VERSAILLES Seine-et-Oise Fan 7
❒ VERSECZ Hun 2
❒ VERTUS Marne Fan 1
❒ VERVIERS Liege Bel 1 14
❒ VERVINS Aisne Fan 7
❒ VESOUL Haute Saone Fan 7 14
❒ VESOUL-GRAY ET LURE Haute Saone Fan 14
❒ VESTER SOTTRUP Den 11
❒ VESZPREM Hun 1
❒ VETRALLA-VITERBO Ita 14
❒ VETSCHAU/ SPREEWALD Brandenburg Ger 1
❒ VEZNESSENSK (Ivanovo-Veznessensk) Rus 1
❒ VEZON Hainaut Bel 1
❒ VIALAR (Tissemsilt) Alg 1
❒ VIANA DO ALENTEJO Evora Por 1 2
❒ VIANA DO CASTELO Viana do Castelo Por 2
❒ VIANNE Lot et Garonne Fan 1
❒ VIAREGGIO Toscana Ita 3
❒ VIATKA (Vjatka) Rus 1
❒ VIATOR Almeria Spa 1
❒ VIAZEMSK (Vyazemski) Rus 1
❒ VIAZMA (Vyazma) Rus 1
❒ VIBORG Den 11 12
❒ VIC Barcelona Spa 1 2
❒ VIC-FEZENSAC Gers Fan 1
❒ VICENZA Ita 3 14
❒ VICHTE West Flanders Bel 1
❒ VICHTENSTEIN OO Aus 1
❒ VICHY Allier Fan 7 11
❒ VIDIGUEIRA Beja Por 1 2
❒ VIDRERES Gerona Spa 1
❒ VIECHTACH Bayern Ger 1 2 6 7
❒ VIECHTWANG OO Aus 1
❒ VIEHBERG OO Aus 1
❒ VIEHDORF NO Aus 1
❒ VIEHOFEN NO Aus 1
❒ VIEIRA DO MINHO Braga Por 2
❒ VIELLA Lerida Spa 1
❒ VIENENBURG/ HARZ Hannover Ger 1 2
❒ VIENNE Isere Fan 1 2 7
❒ VIERSEN Rheinland Ger 1 2
❒ VIERZON Cher Fan 3
❒ VIESALM Luxembourg Bel 1
❒ VIEUX-CONDE Nord Fan 2
❒ VIGAN Gard Fan 7

❒ VIGEVANO Lombardia Ita 3
❒ VIGEVANO Pavio Ita 3
❒ VIGRESTAD Nor 14
❒ VIKEDAL Nor 14
❒ VILA DE REI Castelo Branco Por 1
❒ VILA DE TOLO (Sant Salvador de Tolo) Lerida Spa 1
❒ VILA DO CONDE Porto Por 1 2
❒ VILA DO TOPO Azs 1
❒ VILA FRANCA DE XIRA Lisboa Por 1 2
❒ VILA NOVA DA BARQUINHA Santarem Por 1 2
❒ VILA NOVA DE CERVEIRA Viana do Castelo Por 1
❒ VILA NOVA DE FAMALICAO Braga Por 1 2
❒ VILA NOVA DE FOZCOA Guarda Por 1
❒ VILA NOVA DE GAIA Porto Por 1
❒ VILA NOVA DE OUREM Santarem Por 1
❒ VILA NOVA DE PAIVA Viseu Por 1
❒ VILA POUCA DE AGUIAR Vila Real Por 2
❒ VILA REAL Vila Real Por 1 2
❒ VILA REAL DE SANTO ANTONIO Faro Por 1 2
❒ VILA VERDE Braga Por 2
❒ VILA VICOSA Evora Por 1 2
❒ VILA-RODONA Tarragona Spa 1
❒ VILA-SANA Lerida Spa 1
❒ VILA-SECA DE SOLCINA Tarragona Spa 1
❒ VILABOI (Sant Boi de Llobregat) Barcelona Spa 1 2
❒ VILADA Barcelona Spa 1
❒ VILADECANS Barcelona Spa 1 2
❒ VILADECAVALLS Barcelona Spa 1
❒ VILADEMAT Gerona Spa 1
❒ VILADRAU Gerona Spa 1
❒ VILAFANT Gerona Spa 1
❒ VILAFRANCA DEL PENEDES Barcelona Spa 1 2
❒ VILAJUIGA Gerona Spa 1
❒ VI LALBA DELS ARCS Tarragona Spa 1 2
❒ VILALLER Lerida Spa 1
❒ VILALLONGA DE TER Gerona Spa 1
❒ VILALLONGA DEL CAMP Tarragona Spa 1
❒ VILAMAJOR Barcelona Spa 1
❒ VILANANT Gerona Spa 1
❒ VILANOVA D'ALPIGAT Lerida Spa 2
❒ VILANOVA D'ESCORNALBOU Tarragona Spa 1
❒ VILANOVA D'ESPOIA Barcelona Spa 2
❒ VILANOVA DE BELLPUIG Lerida Spa 1
❒ VILANOVA DE LA AGUDA Lerida Spa 1
❒ VILANOVA DE LA BARCA Lerida Spa 1 2
❒ VILANOVA DE LA MUGA Gerona Spa 2
❒ VILANOVA DE MEIA Lerida Spa 1

❒ VILANOVA DE PRADES Tarragona Spa 1
❒ VILANOVA DE SAU Barcelona Spa 1
❒ VILANOVA DE SEGRIA Lerida Spa 1
❒ VILANOVA DEL VALLES Barcelona Spa 1
❒ VILANOVA I LA GELTRU Barcelona Spa 1
❒ VILAPLANA DEL CAMP Tarragona Spa 1
❒ VILASSAR DE DALT Barcelona Spa 1
❒ VILASSAR DE MAR Barcelona Spa 1
❒ VILATORTA Barcelona Spa 1
❒ VILLA CIDRO Sardegna Ita 3
❒ VILLA DE DON FADRIQUE Toledo Spa 1
❒ VILLA DEL RIO Cordoba Spa 2
❒ VILLABATE Ita 3
❒ VILLACANAS Toledo Spa 1
❒ VILLACARRILLO Jaen Spa 1
❒ VILLACH Kaernten Aus 2 9
❒ VILLACH-TARVIS Aus 9
❒ VILLADOMPARDO Jaen Spa 1 2
❒ VILLAFRANCA DE LOS CABALLEROS Toledo Spa 1
❒ VILLAFRANCA DEL CID Castellon Spa 1
❒ VILLAGARCIA DEL LLANO Cuenca Spa 1
❒ VILLAHERMOSA Ciudad Real Spa 1
❒ VILLAJOYOSA Alicante Spa 1
❒ VILLALBA BAJA Teruel Spa 1
❒ VILLALGORDO DEL JUCAR Albacete Spa 1
❒ VI LLALONGA Valencia Spa 1
❒ VILLAMANRIQUE Ciudad Real Spa 1
❒ VILLAMARCHANTE Valencia Spa 1
❒ VILLAMAYOR DE CALATRAVA Ciudad Real Spa 1
❒ VILLAMAYOR DE SANTIAGO Cuenca Spa 1
❒ VILLANOVA-MONTELEONE Ita 3
❒ VILLANUEVA Murcia Spa 1
❒ VILLANUEVA DE ALCAUDETE Toledo Spa 1
❒ VILLANUEVA DE ALCOLEA Castellon Spa 1
❒ VILLANUEVA DE CASTELLON Valencia Spa 2
❒ VILLANUEVA DE CORDOBA Cordoba Spa 1
❒ VILLANUEVA DE LA JARA Cuenca Spa 1
❒ VILLANUEVA DE LA SERENA Badajoz Spa 1
❒ VILLANUEVA DEL ARZOBISPO Jaen Spa 2
❒ VILLANUEVA DEL DUQUE Cordoba Spa 1
❒ VILLANUEVA LA ROJA Spa 1
❒ VILLAR DE LA LIBERTAD (Villar del Arzobispo) Valencia Spa 1

❒ VILLAR DE LOS NAVARROS Zaragoza Spa 2
❒ VILLAR DE OLALLA Cuenca Spa 1
❒ VILLARALTO Cordoba Spa 1
❒ VILLARET Loire Fan 3 14
❒ VILLARGORDO Jaen Spa 1
❒ VILLARLUENGO Teruel Spa 2
❒ VILLARREAL Castellon Spa 2
❒ VILLARROBLEDO Albacete Spa 1
❒ VILLARRODRIGO Jaen Spa 1
❒ VILLARROYA DE LOS PINARES Teruel Spa 1
❒ VILLARRUBIA DE LOS OJOS Ciudad Real Spa 1
❒ VILLARS Loire Fan 7
❒ VILLARTA Ciudad Real Spa 1
❒ VILLATOBAS Toledo Spa 1
❒ VILLAVERDE DE GUADALIMAR Albacete Spa 1
❒ VILLEBRUMIER Tarn et Gar Fan 1
❒ VILLEFRANCHE S/ SAONE Rhone Fan 1
❒ VILLEFRANCHE-LAURAGEAIS Haute Garonne Fan 1
❒ VILLEMOMBLE Seine et Oise Fan 14
❒ VILLEMUR Haute Garonne Fan 1 7
❒ VILLENA Alicante Spa 2
❒ VILLENEUVE-LES-BOULOC Haute Garonne Fan 2
❒ VILLENEUVE-ST. GEORGES Seine Fan 7
❒ VILLENEUVE-SUR-LOT Lot et Garonne Fan 1 2
❒ VILLE RS Aisne Fan 1
❒ VILLERS-CAMPEAU Nord Fan 1
❒ VILLERS-GUISLAIN Nord Fan 1
❒ VILLERS-LA-TOUR Hainaut Bel 1
❒ VILLERS-LE-BOUILLET Liege Bel 2
❒ VILLERS-LE-SEC Aisne Fan 1
❒ VILLERS-LE-TEMPLE Liege Bel- 1
❒ VILLERS-LES-GUISE Aisne Fan 3
❒ VILLERS-LEZ-CAGNICOURT Pas de Calais Fan 1
❒ VILLERS-NOTRE-DAME Hainaut Bel 1
❒ VILLERS-OUTREAUX Nord Fan 1 2
❒ VILLERS-SAINTCHRISTOPHE Nord Fan 1
❒ VILLERS-SAINT-AMAND Hainaut Bel 1
❒ VILLEUBRANNE Rhone Fan 7
❒ VILLINGEN Baden Ger 1 2 9
❒ VILLORES Castellon Spa 1
❒ VILOSELL Lerida Spa 1
❒ VILOVI D'ONYAR Gerona Spa 1
❒ VILSBIBURG Bayern Ger 1 6 7
❒ VILSECK Bayern Ger 2
❒ VILSHOFEN/ DONAU Bayern Ger 1 2
❒ VILVOORDE Brabant Bel 1 14
❒ VIMBODI Lerida Spa 1 2
❒ VIMOUTIERS Orne Fan 7
❒ VINADIO Cunco Ita 3
❒ VINADIO Piemonte Ita 3
❒ VINAIXA Lerida Spa 1
❒ VINALESA Valencia Spa 2
❒ VINALMONT Liege Bel 1
❒ VINAROZ Castellon Spa 1
❒ VINCENNES Seine Fan 7
❒ VINEBRE Tarragona Spa 1
❒ VINNITZA Rus 1
❒ VINSEBEK Westfalen Ger 1
❒ VIPAVSKO Yug 14
❒ VIRE Calvados Fan 2
❒ VIRTON Luxembourg Bel 1
❒ VIRY-NOUREUIL Aisne Fan 1
❒ VISCO Ita 14
❒ VISEU (Vizeu) Viseu Por 1 2
❒ VISIMO SHAITANSKI (Visim) Rus 1
❒ VISIMO UTKINSK Rus 1
❒ VISO DE LOS PEDROCHES Cordoba Spa 1
❒ VISO DEL MARQUES Ciudad Real Spa 1
❒ VISSELHOEVEDE Hannover Ger 1 2
❒ VITERBO Ita 3
❒ VITIS NO Aus 1
❒ VITRY-EN-ATROIS Pas de Calais Fan 1
❒ VITTORIA Trapani Sicilia Ita 3
❒ VITY Seine Fan 7
❒ VIUZ-EN-SACCAZ (Viuz-en-Sallaz) Haute Savoie Fan 1 2
❒ VIVE-SAINT-ELOI West Flanders Bel 1
❒ VIVEROS Albacete Spa 1
❒ VIVIERS Ardeche Fan 3 7
❒ VLAARDINGEN South Holland Net 8 14
❒ VLADIKAVKAZ (Vladicaucase, Dzaudzhikua) Rus 1
❒ VLADIMIR Rus 1
❒ VLAGTWEDDE Groningen Net 14
❒ VLASIM Cze 1
❒ VLASOV/ DON Rus 1
❒ VLEHARIES Hainaut Bel 1
❒ VLIELAND North Holland Net 14
❒ VLIERZELE East Flanders Bel 1
❒ VLISSINGEN North Brabant Net 1
❒ VLOTHO/ WESER Westfalen Ger 1 2
❒ VLOTSLAVSK (Vloslavsk, Vlotslawsk, Wloclawek, Lesiau) Rus 1
❒ VOECKLABRUCK OO Aus 1
❒ VOECKLAMARKT OO Aus 1
❒ VOEHRENBACH Baden Ger 1
❒ VOELKLINGEN Rheinland Ger 2 7
❒ VOERDE Rheinland Ger 1
❒ VOERDE Westfalen Ger 1 2
❒ VOERDEN Nordrhein-Westfalen Ger 14
❒ VOESLAU NO Aus 1
❒ VOGELBECK Hannover Ger2
❒ VOGELKOJE/ SYLT Schleswig-Holstein Ger 1
❒ VOGELSANG/ HAGEN Westfalen Ger 2 11
❒ VOGHERA Lombardia Ita 3
❒ VOGHERA Pavia Ita 3
❒ VOHWINKEL Rheinland Ger 1 2 6 11
❒ VOIGTSDORF/ ERZGEBIRGE Sachsen Ger 2
❒ VOIGTSTEDT Sachsen Ger 1
❒ VOITHENBERG Bayern Ger 2
❒ VOITSBERG Steiermark Aus 9
❒ VOJENS (Woyens) Den 1
❒ VOLKACH Bayern Ger 6
❒ VOLKEGHEM East Flanders Bel 1
❒ VOLKSTEDT Schwarzburg-Rudolstadt Ger 1
❒ VOLLEN Nor 14
❒ VOLLERUP Den 2
❒ VOLLERUP Schleswig-Holstein Ger 2
❒ VOLMARSTEIN Westfalen Ger 1 2
❒ VOLLMERHAUSEN Rheinland Ger 2 14
❒ VOLMERSWERTH (Duesseldorf) Rheinland Ger 5
❒ VOLOGDA Rus 1
❒ VOLPRIEHAUSEN Hannover Ger 2
❒ VOLTAGGIO Alessandria Ita 3
❒ VOLTAGGIO Piemonte Ita 3
❒ VOLTERRA Pisa Ita 3
❒ VOLTERRA Toscana Ita 3
❒ VOLTREGA Barcelona Spa 1
❒ VOORBURG South Holland Net 8
❒ VORCHDORF OO Aus 1
❒ VORDENBERG Steiermark Aus 9
❒ VORDERSTODER OO Aus 1
❒ VORDINGBORG Den 11
❒ VORHALLE Westfalen Ger 1
❒ VORKLOSTER (Bregenz) Voralberg Aus 9
❒ VORONEZH Rus 1
❒ VORONIKOVSK (Novo-Voronikovsk) Rus 1
❒ VORONTSOVO-ALEXANDOVSKOYE Rus 1
❒ VOROSHILOV (Nikolsk-Ussuriisky) Rus 1
❒ VORST Rheinland Ger 1
❒ VOSNESENSK (Voznesensk) Rus 1
❒ VOSS Nor 14
❒ VOSSELAER Antwerp Bel 1
❒ VOTCHINO Rus 1
❒ VOTICE Cze 1
❒ VOTKINSK (Votkin, Votkinski Zavod) Rus 1
❒ VOUZELA Viseu Por 1
❒ VOYENNES Somme Fan 1
❒ VRACENE East Flanders Bel 1
❒ VRAIGNES-ROISEL Somme Fan 1

❒ VRED Nord Fan 1
❒ VREDEN Westfalen Ger 1 2
❒ VUGHT (s-Hertogenbosch) North Brabant Net 15

W

❒ WAALWIJK North Brabant Net 14
❒ WAASMUNSTER (Waesmunster) East Flanders Bel 1
❒ WACHTEBEKE East Flanders Bel 1
❒ WACHTENDONK Rheinland Ger 1
❒ WACKEN (Wakken) West Flanders Bel 1 14
❒ WADDINXVEEN South Holland Net 8
❒ WADI SEIDNA Aes 14
❒ WADOWICE/ SKAWA (Wadertz, Wadowyce, Frauenstadt) Rpl 1 2
❒ WAECHTERSBACH Hessen-Nassau Ger 1 7
❒ WAERGHEM West Flanders Bel 1
❒ WAERMAERDE West Flanders Bel 1
❒ WAGEMINGEN Net 1
❒ WAGENHAM OO Aus 1
❒ WAGNES Bel 1
❒ WAHA Luxembourg Bel 1
❒ WAHMBECK Hessen-Nassau Ger 3
❒ WAHREN (Leipzig) Sachsen Ger 7
❒ WAIBLINGEN Wuerttemberg Ger 1 2 6 9 13 14
❒ WAIDENDORF OO Aus 1
❒ WAIDHOFEN AN DER YBBS NO Aus 1
❒ WAIDHOFEN/ THAYA NO Aus 1
❒ WAIZENKIRCHEN OO Aus 1
❒ WALBACH (Guensbach) Elsass Ger 1
❒ WALBECK Provinz Sachsen Ger 1 2 7
❒ WALD IM PINZGAU Salzburg Aus 1
❒ WALD/ SOLINGEN Rheinland Ger 1 2 6
❒ WALDBROEHL Rheinland Ger 1
❒ WALDBURG OO Aus 1
❒ WALDDORF Sachsen Ger 1
❒ WALDECK Waldeck Ger 1
❒ WALDENBURG Sachsen Ger 1 2 13
❒ WALDENBURG (Walbrzych) Schlesien Ger 1 2 4 5 6 7 13
❒ WALDENBURG-ALTWASSER (Walbrzych) Schlesien Ger 2
❒ WALDFISCHBACH Pfalz Ger 1
❒ WALDGHEIM (Valdeheim) Rus 1
❒ WALDHAUSEN OO Aus 1
❒ WALDHEIM Sachsen Ger 1 2
❒ WALDHOF/ PFARRKIRCHEN Bayern Ger 7
❒ WALDING OO Aus 1
❒ WALDKIRCH Baden Ger 1 2 7
❒ WALDKIRCHEN Bayern Ger 1 2 7
❒ WALDKIRCHEN AM WESEN OO Aus 1
❒ WALDKIRCHEN/ ZSCHOPAUTAL Sachsen Ger 1
❒ WALDMOHR Pfalz Ger 1 9
❒ WALDMUENCHEN Bayern Ger 1
❒ WALDNEUKIRCHEN OO Aus 1
❒ WALDNIEL Rheinland Ger 1
❒ WALDSASSEN Bayern Ger 1 2
❒ WALDSEE (Bad Waldsee) Wuerttemberg Ger 1 2 6
❒ WALDSHUT (Waldshut-Tiengen) Baden Ger 1 2 5 6 7 14
❒ WALDZELL OO Aus 1
❒ WALEFFES, LES Liege Bel 1
❒ WALHORN Liege Bel 14
❒ WALINCOURT Nord Fan 1
❒ WALLDORF Baden Ger 1
❒ WALLDORF Hessen-Nassau Ger 1 7
❒ WALLDUERN Baden Ger 6
❒ WALLENDORF Sachsen-Meiningen Ger 7
❒ WALLENSEN (Salzhemmendorf) Hannover Ger 7
❒ WALLERN OO Aus 1
❒ WALLERS-TRELON Nord Fan 1
❒ WALLERSDORF Bayern Ger 1
❒ WALLERSTEIN Bayern Ger 7
❒ WALLERTHEIM Hessen Ger 1 7
❒ WALLES Nord Fan 7
❒ WALLHAUSEN-HELME Provinz Sachsen Ger 2
❒ WALLSEE NO Aus 1
❒ WALSRODE Hannover Ger 2 5
❒ WALSRODE & FALLINGSBOSTEL Ger 1 7
❒ WALSTATT-LIEGNITZ (Legnica) Schlesien Ger 14
❒ WALSUM (Duisburg) Rheinland Ger 7
❒ WALTERSDORF Sachsen Ger 1 2
❒ WALTERSHAUSEN Thueringen Ger 1 2
❒ WALTROP Westfalen Ger 1 5
❒ WAMPERSDORF NO Aus 1
❒ WANDERSLEBEN Provinz Sachsen Ger 7
❒ WANDIGNIES-HAMAGE Nord Fan 1
❒ WANDSBEK (Wandsbeck) Schleswig-Holstein Ger 1 2 7 8
❒ WANFRIED Hessen-Nassau Ger 1
❒ WANG NO Aus 1
❒ WANGEN/ ALLGAEU Wuerttemberg Ger 1 2 6
❒ WANGEROOG (Wangerooge) Oldenburg Ger 2 7
❒ WANNE (Herne) Westfalen Ger 1 5 7
❒ WANNE-EICKEL Westfalen Ger 1 14
❒ WANNEGEM-LEDE East Flanders Bel 1
❒ WANSEN (Wiazow) Schlesien Ger 1 6 7
❒ WANZE Liege Bel 1
❒ WANZLEBEN Provinz Sachsen Ger 1
❒ WAPENVELD Gelderland Net 14
❒ WAPIENNO (Kalkbruch, Wielichowo) Posen Ger 7
❒ WARBURG Westfalen Ger 1 6
❒ WARCHIN Hainaut Bel 1
❒ WARDENBURG Oldenburg Ger 2
❒ WAREMME Liege Bel 1
❒ WAREN Mecklenburg-Schwerin Ger 1
❒ WARENDORF Westfalen Ger 1 6 14
❒ WARET-L-EVEQUE Liege Bel 1
❒ WARIN Mecklenburg-Schwerin Ger 1
❒ WARLAING Nord Fan 1
❒ WARMBRUNN, BAD (Cieplice-Zdroj) Schlesien Ger 2 7
❒ WARMING OO Aus 1
❒ WARNEMUENDE Mecklenburg-Schwerin Ger 2 7 10
❒ WARNITZ (Vaernaes, Denmark) Schleswig-Holstein Ger 1
❒ WARNSDORF (Varnsdorf) Boehmen Cze 1
❒ WARSAW/ VISTULA (Warszawa, Varsovie) Rpl 2 14
❒ WARSTEIN Westfalen Ger 1 14
❒ WARTBERG/ AIST OO Aus 1
❒ WARTBERG/ KREMS OO Aus 1
❒ WARTENBURG (Barczewo) Ostpreussen Ger 1 6
❒ WARTHA (Bardo) Schlesien Ger 1
❒ WARTHELAGER (Biedrus) Posen Ger 1 2 3 4 10
❒ WARTIN Pommern Ger 7
❒ WASCHPOINT OO Aus 1
❒ WASMES-AUDEMETZ-BRIFFOEIL Hainaut Bel 1
❒ WASMUEL Hainaut Bel 2
❒ WASPIK North Brabant Net 14
❒ WASSEIGES Liege Bel 1
❒ WASSELNHEIM Elsass Ger 1
❒ WASSENAAR South Holland Net 8
❒ WASSENBERG Rheinland Ger 2
❒ WASSERALFINGEN Wuerttemberg Ger 1 2 6 7
❒ WASSERBURG/ INN Bayern Ger 1 2 6
❒ WASSERLEBEN Provinz Sachsen Ger 1
❒ WASSERMUNGENAU Bayen Ger 7
❒ WASSIGNY Aisne Fan 1
❒ WASSY Haute Marne Fan 1 14
❒ WASUNGEN Thueringen Ger 1 2
❒ WATERLOO Brabant Bel 1
❒ WATERSCHEI Limbourg Bel 14
❒ WATHLINGEN/ CELLE Hannover Ger 2
❒ WATTENSCHEID Westfalen Ger 1 2 5 6
❒ WATTRELOS Nord Fan 1
❒ WATTWEILER Elsass Ger 1

❒ WAUDREZ Hainaut Bel 1
❒ WAXENBERG OO Aus 1
❒ WAZIERS Nord Fan 1
❒ WEBERSTEDT Provinz Sachsen Ger 2
❒ WECHLING NO Aus 1
❒ WECHSELBURG Sachsen Ger 1 2
❒ WECKERSDORF (Krinice) Boehmen Cze 2
❒ WEDAU Rheinland Ger 1
❒ WEDDERSLEBEN Provinz Sachsen Ger 1
❒ WEDEL Schleswig-Holstein Ger 1 2
❒ WEENER/ EMS Hannover Ger 2 6
❒ WEEZE Rheinland Ger 1 3
❒ WEFERLINGEN Provinz Sachsen Ger 1
❒ WEGELEBEN Provinz Sachsen Ger 7
❒ WEGNEZ Liege Bel 1
❒ WEGSCHEID Bayern Ger 2 15
❒ WEGSCHEID BEI LINZ OO Aus 15
❒ WEHL Gelderland Net 14
❒ WEHLEN/ MOSEL Rheinland Ger 2
❒ WEHR Baden Ger 1
❒ WEHRSDORF Sachsen Ger 2
❒ WEHRSTADT Niedersachsen Ger 14
❒ WEIBEK (Vejbaek) Schleswig-Holstein Ger 2
❒ WEIBERN OO Aus 1
❒ WEIDA Thueringen Ger 1 2 6
❒ WEIDEN/ OBERPFALZ Bayern Ger 1 2 3 6
❒ WEIDENAU/ SIEG Westfalen Ger 2
❒ WEIDENBACH-TRIESDORF Bayern Ger 7
❒ WEIGETSCHLAG OO Aus 1
❒ WEIGMANNSDORF Sachsen Ger 1
❒ WEIHERHAMMER Bayern Ger 2
❒ WEIKERSHEIM Wuerttemberg Ger 2
❒ WEIL-FRIEDLINGEN Baden Ger 2
❒ WEILBACH Bayern Ger 1
❒ WEILBACH OO Aus 1
❒ WEILBURG/ LAHN Hessen-Nassau Ger 1 4 6 10
❒ WEILER/ ALLGAEU Bayern Ger 2 6
❒ WEILER/ THANN (Willer) Elsass Ger 1 2 3
❒ WEILHEIM/ AMPER Bayern Ger 1 2 6
❒ WEIMAR Thueringen Ger 1 2 6 7 8 12
❒ WEINBERG Steiermark Aus 1
❒ WEINBOEHLA Sachsen Ger 1
❒ WEINGARTEN Pfalz Ger 1
❒ WEINGARTEN Wuerttemberg Ger 1 2
❒ WEINHEIM UND SCHOENAU Baden Ger 2
❒ WEINHEIM/ BADISCHE Bergstrasse Baden Ger 1 7 8
❒ WEINSBERG Wuerttemberg Ger 1 3

❒ WEINVIERTEL OO Aus 1
❒ WEINZIERL AM WALDE NO Aus 1
❒ WEINZIERL BE] PERG OO Aus 1
❒ WEINZIERL BEI WIESELBURG NO Aus 1
❒ WEIPERT (Vejprty) Boehmen Cze 1
❒ WEISMES (Waimes) Liege Bel 14
❒ WEISSBACH Sachsen Ger 1
❒ WEISSENBACH Kaernten Aus 1
❒ WEISSENBACH BEI MOEDLING NO Aus 1
❒ WEISSENBACH/ TRIESTING NO Aus 1
❒ WEISSENBERG Sachsen Ger 1
❒ WEISSENBORN Sachsen Ger 7
❒ WEISSENBURG Bayern Ger 1 2 6 7
❒ WEISSENBURG (Wissembourg) Elsass Ger 6
❒ WEISSENFELS Provinz Sachsen Ger 1 2 6
❒ WEISSENFELS-NAUMBURG Provinz Sachsen Ger 9
❒ WEISSENHORN Bayern Ger 1
❒ WEISSENKIRCHEN BEI FRANKENMARKT 00 Aus1
❒ WEISSENKIRCHEN IN DER WACHAU NO Aus 1
❒ WEISSENSEE Provinz Sachsen Ger 1 6
❒ WEISSENSTADT Bayern Ger 1 6
❒ WEISSENSTEIN Bayern Ger 2
❒ WEISSENSTEIN/ DRAU Kaernten Aus 1
❒ WEISSKIRCHEN OO Aus 1
❒ WEISSWASSER O.L. (Biala Woda, Weiszwasser) Schlesien Ger 1 2
❒ WEISTRACH NO Aus 1
❒ WEISWEIL Baden Ger 1
❒ WEITEN NO Aus 2
❒ WEITENEGG NO Aus 1
❒ WEITERSFELDEN OO Aus 1
❒ WEITRA NO Aus 1
❒ WEIXDORF/ LAUSA Sachsen Ger 6 13
❒ WEKELSDORF (Teplice nad Metuji) Cze 2
❒ WELDEN East Flanders Bel 1
❒ WELKENRAEDT Liege Bel 1 14
❒ WELLE East Flanders Bel 1
❒ WELLENDORF Hannover Ger 2
❒ WELS OO Aus 1 2
❒ WELSEN Rheinland Ger 5
❒ WELSK (Velsk) Rus 1
❒ WELZHEIM Wuerttemberg Ger 1 2 6
❒ WELZOW N.L. Brandenburg Ger 2
❒ WEMDING Bayern Ger 6
❒ WENDELSTEIN Bayern Ger 2 9
❒ WENDEN (Venden, Cesis) Rus 1
❒ WENDISHAIN/ LEISNIG Sachsen Ger 2

❒ WENDLING OO Aus 1
❒ WENDTHOHE Schaumburg-Lippe Ger 2
❒ WENDUYNE West Flanders Bel 1
❒ WENG OO Aus 1
❒ WENGERN/ HAGEN (Wetter) Westfalen Ger 5
❒ WENNINGSTEDT/ SYLT Schleswig-Holstein Ger 1
❒ WERDAU Sachsen Ger 1 2 6 7 8
❒ WERDEN/ RUHR Rheinland Ger 1 2 3 6 7 8
❒ WERDOHL Westfalen Ger 1 2 7
❒ WERFEN Salzburg Aus 1
❒ WERL Westfalen Ger 1 3 4
❒ WERMELSKIRCHEN Rheinland Ger 2
❒ WERMINGHOFF Grube Schlesien Ger 3
❒ WERMSDORF Sachsen Ger 1 2
❒ WERNBERG Bayern Ger 2
❒ WERNE Westfalen Ger 2 5 6 7
❒ WERNIGERODE Provinz Sachsen Ger 1 2 11
❒ WERNSDORF I E. Sachsen Ger 2
❒ WERNSTEIN OO Aus 1
❒ WERSTE Westfalen Ger 1
❒ WERTHEIM/ MAIN Baden Ger 1 6
❒ WERTHER Westfalen Ger 1
❒ WERTINGEN Bayern Ger 1 7
❒ WERVICQ West Flanders Bel 1
❒ WESEL Rheinland Ger 1 2 5 7 8
❒ WESENBERG Mecklenburg-Strelitz Ger 1
❒ WESSELBUREN/ DITHMARSCHEN Schleswig-Holstein Ger 1
❒ WESSELING Rheinland Ger 1 2
❒ WESSERLING (Huesseren-Wesserling) Elsass Ger 1
❒ WEST STERNBERG (Zielona Gora,Poland) Ger 1
❒ WESTERBOEDEFELD Westfalen Ger 2
❒ WESTERBORK Drenthe Net 15
❒ WESTERBURG Hessen-Nassau Ger 1
❒ WESTEREGELN Provinz Sachsen Ger 2
❒ WESTERHOLT (Herten) Westfalen Ger 1 6
❒ WESTERHORN Schleswig-Holstein Ger 1
❒ WESTERKAPPELN Westfalen Ger 2
❒ WESTERLAND/ SYLT Schleswig-Holstein Ger 1 2
❒ WESTERNBOEDEFELD Westfalen Ger 2
❒ WESTERSTEDE Oldenburg Ger 2
❒ WESTFALEN Westfalen Ger 1 6
❒ WESTHAUSEN Elsass Ger 1 2
❒ WESTHEIM Pfalz Ger 1
❒ WESTHOFEN Hessen-Nassau Ger 7
❒ WESTZAAN North Holland Net 14
❒ WETTER/ RUHR Westfalen Ger 1 2 3 5 6 7
❒ WETTERNE (Wetteren) East Flanders Bel 1

❐ WETTIN
Provinz Sachsen Ger 1
❐ WETZLAR/ LAHN
Rheinland Ger 1 2 4 7 8
❐ WEVELGHEM (Wevelgem)
West Flanders Bel 1 10
❐ WEYER OO Aus 1 2
❐ WEZ-VALVAIN
Hainaut Bel 1
❐ WEZ-VELVAIN BLEHARIES, ERE, ETC. Hainaut Bel 1
❐ WICKEDE-ASSELN Westfalen Ger 2
❐ WICKENDORF OO Aus 1
❐ WICKRATH Rheinland Ger 1 2
❐ WIDAWA/ WIDAWKA
(Widawka) Rpl 2
❐ WIEBELSKIRCHEN
Rheinland Ger 1
❐ WIEDENAU (Vidnava) Cze 1
❐ WIEDENBACH-TRIESDORF Bayern Ger 7
❐ WIEDENBRUECK
Westfalen Ger 1 3
❐ WIEDENEST
Rheinland Ger 1
❐ WIEDENSAHL
Hannover Ger 1
❐ WIEDERAU Sachsen Ger 1 2
❐ WIEDEREST
Rheinland Ger 1
❐ WIEHE
Provinz Sachsen Ger 1 2 7
❐ WIEHL Rheinland Ger 1 2
❐ WIELICHOWO
(Wiesenstadt) Posen Ger 1
❐ WIELICZKA Rpl 1 2
❐ WIELUN (Welun, Welungen) Rpl 2
❐ WIEN OO Aus 1 2 9 11 14
❐ WIENER-NEUDORF
NO Aus 1
❐ WIENER-NEUSTADT
NO Aus 1 9
❐ WIERINGEN
North Holland Net 14
❐ WIESA-ANNABERG
(Zschopautal) Sachsen Ger 1 3
❐ WIESAU/ SAGAN
Bayern Ger 2 7
❐ WIESBADEN
Hessen-Nassau Ger 1 2 6 7 8 10 14
❐ WIESCHOWA
(Wieszowa) Schlesien Ger 12
❐ WIESDORF Rheinland Ger 1
❐ WIESELBURG/ ERLAUF
NO Aus 1 2
❐ WIESEN (Viznov) Cze 2
❐ WIESENBAD/ ERZGEBIRGE Sachsen Ger2
❐ WIESLOCH Baden Ger 1
❐ WIESSENSTADT
Bayern Ger 1 6
❐ WIETZE Hannover Ger 2
❐ WIGGENSBACH
Bayern Ger 14
❐ WIGNEHIES Nord Fan 1
❐ WIJCHEN (Wychen)
Gelderland Net 14
❐ WIJK/ AALBURG
North Brabant Net 14
❐ WILCZAGORA
(Viltchagora) Rpl 1
❐ WILDBAD
Wuerttemberg Ger 1 2 3 13
❐ WILDBERG
Wuerttemberg Ger 1
❐ WILDEMANN
Hannover Ger 3
❐ WILDENFELS
Sachsen Ger 1 2
❐ WILDENSTEIN
(Dietfurt) Bayern Ger 7
❐ WILDENSTEIN Elsass Ger 1
❐ WILDERVANK
Groningen Net 1
❐ WILDESHAUSEN
Oldenburg Ger 1
❐ WILDUNGEN, BAD
Waldeck Ger 1
❐ WILHELMSBURG (Hamburg)
Hannover Ger 1 2 7
❐ WILHELMSBURG NO Aus 1
❐ WILHELMSHAVEN
Hannover Ger 1 2 3 7 12
❐ WILHELMSHAVEN-RUESTRINGEN
Hannover Ger 1 2
❐ WILHELMSHORST
(Kleszczewo) Posen Ger 2
❐ WILHERING OO Aus 1
❐ WILHERMSDORF
Bayern Ger 14
❐ WILISCHTHAL
Sachsen Ger 2
❐ WILKAU Sachsen Ger 1 2 3
❐ WILLEBROEK
(Wilebroeck) Antwerp Bel 1
❐ WILLEMS Nord Fan 1
❐ WILLEMSTAD
North Brabant Net 14
❐ WILLERSHAUSEN
Hannover Ger 2
❐ WILLICH Rheinland Ger 1 2 3 14
❐ WILLINGEN Waldeck Ger 1 3
❐ WILSDRUFF Sachsen Ger 1
❐ WILSELE Brabant Bel 1
❐ WILSNACK
Brandenburg Ger 1 2
❐ WILSTER
Schleswig-Holstein Ger 1
❐ WILTHEN Sachsen Ger 1 2
❐ WIMM OO Aus 1
❐ WIMPASSING/ PIELACH NO Aus 1 2
❐ WIMPFEN/ NECKAR
Wuerttemberg Ger 1
❐ WIMSBACH OO Aus 1
❐ WIMY Fan 1
❐ WINDAU/ VINDAU (Vindau, Vindava) Rpl 1
❐ WINDEGG OO Aus 1
❐ WINDHAAG BEI FREISTADT OO Aus 1
❐ WINDHAAG BEI PERG OO Aus 1
❐ WINDHAAG/ YBBS NO Aus 1
❐ WINDHUK Ged 1 2
❐ WINDISCH-ESCHENBACH
(Windischeschenbach)
Bayern Ger 1 2 7
❐ WINDISCHGARSTEN
OO Aus 1
❐ WINDSHEIM (Bad Windsheim)
Bayern Ger 1 2 7
❐ WINGENDORF/ FRANKENSTEIN
Sachsen Ger 2
❐ WINGENE (Wyngene)
West Flanders Bel 1 14
❐ WINKEL-SAINT-ELOI
West Flanders Bet 1
❐ WINKLARN NO Aus 1
❐ WINNAGORA
(Winenberg) Posen Ger 1 2 7
❐ WINNENDEN
Wuerttemberg Ger 1
❐ WINNWEILER Pfalz Ger 2
❐ WINSEN/ LUHE
Hannover Ger 1
❐ WINTERBERG
Westfalen Ger 1 2
❐ WINTERBORN
Rheinland Ger 2
❐ WINTERLINGEN
Wuerttemberg Ger 1
❐ WINTERSDORF
Sachsen-Altenburg Ger 2 7
❐ WINTERSWIJK
Gelderland Net 8
❐ VVINZELDORF
Schleswig-Holstein Ger 1
❐ WINZIG
(Winsko) Schlesien Ger 2
❐ WIPPENHAM OO Aus 1
❐ WIPPERFUERTH
Rheinland Ger 1 2
❐ WIREK (Antonienhuette)
Schlesien Ger 2
❐ WIRSITZ Posen Ger 1
❐ WISMAR
Mecklenburg-Schwerin Ger 1 2 3
❐ WISSEK
(Wysoka) Posen Ger 1
❐ WISSELS Bel 1
❐ WISSEN/ SIEG
Rheinland Ger 1 7
❐ WISSING
(Seubersdorf) Bayern Ger 6
❐ WITKOWO (Wittkowo, Witkowska) Pose Ger 1 2 7
❐ WITTDUEN
Schleswig-Holstein Ger 1
❐ WITTEN Westfalen Ger 1 2 6 7 11
❐ WITTENBERG (Wittenberg Lutherstadt) Provinz Sachsen Ger 1 2 3 6 7
❐ WITTENBERGE
Brandenburg Ger 1 2 6 7 8
❐ WITTENBURG
Meckienburg-Schwerin Ger 1
❐ WITTENHEIM Elsass Ger 1
❐ WITTERSCHLICK
(Alfter-Witterschlick)
Rheinland Ger 5
❐ WITTGENSDORF/ CHEMNITZ
Sachsen Ger 1 2
❐ WITTGENSTEIN
Westfalen Ger 1
❐ WITTICHENAU O.L.
Schlesien Ger 1
❐ WITTINGEN Hannover Ger 1
❐ WITTLICH Rheinland Ger 1 6
❐ WITTMUND Hannover Ger 2
❐ WITTSTOCK/ DOSSE
Brandenburg Ger 1 7
❐ WITZENHAUSEN
Hessen-Nassau Ger 1
❐ WITZNITZ Sachsen Ger 2
❐ WLADIWOSTOK Rus 1
❐ WLADYSLAWOW
(Osada) Rpl 1
❐ WLOCLAWEK/ VISTULA
(Vlotslawsk, Leslau) Rpl 2
❐ WODECQ Hainaut Bel 1
❐ WOELFERSHEIM
Hessen-Nassau Ger 2
❐ WOELLERSDORF N0 Aus 2
❐ WOERDEN
South HoMand Net 8
❐ WOERGL Tirol Aus 1 2
❐ WOERISHOFEN, BAD Bayern Ger 1

❒ WOERLITZ Anhalt Ger 1
❒ WOERSCHACH Steiermark Aus 1
❒ WOERTH/ DONAU Bayern Ger 1 7
❒ WOERTH/ MAIN Bayern Ger 1 7
❒ WOESENDORF NO Aus 1
❒ WOEVRE, LA Fan 1
❒ WOHLAU (Wolow) Schlesien Ger 1 2 4 6 7
❒ WOHLDORF Schleswig-Holstein Ger 1
❒ WOLDEGK Mecklenburg-Strelitz Ger 1
❒ WOLDENBERG (Neumark; Dobiegniew) Brandenburg Ger 1 6 14
❒ WOLFACH Baden Ger 1 2 6
❒ WOLFEN Provinz Sachsen Ger 2 14
❒ WOLFENBUETTEL Braunschweig Ger 1 2 7 8
❒ WOLFERN OO Aus 1
❒ WOLFHAGEN Hessen-Nassau Ger 1
❒ WOLFMANNSHAUSEN Sachsen-Meiningen Ger 1
❒ WOLFPASSING AM FORST NO Aus 1
❒ WOLFRATSHAUSEN Bayern Ger 1 2
❒ WOLFSBACH NO Aus 1
❒ WOLFSBERG Bayern Ger 14
❒ WOLFSEGG OO Aus 1
❒ WOLFSTEIN Pfalz Ger 1
❒ WOLGAST Pommern Ger 1 7
❒ WOLHYNIE/ VOLHYNIA (Wotyn) Rpl 2
❒ WOLKENBURG Sachsen Ger 2
❒ WOLKENSTEIN Sachsen Ger 1 2
❒ WOLLENTHAL (Wolenthal) Posen Ger 2
❒ WOLLIN (Wolin) Pommern Ger 1 6
❒ WOLLMATINGEN (Konstanz) Baden Ger 1
❒ WOLLSTEIN (Wolsztyn) Posen Ger 1
❒ WOLMIRSTEDT Provinz Sachsen Ger 1
❒ WOLNZACH Bayern Ger 6
❒ WOLPHAARTSDIJRK Zeeland Net 1
❒ WONG ROWITZ (Wagrowiec, Wagrowska) Posen Ger 1 2
❒ WONSAWA (Wonsowo, Wasawa) Posen Ger 7
❒ WORBIS Provinz Sachsen Ger 1
❒ WORMDITT (Orneta) Ostpreussen Ger 1
❒ WORMS Hessen Ger 1 3 4 5 6 7 8 11 12
❒ WORPSWEDE Hannover Ger 1
❒ WORTEGEM (Wortegen) East Flanders Bel 2
❒ WOUDRICHEM North Brabant Net 14
❒ WOYENS (Vojens, Denmark) Schleswig-Holstein Ger 1
❒ WRESCHEN (Wrzesnia) Posen Ger 1
❒ WRIEZEN Brandenburg Ger 1 2
❒ WROBLE/ STRELNO Posen Ger 2
❒ WRONKE (Wronki) Posen Ger 1 2
❒ WRZOSOWA Rpl 2
❒ WRZOSOWA (Yrsozova) Rus 1
❒ WSZEMBORZ/ BORZYKOWO Posen Ger 2
❒ WUELFEL Hannover Ger 7 9
❒ WUELFRATH Rheinland Ger 1 2 3 8
❒ WUELZBURG (Weissenburg) Bayern Ger 3 4
❒ WUENSCHENDORF Sachsen-Weimar-Eisenach Ger 1
❒ WUEN,SCHENDORF Schlesien Ger 1 2
❒ WUENSDORF Brandenburg Ger 2
❒ WUENSTORF Hannover Ger 1 7
❒ WUERNITZ NO Aus 2
❒ WUERNSDORF NO Aus 1
❒ WUERTTEMBERG (Stuttgart) Wuerttemberg Ger 1
❒ WUERTTEMBERG-HOHENZOLLERN Wuerttemberg Ger 14
❒ WUERZBURG Bayern Ger 1 2 3 7 8 12
❒ WUESTEGIERSDORF (Gluszyca) Schlesien Ger 2
❒ WUESTEWALTERSDORF (Walim) Schlesien Ger 1 2 7
❒ WULFEN Westfalen Ger 1
❒ WUNSIEDEL Bayern Ger 1 2 6 7
❒ WUNSTORF Hannover Ger 1 2 7
❒ WURZACH, BAD Wuerttemberg Ger 1 6
❒ WURZBACH Thueringen Ger 1 2 6
❒ WURZEN Sachsen Ger 1 2 8
❒ WUSTERHAUSEN/ DOSSE Brandenburg Ger 1
❒ WUSTROW Mecklenburg-Schwerin Ger 2
❒ WYHLEN (Grenzach-Wyhlen) Baden Ger 1 6
❒ WYK/ FOEHR Schleswig-Holstein Ger 1 2 6
❒ WYPICHOW Rpl 2
❒ WYPICHOW Rus 1
❒ WYRZYSKA (Wirsitz) Rpl 1

X

❒ XANTEN Rheinland Ger 1 2 3
❒ XERTA Tarragona Spa 1
❒ XIONS (Ksiaz) Posen Ger 1

Y

❒ YAKOVLEVKOYE Rus 1
❒ YALTA (lalta) Rus 1
❒ YAMPOL (lampol, Jampol) Rus 1
❒ YANOVKA (lanovka, Janovka) Rus 1
❒ YAROSLAV (laroslav, laroslovl, Jaroslav) Rus 1
❒ YASHKINO (Yaskino, lachkino, Jaschkino) Rus 1
❒ YBBS NO Aus 1
❒ YBBS/ DONAU NO Aus 2
❒ YBBSITZ NO Aus 1
❒ YEBENES Toledo Spa 1
❒ YECLA Murcia Spa 1 2
❒ YEGEN Granada Spa 1
❒ YELNIKI (Elninsk) Rus 1
❒ YENISELISK (Yenakyevo, Enisel, Jenisejsk) Rus 1 2
❒ YEPES Toledo Spa 1
❒ YERNEE-FRAINEUX Liege Bel 1
❒ YESSENTUKI (Essentuki) Rus 1
❒ YESTE Albacete Spa 1
❒ YEVPATORIYA (Eupatoria) Rus 1
❒ YOL Ita 14
❒ YPRES West Flanders Bel 1
❒ YRETTINJE Nor 14
❒ YSPER NO Aus 1
❒ YTTEROEY Nor 14
❒ YUCHNOV (Juchnov) Rus 1
❒ YURIEV-POLSKI (Yuryev-Polski) Rus 1
❒ YUSOVKA (Yuzovka, Stalino, Hughesovka, Donetsk) Rus 1
❒ YVOIR Namur Bel 2

Z

❒ ZAANDAM North Holland Net 8
❒ ZAANSTREEK Net 8
❒ ZABERN (Saverne) Elsass Ger 6 10
❒ ZABKOWICE (Zombkovitsi; Frankenstein) Schlesien Ger 2
❒ ZABORZE Schlesien Ger 1 3 6
❒ ZABRZE (Hindenburg) Schlesien Ger 1 6 7 8
❒ ZAGLEBIE DABROWSKIE (Dombrowskie Kop.) Ger 2
❒ ZAGLEBIE DABROWSKIE (Dabrowskie Zaglebie) Rus 1
❒ ZAGOROW Posen Ger 2
❒ ZAGREB (Agram) Yug 1
❒ ZAGUROV (Zagorow) Rus 1
❒ ZAHNA Provinz Sachsen Ger 1
❒ ZAHRADKA Cze 2
❒ ZAIDA, LA Zaragoza Spa 1
❒ ZAIRKUTNY GORODOK Rus 1 3
❒ ZAKOPANE (Zakopuno) Rpl 2
❒ ZALACSANY Hun 3
❒ ZALAEGERSZEG-TABOR Hun 3
❒ ZALAMEA DE LA SERENA Badajoz Spa 1
❒ ZALENZE (Zaleze) Schlesien Ger 1
❒ ZALESSKI (Pereslav) Rus 1
❒ ZALTBOMMEL Gelderland Net 14
❒ ZAMBERK (Stavba Kasaren) Cze 1 2
❒ ZAMBO Ita 14
❒ ZAMOSC Rpl 1 14
❒ ZANDVOORT North Holland Net 14
❒ ZANIEMYSL (Santomischel) Posen Ger 1 2
❒ ZANTE Gre 14
❒ ZAPORIZHIA (Alexandrovsk, Zaporzhye) Rus 1
❒ ZARA Dalmai Yug
❒ ZARIZYN (Tsaritsin) Rus 1
❒ ZARRA Valencia Spa 2
❒ ZARRENTIN Mecklenburg-Schwerin Ger 1
❒ ZARZA-CAPILLA Badajoz Spa 1
❒ ZAUCH-BELZIG Brandenburg Ger 1

❒ ZAVERTSE (Zawiercie, Warthenau) Rus 1
❒ ZAWADZKI (Zawadzkie) Schlesien Ger 5 7
❒ ZAWIERCIE (Warthenau, Zavertse) Rpl 2
❒ ZAWIERCIE (Zavertse) Rus 1
❒ ZBARAZ (Zbarazh) Rus 1
❒ ZDAR Cze 1
❒ ZDUNSKA WOLA Rpl 1 2
❒ ZDUNSKAYA VOLYA (Zdunska Wola) Rus 1
❒ ZDUNY (Freihaus, Zerkow) Posen Ger 1
❒ ZEA (Zeia, Seja) Rus. 1
❒ ZECHE HOLLAND Ger 3
❒ ZEDELGHEM (Zedelgem) West Flanders Bel 1
❒ ZEELAND Net 14
❒ ZEHDENICK Brandenburg Ger 2
❒ ZEHETGRUB NO Aus 1
❒ ZEILLERN NO Aus 1
❒ ZEILLING OO Aus 1
❒ ZEISELMAUER NO Aus 1
❒ ZEISKAM Pfalz Ger 1
❒ ZEISS OO Aus 1
❒ ZEISSHOLD/ LIEGNITZ Schlesien Ger 5
❒ ZEITHAIN Sachsen Ger 1 2
❒ ZEITZ Provinz Sachsen Ger 1 2 6 7 8
❒ ZELE East Flanders Bel 1
❒ ZELENIN/ BERENT Westpreussen Ger 2
❒ ZELKING NO Aus 1
❒ ZELL AM SEE Salzburg Aus 1
❒ ZELL BEI ZELLHOF OO Aus 1
❒ ZELL-ARZBERG NO Aus 1
❒ ZELL-HARMERSBACH Baden Ger 2
❒ ZELL/ HARMERSBACH (UNTERHARMERSBACH NORDRACH BIBERACH) Baden Ger 1 7
❒ ZELL/ MOOS OO Aus 1
❒ ZELL/ PETTENFUERST OO Aus 1
❒ ZELL/ PRAM OO Aus 1
❒ ZELL/ WIESENTHAL Baden Ger 1 2 6 7
❒ ZELL/ YBBS NO Aus 1
❒ ZELLA (Zella-Mehlis) Sachsen-Coburg-Gotha Ger 7 9
❒ ZELLA ST. BLASII UND MEHLIS Sachsen Ger 1
❒ ZELLA-MEHLIS Sachsen Ger 1 3 7
❒ ZELLA-ST. BLASII Sachsen Ger 1
❒ ZELTINGEN/ MOSEL Rheinland Ger 2
❒ ZELZATE (Sint-Jean-Baptist) Liege Bel 14
❒ ZEMLYANSK Rus 1
❒ ZEMPELBURG (Sepolno) Westpreussen Ger 1
❒ ZENKOV (Sinkov) Rus 1
❒ ZERALDA Alg 7
❒ ZERBST Anhalt Ger 1 2 3 12
❒ ZERKOW (Zlotowski) Posen Ger 1
❒ ZERNICKOW (Seelow) Brandenburg Ger 7
❒ ZERNSDORF Brandenburg Ger 2
❒ ZETHAU Sachsen Ger 1
❒ ZEULENRODA Thueringen Ger 1 2 7 8
❒ ZEVEN Hannover Ger 1
❒ ZEVEN, WILSTEDT UND SITTENSEN Hannover Ger 2
❒ ZEVENBERGEN North Brabant Net 14
❒ ZGERZH (Zgierz) Rus 1
❒ ZHIRARDOV (Zyrardow) Rus 1
❒ ZHITNY Rus 1
❒ ZHITOMIR (Schitomir, Jitomir) Rus 1
❒ ZIEGENHAIN Hessen-Nassau Ger 1 3
❒ ZIEGENHALS (Glucholazy) Schlesien Ger 1 2 6 7 8
❒ ZIEGENRUECK Provinz Sachsen Ger 1 2 6
❒ ZIELENZIG (Sulecin, Poland) Brandenburg Ger 1
❒ ZIELENZIG/ OST-STERNBERG Brandenburg Ger 1
❒ ZIERIKZEE Zeeland Net 8
❒ ZIERSDORF NO Aus 1
❒ ZIESAR Provinz Sachsen Ger 1 2
❒ ZIGUINCHOR Sen 6
❒ ZI LI NA (Zilinska, Sukenna, Tovarna) Cze 1
❒ ZILLERTHAL (Myslakowice) Schlesien Ger 7
❒ ZILLY Provinz Sachsen Ger 1 7 12
❒ ZINNA Sachsen Ger 1
❒ ZINNOWITZ Pommern Ger 1 7
❒ ZINTEN (Korniewo, Karszewo) Ostpreussen Ger 1
❒ ZINTENHOF BEI PERNAU Est 1 2
❒ ZIPSENDORF Provinz Sachsen Ger 2
❒ ZIRNDORF Bayern Ger 1 2 6 8
❒ ZISTERSDORF NO Aus 1
❒ ZITTAU UND BAUTZEN Sachsen Ger 1
❒ ZITTAU/ MAUDAU (Svitavy) Sachsen Ger 1 2 7 8 12
❒ ZLATOUST (Slatoust) Rus 1
❒ ZLOCZOW/ SIERADZ Galicia Rpl 1 2
❒ ZLYNKA Rus 1
❒ ZNIN Posen Ger 1 2 6
❒ ZOBTEN/ BERGE (Sobotka) Schlesien Ger 1 2
❒ ZOEBLITZ Sachsen Ger 1
❒ ZOERBIG Provinz Sachsen Ger 1 2
❒ ZOESCHLINGSWEILER/ DILLINGEN Bayern Ger 2
❒ ZOLDER-VOORT Limbourg Bel 2
❒ ZOMBKOVITSI (Zabkowice) Rus 1
❒ ZONHOVEN Limbourg Bel 1 2
❒ ZONS/ RHEIN Rheinland Ger 1
❒ ZOPPOT/ DANZIG (Sopot) Westpreussen Ger 1 8 13
❒ ZORITA Castellon Spa 2
❒ ZOSSEN Brandenburg Ger 3
❒ ZOSSEN-HALBMONDLAGER Brandenburg Ger 1 3
❒ ZOSSEN-WEINBERGE Brandenburg Ger 3
❒ ZSCHEPKAU Sachsen Ger 2
❒ ZSCHIPKAU (Schipkau) Sachsen Ger 7
❒ ZSCHOPAU Sachsen Ger 1 2
❒ ZUCKMANTEL (Cukmantl, Zlate Hory) Cze 1
❒ ZUELLICHAU (Sulechow) Brandenburg Ger 1 2 6
❒ ZUELZ O.S. (Biala Prudnicka) Schlesien Ger 1
❒ ZUESCHEN Westfalen Ger 2 9
❒ ZUETTLINGEN Wuerttemberg Ger 1
❒ ZUFFENHAUSEN/ STUTTGART Wuerttemberg Ger 1 6 7 8 9
❒ ZURAWNO (Zurawna, Zhuravno, Zuravno) Rpl 2
❒ ZURGENA Almeria Spa 1
❒ ZURGENA DEL RIO Almeria Spa 2
❒ ZVENIGOROD Rus 1
❒ ZWEIBRUECKEN Pfalz Ger 1 2 6 7
❒ ZWEINAUNDORF Sachsen Ger 1
❒ ZWENKAU Sachsen Ger 1
❒ ZWETTL NO Aus 1
❒ ZWETTL IM MUEHLKREIS OO Aus 1
❒ ZWICKAU Sachsen Ger 1 3 4 6 7 8 11 12
❒ ZWIESEL Bayern Ger 1 2 6 7
❒ ZWIJNDRECHT East Flanders Bel 1
❒ ZWIJNDRECHT South Holland Net 14
❒ ZWINGENBERG Hessen Ger 1
❒ ZWISCHENAHN (Bad Zwischenahn) Oldenburg Ger 2 7
❒ ZWITTAU Aus 1
❒ ZWITTAU (Svitavy) Maehren Cze 1 2
❒ ZWOENITZ Sachsen Ger 1 2 7
❒ ZWOTA/ VOGTLAND Sachsen Ger 1
❒ ZYDACZOW (Zhidachov, Zidaccov) Rpl 2
❒ ZYRARDOW Rpl 2
❒ ZYTYN (Zytin, Jitin) Rpl 2
❒ ZYWIEC/ SOLA (Savbusch) Rpl 2

Bibliography

Austria

Richter, Rudolf, *Notgeld Oesterreich (Deutsch-Oesterrich und Nachfolgestaaten mit Nebengebieten ab 1918.* 130 pages, 1993 Gietl Verlag Regenstauf, Germany.

Richter, Rudolf, *Notgeld Oesterreich Oesterreich-Ungarn 1914-1918.* 200 pages, 1996 Gietl Verlag Regenstauf, Germany.

Richter, Rudolf, *Lagergeld (Kriegsgefangenen-, Konsentrations-, Fluechtlings-und Internierlager, 1, und 2.* Weltkrieg. 124 pages, 1997 Gietl Verlag Regenstauf, Germany.

France

Manasselian, Jean, *Les Monnaies de Necessite Francaises et Coloniales.* 266 pages, 1982 Marseille, France.

Gadoury, Victor and Georges Cousinie, *Monnaies Coloniales Francaises 1670-1988,* 552 pages, 1988 Victor Gadoury Monte Carlo, Monaco.

Gadoury, Victor and Raymond Elie, *Monnaies de Necessite Francaises 1789-1990,* 688 pages, Victor Gadoury Monte Carlo, Monaco.

Pirot, Jean, Les Billets des Chambres de Commerce, 192 pages, 1989 La Roche-sur-Yon.

Germany

Bayer, Gerd, *Notgeld von 1918-1923 und 1947 im Gebiet des heutigen Kreises Bernkastel-Wittlich*, 200 pages, 1994 Trierer Muenzfreunde e. V. Trier Germany

Brendel, Lothar, *Das Notgeld in der Vormaligen Residenzstadt Kassel*, 180 pages, 1996 Numismatische Gesellschaft Kassel.

Gerke, Guenter, *Das Geld der mageren Jahre – als alle Milliardaere waren (Bielefelder Notgeld 1917-1924)*, 200 pages, 1998 Sparkasse Bielefeld Germany.

Hasselman, W., *Die Privaten Notmuenzen 1916-1922,* 338 pages, 1985 Holger Rosenberg, Kutenholz-Mulsum, Germany.

Geiger, Anton, *Das deutsche Grossnotgeld 1918-1921*, 256 pages, 1998 Verlag A. Geiger, Frankenthal Germany.

Grabowski, Hans L., *Das Papiergeld der deuschen Laender von 1871 bis 1948,* 600 pages, 1999 Gietl Verlag Regenstauf, Germany.

Kubilas, Aleksandras, *World II War Russian-German Occupations in Lithuania,* 200 pages, 1997 LKA, Vilnius, Lithuania.

Lindman, Kai, *Serienscheine 3rd edition*, 412 pages, 2000 Kolme K – Verlag Sassenburg, Germany

Mehl, Manfred, *Die Notgeldscheine der deutschen Inflation 1922*, 260 pages, 1988 Verlag A. Geiger, Frankenthal, Germany.

Moeller, Ingrid, *Das Mecklenburgische Reutergeld von 1921*, 140 pages, Stock & Stein, Schwerin, Germany.

Mueller, Manfred, *Die Notgeldscheine der deutschen Inflation 1922*, 260 pages, 1998 Verlag A. Geiger, Frankenthal, Germany.

Mueller, Manfred and Anton Geiger, *Das Papiergeld der deutschen Eisenbahnen und der Reichspost*, 268 pages, 200 Verlag A. Geiger, Frankenthal, Germany.

Rupertus, Guenter, *Das Pepiergeld von Baden 1849-1948*, 308 pages, 1988 Weiss + Hameier, KG Ludwigshafen/Rhein, Germany.

Tieste, Reinhard, Katalog des Papiergeldes der deutschen Kriegsgefangenenlager im I. Weltkrieg, 152 pages, 1988 Verlag R. Tieste, Bremen Germany.

General

Campbell, Lance K., *Prisoner of War and Concentration Camp Money of the 20th Century*, 200 pages, BNR Press, Port Clinton, Ohio.

Key to Abbreviations

Anglo-Egyptian Sudan .... (AES)
Algeria .... (ALG)
Angola .... (ANG)
Argentina .... (ARG)
Armenia .... (ARM)
Austrailia .... (AUL)
Austria .... (AUS)
Azores .... (AZS)
Belgium .... (BEL)
Cameroons .... (CAM)
Cape Verde Islands .... (CAV)
Ceylon .... (CEY)
China .... (CHI)
Cyprus .... (CYR)
Czechoslovakia .... (CZE)
Denmark .... (DEN)
Estonia .... (EST)
Ethiopia .... (ETH)
Fiji .... (FIJ)
Finland .... (FIN)
France .... (FAN)
French Equatorial Africa .... (FEA)
French Guiana .... (FGA)
French Indo-China .... (FIC)
French Oceania .... (FOA)
French Somaililand .... (FSL)
French West Africa .... (FWA)
German East Africa .... (GEA)
German New Guinea .... (GEB)
German Samoa .... (GEC)
German Southwest Africa .... (GED)
Germany .... (GER)
Gibraltar .... (GIB)
Grand Comoro .... (GRA)
Great Britain .... (GRB)
Greece .... (GRE)
Greenland .... (GRN)
Hong Kong .... (HKG)
Hungary .... (HUN)
Iceland .... (ICE)
India .... (IND)
Ireland .... (IRE)
Isle of Man .... (ISM)
Italy .... (ITA)
Kenya .... (KEN)
Latvia .... (LAT)
Liechtenstein .... (LIE)
Lithuania .... (LIT)
Luxenburg .... (LUX)
Macao .... (MAC)
Madagascar .... (MAD)
Madeira .... (MAI)
Martinique .... (MAR)
Monaco .... (MCO)
Montenegro .... (MON)
Morocco .... (MOR)
Mozambique .... (MOZ)
Netherlands .... (NET)
New Caledonia .... (NEW)
Norway .... (NOR)
Portugal .... (POR)
Portuquese Guinea .... (PRG)
Reunion .... (REU)
Rhodesia .... (RHD)
Romania .... (ROM)
Russia .... (RUS)
Russian Poland .... (RPL)
St. Thomas & Prince .... (SAP)
Senegal .... (SEN)
Serbia .... (SER)
Spain .... (SPA)
Sudan .... (SUD)
Sweden .... (SWE)
Syria .... (SYR)
Switzerland .... (SWI)
Tunisia .... (TUN)
Uruguay .... (URU)
Yugoslavia .... (YUG)

JOIN THE EXCITING WORLD OF NUMISMATICS

Standard Catalog™ of World Paper Money, Modern Issues 1961 - 2000
Volume III, 6th Edition
edited by Colin R. Bruce II and Neil Shafer
The most comprehensive reference for modern world paper money ever published, this edition includes current market values for more than 10,500 notes in three grades of condition, and over 7,000 photos and illustrations. You get all notes issued from 1961 to present, representing more than 376 note-issuing authorities. Plus prices and photos for new notes issued in 1999, including new U.S. paper money issues. A user's guide, grading terms, dating information, foreign language references, exchange tables, foreign bank index and more help collectors at all levels.
Softcover • 8-1/2 x 11 • 864 pages
7,000 b&w photos
Item# WP06 • $39.95

Standard Catalog™ of World Paper Money, Specialized Issues
Volume I, 8th Edition
by Colin R. Bruce II, Senior Editor/Neil Shafer, Editor
More than 51,000 updated prices for more than 17,000 notes are presented along with more than 8,000 photos of faces AND backs for easy identification. Helpful exchange and translation information lets you tour this special world with ease and accuracy.
Softcover • 8-1/2 x 11
1,184 pages
8,000 b&w photos
Item# PS08 • $60.00

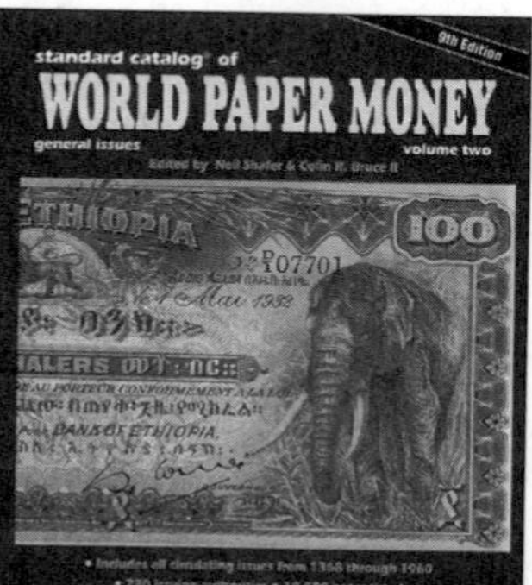

Standard Catalog™ of World Paper Money, General Issues
Volume II, 9th Edition
edited by Colin R. Bruce and Neil Shafer
This is the world's most comprehensive world paper money price guide and reference. The new 9th edition includes 19,000+ listings of paper money circulating worldwide from 1650 through 1960 in three grades of condition and well over 50,000 up-to-date prices that reflect recent market activity. Introductory chapters are updated. An Exotic Language Photo Identification Guide is new to this edition and many photos are incorporated throughout.
Hardcover • 8-1/2 x 11 • 1,144 pages
5,200 b&w photos
Item# PM09 • $65.00

STATE QUARTER COLLECTOR SERIES

by Krause Publications

Join the flurry of excitement that surrounds the new 50 State Quarter Program. Showcasing the state quarters the series combines the fun of collecting with the learning experience of history. Each volume features ten convenient quarter slots in the cover to display your treasures both front and back. You'll love the ten convenient quarter display slots, the ten pages of fascinating reading dedicated to each state and the vivid photography that captures all the charm of this exciting program. Young and old will cherish this extraordinary series for years to come.

Hardcover • 6 x 9 • 64 pages
150 color photos

State Quarter Collector Volume I:
1999 Releases
Item# SQ1999 • $9.95
State Quarter Collector Volume II:
2000 Releases
Item# SQ2000 • $9.95

Standard Guide to Small Size U.S. Paper Money
1928 to Date, 3rd Edition
by Dean Oakes & John Schwartz
The exciting third edition of this numismatic standard is still the most comprehensive listing of small-size U.S. currency available. Newly included in this edition are the 1996 $20 note and the 1996 $50 note. It's easy-to-use format, updated pricing and serial information, and more than 250 photographs make this book a must-have.
Softcover • 6 x 9 • 352 pages
275 b&w photos
Item# HP05 • $24.95

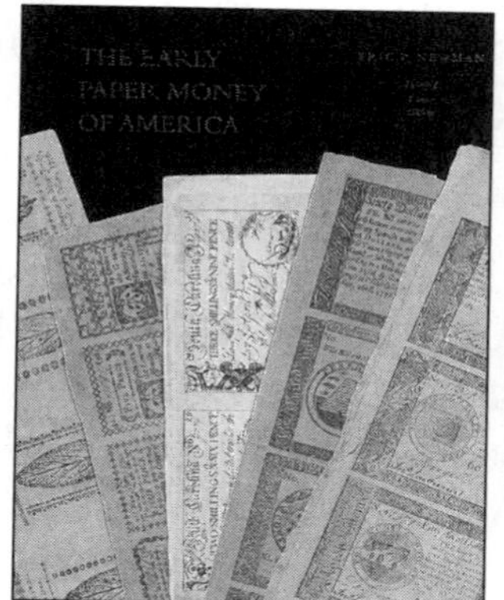

Early Paper Money of America
4th Edition
by Eric P. Newman
Compile historical and descriptive data on American paper currency from 1686 to 1800. Eric P. Newman has completely revised and updated his popular book to include current values of all available bills.
Hardcover • 8-1/2 x 11 • 488 pages
930 b&w photos • 100 color photos
Item# EP04 • $75.00

Shipping and Handling: $3.25 1st book; $2 ea. add'l. Foreign orders $20.95 1st item, $5.95 each add'l.

Sales tax: CA, IA, IL, PA, TN, VA, WA, WI residents please add appropriate sales tax.

To place a credit card order or for a FREE all-product catalog call

800-258-0929 **Offer NUBR**

M-F, 7 am - 8 pm • Sat, 8 am - 2 pm, CST
Krause Publications, Offer NUBR
P.O. Box 5009, Iola, WI 54945-5009
www.krausebooks.com

Satisfaction Guarantee:
If for any reason you are not completely satisfied with your purchase, simply return it within 14 days and receive a full refund, less shipping.

Retailers call toll-free 888-457-2873 ext 880, M-F, 8 am - 5 pm